U0572184

广西铜鼓精华

Bronze Drums in Guangxi

上 册

中国古代铜鼓研究会 编
广西民族博物馆

Compiled by The Chinese Association for Ancient Bronze Drums Research
& Anthropology Museum of Guangxi

覃 溥 主编

Chief Editor　Qin Pu

文物出版社

Cultural Relics Press

图书在版编目（ＣＩＰ）数据

广西铜鼓精华 / 覃溥主编 .— 北京：文物出版社，
2017.12
ISBN 978-7-5010-4856-4

Ⅰ . ①广… Ⅱ . ①覃… Ⅲ . ①铜鼓－广西－图集
Ⅳ . ① K875.52

中国版本图书馆 CIP 数据核字 (2016) 第 302700 号

广 西 铜 鼓 精 华

主　　编：覃　溥
封面设计：王梦祥
责任编辑：窦旭耀
责任印制：张道奇

出版发行：文物出版社
地　　址：北京市东直门内北小街 2 号楼
邮　　编：100007
网　　址：www.wenwu.com
邮　　箱：web@wenwu.com
印　　刷：北京雅昌艺术印刷有限公司
经　　销：新华书店
开　　本：787mm×1092mm　1/8
印　　张：66.5
版　　次：2017 年 12 月第 1 版
印　　次：2017 年 12 月第 1 次印刷
书　　号：ISBN 978-7-5010-4856-4
定　　价：880.00 元（全二册）

本书版权独家所有，非经授权，不得复制翻印

《广西铜鼓精华》编委会

主　编：覃　溥
副主编：王　颋　蒋廷瑜　农学坚　王梦祥
编　委：（按姓氏笔画为序）
　　　　王　颋　王梦祥　农学坚　刘文毅　陆秋燕
　　　　陈　嘉　梁燕理　覃　溥　蒋廷瑜　富　霞
摄　影：王梦祥
翻　译：陆秋燕

Chief Editor: Qin Pu
Subeditor: Wang Wei, Jiang Tingyu, Nong Xuejian, Wang Mengxiang
Editorial Board: Wang Wei, Wang Mengxiang, Nong xuejian, Liu Wenyi, Lu Qiuxia,
　　　　　　　　Chen Jia, Liang Yanli, Qin Pu, Jiang Tingyu, Fu Xia
Photograph: Wang Mengxiang
English Translation: Lu Qiuyan

目录 Index

序

一个民族、一个国家离不开她的文脉传承以及文化的繁荣与发展。文化是民族之魂，是一个地区（或国家）综合竞争力的重要体现，也是推动经济与社会可持续发展的内生动力之源。

广西，是我国古代南方青铜文化繁盛之地。在八桂大地出土了不同年代的铜鼓：在右江河谷田东，先后出土了3面战国时期的万家坝型铜鼓；在贵港罗泊湾西汉墓中出土了石寨山型铜鼓（其中一面定为国宝级文物）；在"俚僚"活跃的"五郡中央"出土了大量北流型、灵山型和冷水冲型铜鼓。2016年刚刚申遗成功的世界文化景观遗产左江花山岩画，留下了战国至东汉时期骆越人敲击铜鼓、祭祀神灵的壮阔恢弘的场景，据统计，左江岩画中有365个铜鼓图形，这一世界文化遗产也为广西是古老的铜鼓之乡提供了历史证据。

以壮族及其先民为主体的各兄弟民族，在广西壮美的土地上共同造就了绵延两千多年采冶铜矿、铸造和使用铜鼓的历史，最终涵育成独树一帜、丰富多彩而又彪炳千秋、影响深远的地域文化——铜鼓文化。正如中国古代铜鼓研究会老会长蒋廷瑜先生在本书《广西铜鼓概述》一文中所说，广西铜鼓"历史文献史不绝书"，"公私收藏，洋洋大观"，"古往今来，多族共有"，"沿江分布，覆盖全区"，"品类齐全，争芳斗艳"，"铜鼓研究，硕果累累"。

广西也是活态铜鼓文化保存最好的区域，特别是红水河流域的壮乡、瑶寨群众手中还存有一千多面清代以前留下来的铜鼓。壮乡东兰县因为铜鼓习俗保护得好被授予铜鼓之乡的称号，以环江县韦启初兄弟为代表的铜鼓铸造工艺在继承传统的工艺基础上又有了新的创发。每年数以百计的新铜鼓不仅在广西畅销，而且远销云南、贵州。河池市一年一度的铜鼓山歌艺术节红红火火，铿锵激越的铜鼓之声依然在壮乡、瑶寨回荡。

正因为广西铜鼓文化底蕴深厚，所以广西铜鼓的精品最多，这本由覃溥会长领衔主编、中国古代铜鼓研究会和广西民族博物馆联合编纂的《广西铜鼓精华》展示了广西出土的万家坝型、石寨山型、冷水冲型、遵义型、麻江型、北流型、灵山型和西盟型八种类型铜鼓的精华，计167面，因为参与调研、拍摄和编辑的人员非常敬业，使得《广西铜鼓精华》也成了精品，高水准摄影使铜鼓图像保真度极高，色彩还原准确，整体与局部皆很清晰。我认为这本《广西铜鼓精华》不仅具有宝贵的史料价值，还具有重要的当代价值。党中央高屋建瓴，在十八届五中全会及时提出了"构建中华优秀传统文化传承体系，加强文化遗产保护"，编者们就是以实际行动响应党中央的号召，诚如覃溥主编所说，"对研究者深入研究和读者拓宽视野，认识海上丝绸之路历史与文化的重要组成之一——铜鼓历史及其文化，无疑是有帮助的"。

广西在过去的几十年中，为保护、传承和发展铜鼓文化做出了重要贡献。我深信，未来广西在以中国为核心的"铜鼓文化圈"研究中一定有所作为，在展示"海上丝绸之路"的历史与现实的辉煌、推动中国对东盟的开放与合作中发挥更大的作用。

万辅彬

2017 年 3 月 20 日

One nation, one country couldn't develop without its cultural inheritance and cultural prosperity. Culture is not only the soul of a nation, but also the important reflection of comprehensive competitive power of one area or one country, and the inner driving force of a sustainable developing economic and society.

Guangxi is the place where bronze culture in ancient south was prosperous. Bronze drums of different eras were discovered in Guangxi: 3 bronze drums of Wanjiaba Type which made in Warring States Period were unearthed at Tiandong, the valley of Youjiang River; in tombs of Western Han at Luopowan, Guigang, unearthed bronze drums of Shizhaishan Type (one of them was evaluated as national treasure; in 'the central of 5 prefectures' where Li and Liao people lived lively, unearthed a lots of bronze drums of Beiliu, Lingshan and Lengshuichong Type. In the Zuojiang rock painting that was just announced the Word Cultural Landscape Heritage, remained huge and grand scenes of beating bronze drums to sacrifice gods by Luoyue People during Warring States Period to Eastern Han dynasty. According to statistics, there are 365 patterns of bronze drum in Zuojiang rock painting, also providing historical evidences of that Guangxi is 'a home of bronze drums' with a long history.

All ethnics, Zhuang people predominantly, created a 2,000 years history of mining and smelting ores, casting and using bronze drums on this beautiful land, and finally fostered the territorial culture which is unique and colourful, shines forever and affects profoundly, that is, bronze drum culture. Just as the former president of Chinese Association for Ancient Bronze Drums Research, Mr. Jiang Tingyu, said in his article REVIEW OF BRONZE DRUMS IN GUANGXI in this book, Guangxi bronze drums were recorded in numerous historical documents, were kept by governments and privates, were owned by many ethnics in history; they distributed along rivers and covered almost the whole province with all types of drum and all the drums owned their beauties; and nowadays, bronze drum research has gained great achievements.

Guangxi, where the living bronze drum cultures keep integrate mostly, there are over 1,000 bronze drums descended from Qing dynasty by Zhuang and Yao people in Hongshui River area. Donglan County, a Zhuang ethnic county, was awarded the title of 'County of Bronze Drums' for its endeavor to preserve bronze drum customs. In Huanjiang County, Wei Qichu and his brother are the representatives of new drum-caster who make new creations on bronze drum cast base on traditional craft. Every year, hundreds of new bronze drums are sold very well not only in Guangxi, but also in Yunnan and Guizhou. In Hechi, a busy festival of bronze drums and folk songs is held every year. The clang and jingle beating of bronze drums are still sounding around Zhuang and Yao ethnic villages.

Base on the solid ground of bronze drum culture, Guangxi has the finest drums in a largest number. This book, BRONZE DRUMS IN GUANGXI, mainly edited by President Qin Pu, compiled by Chinese Association for Ancient Bronze Drums Research and Anthropology Museum of Guangxi, presents 167 finest bronze drums unearthed in Guangxi, which are divided into 8 types: Wanjiaba, Shizhaishan, Lengshuichong, Zunyi, Majiang, Beiliu, Lingshan and Ximeng. Dedicated investigators, photographers and compilers make this book an artwork, with high level pictures of high resolution and accurate colour, which retain the image and colour of bronze drums furthest, including entirety and parts. For me, this book is not only of precious historical value, but also of important present value. On a strategically advantageous position, the Party Central Committee put forward in time to 'construct an inherited system of Chinese traditional culture and strengthen the preservation of cultural heritages' at the fifth Plenary Session of the 18th CPC Central Committee. Compilers of this book are answering the call of the Party with their actual actions. Just as the chief-editor Ms. Qin Pu said, 'It is important for researchers to deepen their research and for readers to widen their vision, to realize bronze drum and its culture—the important part of the history and culture of Maritime Silk Rode.'

Over the past few decades, Guangxi has made great contribution to protect, inherit and develop bronze drum cultures. I firmly believed, Guangxi will do more on the research of Bronze Drum Culture Circle that China as the core, and will play a more important role in presenting the splendid history and a present Maritime Silk Rode, in the open relationship and cooperation between China and ASEAN.

Wan Fubin
March 20th, 2017

前言

　　"弹指一挥间"，上世纪 80 年代初那次由广西牵头、国内 64 个收藏单位参与的全国铜鼓大调查已经过去了三十多年，因诸多原因其成果《中国古代铜鼓实测·记录资料汇编》在去年底终于公开出版，并给正在进行"第一次全国可移动文物普查"的相关博物馆在藏品信息录入时提供了重要参考。2014 年，在国家文物局和广西文物局的同意并资助下，广西民族博物馆会同中国古代铜鼓研究会、广西壮族自治区博物馆组织启动了为期三年包括国际相关收藏机构在内的"世界博物馆收藏铜鼓调查工程"。工程浩大，但千里之行始于足下，对广西境内国有单位收藏铜鼓的调查安排在了第一阶段。在被调查单位的积极响应和配合下，调查组紧凑有序并卓有成效地持续工作，全面调查工作在 2014 年底如期完成。本图集呈现的工作成果，对研究者深入研究和读者拓宽视野，认识海上丝绸之路历史与文化的重要组成部分之一——铜鼓历史及其文化，无疑是有帮助的。

　　对于广西的古代铜鼓，本图集以图文并茂的形式第一次正式向读者传递了它最全面和最新的信息：全世界收藏数量最多、种类最齐全、"大个子"最多；精选的代表性铜鼓具象；铜鼓特有的各种纹饰和立体雕塑装饰；针对性的研究介绍和全部铜鼓的"家"在何方。它对以往工作的最大弥补是，呈献了调查工作借助现代采集器材给予读者提供铜鼓的全彩真实图像与纹饰及雕塑装饰的立体感知，以及因分布全区而呈现的广西古代铜鼓文化的历史生态和今生归宿。关于铜鼓的研究和认识还有很多的方面有待深入和拓展，在这方面本图集将起到"工具"作用，读者可各取所需。

　　图集成果的得来是非常不容易的。广西的气候酷热，尤其是"夏天"漫长，参加调查的虽然大部分是 80 后，但还有三位年逾七十的老专家，群贤毕至，少长咸集。调查组对这项工程抱有很强的使命感，走遍广西铜鼓藏身之地，挥汗努力，尽可能不漏掉每个铜鼓的点滴信息，在室内整理、分类、合成中投入了大量的精力，综合过往成果，以求体系完备。这份成果是心血与汗水换来，弥足珍贵。"世界博物馆收藏铜鼓调查工程"还将继续，因涉及国内外大量收藏，需要耐心、合作和共享精神，要做大量的组织和协调工作。衷心祝愿国内与国际两个阶段的调查顺利，早出成果！

覃 溥

2015 年 9 月 7 日

Time flies. 30 years has passed since the investigation that was organized by Guangxi and taken by 64 domestic cultural institutes in 1980s'. As the achievement of this investigation, for many reasons, *Data Compilation of Chinese Ancient Bronze Drums Measurement* & Recording was eventually published at the end of last year, which provides an important reference to the relevant museums when they were recording information of collections during the first nations' investigation on portable antiquities. In 2014, agreed and founded by National Cultural Relics Bureau and Guangxi Cultural Relics Bureau, Anthropology Museum of Guangxi, The Chinese Association for Ancient Bronze Drums Research and Museum of Guangxi Zhuang Autonomous Region together launched an investigation project of worldwide museums' bronze drum collections, which involves many museums abroad and is predicted to take 3 years to be accomplished. The work is great and large. As the saying goes, "A journey of one thousand miles begins with one step", our first step is to investigate the bronze drum collection of all state-owned cultural institutes in Guangxi Province. Responded positively by these institutes and in close collaboration with them, the investigation team worked orderly, persistently and fruitfully on a compact schedule, and finished the work on time at the end of last year. That is undoubtedly very in time to present the fruits of the investigation in this book, for researchers and readers who want to deepen their studies and expand their visions on bronze drums' history and culture, as the important components of the history and culture of Maritime Silk Road.

This book delivers the most comprehensive and the newest information about Guangxi bronze drums with vivid images and detailed captions to the readers, with accurate data includes: Guangxi Province is the area which has the largest number of bronze drum collection, the most complete types and the largest number of huge drums; all specific information about the selected bronze drums; special decorations and statues; the targeted introduction on research and "the home" of all the bronze drums. Its' most efficient remedy to previous work is to present the colorful images of bronze drums and three-dimensional perceptions of decorations and statues, the historical ecosystem of Guangxi ancient bronze drums because of their province-wide distribution and the preservation situations of these drums to the readers, with the help of modern measuring and recording instruments. There are still lots of researches and knowledge about bronze drums waiting to be deepened and expanded, in this respect, this book will play a role as a "tool", providing what you need.

It was very hard to obtain this achievement. Guangxi has a very long, hot "summer". Even though most of the team members are born after 1980, there are 3 retired expert participants over 70 years old. They feel a very strong sense of mission of this project, went through every place where the bronze drums are preserved in Guangxi, endeavored to record every bit of information of the bronze drums, threw themselves into the reorganization, classification and photos combination, for the purpose to integrate previous fruits and make out a system. That makes the achievement very precious because of all participants' sweat and hard work. The investigation project of worldwide museums' bronze drum collections is to be continued, and it needs collaboration, patience, good control and coordination on the sharing of previous fruits because of involving other countries' institutes. Here, I sincerely wish the two investigative phrases—domestic and abroad—make smooth progress and succeed in research work early.

Qin Pu

September 7th, 2015

广西铜鼓概述

蒋廷瑜

铜鼓作为一种民族民间乐器，大约从公元前 8 世纪起，就在我国云南中部地区产生，嗣后随着民族的迁徙和民族间的文化交流，沿着大江大河分布到我国南方的广西、广东、海南、贵州、四川、重庆、湖南等省和东南亚地区许多国家。

广西历来是少数民族聚居区，壮、瑶、苗、侗及其他民族的先民，世世代代劳动、生息在这块富饶、美丽的土地上，创造了丰富的物质财富和精神财富，给我们留下许多珍贵的文化遗产。铜鼓是这些珍贵文化遗产中最令人敬仰和思慕的伟大杰作，是广西民族文化中最值得骄傲的一宗无价之宝。

广西是古代铜鼓历史文献最丰富、铜鼓收藏历史悠久、使用民族众多、分布面最广的最重要地区。

一、历史文献"史不绝书"

广西之有铜鼓，至少也有两千多年的历史了，田东县锅盖岭春秋战国时期墓葬中所出的铜鼓就是物证。《后汉书·马援列传》说，东汉初伏波将军马援南征交趾"得骆越铜鼓"，其事就可能发生在广西境内。自汉代以后，广西铜鼓之见于文献记载者，真可谓"史不绝书"。

《晋书·食货志》载：

孝武太元三年，诏曰："钱，国之重宝。小人贪利，销坏无已，监司当以为意。广州夷人，宝贵铜鼓，而州境素不出铜，闻官私贾人，皆于此下贪比输钱，斤两差重，以入广州，货与夷人，铸败作鼓。其重为禁制，得者科罪"。

这里讲的是，广州的少数民族"宝贵铜鼓"，由于大量铸造铜鼓，致使铜料乏缺，而"官私贾人"看准了这一点，把视之为"国之重宝"的铜钱运到广州，卖给他们，熔化了，用来铸作铜鼓。孝武帝即东晋司马曜，太元三年即公元 378 年。晋代的广州辖南海、郁林、苍梧、宁浦、高凉、晋宁等郡，包括今广西、广东的绝大部分地区。当时的所谓"夷人"就是生活在两广地区南部的少数民族。后世的考古资料表明，这些地区正是铜鼓分布集中的地区。

《陈书·欧阳頠传》曰：

梁左卫将军兰钦之少也，与頠相善，故頠常随钦征讨，……钦南征夷僚，擒陈文彻，所获不可胜计，献大铜鼓，累代所无，頠预其功。

《南史·欧阳頠传》也有与此相同的记载。

兰钦所征讨的"夷僚"就是《晋书·食货志》上提到的"广州夷人"，他们是拥有"大铜鼓"的民族。"夷僚"也称为"俚"，夷僚首领陈文彻在《梁书·兰钦传》中被称为"俚帅"。而裴渊《广州记》说："俚僚铸铜为鼓，鼓唯高大为贵，面阔丈余。"这种面阔"丈余"的大铜鼓，只有在广西、广东接境的云开大山区才有。所以，《广州记》、《晋书》、《陈书》、《南史》

说到的铜鼓都有广西的铜鼓。

《隋书·地理志》载：

> 自岭以南，二十余郡，……诸獠皆然，并铸铜为大鼓。初成，悬于庭中，置酒以招同类。
> 来者有富豪子女，则以金银为大钗，执以叩鼓。竟，乃留遗主人，名为铜鼓钗。俗好相杀，
> 多构仇怨，欲相攻，则鸣此鼓，到者如云。有鼓者号为都老，群情推服。

这里记载的是铸造铜鼓的一种仪式，存在这种仪式的地点是"自岭以南，二十余郡"，当然其中也包括广西各郡在内。铸铜为大鼓的"诸獠"也就是两广地区南部的少数民族。

唐昭宗时任广州司马的刘恂，到过广西的梧州、容州、廉州、邕州等地，写了《岭表录异》一书。书中记述了一面广西铜鼓：

> 咸通末，幽州张直方贬龚州刺史。到任后，修葺州城，因据土得一铜鼓。载以归京，到襄汉，
> 以为无用之物，遂舍于延庆禅院，用代木鱼，悬于斋室。

唐代的龚州在今广西平南县境，咸通末约公元874年前后。从这段记述可知，在9世纪时，广西已有铜鼓从地下出土的记录，这面铜鼓在当时运到湖北襄汉去了。

到宋代，广西铜鼓从地下出土的机会更多，已引起地方官吏和文人学士的重视。曾在桂林做过广南西路经略安抚使兼静江知府的范成大，在《桂海虞衡志》中说到："铜鼓，古蛮人所用，南边土中时有掘得者。"比范成大稍晚，做过桂林通判的周去非，在《岭外代答》中则把"南边"直接说成"广西"，说："广西土中铜鼓耕者屡得之"。周去非大概在广西亲眼见过不少铜鼓，对铜鼓做了仔细的观察，因而对铜鼓的形制、大小、纹饰能作出详细的描述：

> 其制正圆，而平其面，曲其腰，状若烘篮，又类宣座。面有五蟾，分踞其上。蟾皆累蹲，
> 一大一小相负也。周围款识，其圆纹为古钱，其方纹如织簟，或为人形，或如琰璧，或尖如浮图，
> 如玉林，或斜如象牙，如鹿耳。各以其环成章，合其众纹，大类细画圆阵之形，工巧微密，
> 可以玩好。铜鼓大者阔七尺，小者三尺。所在神祠佛寺皆有之，州县用以更点。……，亦
> 有极小铜鼓，方二尺许者，极可爱玩，类为士大夫搜求无遗矣。

广西出土铜鼓，还作为祥瑞载入《宋史·五行志》：

> 熙宁元年（1068）至元丰元年（1078），横州（今广西横县）共获古铜鼓一十七；元丰……
> （七年）十一月，宾州（今广西宾阳）获铜鼓一。

据《宋史》记载，宋太宗淳化元年（990）广西南丹州的少数民族首领莫洪皓派他的儿子莫淮通向宋王朝进贡方物，其贡品中有铜鼓3面。又据《玉海》记载，宋真宗景德元年（1004）广西象州也曾向中央王朝奉献过铜鼓。由此可见，广西铜鼓在宋代已进入当时的都城汴梁，即今河南开封。

明清以降，正史、野史、笔记、诗词歌赋中有关广西铜鼓的记载更是不胜枚举。明景泰三年（1452）在北流县铜鼓潭获一面铜鼓（光绪《北流县志》），弘治十三年（1494）在博白县马绿堡铜鼓湾又获一面铜鼓（道光《博白县志》）。万历十五年（1618）端阳日，在浔州（今桂平）铜鼓滩和白石山同时各获一面铜鼓（同治《浔州府志》）。清康熙四十年（1701）在岑溪六络山得一面铜鼓，雍正元年（1723）在岑溪封贵洞又得一面铜鼓（民国《岑溪县志》）。雍正八年（1730）在北流得一铜鼓（光绪《北流县志·古迹》），在桂平铜鼓滩又得一铜鼓（同治《浔州府志》）。雍正十年（1732）在玉林县六西村有铜鼓出土（光绪《郁林州志·金石》）。乾隆年间（1736—1795）在邕宁县（民国《邕宁县志》）、玉林北容山（光绪《郁林州志·金石》）也有铜鼓出土。嘉庆二年（1797）在北流石一里庞坡上出土铜鼓（光绪《北流县志·古迹》）、在藤县二十五都祝村出土铜鼓（同治《藤县志·杂记》）。嘉庆三年（1798）在钦州铜鼓岭出土铜鼓，嘉庆六年（1801）在钦州石滩村出土铜鼓（《廉州府志·金石》），嘉庆十年（1805年）在藤县随化里黄坡村出土铜鼓（同治《藤县志·杂记》）。道光元年（1821）在宾阳（民国《宾阳县志》）和博白三瑾堡、蟠龙山（道光《博白县志》），五年（1825）在宜山县交椅村铜鼓岩前田内（道光《庆远府志》），六年（1826）在北流县卞一里，十八年（1838）在北流县扶来里大伦村（《北流县志·古迹》），二十一年（1841）在玉林城荔枝根旺岭山旁（《郁林州志·金石》），二十五年（1845）在扶绥云横山（《同正县志》），二十六年（1846）在玉林腾龙堡，三十年（1850）在北流新圩（光绪《郁林州志·艺文》）也有铜鼓出土记录。同治七年（1868）在玉林镇武山，光绪初年（1875）在灵山牯牛峰，光绪二年（1876）在象州县（民国《象县志·铜鼓》），四至五年（1878—1979）在合浦县白龙烟墩岭下海滩（民国《合浦县志·金石》），二十年（1894）在灵山大化村（民国《灵山县志·金石》），二十四年（1898）在桂平县上秀里旺安村（民国《桂平县志·古迹》），宣统三年（1911）在灵山石塘练竹村（民国《灵山县志·金石》），在钦州（民国《钦县县志》），贵港（民国《贵县志·金石》），还有铜鼓出土的记录。

　　这些史籍，从不同角度记录了铜鼓的发现、使用、流传及其有关风俗民情，展现了广西铜鼓多彩多姿的艺术风貌。

　　二、公私收藏，洋洋大观

　　从地下出土的这些铜鼓，大都被认为是稀有之物，"非人间所宜私宝"（金锹《铜鼓记》）。在古代，出土的铜鼓大部分被没入省、府、州、县的署衙学宫，也有的流入神祠佛寺和士大夫私藏。正如清代平南县举人彭廷椿在一首诗里吟咏的："吾乡铜鼓委林莽，从祠野庙往往觏。"这也可以从各地地方志中看到。如北流县北的铜鼓潭在明弘治己未（1499）出一铜鼓，县人得之，送给苍梧制府。明嘉靖年间，广西南宁"城隍庙后寝有小铜鼓"（嘉靖《南宁府志·地理志》）。

梧州镇左廊悬挂一铜鼓（张穆《异闻录》），桂林府中有铜鼓（魏浚《西事珥》）。又如明万历四十五年（1617）端阳日，在桂平县白石山出土的铜鼓，献入浔州官府后，被放在府城的清风，同时在浔江铜鼓滩捞出的铜鼓，献入官府后被放入府城的文庙（乐明盛《浔州双获铜鼓记》）。徐霞客在南宁见府城城隍庙内有铜鼓，并说"闻制各道亦有一二"（《徐霞客游记》卷四上）。

清初，广西梧州府"旧有铜鼓十数面"（乾隆《梧州府志》）。雍正八年(1730)秋天，桂平浔江铜鼓滩又捞出一面铜鼓，被知府奉送给广西巡抚金鉷，金鉷将这面铜鼓带回桂林，放置在巡抚衙门，以壮军威。到嘉庆四年(1799)谢启昆任广西巡抚时，还专为这面铜鼓盖了一座铜鼓亭。乾隆五年（1740）七月，灵山县村民王邦俊挖获铜鼓，"解贮司库"。乾隆六年（1741）夏六月，合浦县藤黎村民谭海鳌刨获铜鼓，"藏学宫"（道光《廉州府志》）。道光五年（1825）宜山县交椅村民在铜鼓岩前的田内掘得一面铜鼓，太平墟人争购，经宜山县断令，将此铜鼓充公，抬到神庙安置。光绪年间两广盐运司知盐鹾梧州金武祥在《粟香随笔》中说："余道经合浦之六硍圩（今浦北县六硍镇）及博白之六凤圩，庙中皆有铜鼓。"

私家收藏铜鼓也渐成风气。光绪四、五年间，在合浦白龙城南门外烟墩岭脚先后挖出五面铜鼓，除一面送入白龙三清庙，一面给乾体天后宫外，另三面都被私人取走（民国《合浦县志》卷六）。光绪二十年（1894）灵山大化村人掘出铜鼓，被知县阮萃恩购去。宣统二年（1910）朱千岁坟铜鼓、高山大庙铜鼓和新圩文庙铜鼓，都被知县马维骢据为己有(民国《灵山县志》卷二十)。据罗振玉《俑庐日札》所载，周霭曾从广西岑溪得一铜鼓收藏。咸丰时，贺州信都兴安乡社洞村人柳家槐任西隆州（今隆林县）教谕时，从农民手中得一铜鼓，带回信都老家收藏（民国《信都县志》卷五）。据德国学者弗朗西·黑格尔托人在中国调查，梧州一位官员藏有铜鼓（《东南亚古代金属鼓》，1902 年莱比锡出版）。钦州大寺冯敏昌家藏铜鼓六七面，冯树荫堂、冯树茂堂、冯荣喜堂、冯坡研斋都有铜鼓（民国《钦县县志·金石》）。

只要稍稍翻阅广西的地方志，就可看到有清一代铜鼓散存于广西各地神佛寺的盛况。郁林一县（今属玉林市玉州区），城东印岭村寒山庙，城西南高沙堡流表村尚书庙，城西荔枝根蔻峒寺，城西北馒头圩金顺庙、文昌阁，城北旺水玉皇庙，谷山村三教堂、蒲堂寒山庙、抚康圆珠寺、豸塘岭北帝庙、石脚堡岩岭庙等，都有铜鼓（《郁林州志·铜鼓》）。北流县的扶来里城隍庙，波一里龙虎寨将军庙，石一里河村泗洲庵、下三里水埇村宝兔庵，卞一里岭峒龙山寺，沙坡村护龙寺，新圩玉虚宫，禄厚村三教堂，都有铜鼓（光绪《北流县志》）。平南县的乌江伏波庙、西村永隆寺、六乌圩庙、韦村庙、大中圩观音庙、蓝峒三甲庙等，也都有铜鼓（光绪《平南县志·金石略》）；博白县新文阁、攀龙庙（道光《博白县志·金石》），容县南门外水月宫（光绪《容县志·金石志》），桂平甘王庙（民国《桂平县志》），崇左城隍庙（雍正《太平府志·崇善古迹》），龙州玄协寺（民国《龙津县志·金石》）等，也有铜鼓；上林县的五显庙、三圣宫、三教寺、清平寺、莲花寺、演德庵，都藏有铜鼓（民国《上林县志·寺观》）。

辛亥革命以后，散见于各地寺庙的铜鼓更多，除上述一些寺庙里的铜鼓有的继续保存之外，还有北流北一里北容高山庙、罗片那排庵、下二里社峒水口禄隆寺、扶来大嵛冲天观、新圩小学等，也藏有铜鼓（民国《北流县志》）。陆川上垌庙（民国《陆川县志·坛庙》），贵县北里上龙寺、怀西里永兴寺（民国《贵县志·金石》），岑溪关帝庙、归义文庙、南渡邓公庙（民国《岑溪县志·杂记篇》），钦州文庙、马侯庙、李家祠（民国《钦州县志·金石》），灵山高山大庙、烟墩圩文武庙、茅金圩文武庙、新圩文武庙、平山练阳山盘古庙、镇南圩庙、宋泰练仇介祠、平力村福成六峰山三清殿（民国《灵山县志·金石类》），合浦福旺圩护民庙、白龙三清庙、天后宫（民国《合浦县志·金石·汉铜鼓》），防城清惠宫（民国《防城县志初稿·金石》），象州五显庙（民国《象县志·金石》），宾阳盐仓岭贤良祠（民国《宾阳县志》），隆安乔建圩雷霆庙（民国《隆安县志·古迹》）都有铜鼓收藏。

据广西省博物馆在 1935 年向 11 个县作的书面调查，当年尚存的铜鼓，桂林县有 7 面，天河县（今罗城县）有 3 面，邕宁县有 2 面，岑溪、陆川、桂平、融县（今融水）、凌云、西隆（今隆林）、凭祥县各有 1 面。

1949 年中华人民共和国成立后，人民政府高度重视少数民族的文化遗产，花了大量的人力、财力，将各地零星出土的或散存于民间的铜鼓认真搜集，妥善保管，并有档案记录，尤其一些考古发现更受到重视。1955 年为配合黎塘至湛江的铁路建设，考古工作者发掘广西贵县（今贵港市）古墓群，从贵县高中 8 号土坑木椁墓中挖出 1 面铜鼓；1972 年在西林县普驮粮站开辟晒场时掘出 4 面铜鼓；1976 年秋发掘贵县罗泊湾 1 号汉墓出土 3 面铜鼓（其中 1 面已改制成铜案）；1977 年在田东县祥周锅盖岭战国墓出土 1 面铜鼓；1991 年在贺县沙田乡（今贺州市八步区沙田镇）龙中村一岩洞葬中发现 1 面铜鼓；1993 年 3 月田东县祥周镇南哈坡战国早期墓出土 2 面铜鼓；1994 年 6 月田东县林逢镇大岭坡春秋晚期墓出土 1 面铜鼓。这两次发现的铜鼓都是万家坝型，填补了广西铜鼓类型的空白。

据不完全统计，到目前为止，收藏于广西各级文物管理部门的铜鼓总数已达 772 面，其中广西民族博物馆 345 面，广西壮族自治区博物馆 15 面，桂林博物馆 34 面，柳州市博物馆 38 面，百色右江革命文物馆 18 面，南宁市博物馆 17 面、贵港市博物馆 10 面，玉林市博物馆 9 面，钦州市博物馆 6 面，右江民族博物馆 5 面，梧州市博物馆、崇左市博物馆、北海市文物管理所各 3 面，贺州市博物馆 1 面，北流市博物馆馆 35 面，灵山县博物馆 26 面，桂平市博物馆 25 面，平南县博物馆 17 面，浦北县博物馆 17 面，陆川县文物管理所 12 面，藤县文物管理所 10 面，博白县博

物馆9面，上林县文物管理所、武鸣县文物管理所各7面，容县博物馆6面，西林县博物馆、象州县文物管理所、横县博物馆、隆林民族博物馆各5面，田东县博物馆、都安瑶族自治县文物馆、西林县博物馆、广西民族大学文物陈列室各4面，大新县博物馆、邕宁区文物管理所、宜州市文物管理所、鹿寨县文物管理所、岑溪市文物管理所、广西师范大学文物陈列室各3面，龙州博物馆、那坡县博物馆、合浦县博物馆、柳江县文物管理所、宾阳县文物管理所、苍梧县文物管理所、蒙山县文物管理所、龙胜各族自治县文物管理所、田阳县博物馆、乐业县文物管理所、上思县博物馆各2面，凌云县文物管理所、靖西县博物馆、马山县文物管理所、武宣县文物管理所、兴宾区文物管理所各1面。地下埋藏的铜鼓每年都有出土。而生活在广西境内的壮、瑶、苗、侗、彝等各少数民族人民至今仍在使用铜鼓。民间使用的铜鼓数量惊人，1991—1993年河池地区文物管理站组织所属11个县市的文物工作者作了一次民间传世铜鼓专题调查，登记到的传世铜鼓1417面。其中东兰县538面，南丹县380面，大化瑶族自治县247面，巴马瑶族自治县141面，天峨县41面，凤山县16面，都安瑶族自治县16面，罗城仫佬族自治县2面。田林、那坡等县民间也有铜鼓。每当欢度新春，或婚嫁丧祀之日，广西山区的许多村寨都会听到铜鼓声。

三、古往今来，多族共有

从使用铜鼓的民族来说，历史上生活在广西的民族，包括汉代及其以后的骆越、句町、乌浒、俚、僚，唐宋及其以后的壮、苗、瑶、彝、侗、水等，成分极为复杂。这些错综复杂的情况，给人呈现出各民族间经济、文化互相交融的多彩图景。

古代文献中最早提到铜鼓族属的当推《后汉书》。《后汉书·马援传》中说，马援"于交趾得骆越铜鼓"。马援所得铜鼓冠以"骆越"二字，表明这类铜鼓是从骆越人手上获得的，或者是骆越人制造或使用的铜鼓。万家坝型铜鼓和石寨山型铜鼓就是战国时期至汉代骆越人使用的铜鼓。

汉晋时代活跃在广西的乌浒人、俚人也铸造和使用铜鼓。乌浒又称乌浒蛮、乌蛮，是西瓯骆越人的后裔。李贤注《后汉书》集解沈钦韩曰："乌浒山在南宁府横州东南六十里，昔乌浒蛮所居之地。"明人魏浚《峤南琐记》说："异物志称，乌蛮在南海郡之西，安南都流司之北，即乌浒蛮也。"乌浒的活动，主要见于东汉时期。乌浒人有使用铜鼓的习俗。俚人是东汉至南北朝时期岭南地区的民族。史籍中常以"俚僚"称之。岭南地区的俚僚，实际上就是俚人。俚是由乌浒发展而来的。乌浒—俚人铸造和使用的铜鼓应是北流型铜鼓和灵山型铜鼓。同时期生活在郁江—浔江流域的夷僚使用冷水冲型铜鼓。

隋唐五代广西的少数民族被称为夷、蛮，主要铸造和使用遵义型、麻江型铜鼓。明清以后当地民族仍使用铜鼓，壮族的青蛙节，彝族的跳弓节，瑶族的祝著节，白裤瑶族的砍牛送葬，等等，都是使用铜鼓传统习俗的历史长河沉淀下来的"活化石"。

四、沿江分布，覆盖全区

铜鼓在广西境内分布广泛。桂东南、桂西南各县都有铜鼓流传和使用，桂东北自贺州、昭平、蒙山以南都有铜鼓出土，桂西北自龙胜、三江沿桂黔、桂滇边境各县，晚近时期仍有不少民族使用铜鼓。只有桂北少数几个县不是铜鼓的分布区。出土铜鼓最密集的地区是玉林、贵港、钦州、南宁，梧州南部、来宾、柳州等地区，传世铜鼓最多的是河池和百色。

战国时期的铜鼓在广西境内主要分布在右江流域，集中在骆越人活动的田东县。汉代铜鼓则沿南盘江、右江东下，到达郁江、浔江流域，分布于西林、隆林、百色、贵港、桂平、藤县。三国两晋南北朝至隋唐是广西铜鼓大发展时期，铜鼓遍布广西各地，形成浔江两岸、云开大山区、六万大山区几个分布中心，巨形铜鼓竞相鼓铸。宋以后铜鼓文化向西转移，回流到河池、百色，积淀于红水河流域。

铜鼓地名大都因出土铜鼓而得。清屈大均《广东新语》说：廉州有铜鼓塘，钦州有铜鼓村，灵山有铜鼓岭，文昌万州亦有铜鼓岭，"皆以掘得铜鼓而名"。桂平的铜鼓滩，宋代已有其名，明万历四十五年（1617）、清雍正八年（1730）渔人又两次从其滩捞出铜鼓；称它为铜鼓滩，更是名副其实。北流的铜鼓潭，因明景泰三年（1452）出过铜鼓，博白的铜鼓湾，因在明弘治十二年（1499）乡人于其地获一铜鼓而得名。钦州的铜鼓岭，因嘉庆二年（1798）在岭下掘得铜鼓。宜州的铜鼓岩，因清代村民在岩前田内掘得铜鼓等等。

灵山县现有铜鼓地名 23 处，其中铜鼓村 3 处、铜鼓塘村 2 处、铜鼓塘 5 处、铜鼓岭 5 处、铜鼓麓 2 处、铜鼓顶、铜鼓江、铜鼓湾、铜鼓滩各 1 处，都因出土铜鼓得名。平南县现有铜鼓地名 7 处，其中铜鼓村 2 处、铜鼓塘 2 处、铜鼓岭 2 处、铜鼓脚 1 处，也因曾出土铜鼓得名。

广西铜鼓很大部分有明确的发现地点。有的有丰富的共存遗物，有的有明显的年代标识，为铜鼓的断代提供了可靠的标尺。

1993 年 4 月在田东县祥周镇联福村联合小学大门前南哈坡发现二面原始形态铜鼓，伴出铜罍一件和铜錾钉、玉管、玉玦、玉钏等物，可断定为战国时代早期；1994 年 6 月在田东县林逢镇和同村大坡岭发现一面原始形态铜鼓，同出一件春秋战国时期的越式甬钟，也可以作断代依据。

1977 年在田东县祥周锅盖岭出土一面残铜鼓，伴出有铜剑、铜戈、铜矛、铜斧等，其中剑、戈、矛都有明显的时代特征，可以推定这些器物同出于一座战国时代墓；1991 年 7 月在贺州市沙田镇龙中村的红朱岩出土一面饰船纹和牛纹的石寨山型铜鼓，同出铜牺尊、铜兽首盉、蟠螭纹铜罍、铜箕形器、风字形铜钺、铜环形器、铜鼎、勾形器、叉形器等，可以断定其年代为战国晚期。1976 年秋在贵县罗泊湾一号墓出土完整的铜鼓二面和已改制成铜案的铜鼓一面，与它们共存的遗物一千多件，可以确定这座墓的时代为西汉前期。1972 年在西林县普驮屯出土铜鼓四面，同时伴出青铜器，玉石器 400 多件，通过对比研究，确定它们属西汉前期。1955 年春，在贵县高中一座土坑木椁墓出土铜鼓一面，同出的随葬品有铜壶、铜鉴、铜博山炉、铜戟、陶壶、五珠钱等，可以确定为西汉晚期。

1953 年在岑溪县城出土一面鼓面和鼓身都印制有五珠钱纹带的北流型铜鼓，可为同类铜鼓的断代作参考；1970 年在横县云表六合村凤山出土一面北流型铜鼓，鼓内有南朝黄釉陶瓷碎片；1975 年 3 月玉林镇新民村东南出土一面北流型铜鼓，内有一件隋唐时期的敞口铜锅。

1962 年在灵山县绿水村出土一面灵山型铜鼓，鼓内有一枚唐代"开元通宝"钱，说明这面铜鼓是唐代开元年间或其以后才埋入地下的。

1975 年 1 月在藤县濛江镇冷水冲出土一面铜鼓，鼓内有一件复系四耳陶罐，这种陶罐在广西东汉早期墓葬中也有出土，可以推定这面铜鼓是东汉初期或其后入土的；1982 年桂平县金田乡理村出土一面冷水冲型铜鼓，鼓内放置四件铜洗，内底饰有东汉流行的双鱼纹；1991 年 10 月桂平县木根镇秀南村出土一面冷水冲型大铜鼓，腹内倒置一件饰弦纹和水波纹四系灰陶罐，时代为东汉晚期至南朝之间；1956 年在金秀瑶族自治县平道乡出土一面冷水冲型铜鼓，鼓内有一件南朝时期的陶碗；1997 年 2 月横县附城镇清江村村民在清江打捞出一面冷水冲型铜鼓，腹内置一件隋唐时期的六系陶罐。

这些都可以作断代的参考。有的麻江型铜鼓上还有年款铭文，如"道光年建立"、"道光二年建立"、"道光六年建立"，"道光八年建立"等等，更能确定它们铸造和流行的时代。

如果将出土铜鼓和流传铜鼓的地点填入广西地图，铜鼓分布面几乎覆盖了整个广西，若以县、市（区）为单位计算，曾经出土或使用过铜鼓的县、市（区）已达 85 个，占总数 80％。宋代以前的铜鼓，以左江—邕江—郁江—浔江两岸及其以南地区最集中，宋代及其以后各个时期的铜鼓，多集中于桂西和桂黔、桂滇交界的大山区，只有桂东北角少数几个县与铜鼓无缘。

五、品类齐全，争芳斗艳

自 20 世纪 80 年代以来，我国学者将中国境内的铜鼓划分为两大系统 8 个类型，分别称为滇桂系统万家坝型、石寨山型、冷水冲型、遵义型和麻江型，粤桂系统北流型、灵山型、西盟型。滇桂系统是指分布在云南、广西、贵州、四川、湖南的铜鼓；粤桂系统是指分布于广东、广西、海南的铜鼓。广西西靠云南，东联广东，两个系统 8 个类型的铜鼓兼而有之。

（一）万家坝型铜鼓

万家坝型铜鼓，以云南省楚雄万家坝春秋战国时期墓葬出土的一批铜鼓为代表，是原始形态的铜鼓。鼓面特别小，鼓胸特别外凸，鼓腰极度收束，鼓足很矮，但足径大，足沿内有一周折边，胸腰之际有四只小扁耳；花纹特点是简单、古朴，有一种稚拙味，给予人以稳重感。鼓面的太阳纹有的仅有光体而无光芒，有的有光芒，而芒数无定。鼓胸和鼓足都素面无纹，腰部也只是由几条纵线划分成几个空格。这类铜鼓主要流行于春秋战国时期。广西田东县林逢镇和同村大岭坡、田东县祥周镇联福村南哈坡都出土过这类铜鼓。

（二）石寨山型铜鼓

以云南省晋宁石寨山汉代墓葬出土的一批铜鼓为代表，是成熟期铜鼓。这类铜鼓面部宽大，胸部突出，腰部呈梯形，足部短而直，布局对称，纹饰丰富华丽。鼓面中心是太阳纹，光体与光芒浑然一体，三角光芒之间填以斜线，太阳纹之外是一道道宽窄不等的晕圈，窄晕中饰锯齿纹、圆圈纹、点纹等构成的花纹带。宽晕是主晕，饰以旋转飞翔的鹭鸟。胸部也饰与面部相同的几何纹带，其主晕则是人物划船的写实画像。腰部除晕圈组成的纹带之外，还有由竖直纹带分隔成的方格，方格中饰以牛纹或用羽毛装饰的人跳舞的图像。此类铜鼓造型较雄伟，而纹饰刻划细腻。贵港罗泊湾西汉墓、西林普驮西汉铜鼓墓出土的铜鼓都属此类，田东祥周、百色龙川、隆林共和也出土过此类铜鼓。此类铜鼓流行年代是从战国时期至东汉初期，前后延续了大约500多年。

（三）冷水冲型铜鼓

以藤县濛江乡横村冷水冲出土的铜鼓为代表，是发展期铜鼓。这类铜鼓体型高大轻薄，鼓面宽大，但不出沿或稍稍出沿。鼓胸略大于面径或与面径相等，稍微膨胀，不很凸出，鼓腰上部略直，最小径在中部，鼓足较高，与胸部高度略等，鼓耳宽扁，饰辫纹，有的在四耳之外，还有半圆茎拱形小耳一对。纹饰总的特点是瑰丽而繁缛。鼓面中心太阳纹基本固定为12芒，芒间夹实心双翎眼坠形纹，鼓面边沿有立体青蛙，有的在青蛙之间再饰马、骑士、牛橇、水禽、龟、鱼等动物塑像，鼓面、鼓身遍布各种图案花纹。鼓面主晕为高度图案化的变形翔鹭纹，有一晕勾连雷纹及由此衍变而来的复线交义纹。鼓胸多有图案化的变形船纹，鼓腰有变形舞人图案和细方格纹，鼓足多有圆心垂叶纹，这些都是匠人精雕细刻的结果，有着一种纤巧的美。冷水冲型铜鼓以桂平、平南、藤县一带最集中，分布于邕江—郁江—浔江—西江两岸，遍布大半个广西。流行年代为东汉晚期至隋唐，以两晋南朝时期最为繁盛。

（四）遵义型铜鼓

以贵州省遵义市南宋播州土司杨粲夫妇墓出土的铜鼓为代表。这类铜鼓的特点，鼓面无蛙，面沿略伸于鼓颈之外，面径、胸径、足径相差甚微；胸、腰、足各部的高度相当接近，胸腰间缓慢收缩，无明显分界线，胸腰际附大跨度扁耳两对，鼓面边缘无青蛙塑像，但有蛙趾装饰。纹饰简单，几何纹用同心圆纹、连续角形图案、羽状纹、雷纹构成，主纹则是一种由一个圆圈缀两条飘动的带子组成的游旗纹。此类铜鼓数量较少，主要发现于贵州、云南，广西也有出土。

（五）麻江型铜鼓

以贵州省麻江县谷峒火车站一座古墓中出土的铜鼓为代表。这类铜鼓的特点是，体形小而扁矮，鼓面略小于鼓胸，面沿微出于颈外，鼓身胸、腰、足间的曲线柔和，无分界标志，腰中部起凸棱一道，将鼓身分为上下两节，胸部有大跨度的扁耳两对。现在民间使用的铜鼓绝大多数都是麻江型铜鼓。

（六）北流型铜鼓

以北流出土的铜鼓为代表。这类铜鼓，形体硕大厚重，鼓面宽大，边缘伸出鼓颈之外，有的边缘下折成"垂檐"，胸壁斜直外凸，最大径偏下，腰呈反弧形收束，胸腰间斜度平缓，只有一道凹槽分界，腰足间以一道凸棱分界，鼓足外侈，与面径大小相当，鼓耳结实，多为圆茎环耳，鼓面青蛙塑像小而朴实，太阳纹圆凸如饼，以八芒居多，装饰纹样多为云雷纹。在西方学者的分类系统中，把这类铜鼓列为Ⅱ型。以高大著称，原存北流县六靖乡水埇庵的大铜鼓面径165厘米，残重299千克，是迄今所知最大的一面铜鼓，被誉为"铜鼓之王"。上海博物馆所藏6597号铜鼓面径145厘米，高78.8厘米，排列第2；广州南海神庙铜鼓，面径138厘米，高77.4厘米，列为第3；桂平麻垌小学铜鼓，面径137.8厘米，高72.5厘米，列为第4；玉林、北流、平南都出土过面径超过122.2厘米的北流型大铜鼓。鼓面大于鼓身，鼓面边缘都伸出鼓胸之外，其中很大一部分北流铜鼓的边缘下折，形成"裙边"（垂檐）。腰胸之际都有两对提耳，除了少数也是扁耳外，绝大多数为圆茎环耳。耳身是实心圆柱形，呈环状或半环状固定在胸腰之间，耳身表面饰一道道细密的缠丝纹，脊背上凸起有节，粗看象蛇，有人称之为蛇纹环耳。耳根饰有三爪，增加了与鼓身的接触面。环耳比起扁耳来，更为强固有力，有的铜鼓除了两对环耳之外，还在相对应的位置上另铸两只小环耳。鼓面中心受击处的太阳纹，光体都呈圆饼状突起。光芒辐射四出，细长如针，常常穿透一二道晕圈，有的芒端还开叉。光芒的道数，绝大部分为8芒，极少数为12芒、10芒、6芒的。鼓面和鼓身的纹饰分晕，都以三道弦纹为一组来分隔，一般来说，鼓面晕圈宽而疏朗，晕圈宽窄相等，少数略有宽窄之分；鼓身晕圈则窄而密集，也是宽窄相等。无论鼓面和鼓身，晕圈内的纹样主要是以单线或复线圆圈、方格、菱格、三角、半圆以及圆点、圆涡、斜方格、方勾等等为基础的多种形式的云雷纹。流行于汉至唐代，主要分布于广西的东南部和广东的西南部以及海南，范围十分集中，以今日广西玉林地区为其分布中心，次为广西钦州地区和广东湛江地区，特别是以广西北流和广东信宜为中心的云开大山区的几个县最为密集，云开大山区是北流型铜鼓的大本营。

（七）灵山型铜鼓

以灵山县出土的铜鼓为代表。形制接近北流型，外观上，体型凝重，形象精巧。鼓面平展，稍广于或等于鼓身，边缘伸出，但不下折，胸壁微凸，最大径居中；胸以下逐渐收缩成腰；胸腰间仅以细线为界；附于胸腰之际的鼓耳均为带状叶脉纹扁耳；鼓面所饰青蛙塑像都是后面两足并拢为一的"三足蛙"，蛙背上饰划线纹或圆涡纹，装饰华丽，有的青蛙背上又有小青蛙，即成"累蹲蛙"；青蛙的数目一般为6只，有的6只全是累蹲蛙，但大多数3只单蛙与3只累蹲蛙相间排列，而且绝大多数为逆时针方向环列；鼓面中心太阳纹光体圆凸如饼，光芒细长如针，芒数不一，但以10芒和12芒为多，也有7芒、8芒、9芒、11芒的，有的芒端开叉；装饰花纹多以二弦分晕，鼓面和身各有三道较宽的主晕，以骑兽纹、兽形纹、鹭鸟纹（或鹭鸶含鱼纹、鸟形纹）为主体纹样，其他晕圈云纹、雷纹、半圆纹、半圆填线纹、席纹、四瓣花纹、"四出"钱纹、连钱纹、虫形纹、水波纹、蝉纹等；蝉纹一般作边饰。其中一些鼓的鼓耳下方接近鼓足处，装饰动物塑像，常见的是一对（或一只）小鸟，也有饰牛、羊等动物塑像者，这些动物都是头朝下。流行的年代是汉至唐代，主要分布中心是灵山县及与之毗邻的横县和浦北县，即六万大山西侧至郁江横县段的两岸。在此范围之外，只有零星散布。散布范围，最东到高州，南到合浦，西到上思在妙、龙州武德，在越南谅山也有出土；北到桂平大洋。这个分布带，正是北流型铜鼓分布区的西侧和冷水冲型铜鼓分布区的西南方，是晋、南朝至唐代乌浒—俚人活动的地盘。

（八）西盟型铜鼓

以云南省西盟佤族地区仍在使用的铜鼓为代表。这类铜鼓器身轻薄，形体高瘦，鼓面宽大，边沿向外伸出，鼓身为上大下小的直筒形，胸、腰、足没有分界线，鼓面太阳纹一般为8芒或12芒，三弦分晕，晕圈多而密，纹饰多小鸟、鱼、圆形多瓣的团花、米粒纹。鼓面有立体青蛙，常见二蛙或三蛙甚至四蛙叠踞。有的鼓身纵列立体的象、螺蛳、玉树等塑像。黑格尔称为Ⅲ型鼓。他说："人们可以把它叫作克伦鼓，因为所有的Ⅲ型鼓都是来自后印度的红、白克伦族，但也许更确切地说，它应该叫掸型。大量消息说明这些鼓是当时印度支那的掸邦制造的。"但他不知道中国境内也有这种鼓。广西只有龙州、靖西靠近中越边境地区出土过这类铜鼓的早期类型。

这八个类型中，冷水冲型、北流型、灵山型三个类型是以广西出土地名命名的，而且以广西为分布重心。

在两千多年铜鼓发展的历史长河中，广西铜鼓在整个铜鼓大家族中占据何种地位呢？如果说，云南中部偏西地区因为出土了大量时代古老、形态古朴的原始类型铜鼓，而被确认为古代铜鼓的发祥地的话，那么地处五岭之南，连接云贵高原与南海之滨的广西，因其蕴藏铜鼓数量之、类型之全，而称之为古代铜鼓的大本营，也应是当之无愧的。

六、铜鼓研究，硕果累累

如此丰富的铜鼓资料，早已引起民族学、考古学方面的重视。明清以来的地方志书，很注意铜鼓资料的搜集和记录，不少修志者对当地的铜鼓作过细心观察，并将观察到的现象忠实记录下

来，对有关传闻和文献广泛搜罗，认真辑录，保存了许多珍贵的资料。清嘉庆年间做广西巡抚的谢启昆，在编修《广西通志》时，亲自撰写了《粤西金石略》一书，其中专辟《铜鼓考》一章，辑录了许多铜鼓文献，对当时流行的铜鼓首创于马援或者诸葛亮的说法提出异议，指出："自石湖（案：即宋代范成大）有'伏波所遗'一语，后人遂误为伏波所制，且因伏波附会于诸葛，至谓大者为伏波鼓，小者为诸葛鼓，真误中之误矣。"为了观察铜鼓，谢启昆还在巡抚衙署旁边盖了一座铜鼓亭，把雍正八年（1730）从桂平浔江铜鼓滩捞出来的铜鼓放在亭中，并写了一首长达58句的《铜鼓歌》，刻石嵌在墙上。这首《铜鼓歌》也就是对铜鼓有关知识的宣传。道光十七年（1837）新任广西巡抚梁章钜又将桂林知府许芳友所献铜鼓并列亭中，并拓取《铜鼓歌》诗刻，邀约同僚部属次韵长歌，前后和诗者四十余人，辑录成一部《铜鼓联吟集》，对铜鼓的来源、用途作了探讨。

1933年，民族学家刘锡蕃将他在苗山见到铜鼓的事写入《岭表纪蛮》一书。

民族学家徐松石在1927年、1935年和1938年，多次到广西各地考察，目验铜鼓五十多面，1938年冬出版《粤江流域人民史》，书中专辟第二十二章为《铜鼓研究》。对铜鼓的起源、创始铜鼓的民族、铜鼓的用途和铜鼓出土的情况，作了简略的介绍。徐松石认为铜鼓是壮族的祖先骆越人在秦汉之间创造的。后来他又在《泰族僮族粤族考》中专辟一节为"铜鼓与岭南僮族"，坚持"铜鼓乃岭南僮族所创造"的观点。

1943年，陈志良查遍了广西的省、府、县志，并向少数民族青年调查过铜鼓的使用情况，发表长文《铜鼓研究发凡——广西古代文化探讨之一》，列举18个县份中的铜鼓资料，对使用铜鼓的民族，对铜鼓的形状、纹饰和虾蟆塑像都有专门的分析。他认为铜鼓并非铸于一时，历代都有制造，现代主要用于祭祀和娱乐。

1948年《宾阳县志》刊出朱昌奎《铜鼓考》，说他在做罗城知县时，深入瑶山，与诸苗瑶来往极密，见其宴会祭祀，均用铜鼓、杂吹芦笙以助兴。他认为铜鼓是苗瑶酋长所有物，谓为伏波、孔明鼓者，均不足置信。同年《防城县志稿》作者对铜鼓也发表不少议论，其中谈到铜鼓的用途，他反对军用说，认为铜鼓实为民间通用之物，自古南方信巫鬼，铸鼓为祭祀用，而祀田祖用之尤为普遍。耕稼社会开始之时，岁时祈祷丰稔。……特以南徼烟瘴潮湿，皮鼓润软而声不亮，祀神乐器特创制铜鼓以利用。南徼渔猎演进而耕稼之时，陇亩之间，处处祈年，故处处有鼓。

1949年，中华人民共和国成立，为铜鼓研究开创了新局面。1955年2—3月，广西省文物管理委员会在贵县中学高中部发现一座汉代木椁墓，在墓坑内左边与铜壶、釜、盒、博山炉、陶坛、长颈瓶一起有一面铜鼓。鼓面完整，鼓身已残。这是考古工作者第一次发掘到铜鼓，意义非同寻常。1955年《文物参考资料》第7期发表谭毅然的报道《广西贵县古墓中发现铜鼓》，公布了鼓面拓本。接着黄增庆在《考古通讯》1956年第4期发表《广西贵县汉木椁墓清理简报》，详细报道这座墓的情况，也公布了铜鼓鼓面拓本。《考古学报》1957年第1期发表广西省文物管理委员会的《广西贵县汉墓的清理》，又公布了这面铜鼓的鼓面拓本，并把它的年代定在东汉时期。

1962年7月，云南大学历史系教授江应梁来南宁，参观了广西壮族自治区博物馆库房中的铜鼓，深感这些铜鼓是广西地方民族历史文化中的一宗无价之宝，于是撰文在《广西日报》发表，呼吁各界珍视广西出土的铜鼓。建议政府订出计划，拨出专款搜集铜鼓，鼓励学术界从事铜鼓研究。1963年春，著名历史学家、考古学家郭沫若来南宁出席广西历史学会成立大会，参观了广西壮族自治区博物馆的馆藏铜鼓，填写了著名的《满江红》词，称"铜鼓云屯，欣赏了壮家文化"。同来的著名历史学家、北京大学副校长翦伯赞在广西历史学会成立大会作报告时也强调广西博物馆收集的数以百计的各式各样的铜鼓和新发现的花山壁画，是研究广西境内少数民族历史最珍贵的资料，建议绘成图谱，早日出版。这些都鼓舞着民族学、考古学、历史学工作者投身铜鼓研究。

1964年黄增庆发表《广西出土铜鼓初探》，将广西铜鼓区分为四大类型，分属两个系统：一个以云雷纹发展到虫鸟花纹为主；一个以鹭纹、羽人纹发展到游旗纹、十二生肖纹为主。指出两个系统分布地区不同，可能分别属于两个不同的部族。

1972年秋，广西壮族自治区博物馆组织专题研究，写出《广西古代铜鼓研究》一文，对广西古代铜鼓的研究作了科学的总结，就广西铜鼓的发现、类型、历史分期和年代，广西铜鼓的系统、纹饰和铜鼓的作用，作了精辟的论述。将广西铜鼓分为4型20式。甲型，即后来通行的北流型；乙型，即后来通行的灵山型；丙型，分为7式，其中Ⅰ、Ⅱ式即石寨山型，Ⅲ式至Ⅴ式是冷水冲型，Ⅵ、Ⅶ式为遵义型；丁型，即后来通称的麻江型。

1980年3—4月在南宁召开了第一次古代铜鼓学术讨论会，与会学者全面讨论了铜鼓的起源、分类、分布、年代、族属、用途等问题，会后出版了《古代铜鼓学术讨论会论文集》，同时出版了蒋廷瑜《铜鼓史话》通俗读物。1988年10月中国古代铜鼓研究会编著的《中国古代铜鼓》出版，全面、系统地论述了中国古代铜鼓的起源、类型、分布、年代、族属、纹饰、用途和铸造工艺等问题。同时出版了蒋廷瑜著《铜鼓艺术研究》，对铜鼓的造型艺术、雕塑艺术、画像艺术、宗教意识、世俗观念、汉字铭文、音乐、舞蹈等专题都有深刻的阐述。

1988年底在昆明举行的中国南方及东南亚地区古代铜鼓和青铜文化国际会议，姚舜安、蒋廷瑜、万辅彬宣读了《论灵山型铜鼓》论文，1990年12月出版了姚舜安、万辅彬、蒋廷瑜合著《北流型铜鼓探秘》。1991年广西壮族自治区博物馆编辑出版了《广西铜鼓图录》，广西收藏铜鼓得到全面公布。

1992年10月万辅彬等著《中国古代铜鼓科学研究》出版，是主要从自然科学的角度研究铜鼓的第一本著作。随后出版蒋廷瑜《古代铜鼓通论》、《壮族铜鼓研究》、《铜鼓文化》、《大器铜鼓》等专著。广西铜鼓研究在国内外处于领先水平。

铜鼓是铸造和使用铜鼓的民族的综合艺术品，它从各个不同侧面，反映了这些民族历史上在冶金、铸造、音乐、美术、舞蹈、宗教等经济、科技和文化方面的成就，是研究这些民族历史的"百科全书"。

广西成为各种类型铜鼓的荟萃之地，铜鼓数量之众多，品类之齐全，资料之丰富，已为世人所瞩目。

铜鼓以它深藏着的无穷奥秘不断诱发人们去思考和探索，使得一代又一代的专门学者为它上下求索。正因为如此，铜鼓研究的课题始终充满魅力，一直延续下去，将成为千古常青的话题。

Jiang Tingyu

An Overview of Guangxi Bronze Drums

As a folk musical instrument of minorities, bronze drum has its' origin in central Yunnan province about 800 B.D ago, and then scattered to southern areas of China, such as Guangxi, Guangdong, Hainan, Guizhou, Sichuan, Chongqing, Hunan, and many countries of south-east Asia along with long big rivers as well as ethnic migration and interchange.

Guangxi has historically been the habitation of ethnic groups like Zhuang, Yao, Miao, Dong and other people who lived and worked on this beautiful and fertile land for generations, created plentiful material and spiritual wealth, left behind lots of precious heritages. Bronze drums are the most respectable and admirable masterpieces of it all, the invaluable assets to be mostly proud of as part of Guangxi ethnic culture.

Guangxi is the most important area for its most abundant historical documents, the long history of collecting, the plentiful ethnic users and the widest distribution area, of bronze drums.

I Guangxi bronze drums were recorded in numerous historical documents.

Guangxi has a two-millennium history of bronze drums, witnessed by a bronze drum which was unearthed in the tombs at Guogai Ling, Tiandong County, made during Spring and Autumn to Warring States Period. According to *The Book of Later Han•Collected Biographies of Ma Yuan*, at the beginning of East-Han Dynasty, General "Wave-Conquer" Ma Yuan fought battles in the south and got a bronze drum at Jiaozhi, where the book means probably Guangxi. From Han Dynasty, there were numerous records about Guangxi bronze drums on historical documents.

According to *The Book of Jin Dynasty•Monograph on Food and Currency*, ethnics in Guangzhou treasured bronze drums very much, and made bronze drums in large quantities. Soon the copper was short of and that provided a chance to the copper dealers, they transferred bronze coins that were treasured by the government to Guangzhou, sold them to the ethnics to melt and made bronze drums. It took place in 378 A.D, during the Empire Xiaowu regime of Dong Jin Dynasty(Empire Xiaowu was also named Sima Yao). At that time, Guangzhou governed many counties like Nanhai, Yulin, Cangwu, Ningpu, Gaoliang and Jinning, including most regions of nowadays Guangxi and Guangdong Province. Yi people was the ethnic who lived in the southern regions of Guangxi and Guangdong. According to the subsequent documents, these regions above were the intensive distribution areas of bronze drums.

The Book of Chen Dynasty•Biography of Ouyang Wei and *The History of Southern Dynasty•Biography of Ouyang Wei* told a same story: When Lan Qin, the Genenal Zuowei of Liang Dynasty was young, Ouyang Wei was treated good by him, so they used to fought battles together. Lan Qin fought battles with Yi and Liao people and captured their chief Chen Wenche. They gained countless spoils of war and parts of them were huge bronze drums that had been never seen, and of course, Ouyang Wei also made contributions to this.

The people Yi and Liao,ethnics conquered by Lan Qin, were Guangzhou Yi people who was mentioned in *The Book of Jin Dynasty•Monograph on Food and Currency* and owed the huge bronze drums. Yi and

Liao had the other name Li, and their chief Chen Wenche was called Marshal Li in *The Book of Liang Dynasty•Biography of Lan Qin*. And in the book *Annals of Guangzhou*, wrote by Pei Yuan, Li and Liao melt copper to made drums, and only the huge one was treasured, which usually with a big wide drum face. Those huge drums with big wide face were only discovered in Yunkai Mountainous Area where the junction of Guangxi and Guangdong. Part of the bronze drums mentioned in *Annals of Guangzhou, The Book of Chen Dynasty, The History of Nan Dynasty* were Guangxi bronze drums.

One ceremony of casting bronze drums was put down in *The Book of Sui Dynasty•Geography:* The ceremony was held in more than twenty counties where in the south to Wuling, including all counties of Guangxi. All of Liao people who cast big drums were ethnics in south regions of Guangxi and Guangdong. Liao people cast and hung big bronze drums in the middle of their yell, prepared a feast to entertain people who had the same customs. Among those people, rich people preferred to click the drum with a big golden or silver hair-pin named Bronze Drum Pin, and left it to the feast host. Liao people had a custom of fights, which made them many enemies. When they wanted to attack each other, they beat drums and soon people crowded. The person who owed bronze drum was called Du Lao, admired by others beyond any doubts.

Liu Xun, the chief executive of Guangzhou during the reign of Emperor Tang Zhaozong, had been to Wuzhou, Rongzhou, Liangzhou and Yongzhou of Guangxi, wrote a book named *Strangeness in Wuling Region,* recorded a story of bronze drum in it:

At the end of Xiantong Emperor's reign, Zhangzhifang, the executive of Youzhou, was demoted Cishi to Gongzhou. After he took office, he made the city-wall repaired and dug out a bronze drum. He carried it to the capital, but it was thought useless and hung in the feast chamber of Yanqing Buddhist Hall for the substitute of woodblock in Xianghan.

In the story, Gongzhou was a county name in Tang Dynasty and now Pingnan County, Guangxi, at the end of Xiantong Emperor's reign(about 874A.D.). According to the story, in 9 centuries A.D., there already were records about unearthed bronze drum and it was transferred to Xianghan, Hubei Province. In Song Dynasty, more bronze drums were unearthed in Guangxi, and that caused the attention of local government officials and scholars. Fan Chengda, who once was the chief official of Guangnan Xilu and Jingjiang, Guilin, said in his book *Customs of Guilin(Chinese name GUI HAI YU HENG ZHI):* bronze drums were used by ethnics in ancient time and often be dug out in the earth of southern region. After him, Zhou Qufei, once the important official of Guilin, took the 'southern region' as 'Guangxi' in his book *Question and Answers on Wuling Region(Chinese name LING WAI DAI DA),* and said bronze drums were often dug out by farmers in Guangxi. Probably Zhou had seen many bronze drums by himself in Guangxi, he did a carefully observation on bronze drums, and made the detail narrations about the shape, size and patterns:

The drums were round, with a flat face, curving waist, like a basket or a stool. Five frogs on the drum face at five corners. The frogs were all overlap and the small one was on the bigger one. Motifs around the body includes round coins, square mats, or sharp human-like motifs, jade, pagoda and stone forest, or ivories and deer horns. Different motifs were connected end-to-end into rings, exquisite and close-set, good for enjoying the sight of them. The big bronze drum was of a diameter over 7 Chi(one kind of length UOM in ancient China,1Chi=31CM), and the small one is of a diameter of 3 Chi. They were kept in every ancestral temple or Buddhist temple, and were used to announce time in prefectures and counties. There were also some tiny bronze drums with a 2 Chi diameter collected and toyed preciously by literati and officialdom.

Furthermore, unearth a bronze drum was thought as the lucky sigh in Guangxi, that was wrote down in *The History of Song Dynasty•Chorography of The Five Elements:* From the reign years of Xining to Yuanfeng (1068-1078 A.D.), 17 bronze drums were discovered in Hengzhou; 1 was discovered in Binzhou(now Binyang County of Guangxi) in November, the 7th year of Yuanfeng.

According to *The History of Song Dynasty,* in the first year of Chunhua(the title of the reign of Emperor Song Tai Zong, 990A.D.), Mo Honghao, the chief of the ethnics in Nandang County, Guangxi, dispatched his son Mo Huaitong to pay tribute to Song Dynasty, with 3 bronze drums. Another record in *Jade Sea* was said that in the first year of Jingde(the title of the reign of Emperor Song Jingzong,1004A. D.), Xiangzhou County of Guangxi also paid tribute to the central dynasty. It shows that at that time, Guangxi bronze drums had entered into Bianliang(now Kaifeng City, Henan Province), the capital of Song Dynasty.

After Ming and Qing Dynasty, numerous records about Guangxi bronze drums were put down in official historical books, unofficial historical books, notes and poetry. Here is a list of the discoveries of bronze drums in Guangxi below: the 3rd reign year of Jingtai, Ming Dynasty(1452A.D.), one bronze drum was discovered in Bronze Drum Pond, Beiliu County(according to Annals of *Beiliu County*); the 13th reign year of Hongzhi(1494A.D.),one at Bronze Drum Bay, Fort Malv, Bobai County(*Annals of Bobai,*Daoguang Years);on the Dragon Boat Festival of the 15th reign year of Wanli(1618A.D.), 2 were respectively found at Bronze Drum Riffle and Baishi Hill in Xunzhou(Now Guiping City, according to *Annals of Xunzhou,*Tongzhi Years; the 40th reign year of Kangxi(1701A.D.), Qing Daynasty, one was found at Liuluo Mountain, Cenxi; and in the first reign year of Yongzheng(1723A.D.), another was found at Fenggui Cave, Cenxi again(*Annals of Cenxi,*the Republic of China). In the 8th reign year of Yongzheng(1730A.D.), one was found in Beiliu(*Annals of Beiliu•Historical Sites,* Guangxu Years), and one at Bronze Drum Riffle of Guiping(*Annals of Xunzhou,*Tongzhi Years). In the 10th reign year of Yongzheng(1732 A.D.), bronze drum was found at Liuxi Village, Yulin County(*Annals of Yulin•Metal and Stone,* Guangxu Years). In the reign year of Qianlong(1736A.D.-1795A.D.), bronze drums were found in Yongning County(*Annals of Yongning,* the Republic of China), and Beirong Mountain of Yulin(*Annals of Yulin•Metal and Stone,* Guangxu Years). In the 2nd reign year of Jiaqing(1797A.D.), bronze drums were found at Pangpo, Shiyili, Beiliu(*Annals of Beiliu•Historical Sites,* Guangxu Years) and Ershiwuduzhu Village of Teng County(*Annals of Teng County•Miscellany,* Tongzhi Years). In the 3rd reign year of Jiaqing(1798A.D.), bronze drum was found at Bronze Drum Hill of Qinzhou; in the 6th reign year(1801A.D.), one was found at Shitan Village of Qinzhou(*Annals of Lianzhou•Metal and Stone*); In the 10th reign year(1805A.D.), one was found at Huangpo Village, Suihua Li, Teng County(*Annals of Teng County•Miscellany,* Tongzhi Years). In the first reign year of Daoguang(1821A.D.), bronze drums were found in Binyang(*Annals of Binyang,* the Republic of China), Fort Sanjin and Panlong Hill of Bobai(*Annals of Bobai,* Daoguang Years);the 5th reign year(1825A.D.), in the fields in front of Bronze Drum Cliff, Jiaoyi Village, Yishan County(*Annals of Qingyuan,* Daoguang Years); the 6th reign year(1826A.D.), at Bianyi Li of Beiliu County;the 18th reign year(1838A.D.), at Dalun Village, Fulaili, Beiliu County(*Annals of Beiliu County•Historical Sites*);the 21st reign year(1841A.D.), next to Wangling Hill, Lichi Gen, Yulin Town(*Annals of Yulin•Metal and stone*);the 25th reign year(1845A.D.), at Yunheng Hill, Fusui(*Annals of Tongzheng County*); the 26th year(1846A.D.), at Fort Tenglong of Yulin; In the 30th year(1850A.D.), at Xinxu of Beiliu(*Annals of Yulin•Art and Literature,* Guangxu Years), the excavations of bronze drums were recorded. The 7th reign year of Tongzhi(1868A. D.) at Zhenwu Hill of Yulin; the first reign year of Guangxu(1875A.D.) at Guniu Hill of Lingshan; the 2nd reign year of Guangxu(1876A.D.) in Xiangzhou County(*Annals of Xiangzhou•Bronze Drums,* the Republic of China); the 4th to 5th reign year (1878A.D.-1879A.D.) at Xiahai Riffle, Yandun Ling, Bailong, Hepu County(*Annals of Hepu•Metal and Stone*, the Republic of China); the 20th reign year(1894A. D.) at Dahua Village, Lingshan(*Annals of Lingshan County•Metal and Stone*, the Republic of China);the 24th reign year(1898A.D.) at Wang'an Village, Shangxiu Li, Guiping County(*Annals of Guiping County•Historical Sites*, the Republic of China); the 3rd reign year of Xuantong(1911A.D.) at Lianzhu Village, Shitang, Lingshan(*Annals of Lingshan•Metal and Stone*, the Republic of China), and in other county annals such as *Annals of Qinzhou County(Annals of Gui County•Metal and stone*, the Republic of China), much more records about the unearthed bronze drums were kept down.

These historical records listed above show us the different conditions of discovery, employ, transition and relevant customs of bronze drums in Guangxi.

II A large number of drums stocked by private and government

Most of unearthed bronze drums were cherished, and were regarded as "the treasures" not belonging to private individuals (as *Bronze Drum Record* by Jin Hong). In ancient times, the majority of unearthed bronze drums were confiscated to governmental academies of all levels, and some of them were stocked by shrines, temples and local government offices. Just as the poem wrote by Peng Tingchun, a "Juren"of Qing Dynasty in Pingnan County:"*Our bronze drums were hided in forest, but you could always see them in shrines and wrecked temples.*" Same records could be found in many local chronicles, such as a bronze drum was unearthed in Bronze Drum Pound in the north of Beiliu County in 1499(Ming Dynasty, the Year Siwei of Hongzhi), and was handed in to Cangwu government by county men. During the Jiajing Years of Ming Dynasty, "there was a Small bronze drum in the back bedroom of Chenghuang Temple" in Nanning, Guangxi(*Nanning Chronicle•Geographical Annals*, Jiajing Years).A bronze drum was hung in the left corridor of Wuzhou Town Hall (*Strange Events*, by Zhangmu), and a small bronze drum was kept in Guilin government office (*The Western Events*, by Weijun). And for other examples, the bronze drum found at Baishi Hill of Guiping County on the Dragon Boat Festival of the 45th reign year of Wanli(1617A.D.), was put in Qingfeng temple of the city town after handed in; the bronze drum found at Bronze Drum Cliffle of Xunjing River was put in the Confusion Temple in city town after handed in(*Two Bronze Drums Were found in Xunzhou*, by Le Mingsheng). Xu Xiake wrote the sentence " There is one or two bronze drums keeping in every city town"(*Travels of Xu Xiake*, Roll 4 Volum 1) after he saw some bronze drums in the Town's God Temple in Nanning.

At the early Qing Dynasty, over 10 bronze drums were kept in the government office of Wuzhou, Guangxi (*Annals of Wuzhou*, Qianlong Years). In the autumn of the 8th reign year of Yongzheng(1730A. D.), a bronze drum was found at Bronze Drum Riffle of Xunjiang River, Guiping, and was presented by the magistrate of Guiping to Jin Hong, the grand coordinator of Guangxi. Jin Hong brought this drum to Guilin and put it in the government office to encourage his army. When Xie Qikun held the post of the grand coordinator of Guangxi in the 4th reign year of Jiaqing(1799A.D.), he built a pavilion for the drum specially. In July of the 5th reign year of Qianlong (1740A.D.), Wang Bangjun, a villager of Lingshan County, dug out a bronze drum and handed it in to the government; in June of the 6th reign year of Qianlong (1741A.D.), Tan Hai'ao, a villager of Tengli, Hepu County, unearthed a bronze drum too, and it was stocked at the school office (*Annals of Lianzhou*, Daoguang Years). In the 5th reign year of Daoguang (1825A.D.), a villager of Jiaoyi, Yishan County dug out a bronze drum in the fields in front of Bronze Drum Cliff. People from Taiping Xu rushed to there for purchasing this drum. But it was confiscated by the government of Yishan County and was put in a temple. During Guangxu reign period, Jin Wuxiang, the official of Wuzhou Salt Management Department which attached to the Salt

Transportation Department of Guangdong and Guangxi, said in a book *The Fragrance of Millet Notes*: "I saw bronze drums in temples as I passed by Liuyin Xu of Hepu (Now Liuyin Town, Hepu county) and Liufeng Xu of Bobai."

To make a collection of bronze drums by private person was becoming popular. During the 4th to the 5th reign year of Guangxu, 5 bronze drums were dug out at the hill foot of Yandun Ling, out of the south gate of Bailong City, Hepu. Except for one was sent to Bailong Sanqing Temple and one to Qianti Temple of the Queen of Heaven, the others were took away by private persons (*Annals of Hepu, Roll 6*, the Republic of China). In the 20th reign year of Guangxu (1894A.D.), a villager of Dahua, Lingshan dug out bronze drum and it soon was purchased by the magistrate, Ruan Cui'en; in the 2nd reign year of Xuantong (1910A.D.), the bronze drums from Zhuqiansui Fen, Gaoshan Temple and the Confusion Temple of Xinxu were all possessed by the magistrate Ma Weicong (*Annals of Lingshan, Roll 20*, the Republic of China). According to Luo Zhenyu's book *The Diary of Yonglu*, a person named Zhou Ai once had gained a bronze drum for his private stock from Guangxi Cenxi. During Xianfeng Years, when Liu Jiahuai-who came from Shedong Village, Xing'an, Xindu of Hezhou-was at his post of the educational official in Xilong (now Longlin County), he bought a drum from the villagers and brought it back to his hometown Xindu as his collection(*Annals of Xindu, Roll 5*,the Republic of China). According to the investigation took in China assigned by Austria scholar Franz Heger, an official of Wuzhou government stocked many drums (*The Ancient Bronze Drums in Southeast Asia*, Leipzig, 1902). A person named Feng Minchang who lived in Qinzhou Dasi, had 6 or 7 drums stocked in his house, and other places such as Feng Shuyin House, Feng Shumao House, Feng Rongxi House and Feng Poyan Abstinence Hall all had drums in their stocks (*Annals of Qin County•Metal And Stone*, the Republic of China).

If you look up the annals of Guangxi, you will find numerous records about bronze drums that were kept in Buddhist temples all over Guangxi during Qing Dynasty: in the first county of Yulin(now Yuzhou District of Yulin City), there were Hanshan Temple at Yinling Village in the east; Shangshu Temple at Liubiao Village of Gaosha Pu in the southwest; Koudong Temple at Lizhigen in the west; Jinshun Temple and Wenchang Ge at Mantou Xu in the northwest; Yuhuang Temple at Wangshui, Taoist Hall at Gushan Village, Hanshan Temple at Putang, Yuanzhu Temple at Fukang in the north; and Beidi Temple at Shitang Ling, Yanling Temple at Shijiao Pu and etc., all were keeping bronze drums(*Annals of Yulin•Bronze Drums*). In Beiliu County, bronze drums were kept in the Town God's Temple, General Temple at Longhu Zhai of Boyili, Sizhou Nunnery at Hecun of Shiyili, Baotu Nunnery at Shuiyong Village of Biansanli, Longshan Temple at Lingdong of Bianyili, Hulong Temple at Shahu Village, Yuxu Taoist Temple, the Taoist Hall at Luhou Village and so on(*Annals of Beiliu*, Guangxu Years). In Pingnan County, temples stocking bronze drums were: Fubo Temple at Wujiang, Yonglong Temple at West Village, Liuwuxu Temple, Weicun Temple, Guanyin Temple at Dazhong Xu, Sanjia Temple at Landong(*Annals of Pingnan•Metal and Stone*, Guangxu Years). In Bobai County, the places were Xinwen Ge, Panlong Temple(*Annals of Bobai•Metal and Stone*, Daoguang Years). And Shuiyue Palace out of the south gate of Rong County(*Annals of Rong County•Metal and Stone*, Guangxu Years), Ganwang Temple in Guiping(*Annals of Guiping County*,the Repubic of China), the Town God's Temple of Chongzuo(*Annals of Taiping Fu•Historical Sites in Congguang*, Yongzheng Years), Xuanxie Temple in Longzhou(*Annals of Longjin County•Metal and Stone*, the Republic of China), and in Shanglin County, Wuxian Temple, Sansheng Palace, Taoist Temple, Qingping Temple, Lotus Temple, Yande Nunnery and so on, had bronze drums(*Annals of Shanglin County•Buddhist and Taoist Temple*,the Republic of China).

After the Revolution in 1911, more bronze drums were kept in temples all over Guangxi. Except those temples listed above, other places such as Gaoshan Temple at Beirong, Beiyili of Beiliu, Napai Nunnery at Luopian, Lulong Temple at Shuikou, Shedong of Bianerli, Chongtian Taoist Temple at Dayu of Fulai, Xinxu Primary School and etc., were keeping bronze drums(*Annals of Beiliu*,the Republic of China). More records were wrote down in local annals: Shangdong Temple in Luchuan(*Annals of Luchuan•Altar and Temple*, the Republic of China) ; Shanglong Temple at Beili and Yongxing Temple at Huixili, Guigang (*Annals of Guigang•Metal and Stone,* the Republic of China); Guandi Temple, Guiyi Confusion Temple and Nandu Denggong Temple in Cenxi (*Annals of Cenxi•Notes*,the Republic of China); Confusion Temple, Mahou Temple and Li's Ancestral Temple in Qinzhou(*Annals of Qinzhou•Metal and Stone*,the Republic of China); In Lingshan County, there was Gaoshan Grand Temple, Wenwu Temple at Yandunxu, Maojinxu and Xinxu, Pangu Temple at Lianyang Hill of Pingshan, Zhennanxu Temple, Qiujie Ancestral Temple of Song Tailian, and Sanqing Palace at Liufeng Hill, Fucheng of Pingli Village(*Annals of Lingshan•Metal and Stone*, the Republic of China); the village's temple of Xuhu, Fuwang, Sanqing Taoist Temple at Bailong and Palace of Queen of Heaven in Hepu(*Annals of Hepu•Metal and Stone•Bronze Drums of Han Dynasty*,the Republic of China); Qinghui Palace in Fangcheng(the first draft of *Annals of Fangcheng•Metal and Stone*,the Republic of China); Wuxian Temple in Xiangzhou(*Annals of Xiangzhou•Metal and Stone*,the Republic of China); Xianliang Shrine at Yancangling in Binyang(*Annals of Binyang*,the Republic of China); Leiting Temple at Qiaojianxu in Longan(*Annals of Longan•Historical Sitesthe*,the Republic of China).

According to Guangxi Province Museum's paper investigation which faced to 11 counties in 1935, the situation of bronze drums preservation in that very year was: 7 in Guilin County, 3 in Tianhe County (now Luocheng County), 2 in Yongning County, Cenxi, Luchuan, Guiping, Rong County (now Rongshui), Lingyun, Xilong (now Longlin) and Pingxiang, each county had one.

After the foundation of People's Republic of China in 1949, the government paid high attention to cultural heritage of ethnic groups and spent a great deal of human and financial resources to collect, preserve properly and record the bronze drums that were unearthed or were stocked in privates, especially the archaeological discoveries. In 1955, for the railway construction of Litang to Zhanjiang, the archaeological workers excavated ancient tombs in Gui County (now Guigang City), unearthed one drum from No.8 Tomb which of earth pit and wooden outer coffin at Gui County High School; in 1972, 4 drums were dug out from Putuo Grain Station of Xilin when the grain-sunning ground was opening up; in the autumn of 1976, 3 drums were excavated from No.1 Han Tomb of Luopowan, Gui County (one of them had been transformed to a bronze table); in 1977, one was unearthed from Guogailing Warring State Tomb, Xiangzhou, Tiandong County; in 1991, one was found in a cave burial site at Longzhong Village, Shatian, He County(now Shatian Town, Babu District, Hezhou City); in March of 1993, 2 was unearthed from an early Warring State Tomb in Nanhapo, Xiangzhou, Tiandong county; in June, 1994, one was unearthed from Dalingpo late Spring and Autumn Tomb in Linfeng Town, Tiandong County. The drums found in 1993 and 1994 are all Wanjiaba Type, which filled up the blank of bronze drum types of Guangxi.

According to incomplete statistics, the number of bronze drums that were collected in different levels of cultural relic administration departments in Guangxi has reached 772, includes: 345 in Anthropology Museum of Guangxi 15 in Museum of Guangxi Zhuang Autonomous Region, 34 in Guilin Museum, 38 in Liuzhou Museum, 18 in Baise Youjiang Revolution Cultural Relic House, 17 in Nanning Museum, 10 in Guigang Museum, 9 in Yulin Museum, 6 in Qinzhou Museum, 5 in Youjiang Museum of Nationalities, 3 each in Wuzhou Museum, Chongzuo Museum and Beihai Cultural Relic Administration, 1 in Hezhou Museum, 35 in Beiliu Museum, 26 in Lingshan County Museum, 25 in Guiping Museum,

17 in Pingnan County Museum, 17 in Pubei County Museum, 12 in Luchuan County Cultural Relic Administration, 10 in Teng County Cultural Relic Administration, 9 in Bobai County Museum, 7 each in Shanglin and Wuming County Cultural Relic Administration, 6 in Rong County Museum, 5 each in Xilin County Cultural Relic Administration, Xiangzhou Cultural Relic Administration, Heng County Museum and Longlin County Museum of Nationalities, 4 each in Tiandong County Museum, Du'an Yao Autonomous County Relic Administration, Xilin County Museum and the cultural relic exhibition hall of Guangxi University for Nationalities, 3 each in Daxin County Museum, Yongning District Cultural Relic Administration, Yizhou City Cultural Relic Administration, Luzhai County Cultural Relic Administration Cenxi City Cultural Relic Administration, and the cultural relic exhibition hall of Guangxi Normal University, 2 each in Longzhou Museum, Napo County Museum, Hepu County Museum, Liujiang County Cultural Relic Administration, Binyang County Cultural Relic Administration, Cangwu County Cultural Relic Administration, Mengshan County Cultural Relic Administration, Longsheng Autonomous County Cultural Relic Administration, Tianyang County Museum and Leye County Cultural Relic Administration, Shangsi County Museum, 1 each in Lingyun County Cultural Relic Administration, Jingxi County Museum, Mashan County Cultural Relic Administration, Wuxuan County Cultural Relic Administration and Xinbin District Cultural Relic Administration. Bronze drums under the earth were unearthed every year. Ethnic groups live in Guangxi such as Zhuang, Yao, Miao, Dong, Yi people still use bronze drums nowadays. The number of bronze drums for folk use is surprising. According to the special investigation on hand-down bronze drums in folk which covered11 counties attached to Hechi Area Cultural Relic Administration in 1991~1993, the number of folk drums has reached to 1417. Among them, 538 in Donglan County, 380 in Nandan County, 247 in Dahua Yao Autonomous County, 141 in Bama Yao Autonomous County, 41 in Tian'e County, 16 in Fengshan County, 16 in Du'an Yao Autonomous County, and 2 in Luocheng Mulao Autonomous County. There are bronze drums in Tianlin, Napo County too. Every Spring Festival, and as people holding a wedding or funeral, drumbeat will be heard in many villages in the mountain areas of Guangxi.

III Go through the ages, owned by ethnics

Components of the ethnic users of bronze drums were very complicated. It included the groups such as Luoyue, Gouding, Wuhu, Li and Liao, who lived in Guangxi since Han Dynasty in history, and the groups such as Zhuang, Miao, Yao, Yi, Dong, Shui since Tang Dynasty. These intricate conditions demonstrate a colorful scene of economic and cultural fusion of the multi-ethnic area.

The Book of Later Han is the earliest literature to mention the users of bronze drums. According to *The Book of Later Han•Collected Biographies of Ma Yuan*, Ma Yuan got a Luoyue bronze drum at Jiaozhi. The drums' name Luoyue indicated that it was got from Luoyue people, or made and used by them. Bronze drums of Wanjiaba and Shizhaishan Type were employed by Luoyue people from Warring State Period to Han Dynasty.

Wuhu and Li people who lived in Guangxi during Han and Jin Dynasty also cast and used bronze drums. Wuhu had other names like Wuhu Man and Wu Man, and they were the descendant of Xi'ou and Luoyue. In Li Xian's annotated edition of *The Book of Later* Han, Shen Qinhan said: "Wuhu Hill is 60Li in southeast to Hengzhou, Nanning, where the living place for Wuhu Man." In Ming Dynasty, Wei Jun said in *Qiaonan Notes*: "According to *The Strange Thing Annals*, Wu Man was in west to Nanhai Jun, in north to Duliusi, Annan, and were called Wuhu Man either." Wuhu was active during Eastern Han Dynasty, with a custom of employing bronze drums. Li people was an ethnic group in Lingnan area from Eastern Han to Northern-Southern Dynasties. In historical books they were called "Liliao". "Liliao" in Lingnan

area was Li people in fact. Li was descended from Wuhu. The bronze drums that Wuhu-Li people cast and employed should be Beiliu and Lingshan Type. Contemporaneously, Yiliao people who lived along Yujiang-Xunjiang River employed bronze drums of Lengshuichong Type.

In Sui, Tang and Wudai Dynasties, ethnic groups in Guangxi were called Yi, Man, and they mainly cast and employ bronze drums of Zunyi and Majiang Type. They still use those drums after Ming and Qing Dynasties in their special festivals or on some formal occasions, such as Zhuang's Frog Festival, Yi's Tiaogong Festival, Yao's Zhuzhu Festival, and Baiku Yao's funerals, which are all the "living fossils" of the long employing history of bronze drums.

IV Distribute along rivers, all over the province

Bronze drums have a wide area distribution around Guangxi Province. Bronze drums are spread and employed in the southeast and southwest of Guangxi; in the northeast, south to Hezhou, Zhaoping and Mengshan, bronze drums were unearthed in all counties; in the northwest, from Longsheng in north to Sanjiang, ethnic groups of many counties along the boundaries between Guangxi and Guizhou, Guangxi and Yunan, still use bronze drums till nowadays. Only several counties in the north of Guangxi are not the distribution area of bronze drums. Bronze drums were unearthed mostly in Yulin, Guigang, Qinzhou, Nanning, southern Wuzhou, Laibin and Liuzhou, but most of the extant drums handed down from ancient times are preserved in Hechi and Baise city.

During the Warring State Period, bronze drums in Guangxi mainly distributed in Youjiang River basin, especially Tiandong County, where was the active area of Luoyue people. In Han Dynasty, bronze drums were spread along Nanpanjiang and Youjiang River to Yujiang and Xunjiang River basins, scattered at Xilin, Longlin, Baise, Guigang, Guiping and Teng County. In Guangxi, three Kingdoms Period, Liang-Jin and Northern-Southern Dynasties, Sui and Tang Dynasties were the blooming times for bronze drums. They were cast and employed everywhere, especially in several distribution centers such as shores of Xunjiang River, Yunkai Mountain Area and Liuwan Mountain Area, where huge size of bronze drums were made vying with one another. After Song Dynasty, bronze drums culture transferred to the west, back to Hechi and Baise, the Hongshuihe River basin.

A place was named after bronze drum mostly because it had once unearthed bronze drums. In Qing Dynasty, Qu Dajun said in his *New Talk about Guangdong*: "All the places named after 'bronze drum' just because bronze drums were dug out there." The Bronze Drum Riffle in Guiping got its name in Song Dynasty, then in the 45th reign year of Wanli of Ming Dynasty (1617A.D.), the 8th reign year of Yongzheng of Qing Dynasty (1730A.D.), 2 drums were got by fishing man from there again, so it was an actual "Bronze Drum Riffle". The Bronze Drum Bond in Beiliu, one drum was got under water in the 3rd reign year of Jingtai of Ming Dynasty(1452A.D.); The Bronze Drum Bay in Bobai, got its name for a drum was unearthed from there by a villager in the 12th reign year of Hongzhi of Ming Dynasty(1499A.D.); The Bronze Drum Hill in Qinzhou, got its name for one drum was unearthed at the hill foot in the 2nd reign year of Jiaqing(1798A.D.); The Bronze Drum Cliff in Yizhou, was named this name for the villagers in Qing Dynasty dug out bronze drum in the fields in front of the cliff.

23 places named after bronze drum in Lingshan County, includes: 3 Bronze Drum Villages, 2 Bronze Drum Pond Villages, 3 Bronze Drum Ponds, 5 Bronze Drum Lings, 2 Bronze Drum Hillsides, 1 for Bronze Drum Top, Bronze Drum River, Bronze Drum Bay, Bronze Drum Riffle, all because of the unearthed drums. 7 places named after bronze drum in Pingnan County, includes: 2 Bronze Drum Villages, 2 Bronze Drum Ponds, 2 Bronze Drum Lings and 1 Bronze Drum Foot, also got their names for the unearthed drums.

Large part of Guangxi bronze drums has exact unearthed location. Some has abundant coexistent items, some has the apparent age indicators, and that provide the reliable scale plate for the chronology of bronze drums.

In April, 1993, 2 bronze drums of primitive form were found in front of the gate of Lianfu Village Primary School, Xiangzhou Town, Tiandong County, coexisting with bronze and jade items such as bronze"Lei", bronze"Banding", jade tube, jade "Jue", and jade "Chuan". The age of them was inferred to be early Warring State Period; in June, 1994, the other primitive form drum was found at Dapoling, Hetong Village, Linfeng Town, Tiandong County again, coexisting with a bronze bell of Spring-Autumn to Warring State Period in Yue style which could be the chronology basis.

In 1977, one bronze drum was unearthed at Guogailing, Xiangzhou, Tiandong County, coexisting with some bronze weapons like sword, dagger, spear and axes. According to these weapons' apparent era characteristics, it can be inferred that they were from the same tomb of the Warring State Period; in July of 1991, one bronze drum in Shizhaishan Type decorated with boats and cattle motifs was unearthed at Hongzhu Cliff, Longzhong Village, Shatian Town, Hezhou City, coexisting with many bronze wares which suggests an age of late Warring State Period. In autumn of 1976, two complete bronze drums and one bronze table transformed from a drum were unearthed in No.1 Tomb of Luobowan, Gui County, with over one thousand of coexistent items together, suggesting an age of early Western Han Dynasty. In 1972, four bronze drums were found at Putuo Tun, Xilin County, coexisting with bronze wares and over 4oo jade wares. Its' age conclusion of Western Han Dynasty can be drew out through comparing studies. In spring of 1955, one bronze drum was unearthed in a tomb with earth pit and wooden outer coffin, coexisting with some bronze wares, potteries and coins, and the chronology is late Western Han Dynasty.

In 1953, one Beiliu Type drum decorated with Wuzhu Coins motifs was unearthed in Cenxi County town, which could be a scale plate for the history division of the same type drums; in 1970, one Beiliu Type drum was unearthed at Fengshan, Liuhe Village, Yunbiao town, Heng County, with some pieces of yellow glaze pottery of Southern Dynasty inside; in March, 1975, one Beiliu Type drum was unearthed in southeast to Xinmin Village, Yulin Town, with a bronze caldron of Sui and Tang Dynasties.

In 1962, one Lingshan Type drum was unearthed at Lvshui Village, Lingshan County, coexisting with a coin carved " 开元通宝 "characters , which indicates the drum was buried during or after Kaiyuan Years of Tang Dynasty.

In January, 1975, one drum was unearthed at Lengshuichong, Mengjiang Town, Teng County, with a 4-handle pottery pot inside which was unearthed in tombs of early Eastern Han Dynasty too, so it could be inferred that the drum was buried during or after Eastern Han Dynasty; in 1982, one Lengshuichong Type drum was unearthed at Licun, Jintian, Guiping County, with 4 bronze basins inside which decorated with double fishes on the basin bottom; in October, 1991, one huge Lengshuichong Type drum was unearthed at Xiunan Village, Mugen Town, Guiping County, coexisting with a 4-handle pottery pot, bottom up, decorated with string and water wave motifs, and it indicates an age of Eastern Han Dynasty to Southern Dynasty; in 1956, one Lengshuichong Type drum was unearthed at Pingdao, Jinxiu Yao Autonomous County, with a pottery bowl of Southern Dynasty; in February, 1997, one Lengshuichong Type drum was fished up from Qingjiang River by the village of Qingjiang, Fucheng Town, Heng County, which with a 6-handle pottery pot of Sui and Tang Dynasties.

All of these drums above could be the scale plate of chronology. Some Majiang Type drums carved with their cast years, such as " Cast in Daoguang Years", "Cast in the 2nd reign year of Daoguang", "Cast in the 6th reign year of Daoguang", " Cast in the 8th reign year of Daoguang" and etc., provide more clear clues to infer their cast and popular times.

If we filled all spots of the unearthed and handed down drums into the Guangxi map, distribution of bronze drums covers almost the whole Guangxi. If we counted in unit of county and city (district), the number of counties and cities unearthed and employ bronze drums has reach 85, taking up a proportion of 80%. The drums cast before Song Dynasty distribute intensively along both shores of Zuojiang-Yongjiang-Yujiang-Xunjiang and the southern areas; bronze drums cast after Song Dynasty mostly concentrated in western Guangxi and the mountain areas between Guangxi and Yunan; only several counties in northern Guangxi has no relations with bronze drums.

V All types contending in their beauty

Chinese scholars divide Chinese bronze drums into 2 systems and 8 types since 1980s'. The 2 systems are Dian(Yunnan)-Gui(Guangxi) system, including 5 types of Wanjiaba, Shizhaishan, Lengshuichong, Zunyi and Majiang; Yue(Guangdong)-Gui(Guangxi) system, including 3 types of Beiliu, Lingshan and Ximeng. Bronze drums of Dian-Gui system distribute in Yunnan, Guangxi, Guizhou, Sichuan and Hunan provinces; bronze drums of Yue-Gui system distribute in Guangdong, Guangxi and Hainan provinces. Guangxi is very special with Yunnan in the west and Guangdong in the east, so it has 2 systems and all of the 8 type drums.

1.Wanjiaba Type

Bronze drums of Wanjiaba Type are in primitive forms, represented by the drums unearthed in the tombs of Spring-Autumn and Warring State Period at Wanjiaba, Chuxiong, Yunnan Province. This type has a small drum face, remarkable arch chest, slender waist, and a short, big round lower part with its' edge fold inside. 4 small flat handles are between chest and waist. The motif features are simple, nature, kind of uncomplicated, and comes on steady feeling. On the drum face, some sun motifs have only the cake shape and no rays, some have rays but not in a regular number. No patterns on chest and foot, only a few of lengthwise cutting lines mark off several blanks. Wanjiaba Type drums were popular during the Spring-Autumn and Warring State Period. In Guangxi, this type drums have been unearthed at Dalingpo, Hetong Village, Linfeng Town, Tiandong County, and Nanhapo, Lianfu Village, Xiangzhou Town, Tiandong County.

2.Shizhaishan Type

Drums of this type are in the maturation stage of bronze drum arts, presented by the drums unearthed from the tombs of Han Dynasty at Shizhaishan, Jinning, Yunnan Province. This type has a larger face, arch chest, trapezoidal waist, short and straight foot, with a symmetrical motif arrangement and plentiful motifs. Sun motif is still in the central part of the face; the sun body and the rays are integrated, filled with oblique lines between the triangular rays. Wide and narrow loops are outside of sun, and motifs of saw tooth, circle and dot in the narrow loops; the wide loops are major, with awing herons inside. The ribbons of same geometric motifs are on chest and face, with realist image of people boating as the major loops. On the waist, except the loops, there are blanks divided by vertical ribbons, decorated with cattle or dancing-feathermen (dancers with feather cap on head). Drums of this type are of vigorous form and exquisite decorations. They used to be found in the tomb of Western Han Dynasty at Luobowan, Guigang and Putuo, Xilin County; and to be found at Xiangzhou of Tiandong, Longchuan of Baise, Gonghe of Longlin, too. Popular time of this type drums was from the Warring State Period to Eastern Han Dynasty, lasting for over 500 years.

3.Lengshuichong Type

Lengshuichong Type is in the development stage of bronze drum arts, presented by the drums unearthed at Lengshuichong, Heng Village, Mengjiag, Teng County. This type has a tall and thin form, large face and its' edge not or just a little projecting out. The chest is a bit larger than the face or as large as the face, slightly arch but not projecting out; the upper waist is kind of straight. The minimum caliber is on the drums' middle part. The foot is as high as the chest; handles are flat, decorated with braid motifs. Some drums have semi-ring attached handles besides the 4 flat handles. Character of the decorations is magnificent and complex in general. The rays of the sun were fixed to 12, with double heart-shape motifs between the rays. Frog statues stand on the edge of the face, between the frogs, sometimes there are more statues such as horse, horse-riders, cattle and plough, water bird, tortoise and fish. Motifs decorations are all over the face and the body. The major loop on drum face decorated with highly patterning transformed herons, supplemented by one loop of hooked thunder motifs and its' transformed motif--the multiple crossed lines. Transformed boating motifs are always on the chest, transformed dancers and thin blanks on the waist, and leaf-shape motifs with circles on the foot. All these were made by the sculptors with great care that brought delicate beauty to the bronze drums. Lengshuichong Type mostly distributes in Guiping, Pingnan and Teng County, along with Yongjiang-Yujiang-Xunjiang-Xijiang River, covering half of Guangxi. Its' popular times was from Eastern Han Dynasty to Sui and Tang Dynasties, especially Liang-Jin and Northern-Southern Dynasties.

4.Zunyi Type

This type is represented by the drums unearthed from the tomb of Yangcan couple, the minority headmen of Bozhou, Zunyi, Guizhou Province in Southern Song Dynasty. The most obvious characteristic of this type is no frog statues on the drum face. The face edge is slightly projecting out of the chest. The diameters and heights of face, chest and foot are almost equal. Chest contracts gradually to waist and there is no apparent boundary. Two pairs of large-span flat handles are between chest and waist. Frog claws decoration is still on the edge of drum face even though there are no frog statues. The whole decoration is simple, with geometric motifs composed of concentric circles, triangle train, feather and thunder. Major loop is composed of Youqi motif (one circle and two fluttering ribbons). Excavation of this type is scarce, mainly unearthed in Guizou, Yunnan and Guangxi.

5.Majiang Type

This type is represented by the drums unearthed from an ancient tomb at Gudong Railway Station, Majiang County, Guizhou Province. It has a short and small form, smaller face comparing to the chest, and the face edge projecting out of the chest. It has soft curves of chest, waist and foot, without any boundaries, only one raise ridge divides the body into the upper and the lower. Two pairs of large-span flat handle on the chest. Most of the bronze drums being used in folk now are Majiang Type.

6.Beiliu Type

This type is represented by the drums unearthed at Beiliu County. It has a huge and thick form, large face, projecting face edge, and caving edge sometimes. The chest arch out straightly, with the largest diameter a little bit below. The waist contracts in reverse arch, with a gentle slope between waist and chest and the boundary is a carved line. On the other hand, the boundary between waist and foot is a raise ridge. The foot arches out and forms a diameter as large as the face. The round stem handles are firm, usually in ring form. Frog statues on the face are small and simple. The sun body like a round cake standing out, with the routine 8 rays. Most part of the decorations are clouds and thunder motifs. In the western scholars' division system on bronze drums, Beiliu Type is called Heger TypeII, and is knew as its' huge and tall. The biggest bronze drum has been ever known was kept in Shuiyong Nunnery, Liujing Xiang, Beiliu County originally, has a face diameter of 165cm and a weight of 299kg, making it "the king of bronze drums". The second huge one is in the collection of Shanghai Museum, No.6597, has a face diameter of 145cm, a height of 78.8cm; the third one is kept in Guangzhou Nanhai God's Temple, has a face diameter of 138cm, a height of 77.4cm; the fourth one was unearthed at Guiping Madong Primary School, with a face diameter of 137.8cm, a height of 72.5cm; in Yulin, Beiliu and Pingnan, bronze drums of Beiliu Type with a face diameter over 122.2cm have been unearthed. The features of this type include: face is bigger than body, all drums' edge sticking out of chest, and most of them have a curving edge that is called "drum face skirt". Two pairs of handles are between chest and waist, except for a few of drums (which have flat handles), most of them having round stem and ring form handles. The handles' body is solid cylinder, in ring or semi-ring form fixed between chest and waist, decorated with circles like twisted silks and a raise ridge like snake, so this kind of handles is also called "snake ring handles". Three-claw motif is on the roots of these handles, which could expand the contact area with drum body, and what's more, ring handles are stronger than flat handles. Some drums have two more little ring handles on corresponding position. Sun pattern is on the central part of drum face, where the beat-bearing position, and its' body is like a round cake and sticking out. sun rays radiate into different directions, thin and long, like needles, some with forfications on the tops, usually penetrating one or two loops. Most of the drums have 8 rays, and the few have 12, 10 or 6 rays. Motifs on drum face and drum body are divided by three strings, and usually, loops on face are wide and sparse in a same size, a few of them in different sizes; loops on body are narrow and intense, all in a same size. Both face or body, the motifs in loops mainly are cloud and thunder that base on forms of single line or multiple line circles, squares, lozenges, triangles, semi-rounds, dots, whirlpools, oblique squares and square hooks. The popular time of Beiliu Type was from Han to Tang Dynasty. It has an intense distribution in the southeast of Guangxi, southwest of Guangdong and Hainan province, focus on Yulin of Guangxi Province, then Qinzhou of Guangxi, Zhanjiang of Guangdong, specially several counties in Yunkai mountain area which including Beiliu County of Guangxi and Xinyi of Guangdong. Yunkai mountain area is the center of Beiliu Type drums.

7.Lingshan Type

This type is represented by drums unearthed at Lingshan County, Qinzhou City. It has an imposing form very similar to Beiliu Type, with delicate decorations. The drum face is flat, with a diameter as large as the chest, and the edge sticking out but not curving. The chest arches out slightly, with a largest diameter on the middle of it. The chest contracts gradually into the waist below, a string between them as the boundary. All handles across chest and waist are flat and in plate form decorated with leaf vein patterns. All frog statues on drum face are "three-leg frogs" with their two hind legs combining to each other. Gorgeous decorations are on frogs' back of carved lines and whirlpools pattern. Some drums have "overlap frogs" (the little frog overlaps on the big one). In general, frogs are 6, sometimes all are overlap frogs, but in most cases 3 single frogs and 3 overlap frogs array phase to phase counterclockwise. On the central part of drum face, sun pattern has a cake-like standing out body, and different numbers of needle-like thin long rays, usually 10 or 12, sometimes 7, 8, 9, or 11 with the fork-like rays' tails. Motifs are divided by 2 strings. There are always 3 major loops both on drum face and drum body, mainly composed of motifs like beast-rider, beast, heron(with fish in mouth, birds),cloud, thunder, semi-circle, semi-circle filled with straight lines, woven mat, quatrefoil, coin with quadrangle inside, coins part of overlap, insect, water wave and cicada that is usually on the edge in the other loops. Near the drum foot, below the handles, some drums are decorated with animal statues like bird or a couple birds, ox or sheep, with their heads toward the drum foot. The popular times of this type is from Han to Tang Dynasty, with a distribution center of Lingshan County and the neighboring counties like Heng County and Pubei County, in other words from western Liuwan Mountain to shores of Heng County section of Yujiang River. Besides these areas, they scatter sporadically here and there, east to Gaozhou, south to Hepu, west to Zaimiao of Shangsi and Wude of Longzhou, even were unearthed in Liangshan, Vietnam, north to Dayang of Guiping. distribution area of Lingshan Type which in the west of Beiliu Type's distribution area and in the southwest of Lengshuichong Type's distribution area, was also the activity sphere of Wuhu-Li people from Jin and Southern Dynasty to Tang Dynasty.

8.Ximeng Type

This type is represented by the drums that are still used by Wa people in Ximeng area, Yunnan Province. This type has a light, tall form with thin wall, large drum face with its edge sticking out, in a shape of the big end up and the small end down, with no boundaries between chest and waist, waist and foot. sun pattern on drum face usually of 8 or 12 rays; decorations of bird, fish, round and polypetalous mission–flower and rice ear motifs are divided into dense loops by 3 strings. Frog statues on drum face are always in overlap and 3 overlap frogs shape, even 4 overlaps. Some drums have statues like elephants, field snails and trees, arraying vertically on its body. Ximeng Type was named Type III by Heger. As he said, " You can call it Karen Drum, because all of the drums of Type III came from Red and White Karen people in post-India; But to be more precise, it should be called the Shan Type. Lots of information support that these drums were cast by Shan people in Indochina." He didn't know there were drums of this type in China when he made such above comments. In Guangxi, only a few of countries where next to the China-Vietnam boundary where were found this type drums, all in their early forms.

Among the 8 types, Lengshuichong, Beiliu and Lingshan were named after the standard drum's unearthed spot in Guangxi, and mainly distribute in Guangxi.

During the over 2,000 years' history of bronze drums, what position did the bronze drums of Guangxi take in the whole bronze drum family? If central-western Yunnan was concerned the original place of ancient bronze drums for a large number of ancient, primary type drums unearthed there, then Guangxi, which locates in the south to Wuling connects Yungui highland and the blank of South China Sea, totally deserves the name of "the supreme center of bronze drums" for its huge number of collections and complete types.

VI Abundant fruits of bronze drum research

Ethnologists and archaeologists have paid attention on the plentiful bronze drums a long time ago. Since Ming and Qing Dynasties, materials about bronze drums were collected and recorded in local annals. Annals editors observed local bronze drums prudentially and kept their observations down faithfully. They widely collected the relevant rumors and documents, seriously edited them, and made lots of precious materials handed down. In Jiaqing Years of Qing Dynasty, Xie Qikun, the coordinator of Guangxi, wrote a book named *Metal and Stone in Yuexi* when he edited *The General Annals of Guangxi*. In his book, he took down many documents in a special chapter of *Bronze Drum Explanations*, and brought out objection to the popular statements at that time that bronze drums were invented by Ma Yuan and Zhuge Liang. He said, "Since Shi Hu(Fan Chengda, a scholar of Song Dynasty) said the bronze drums were cast by Ma Yuan, later points were misled to regard bronze drums as the invention of Ma Yuan, and then they made a strained interpretation that the big drums were cast by Ma Yuan, the smaller ones were cast by Zhuge Liang. What a mistake it is!" In order to observe bronze drums, Xie Qikun built a bronze drum pavilion beside his government office, and put the drum which was fished out from Bronze Drum Riffle, Xunjiang River of Guiping in it. He wrote a 58-sentence long poem named *Bronze Drum Poem*, and carved it on the wall. This was an advertisement about the knowledge of bronze drums. In the 17th reign year of Daoguang, Liang Zhangju, the new coordinator of Guangxi, put another drum that presented by Xu Shaoyou, the magistrate of Guilin, into the pavilion, and rubbed a copy of Bronze Drum Poem, invited more than 40 colleges and friends to write new songs about bronze drums, then edited a poem book named *Bronze Drum Poems Album*, discussing the origin and usage of bronze drums.

In 1933, ethnologist Liu Xifan wrote down what he saw and heard in Miao ethnic mountain area in the book *Ling Biao Ji Man*.

Ethnologist Xu Songshi, had been to Guangxi many times in 1927, 1935 and 1938. In Guangxi, he observed more than 50 bronze drums and wrote a book named *Peoples' History of Yuejiang Basin*, which included the 22nd chapter of *Research on Bronze Drums*, published in the winter of 1938. In this chapter, he introduced the origin of bronze drums, the ethnic groups who initiated the drums, the usages and the excavations of bronze drums briefly. To Xu, he regarded bronze drums as the invention of Luoyue who the ancestor of Zhuang people during Qin and Han Dynasty. Then he wrote a section of *Bronze drums and Lingnan Zhuang people* in his another book *Tai, Zhuang and Yue People*, insisting that bronze drums were invented by Zhuang People in Lingnan area.

In 1943, Chen Zhiliang combed through all the local annals in Guangxi, and investigated some ethnic young people on employ situations of bronze drums. He published a long article, *To Start the Research on Bronze Drums-One of the Discussions on Ancient Culture of Guangxi*, sited out the materials of bronze drums in 18 counties, including the analysis of drum-using ethnic groups, drums' form, decorations and the frog statues. As his point, bronze drums were not all cast in the same time but in different dynasties, and they are used for funerals and entertainments in modern times.

In 1948, Zhu Changkui published his article *Research on Bronze Drums on Annals of Binyang*, which mentioned that when he was the magistrate of Luocheng County, he went into Yao mountain area, communicating with Miao and Yao people and seeing them used bronze drums and Lusheng for entertainments in banquets or sacrifices. He considered that bronze drums were the possessions of Miao and Yao chiefs, and it was ridiculous to take them as the inventions of Ma Yuan and Zhuge Liang. In the same year, the writer of *Annals of Fangcheng County* added some comments about the usages of bronze drums. He objected the opinions that bronze drums were used for war, but thought that bronze drums were used in folk for southern areas people who believed in witchcraft and ghost, so they cast drums for sacrifices, especially the sacrifices for harvest and ancestor. At the beginning of agriculture, people prayed for harvest when the new year coming. In southern areas, the wet weather makes feather drums soft and sound low, so people invented bronze drums as the sacrifice instrument. Because people in southern areas prayed for harvest everywhere when their society developed from fishing-hunting society to agricultural society, so there are bronze drums unearthed everywhere.

In 1949, Peoples' Republic of China was established and opened up new situations of research on bronze drums. During February to March of 1955, Guangxi Cultural Relics Management Committee excavated a wooden outer coffin of Han Dynasty at Gui County High School. On the left side of this tomb, a bronze drum was found together with other bronze wares and potteries. Tan Yiran, one of the excavators, published his report, *Bronze Drum Was Found in an Ancient Tomb of Gui County, Guangxi* on the 7th issue of *Cultural Relics References* in 1955, and the rubbings of the drums' face were published together. Consequently, Huang Zengqing published his report, *Sorting Report of the Wooden Outer Coffin of Han Dynasty in Gui County, Guangxi*, on the 4th issue of Archaeology Message in 1956, revealing some details of this tomb, and published the rubbings of drum face as well. On the first issue of *Archaeology Journal* in 1957, an article named *Sorting of the Han Dynasty Tomb in Guangxi Gui County* was published with the rubbings of drum face, and its' casting time was concluded to be Eastern Han Dynasty.

In July of 1962, Jiang Yingliang, history professor of Yunnan University, came to Nanning and visited the bronze drums which preserved in the storeroom of Museum of Guangxi Zhuang Autonomous Region, feeling that bronze drums were priceless treasures of Guangxi local culture and history. After then, he wrote an article on *Guangxi Daily*, appealing to the public to treasure the bronze drums that were unearthed all over Guangxi. He suggested that the government should make plans and appropriate funds to collect the drums, and encourage scholars to do research. In spring of 1963, the famous historian and archaeologist Guo Moruo came to Naning to attended the founding conference of Guangxi History Academy, visited the bronze drums stored in Museum of Guangxi Zhuang Autonomous Region, composed a well-know poem to the given tune of *Man Jiang Hong*, with the sentence of " Numerous bronze drums, I appreciated the Zhuang Culture." His accompany Jian Bozan, the famous historian and the vice-principal of Peking University, emphasized that the varied and hundreds of bronze drums which preserved in Museum of Guangxi Zhuang Autonomous Region and the cliff arts which was newly found at Huashan were the most precious materials for the studies on the history of ethnic groups in Guangxi. He suggested that the drawing volumes should be worked out and published earlier. All of these encouraged ethnologists, archaeologists and historians to throw themselves into the study of bronze drums.

In 1964, Huang Zengqing published his article *The First Discussion on the Bronze Drums Unearthed in Guangxi*, divided Guangxi bronze drums into 4 types and 2 systems: one has a decoration development from cloud-thunder pattern to insect, bird and flower, and the other developed from heron, feathermen to fluttering flag and zodiac. He pointed out that these two systems distributed in different areas and maybe they belonged to two tribes.

In autumn of 1972, Museum of Guangxi Zhuang Autonomous Region organized a special research on bronze drums, and wrote out the article *Research on the Ancient Bronze Drums of Guangxi*, made a conclusion of the researches on Guangxi ancient bronze drums scientifically, and the incisive dissertation about the excavations, types, historical division and times, the systems, decorations and the usages of bronze drums. This article divided Guangxi bronze drums into 4 types and 20 forms. Type Jia is now Beiliu Type; Type Yi, now Lingshan Type; Type Bing had 7 forms, the first and the second form are now Shizhaishan Type, the third to the fifth are now Lengshichong Type, the sixth and the seventh are now Zunyi Type; Type Ding, is now Majiag Type.

During March to April of 1980, the first symposium about ancient bronze drums was held in Nanning. On this symposium, participants discussed the origin, types, distribution, times, ethnic belongingness and usages of bronze drums, and published *The Conference Proceedings of Ancient Bronze Drums Academic Symposium* and the popular reading *The Historical Stories of Bronze Drums by* Jiang Tingyu. In October of 1988, The Chinese Association for Ancient Bronze Drums Research published *Chinese Ancient Bronze Drums*, completely and systematically expounded the origin, types, distribution, times, ethnic belongingness, decorations, usages and casting crafts. Meanwhile, *Research on Bronze Drums' Art* by Jiang Tingyu was published, profoundly explained arts of formation, statue, religion thoughts, common sense, Chinese inscriptions, music and dancing about bronze drums.

In 1988, on the international conference of ancient bronze drums and bronze culture in Southern China and Southeast Asia that was held in Kunming, Yao Shun'an, Jiang Tingyu and Wan Fubin read out their thesis *The Discussions on Lingshan Type Bronze Drums*. In December of 1990, their book *Discovery in Beiliu Type Bronze Drums* was published. In 1991, Catalogue of Guangxi Bronze Drums was edited and published by Museum of Guangxi Zhuang Autonomous Region, publishing all the collections of bronze drums in Guangxi cultural institutes.

In October, 1992, *Scientific Research on Chinese Ancient Bronze Drums* by Wan Fubin was published, which was the first book to study bronze drums from the perspective of natural science. Consequently, several books wrote by Jiang Tingyu were published, including *Introduction to Ancient Bronze Drums*, *Research on the Bronze Drums of Zhuang People*, *Culture of Bronze Drums*, *The Great Bronze Drums*, and so on. Bronze drum study in Guangxi was in a world leading level.

Bronze drum is an integrated art work of nationalities that cast and used them, reflecting the achievements gained by these nationalities in economic, science& technology and culture fields of metallurgy, casting, music, art, dance and religion in history. It is an encyclopaedia for the study on these peoples' history.

As an assembling center of bronze drums, Guangxi is drawing attentions for its' large numbers of collection, complete types and abundant materials.

The indefinite mysteries contained in bronze drums induce people to keep thinking and exploring, appealing to scholars from generation to generation. Just because of this reason , the study of bronze drums is full of charming and will be continued in the future.

2014年广西铜鼓调查综述

农学坚

《广西铜鼓精华》顺利出版，是得益于2014年"广西铜鼓调查"项目的实施完成。它是在广西壮族自治区文化厅、文物局直接领导和大力支持下，项目组和全区铜鼓收藏单位通力合作的成果。这次的铜鼓调查，主要是围绕广西各级文物收藏单位的铜鼓开展，其工作内容是对广西14个设区市、57个县（市、区）共62家文物收藏单位的772面铜鼓进行实地调查，包括多角度拍照、实测和描述记录、资料建档和数据储存。通过这次调查，全面、真实地摸清了广西馆藏铜鼓的家底，获得了珍贵的资料，对于铜鼓研究、保护利用和优秀民族文化的传承与弘扬具有十分重要的意义。

一、项目的必要性

铜鼓调查，是一项非常重要的基础性工作。不论是铜鼓研究，还是与铜鼓文化有关的陈列展览，都离不开对铜鼓的收藏、来源以及铜鼓本体状貌的记录。

1979年至1980年，广西博物馆铜鼓调查组在广东、云南、四川、贵州、湖南、湖北、江苏、浙江、上海、北京等省、市铜鼓收藏单位的大力支持下，开展了一次全国性的铜鼓资料大普查，实测记录铜鼓1383面，其中广西各级文物单位所藏铜鼓503面，第一次摸清了全国铜鼓收藏的基本情况。后来由广西、广东、云南、贵州、四川五省（区）博物馆合作，将这些资料汇编成《中国古代铜鼓实测记录资料汇编》，为日后进一步研究铜鼓打下了坚实的基础。1991年，广西博物馆为编写《广西铜鼓图录》又对全区馆藏铜鼓进行过补充调查和统计，当时全区各级文物单位共收藏铜鼓629面，数量上比第一次全国普查时增加了126面。

上述两次铜鼓调查及其资料的编印发行，直接助推了铜鼓研究的深入开展，使中国古代铜鼓研究在上世纪末、本世纪初取得了令人瞩目的成就。然而，略有遗憾的是，由于条件所限，当时所拍摄的铜鼓照片绝大多数是黑白照片，且有部分铜鼓尚缺照片或详细资料。二十多年来，各地出土或征集的铜鼓也有所增加，尚无记录资料面世。那么，数十年过去了，随着铜鼓研究领域的纵深拓展，对于全面掌握铜鼓收藏情况和建立完备的铜鼓资料库就显得十分必要。

2012年2月，中国古代铜鼓研究会在南宁召开了驻邕理事会议，会议选举产生了新一届负责人，并决定将本会的秘书处由广西壮族自治区博物馆迁至广西民族博物馆。同年，在理事长覃溥女士（时任广西文化厅副厅长）的倡导和支持下，世界铜鼓调查项目也开始启动，而"广西馆藏铜鼓调查"便是这一项目的首期工作。广西馆藏铜鼓占全国馆藏铜鼓总数的三分之一强，而且两个系统、八大类型铜鼓在广西均有发现，因此，做好广西铜鼓调查，建立完备的广西铜鼓数据库，这对于下一步开展全国乃至世界铜鼓调查工作具有相当重要的铺垫作用和借鉴意义。

二、项目的周密筹划

为了确保广西馆藏铜鼓调查工作顺利、高效开展，承担中国古代铜鼓研究会日常工作的广

西民族博物馆研究三部为此做了详细的计划和准备。

首先，成立了由广西民族博物馆和广西博物馆相关人员组成的项目组，项目组负责人由覃溥副厅长担任。成员及其主要分工是：蒋廷瑜、农学坚负责业务指导，王梦祥、刘文毅负责摄影摄像，梁燕理、陆秋燕、陈嘉负责文字记录，吴崇基、罗坤馨、蔡荭负责装饰艺术考察，李永春、邹桂森负责铸造工艺考察。

第二，办理项目手续。为了取得铜鼓调查工作的合法性，也为了取得全区文博单位的大力支持，2014 年 4 月，项目组向自治区文化厅呈报了《广西馆藏铜鼓调查方案》，很快获得了批准。自治区文化厅还为此下发了通知，要求各地文博单位全力协助此项工作。

第三，掌握线索，做好行动计划。项目组根据蒋廷瑜先生所掌握的全区 600 余面馆藏铜鼓的资料和线索，结合广西文物信息中心提供的全区珍贵文物数据库 667 条铜鼓信息，制订了分片区、分阶段的铜鼓实地调查线路与步骤。

第四，制定详细的记录指标项和描述标准。此次调查，是采纳以往中国铜鼓学界一贯采用的标准器地名命名的八大类型分类法，并参照第一次全国铜鼓普查时采用的铜鼓造型与纹饰的记录描述，同时也参考了上世纪 90 年代末期中日合作项目"北流、灵山铜鼓调查研究"所制定的《铜鼓调查登记表》，制定了此次铜鼓调查的记录指标项和文字描述标准。另外，照片拍摄则参照第一次全国可移动文物普查的标准实施。

三、项目的具体实施

经过充分准备，铜鼓实地调查终于在 2014 年 4 月 21 日拉开序幕。实地调查行程如下：

第一阶段（4 月 21 日至 29 日），到武鸣、横县、宾阳、上林、马山的 6 个文博馆所，共调查铜鼓 23 面。

第二阶段（5 月 6 日至 14 日），到崇左、钦州、北海三市的 9 个文博馆所，共调查铜鼓 67 面。

第三阶段（5 月 22 日至 26 日），到来宾、柳州两市的 6 个文博馆所，共调查铜鼓 50 面。

第四阶段（6 月 10 日至 7 月 20 日），先到玉林市 5 个文博馆所，共调查铜鼓 70 面，继而对广西民族博物馆 100 面麻江型铜鼓进行了数据采集。

第五阶段（7 月 23 日至 8 月 2 日），到贵港、梧州两市 8 个文博馆所，共调查铜鼓 70 面。

第六阶段（8 月 11 日至 19 日），到桂林、贺州、河池三市 11 个文博馆所，共调查铜鼓 64 面。

第七阶段（8 月 26 日至 9 月 2 日），到百色市 12 个文博馆所，共调查铜鼓 51 面。

第八阶段（9 月 15 日至 11 月 30 日），在广西民族博物馆、广西博物馆、南宁市博物馆、南宁孔庙 4 个文博馆所，共调查铜鼓 276 面。

第九阶段（12 月 8 日至 12 月 12 日），调查东兰县革命纪念馆 1 面麻江型铜鼓，并考察了东兰县罗明金铜鼓铸造厂和环江县韦启初铜鼓铸造厂，观摩记录了当代铜鼓制作技艺。

铜鼓实地调查至此圆满完成。此后大约半年时间，项目组对铜鼓调查所得资料进行了整理和建档，顺利完成了广西馆藏铜鼓数据库的建立。

四、项目成果

此次广西馆藏铜鼓调查，正如下表所反映的，摸清了广西馆藏铜鼓的家底，弄清了广西馆藏铜鼓的分布和保存状况，掌握了所有相关的资料。对于772面馆藏铜鼓，每面均有整体和局部高清晰度数码照片，有包括造型、尺寸、铸造工艺特征、完残情况、纹饰布局、出土或征集等完备的文字记录。所获资料，全部分门别类地建立档案，建成了方便于研究利用的广西馆藏铜鼓数据库。

五、小结

广西馆藏铜鼓调查的完成，实属不易。它体现了自治区文化厅领导的英明决策，体现了全区文物工作者无私奉献的协作精神，体现了项目组全体工作人员不辞辛劳、忘我工作的使命感。项目组的蒋廷瑜、吴崇基、王梦祥、罗坤馨四位老前辈，虽然年事已高，但都能自始至终和年轻人一起，日夜兼程，长途跋涉，亲赴全区各地实地考察，和年轻人一起挥汗作业。项目组的年轻人，非常珍惜这一次全区铜鼓调查的机会，他们勤学好问，在现场向老专家请教，实实在在地学到了很多知识。就是这样一个老中青结合的集体，在短短的半年时间里，辗转全区各地，团结协作，完成了几代人建立广西铜鼓数据库的夙愿。这一成果，必将有助于新一轮铜鼓研究高潮的掀起，铜鼓文化遗产的保护和利用也将会迈上新的台阶。

广西各地馆藏铜鼓统计											
	万家坝型	石寨山型	冷水冲型	遵义型	麻江型	北流型	灵山型	西盟型	异型	越南芒鼓	不明类型	合计
百色起义纪念馆		1			16							17
北海市文管所						2	1					3
北流市博物馆			1			32	2					35
宾阳县博物馆							1					1
博白县文管所						4	4					8
苍梧县文管所						1						1
岑溪市文管所						3						3
崇左市博物馆							1			2		3
大新县博物馆			1		2							3
贵港市博物馆			8			1	1					10
桂林市博物馆			2		32							34
桂平市博物馆			21	1		3						25
合浦县博物馆							2					2
河池市文管所					13							13
贺州市博物馆		1										1
横县博物馆			3				2					5
环江县博物馆					1							1
金城江文管所					1							1
乐业县文管所			1		1							2
灵山县博物馆			1		1	2	21		1			26
凌云县博物馆					1							1
柳江县文管所			2									2

	万家坝型	石寨山型	冷水冲型	遵义型	麻江型	北流型	灵山型	西盟型	异型	越南芒鼓	不明类型	合计
柳州市博物馆			6		28		1	1	2			38
龙胜县文管所					2							2
龙州红八军纪念馆			1				1					2
隆林县博物馆		1			6							7
陆川县文管所						9	3					12
鹿寨县文管所			3									3
马山县文管所			1									1
蒙山县文管所			1		1							2
那坡县博物馆			1		1							2
南丹县文管所					1							1
南宁市博物馆			1	1	10		1					13
平果县博物馆					2							2
平南县博物馆			13			2						15
浦北县博物馆			1			4	12					17
钦州市博物馆					1	1	5					7
容县博物馆			1			3	1	1				6
融水县博物馆					4							4
上林县文管所			7									7
上思县博物馆							2					2
藤县博物馆			5		1	3	1					10
田东县博物馆	3	1										4
田阳县博物馆			1	1								2
梧州市博物馆			2		1	1						4

	万家坝型	石寨山型	冷水冲型	遵义型	麻江型	北流型	灵山型	西盟型	异型	越南芒鼓	不明类型	合计
武鸣县文管所			6		1							7
武宣县博物馆			1									1
西林县博物馆					5							5
象州县博物馆			5									5
来宾市兴宾区文管所			1									1
宜州市博物馆			3		2							5
邕宁县文管所							3					3
右江革命纪念馆			1									1
右江民族博物馆					7							7
玉林市文管所						5	4					9
广西博物馆		4	5		5	1						15
东兰县文管所					2							2
巴马县文管所					1							1
南宁市孔庙博物馆					5							5
广西民族博物馆	1		46	2	221	30	30	3	2		10	345
合计	4	8	152	5	375	107	99	5	5	2	10	772

Nong Xuejian

Review of the Investigation
on Guangxi Bronze Drums in 2014

The successful publication of BRONZE DRUMS IN GUANGXI that benefited from the accomplishment of Project Investigation on Bronze Drums in Guangxi 2014, which was directly organized and supported by Guangxi Zhuang Autonomous Region Department of Culture and Guangxi Zhuang Autonomous Region Administration of Cultural Heritage, and was the outcome of the cooperation between the project team and bronze drums collection institutions in Guangxi. This investigation mainly focused on the bronze drums collected by cultural units of different levels in Guangxi, includes field survey, photos in diverse angles, recordings of measure and description, documents and data works on 772 bronze drums preserved at 62 cultural units in 57 counties that belonged to 14 cities of divided districts in Guangxi. Through this investigation, we possess the comprehensive, actual information and precious data of bronze drums collections of cultural heritage institutions in Guangxi, which being of important meaning to bronze drum research and the protection, usage, inheritance and development of excellent national culture.

I Necessity

Bronze drum investigation, composing of the survey on collection information, origins and figure recordings of bronze drums, is one of the very important base works no matter to do the bronze drum research or to hold exhibitions about bronze drum culture.

1979-1980, under the support of bronze drum collection institutions in Guangdong, Yunnan, Sichuan, Guizhou, Hunan, Hubei, Jiangsu, Zhejiang, Shanghai and Beijing, Museum of Guangxi Zhuang Autonomous Region conducted an investigation on national scale, measured and took recordings of 1383 bronze drums, including 503 collected in all levels of cultural heritage institutions. That was the first time to get a clear picture of the general situation of nationwide bronze drum collections. Then these data were compiled and published as the book Data Compilation of Chinese Ancient Bronze Drum Measurement& Recording, which laid a solid foundation for further research of bronze drums. In 1991, Museum of Guangxi Zhuang Autonomous Region implemented a supplementary investigation and calculation for the compilation of the book Catalog of Guangxi Bronze Drums. According to the statistic, the number of bronze drums collected by all levels of cultural heritage institutions in Guangxi was 629, 126 more than the 1979-1980 investigation.

These two investigations and publications pushed the research on bronze drums ahead directly, and gained remarkable achievements. How ever, it was a pity that the instruments of those investigations were not so fine because of the limits of conditions. Photos were filmed in black and white, as well as a part of the drums were lack of photos and detail information. What's more, the collection situations have changed during the last two decades as more drums were unearthed and collected but no new information was published. Therefore, along with the further researching, it seems very necessity to fully master the collection situations all over Guangxi and to establish a complete data base of bronze drums. In February, 2012, the Chinese Association for Ancient Bronze Drums Research held a council meeting of representatives in Nanning. The meeting brought in a new leader, and decided to relocate the Secretariat from Museum of Guangxi Zhuang Autonomous Region to Anthropology Museum of Guangxi. In the same year, under the proposition and support of Council Director Ms.Qin Pu, who the vice director of Guangxi Zhuang Autonomous Region Department of Culture at that time, the world-wide investigation on bronze drums started, and its first step is to accomplish the investigation on Guangxi preserved bronze drums. Bronze drums preserved in Guangxi takes up one third of national preserved drums, what's more, two systems and 8 types of bronze drums were all discovered in Guangxi, therefore, to make a good investigation on Gunagxi bronze drums and establish a complete database will play an important role and have reference significance to the next stage work of national and global investigation on bronze drums.

II Preparation

In order to insure a smooth and effective investigation on bronze drums collected in Guangxi cultural heritage institutions, the Third Research Department of Anthropology Museum of Guangxi, which undertake the daily work of the Chinese Association for Ancient Bronze Drums Research, made a thorough plan and preparation.

Firstly, a project team constituted of members from Anthropology Museum of Guangxi and Museum of Guangxi Zhuang Autonomous Region was established, with the vice director of Guangxi Zhuang Autonomous Region Department of Culture as project leader, Ms. Qin Pu. Work division of the members were as following: professional guidance by Jiang Tingyu and Nong Xuejian; photography and video recording by Wang Mengxiang, Liu Wenyi; textual recording by Liang Yanli, Lu Qiuyan and Chen Jia; decoration arts survey by Wu Chongji, Luo Kunxin and Cai Hong; casting craft survey by Li Yongchun and Zou Guisen.

Secondly, the project procedures were went through quickly. In order to gain legitimacy of this project and the support of cultural heritage institutions all over Guangxi, in April, 2014, the project team presented an Investigation Plan for Bronze Drums Collected by Cultural Heritage Institutions in Guangxi to Guangxi Zhuang Autonomous Region Department of Culture, and got permission soon. The Department issued a notice document specially to require all the cultural heritage institutions in Guangxi to fully assist this investigation.

Thirdly, they kept track of clues of bronze drums and made a good plan. According to the materials and clues (provided by Mr. Jiang Tingyu) of over 600 bronze drums collected by Guangxi cultural heritage institutions, combined with 667 bronze drums information provided by Guangxi Cultural Heritage Information Center, the project team arranged survey routes for several districts and a schedule for stages.

Fourthly, the detailed items and description standards for recording were prepared. This investigation adopted the 8-types classification method that prevails in China, according to the description recordings of bronze drum shape and decorations that were adopted during the first national bronze drum survey, as well as the recording items and textual description standards according to the contents of Bronze Drum Survey Form used in the cooperation project INVESTIGATION ON BRONZE DRUMS OF BEILIU & LINGSHAN TYPE between China and Japan at the end of 1990's. What's more, photography was conducted according to the standards of the first national survey on portable antiquities.

III Specific implementation

Under the well preparation, field survey started on 21st, April, 2014. Schedule of this survey is as listed below:

The first stage (21st-29th, April), investigated 23 bronze drums preserved in 6 cultural heritage institutions of Wuming, Heng, Binyang, Shanglin and Mashan county.

The second stage (6th-14th, May), investigated 67 bronze drums preserved in 9 cultural heritage institutions of Congzuo, Qinzhou and Beihai city.

The third stage (22nd-26th, May), investigated 50 bronze drums preserved in 6 cultural heritage institutions of Laibin and Liuzhou city.

The fourth stage (10th, June-20th, July), after the investigation on 70 bronze drums preserved in 5 cultural heritage institutions of Yulin city, the project team collected data from 100 bronze drums of Majiang Type which preserved in Anthropology Museum of Guangxi.

The fifth stage (23rd, July-2nd, August), investigated 70 bronze drums preserved in 8 cultural heritage institutions of Guigang and Wuzhou city.

The sixth stage (11th-19th, August), investigated 64 bronze drums preserved in 11 cultural heritage institutions of Guilin, Hezhou and Hechi city.

The seventh stage (26th, August -2nd, September), investigated 51 bronze drums preserved in 12 cultural heritage institutions of Baise city.

The eighth stage (15th, September-30th, November), investigated 276 bronze drums preserved in Anthropology Museum of Guangxi, Museum of Guangxi Zhuang Autonomous Region, Nanning Museum and Nanning Confusion Temple in Nanning city.

The ninth stage (8th-12th, December), investigated 1 bronze drum preserved in Revolution Memorial Museum of Donglan County, and surveyed two bronze drum cast workshops – Donglan County Luo Mingjin Bronze Drum Cast Plant and Huanjiang County Wei Qichu Bronze Drum Cast Plant, surveyed and recorded the cast craft of modern bronze drums.

Until this, field survey of the investigation had been finished. Half a year later, project team sorted and collated materials got from this investigation, and set up a database, succeeded in the construction of Guangxi Preserved Bronze Drum Database.

IV Achievements

This investigation on Guangxi preserved bronze drums, showed as the following table, made the real situations of Guangxi preserved bronze drums clear, including the situations of distribution and preservation conditions, and made us mastered all the relevant materials. For each one of 772 bronze drums, there are high-resolution digital photos of entirety and parts, and complete textual recordings constitute of information of form, size, cast characters, damage situation, patterns layout, excavation or collection origin. All the materials have been sorted to create files, and established a database of Guangxi preserved bronze drums for further research.

V Summary

It's not easy to accomplish this investigation. It shows the brilliant decision of Guangxi Zhuang Autonomous Region Department of Culture, the team cooperation of self-giving antiquarian all over Guangxi, and the mission sense of hardworking and selfless team members. Although they were already of advanced years, the 4 senior researchers in project team – Jiang Tingyu, Wu Chongji, Wang Mengxiang and Luo Kunxin – worked all along with the young night and day, got through the long and hard journey to do field survey everywhere. The elder and the younger, they sweated together. Young people in the project team cherished this opportunity very much. They were inquisitive and hardworking, raised many on-site consultations to the experts, which made them learn much more knowledge about bronze drums. In the short half of year, this group that composes of the old, the middle aged and the young, traveled all over the province, collaborated with each other, fulfilled the wish of generations to establish a bronze drum database of Guangxi. This achievement is sure to be helpful for a new research enthusiasm, as well as to push the protection and usage of bronze drum cultural heritage into a new stage.

	Wanjiaba Type	Shizhaishan Type	Lengshui-Chong Type	Zunyi Type	Majiang Type	Beiliu Type	Lingshan Type	Ximeng Type	Abnormal shape	Mang Type of Vietnam	Unclear Type	total
Baise Uprising Memorial Hall		1			16							17
Beihai City Cultural Relics Administration						2	1					3
Beiliu City Museum			1			32	2					35
Binyang County Museum							1					1
Bobai CountyCultural Relics Administration						4	4					8
Cangwu County Cultural Relics Administration						1						1
Cenxi City Cultural Relics Administration						3						3
Chongzuo City Museum							1			2		3
Daxin County Museum			1	2								3
Guigang City Museum			8			1	1					10
Guilin City Museum			2		32							34
Guiping City Museum			21	1		3						25
Hepu Museum							2					2
Hechi City Cultural Relics Administration			13									13

	Wanjiaba Type	Shizhaishan Type	Lengshui-Chong Type	Zunyi Type	Majiang Type	Beiliu Type	Lingshan Type	Ximeng Type	Abnormal shape	Mang Type of Vietnam	Unclear Type	total
Hezhou City Museum		1										1
Heng County Museum			3				2					5
Huanjiang County Museum					1							1
Jinchengjiang Cultural Relics Administration					1							1
Leye County Cultural Relics Administration			1		1							2
Lingshan County Museum			1		1	2	21		1			26
Lingyun County Museum					1							1
Liujiang County Museum			2									2
Liuzhou City Museum			6		28		1	1	2			38
Longsheng County Cultural Relics Administration					2							2
Longzhou Memorial Hall for the Eighth Red Army			1				1					2
Longlin County Museum	1				6							7
Luchuan County Cultural Relics Administration						9	3					12
Luzhai County Cultural Relics Administration			3									3
Mashan County Cultural Relics Administration			1									1
Mengshan County Cultural Relics Administration			1		1							2
Napo County Museum			1		1							2

	Wanjiaba Type	Shizhaishan Type	Lengshui-Chong Type	Zunyi Type	Majiang Type	Beiliu Type	Lingshan Type	Ximeng Type	Abnormal shape	Mang Type of Vietnam	Unclear Type	total
Nandan County Cultural Relics Administration					1							1
Nanning City Museum			1	1	10		1					13
Pingguo County Museum					2							2
Pingnan County Museum			13			2						15
Pubei County Museum			1			4	12					17
Qinzhou City Museum					1	1	5					7
Rong County Museum			1			3	1	1				6
Rongshui County Museum					4							4
Shanglin County Cultural Relics Administration			7									7
Shangsi County Museum							2					2
Teng County Museum			5		1	3	1					10
Tiandong County Museum	3	1										4
Tianyang County Museum			1	1								2
Wuzhou City Museum			2		1	1						4
Wuming County Cultural Relics Administration			6		1							7
Wuxuan County Museum			1									1
Xilin County Museum					5							5
Xiangzhou County Museum			5									5

	Wanjiaba Type	Shizhaishan Type	Lengshui-Chong Type	Zunyi Type	Majiang Type	Beiliu Type	Lingshan Type	Ximeng Type	Abnormal shape	Mang Type of Vietnam	Unclear Type	total
Xingbin District Cultural Relics Administration of Laibin City			1									1
Yizhou City Museum			3		2							5
Yongning County Cultural Relics Administration							3					3
Youjiang Revolution Memorial Museum			1									1
Youjiang Museum of Nationalities					7							7
Yulin City Cultural Relics Administration						5	4					9
Museum of Guangxi Zhuang Autonomous Region	4		5		5	1						15
Donglan County Cultural Relics Administration					2							2
Bama County Cultural Relics Administration					1							1
Nanning City Museum of Confusion Temple					5							5
Anthropology Museum of Guangxi	1		46	2	221	30	30	3	2		10	345
Summary	4	8	152	5	375	107	99	5	5	2	10	772

万家坝型铜鼓
Wanjiaba Type

以云南省楚雄彝族自治州万家坝墓葬出土的一批铜鼓为代表，流行年代为春秋战国时期（约公元前 8 世纪至公元前 5 世纪）。主要分布于云南省中部偏西地区、广西西部、越南西北部和泰国北部。历史上铸造和使用该型铜鼓的民族有濮和骆越。其特点是体型小而略扁，鼓面窄小，鼓胸特别凸出，鼓面至鼓胸自然过渡，形成同一弧线，鼓腰极度收束，鼓足短，足径大，足沿内有一周折边；器壁浑厚，器表粗糙，部分通体无纹，部分装饰稚拙简朴的花纹；鼓腰之际有四小扁耳。此型是原始形态的铜鼓。

The bronze drums unearthed in Wanjiaba Tombs of Chuxiong Yi Autonomous Prefecture, Yunnan province are the representatives of this type, which was popular from Spring and Autumn Period to Warring States Period (about 8 C.B.C.–5 C.B.C.) and mainly scattered in the central or west Yunnan, west Guangxi, northwest Vietnam and north Thailand. Pu and Luoyue people cast and used this type of bronze drums in history. This type has a small drum face, remarkable arch chest; there is a natural transition from face to chest, forming an arc;slender waist and a short, foot big round lower part with its edge fold inside. The motif features are simple, nature, kind of uncomplicated, and comes on steady feeling. Some of this type drums have no patterns, some are decorated by simple patterns. 4 small flat handles are between chest and waist. Wanjiaba Type is the most primitive type of bronze drums.

1

总号 005044，分类号 0331，素纹铜鼓，出土于云南西部地区，1984 年广西壮族自治区博物馆与云南省博物馆交换得来，2007 年由广西壮族自治区博物馆拨交广西民族博物馆，现存广西民族博物馆。面径 36—37 厘米，身高 31.8 厘米。

Bronze Drum with no patterns(No.005044, CN: 0331), unearthed in western area of Yunnan Province, exchanged from Yunnan Museum by Museum of Guangxi Zhuang Autonomous Region in 1984, and was allotted to Anthropology Museum of Guangxi in 2007. Now it is preserved at Anthropology Museum of Guangxi.
Face Diameter: 36−37cm, Height:31.8cm

2

总号 000020，南哈坡鼓（A），1993 年 3 月 17 日出土于百色市田东县祥周乡联福村南哈屯联合中心小学，现存田东县博物馆。面径 49—50 厘米，身高 31.2 厘米。

Bronze Drum Nanha Po(A) (No.000020), unearthed at the Central Elementary School, Nanha Tun, Lianfu Village, Xiangzhou, Tiandong County, Baise City on March 17th ,1993. Now it is preserved at Tiandong Museum. Face Diameter: 49-50cm, Height:31.2cm

鼓面细部

鼓耳

鼓足细部

3

总号 000021，南哈坡鼓（B），1993 年 3 月 18 日出土于百色市田东县祥周乡联福村南哈屯联合中心小学，现存田东县博物馆。面径 47.5—48 厘米，身高 36.5—37.5 厘米。

Bronze Drum Nanha Po(B) (No.000021), unearthed at the Central Elementary School, Nanha Tun, Lianfu Village, Xiangzhou, Tiandong County, Baise City on March 18th ,1993. Now it is preserved at Tiandong Museum. Face Diameter: 47.5−48cm, Height:36.5−37.5cm

鼓耳

鼓面太阳纹饰

鼓腰纹饰

4

总号 000025，大岭坡鼓，1994
年 6 月 14 日出土于百色市田东
县林逢乡和同村小沙屯大岭坡，
伴随出土的有铜编钟，现存田东
县博物馆。面径 33.7—35 厘米，
身高 29.5 厘米。

Bronze Drum Daling Po
（No.000025), unearthed at Daling
Po, Xiaosha Tun, Hetong Village,
Linfeng, Tiandong County, Baise
City on June 14th,1994,along
with a bronze bell. Now it is
preserved at Tiandong Museum.
Face Diameter: 33.7-35cm,
Height:29.5cm

鼓面

鼓耳

鼓腰纹饰

石寨山型铜鼓
Shizhaishan Type

以云南省晋宁县石寨山墓葬出土的一批铜鼓为代表。流行年代为战国至汉代（约公元前5世纪至公元1世纪）。该型铜鼓分布以云南为中心，北到四川南部，东北到贵州毕节，东南到广西贵港，并普遍流行于东南亚地区，最南至印度尼西亚。历史上铸造和使用该型铜鼓的民族有滇、骆越、劳浸、靡莫、夜郎和句町等。其特点是鼓面大于鼓腰，鼓胸凸出，腰部横截面呈梯形，鼓足较高，纹饰丰富华丽。翔鹭纹、牛纹、羽人划船纹、羽人舞蹈纹、砍牛祭祀等写实图案再现了古代南方民族的社会生活。此型是成熟期铜鼓，由万家坝型发展而来。

This type was represented by the drums unearthed from the tombs at Shizhaishan, Jinning, Yunnan province. Its popular time was from the Warring State Period to Han Dynasty (about 5 C.B.C.–1 C.A.C.). Centered on Yunnan, it scattered over a big area: north to south Sichuan, northeast to Bijie of Guizhou, southeast to Guigang of Guangxi, prevailing over Southeast Asia, and the most south to Indonesia. Dian, Luoyue, Laojin, Mimo, Yelang and Gouding cast and used this type of bronze drums in history. Characters of this type are: face larger than waist, chest arching out, trapezoidal cross–section of waist, a higher foot and gorgeous decorations. The realist images of flying herons, cattle, feathermen boating, feathermen dancing and cutting cattle for sacrifice, make the social life of ancient southern ethnic reappear. This type was in the maturation stage of bronze drum arts, and was developed from Wanjiaba Type.

1

参 0003，2012 年购于靖西，现存广西民族博物馆。面径 68.7—69.7 厘米，残高 22.3 厘米。

Bronze Drum CN.0003, collected in Jingxi County in 2012, now is preserved at Anthropology Museum of Guangxi.
Face Diameter: 68.7−69.7cm, Remained Height:22.3cm

鼓胸羽人划船纹

鼓胸鱼纹

鼓胸鸟纹

2

总号 08329，上 1611，翔鹭纹铜鼓（又名贵港高中鼓），1955 年出土于贵县高中 8 号墓，现存广西壮族自治区博物馆。面径 42.3—42.5 厘米，身高 24.5 厘米。

Bronze Drum with flying heron patterns(No.08329, EN:1611, alternate name The drum of Guigang High School), unearthed in Gui County High School Tomb(Han) No.8 in 1955. Now it is preserved at Museum of Guangxi Zhuang Autonomous Region. Face Diameter: 42.3–42.5cm, Height:24.5cm

鼓面细部纹饰

鼓腰纹饰

3

总号19488，土10847，翔鹭纹铜鼓（又名罗泊湾M1:10号鼓），1976年出土于贵县罗泊湾一号汉墓，现存广西壮族自治区博物馆。面径56.2厘米，身高36.8厘米。

Bronze Drum with flying heron patterns (No.19488, EN:10847, alternate name The drum of Luobo Wan No.M1:10), unearthed in Luobo Wan Tomb(Han) No.1 in 1976. Now it is preserved at Museum of Guangxi Zhuang Autonomous Region.
Face Diameter:56.2cm, Height:36.8cm

鼓面

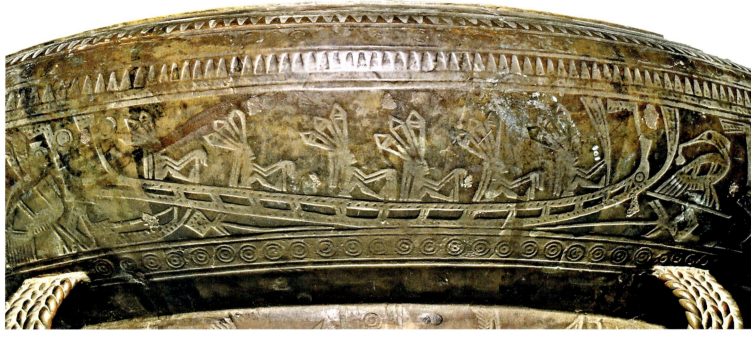

鼓面纹饰细部

鼓足铭文

鼓胸羽人划船纹

鼓腰羽人舞蹈纹

4

总号 19785，土 10992，羽人划船纹栉纹铜鼓（又名罗泊湾 M1:11 号鼓），1976 年出土于贵县罗泊湾一号汉墓，现存广西壮族自治区博物馆。面径 28.8 厘米，身高 24.4 厘米。

Bronze Drum with feathermen rowing and comb patterns(No.19785, EN:10992, alternate name The drum of Luobo Wan Tomb No.M1:11), unearthed in Luobo Wan Tomb(Han) No.1, Gui County in 1976. Now it is preserved at Museum of Guangxi Zhuang Autonomous Region.
Face Diameter:28.8cm, Height:24.4cm

鼓胸划船纹拓片

5

总号 09987，土 3269，锯齿纹小铜鼓（又名田东锅盖岭鼓），1977 年 8 月出土于百色市田东县祥周公社甘蓬大队锅盖岭一号墓，现存广西壮族自治区博物馆。面径 23.4 厘米，残高 11.8 厘米。

Bronze Drum with sawtooth patterns(No.09987, EN:3269, alternate name The drum of Tiandong Guogai Ling), unearthed at Guogai Ling Tomb No.1, Ganpeng Village, Xiangzhou Commune, Tiandong County, Baise City in August, 1977. Now it is preserved at Museum of Guangxi Zhuang Autonomous Region.
Face Diameter:23.4cm Remained, Height:11.8cm

鼓面局部

6
总号 06998，土 0280，翔鹭纹铜鼓（又名西林 280 号鼓），1972 年出土于西林普驮粮站，现存广西壮族自治区博物馆。面径 77.5—78.2 厘米，身高 49.5 厘米。

Bronze Drum with flying heron patterns (No.06998, EN:0280, alternate name The drum of Xilin No.281), unearthed at Putuo Grain Supply Center, Xilin County, Baise City in 1972. Now it is preserved at Museum of Guangxi Zhuang Autonomous Region.
Face Diameter:77.5−78.2cm, Height:49.5cm

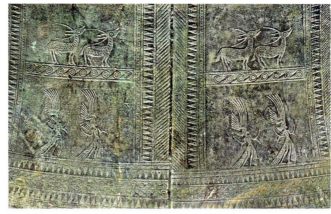

鼓腰局部

鼓腰羽人纹鹿纹

鼓胸羽人划船纹

鼓面

7

总号 07000，土 0282，翔鹭纹铜鼓（又名西林 282 号鼓），1972 年 7 月出土于百色市西林县普驮粮站，现存广西壮族自治区博物馆。面径 57.2—57.5 厘米，残高 16.5 厘米。

Bronze Drum with flying heron patterns(No.07000, EN:0282, alternate name The drum of Xilin No.282), unearthed at Putuo Grain Supply Center, Xilin County, Baise City in July, 1972. Now it is preserved at Museum of Guangxi Zhuang Autonomous Region. Face Diameter: 57.2−57.5cm, Height:16.5cm

鼓面太阳纹局部

鼓面纹饰细部

8
总号 07001、土 0283、翔鹭纹铜鼓（又名西林 283 号鼓），1972 年 7 月出土于百色市西林县
普驮粮站，现存广西壮族自治区博物馆。面径 51.6—52 厘米，身高 40.2 厘米。

Bronze Drum with flying heron patterns, (No.07001, EN:0283, alternate name The drum of Xilin
No.283), unearthed at Putuo Grain Supply Center, Xilin County, Baise City in July, 1972. Now it is
preserved at Museum of Guangxi Zhuang Autonomous Region.
Face Diameter: 51.6—52cm, Height:40.2cm

鼓面局部

鼓足立饰

9

总号001047，百色龙川鼓，1977年出土于百色龙川公社合乐大队，现存百色起义纪念馆。面径40.8—41.3厘米，身高29.7厘米。

Bronze Drum Longchuan (No.001047), unearthed at Hele Village, Longchuan Commune, Baise City in 1977. Now it is preserved at Baise Uprising Memorial Hall.
Face Diameter:40.8—41.3cm, Height:29.7cm

鼓面

鼓腰

鼓耳

10

总号 000260，共和村鼓，1990 年 9 月出土于百色市隆林县扁牙乡共和村河岸，现存隆林县博物馆。面径 44.5 厘米，身高 28.5。

Bronze Drum Gonghe Cun(No.000260), unearthed at river bank of Gonghe Village, Bianya, Longlin County, Baise City in September, 1990. Now it is preserved at Longlin Museum.

Face Diameter:44.5cm, Height:28.5cm

鼓耳

鼓腰牛纹

鼓面

11

战国竞渡纹牛纹铜鼓，
1991 年 7 月 18 日出土于
贺县（现贺州市）沙田龙
中村，现存贺州市博物
馆。面径36.4—36.5厘米，
身高 27.5 厘米。

Bronze Drum with boat
racing and cattle patterns,
made in Warring States
Period, unearthed at
Longzhong Village,
Shatian, He County on
July 18th, 1991. Now it
is preserved at Hezhou
Museum.
Face Diameter:36.4−36.5cm,
Height:27.5cm

鼓胸竞渡纹

鼓腰局部

鼓腰牛纹

12

西林 281 号铜鼓，1972
年 7 月出土于百色市西
林县普驮村铜鼓墓葬，
现存北京民族文化宫。
面径 72 厘米，身高 49
厘米。

Bronze Drum Xilin
(No.281), unearthed in
tombs of Putuo Village,
Baise city on July, 1972.
Now it is preserved at
The Cultural Palace of
Nationalities of Beijing.
Face Diameter:72cm,
Height:49cm

鼓耳

鼓腰羽人纹

鼓腰羽人纹

鼓面

冷水冲型铜鼓
Lengshuichong Type

以广西藤县濛江镇横村冷水冲出土的铜鼓为代表。流行年代为东汉至北宋（约公元 1 世纪至公元 12 世纪）。主要分布于广西的左右江、黔江、郁江、浔江沿岸一带，西到云南陆良，北达四川古蔺，南至越南北部的红河流域及泰国。历史上铸造和使用该型铜鼓的民族是僚。其特点是形体高大而壁薄，鼓面不出沿或略出沿，鼓胸直径略大于或等于鼓面直径，鼓腰上部内收成筒形，鼓足较高，鼓耳宽大，多饰辫纹。纹饰密集且高度图案化，立体装饰丰富，多为青蛙，部分还饰乘骑、马、鸟、龟等立体装饰。此型为石寨山型铜鼓发展而成。

This type was represented by the drums unearthed at Lengshuichong, Heng Village, Mengjiag, Teng County. The popular time was from the Eastern Han to the Northern Song (about 1 C.A.C.–12 C.A.C.). Lengshuichong Type mostly distributes in the areas along with Zuoyoujiang, Qianjiang, Yujiang, Xunjiang River, west to Luliang of Yunnan, north to Gulin of Sichuan, south to the Red River in Northern Vietnam and Thailand. Liao people cast and used this type of bronze drums in history. This type has a tall and thin form, large face and its' edge not or just a little projecting out. The chest is a bit larger than the face or as large as the face, slightly arch but not projecting out; the upper waist is kind of tubular. The foot is as high as the chest; handles are big and flat, decorated with braid motifs. Character of the decorations is magnificent and complex in general; various statues, most of them are frog statues; between the frogs, sometimes there are more statues such as horse, horse-riders, bird, tortoise, and so on. This type was developed from Shizhaishan Type.

1

总号 004824，族鼓 0100 号，乘骑饰变形羽人纹铜鼓（又名 100 号鼓），1975 年出土于梧州市藤县蒙江镇横村冷水冲，现存广西民族博物馆。面径 83—83.6 厘米，身高 60.3 厘米。

Bronze drum with transformed feathermen patterns and horse rider statues(No.004824, ZG No.0100), unearthed at Lengshuichong, Heng Village, Mengjiang Town, Teng County, Wuzhou City in1975. Now it is preserved at Anthropology Museum of Guangxi. Face Diameter: 83–83.6cm, Height:60.3cm

鼓面乘骑立饰

鼓面蛙饰

鼓耳

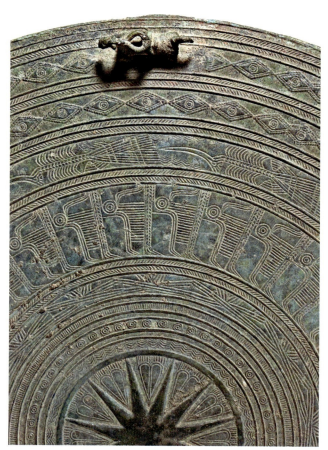

鼓面局部

2

总号 004826，族鼓 0102 号，乘
骑水鸟饰变形羽人纹铜鼓（又名
102 号鼓），20 世纪 50 年代初
出土于梧州市藤县和平区古竹
乡，现存广西民族博物馆。面径
87.8—89 厘米，身高 66.5 厘米。

Bronze drum with transformed
feathermen patterns and
horse rider mixed waterfowl
statues(No.004826, ZG No.0102),
unearthed at Guzhu, Heping
District of Teng County,
Wuzhou City in the 50s' of the
last century. Now it is preserved
at Anthropology Museum of
Guangxi.
Face Diameter: 87.8−89cm,
Height:66.5cm

鼓面蛙饰

鼓面单乘骑立饰

鼓面水鸟立饰

鼓面

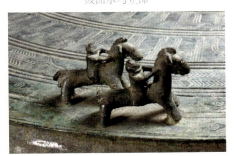

鼓面双乘骑立饰

3

总号 004827，族鼓 0103，牛拉橇饰变形羽人纹铜鼓（又名 103 号鼓），1954 年征集于桂平县，现存广西民族博物馆。面径 82—82.7 厘米，身高 59.5 厘米。

Bronze drum with transformed feathermen patterns and cart-dragging ox statutes(No.004827,ZG No.0103), collected in Guiping County in 1954. Now it is preserved at Anthropology Museum of Guangxi. Face Diameter: 82—82.7cm, Height:59.5cm

鼓面牛拉撬立饰（侧）

鼓面牛拉撬立饰（正）

鼓身

鼓面

4

总号 004834，族鼓 0110 号，乘骑饰变形羽人纹铜鼓（又名 110 号鼓），1956 年出土于广西来宾市金秀瑶族自治县平道乡。现存广西民族博物馆。面径 62.2—63.5 厘米，身高 41.8 厘米。

Bronze drum with transformed feathermen patterns and horse rider statues(No.004834,ZG No.0110), unearthed at Pingdao, Jinxiu Yao Autonomous County, Laibin City in 1956. Now it is preserved at Anthropology Museum of Guangxi.
Face Diameter: 62.2−63.5cm,
Height:41.8cm

鼓面局部

鼓面乘骑立饰 2

鼓面乘骑立饰 1

5

总号004835，族鼓0111号，鸟饰变形羽人纹铜鼓（又名111号鼓），20世纪50年代初出土于梧州市藤县和平区，现存广西民族博物馆。面径80—80.5厘米，身高55.2厘米。

Bronze drum with transformed feathermen patterns and bird statutes(No.004835, ZG No.0111), unearthed in Heping District of Teng County, Wuzhou City in the 50s' of the last century. Now it is preserved at Anthropology Museum of Guangxi.
Face Diameter: 80−80.5cm, Height:55.2cm

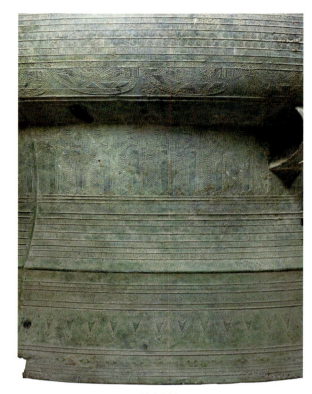

鼓身局部

鼓面鸟立饰

鼓面乘骑立饰

鼓面

6

总号 04840，族鼓 0117。乘骑饰变形羽人纹铜鼓，来源不详，原存广西壮族自治区博物馆，现存广西民族博物馆。面径 72.5—73.3 厘米，身高 51 厘米。

Bronze drum with transformed feathermen patterns and horse rider statues(No.04840, ZG No.0117), the unearthed source unknown. It was originally preserved at Museum of Guangxi Zhuang Autonomous Region, and now at Anthropology Museum of Guangxi.
Face Diameter: 72.5−73.3cm, Height:51cm

鼓面乘骑立饰

鼓耳

鼓面

7

总号004846，族鼓0123号，下渡铜鼓，
1958年冬出土于贵港市平南县上渡
公社下渡水闸，原存广西壮族自治
区，现存广西民族博物馆。面径76.3
厘米，身高52.9厘米。

Bronze Drum Xiadu(No.004846, ZG
No.0123), unearthed at a water gate
of Xiadu Commune, Pingnan County,
Guigang City in the winter of 1958. It
was originally preserved at Museum of
Guangxi Zhuang Autonomous Region
and now at Anthropology Museum of
Guangxi.
Face Diameter: 76.3cm,
Height:52.9cm

鼓面

鼓面蛙饰

鼓面蛙饰2

8

总号 004884，族鼓 0166 号，变形羽人纹铜鼓（又名 166 号鼓），
1957 年征集于广西横县陶圩乡大塘村，现存广西民族博物馆。面
径 72.5—73.5 厘米，身高 52 厘米。

Bronze drum with transformed feathermen patterns(No.004884,ZG
No.0166), collected at Datang Village, Taoxu, Heng County in1957.
Now it is preserved at Anthropology Museum of Guangxi.
Face Diameter: 72.5−73.5cm, Height:52cm

鼓面局部

鼓身局部

9

总号05033，族鼓0320号，覃村铜鼓，1974
年出土于南宁市宾阳县卢圩公社覃村二
队，现存广西民族博物馆。面径81—82.5厘
米，身高58.5厘米。

Bronze Drum Qincun(No.05033, ZG
No.0320), unearthed at the 2nd group of
Qincun Village, Luxu Commune, Binyang
County, Nanning City in 1974. Now it is
preserved at Anthropology Museum of
Guangxi.
Face Diameter: 81−82.5cm, Height: 58.5cm

鼓面蛙饰

鼓面

10

总号05037，族鼓0324号，变形羽人纹铜鼓，1983年出土于宾阳县，7月从宾阳县文化馆运回广西壮族自治区博物馆，现存广西民族博物馆。面径70.5厘米，身高46.8厘米。

Bronze drum with transformed feathermen patterns(No.05037, ZG No.0324), unearthed in Binyang County, Nanning City in 1983 and was transported to Museum of Guangxi Zhuang Autonomous Region. Now it is preserved at Anthropology Museum of Guangxi.
Face Diameter: 70.5cm,
Height:46.8cm

鼓面动物立饰

鼓面蛙饰

鼓面

11

总号 0058，崇丘鼓（又名武鸣 01 号鼓），1975 年 5 月 22 日，武鸣县两江镇三联村村民在那阮屯附近的崇丘坡开荒时发现，现存武鸣县文物管理所。

面径 65—70 厘米，残高 46.5 厘米。

Bronze Drum Dongqiu(No.0058,alternated name Wuming No.01), unearthed by villagers of Sanlian Village, Liangjiang Town, Wuming County, Nanning City when they were cultivating the wasteland on Dongqiu Hill, near Naruan Tun Village on May 22nd,1975. Now it is preserved at Wuming County Cultural Relics Administration. Face Diameter:65−70cm, Height:46.5cm

鼓面

12

凤林村鼓。2014 年 6 月出土于武鸣县罗波镇凤林村，现存武鸣县文物管理所。面径 78.6—80 厘米，身高 55 厘米。

Bronze Drum Fenglin Cun, unearthed at Fenglin Village, Luobo Town, Wuming County, Nanning City in June, 2014. Now it is preserved at Wuming County Cultural Relics Administration.
Face Diameter:78.6—80cm, Height:55cm

鼓面蛙饰

鼓面局部

13

总号 0205，云聪一号鼓，1992 年 5
月 18 日，韦好良用金属探测仪在南
宁市上林县三里屯双罗村云聪屯共
探掘出四面铜鼓，此鼓为其中一面，
5 月 29 日移交县文物管理所收藏，
现存上林县文物管理所。面径 80—
80.8 厘米，身高 61.6 厘米。

Bronze Drum Yuncong No.1(No.0205),
one of the four drums which were
unearthed by Wei Haoliang with
a metal detector at Yuncong Tun,
Shuangluo Village, Sanli Tun, Shanglin
County, Nanning City on May 18th,
1992. He turned them over to County
Cultural Relics Administration on
May 29th, 1992. Now it is preserved
at Shanglin County Cultural Relics
Administration.
Face Diameter:80—80.8cm,
Height:61.6cm

鼓面动物立饰

鼓面蛙饰

鼓面局部

鼓面蛙饰

14

总号 0207，云聪三号鼓，1992 年 5 月 18 日，韦好良用金属探测仪在南宁市上林县三里屯双罗村云聪屯共探掘出四面铜鼓，此鼓为其中一面，5 月 29 日移交县文物管理所收藏，现存上林县文物管理所。面径 78.2—78.5 厘米，身高 58.2 厘米。

Bronze Drum Yuncong No.3(No.0207), one of the four drums which were unearthed by Wei Haoliang with a metal detector at Yuncong Tun, Shuangluo Village, Sanli Tun, Shanglin County, Nanning City on May 18th, 1992. He turned them over to County Cultural Relics Administration on May 29th, 1992. Now it is preserved at Shanglin County Cultural Relics Administration. Face Diameter:78.2−78.5cm, Height:58.2cm

鼓面

鼓面蛙饰

15

总号0208，云聪四号鼓，1992
年5月18日，韦好良用金属探
测仪在南宁市上林县三里屯双罗
村云聪屯共探掘出四面铜鼓，此
鼓为其中一面，5月29日移交
县文物管理所收藏，现存上林县
文物管理所。面径74—75.6厘米，
身高50厘米。

Bronze Drum Yuncong
No.4(No.0208), one of the four
drums which were unearthed
by Wei Haoliang with a metal
detector at Yuncong Tun,
Shuangluo Village, Sanli Tun,
Shanglin County, Nanning City
on May 18th, 1992. He turned
them over to County Cultural
Relics Administration on May
29th, 1992. Now it is preserved at
Shanglin County Cultural Relics
Administration.
Face Diameter:74−75.6cm,
Height:50cm

鼓面立饰

鼓胸船纹

鼓面

16

下康鼓，1993 年 9 月 2 日，南宁市马山县合群乡造华村下康屯村民蓝贵斌在村口一水塘边挖得。现存马山县文物管理所。面径 69.8—70.5 厘米，身高 43 厘米。

Bronze Drum Xiakang, unearthed by Lan Guibin, a villager of Xiakangtun, Zaohua Village, Hequn, Mashan County, Nanning City in a pond beside the village entrance on September 2nd, 1993. Now it is preserved at Mashan County Cultural Relics Administration.
Face Diameter:69.8—70.5cm, Height:43cm

鼓面蛙饰

鼓面

17

Hg00015 号，乘骑铜鼓 I（又名
柳州 640490 号鼓），1973 年 9
月在柳州二级站拣选，现存柳州
市博物馆。面径 73.6—74.9，身
高 54 厘米。

Bronze Drum with horse rider
statues I (Hg00015, alternate name
Liuzhou No.640490), collected
at the Second Metal Station of
Liuzhou in September,1973. Now
it is preserved at Liuzhou Museum.
Face Diameter:73.6—74.9cm,
Height:54cm

鼓面蛙饰

鼓耳

鼓面乘骑立饰

18

Hg00021 号，东汉观斗蛙变形
羽人纹铜鼓（又名武宣 1 号
鼓），1966 年出土于武宣县
车渡码头，1980 年 1 月 6 日
武宣县文化馆征集。现存柳州
市博物馆。面径 89—89.5 厘米，
身高 66 厘米。

Bronze drum with transformed
feathermen patterns and
frog−fight−onlooker statues
(Hg00021, alternate name
Wuxuan No.1), was made
in East Han Dynasty. It was
unearthed at Chedu Dock,
Wuxuan County, in 1966,
collected by Wuxuan County
Culture House on January 6th,
1980, and now it is preserved at
Liuzhou Museum
Face Diameter:89−89.5cm,
Height:66cm

鼓面斗蛙立饰

鼓耳

鼓身局部

鼓面

19

总号 110，分号 007，流塘村铜鼓，
1993 年出土于柳州市柳江县流山乡
流塘村，现存柳江县文物管理所。面
径 62.5—65.6 厘米，身高 48 厘米。

Bronze Drum Liutang(No.110,
CN:007), unearthed at Liutang Village,
Liushan, Liujiang County, Liuzhou City
in 1993. Now it is preserved at Liujiang
County Cultural Relics Administration.
Face Diameter:62.5—65.6cm,
Height:48cm

鼓面乘骑立饰

鼓面蛙饰

鼓耳

鼓面

20

广崖山铜鼓，1985 年出上于鹿
寨县中渡镇广崖山，现存鹿寨县
文物管理所。面径 65.5—68.5 厘
米，残高 45 厘米。

Bronze Drum Guangya Shan,
unearthed at Guangya Hill,
Zhongdu Town, Luzhai County
in 1985. Now it is preserved at
Luzhai County Cultural Relic
Administration.
Face Diameter:65.5−68.5cm,
Remained Height:45cm

鼓面蛙饰

鼓耳

鼓面乘骑立饰

21

藤 03 号，平福鼓（又名藤县 3
号鼓），1974 年出土于藤县平
福乡四方村，现存藤县博物馆。
面径 82.1—83.8 厘米，身高 60.2
厘米。

Bronze Drum Pingfu(Teng
No.03,alternate name Teng
County No.3), unearthed at Sifang
Village, Pingfu, Teng County
in1974. Now it is preserved at Teng
County Museum.
Face Diameter:82.1−83.8cm,
Height:60.2cm

鼓面

鼓面龟饰

鼓身局部

22

藤 04 号，濛江镇鼓。1964 年出
土于藤县濛江镇西山坡，现存藤
县博物馆。面径 68.3—69.4 厘米，
身高 48 厘米。

Bronze Drum Mengjiang
Zhen(Teng No.04), unearthed
on the slope of the West Hill,
Mengjiang Town, Teng County in
1964. Now it is preserved at Teng
County Museum.
Face Diameter:68.3~69.4cm,
Height:48cm

鼓面火灶立饰

鼓耳

鼓面

23

藤 05 号，志成村鼓，1951
年出土于藤县和平镇志成
村山坡，现存藤县博物馆。
面径 63.3—64.1 厘米，残
高 38.5 厘米。

Bronze Drum Zhicheng
Cun(Teng No.05),
unearthed on a hill of
Zhicheng Village, Heping
Town, Teng County
in1951. Now it is preserved
at Teng County Museum.
Face Diameter:63.3−64.1cm,
Height:38.5cm

鼓面动物立饰

鼓面乘骑立饰

鼓耳

鼓面局部

鼓面

24

总号 02，高堆村鼓，1990 年 9 月出土于蒙山西河镇高堆村德梗组营盘岭，现存蒙山县文物管理所。面径 69.4—70.8 厘米，身高 47 厘米。

Bronze Drum Gaodui Cun(No.02), unearthed at Yingpan Ling, Degeng, Gaodui Village, Xihe Town, Mengshan County in September,1990. Now it is preserved at Mengshan County Cultural Relics Adiministrtion. Face Diameter:69.4-70.8cm, Height:47cm

鼓面乘骑立饰

鼓面蛙饰

鼓耳

25

总号545，万新村铜鼓（又名贵港696号鼓），1978年出土于贵港庆丰乡万新村西南约300米处，现存贵港市博物馆。面径76—77.7厘米，身高52.6厘米。

Bronze Drum Wanxin Cun(No.545, alternate name The drum of Guigang No.696), unearthed at the southwest of 300m to Wanxing Village, Qingfeng, Guigang City in 1978. Now it is preserved at Guigang Museum.
Face Diameter:76—77.7cm, Height:52.6cm

鼓面局部

鼓面乘骑立饰

鼓腰

鼓胸

鼓面局部

26

总号 580，长岭铜鼓，1982 年 4 月出土于贵港东龙镇柳蓬村东北长岭，现存贵港市博物馆。面径 79.4—79.7 厘米，残高 48 厘米。

Bronze Drum Changling(No.580), unearthed at the northeast of Changling, Liupeng Village, Donglong Town, Guigang City in April 1982. Now it is preserved at Guigang Museum.
Face Diameter:79.4–79.7cm,
Remained Height:48cm

鼓面蛙饰

27

总号 01，东胜屯铜鼓，
1979 年 2 月出土于平南
官城镇八宝村东胜屯坡
地，现存平南县博物馆。
面径 86.3—87.5 厘米，身
高 59.5 厘米。

Bronze Drum Dongsheng
Tun(No.01), unearthed on
a slope of Dongsheng Tun,
Babao Village, Guancheng
Town, Pingnan County
in Feburary,1979. Now it
is preserved at Pingnan
Museum.
Face Diameter:86.3–87.5cm,
Height:59.5cm

鼓面局部

鼓面蛙饰

鼓身局部

28

总号 02，古蓬坪铜鼓（又名平南 2 号鼓），1979 年 3 月出土于平南同和镇陈龙村古蓬坪屯溷勒冲白坟坪西坡，现存平南县博物馆。面径 69.8—71.5 厘米，身高 47.7 厘米。

Bronze Drum Gupengping(No.02,alternate name The drum of Pingnan No.2), unearthed on the west slope of Baifenping, Hunleichong, Gupengpingtun, Chenlong Village, Tonghe Town, Pingnan County in March,1979. Now it is preserved at Pingnan Museum.
Face Diameter:69.8—71.5cm,
Height:47.7cm

鼓面蛙饰

鼓面动物立饰 1

鼓面动物立饰 2

鼓耳

鼓胸变形船纹

鼓足细部

29

总号 1304，深塘村铜鼓（又名
平南 1304 号鼓），1981 年 11 月
出土于平南官城镇八宝村深塘村
（屯）西北面中央冲鲶鱼岭西北
坡，现存平南县博物馆。面径
63.5 厘米，身高 43 厘米。

Bronze Drum Shentang
Cun(No.1304, alternate name
Pingnan No.1304), unearthed on
the northwest slope of Nianyuling,
Zhongyangchong, the northwest
of Shentang Village, Babao,
Guancheng Town, Pingnan
County in November, 1981. Now it
is preserved at Pingnan Museum.
Face Diameter:63.5cm,
Height:43cm

鼓面动物立饰

鼓面谷仓立饰

鼓身

30

总号 2404，大岭铜鼓，
1991 年 7 月出土于平南
安怀镇高荔村莲塘屯大
岭顶上，现存平南县博
物馆。面径 67—68.2 厘
米，身高 46.2 厘米。

Bronze Drum
Daling(No.2404),
unearthed on the top of
Daling Hill, Liantang
Tun of Gaoli Village,
Anhuai Town, Pingnan
County in July,1991. Now
it is preserved at Pingnan
Museum.
Face Diameter:67—68.2cm,
Height:46.2cm

鼓面局部

鼓面动物立饰

鼓耳

31

总号 2406，武多鼓，2003
年 10 月出土于平南同和
镇武全村武多屯六振冲半
山村道旁，现存平南县
博物馆。面径 68.5—69.4
厘米，身高 48 厘米。

Bronze Drum
Wuduo(No.2406),
unearthed beside the
village road lies in
Liuzhenchong, Wuduo
Tun of Wuquan Village,
Tonghe Town, Pingnan
County in October, 2003.
Now it is preserved at
Pingnan Museum.
Face Diameter:68.5-69.4cm,
Height:48cm

鼓面田螺立饰 1

鼓面田螺立饰 2

鼓耳

鼓面蛙饰

鼓腰

32

总号 000436，樟村铜鼓（又名桂平 3 号鼓），1972 年出土于桂平西山镇渡头村樟村屯西浔江岸台，现存桂平市博物馆。面径 85—85.5 厘米，身高 62 厘米。

Bronze Drum Zhangcun(No.000436,alternate name Guiping No.3), unearthed at the bank of Xunjiang River, the west of Zhangcun Tun, Dutou Village, Xishan Town, Guigping City in 1972. Now it is preserved at Guiping Museum.
Face Diameter:85–85.5cm,
Height:62cm

鼓面龟饰

鼓面蛙饰

鼓耳

鼓面

33

总号 000439，朱冲铜鼓，1978 年出土于
桂平油麻镇六平村南约 80 米的朱冲山上，
现存桂平市博物馆。面径 69.8—71 厘米，
身高 44.4 厘米。

Bronze Drum Zhuchong(No.000439),
unearthed at the south of 80m to Liuping
Village, Youma Town, Guigping City
in1978. Now it is preserved at Guiping
Museum.
Face Diameter:69.8—71cm, Height:44.4cm

鼓面局部

鼓腰局部

鼓耳

34

总号 000445，石鼓岭铜鼓（又名桂平 12 号鼓），1972 年出土于贵港市桂平石咀镇石鼓岭村西南河边水田，现存桂平市博物馆。面径 73.3—74.3 厘米，身高 48.3 厘米。

Bronze Drum Shiguling(No.000445,alternate name The drum of Guiping No.12), unearthed in paddy field beside the river at the southwest of Shiguling Village, Shizui Town, Guigping City in 1972. Now it is preserved at Guiping Museum. Face Diameter:73.3~74.3cm, Height:48.3cm

鼓面乘骑立饰

鼓面花树立饰

鼓耳

鼓面

35

总号000447，鹤岭铜鼓（又名桂平13号鼓），1980年6月出土于桂平西山乡福山村东屯西南约一公里的鹤岭，现存桂平市博物馆。面径80.3—80.8厘米，身高58.7厘米。

Bronze Drum Heling(No.000447,alternate name The drum of Guiping No.13), unearthed at He-ling, the southwest of 1km to Dong Tun, Fushan Village, Xishan town, Guigping City in June,1980. Now it is preserved at Guiping Museum.
Face Diameter:80.3—80.8cm, Height:58.7cm

鼓面局部

鼓面女童喂马立饰 2

鼓面女童喂马立饰 1

鼓面蛙饰

36

总号 000449，寻旺村鼓（又名桂平 449 号鼓），1983 年 3月 24 日出土于桂平寻旺村西南，现存桂平市博物馆。面径72.673.8 厘米，残高 40 厘米。

Bronze Drum
XunWangcun(No.000449,alternate
name The drum of Guiping
No.449), unearthed at the
southwest of Xunwang Village,
Guigping City on March 24th,
1983. Now it is preserved at
Guiping Museum.
Face Diameter:72.6—73.8cm.
Remained Height:40cm

鼓面乘骑立饰

鼓面蛙饰

鼓面动物立饰

鼓面

37

总号 000451，理村铜鼓（又名
桂平 451 号鼓），1982 年出土于
桂平垌心乡理村北约 50 米坡地，
现存桂平市博物馆。面径 36.5—
37 厘米。

Bronze Drum
Licun(No.000451,alternatd name
The drum of Guiping No.451),
unearthed at the north of 50m to
Licun Village, Dongxin, Guigping
City in 1982. Now it is preserved at
Guiping Museum.
Face Diameter:36.5−37cm

鼓面纹饰细部 1   鼓面纹饰细部 2

鼓面

38

总号：000613，张凌彭铜鼓，1993 年 1 月 31 日出土于桂平金田镇狮燕村张凌彭村南约 50 米处，现存桂平市博物馆。面径 73—74 厘米，身高 48.8 厘米。

Bronze Drum Zhanglingpeng(No.000613), unearthed in the south of 50m to Zhanglingpeng, Xinyan Village, Jintian Town, Guiping City on January 31st, 1993. Now it is preserved at Guiping Museum.
Face Diameter:73—74cm, Height:48.8cm

鼓面立饰 2

鼓面立饰 1

鼓面蛙饰

鼓面

39

汉行走鹭纹铜鼓（小），宜州市
西郊约 20 公里怀远镇冲英屯村
民潘立敏葬祖取土时在村后山脚
挖出大小两面相套和的铜鼓，
此为其中一面较小的铜鼓，1995
年上交，现存宜州市博物馆。面
径33.2—33.8厘米，身高24.6厘米。

Bronze drum with walking heron
patterns(smaller), unearthed at
the foot of a mountain behind
Chongying Tun Village of
Huaiyuan Town, the western
suburbs of 20km from Yizhou City,
by a villager named Pan Limin
when he was digging the earth in
his ancestor's burial. This is the
smaller one of the two bronze
drums which were dug out one
inside the other. It was turned over
in 1995. Now it is preserved at
Yizhou Museum.
Face Diameter:33.2–33.8cm,
Height:24.6cm

鼓面

鼓面细部　　　　　　鼓身

40

东汉蹲蛙翔鹭纹铜鼓，70 年
代原宜山县矮山乡良山冲屯
（今宜州市庆远镇良山冲屯）
潘姓农民耙玉米地时发现，现
存宜州市博物馆。面径 66.4—
66.8 厘米，身高 44.7 厘米。

Bronze drum with flying heron
patterns and frog statutes,
unearthed by Pan, a villager of
Liangshanchong Tun, Qingyuan
Town, Yizhou City when he was
harrowing his cornfields in the
70s' of the last century. Now it is
preserved at Yizhou Museum.
Face Diameter:66.4－66.8cm,
Height:44.7cm

鼓面蛙饰

鼓耳

鼓足

鼓面局部

41

古防鼓，1989 年 7 月出
土于来宾县北五乡白山
上马寨村西北古防崖榕
村山东坡，现存来宾市
兴宾区文物管理所。面
径 80—81.7 厘米，身高
54.2 厘米。

Bronze Drum Gufang,
unearthed at a hill named
Shandong Po, which lies
in Rongcun, Gufang Cliff,
the northwest of Baishan
Shangmazhai Village,
Beiwu, Laibin County
in July, 1989. Now it is
preserved at Xingbin
District Cultural Relics
Administration of Laibin
City.
Face Diameter: 80—81.7cm,
Height:54.2cm

鼓面鱼纹

鼓面蛙饰

鼓身

42

总号 0061，分号 036，崇山鼓，1974 年 4 月 7 日出土于象州县寺村镇崇山村崇山南约 700 米，现存象州县博物馆。面径 75.5—76.4 厘米，身高 52.5 厘米。

Bronze Drum Chongshan(No.0061, CN:036), unearthed at the south of 700m to the Chongshan Hill of Chongshan Village, Sicun Town, Xiangzhou County on April 7th, 1974. Now it is preserved at Xiangzhou Museum.
Face Diameter: 75.5–76.4cm, Height:52.5cm

鼓面乘骑立饰

鼓面局部

鼓耳

43

总号 0727，分号 048，罗汉村鼓，1976 年 12 月出土于象州县中平乡罗汉村南约 500 米水田中，现存象州县博物馆。面径 88.3—89 厘米，残高 53.5 厘米。

Bronze Drum Luohan Cun(No.0727, CN:048), unearthed in the paddy field at the south of 500m to Luohan Village, Zhongping, Xiangzhou County in December,1976. Now it is preserved at Xiangzhou Museum. Face Diameter: 88.3−89cm, Remained Height:53.5cm

鼓面乘骑立饰

鼓面蛙饰

鼓耳

鼓面乘骑立饰 2

鼓面动物立饰

44

总号 0751，分号 050，大普化村鼓，1991 年 11 月 20 日出土于象州县中平乡大普化村北约 100 米，现存象州县博物馆。面径 81.6—82 厘米，身高 57.5 厘米。

Bronze Drum Dapuhua Cun(No.0751, CN:050), unearthed at the north of 100m to Dapuhua Village, Zhongping, Xiangzhou County on November 20th, 1991. Now it is preserved at Xiangzhou Museum.
Face Diameter: 81.6−82cm, Height:57.5cm

鼓面鱼饰

鼓面蛙饰

鼓胸船纹

45

总号 0834，分号 0030，石崖村鼓，1988 年 1 月出土于武宣县东乡乡石崖村北，现存武宣县博物馆。面径 72.1—72.7 厘米，身高 53.4 厘米。

Bronze Drum Shiya Cun(No.0834, CN:0030), unearthed at the north of Shiya Village, Dongxiang, Wuxuan County on January, 1988. Now it is preserved at Wuxuan Museum.
Face Diameter: 72.1—72.7cm, Height:53.4cm

鼓面局部

鼓面动物立饰

鼓耳

46

总号 000050，慢侣鼓，1993 年 10 月 22 日，崇左市大新县桃城镇大塘村慢侣屯村民赵金芬在屯头大路行走时发现地表弧形金属圈，随即挖出，现存大新县博物馆。面径 69—70 厘米，身高 47 厘米。

Bronze Drum Manlv(No.000050), discovered by Zhao Jinfen, the villager of Manlv, Datang Village, Taocheng Town, Daxin County, Chongzuo City on October 22nd, 1993, when she was walking on the village road. She found a curved metal ring out of the earth and dug it out at once. Now it is preserved at Daxin Museum. Face Diameter: 69−70cm, Height:47cm

鼓面蛙饰

鼓身局部

鼓面

47

乘骑变形羽人纹铜鼓，现存北京
民族文化宫。面径 77.5 厘米，
身高 53.5 厘米。

Bronze Drum with transformed
feathermen patterns and horse
rider statues. Now it is preserved
at The Cultural Palace of
Nationalities in Beijing.
Face Diameter: 77.5cm,
Height:53.5cm

鼓身局部

鼓身蛙饰

附耳

鼓面乘骑立饰 1

鼓面乘骑立饰 2

遵义型铜鼓
Zunyi Type

以贵州省遵义市南宋播州土司杨粲夫妇墓出土的铜鼓为代表。流行年代为宋元时期（约公元10世纪至公元14世纪）。主要分布在贵州、广西、云南、四川和越南北部。历史上铸造和使用该型铜鼓的民族是僚。其特点是鼓面略大于鼓胸，鼓面、鼓胸和鼓足的直径相当，鼓胸和鼓腰无明显分界线，纹饰简单，主纹饰是一种由圆圈和飘带组成的游旗纹，鼓面青蛙塑像消失，部分以蛙趾代之。此型是冷水冲型发展到麻江型的过渡期铜鼓。

This type was represented by the drums unearthed in the tomb of Yangcan couple, the minority headmen of Bozhou, Zunyi, Guizhou Province in Southern Song Dynasty. The popular time was from Song to Yuan Dynasty (about 10 C.A.C.–14 C.A.C.). They were mainly found in Guizhou, Guangxi, Yunnan, Sichuan and North Vietnam. Liao people cast and used this type of bronze drums in history. The face edge is slightly projecting out of the chest; the diameters and heights of face, chest and foot are almost equal; chest contracts gradually to waist and there is no apparent boundary. The whole decoration is simple, and the major loop is composed of Youqi motif (one circle and two fluttering ribbons). The most obvious characteristic of this type is no frog statues on the drum face, only claws decoration still on the edge of drum face. This type was the transitional type between Lengshuichong and Majiang.

1

总号004874，族鼓0155号，铜鼓，来源不详，原存广西壮族自治区博物馆，现存广西民族博物馆。面径55.8—56厘米，身高35.8厘米。

Bronze drum (No.004874, ZGNo.0155), origin resource unknow. Preserved at Museum of Guangxi Zhuang Autonomous Region, now it is preserved at Anthropology Museum of Guangxi.
Face Diameter: 55.8-56cm, Height:35.8cm

鼓耳

鼓面局部

2

总号 004903，族鼓 0186 号，蛙趾纹变形羽人纹铜鼓（又名 186 号鼓）。
20 世纪 50 年代征集于容县城厢镇。现存广西民族博物馆。面径 61.3 厘米，
身高 28 厘米。

Bronze drum with transformed feathermen mixed frog claws pattern(No.004903,
ZGNo.0186), collected at Chengxiang Town, Rong County in 1950s'. Now it is
preserved at Anthropology Museum of Guangxi.
Face Diameter: 61.3cm, Height:28cm

鼓面局部

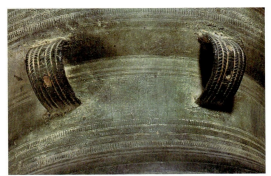

鼓耳

鼓足局部

3

总号 000444 号，蛙趾游旗纹铜鼓，旧藏，现存桂平市博物馆。面径 61 厘米，身高 35 厘米。

Bronze drum with frog claws & flying flag patterns(No.000444). Now it is preserved at Guiping City Museum.
Face Diameter: 61cm,
Height:35cm

鼓身铭文

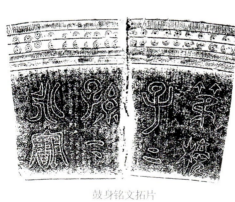

鼓身铭文拓片

鼓面局部

鼓身局部

4

总号 000595，宋十二芒同心圆纹鼓，1991 年 2 月那坡县公安局移交，现存那坡具博物馆。面径 57 厘米，身高 36 厘米。

Bronze drum with 12-rays and concentric circles and dot patterns(Song Dynasty, No.000595), handed over by Napo County Public Security Bureau in February, 1991.Now it is preserved at Napo County Museum. Face Diameter: 57cm, Height:36cm

鼓耳

鼓面局部

鼓面

麻江型铜鼓
Majiang Type

以贵州省麻江县谷峒火车站一座古墓出土的铜鼓为代表。流行年代为南宋至清代末期（约公元12世纪至公元19世纪）。分布于我国南方广大地区至越南北部，现存数量最多。当代壮、瑶、苗、侗、水、彝、布依等民族仍在使用此型铜鼓。其特点是鼓型矮扁，鼓胸、鼓腰、鼓足无明显分界，而在鼓腰处起一周凸棱将鼓身分为上下两部分，主要纹饰为游旗、符箓、云雷、十二生肖、人物和花草纹等，部分有吉祥语和纪年铭文，受汉文化影响较明显。

This type was represented by the drums unearthed in an ancient tomb at Gudong Railway Station, Majiang County, Guizhou province. The popular time was from Southern Song dynasty to late Qing dynasty (about 12 C.A.C.–19 C.A.C.). This type of bronze drum scatters in many areas in southern China and northern Vietnam, with a biggest quantity on hand. Ethnics such as Zhuang, Yao, Miao, Dong, Shui, Yi and Buyi are still using bronze drums of this type nowadays. It has a short and small form; chest, waist and foot without any boundaries, only one raise ridge divides the body into the upper and the lower. The main decorations are flying flags, Ofuda, cloud& thunder, zodiac, man figures and plants. Some of them were decorated by auspicious words and cast year, influenced by Han culture apparently.

1

族鼓0015号，游旗纹铜鼓，1971年3月收购于南宁废品公司，现存广西民族博物馆。面径49.5厘米，身高25.8厘米。

ZG No.0015, Bronze Drum with flying flag pattern, collected at Nanning Waste Recycle Company in March, 1971. Now it is preserved at Anthropology Museum of Guangxi.
Face Diameter: 49.5cm, Height: 25.8cm

鼓面局部

鼓面

2

族鼓 0017 号，四鱼纹铜鼓，1971 年 3 月收购于南宁废品公司，现存广西民族博物馆。面径 47.5 厘米，身高 25.5 厘米。

ZG No.0017, Bronze Drum with 4-fish pattern, collected at Nanning Waste Recycle Company in March, 1971. Now it is preserved at Anthropology Museum of Guangxi.
Face Diameter: 47.5cm, Height: 25.5cm

鼓面鱼纹

鼓面铭文

鼓面局部

3

族鼓 0019 号，符箓纹铜鼓，1971 年 3 月收购于南宁废品公司，现存广西民族博物馆。面径 46—46.3 厘米，身高 26 厘米。

ZG No.0019, Bronze Drum with Ofuda pattern, collected at Nanning Waste Recycle Company in March, 1971. Now it is preserved at Anthropology Museum of Guangxi. Face Diameter: 46—46.3cm, Height: 26cm

鼓面

鼓耳

鼓面符箓纹

鼓足细部

4

族鼓 0023 号，符箓纹铜鼓，1971 年 3 月收购于南宁废品公司，现存
广西民族博物馆。面径 49.3—50 厘米，身高 26.5 厘米。

ZG No.0023, Bronze Drum with Ofuda pattern, collected at Nanning Waste
Recycle Company in March, 1971. Now it is preserved at Anthropology
Museum of Guangxi.
Face Diameter: 49.3—50cm,
Height: 26.5cm

鼓面局部

5

族鼓 0041 号，游旗纹铜鼓，1972 年收购于南宁市废品仓库。现存广西民族博物馆。面径 46.7 厘米，身高 27 厘米。

ZG No.0041, Bronze Drum with flying flag pattern, collected at Nanning Waste Storage in 1972. Now it is preserved at Anthropology Museum of Guangxi. Face Diameter: 46.7cm, Height: 27cm

鼓面局部

鼓耳

鼓面游旗纹

鼓足细部

6

族鼓 0049 号，鱼纹马纹铜鼓，
1972 年收购于南宁市废品仓
库，现存广西民族博物馆。面径
46.6—46.8 厘米，身高 27 厘米。

ZG No.0049, Bronze Drum with
fish& horse pattern, collected
at Nanning Waste Storage
in1972. Now it is preserved
at Anthropology Museum of
Guangxi.
Face Diameter: 46.6–46.8cm,
Height: 27cm

鼓面

鼓胸马纹

鼓面鱼纹

鼓面马纹

7

族鼓 0052 号，四龙双印纹铜鼓，1972 年收购于南宁市废品仓库，现存广西民族博物馆。面径 49—49.5 厘米，身高 26 厘米。

ZG No.0052, Bronze Drum with 4-dragon& 2-stamp pattern, collected at Nanning Waste Storage in1972. Now it is preserved at Anthropology Museum of Guangxi.
Face Diameter: 49–49.5cm, Height: 26cm

鼓面印章

鼓面细部

鼓面四龙双印纹

8

族鼓 0063 号，"道光八年"铭双龙团寿纹铜鼓，收购于河池地区（现河池市），现存广西民族博物馆。面径 46.9—47.4 厘米，身高 26.5 厘米。

ZG No.0063, Bronze Drum with 道光八年 & 寿 -character and 2-dragon pattern, collected in Hechi Area(Now Hechi City). Now it is preserved at Anthropology Museum of Guangxi.
Face Diameter: 46.9–47.4cm,
Height: 26.5cm

鼓身局部

鼓面双龙团寿纹

鼓面

9

族鼓 0065 号，"天元孔明"铭坎卦铜鼓，1973 年收购于河池废品公司，现存广西民族博物馆。面径 47.5—48.2 厘米，身高 27.8 厘米。

ZG No.0065, Bronze Drum with 天元孔明 -character and Ofuda pattern, collected at Hechi Waste Recycle Company in 1973. Now it is preserved at Anthropology Museum of Guangxi.
Face Diameter: 47.5—48.2cm,
Height: 27.8cm

鼓面铭文 2

鼓面坎卦纹

鼓面铭文 1

10

族鼓 0066 号、双龙团寿纹铜鼓，
1973 年收购于河池废品公司，
现存广西民族博物馆。面径 48
厘米，身高 27 厘米。

ZG No.0066, Bronze Drum
with 寿 -character and 2-dragon
pattern, collected at Hechi Waste
Recycle Company in 1973. Now
it is preserved at Anthropology
Museum of Guangxi.
Face Diameter: 48cm,
Height: 27cm

鼓面双龙团寿纹

鼓面铭文 1

鼓面铭文 2

鼓面

11

族鼓 0068 号，人物走兽纹铜鼓，
1973 年收购于河池废品公司，
现存广西民族博物馆。面径 44.5
厘米，身高 25 厘米。

ZG No.0068, Bronze Drum
with human figures and beasts
pattern, collected at Hechi Waste
Recycle Company in 1973. Now
it is preserved at Anthropology
Museum of Guangxi.
Face Diameter: 44.5cm,
Height: 25cm

鼓面

鼓面局部

12

族鼓 0083 号，八人符箓纹铜鼓。
1973 年收购于河池废品公司，
现存广西民族博物馆。面径 45
厘米，身高 27 厘米。

ZG No.0083, Bronze Drum with
8-person and Ofuda pattern,
collected at Hechi Waste Recycle
Company in 1973. Now it is
preserved at Anthropology
Museum of Guangxi.
Face Diameter: 45cm,
Height: 27cm

鼓面

鼓面局部

13

族鼓 0085 号，双龙游旗纹铜鼓，来源不详，现存广西民族博物馆。面径 49—49.2 厘米，身高 26.5 厘米。

ZG No.0085, Bronze Drum with 2-dragon& flying flag pattern, collected source is unclear. Now it is preserved at Anthropology Museum of Guangxi.
Face Diameter: 49-49.2cm, Height: 26.5cm

鼓面

鼓面局部

鼓耳

14

族鼓 0202 号，游旗纹铜鼓，1964
年收购于柳州二级站，现存广西
民族博物馆。面径 45 厘米，身高
26 厘米。

ZG No.0202, Bronze Drum with
flying flag pattern, collected at
Liuzhou Second Waste Station
in 1964. Now it is preserved
at Anthropology Museum of
Guangxi.
Face Diameter: 45cm,
Height: 26cm

鼓面

鼓耳

鼓面局部

15

族鼓 0211 号，寿字纹铜鼓，来源不详，现存广西民族博物馆。面径 46.5—46.7 厘米，身高 27.5 厘米。

ZG No.0211, Bronze Drum with 寿 -character, collected source is unclear. Now it is preserved at Anthropology Museum of Guangxi.
Face Diameter: 46.5–46.7cm, Height: 27.5cm

鼓足细部

鼓面局部

16

族鼓 0213 号，十二生
肖纹铜鼓，1962 年收购
于柳州市收购站，现存
广西民族博物馆。面径
50 厘米，身高 28 厘米。

ZG No.0213, Bronze
Drum with Zodiac
pattern, collected at
Liuzhou Waste Station in
1962. Now it is preserved
at Anthropology Museum
of Guangxi.
Face Diameter: 50cm,
Height: 28cm

鼓足细部

鼓腰细部

鼓面局部

17

族鼓 0215 号，游旗纹铜鼓，来源不详，现存广西民族博物馆。面径 47—47.5 厘米，身高 27 厘米。

ZG No.0215, Bronze Drum with flying flag pattern, collected source is unclear. Now it is preserved at Anthropology Museum of Guangxi.
Face Diameter: 47—47.5cm, Height: 27cm

鼓足细部

鼓面局部

18

族鼓 0220 号，二龙戏珠纹铜
鼓，1962 年征集于柳州市，
现存广西民族博物馆。面径
55—57 厘米，身高 28 厘米。

ZG No.0220, Bronze Drum
with 2-dragon playing pearl
pattern, collected at Liuzhou
City in 1962. Now it is
preserved at Anthropology
Museum of Guangxi.
Face Diameter: 55−57cm,
Height: 28cm

鼓面

鼓面二龙双珠纹

鼓耳

19

族鼓 0234 号，钱纹铜鼓，征
集于柳州市收购站，现存广
西民族博物馆。面径 48.5 厘
米，身高 26 厘米。

ZG No.0234, Bronze Drum
with coins pattern, collected at
Liuzhou Waste Station. Now
it is preserved at Anthropology
Museum of Guangxi.
Face Diameter: 48.5cm,
Height: 26cm

鼓面局部

鼓面螃蟹纹

20

族鼓 0284 号，游旗纹铜鼓，1958 年征集于柳州市收购站，现存广西民族博物馆。面径 48.6—48.8 厘米，身高 28 厘米。

ZG No.0284, Bronze Drum with flying flag pattern, collected at Liuzhou Waste Station in 1958. Now it is preserved at Anthropology Museum of Guangxi. Face Diameter: 48.6—48.8cm, Height: 28cm

鼓耳

鼓足细部

鼓面局部

21

族鼓0296号，寿字纹铜鼓，1958年征集于柳州市收购站，
现存广西民族博物馆。面径47.3厘米，身高27.3厘米。

ZG No.0296, Bronze Drum with 寿 -character, collected
at Liuzhou Waste Station in 1958. Now it is preserved at
Anthropology Museum of Guangxi.
Face Diameter: 47.3cm,
Height: 27.3cm

鼓耳

鼓面局部

22

族鼓 0310 号，龙纹鱼纹铜鼓，1977 年征集于河池市东兰县，现存广西民族博物馆。面径 48.3 厘米，身高 27.2 厘米。

ZG No.0310, Bronze Drum with dragon& fish pattern, collected at Donglan County, Hechi City in 1977. Now it is preserved at Anthropology Museum of Guangxi. Face Diameter: 48.3cm, Height: 27.2cm

鼓面鱼纹

鼓面龙纹

鼓面

23

族鼓 0341 号，"未"字款铜鼓，1984 年征集于南宁市，现存广西民族博
物馆。面径 46.5 厘米，身高 29.5 厘米。

ZG No.0341, Bronze Drum with 未 -character, collected in Nanning City in
1984. Now it is preserved at Anthropology Museum of Guangxi.
Face Diameter: 46.5cm,
Height: 29.5cm

鼓面

鼓面 "未" 字

24
Hg00031 号，清鱼龙纹铜鼓，1997 年 1 月征集于广西南丹县三口林场，现
存柳州市博物馆。面径 36.2—36.5 厘米，身高 26.5 厘米。

Hg00031, Bronze Drum with dragon& fish pattern of Qing Dynasty, collected
at Sankou Tree Farm, Nandan County in January, 1997. Now it is preserved at
Liuzhou Museum.
Face Diameter: 36.2—36.5cm, Height: 26.5cm

鼓面鱼纹

鼓面龙纹

鼓内铭文

鼓耳

鼓面局部

25

Hg00037 号，清牛耕纹游旗纹铜鼓（有铭文），2008
年 3 月 4 日征集于广西环江，现存柳州市博物馆。面径
51.8—52 厘米，身高 27 厘米。

Hg00037, Bronze Drum with dragon& flying flag pattern
of Qing Dynasty(with characters also), collected at
Huanjiang County on March 4th, 2008. Now it is preserved
at Liuzhou Museum.
Face Diameter: 51.8–52cm,
Height: 27cm

鼓内铭文

鼓面

26

融水小铜鼓，90 年代广西融水县志办移交，现存融水苗族自治县博物馆。面径32.6—32.9厘米，身高 19.2 厘米。

Rongshui Bronze Drum in small size, allocated by Rongshui Annals Office in 1990s'. Now it is preserved at Rongshui Museum of Miao.
Face Diameter: 32.6–32.9cm, Height: 19.2cm

鼓身局部

鼓面内纹饰线描图

鼓面内晾谷架纹饰

鼓面内人物纹

鼓面内谷仓纹饰

鼓面内鱼纹龙纹鸟纹

鼓面内房屋纹

鼓面内鱼纹龙纹

27

总 1778 号，清梅花图案纹铜鼓，1964 年购于隆林废品收购站，现存桂林市博物馆。面径 47.5 厘米，身高 26.5 厘米。

No.1778, Bronze Drum with plum blossom pattern of Qing Dynasty, collected at Longlin County Waste Station in 1964. Now it is preserved at Guilin Museum.
Face Diameter: 47.5cm, Height: 26.5cm

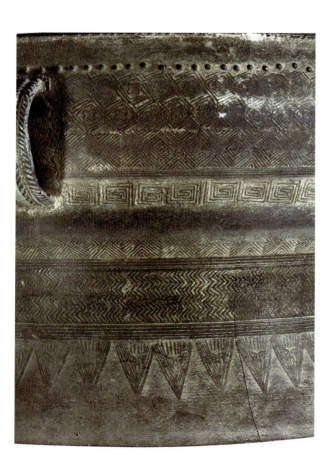

鼓身局部

鼓面

28

总 1779 号，清杂宝花草纹铜鼓，1964 年购于隆林废品收购站，
现存桂林市博物馆。面径 45.5 厘米、身高 25.3 厘米。

No.1779, Bronze Drum with treasure& plant pattern of Qing Dynasty,
collected at Longlin County Waste Station in 1964. Now it is preserved
at Guilin Museum.
Face Diameter: 45.5cm, Height: 25.3cm

鼓面局部

鼓面杂宝纹 1

鼓面杂宝纹 2

29
总 1781 号，清游旗纹铜鼓（有铭文），1964 年购于隆林废品收购站，现存桂林市博物馆。面径 48 厘米，身高 26.5 厘米。

No.1781, Bronze Drum with flying flag pattern of Qing Dynasty(with character also), collected at Longlin County Waste Station in 1964. Now it is preserved at Guilin Museum.
Face Diameter: 48cm, Height: 26.5cm

鼓面内铭文 1

鼓面内铭文 2

鼓面内铭文 3

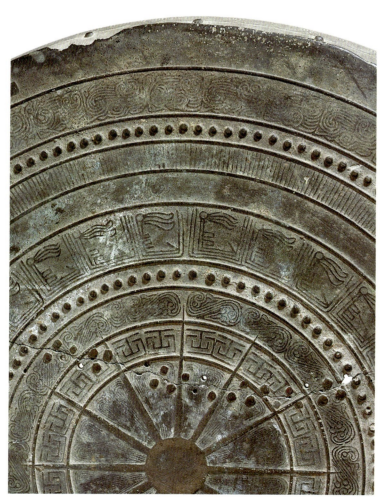
鼓面局部

30

总 1794 号，清卷草纹
铜鼓，1964 年购于隆林
废品收购站，现存桂林
市博物馆。面径 47.5 厘
米，身高 27.5 厘米。

No.1794, Bronze Drum
with twisted plant
pattern of Qing Dynasty,
collected at Longlin
County Waste Station in
1964. Now it is preserved
at Guilin Museum.
Face Diameter: 47.5cm,
Height: 27.5cm

鼓面卷草纹

鼓面

31

总 1805 号，明"王魁"
铭符箓纹铜鼓，1982 年
桂林市文管会拨交，现存
桂林市博物馆。面径 49
厘米，身高 27.2 厘米。

No.1805, Bronze Drum
with 王魁 -character of
Ming Dynasty, allocated
by Guilin Cultural Relic
Administration in 1982.
Now it is preserved at
Guilin Museum.
Face Diameter: 49cm,
Height: 27.2cm

鼓面铭文 1

鼓面铭文 2

鼓面铭文 3

鼓面

32

总01995号，"万宝家财"铭文铜鼓，1960年征集于广西梧州市废品收购站，现存梧州市博物馆。面径48.8—49.3厘米，身高27.4厘米。

No.01995, Bronze Drum with 万宝家财 -character, collected at Wuzhou Waste Station in 1960. Now it is preserved at Wuzhou Museum. Face Diameter: 48.8– 49.3cm, Height: 27.4cm

鼓面铭文 1

鼓面铭文 2

鼓足细部

鼓面

33

总 001049 号，清耕田奔马图铜鼓，1976 年征集于广西西林县马蚌公社马桑大队田湾志村，现存百色起义纪念馆。面径 47.3—47.6 厘米，身高 27.2 厘米。

No.001049, Bronze Drum with man-ploughing& galloping-horse pattern of Qing Dynasty, collected at Tianwanzhi Village, Masang Team, Mabang Commune, Xilin County in 1976. Now it is preserved at Baise Uprising Memorial Hall. Face Diameter: 47.3−47.6cm, Height: 27.2cm

鼓面

鼓胸牛耕图

鼓胸马纹 1

鼓身局部

34

总000168号，清乳钉
卷花纹铜鼓，1990年
百色市中级法院没收
并转交，现存右江民
族博物馆。面径47.8
厘米，身高27厘米。

No.000168, Bronze
Drum with nipple-
protrusion& twisted-
plant pattern of Qing
Dynasty, transferred
by Baise Intermediate
Court in 1990. Now
it is preserved at
Youjiang Museum of
Nationalities.
Face Diameter: 47.8cm,
Height: 27cm

鼓耳

鼓足细部

鼓面局部

35

总 000857 号，清"盘古至今人旺财兴"铭文铜鼓，2004 年征集于广西隆林县天生桥，现存右江民族博物馆。面径 47.2 厘米，身高 27.2 厘米。

No.000857，Bronze Drum with 盘古至今人旺财兴 -character of Qing Dynasty, collected at Tiansheng qiao, Longlin County in 2004. Now it is preserved at Youjiang Museum of Nationalities. Face Diameter: 47.2cm, Height: 27.2cm

鼓面铭文 1

鼓面铭文 2

鼓胸花纹

鼓胸龙纹

鼓身局部

36

总 000166 号，"虎"字纹铜鼓，1996 年征集于广西隆林县德峨乡，现存隆林县博物馆。面径 45 厘米，身高 27 厘米。

No.000166, Bronze Drum with, 虎 -character, collected at De'e, Longlin County in 1996. Now it is preserved at Longlin Museum.
Face Diameter: 45cm,
Height: 27cm

鼓面"虎"字

鼓面局部

鼓身局部

37

旧01号，游旗窗花纹铜鼓，来源不明，现存西林县博物馆。面径48厘米，身高28厘米。

Old No.01, Bronze Drum with flying flag& window lattice, collected source is unclear. Now it is preserved at Xilin County Museum.
Face Diameter: 48cm,
Height: 28cm

鼓身局部

鼓面局部

鼓面

38

河池 031 号，明八蛙饰
回纹铜鼓，20 世纪 90
年代中期征集于广西河
池凤山县砦牙乡拉英村
那田屯，现存河池市文
物站。面径 48.7—49 厘
米，身高 27.7 厘米。

No.031, Bronze
Drum with 8-frog and
回 -character of Ming
Dynasty, collected at
Natian Tun, Laying
Village, Zhaiya, Fengshan
County, Hechi City in
middle 1990s. Now it
is preserved at Hechi
Cultural Relic Station.
Face Diameter: 48.7–
49cm,
Height: 27.7cm

鼓面

鼓面蛙饰

鼓身局部

39

都安代 029 号，荷耙人纹铜鼓，广西都安文物馆委托代管，现存河池市文物站。面径 45 厘米，身高 26.7 厘米。

(Du'an Dai)No.029, Bronze Drum with hoer pattern. Now it is preserved at Hechi Cultural Relic Station by the authorization of Du'an Cultural Relic House.
Face Diameter: 45cm,
Height: 26.7cm

鼓面

鼓面荷耙人纹

40

兰阳一号铜鼓，广西东兰县长江乡兰阳村 韦克锋私藏，面径 45.5 厘米，身高 27.5 厘米。

Bronze Drum Lanyang No.1, the private collection of Wei Kefeng, a villager of Lanyang Village, Changjiang, Donglan County.
Face Diameter: 45.5cm, Height: 27.5cm

鼓面内部

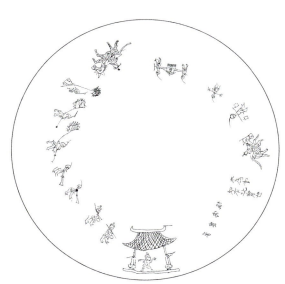

鼓面内部线描图

鼓面

北流型铜鼓
Beiliu Type

以广西北流市出土的一批铜鼓为代表。流行年代为西汉至唐代（约公元 1 世纪至公元 8 世纪）。主要分布于两广地区及海南省，尤以桂东南和粤西南的云开大山周围分布最为密集。历史上铸造和使用该型铜鼓的民族是西瓯、骆越及其后裔乌浒、俚等。其特点是形体硕大厚重，鼓面径大于鼓胸，部分面沿下折形成"垂檐"，中心太阳纹多为八芒，光体圆凸，鼓腰逐渐收缩，鼓耳多为圆茎环耳。通体多饰精细的云雷纹等几何形纹。鼓面立体青蛙一般瘦小无纹，背部多有调音铲痕。

This type was represented by the drums unearthed at Beiliu County. The popular time was from the Western Han to Tang dynasty (about 1 C.A.C.–8 C.A.C.). It has an intense distribution in Guangxi, Guangdong and Hainan province, especially several counties in Yunkai mountain area which including southeast Guangxi and southwest Guangdong. Xiou, Luoyue and their descendant Wuhu and Li cast and used this type of bronze drum in history. It has a huge and thick form, face larger than chest, all drums' edge sticking out of chest, and most of them have a curving edge that is called "drum face skirt". The sun body like a round cake standing out, with the routine 8 rays. The waist contracts in reverse arc and most of the handles are usually in ring form. Clouds and thunder motifs are usually decorated over the whole drum body. Frog statues on the face are small, simple, without patterns. On the reverse side of drum face, there always are the scratching marks for tone tuning.

1

总号 004825，族鼓 0101，云雷纹大铜鼓（原名 101 号鼓），原存北流市六靖镇水埇庵，1955 年北流县（现北流市）拨交给广西壮族自治区博物馆，现存广西民族博物馆。面径 163.5—164.8 厘米，残高 63.5 厘米。

Bronze drum with cloud and thunder patterns(No.004825, ZG No.0101), originally preserved at Shuiyong Nunnery, Liujing Town, Beiliu City and was allotted to Museum of Guangxi Zhuang Autonomous Region by Beiliu County(now Beiliu City) in 1955. Now it is preserved at Anthropology Museum of Guangxi.
Face Diameter: 163.5−164.8cm,
Remained Height:63.5cm

鼓耳

鼓面局部

鼓身细部

2

总号 004829，族鼓 0105，钱
纹席纹铜鼓，1954 年征集于
钦州市灵山县，原存广西壮族
自治区博物馆，现存广西民族
博物馆。面径 100—104.5 厘
米，身高 54 厘米。

Bronze drum with coins and
woven patterns(No.004829,
ZGNo.0105), collected
at Lingshan County,
Qinzhou City in 1954. It
was originally preserved at
Museum of Guangxi Zhuang
Autonomous Region and now
at Anthropology Museum of
Guangxi.
Face Diameter: 100−104.5cm,
Height:54cm

鼓面细部

鼓面蛙饰

鼓耳

鼓身细部

3

总号 004831，族鼓 0107，雷纹铜鼓（原名 107 号鼓），1952 年出土于贵港市桂平县麻垌村，原存广西壮族自治区博物馆，现存广西民族博物馆。面径 134.5—138 厘米，身高 72.5 厘米。

Bronze drum with thunder patterns(No.004831, ZGNo.0107), unearthed at Madong Village, Guiping County, Guigang City in 1952. It was originally preserved at Museum of Guangxi Zhuang Autonomous Region and now at Anthropology Museum of Guangxi.
Face Diameter: 134.5−138cm, Height:72.5cm

鼓面蛙饰

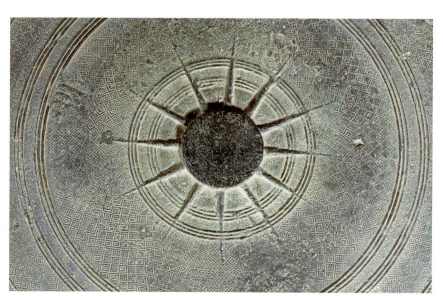

鼓面细部

鼓耳

4

总号 004832，族鼓 0108，雷纹填线纹铜鼓（原名 108 号鼓），20 世纪 50 年代征集于北海市合浦县，原存广西壮族自治区博物馆，现存广西民族博物馆。面径 90.5 厘米，身高 54 厘米。

Bronze drum with thunder mixed straight line patterns(No.004832, ZG No.0108), collected in Hepu County, Beihai City in 1950s'. It was originally preserved at Museum of Guangxi Zhuang Autonomous Region and now at Anthropology Museum of Guangxi. Face Diameter: 90.5cm, Height:54cm

鼓面细部

鼓面蛙饰

鼓面内部调音铲痕

鼓耳

5

总号 004858，族鼓 0137，云雷纹铜鼓（原名 137 号鼓），1954 年征集于梧州市岑溪县，原存广西壮族自治区博物馆，现存广西民族博物馆。面径 93—94.4 厘米，身高 53.8 厘米。

Bronze drum with clouds and thunder patterns(No.004858, ZGNo.0137), collected at Cenxi County, Wuzhou City in 1954. It was originally preserved at Museum of Guangxi Zhuang Autonomous Region and now at Anthropology Museum of Guangxi. Face Diameter: 93−94.4cm, Height:53.8cm

鼓耳

鼓面细部

鼓面蛙饰

鼓身细部

6

总 号 004861，族 鼓 0140，云雷纹铜鼓，采集于玉林市博白县，原存广西壮族自治区博物馆，现存广西民族博物馆。面径 114.5—115.3 厘米、身高 63.5 厘米。

Bronze drum with clouds and thunder patterns(No.004861, ZGNo.0140), collected at Bobai County, Yulin City. It was originally preserved at Museum of Guangxi Zhuang Autonomous Region and now at Anthropology Museum of Guangxi.
Face Diameter: 114.5–115.3cm, Height:63.5cm

鼓面蛙饰

鼓身细部

鼓面

7

总号 005029，族鼓 0316，人形
图案云雷纹铜鼓（原名 316 号
鼓），1976 年 11 月出土于玉林
市陆川县何莫村，原存广西壮族
自治区博物馆，现存广西民族博
物馆。面径 104.2－106 厘米，
身高 55.5 厘米。

Bronze drum with clouds
and thunder patterns mixed
人 -shape character (No.005029,
ZGNo.0316), unearthed at Hemo
Village, Luchuan County, Yulin
City in November 1976. It was
originally preserved at Museum
of Guangxi Zhuang Autonomous
Region and now at Anthropology
Museum of Guangxi.
Face Diameter: 104.2－106cm,
Height:55.5cm

鼓面蛙饰

鼓面蛙饰

鼓耳

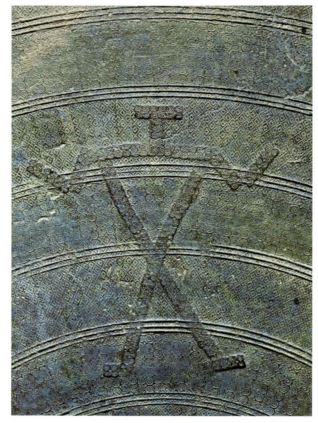

鼓面人形图案

8

总号 00069，富华铜鼓（苍梧
01），1973 年 6 月出土于梧
州市苍梧县大坡镇马王村富华
屯村边山坡，现存梧州市博物
馆。面径 71—71.5 厘米，身
高 41 厘米。

Bronze Drum Fuhua(No.00069,
CangwuNo.01), unearthed at
the hillside beside Fuhua Tun,
Mawang Village, Dapo Town,
Cangwu County, Wuzhou City
in June 1973. Now it is preserved
at Wuzhou Museum.
Face Diameter: 71−71.5cm,
Height:41cm

鼓面牛饰

鼓面细部

9

红九匡鼓，1994 年 5 月
25 日出土于北海市铁山
港区营盘镇白龙村委坪
底村红九匡海边沙滩，
现存北海市文物局。面
径 74.6 厘米，身高 39 厘
米。

Bronze Drum
Hongjiukuang,
unearthed at the beach
of Hongjiukuang, Pingdi
Village, Bailong, YingPan
Town, Tieshangang
District of Beihai City
on May 25th,1994. Now
it is preserved at Beihai
Cultural Relics Bureau.
Face Diameter: 74.6cm,
Height:39cm

鼓耳、鼓身细部

鼓面蛙饰

10

崇表岭鼓，1993 年元月出土于北海市西塘乡禾沟村崇表
岭屯东约 1 公里海滩，现存北海市文物局。面径 81.5—
83 厘米，身高 47 厘米。

Bronze Drum Chongbiao Ling, unearthed at the beach in the
east of 1km to Chongbiao Ling Tun, Hegou Village, Xitang,
Beihai City in Juanuary,1993. Now it is preserved at Beihai
Cultural Relics Bureau.
Face Diameter: 81.5−83cm, Height:47cm

鼓耳

鼓面细部

11

总号 0066，灵山 16 号，富致岭鼓，1987 年 8 月 1 日出土于钦州市灵山县旧州镇青松村富致岭屯大坑口，现存灵山县博物馆。面径 74.3—75 厘米，身高 42.5 厘米。

Bronze Drum Fuzhi Ling(No.0066, Lingshan No.16), unearthed at Dakengkou, Fuzhi Ling Tun, Qingsong Village, Jiuzhou Town, Lingshan County, Qinzhou City on August 1st,1987. Now it is preserved at Lingshan County Museum. Face Diameter: 74.3−75cm, Height:42.5cm

鼓面细部

鼓面蛙饰

鼓面内部调音铲痕

12
玉 01 号，新民村铜鼓，1975 年 3 月出土于玉林县
玉林镇新民村东南约 150 米处，现存玉林市博物馆。
面径 59.3—60.3 厘米，残高 30 厘米。

Bronze Drum Xinmin Cun (Yu No.1), unearthed at
the southeast of 150m to Xinmin Village, Yulin Town,
Yulin County in March, 1975. Now it is preserved at
Yulin Museum.
Face Diameter: 59.3−60.3cm, Remained Height:30cm

鼓面蛙饰

鼓面细部

13

总号 00625，浪平鼓，1991 年 3 月 21 日出土于玉林市兴业县小平山乡浪平屯东约 2.5 公里，现存玉林市博物馆。面径 123.6—124.6 厘米，身高 66.5 厘米。

Bronze Drum Langping(No.00625), unearthed in the east of 2.5km to Langping Tun, Xiaopingshan, Xingye County, Yulin City on March 21st,1991. Now it is preserved at Yulin Museum.
Face Diameter: 123.6–124.6cm,
Height:66.5cm

鼓面装饰

鼓面蛙饰

鼓面动物纹饰

14

容 04 号，三夯山铜鼓，1990 年 7 月 4 日出土于玉林市容县黎村镇
六振村南约 50 米三夯山，现存容县博物馆。面径 100.4—102.5 厘
米，身高 56.8 厘米。

Bronze Drum Sanduoshan(RongNo.04),unearthed at Sanduoshan, the
hill in the south of 50m to Liuzhen Village, Licun Town, Rong County,
Yulin City on July 4th,1990. Now it is preserved at Rong County Museum.
Face Diameter: 100.4−102.5cm, Height:56.8cm

鼓面蛙饰

鼓面细部

鼓耳

15

独山岭鼓，2010 年 4 月玉林市容县灵山镇六良村村民朱金生在独山岭木茹地除草时发现，现存容县博物馆。面径 82.2—84 厘米，身高 46.2 厘米。

Bronze Drum Dushan Ling, unearthed by Zhu Jinsheng, a villager of Liuliang Village, Lingshan Town, Rong County, Yulin City when he was weeding out grass on Dushan Ling in April, 2010. Now it is preserved at Rong County Museum. Face Diameter: 82.2−84cm, Height:46.2cm

鼓耳、鼓身细部

鼓面细部

鼓面内部调音铲痕

16

00004 号，雅松鼓，1977 年出土于玉林市陆川县大桥镇雅松村，陆川县文化馆征集，现存陆川县文管所。面径
71—72.5 厘米，身高 45 厘米。

Bronze Drum Yasong(No.00004), unearthed at Yasong Village, Daqiao Town, Luchuan County, Yulin City in 1977 and
collected by Luchuan County Cultural House. Now it is preserved at Luchuan County Museum.
Face Diameter: 71－72.5cm, Height:45cm

鼓耳   鼓面细部

17

北流 01 号，下浪湾铜鼓，1964 年出土于北流市白马镇大伦农场下浪湾山腰，现存北流市博物馆。面径 90.5—91.5 厘米，身高 53 厘米。

Bronze Drum Xialan gwan(BeililuNo.01),un earthed at the hillside of Xialangwan, Dalun Farm, Baima Town, Beiliu City in 1964. Now it is preserved at Beiliu Museum.
Face Diameter: 90.5－91.5cm, Height:53cm

鼓面细部

鼓面蛙饰

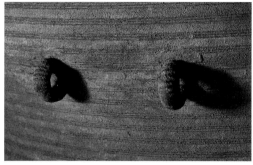

鼓耳

18

北流 06 号，大屋铜鼓，1974 年
11 月出土于北流市六靖镇水冲
村大屋屯南 60 米岭脚，现存北
流市博物馆。面径 91.2—92.5
厘米，身高 54 厘米。

Bronze Drum
Dawu(BeiliuNo.06),unearthed
at the foot of a hill, south of
60m to Dawu Tun, Shuichong
Village, Liujing Town, Beiliu
City in November,1974. Now it is
preserved at Beiliu Museum.
Face Diameter: 91.2—92.5cm,
Height:54cm

鼓耳

鼓面蛙饰

鼓身细部

19

北流 21 号，垌尾铜鼓，
1982 年 1 月 7 日北流市
白马镇黄金村垌尾屯，
村民李荣清在其屋后果
园锄地挖得，现存北流
市博物馆。面径 103.5—
105 厘米，身高 58 厘米。

Bronze Drum
Dongwei(BeiliuNo.21),
unearthed by Li Rongqing,
a villager of Dongwei
Tun, Huangjin Village,
Baima Town, Beiliu City
on January 7th,1982,
when he was hoeing up
the orchard after his
house. Now it is preserved
at Beiliu Museum.
Face Diameter: 103.5−
105cm，Height:58cm

鼓面蛙饰

鼓面内部调音铲痕

鼓面

20

北流 22 号，寨顶铜鼓，1983 年 1 月 20 日北流市平政镇六沙村寨顶屯西南约 100 米处，村民陈开宫锄宅基地时挖出，现存北流市博物馆。面径 89.5—90.5 厘米，身高 51.3 厘米。

Bronze Drum Zhaiding(BeiliuNo.22), unearthed by a villager Chen Kaigong, when he was hoeing up his house site in the southwest of 100m to Zhaiding Tun, Liusha Village, Pingzheng Town, Beiliu City on January 20th,1983. Now it is preserved at Beiliu Museum.
Face Diameter: 89.5—90.5cm, Height:51.3cm

鼓身细部

鼓面蛙饰

21

北流 23 号，六月化岭铜鼓，
1983 年 5 月中旬北流市石窝镇
煌炉村旺祖屯西北 1.5 公里，村
民吕培雄在六月化岭除木茹草时
挖得，现存北流市博物馆。面径
111.1—113 厘米，身高 59.8 厘米。

Bronze Drum Liuyuehua
Ling(BeiliuNo.23), unearthed by
Lv Peixiong, when he was weeding
out grass on Liuyuehua Ling, a
hill in the northwest of 1.5km to
Wangzu Tun, Huanglu Village,
Shiwo Town, Beiliu City in the
middle of May,1983. Now it is
preserved at Beiliu Museum.
Face Diameter: 111.1−113cm,
Height:59.8cm

鼓面蛙饰

鼓耳、鼓身细部

鼓面内部调音铲痕

22

北流 30 号，大坡外铜鼓，1995 年 5 月 17 日大坡外镇大坡外村村民李成枝夫妇在本鸡岭半山坳挖瓷土时挖出，现存北流市博物馆。面径 103.2—104.2 厘米，身高 56.7 厘米。

Bronze Drum Dapowai(BeiliuNo.30), unearthed by Li Chengzhi and his wife when they were taking china clay at the hillside of Muji Ling, a hill of Dapowai Village, Dapowai Town, Beiliu City on May 17th,1995. Now it is preserved at Beiliu Museum. Face Diameter: 103.2−104.2cm, Height:56.7cm

鼓面蛙饰

鼓耳

鼓足动物纹饰

鼓面细部

23

北流 33 号，南蛇岭铜鼓，1997 年 3 月 5 日北流市六麻镇大旺村南蛇岭，村民樊惠芳在自家后山南蛇岭半山腰开荒时挖出，现存北流市博物馆。面径 77—77.6 厘米，身高 46 厘米。

Bronze Drum Nansheling(BeiliuNo.33),unearthed by Fan Huifang, when she was cultivating wasteland behind her house at the hillside of Nanshe Ling, a hill of Dawang Village, Liuma Town, Beiliu City on March 5th,1997. Now it is preserved at Beiliu Museum.
Face Diameter: 77–77.6cm, Height:46cm

鼓面蛙饰

鼓面细部

24
五铢钱纹铜鼓，1953 年 3 月 5
日出土于广西岑溪县，现存中
国国家博物馆。面径 90 厘米，
身高 53 厘米。

Bronze Drum with WuZhu Coin
pattern, unearthed at CenXi
county, Guangxi province 1953,
Now it is preserved at National
Museum of China .
Face Diameter: 90cm,
Height:53cm

鼓面蛙饰

鼓面线描图

鼓耳

鼓身五铢钱纹

灵山型铜鼓
Lingshan Type

以广西钦州市灵山县出土的一批铜鼓为代表。流行年代在东汉至唐代（约公元 3 世纪至公元 10 世纪）。主要分布于广西东南部，以灵山县及周边地区为分布重心。历史上铸造和使用该型铜鼓的民族是乌浒和俚等。其形制与北流型铜鼓较为接近，但鼓壁较薄，鼓胸圆鼓，鼓身一律附以扁耳，鼓面中心太阳纹多为十芒或十二芒，立体青蛙后足合并，形成三足，蛙背有纹饰，多见累蹲蛙。装饰花纹主要为钱纹、变形羽人纹、虫纹、鸟纹、兽纹、四瓣花纹、蝉纹、席纹等，种类繁多，有主次之分；部分鼓足或鼓腔内有立体动物装饰，部分鼓面背部有调音铲痕。

This type was represented by drums unearthed at Lingshan county, Qinzhou City. The popular time was from the Eastern Han to Tang dynasty (about 3 C.A.C.－10 C.A.C.). This type scatters mainly in southeast Guangxi, centers on Lingshan county and the surrounding areas. Wuhu and Li people casted and used bronze drums of this type in history. It has an imposing form very similar to Beiliu Type, with thinner well. The chest arches out slightly; all handles across chest and waist are flat and in plate form; on the central part of drum face, the sun pattern has different numbers of needle-like thin long rays, usually 10 or 12. All frog statues on drum face are "three-leg frogs" with their two hind legs combining to each other. Gorgeous decorations are on frogs' back composing of carved lines and whirlpools pattern. Some drums have "overlap frogs" (the little frog overlaps on the big one). The decorations mainly include motifs such ascoins, transform feathermen, insects, birds, beasts, quatrefoils, cicadas, woven mats and so on, in a wide range and in primary and secondary order. Some of them have animal statues on the foot or inside the drum, some have scratching marks for tone tuning on the reverse of drum face.

1

总号 04830，族鼓 0106，变形羽人纹鸟纹铜鼓（又名 106 号鼓），50 年代广西省文化局拨交广西壮族自治区博物馆，现存广西民族博物馆。面径 70—70.5 厘米，身高 41.4 厘米，一侧鼓耳下鼓足位置饰立体鸟一只。

Bronze drum with transformed feathermen patterns(No.04830,ZG No.0106),with a bird statute on the foot under one of the four handles, allotted to Museum of Guangxi Zhuang Autonomous Region in 1950s' by Guangxi Cultural Bureau. Now it is preserved at Anthropology Museum of Guangxi.
Face Diameter: 70−70.5cm, Height:41.4cm

鼓足动物纹饰

鼓面内部调音铲痕

鼓面细部

鼓身细部

2

总号 04850，族鼓 0128，安矿
村铜鼓，1966 年 1 月 31 日出土
于玉林市陆川县平乐八晋安矿
村，现存广西民族博物馆。面径
93.5—95 厘米，身高 52 厘米。

Bronze Drum Ankuang
Cun(No.04850, ZG No.0128),
unearthed at Ankuang Village,
Bajin, Pingle Town, Luchuan
County, Yulin City on January
31st,1966. Now it is preserved
at Anthropology Museum of
Guangxi.
Face Diameter: 93.5−95cm,
Height:52cm

鼓面蛙饰

鼓耳、鼓身细部

鼓面

3

总号 004856，族鼓 0135，鹭含鱼纹鸟纹铜鼓，来源不详，现存广西民族博物馆。面径 78—78.8 厘米，身高 49 厘米。

Bronze drum with patterns of heron with fish in mouth(No.004856, ZG No.0135), unearthed source unknown. Now it is preserved at Anthropology Museum of Guangxi. Face Diameter: 78−78.8cm, Height:49cm

鼓面蛙饰

鼓面鹭含鱼纹

鼓身细部

4

总号 004862，族鼓 0141，
骑士纹"五"字钱纹铜鼓（又
名 141 号鼓），来源不详，
现存广西民族博物馆。面径
85.2—86 厘米，身高 50.8
厘米。

Bronze drum with rider and
五 -character-inside coin
patterns(No.004862, ZG
No.0141),unearthed source
unknown. Now it is preserved
at Anthropology Museum of
Guangxi.
Face Diameter: 85.2—86cm,
Height:50.8cm

鼓面蛙饰

鼓面细部

鼓面骑士纹、"五"字钱纹

5

总号 005019，族鼓 0306，鸟纹钱纹铜鼓，
1964 年出土于南宁市横县广龙公社水村，
现存广西民族博物馆。面径 79.6—80 厘米，
身高 46.8 厘米，一侧鼓耳下鼓足位置饰立
体鸟一只。

Bronze drum with bird and coin patterns
(No.005019, ZG No.0306), with a bird statute
on the foot under one of the four handles
unearthed at Shui Village, Guanglong
Commune, Heng County, Nanning City in
1964. Now it is preserved at Anthropology
Museum of Guangxi.
Face Diameter: 79.6−80cm, Height:46.8cm

鼓耳、鼓身细部　　　　　　鼓面细部

鼓面蛙饰

6

总号 005039，族鼓 0326，牛塑饰四出钱纹铜鼓（又名 326 号鼓），1982 年 11 月出土于钦州市灵山县石塘公社红星大队乐彩村，现存广西民族博物馆。面径 87.5—87.8 厘米，身高 52.3 厘米，一侧鼓耳下鼓足位置饰立体鸟一只，鼓胸内壁饰一立体牛塑。

Bronze drum with quadrangle-inside-a-circle coin patterns and ox statutes(No.005039, ZG No.0326),with a bird statute on the foot under one of the four handles and an ox on the breast inside, unearthed at Lecai Village, Hongxing Group, Shitang Commune, Lingshan County, Qinzhou City in November,1982. Now it is preserved at Anthropology Museum of Guangxi.
Face Diameter: 87.5−87.8cm,
Height:52.3cm

鼓面蛙饰

鼓足动物纹饰

鼓胸内部牛饰

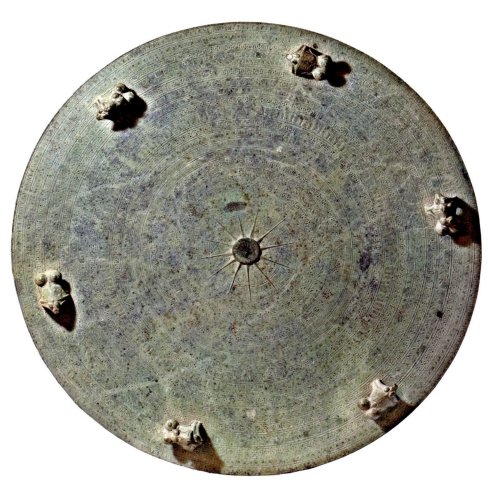

鼓面

7

总号 005051，族鼓 0338，鸟纹变形羽人纹铜鼓（又名 338 号鼓），1976 年出土于南宁市横县良圻公社藤山村，现存广西民族博物馆。面径 95.8—98.5 厘米，身高 56 厘米，一侧鼓耳下鼓足位置饰立体鸟一只。

Bronze drum with transformed feathermen and bird patterns (No.005051, ZG No.0338),with a bird statute on the foot under one of the four handles, unearthed at Tengshan Village, Liangqi Commune, Heng County, Nanning City in 1976. Now it is preserved at Anthropology Museum of Guangxi.
Face Diameter:95.8–98.5cm, Height:56cm

鼓足动物装饰

鼓面蛙饰

鼓面蛙饰

鼓面细部

鼓身细部

8

总号 05056，族鼓 0344，骑兽纹
四出钱纹铜鼓（又名344号鼓），
1989 年 2 月 19 日出土于南宁市
邕宁县吴圩镇敢绿村，现存广西
民族博物馆。面径 91.5 厘米，
身高 55 厘米，一侧鼓耳下鼓腰
位置饰立体乘骑一组。

Bronze drum with beast rider
and quadrangle-inside-a-circle
coin patterns(No.05056, ZG
No.0344),with a horse rider statute
on the waist under one of the
four handles, unearthed at Ganlv
Village, Wuxu Town, Yongning
County, Nanning City on February
19th,1989. Now it is preserved
at Anthropology Museum of
Guangxi.
Face Diameter:91.5cm,
Height:55cm

鼓面蛙饰

鼓腰乘骑装饰

鼓面细部

9

和同村鼓，2003 年出土于南宁市江西镇和同村，现存南宁市博物馆。面径
93—94 厘米，身高 54.9 厘米。

Bronze Drum Hetong Cun, unearthed at Hetong Village, Jiangxi Town,
Nanning City in 2003. Now it is preserved at Nanning Museum.
Face Diameter:93—94cm, Height:54.9cm

鼓耳

鼓面细部

鼓身细部

10

子鹤山鼓，1988 年 6 月出土于南
宁市邕宁县吴圩镇那佳村子鹤山
上，现存邕宁县文物管理所。面
径 81 厘米，身高 48 厘米，一侧
鼓耳下鼓足位置饰立体鸟一只，
鼓内胸部位置饰立体青蛙两只。

Bronze Drum Zihe Shan, with a bird
statute on the foot under one of the
four handles and two frogs statutes
on the chest inside, unearthed at
Zihe Hill, Najia Village, Wuxu Town,
Yongning County, Nanning City in
June 1988. Now it is preserved at
Yongning County Cultural Relics
Administration.
Face Diameter:81cm，Height:48cm

鼓胸内部蛙饰

鼓面蛙饰

鼓足动物纹饰

鼓面内部调音铲痕

11

那口岭鼓，1989 年 5 月出土于南宁市邕宁县吴圩镇那德村那审坡那口岭北麓半山腰畲地上，现存邕宁县文物管理所。面径 79 厘米，身高 48 厘米，一侧鼓耳下鼓足位置饰立体鸟一只。

Bronze Drum Nakou Ling, with a bird statute on the foot under one of the four handles, unearthed in the fire fields of the north hillside of Nakouling Hill, Nashenpo, Nade Village, Wuxu Town, Yongning County, Nanning City in May 1989. Now it is preserved at Yongning County Cultural Relics Administration.
Face Diameter:79cm,
Height:48cm

鼓身细部

鼓足动物纹饰

12
圭壁鼓，1988 年 4 月 4 日出土于南宁市横县板露乡圭壁村，现存横县博物馆。面径 118 厘米，身高 64 厘米，一侧鼓耳下鼓足位置饰立体四人乘双翼兽一组。

Bronze Drum Guibi, with a statute of four men on a bi-wing monster on the foot under one of the four handles, unearthed at Guibi Village, Banlu, Heng County, Nanning City on April 4th, 1988. Now it is preserved at Heng County Museum.
Face Diameter:118cm, Height:64cm

鼓足装饰

鼓身细部

鼓面蛙饰

鼓耳

附耳

13

新宁村鼓，1999 年出土于南宁市宾阳县甘棠镇新宁村，现存宾阳县文物管理所。面径 79.8—80.1 厘米，身高 45.5 厘米，一侧鼓耳下鼓足位置饰立体鸟一只。

Bronze Drum Xinning Cun, with a bird statute on the foot under one of the four handles, unearthed at Xinning Village, Gantang Town, Binyang County, Nanning City in 1999. Now it is preserved at Binyang County Cultural Relics Administration.
Face Diameter:79.8−80.1cm,
Height:45.5cm

鼓面蛙饰

鼓面蛙饰

鼓足动物装饰

14

竹林村铜鼓，2011 年 4 月 7 日出土于北海市银海区福成镇竹林村，现存北海市文物局。面径 79.7—80 厘米，身高 43 厘米，鼓内饰立体牛一只。

Bronze Drum Zhulin Cun, with an ox statue inside, unearthed at Zhulin Village, Fucheng Town, Yinhai District of Beihai City on April 7th, 2011. Now it is preserved at Beihai City Cultural Relics Bureau.
Face Diameter:79.7−80cm, Height:43cm

鼓面蛙饰

鼓耳

鼓胸内部动物纹饰

15

那凤铜鼓，出土于防城港市上思县在妙镇那凤屯，现存上思县博物馆。面径 76.8—77.2 厘米，身高 46.4 厘米。

Bronze Drum Nafeng, unearthed at Nafeng Tun, Zaimiao Town, Shangsi County, Fangchenggang City. Now it is preserved at Shangsi County Museum.
Face Diameter:76.8—77.2cm, Height:46.4cm

鼓面细部

鼓面蛙饰

鼓身细部

16

094 号，新塘鼓，1993 年出土于
钦州市板城镇城垇北一公里新
塘村麓山，现存钦州市博物馆。
面径 79.3 厘米，身高 47.5 厘米，
一侧鼓耳下鼓足位置饰立体鸟
一只。

Bronze Drum Xintang(No.094),
with a bird on the foot under one
of the four handles, unearthed at
Lushan Hill of Xintang Village,
the north of 1km to Chengxu,
Bancheng Town, Qinzhou City
in 1993. Now it is preserved at
Qinzhou Museum.
Face Diameter:79.3cm,
Height:47.5cm

鼓面内部调音铲痕

鼓面蛙饰

鼓足动物纹饰

17

总号 0019，原灵山 07 号，
石塘鼓，1984 年钦州市
灵山县文化馆征集，现
存灵山县博物馆。面径
79.3—80.6 厘米，身高 44
厘米，一侧鼓耳下鼓足位
置饰立体乘骑两组，鼓胸
内壁饰一立体牛塑。

Bronze Drum
Shitang(No.0019, original
name Lingshan No.07)
,with two horse-rider
statues on the foot under
one of the four handles and
an ox on the breast inside,
collected by Lingshan
County Cultural House,
Qinzhou City in 1984.
Now it is preserved at
Lingshan County Museum.
Face Diameter:79.3−
80.6cm, Height:44cm

鼓面细部

鼓内动物纹饰

鼓面蛙饰

鼓足乘骑装饰

18

总号 0143，原灵山 19 号，天顶山鼓，1990 年 3 月出土于钦州市灵山县檀圩镇东岸村天顶山屯六局塘岭，现存灵山县博物馆。面径 80—80.5 厘米，身高 48.5 厘米，一侧鼓耳下鼓足位置饰立体鸟一只。

Bronze Drum Tiandingshan(No.0143, original name Lingshan No.19) ,with a bird statues on the foot under one of the four handles, unearthed at Liujutang Hill, Tiandingshan Tun, Dong'an Village, Tanxu Town, Lingshan County, Qinzhou City in March,1990. Now it is preserved at Lingshan County Museum.
Face Diameter:80—80.5cm, Height:48.5cm

鼓面蛙饰

鼓面蛙饰

鼓足动物装饰

鼓耳

鼓面内部调音铲痕

19

总号 0015，石基鼓，1984 年 4 月 7 日出土于贵港市平南县石基村石基屯，现存灵山县博物馆。面径 88.5—89 厘米，身高 52.4 厘米，一侧鼓耳下鼓足位置饰立体鸟一只，鼓胸内壁饰一立体牛塑。

Bronze Drum Shiji(No.0015), with a bird statues on the foot under one of the four handles, and an ox statue inside the chest unearthed at Shiji Tun, Shiji Village, Pingnan County, Guigang City on April 7th ,1984. Now it is preserved at Lingshan County Museum. Face Diameter:88.5−89cm, Height:52.4cm

鼓足动物装饰

鼓面蛙饰

鼓内牛装饰

鼓面内部调音铲痕

20

总号0183，原灵山01号，双凤鼓，1973年出土于钦州市灵山县旧州镇双凤村北约150米处，现存灵山县博物馆。面径103—103.5厘米，身高62厘米。

Bronze Drum Shuangfeng(No.0183, original name Lingshan No.01), unearthed in the north of 150m to Shuangfeng Village, Jiuzhou Town, Lingshan County, Qinzhou City in 1973. Now it is preserved at Lingshan County Museum. Face Diameter:103—103.5cm, Height:62cm

鼓面蛙饰

鼓面细部

21

总号0040，原灵山13号，大丰鼓，1986年6月1日出土于钦州市灵山县丰塘镇大丰村大丰屯猫岭，现存灵山县博物馆。面径99—100.5厘米，身高59.3厘米，一侧鼓耳下鼓足位置饰立体鸟一对。

Bronze Drum Dafeng(No.0040, original name Lingshan No.13),with a pair of birds statute on the foot under one of the four handles, unearthed at Maoling, Dafeng Tun, Dafeng Village, Fengtang Town, Lingshan County, Qinzhou City on June 1st, 1986. Now it is preserved at Lingshan County Museum. Face Diameter:99− 100.5cm, Height:59.3cm

鼓面蛙饰

鼓耳

鼓足动物装饰

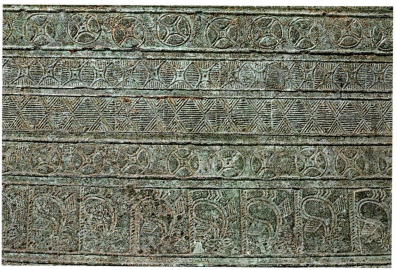

鼓身细部

鼓面细部

22

总号 0036，原灵山 12 号，白木鼓，1986 年 2 月 5 日出土于钦州市灵山县三海乡白木村屋背岭，现存灵山县博物馆。面径 103.9—104.6 厘米，身高 64 厘米，一侧鼓耳下鼓足位置饰立体羊两只。

Bronze Drum Baimu(No.0036, original name Lingshan No.12), with a pair of sheep statutes on the foot under one of the four handles, unearthed Wubeiling Hill, Baimu Village, Sanhai, Lingshan County, Qinzhou City on February 5th, 1986. Now it is preserved at Lingshan County Museum. Face Diameter:103.9—104.6cm, Height:64cm

鼓足动物装饰

鼓面蛙饰

鼓面蛙饰

23

总号 0124，原灵山 21 号，六颜
鼓，1987 年出土于钦州市灵山
县丰塘乡六颜村，现存灵山县博
物馆。面径 81—81.3 厘米，身
高 50 厘米。

Bronze Drum Liuyan(No.0124,
original name Lingshan No.21),
unearthed at Liuyan Village,
Fengtang, Lingshan County,
Qinzhou City in 1987. Now it is
preserved at Lingshan County
Museum.
Face Diameter:81—81.3cm,
Height:50cm

鼓面蛙饰

鼓面细部

24

总号 0018，原灵山 06 号，稔坡村鼓，50 年代出土于钦州市灵山县新圩
镇稔坡村，1984 年 9 月 24 日移交灵山县博物馆，现存灵山县博物馆。
面径 69.9—70.2 厘米，身高 42.5 厘米，一侧鼓耳下鼓足位置饰立体鸟一对。

Bronze Drum Renpo Cun(No.0018, original name Lingshan No.06),with a
pair of bird statutes on the foot under one of the four handles, unearthed at
Renpo Village, Xinxu Town, Lingshan County, Qinzhou City in the 50s' of
last century, and was transferred to Lingshan County Museum on September
24th,1984. Now it is preserved at Lingshan County Museum.
Face Diameter:69.9-70.2cm, Height:42.5cm

鼓面蛙饰

鼓足动物装饰

鼓面细部

鼓耳、鼓身细部

25

总号 000584，上柿子村鼓，1995 年 2 月 18 日出土于钦州市浦北县乐民镇西角上柿子村，现存浦北县博物馆。面径 89.5—90 厘米，身高 56 厘米。

Bronze Drum Shangshizi Cun(No.000584), unearthed at Shangshizi Village, west to Lemin Town, Pubei County, Qinzhou City on February 18th ,1995. Now it is preserved at Pubei County Museum.
Face Diameter:89.5—90cm, Height:56cm

鼓面细部

鼓耳

鼓面蛙饰

鼓身细部

26

总号 1878，石卡铜鼓，1995 年
12 月出土于贵港市覃塘区石卡
镇凤凰林场，现存贵港市博物
馆。面径 118.5—119.8 厘米，身
高 66.4 厘米。一侧鼓耳下鼓足
位置饰立体鸟一对。

Bronze Drum Shika(No.1878),with
a pair of bird statutes on the foot
under one of the four handles,
unearthed at Fenghuang Tree
Farm, Shika Town, Qintang
District of Guigang City in
December 1995. Now it is
preserved at Guigang Museum.
Face Diameter:118.5—119.8cm,
Height:66.4cm

鼓足动物纹饰

鼓面蛙饰

鼓身细部

鼓面太阳纹

27
总号 000759，莲塘坪鼓，1993
年 2 月出土于玉林市沙田镇六龙
村莲塘坪南约一公里十五冲山
上，现存玉林市博物馆。面径
126.2—133.5 厘米，身高 66.5 厘
米，一侧鼓耳下鼓足位置饰立体
虎一只。

Bronze Drum Liantang
Ping(No.000759), with a tiger
statute on the foot under one of
the four handles, unearthed at
Shiwuchong Hill, the south of 1km
to Liantang Ping, Liulong Village,
Shatian Town, Yulin City in
February 1993. Now it is preserved
at Yulin Museum.
Face Diameter:126.2—133.5cm,
Height:66.5cm

鼓面蛙饰

鼓面蛙饰

鼓足虎立饰

鼓耳

28

总号 000442，三龙铜鼓，1984
年 5 月出土于玉林市石南镇东
龙村三龙屯东南约 100 米处，现
存玉林市博物馆。面径 95.2—96
厘米，身高 52 厘米。

Bronze Drum Sanlong(No.000442),
unearthed in the southeast of
100m to Sanlong Tun, Donglong
Village, Shinan Town, Yulin City
in May 1984. Now it is preserved
at Yulin Museum.
Face Diameter:95.2—96cm,
Height:52cm

鼓面蛙饰

鼓面蛙饰

鼓耳

29

总号 00002，李屋鼓，1976 年出土于玉林市米场镇李屋村，现存陆川县文物管理所。面径 118—121 厘米，残高 60.5 厘米。

Bronze Drum Liwu(No.00002), unearthed at Liwu Village, Michang Town, Yulin City in 1976. Now it is preserved at Luchuan County Cultural Relics Administration. Face Diameter:118–121cm, Remained Height:60.5cm

鼓面蛙饰

鼓耳

鼓内调音铲痕

30

总号 00005，牛角冲鼓，1991 年
10 月 28 日出土于玉林市陆川县
沙坡镇北安村风塘屯牛角冲，
现存陆川县文物管理所。面径
100.5—102 厘米，身高 56 厘米。

Bronze Drum
Niujiaochong(No.00005),
unearthed at Niujiaochong,
Fengtang Tun, Bei'an Village,
Shapo Town, Yulin City on
October 28th,1991. Now it is
preserved at Luchuan County
Cultural Relics Adiministration.
Face Diameter:100.5−102cm,
Height:56cm

鼓面细部　　　　　鼓面蛙饰

31

016 号，莫屋铜鼓，1982
年 11 月出土于玉林市博
白县宁潭镇大车塘村莫屋
屯，现存博白县博物馆。
面径 83.9—84.2 厘米，身
高 49.7 厘米，鼓胸内壁
饰立体蛙一对。

Bronze Drum
Mowu(No.016), With a pair
of frogs inside the chest,
unearthed at Mowu Tun,
Dachetang Village, Ningtan
Town, Bobai County, Yulin
City in November, 1982.
Now it is preserved at
Bobai County Museum.
Face Diameter:83.9–
84.2cm, Height:49.7cm

鼓面蛙饰

鼓面蛙饰

鼓身细部

鼓内蛙饰

鼓面太阳纹

鼓面内部调音铲痕

32

总号 020，亚山铜鼓，1986年 3 月出土于玉林市博白县亚山镇西约 3 公里的农场，现存博白县博物馆。面径 76.3—76.8 厘米，身高 46 厘米。一侧鼓耳下鼓足位置饰立体鸟一对。

Bronze Drum Yashan(No.020),with a pair of bird statutes on the foot under one of the four handles, unearthed at a farm in the west of 3km to Yashan Town, Bobai County, Yulin City in March 1986. Now it is preserved at Bobai Museum. Face Diameter:76.3~76.8cm, Height:46cm

鼓耳

鼓足动物装饰

鼓面蛙饰

鼓身细部

鼓面细部

33

咘罗鼓，1973年出土于崇左市江州区，现存崇左市博物馆。面径59—59.5厘米，身高35.3厘米，一侧鼓耳下鼓足位置饰立体鸟一只。

Bronze Drum Buluo, with a bird statue on the foot under one of the four handles, unearthed at Jiangzhou District of Chongzuo City in 1973. Now it is preserved at Chongzuo Museum.
Face Diameter:59—59.5cm, Height:35.3cm

鼓身细部

鼓面蛙饰

鼓足动物装饰

鼓面细部

西盟型铜鼓
Ximeng Type

以云南省西盟佤族自治县地区仍在使用的铜鼓为代表。铸造年代在唐代中期至清代末叶（公元8世纪至公元20世纪）。该型早期鼓在广西西南的龙州和靖西有所发现，中、晚期鼓主要分布于云南西南部及其毗邻的缅甸、老挝和泰国。使用该型铜鼓的民族，在中国境内有傣族和佤族，东南亚有缅甸的克伦族、老挝的卡族和泰国的泰族。其特点是：器壁轻薄，形体高瘦，鼓身近乎直筒形，晕多而密。主要纹饰有双眼条花纹、团花纹、小鸟纹、鱼纹、雷纹和米粒纹等。鼓面常见二、三蛙累蹲，部分鼓身纵列立体的象、螺蛳和玉树等。

This type was represented by the drums that are still used by Wa people in Ximeng area, Yunnan province. The cast time could be dated from middle Tang dynasty to late Qing dynasty (about 8 C.A.C.-20 C.A.C.). Early form of this type was found in Longzhou and Jingxi, the Southwestern areas of Guangxi; its middle and late forms were found mainly in southwest Yunnan, and the neighboring areas such as Burma, Laos and Thailand. Dai and Wa people in China, Karen people in Burma, Ka people in Laos, Thai people in Thailand use this type of bronze drums. This type drum has a light, tall form with thin wall, almost in a shape ofstraight cylinder, decorated by numerous and intensive loops. Main motifs includes eyes&flowers, flower clusters, birds, fishes, thunders and rices. Frog statues on drum face are always in overlap and 3 overlap frogs shape. Some drums have statues like elephants, field snails and trees, arraying vertically on the drum body.

1

总号 004757，族鼓 0031 号，变形羽人纹鸟纹铜鼓（又名 031 号鼓），1971 年 2 月出土于龙州响水公社龙江大队派良屯，现存广西民族博物馆。面径 49.7—50 厘米，身高 33.4 厘米。

Bronze drum with bird and transformed feathermen patterns(No.004757, ZGNo.0031), unearthed at Pailiang Tun, Longjiang Group, Xiangshui Commune, Longzhou County in February 1971. Now it is preserved at Anthropology Museum of Guangxi. Face Diameter:49.7－50cm, Height:33.4cm

鼓面蛙饰

鼓耳

鼓面细部

鼓身细部

2

总号 005045，族鼓 0332，
鱼纹鸟纹菊花纹铜鼓，出
土于云南西部地区，1984
年云南省博物馆移交广西
壮族自治区博物馆，现存
广西民族博物馆。面径
53.4 厘米，身高 41 厘米。

Bronze drum with fish,
bird and chrysanthemum
patterns(No.005045,
ZGNo.0332), unearthed in
the western region of Yunnan
Province, and was handed
over to Museum of Guangxi
Zhuang Autonomous Region
in 1984. Now it is preserved
at Anthropology Museum of
Guangxi.
Face Diameter:53.4cm,
Height:41cm

鼓面细部

鼓面太阳纹

鼓耳

3

Hg00038 号，东汉立蛙鼓，2008 年 7 月购买，现存柳州市博物馆。面径
43—43.5 厘米，身高 28 厘米。

Bronze drum with frog statutes(East Han Dynasty, Hg00038), collected in July,
2008. Now it is preserved at Liuzhou Museum.
Face Diameter:43-43.5cm，Height:28cm

鼓面蛙饰

鼓面细部

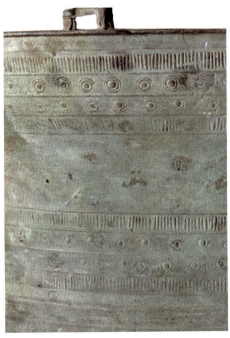

鼓面细部

广西铜鼓精华

Bronze Drums in Guangxi

下　册

中国古代铜鼓研究会　编
广西民族博物馆

Compiled by The Chinese Association for Ancient Bronze Drums Research
& Anthropology Museum of Guangxi

覃　溥　主编
Chief Editor　Qin Pu

文物出版社
Cultural Relics Press

广西馆藏铜鼓一览表

序号 NO.	原编号及鼓名 Stock Number & Name	收藏单位 Museum	出土（征集）时间、地点 Time & Spot for discovered or collected	主要装饰 Main Decorations	尺寸（厘米）Size(cm)		类型 Type	图片 Picture
					面径 Face Diameter	身高 Height		
1	族鼓 0001 游旗纹铜鼓 ZG No.0001 Bronze Drum with flying flag patterns	广西民族博物馆 Anthropology Museum of Guangxi	1971 年 5 月收购于南宁废品公司 Collected at Nanning Waste Recycle Company in May, 1971	鼓面：太阳纹（12 芒）、西字纹、S 云纹、乳钉纹、游旗纹、栉纹、兽面云纹、卦纹；鼓身：乳钉纹、回形雷纹、如意云纹、栉纹、云纹、复线三角纹；扁耳两对饰回形雷纹、辫纹 Drum face: patterns of sun(12rays), 西 -character, S-shape cloud, nipple protrusion, flying flag, comb line, beast-face cloud, divinatory symbol; Drum body: patterns of nipple protrusion, 回 -shape thunder, Ruyi-shape cloud, comb line, cloud, double line triangle; 回 -shape thunder and braid patterns on 2 pairs of flat handles.	47–47.4	27	麻江型 Majiang Type	
2	族鼓 0002 游旗纹铜鼓 ZG No.0002 Bronze Drum with flying flag patterns	广西民族博物馆 Anthropology Museum of Guangxi	1971 年 3 月收购于南宁废品公司 Collected at Nanning Waste Recycle Company in March, 1971	鼓面：太阳纹（12 芒）、西字纹、栉纹、乳钉纹、菱形纹、游旗纹、五瓣花纹、S 云纹、云纹；鼓身：栉纹、乳钉纹、游旗纹、复线三角纹；扁耳两对饰辫纹 Drum face: patterns of sun(12rays), 西 -character, comb line, nipple protrusion, joint-diamond, flying flag, cinquefoil, S-shape cloud, cloud; Drum body: patterns of comb line, nipple protrusion, flying flag, double line triangle; Braid patterns on 2 pairs of flat handles.	48.2–48.4	27.5	麻江型 Majiang Type	
3	族鼓 0003 游旗纹铜鼓 ZG No.0003 Bronze Drum with flying flag patterns	广西民族博物馆 Anthropology Museum of Guangxi	1971 年 3 月收购于南宁废品公司 Collected at Nanning Waste Recycle Company in March, 1971	鼓面：太阳纹（12 芒）、西字纹、S 云纹、乳钉纹、栉纹、游旗纹、云纹；鼓身：乳钉纹、如意云纹、回形雷纹、栉纹、云纹、复线三角纹；扁耳两对饰辫纹 Drum face: patterns of sun(12rays), 酉 -character, S-shape cloud, nipple protrusion, comb line, flying flag, cloud; Drum body: patterns of nipple protrusion, Ruyi-shape cloud, 回 -shape thunder, comb line, cloud, double line triangle; Braid patterns on 2 pairs of flat handles.	47.2–47.4	26	麻江型 Majiang Type	

序号 N0.	原编号及鼓名 Stock Number & Name	收藏单位 Museum	出土（征集）时间、地点 Time & Spot for discovered or collected	主要装饰 Main Decorations	尺寸（厘米）Size(cm)		类型 Type	图片 Picture
					面径 Face Diameter	身高 Height		
4	族鼓 0004 游旗纹铜鼓 ZG No.0004 Bronze Drum with flying flag patterns	广西民族博物馆 Anthropology Museum of Guangxi	1971 年 3 月收购于南宁废品公司 Collected at Nanning Waste Recycle Company in March, 1971	鼓面：太阳纹（12 芒）、酉字纹、S 云纹、乳钉纹、游旗纹、栉纹、兽形云纹；鼓身：乳钉纹、如意云纹、回形雷纹、云纹、复线三角纹；扁耳两对饰辫纹 Drum face: patterns of sun(12rays), 酉 -character, S-shape cloud, nipple protrusion, flying flag, comb line, beast-shape cloud; Drum body: patterns of nipple protrusion, Ruyi-shape cloud, 回 -shape thunder, cloud, double line triangle; Braid patterns on 2 pairs of flat handles.	49	26	麻江型 Majiang Type	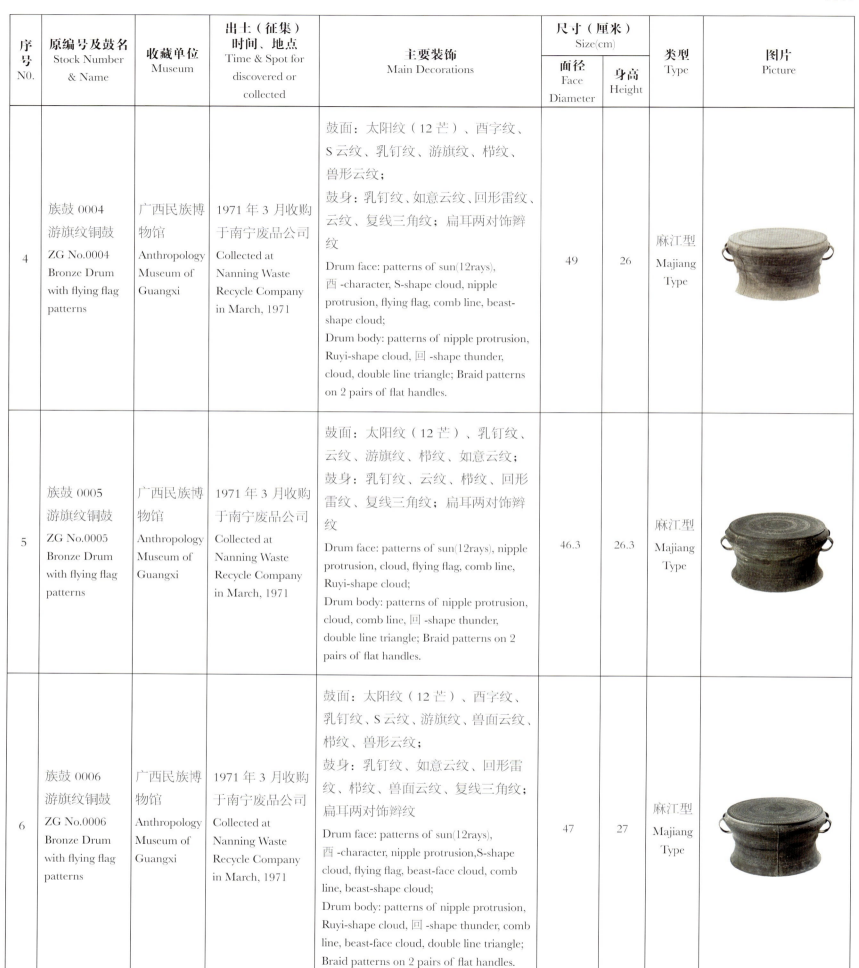
5	族鼓 0005 游旗纹铜鼓 ZG No.0005 Bronze Drum with flying flag patterns	广西民族博物馆 Anthropology Museum of Guangxi	1971 年 3 月收购于南宁废品公司 Collected at Nanning Waste Recycle Company in March, 1971	鼓面：太阳纹（12 芒）、乳钉纹、云纹、游旗纹、栉纹、如意云纹；鼓身：乳钉纹、云纹、栉纹、回形雷纹、复线三角纹；扁耳两对饰辫纹 Drum face: patterns of sun(12rays), nipple protrusion, cloud, flying flag, comb line, Ruyi-shape cloud; Drum body: patterns of nipple protrusion, cloud, comb line, 回 -shape thunder, double line triangle; Braid patterns on 2 pairs of flat handles.	46.3	26.3	麻江型 Majiang Type	
6	族鼓 0006 游旗纹铜鼓 ZG No.0006 Bronze Drum with flying flag patterns	广西民族博物馆 Anthropology Museum of Guangxi	1971 年 3 月收购于南宁废品公司 Collected at Nanning Waste Recycle Company in March, 1971	鼓面：太阳纹（12 芒）、酉字纹、乳钉纹、S 云纹、游旗纹、兽面云纹、栉纹、兽形云纹；鼓身：乳钉纹、如意云纹、回形雷纹、栉纹、兽面云纹、复线三角纹；扁耳两对饰辫纹 Drum face: patterns of sun(12rays), 酉 -character, nipple protrusion,S-shape cloud, flying flag, beast-face cloud, comb line, beast-shape cloud; Drum body: patterns of nipple protrusion, Ruyi-shape cloud, 回 -shape thunder, comb line, beast-face cloud, double line triangle; Braid patterns on 2 pairs of flat handles.	47	27	麻江型 Majiang Type	

续表

序号 NO.	原编号及鼓名 Stock Number & Name	收藏单位 Museum	出土（征集） 时间、地点 Time & Spot for discovered or collected	主要装饰 Main Decorations	尺寸（厘米） Size(cm)		类型 Type	图片 Picture
					面径 Face Diameter	身高 Height		
7	族鼓 0007 游旗纹铜鼓 ZG No.0007 Bronze Drum with flying flag patterns	广西民族博物馆 Anthropology Museum of Guangxi	1971 年 3 月收购于南宁废品公司 Collected at Nanning Waste Recycle Company in March, 1971	鼓面：太阳纹（12 芒）、酉字纹、S 云纹、乳钉纹、游旗纹、栉纹、兽形云纹； 鼓身：乳钉纹、如意云纹、回形雷纹、栉纹、云纹、复线三角纹；扁耳两对饰辫纹 Drum face: patterns of sun(12rays), 酉-character, S-shape cloud,nipple protrusion,flying flag, comb line, beast-shape cloud; Drum body: patterns of nipple protrusion, Ruyi-shape cloud, 回-shape thunder, comb line, cloud, double line triangle;Braid patterns on 2 pairs of flat handles.	46.5	26.5	麻江型 Majiang Type	
8	族鼓 0008 游旗纹铜鼓 ZG No.0008 Bronze Drum with flying flag patterns	广西民族博物馆 Anthropology Museum of Guangxi	1971 年 3 月收购于南宁废品公司 Collected at Nanning Waste Recycle Company in March, 1971	鼓面：太阳纹（12 芒）、酉字纹、S 云纹、乳钉纹、游旗纹、栉纹、兽面云纹； 鼓身：梅花状乳钉纹、如意云纹、回形雷纹、栉纹、复线三角纹；扁耳两对饰辫纹 Drum face: patterns of sun(12rays), 酉-character, S-shape cloud,nipple protrusion,flying flag, comb line, beast-face cloud; Drum body: patterns of nipple protrusion in plum blossom shape, Ruyi-shape cloud, 回-shape thunder, comb line, double line triangle;Braid patterns on 2 pairs of flat handles.	47—47.2	26.3	麻江型 Majiang Type	
9	族鼓 0009 符箓纹铜鼓 ZG No.0009 Bronze Drum with Ofuda patterns	广西民族博物馆 Anthropology Museum of Guangxi	1971 年 3 月收购于南宁废品公司 Collected at Nanning Waste Recycle Company in March, 1971	鼓面：太阳纹（12 芒）、同心圆纹、回形雷纹、乳钉纹、符箓纹、云纹； 鼓身：乳钉纹、如意云纹、复线三角纹；扁耳两对饰辫纹 Drum face: patterns of sun(12rays), concentric circle, 回-shape thunder,nipple protrusion, Ofuda, cloud; Drum body: patterns of nipple protrusion, Ruyi-shape cloud,double line triangle;Braid patterns on 2 pairs of flat handles.	47.3—48	26.7	麻江型 Majiang Type	

序号 N0.	原编号及鼓名 Stock Number & Name	收藏单位 Museum	出土（征集） 时间、地点 Time & Spot for discovered or collected	主要装饰 Main Decorations	尺寸（厘米） Size(cm)		类型 Type	图片 Picture
					面径 Face Diameter	身高 Height		
10	族鼓 0010 游旗纹铜鼓 ZG No.0010 Bronze Drum with flying flag patterns	广西民族博物馆 Anthropology Museum of Guangxi	1971 年 3 月收购于南宁废品公司 Collected at Nanning Waste Recycle Company in March, 1971	鼓面：太阳纹（12 芒）、酉字纹、S 云纹、乳钉纹、游旗纹、栉纹、云纹、兽面云纹； 鼓身：乳钉纹、如意云纹、回形雷纹、栉纹、云纹、复线三角纹；扁耳两对饰回形雷纹、辫纹 Drum face: patterns of sun(12rays), 酉 -character, S-shape cloud, nipple protrusion, flying flag,comb line, cloud, beast-face cloud; Drum body: patterns of nipple protrusion, Ruyi-shape cloud, 回 -shape thunder, comb line, cloud, double line triangle; 回 -shape thunder and braid patterns on 2 pairs of flat handles.	46.5-46.8	26.2	麻江型 Majiang Type	
11	族鼓 0011 游旗纹铜鼓 ZG No.0011 Bronze Drum with flying flag patterns	广西民族博物馆 Anthropology Museum of Guangxi	1971 年 3 月收购于南宁废品公司 Collected at Nanning Waste Recycle Company in March, 1971	鼓面：太阳纹（12 芒）、酉字纹、S 云纹、乳钉纹、游旗纹、栉纹、云纹； 鼓身：乳钉纹、如意云纹、回形雷纹、栉纹、云纹、复线三角纹；扁耳两对饰辫纹 Drum face: patterns of sun(12rays), 酉 -character, S-shape cloud, nipple protrusion, flying flag,comb line, cloud; Drum body: patterns of nipple protrusion, Ruyi-shape cloud, 回 -shape thunder, comb line, cloud, double line triangle;Braid patterns on 2 pairs of flat handles.	48	26	麻江型 Majiang Type	
12	族鼓 0012 游旗纹铜鼓 ZG No.0012 Bronze Drum with flying flag patterns	广西民族博物馆 Anthropology Museum of Guangxi	1971 年 3 月收购于南宁废品公司 Collected at Nanning Waste Recycle Company in March, 1971	鼓面：太阳纹（12 芒）、乳钉纹、酉字纹、游旗纹、菱形填四瓣花纹、回形雷纹； 鼓身：乳钉纹、羽纹、雷纹、水波纹、雷／虫形纹、四瓣花纹、雷纹、虫形纹、倒复线三角纹；扁耳两对饰凸棱纹 Drum face: patterns of sun(12rays), nipple protrusion, 酉 -character, flying flag, diamond filled with quatrefoil, 回 -shape thunder; Drum body: patterns of nipple protrusion, feather thunder, water wave, thunder & insect, quatrefoil, thunder, insect, reverse double line triangle; raise ridges on 2 pairs of flat handles.	48	27	麻江型 Majiang Type	

序号 N0.	原编号及鼓名 Stock Number & Name	收藏单位 Museum	出土（征集）时间、地点 Time & Spot for discovered or collected	主要装饰 Main Decorations	尺寸（厘米）Size(cm)		类型 Type	图片 Picture
					面径 Face Diameter	身高 Height		
13	族鼓 0013 回纹铜鼓 ZG No.0013 Bronze Drum with 回-shape motif patterns	广西民族博物馆 Anthropology Museum of Guangxi	1971 年 3 月收购于南宁废品公司 Collected at Nanning Waste Recycle Company in March, 1971	鼓面：太阳纹（12 芒）、乳钉纹、回形纹、水波纹、羽纹、S 云纹、绚纹；鼓身：乳钉纹、云朵纹、回形纹、水波纹、复线三角纹；扁耳两对饰弦纹 Drum face: patterns of sun(12rays), nipple protrusion, 回-shape motif, water wave, feather, S-shape cloud, twisted rope; Drum body: patterns of nipple protrusion, cloud, 回-shape motif, water wave, double line triangle; strings on 2 pairs of flat handles.	48–48.2	27	麻江型 Majiang Type	
14	族鼓 0014 游旗纹铜鼓 ZG No.0014 Bronze Drum with flying flag patterns	广西民族博物馆 Anthropology Museum of Guangxi	1971 年 3 月收购于南宁废品公司 Collected at Nanning Waste Recycle Company in March, 1971	鼓面：太阳纹（12 芒）、四出钱纹、S 云纹、乳钉纹、游旗纹、栉纹、兽形云纹；鼓身：乳钉纹、如意云纹、回纹、回形雷纹、栉纹、S 云纹、复线三角纹；扁耳两对饰龙首凸棱纹 Drum face: patterns of sun(12rays), coin with quadrangle inside, S-shape cloud, nipple protrusion, flying flag, comb line, beast-shape cloud; Drum body: patterns of nipple protrusion, Ruyi-shape cloud, 回-shape motif, 回-shape thunder, S-shape cloud, double line triangle; raise ridges with dragon head on 2 pairs of flat handles.	46.7–47	26.6	麻江型 Majiang Type	
15	族鼓 0015 游旗纹铜鼓 ZG No.0015 Bronze Drum with flying flag patterns	广西民族博物馆 Anthropology Museum of Guangxi	1971 年 3 月收购于南宁废品公司 Collected at Nanning Waste Recycle Company in March, 1971	鼓面：太阳纹（12 芒）、乳钉纹、雷纹、雷纹填十字纹、游旗纹、回形雷纹、同心圆纹；鼓身：乳钉纹、绚纹、回形雷纹、雷纹、复线三角纹、同心圆纹；扁耳两对饰凸棱纹 Drum face: patterns of sun(12rays), nipple protrusion, thunder, thunder filled with cross, flying flag, 回-shape thunder, concentric circle; Drum body: patterns of nipple protrusion, twisted rope, 回-shape thunder, thunder, double line triangle, concentric circle; Raise ridges on 2 pairs of flat handles.	49.5	25.8	麻江型 Majiang Type	

序号 N0.	原编号及鼓名 Stock Number & Name	收藏单位 Museum	出土（征集）时间、地点 Time & Spot for discovered or collected	主要装饰 Main Decorations	尺寸（厘米）Size(cm)		类型 Type	图片 Picture
					面径 Face Diameter	身高 Height		
16	族鼓 0016 游旗纹铜鼓 ZG No.0016 Bronze Drum with flying flag patterns	广西民族博物馆 Anthropology Museum of Guangxi	1971 年 3 月收购于南宁废品公司 Collected at Nanning Waste Recycle Company in March, 1971	鼓面：太阳纹（12 芒）、钱纹、S云纹、乳钉纹、游旗纹、栉纹、兽形云纹； 鼓身：乳钉纹、如意云纹、回形雷纹、栉纹、云纹、复线三角纹；扁耳两对饰辫纹 Drum face: patterns of sun(12rays), coin, S-shape cloud,nipple protrusion,flying flag, comb line, beast-shape cloud; Drum body: patterns of nipple protrusion, Ruyi-shape cloud, 回 -shape thunder, comb line, cloud,double line triangle; Braid patterns on 2 pairs of flat handles.	46.3	26.5	麻江型 Majiang Type	
17	族鼓 0017 四鱼纹铜鼓 ZG No.0017 Bronze Drum with 4-fish patterns	广西民族博物馆 Anthropology Museum of Guangxi	1971 年 3 月收购于南宁废品公司 Collected at Nanning Waste Recycle Company in March, 1971	鼓面：太阳纹（12 芒）、乳钉纹、四瓣花纹、双鱼间八宝纹、波浪纹、回形雷纹、同心圆纹、有"富贵"二字铭文； 鼓身：乳钉纹、雷纹、复线三角纹、缠枝花纹、回形雷纹、S 勾纹、复线三角间乳钉纹；扁耳两对（已失） Drum face: patterns of sun(12rays), nipple protrusion,quatrefoil, 2 fishes mixed 8 Buddhist Treasures, water wave, 回 -shape thunder, concentric circle，" 富贵 "-character; Drum body: patterns of nipple protrusion, thunder, double line triangle, twisted branches, 回 -shape thunder, S-shape hook, double line triangle mixed nipple protrusion; 2 pairs of flat handles(lost).	47.5	25.5	麻江型 Majiang Type	
18	族鼓 0018 鱼纹铜鼓 ZG No.0018 Bronze Drum with fish patterns	广西民族博物馆 Anthropology Museum of Guangxi	1971 年 3 月收购于南宁废品公司 Collected at Nanning Waste Recycle Company in March, 1971	鼓面：太阳纹（12 芒）、同心圆纹、回形雷纹、乳钉纹、鱼纹、云纹、4组同心圆纹间回形雷纹； 鼓身：乳钉纹、同心圆纹、回形雷纹、云纹、如意云纹、复线三角纹；扁耳两对饰辫纹 Drum face: patterns of sun(12rays), concentric circle, 回 -shape thunder,nipple protrusion, fish, cloud, 4 groups of concentric circle mixed 回 -shape thunder; Drum body: patterns of nipple protrusion, concentric circle, 回 -shape thunder, cloud, Ruyi-shape cloud, double line triangle; Braid on 2 pairs of flat handles.	45.5－45.8	27.5	麻江型 Majiang Type	

续表

序号 NO.	原编号及鼓名 Stock Number & Name	收藏单位 Museum	出土（征集）时间、地点 Time & Spot for discovered or collected	主要装饰 Main Decorations	尺寸（厘米）Size(cm)		类型 Type	图片 Picture
					面径 Face Diameter	身高 Height		
19	族鼓 0019 符箓纹铜鼓 ZG No.0019 Bronze Drum with Ofuda patterns	广西民族博物馆 Anthropology Museum of Guangxi	1971 年 3 月收购于南宁废品公司 Collected at Nanning Waste Recycle Company in March, 1971	鼓面：太阳纹（12 芒）、梅花状圆圈纹、乳钉纹、水波纹、符箓纹、如意云纹、勾形纹、窗花纹、勾连雷纹；鼓身：乳钉纹、窗花纹、缠枝纹、如意纹、勾连雷纹、垂穗纹；扁耳两对饰凸棱纹 Drum face: patterns of sun(12rays), plum-blossom-shape circles, nipple protrusion, water wave, Ofuda, Ruyi-shape cloud, hook, window lattices, hooked thunder; Drum body: patterns of nipple protrusion, window lattices, twisted branches, Ruyi-shape cloud, hooked thunder, rice ear pendant; Raise ridges on 2 pairs of flat handles.	46－46.3	26	麻江型 Majiang Type	
20	族鼓 0020 行马走山纹铜鼓 ZG No.0020 Bronze Drum with horse-walking-on-hills patterns	广西民族博物馆 Anthropology Museum of Guangxi	1971 年 3 月收购于南宁废品公司 Collected at Nanning Waste Recycle Company in March, 1971	鼓面：太阳纹（12 芒）、乳钉纹、复线三角纹、梅兰竹菊纹、行马走山纹、绹纹；鼓身：乳钉纹、缠枝纹、如意纹、行马走山纹、复线三角纹；扁耳两对饰凸棱纹 Drum face: patterns of sun(12rays),nipple protrusion, double line triangle, pattern group of plum blossom, orchid, bamboo and chrysanthemum, horse walking on mountains, twisted rope; Drum body: patterns of nipple protrusion, twisted branches, Ruyi, horse walking on mountains, double line triangle; raise ridges on 2 pairs of flat handles.	46.3－28	28	麻江型 Majiang Type	
21	族鼓 0021 十二生肖纹铜鼓 ZG No.0021 Bronze Drum with zodiac patterns	广西民族博物馆 Anthropology Museum of Guangxi	1971 年 3 月收购于南宁废品公司 Collected at Nanning Waste Recycle Company in March, 1971	鼓面：太阳纹（12 芒）、栉纹、蝉纹、羽纹、绹纹、十二生肖纹、游旗纹、回形雷纹、云纹；鼓身：勾云纹、乳钉纹、回形雷纹、复线三角纹；扁耳两对饰凸棱纹 Drum face: patterns of sun(12rays), comb line, cicada, feather, twisted rope, zodiac, flying flag, 回 -shape thunder,cloud; Drum body: patterns of hooked cloud, nipple protrusion, 回 -shape thunder, double line triangle; Raise ridges on 2 pairs of flat handles.	49－49.4	30	麻江型 Majiang Type	

序号 NO.	原编号及鼓名 Stock Number & Name	收藏单位 Museum	出土（征集）时间、地点 Time & Spot for discovered or collected	主要装饰 Main Decorations	尺寸（厘米）Size(cm)		类型 Type	图片 Picture
					面径 Face Diameter	身高 Height		
22	族鼓 0022 游旗纹铜鼓 ZG No.0022 Bronze Drum with flying flag patterns	广西民族博物馆 Anthropology Museum of Guangxi	1971 年 3 月收购于南宁废品公司 Collected at Nanning Waste Recycle Company in March, 1971	鼓面：太阳纹（12 芒）、酉字纹、S 云纹、乳钉纹、游旗纹、栉纹、兽形云纹； 鼓身：乳钉纹、如意云纹、回形雷纹、栉纹、复线三角纹；扁耳两对饰辫纹 Drum face: patterns of sun(12rays), 酉 -character, S-shape cloud,nipple protrusion,flying flag, comb line, beast-shape cloud; Drum body: patterns of nipple protrusion, Ruyi-shape cloud, 回 -shape thunder, comb line, double line triangle; Braid patterns on 2 pairs of flat handles.	47.4	25.5	麻江型 Majiang Type	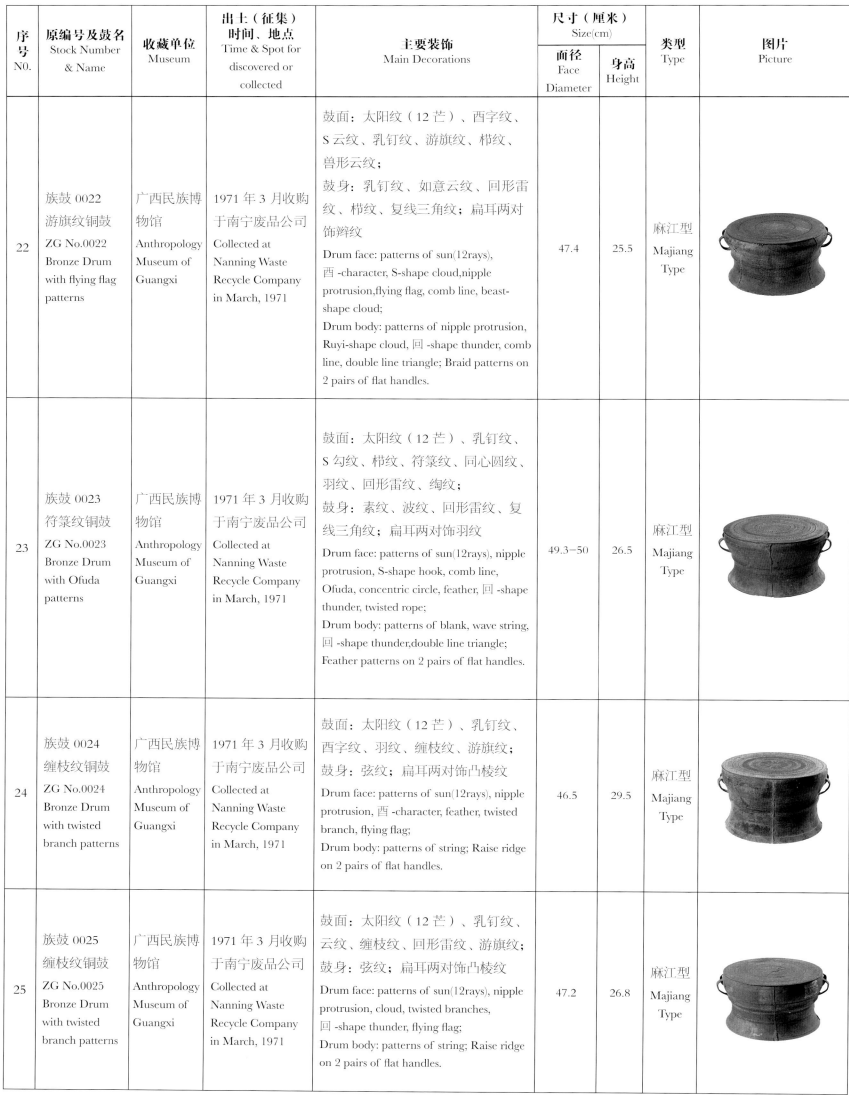
23	族鼓 0023 符箓纹铜鼓 ZG No.0023 Bronze Drum with Ofuda patterns	广西民族博物馆 Anthropology Museum of Guangxi	1971 年 3 月收购于南宁废品公司 Collected at Nanning Waste Recycle Company in March, 1971	鼓面：太阳纹（12 芒）、乳钉纹、S 勾纹、栉纹、符箓纹、同心圆纹、羽纹、回形雷纹、绚纹； 鼓身：素纹、波纹、回形雷纹、复线三角纹；扁耳两对饰羽纹 Drum face: patterns of sun(12rays), nipple protrusion, S-shape hook, comb line, Ofuda, concentric circle, feather, 回 -shape thunder, twisted rope; Drum body: patterns of blank, wave string, 回 -shape thunder,double line triangle; Feather patterns on 2 pairs of flat handles.	49.3—50	26.5	麻江型 Majiang Type	
24	族鼓 0024 缠枝纹铜鼓 ZG No.0024 Bronze Drum with twisted branch patterns	广西民族博物馆 Anthropology Museum of Guangxi	1971 年 3 月收购于南宁废品公司 Collected at Nanning Waste Recycle Company in March, 1971	鼓面：太阳纹（12 芒）、乳钉纹、酉字纹、羽纹、缠枝纹、游旗纹； 鼓身：弦纹；扁耳两对饰凸棱纹 Drum face: patterns of sun(12rays), nipple protrusion, 酉 -character, feather, twisted branch, flying flag; Drum body: patterns of string; Raise ridge on 2 pairs of flat handles.	46.5	29.5	麻江型 Majiang Type	
25	族鼓 0025 缠枝纹铜鼓 ZG No.0025 Bronze Drum with twisted branch patterns	广西民族博物馆 Anthropology Museum of Guangxi	1971 年 3 月收购于南宁废品公司 Collected at Nanning Waste Recycle Company in March, 1971	鼓面：太阳纹（12 芒）、乳钉纹、云纹、缠枝纹、回形雷纹、游旗纹； 鼓身：弦纹；扁耳两对饰凸棱纹 Drum face: patterns of sun(12rays), nipple protrusion, cloud, twisted branches, 回 -shape thunder, flying flag; Drum body: patterns of string; Raise ridge on 2 pairs of flat handles.	47.2	26.8	麻江型 Majiang Type	

序号 NO.	原编号及鼓名 Stock Number & Name	收藏单位 Museum	出土（征集）时间、地点 Time & Spot for discovered or collected	主要装饰 Main Decorations	尺寸（厘米） Size(cm)		类型 Type	图片 Picture
					面径 Face Diameter	身高 Height		
26	族鼓 0026 缠枝纹铜鼓 ZG No.0026 Bronze Drum with twisted branch patterns	广西民族博物馆 Anthropology Museum of Guangxi	1971 年 3 月收购于南宁废品公司 Collected at Nanning Waste Recycle Company in March, 1971	鼓面：太阳纹（12 芒）、乳钉纹、水波纹、异形游旗纹、羽纹、缠枝纹； 鼓身：乳钉纹、弦纹；扁耳两对饰凸棱纹 Drum face: patterns of sun(12rays), nipple protrusion, water wave, transformed flying flag, feather, twisted branches; Drum body: patterns of nipple protrusion string; Raise ridge on 2 pairs of flat handles.	47–47.5	27	麻江型 Majiang Type	
27	族鼓 0027 符箓纹铜鼓 ZG No.0027 Bronze Drum with Ofuda patterns	广西民族博物馆 Anthropology Museum of Guangxi	1971 年 3 月收购于南宁废品公司 Collected at Nanning Waste Recycle Company in March, 1971	鼓面：太阳纹（12 芒）、S 云纹、同心圆纹、乳钉纹、符箓纹、回形雷纹； 鼓身：梅花状乳钉纹间单乳钉纹、翎眼纹、回形雷纹、如意云纹、雷纹、云纹、复线三角纹；扁耳两对饰凸棱纹 Drum face: patterns of sun(12rays), S-shape cloud, concentric circle, nipple protrusion, Ofuda, 回 -shape thunder; Drum body: patterns of nipple protrusion in plum-blossom shape mixed single nipple protrusion, peacock feather, 回 -shape thunder, Ruyi-shape cloud, thunder, cloud, double line triangle; Raise ridges on 2 pairs of flat handles.	42.6–43	26	麻江型 Majiang Type	
28	族鼓 0028 泉素铜鼓 ZG No.0028 Bronze Drum Quansu	广西民族博物馆 Anthropology Museum of Guangxi	1965 年出土于泉素大队水利工地 Unearthed at Quansu Team Irrigation Works Filed in 1965	鼓面：太阳纹（12 芒）、羽纹、栉纹、切线同心圆纹、复线交叉纹、变形羽人纹、变形翔鹭纹间定胜纹，鼓面边缘饰四只逆时针四足素面立体青蛙； 鼓身：羽纹、栉纹、切线同心圆纹、羽纹栉纹切线同心圆纹垂直纹带、圆心三角垂叶纹；扁耳两对饰辫纹 Drum face: patterns of sun(12rays), feather, comb line, tangent concentric circles, crossed double lines, transformed feathermen,transformed flying heron mixed Dingsheng, 4 frog statues of 4 feet and blank back anticlockwise stand on the edge of drum face; Drum body: patterns of feather, comb line, tangent concentric circles, vertical ribbon of feather, comb line and tangent concentric circles, leaf-shape triangle with concentric circles in the middle; Braids pattern on 2 pairs of flat handles.	62.8–64	37.8 （残） Incomplete	冷水冲型 Lengshui-chong Type	

序号 N0.	原编号及鼓名 Stock Number & Name	收藏单位 Museum	出土（征集） 时间、地点 Time & Spot for discovered or collected	主要装饰 Main Decorations	尺寸（厘米） Size(cm)		类型 Type	图片 Picture
					面径 Face Diameter	身高 Height		
29	族鼓 0029 寻旺铜鼓 ZG No.0029 Bronze Drum Xunwang	广西民族博 物馆 Anthropology Museum of Guangxi	1966 年出土于桂 平县（现桂平市） 寻旺公社 Unearthed at Xunwang Community, Guiping County in 1966	鼓面：太阳纹（12 芒）、栉纹、同心圆纹、复线交叉纹、变形羽人纹、变形翔鹭纹间定胜纹，鼓面边缘饰四只逆时针四足素面立体青蛙； 鼓身：栉纹、同心圆纹、素纹栉纹同心圆纹垂直纹带、圆心三角垂叶纹；扁耳两对饰辫纹 Drum face: patterns of sun(12rays), comb line, concentric circles, crossed double lines, transformed feathermen, transformed flying heron mixed Dingsheng;4 frog statues of 4 feet and blank back anticlockwise stand on the edge of drum face; Drum body: patterns of comb line, concentric circles, vertical ribbon of blank, straight line and concentric circles, leaf-shape triangle with concentric circles in the middle; Braids pattern on 2 pairs of flat handles.	58.5-58.5	39.5	冷水冲型 Lengshui-chong Type	
30	族鼓 0030 钱纹铜鼓 ZG No.0030 Bronze Drum with coin patterns	广西民族博 物馆 Anthropology Museum of Guangxi	1966 年出土于桂 平县（现桂平市） 寻旺公社 Unearthed at Xunwang Community, Guiping County in 1966	鼓面：太阳纹（12 芒）、蝉纹、四出钱纹、鸟纹、雷纹填线纹、连钱纹、席纹、四出钱纹、四瓣花填线纹、虫形纹、变形羽人纹，鼓面边缘饰六只逆时针三足螺旋纹立体青蛙； 鼓身：蝉纹、连钱纹、席纹、四出钱纹、鸟纹、雷纹填线纹、四瓣花填线纹、虫形纹、变形羽人纹；扁耳两对 Drum face: patterns of sun(12 rays), cicada, coin with quadrangle inside, bird, thunder filled with straight line, coins part of overlap, woven mat, coin with quadrangle inside, quatrefoil filled with straight line, insect, transformed feathermen;6 frogs with 3 feet and spiracle on their backs anticlockwise stand on the edge; Drum body: patterns of cicada, coins part of overlap, woven mat,coin with quadrangle inside, bird, thunder filled with straight line, quatrefoil filled with straight line, insect-shape motif, transformed feathermen; 2 pairs of flat handles.	120.5-122	64	灵山型 Lingshan Type	

序号 N0.	原编号及鼓名 Stock Number & Name	收藏单位 Museum	出土（征集）时间、地点 Time & Spot for discovered or collected	主要装饰 Main Decorations	尺寸（厘米）Size(cm)		类型 Type	图片 Picture
					面径 Face Diameter	身高 Height		
31	族鼓 0031 变形羽人纹鸟纹铜鼓 ZG No.0031 Bronze Drum with transformed feathermen and bird patterns	广西民族博物馆 Anthropology Museum of Guangxi	1971 年 2 月出土于崇左市龙州县响水公社龙江大队派良屯 Unearthed at Pailiang Tun, Xiangshui Community, Longzhou County, Chongzuo City in February, 1971	鼓面：太阳纹（7 芒）、栉纹、雷纹填线纹、同心圆纹、变形羽人纹、鸟纹、鸟纹间定胜纹雷纹，鼓面边缘饰四只逆时针四足素面立体青蛙；鼓身：栉纹、同心圆纹、圆心三角垂叶纹；扁耳两对饰羽纹 Drum face: patterns of sun(7rays), comb line, thunder filled with comb line, concentric circle, transformed feathermen, bird, bird mixed Dingsheng; 4 frog statues of 4 feet and blank back anticlockwise stand on the edge of drum face; Drum body: patterns of comb line, concentric circles, leaf-shape triangle with concentric circles in the middle; Feather pattern on 2 pairs of flat handles.	49.7–50	33.4	西盟型 Ximeng Type	
32	族鼓 0032 灯草塘铜鼓 ZG No.0032 Bronze Drum Dengcao Tang	广西民族博物馆 Anthropology Museum of Guangxi	1959 年出土于梧州市岑溪县樟木公社灯草塘 Unearthed at Dengcao Tang, Zhangmu Community, Cenxi County, Wuzhou City in 1959	鼓面：太阳纹（8 芒）、云纹、雷纹，鼓面边缘饰四只顺时针四足素面立体青蛙；鼓身：雷纹；环耳两对饰缠丝纹 Drum face: patterns of sun(8rays), cloud, thunder; 4 frog statues of 4 feet and blank back clockwise stand on the edge of drum face; Drum body: patterns of thunder; silk-like patterns on 2 pairs of ring handles.	90.2–91.7	52.8	北流型 Beiliu Type	
33	族鼓 0033 肖屋园铜鼓 ZG No.0033 Bronze Drum Xiaowuyuan	广西民族博物馆 Anthropology Museum of Guangxi	1971 年 9 月出土于北流县（现北流市）府城公社松花大队肖屋园 Unearthed at Xiaowuyuan, Songhua Team, Fucheng Community, Beiliu County in September, 1971	鼓面：太阳纹（8 芒）、云纹、席纹、雷纹填线纹、雷纹，鼓面边缘饰六只顺时针三足素面青蛙（一只已失）；鼓身：雷纹、小太阳纹、席纹、雷纹填线纹、连钱纹、半圆填线纹、花纹；扁耳两对 Drum face: patterns of sun(8 rays), cloud, woven mat, thunder filled with straight line, thunder; 6 frogs with 3 feet and blank back clockwise stand on the edge(one lost); Drum body: patterns of thunder, small sun, woven mat, thunder filled with straight line, coins part of overlap, semicircle filled with straight line, flower;2 pairs of flat handles.	65–66.2	38.5	灵山型 Lingshan Type	

序号 N0.	原编号及鼓名 Stock Number & Name	收藏单位 Museum	出土（征集）时间、地点 Time & Spot for discovered or collected	主要装饰 Main Decorations	尺寸（厘米）Size(cm)		类型 Type	图片 Picture
					面径 Face Diameter	身高 Height		
34	族鼓 0034 云雷纹铜鼓 ZG No.0034 Bronze Drum with cloud & thunder patterns	广西民族博物馆 Anthropology Museum of Guangxi	1972 年 3 月征购于北流县（现北流市）废品仓库 Collected at Beiliu County Waste Storage in March, 1972	鼓面：太阳纹（8 芒）、云纹、雷纹，鼓面边缘饰四只逆时针方向立体青蛙；鼓身：雷纹；环耳两对 Drum face: patterns of sun(8rays), cloud, thunder; 4 frog statues stand anticlockwise on the edge of drum face; Drum body: patterns of thunder; 2 pairs of ring handles.	74.3~74.5	43.5（残）Incomplete	北流型 Beiliu Type	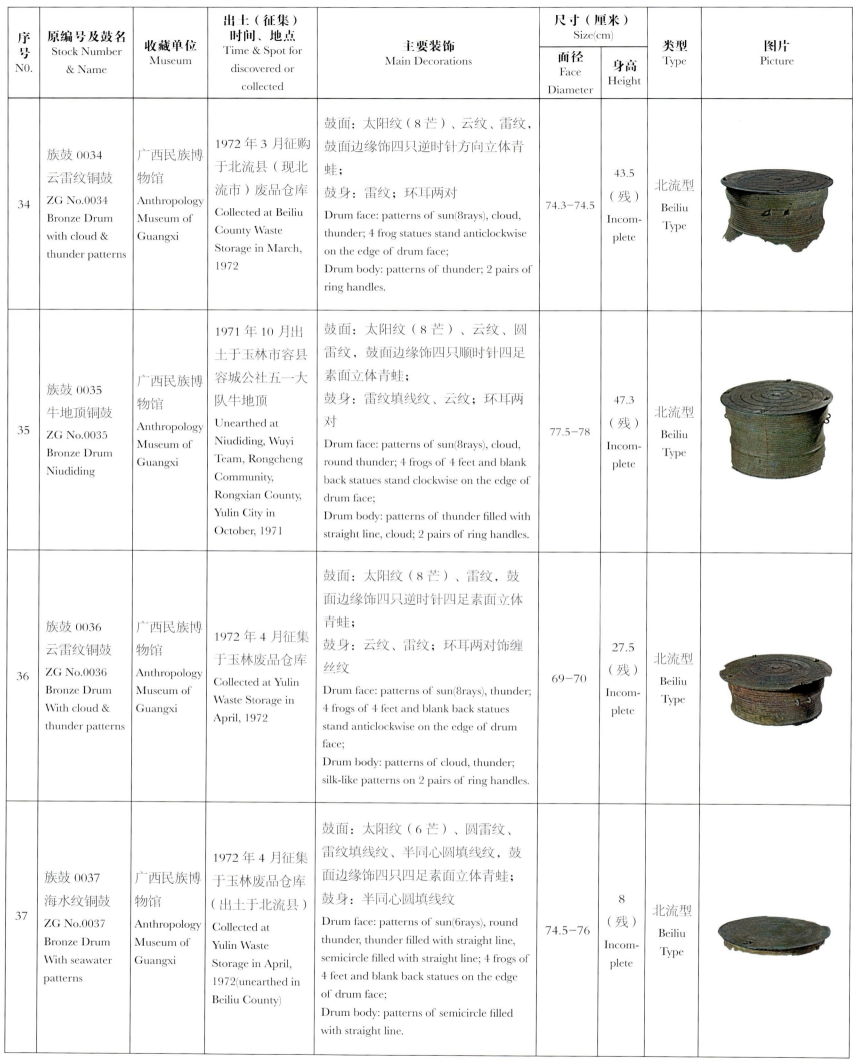
35	族鼓 0035 牛地顶铜鼓 ZG No.0035 Bronze Drum Niudiding	广西民族博物馆 Anthropology Museum of Guangxi	1971 年 10 月出土于玉林市容县容城公社五一大队牛地顶 Unearthed at Niudiding, Wuyi Team, Rongcheng Community, Rongxian County, Yulin City in October, 1971	鼓面：太阳纹（8 芒）、云纹、圆雷纹，鼓面边缘饰四只顺时针四足素面立体青蛙；鼓身：雷纹填线纹、云纹；环耳两对 Drum face: patterns of sun(8rays), cloud, round thunder; 4 frogs of 4 feet and blank back statues stand clockwise on the edge of drum face; Drum body: patterns of thunder filled with straight line, cloud; 2 pairs of ring handles.	77.5~78	47.3（残）Incomplete	北流型 Beiliu Type	
36	族鼓 0036 云雷纹铜鼓 ZG No.0036 Bronze Drum With cloud & thunder patterns	广西民族博物馆 Anthropology Museum of Guangxi	1972 年 4 月征集于玉林废品仓库 Collected at Yulin Waste Storage in April, 1972	鼓面：太阳纹（8 芒）、雷纹，鼓面边缘饰四只逆时针四足素面立体青蛙；鼓身：云纹、雷纹；环耳两对饰缠丝纹 Drum face: patterns of sun(8rays), thunder; 4 frogs of 4 feet and blank back statues stand anticlockwise on the edge of drum face; Drum body: patterns of cloud, thunder; silk-like patterns on 2 pairs of ring handles.	69~70	27.5（残）Incomplete	北流型 Beiliu Type	
37	族鼓 0037 海水纹铜鼓 ZG No.0037 Bronze Drum With seawater patterns	广西民族博物馆 Anthropology Museum of Guangxi	1972 年 4 月征集于玉林废品仓库（出土于北流县）Collected at Yulin Waste Storage in April, 1972(unearthed in Beiliu County)	鼓面：太阳纹（6 芒）、圆雷纹、雷纹填线纹、半同心圆填线纹，鼓面边缘饰四只四足素面立体青蛙；鼓身：半同心圆填线纹 Drum face: patterns of sun(6rays), round thunder, thunder filled with straight line, semicircle filled with straight line; 4 frogs of 4 feet and blank back statues on the edge of drum face; Drum body: patterns of semicircle filled with straight line.	74.5~76	8（残）Incomplete	北流型 Beiliu Type	

续表

序号 NO.	原编号及鼓名 Stock Number & Name	收藏单位 Museum	出土（征集）时间、地点 Time & Spot for discovered or collected	主要装饰 Main Decorations	尺寸（厘米） Size(cm)		类型 Type	图片 Picture
					面径 Face Diameter	身高 Height		
38	族鼓 0038 变形羽人纹铜鼓 ZG No.0038 Bronze Drum With transformed feathermen patterns	广西民族博物馆 Anthropology Museum of Guangxi	1972 年出土于宾阳县思陇公社六谷村 Unearthed at Liugu Village, Silong Community, Binyang County in 1972	鼓面：太阳纹（13 芒）、叶脉纹、栉纹、同心圆纹、复线交叉纹、变形羽人纹、变形翔鹭纹，鼓面边缘饰四只逆时针四足线条几何纹立体青蛙； 鼓身：叶脉纹、栉纹、同心圆纹、四角填花纹、变形羽人纹、圆心三角垂叶纹间四角填花纹；扁耳两对饰辫纹 Drum face: patterns of sun(13rays), leaf vein, comb line, concentric circles, crossed double lines, transformed feathermen, transformed flying heron;4 frog statues of 4 feet and geometry grains on back anticlockwise stand on the edge of drum face; Drum body: patterns of leaf vein, comb line, concentric circles, quadrangle filled with flowers, transformed feathermen, leaf-shape triangle with concentric circles in the middle mixed quadrangle filled with flowers inside; Braids pattern on 2 pairs of flat handles.	83.5−84	59	冷水冲型 Lengshui-chong Type	
39	族鼓 0039 十二牲畜纹铜鼓 ZG No.0039 Bronze Drum With 12-animal patterns	广西民族博物馆 Anthropology Museum of Guangxi	1972 年收购于南宁市废品仓库 Collected at Nanning Waste Storage in 1972	鼓面：太阳纹（12 芒）、同心圆纹、回形雷纹、乳钉纹、四鱼戏双珠纹间 S 云纹回形雷纹蒲叶纹、牛纹、狗纹、猪纹、兔纹、S 云纹； 鼓身：乳钉纹、可辨圆形纹、回形雷纹、蒲叶纹、S 云纹、复线三角纹；扁耳两对饰辫纹、回形雷纹 Drum face: patterns of sun(12rays), concentric circles, 回 -shape thunder,nipple protrusion, 4 fishes playing 2 pearls mixed S-shape cloud, 回 -shape thunder and cattail, pattern group of ox, dog, pig and rabbit, S-shape cloud; Drum body: patterns of nipple protrusion, only circle, 回 -shape thunder, cattail, S-shape cloud, and double line triangle are recognized; Braid and 回 -shape thunder on 2 pairs of flat handles.	44−46	27.5	麻江型 Majiang Type	

续表

序号 N0.	原编号及鼓名 Stock Number & Name	收藏单位 Museum	出土（征集）时间、地点 Time & Spot for discovered or collected	主要装饰 Main Decorations	尺寸（厘米）Size(cm)		类型 Type	图片 Picture
					面径 Face Diameter	身高 Height		
40	族鼓 0040 符箓纹铜鼓 ZG No.0040 Bronze Drum With Ofuda patterns	广西民族博物馆 Anthropology Museum of Guangxi	1972 年收购于南宁市废品仓库 Collected at Nanning Waste Storage in 1972	鼓面：太阳纹（12 芒）、同心圆纹、回形雷纹、乳钉纹、符箓纹、云纹；鼓身：乳钉纹、云纹、如意云纹、回形雷纹、同心圆纹、复线三角纹；扁耳两对饰凸棱纹 Drum face: patterns of sun(12rays), concentric circle, 回 -shape thunder, nipple protrusion, Ofuda, cloud; Drum body: patterns of nipple protrusion, cloud, Ruyi-shape cloud, 回 -shape thunder, concentric circle, double line triangle;Raise ridges on 2 pairs of flat handles.	42.8	26	麻江型 Majiang Type	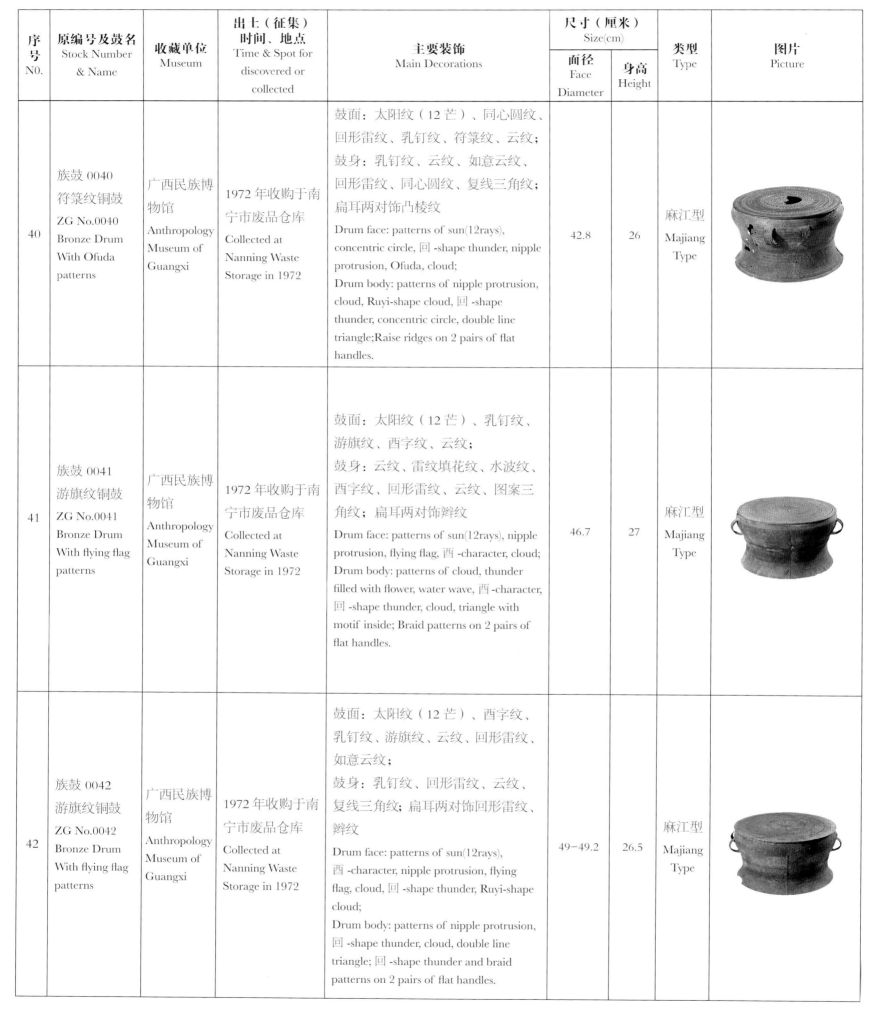
41	族鼓 0041 游旗纹铜鼓 ZG No.0041 Bronze Drum With flying flag patterns	广西民族博物馆 Anthropology Museum of Guangxi	1972 年收购于南宁市废品仓库 Collected at Nanning Waste Storage in 1972	鼓面：太阳纹（12 芒）、乳钉纹、游旗纹、西字纹、云纹；鼓身：云纹、雷纹填花纹、水波纹、西字纹、回形雷纹、云纹、图案三角纹；扁耳两对饰辫纹 Drum face: patterns of sun(12rays), nipple protrusion, flying flag, 西 -character, cloud; Drum body: patterns of cloud, thunder filled with flower, water wave, 西 -character, 回 -shape thunder, cloud, triangle with motif inside; Braid patterns on 2 pairs of flat handles.	46.7	27	麻江型 Majiang Type	
42	族鼓 0042 游旗纹铜鼓 ZG No.0042 Bronze Drum With flying flag patterns	广西民族博物馆 Anthropology Museum of Guangxi	1972 年收购于南宁市废品仓库 Collected at Nanning Waste Storage in 1972	鼓面：太阳纹（12 芒）、西字纹、乳钉纹、游旗纹、云纹、回形雷纹、如意云纹；鼓身：乳钉纹、回形雷纹、云纹、复线三角纹；扁耳两对饰回形雷纹、辫纹 Drum face: patterns of sun(12rays), 西 -character, nipple protrusion, flying flag, cloud, 回 -shape thunder, Ruyi-shape cloud; Drum body: patterns of nipple protrusion, 回 -shape thunder, cloud, double line triangle; 回 -shape thunder and braid patterns on 2 pairs of flat handles.	49—49.2	26.5	麻江型 Majiang Type	

续表

序号 NO.	原编号及鼓名 Stock Number & Name	收藏单位 Museum	出土（征集） 时间、地点 Time & Spot for discovered or collected	主要装饰 Main Decorations	尺寸（厘米） Size(cm)		类型 Type	图片 Picture
					面径 Face Diameter	身高 Height		
43	族鼓 0043 游旗纹铜鼓 ZG No.0043 Bronze Drum With flying flag patterns	广西民族博物馆 Anthropology Museum of Guangxi	1972 年收购于南宁市废品仓库 Collected at Nanning Waste Storage in 1972	鼓面：太阳纹（12 芒）、酉字纹、云纹、乳钉纹、游旗纹、栉纹、兽形云纹； 鼓身：乳钉纹、云纹、回形雷纹、栉纹、复线三角纹；扁耳两对饰辫纹 Drum face: patterns of sun(12rays), 酉-character, cloud, nipple protrusion, flying flag, comb line, beast-shape cloud; Drum body: patterns of nipple protrusion, cloud, 回-shape thunder, comb line, double line triangle; Braid patterns on 2 pairs of flat handles.	46.5	26.5	麻江型 Majiang Type	
44	族鼓 0044 游旗纹铜鼓 ZG No.0044 Bronze Drum With flying flag patterns	广西民族博物馆 Anthropology Museum of Guangxi	1972 年收购于南宁市废品仓库 Collected at Nanning Waste Storage in 1972	鼓面：太阳纹（12 芒）、乳钉纹、游旗纹、缠枝纹； 鼓身：素面；扁耳两对饰凸棱纹 Drum face: patterns of sun(12rays), nipple protrusion, flying flag, twisted branches Drum body: all blank; Raise ridges on 2 pairs of flat handles.	47−47.8	27.5	麻江型 Majiang Type	
45	族鼓 0045 游旗纹铜鼓 ZG No.0045 Bronze Drum With flying flag patterns	广西民族博物馆 Anthropology Museum of Guangxi	1972 年收购于南宁市废品仓库 Collected at Nanning Waste Storage in 1972	鼓面：太阳纹（12 芒）、乳钉纹、栉纹、异形游旗纹、羽纹； 鼓身：素面；扁耳两对饰凸棱纹 Drum face: patterns of sun(12rays), nipple protrusion, comb line, transformed flying flag, feather; Drum body: all blank; Raise ridges on 2 pairs of flat handles.	47−47.5	27.5	麻江型 Majiang Type	
46	族鼓 0046 乳钉纹铜鼓 ZG No.0046 Bronze Drum With nipple protrusion patterns	广西民族博物馆 Anthropology Museum of Guangxi	1972 年收购于南宁市废品仓库 Collected at Nanning Waste Storage in 1972	鼓面：太阳纹（12 芒）、乳钉纹（其余磨蚀）； 鼓身：纹饰磨蚀；扁耳两对饰凸棱纹 Drum face: patterns of sun(12rays), nipple protrusion(the other patterns are obscure); Drum body: all are obscure; Raise ridges on 2 pairs of flat handles.	50.3−50.5	27	麻江型 Majiang Type	

序号 N0.	原编号及鼓名 Stock Number & Name	收藏单位 Museum	出土（征集）时间、地点 Time & Spot for discovered or collected	主要装饰 Main Decorations	尺寸（厘米） Size(cm)		类型 Type	图片 Picture
					面径 Face Diameter	身高 Height		
47	族鼓 0047 游旗纹铜鼓 ZG No.0047 Bronze Drum With flying flag patterns	广西民族博物馆 Anthropology Museum of Guangxi	1972 年收购于南宁市废品仓库 Collected at Nanning Waste Storage in 1972	鼓面：太阳纹（12 芒）、乳钉纹、栉纹、云纹（其余磨蚀）；鼓身：乳钉纹、同心圆纹、动物纹、缠枝纹、栉纹、回形雷纹、云纹、钱纹、圆心三角垂叶纹；扁耳两对饰辫纹 Drum face: patterns of sun(12rays), nipple protrusion, comb line, cloud (the other patterns are obscure); Drum body: patterns of nipple protrusion, concentric circle, animal, twisted branches, comb line, 回 -shape thunder, cloud, coin, leaf-shape triangle with concentric circles in the middle; Braid patterns on 2 pairs of flat handles.	46.3−46.8	27.7	麻江型 Majiang Type	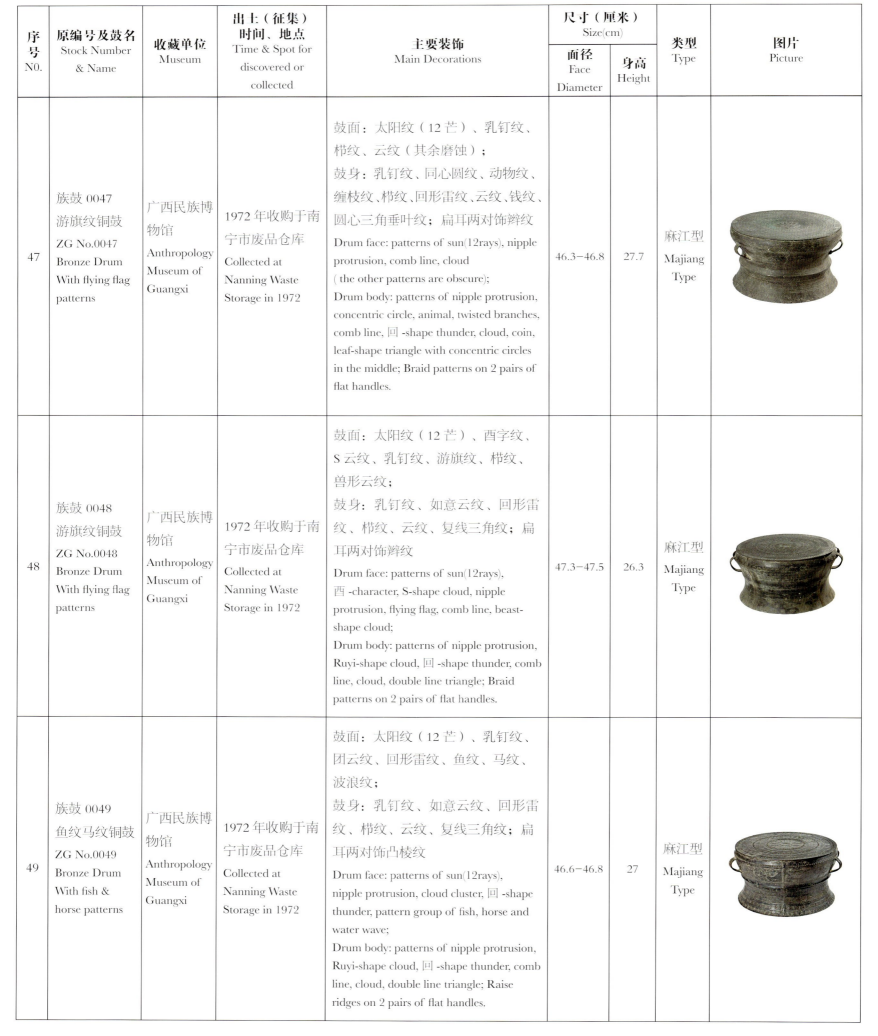
48	族鼓 0048 游旗纹铜鼓 ZG No.0048 Bronze Drum With flying flag patterns	广西民族博物馆 Anthropology Museum of Guangxi	1972 年收购于南宁市废品仓库 Collected at Nanning Waste Storage in 1972	鼓面：太阳纹（12 芒）、酉字纹、S 云纹、乳钉纹、游旗纹、栉纹、兽形云纹；鼓身：乳钉纹、如意云纹、回形雷纹、栉纹、云纹、复线三角纹；扁耳两对饰辫纹 Drum face: patterns of sun(12rays), 酉 -character, S-shape cloud, nipple protrusion, flying flag, comb line, beast-shape cloud; Drum body: patterns of nipple protrusion, Ruyi-shape cloud, 回 -shape thunder, comb line, cloud, double line triangle; Braid patterns on 2 pairs of flat handles.	47.3−47.5	26.3	麻江型 Majiang Type	
49	族鼓 0049 鱼纹马纹铜鼓 ZG No.0049 Bronze Drum With fish & horse patterns	广西民族博物馆 Anthropology Museum of Guangxi	1972 年收购于南宁市废品仓库 Collected at Nanning Waste Storage in 1972	鼓面：太阳纹（12 芒）、乳钉纹、团云纹、回形雷纹、鱼纹、马纹、波浪纹；鼓身：乳钉纹、如意云纹、回形雷纹、栉纹、云纹、复线三角纹；扁耳两对饰凸棱纹 Drum face: patterns of sun(12rays), nipple protrusion, cloud cluster, 回 -shape thunder, pattern group of fish, horse and water wave; Drum body: patterns of nipple protrusion, Ruyi-shape cloud, 回 -shape thunder, comb line, cloud, double line triangle; Raise ridges on 2 pairs of flat handles.	46.6−46.8	27	麻江型 Majiang Type	

续表

序号 NO.	原编号及鼓名 Stock Number & Name	收藏单位 Museum	出土（征集） 时间、地点 Time & Spot for discovered or collected	主要装饰 Main Decorations	尺寸（厘米） Size(cm)		类型 Type	图片 Picture
					面径 Face Diameter	身高 Height		
50	族鼓 0050 游旗纹铜鼓 ZG No.0050 Bronze Drum With flying flag patterns	广西民族博物馆 Anthropology Museum of Guangxi	1972 年收购于南宁市废品仓库 Collected at Nanning Waste Storage in 1972	鼓面：太阳纹（12 芒）、乳钉纹、S 云纹、羽纹、栉纹、游旗纹、绚纹； 鼓身：乳钉纹、回形雷纹、羽纹、云纹、酉字纹、同心圆纹、雷纹、S 云纹、复线三角纹；扁耳两对饰凸棱纹 Drum face: patterns of sun(12rays), nipple protrusion, S-shape cloud, feather, twisted rope; Drum body: patterns of nipple protrusion, 回 -shape thunder, feather, cloud, 酉 -character, concentric circle, thunder, S-shape cloud, double line triangle; Raise ridges on 2 pairs of flat handles.	47.3	26.5	麻江型 Majiang Type	
51	族鼓 0051 缠枝纹铜鼓 ZG No.0051 Bronze Drum With twisted branches pattern	广西民族博物馆 Anthropology Museum of Guangxi	1972 年收购于南宁市废品仓库 Collected at Nanning Waste Storage in 1972	鼓面：太阳纹（残）、乳钉纹、（其余磨蚀）； 鼓身：素面；扁耳两对饰凸棱纹 Drum face: patterns of sun(incomplete), nipple protrusion(the other patterns are obscure); Drum body: all are blank; Raise ridges on 2 pairs of flat handles.	47.5	27.5	麻江型 Majiang Type	
52	族鼓 0052 四龙双印铜鼓 ZG No.0052 Bronze Drum With 4-dragons and 2-stamps patterns	广西民族博物馆 Anthropology Museum of Guangxi	1972 年收购于南宁市废品仓库 Collected at Nanning Waste Storage in 1972	鼓面：太阳纹（12 芒）、酉字纹、S 云纹、乳钉纹、双龙间文字印章、云纹、回形雷纹、羊纹； 鼓身：乳钉纹、回形雷纹、云纹、复线三角纹；扁耳两对饰辫纹、回形雷纹 Drum face: patterns of sun(12rays), 酉 -character, S-shape cloud, nipple protrusion, 2 dragons with a character stamp, cloud, 回 -shape thunder, goat; Drum body: patterns of nipple protrusion, 回 -shape thunder, cloud, double line triangle; Braid and 回 -shape thunder on 2 pairs of flat handles.	49~49.5	26	麻江型 Majiang Type	

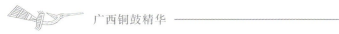

序号 N0.	原编号及鼓名 Stock Number & Name	收藏单位 Museum	出土（征集）时间、地点 Time & Spot for discovered or collected	主要装饰 Main Decorations	尺寸（厘米）Size(cm)		类型 Type	图片 Picture
					面径 Face Diameter	身高 Height		
53	族鼓 0053 变形羽人纹铜鼓 ZG No.0053 Bronze Drum With transformed feathermen patterns	广西民族博物馆 Anthropology Museum of Guangxi	1972 年收购于南宁市废品仓库 Collected at Nanning Waste Storage in 1972	鼓面：太阳纹（12 芒）、栉纹、同心圆纹、复线交叉纹、变形翔鹭间定胜纹、变形羽人纹，鼓面边缘饰四只四足立体青蛙（已失）；鼓身：栉纹、同心圆纹、素纹栉纹同心圆纹垂直纹带；扁耳两对饰辫纹 Drum face: patterns of sun(12rays), comb line, concentric circles, crossed double lines, transformed flying heron mixed Dingsheng; transformed feathermen, 4 frog statues of 4 feet stand on the edge of drum face(lost); Drum body: patterns of comb line, concentric circles, vertical ribbon of straight line, blank and concentric circles; Braids pattern on 2 pairs of flat handles.	68.9－69.5	36 （残）Incomplete	冷水冲型 Lengshuichong Type	
54	族鼓 0054 变形羽人纹铜鼓 ZG No.0054 Bronze Drum With transform feathermen patterns	广西民族博物馆 Anthropology Museum of Guangxi	1972 年收购于南宁市废品仓库 Collected at Nanning Waste Storage in 1972	鼓面：太阳纹（10 芒）、水波纹、栉纹、同心圆纹、眼纹、变形羽人纹、变形翔鹭纹，鼓面边缘饰四只逆时针四足素面立体青蛙；鼓身：栉纹、同心圆纹 Drum face: patterns of sun(10rays), water wave, comb line, concentric circles, diamond-shape eye, transformed feathermen, transformed flying heron; 4 frog statues of 4 feet and blank back stand anticlockwise on the edge of drum face; Drum body: patterns of comb line, concentric circles.	74－76	10.8 （残）Incomplete	冷水冲型 Lengshuichong Type	
55	族鼓 0055 万丈越种塘铜鼓 ZG No.0055 Bronze Drum Wanzhangyue Zhongtang	广西民族博物馆 Anthropology Museum of Guangxi	1970 年 11 月出土于玉林市陆川县城厢公社万丈越种塘社 Unearthed at zhongtang, Wanzhangyue, Chengxiang Community, Luchuan County, Yulin City in November, 1970	鼓面：太阳纹（8 芒）、圆雷纹，鼓面边缘饰四只逆时针四足素面立体青蛙；鼓身：雷纹填线纹；环耳两对饰缠丝纹 Drum face: patterns of sun(8rays), all are round thunders; 4 frog statues of 4 feet and blank back anticlockwise stand on the edge of drum face; Drum body: all are thunder filled with straight line; Silk-like patterns on 2 pairs of flat handles.	70.2－70.8	35 （残）Incomplete	北流型 Beiliu Type	

序号 NO.	原编号及鼓名 Stock Number & Name	收藏单位 Museum	出土（征集） 时间、地点 Time & Spot for discovered or collected	主要装饰 Main Decorations	尺寸（厘米） Size(cm)		类型 Type	图片 Picture
					面径 Face Diameter	身高 Height		
56	族鼓 0056 云雷纹水波纹铜鼓 ZG No.0056 Bronze Drum with cloud & thunder, water wave patterns	广西民族博物馆 Anthropology Museum of Guangxi	1972 年出土于玉林市陆川县良田西十村 Unearthed at Xishi Village, Liangtian, Luchuan County, Yulin City in 1972	鼓面：太阳纹（8 芒）、雷纹、水波纹、鼓面边缘饰四只两两相对四足素面立体青蛙； 鼓身：半同心圆纹、雷纹、云纹、水波纹、四瓣花纹、半同心圆填线纹、四出钱纹；环耳两对饰缠丝纹 Drum face: patterns of sun(8rays), thunder, water wave; 4 frog statues of 4 feet and blank back stand on the edge of drum face, face to each other in pairs; Drum body: patterns of semi-concentric circle, thunder, cloud, water wave, quatrefoil, semi-concentric circle filled with straight line, coin with quadrangle inside; Silk-like patterns on 2 pairs of blank flat handles.	102.5–103.6	60	北流型 Beiliu Type	
57	族鼓 0058 龟饰变形羽人纹铜鼓 ZG No.0058 Bronze Drum with transformed feathermen patterns& tortoise statue	广西民族博物馆 Anthropology Museum of Guangxi	1972 年 12 月贵港市平南县大新公社供销社出土 Unearthed at Daxin Community Supply & Marketing Cooperative, Pingnan County, Guigang City in December, 1972	鼓面：太阳纹（14 芒）、水波纹、栉纹、同心圆纹、复线交叉纹、羽纹、变形羽人纹、变形翔鹭纹、眼纹、鼓面边缘饰四只逆时针四足谷穗纹立体青蛙，蛙背各负一龟，蛙间饰龟，龟背饰网格纹； 鼓身：水波纹、同心圆纹、船纹、变形羽人纹、羽纹、网纹、栉纹、圆心三角垂叶纹、眼纹；扁耳两对饰辫纹 Drum face: patterns of sun(14rays), water wave, comb line, concentric circles, crossed double lines, feather, transformed feathermen, transformed flying heron, diamond-shape eye; 4 frog statues of 4 feet and rice ears on back anticlockwise stand on the edge of drum face, all of them carrying a tortoise; a tortoise statue with grids pattern on back between the frogs; Drum body: patterns of water wave, concentric circles, boat, transformed feathermen, feather, net, comb line, leaf-shape triangle with circle in the middle, diamond-shape eye; braid patterns on 2 pairs of flat handles.	76–77	55	冷水冲型 Lengshui-chong Type	

序号 N0.	原编号及鼓名 Stock Number & Name	收藏单位 Museum	出土（征集） 时间、地点 Time & Spot for discovered or collected	主要装饰 Main Decorations	尺寸（厘米） Size(cm)		类型 Type	图片 Picture
					面径 Face Diameter	身高 Height		
58	族鼓 0059 翔鹭纹铜鼓 ZG No.0059 Bronze Drum with flying heron patterns	广西民族博物馆 Anthropology Museum of Guangxi	1972 年收购于贵港市平南县丹竹公社供销社 Collected at Danzhu Community Supply & Marketing Cooperative, Pingnan County, Guigang City in 1972	鼓面：太阳纹（12 芒）、水波纹、同心圆纹、复线交叉纹、变形羽人、变形翔鹭纹、眼纹，鼓面边缘饰四只逆时针四足谷穗纹立体青蛙、蛙间饰乘骑、马立饰； 鼓身：水波纹、栉纹、同心圆纹、羽纹、船纹、变形羽人纹、网纹；扁耳两对饰辫纹 Drum face: patterns of sun(12rays), water wave, concentric circles, crossed double lines, transformed feathermen, transformed flying heron, diamond-shape eye; 4 frog statues of 4 feet and rice ears on back anticlockwise stand on the edge of drum face; a horse-rider and a horse statues between the frogs; Drum body: patterns of water wave, comb line, concentric circles, feather, boat, transformed feathermen, net; Braid patterns on 2 pairs of flat handles.	87.8—88.5	45.8 （残） Incomplete	冷水冲型 Lengshui-chong Type	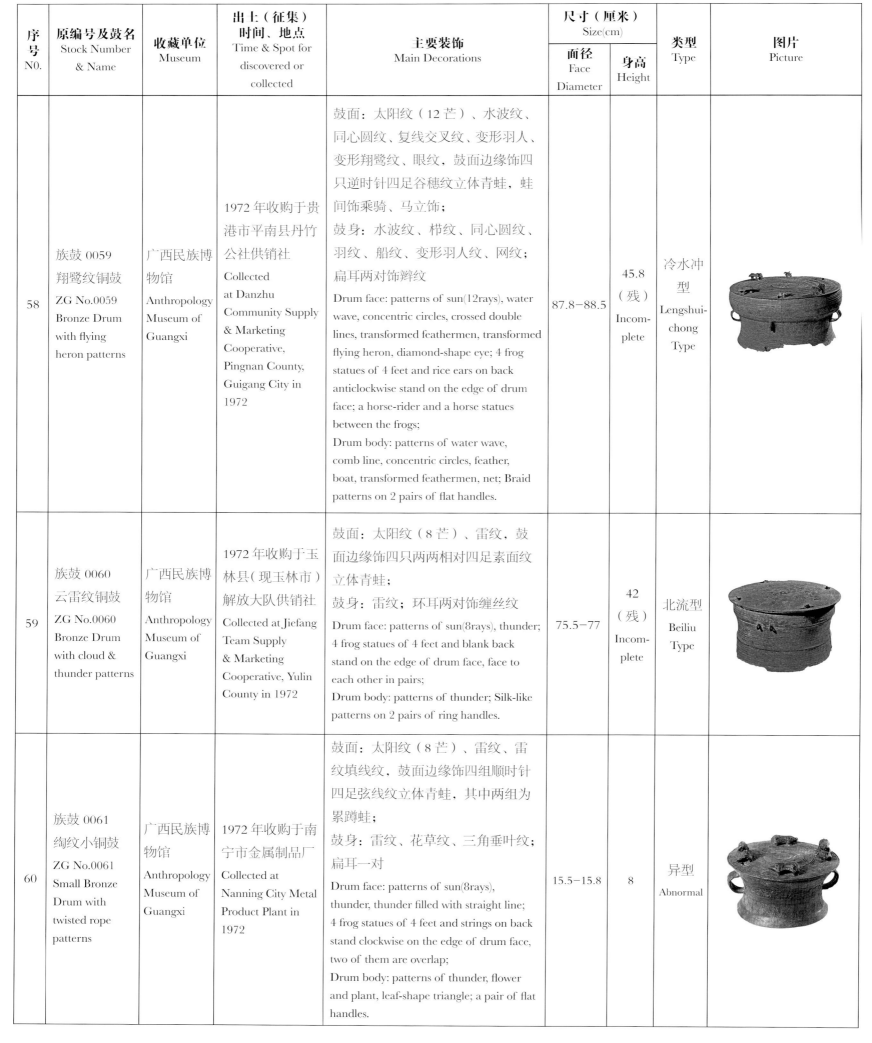
59	族鼓 0060 云雷纹铜鼓 ZG No.0060 Bronze Drum with cloud & thunder patterns	广西民族博物馆 Anthropology Museum of Guangxi	1972 年收购于玉林县（现玉林市）解放大队供销社 Collected at Jiefang Team Supply & Marketing Cooperative, Yulin County in 1972	鼓面：太阳纹（8 芒）、雷纹，鼓面边缘饰四只两两相对四足素面纹立体青蛙； 鼓身：雷纹；环耳两对饰缠丝纹 Drum face: patterns of sun(8rays), thunder; 4 frog statues of 4 feet and blank back stand on the edge of drum face, face to each other in pairs; Drum body: patterns of thunder; Silk-like patterns on 2 pairs of ring handles.	75.5—77	42 （残） Incomplete	北流型 Beiliu Type	
60	族鼓 0061 绹纹小铜鼓 ZG No.0061 Small Bronze Drum with twisted rope patterns	广西民族博物馆 Anthropology Museum of Guangxi	1972 年收购于南宁市金属制品厂 Collected at Nanning City Metal Product Plant in 1972	鼓面：太阳纹（8 芒）、雷纹、雷纹填线纹，鼓面边缘饰四组顺时针四足弦线纹立体青蛙，其中两组为累蹲蛙； 鼓身：雷纹、花草纹、三角垂叶纹；扁耳一对 Drum face: patterns of sun(8rays), thunder, thunder filled with straight line; 4 frog statues of 4 feet and strings on back stand clockwise on the edge of drum face, two of them are overlap; Drum body: patterns of thunder, flower and plant, leaf-shape triangle; a pair of flat handles.	15.5—15.8	8	异型 Abnormal	

续表

序号 NO.	原编号及鼓名 Stock Number & Name	收藏单位 Museum	出土（征集） 时间、地点 Time & Spot for discovered or collected	主要装饰 Main Decorations	尺寸（厘米） Size(cm)		类型 Type	图片 Picture
					面径 Face Diameter	身高 Height		
61	族鼓 0062 钱纹铜鼓 ZG No.0062 Bronze Drum with coin patterns	广西民族博物馆 Anthropology Museum of Guangxi	1973 年 3 月南宁市刑警大队拨交 Transferred by Nanning City Criminal Police Team in March, 1973	鼓面：太阳纹（10 芒）、兽面纹、虫形纹、鸟纹、四出钱纹、连钱纹、变形羽人纹、蝴蝶纹、蝉纹，鼓面边缘饰六组逆时针三足螺旋纹立体青蛙组，其中三组为累蹲蛙； 鼓身：蝉纹、连钱纹、鸟纹、四出钱纹、虫形纹、兽面纹、蝴蝶纹； Drum face: patterns of sun(10 rays), beast face, insect, bird, coin with quadrangle inside, coins part of overlap, transformed feathermen, butterfly, cicada; 6 frogs with 3 feet and spiracle on their backs stand anticlockwise on the edge, three of them are overlap; Drum body: patterns of cicada, coins part of overlap, bird, coin with quadrangle inside, insect-shape motif, beast face, butterfly.	72−72.4	17.5（残） Incomplete	灵山型 Lingshan Type	
62	族鼓 0063 "道光八年"铭双龙闹寿纹铜鼓 ZG No.0063 Bronze Drum with "道光八年"–character, 2 dragons and round 寿 –character	广西民族博物馆 Anthropology Museum of Guangxi	收购于河池地区（现河池市） Collected in Hechi area	鼓面：太阳纹（12 芒）、西字纹、乳钉纹、双龙闹寿纹、窗花纹、"道光八年建立，永世家财，万代进宝"铭文、云纹、双龙闹寿纹、如意纹； 鼓身：乳钉纹、回形雷纹、云纹、复线三角纹；扁耳两对饰辫纹 Drum face: patterns of sun(12 rays), 西 -character, nipple protrusion, pattern group of 2 dragons mixed round 寿 -character, window lattices, "道光八年建立，永世家财，万代进宝"-character, cloud & 2 dragons mixed round 寿 -character, Ruyi-shape cloud; Drum body: patterns of nipple protrusion & 回 -shape thunder, cloud, double line triangle; Braid and strings on 2 pairs of flat handles.	46.9−47.4	26.5	麻江型 Majiang Type	

续表

序号 N0.	原编号及鼓名 Stock Number & Name	收藏单位 Museum	出土（征集）时间、地点 Time & Spot for discovered or collected	主要装饰 Main Decorations	尺寸（厘米）Size(cm)		类型 Type	图片 Picture
					面径 Face Diameter	身高 Height		
63	族鼓 0064 ZG No.0064 双龙团寿纹铜鼓 Bronze Drum with 2 dragons& round "寿" −character	广西民族博物馆 Anthropology Museum of Guangxi	1973 年征集于河池地区废品公司 Collected at Hechi Waste Recycle Company in 1973	鼓面：太阳纹（12 芒）、酉字纹、乳钉纹、双龙团寿纹间铭文"福如东海""寿比南山""道光 年建立"、云纹；鼓身：乳钉纹、云纹、回纹、复线三角纹、扁耳两对饰辫纹 Drum face: patterns of sun(12rays), 酉 -character, nipple protrusion, pattern group of 2 dragons mixed round 寿 -character, " 福如东海 "" 寿比南山 "" 道光 年建立 "-character, cloud; Drum body: patterns of nipple protrusion, cloud, 回 -shape thunder, double line triangle; Braid and strings on 2 pairs of flat handles.	46.8	26.5	麻江型 Majiang Type	
64	族鼓 0065 天元孔明铭坎卦铜鼓 ZG No.0065 Bronze Drum with "天元孔明" −character	广西民族博物馆 Anthropology Museum of Guangxi	1973 年收购于河池废品公司 Collected at Hechi Waste Recycle Company in 1973	鼓面：太阳纹（14 芒）、酉字纹、桃符纹、乳钉纹、"天元孔明、寿福进宝"铭文、同心圆纹、乳钉纹、羽纹、卦纹；鼓身：梅花状乳钉纹、羽纹间花瓣纹、桃符纹、复线三角纹；扁耳两对饰辫纹 Drum face: patterns of sun(14rays), 酉 -character, Ofuda, nipple protrusion, " 天元孔明、寿福进宝 "-character, concentric circle & nipple protrusion, feather, divinatory symbol; Drum body: patterns of nipple protrusion in plum-blossom shape, feather mixed flower petals, Ofuda, double line triangle; Braid and strings on 2 pairs of flat handles.	47.5−48.2	27.8	麻江型 Majiang Type	
65	族鼓 0066 双龙团寿纹铜鼓 ZG No.0066 Bronze Drum with 2 dragons& round "寿" −character	广西民族博物馆 Anthropology Museum of Guangxi	1973 年河池征集 Collected in Hechi area in 1973	鼓面：太阳纹（12 芒）、酉字纹、素纹、乳钉纹、双龙团寿纹间"永世家财、万代进宝铭文"、云纹、回形纹；鼓身：梅花状乳钉纹、回形雷纹、云纹、复线三角纹；扁耳两对饰辫纹 Drum face: patterns of sun(12rays), 酉 -character, blank, nipple protrusion, 2 dragons& round " 寿 "-character, " 永世家财、万代进宝 "-character, cloud, 回 -character; Drum body: patterns of nipple protrusion in plum-blossom shape, 回 -shape thunder, cloud, double line triangle; Braid and strings on 2 pairs of flat handles.	46.8− 47	26.7	麻江型 Majiang Type	

序号 N0.	原编号及鼓名 Stock Number & Name	收藏单位 Museum	出土（征集） 时间、地点 Time & Spot for discovered or collected	主要装饰 Main Decorations	尺寸（厘米） Size(cm)		类型 Type	图片 Picture
					面径 Face Diameter	身高 Height		
66	族鼓 0067 云雷纹铜鼓 ZG No.0067 Bronze Drum with cloud& thunder patterns	广西民族博物馆 Anthropology Museum of Guangxi	1973 年收购于河池废品公司 Collected at Hechi Waste Recycle Company in 1973	鼓面：太阳纹（12 芒）、S 云纹、西字纹、乳钉纹、云纹； 鼓身：乳钉纹、回形雷纹、云纹、复线三角纹；扁耳两对饰辫纹、回形雷纹 Drum face: patterns of sun(12rays), S-shape cloud, 西-character, nipple protrusion, cloud; Drum body: patterns of nipple protrusion, 回-shape thunder, cloud, double line triangle; Braid and 回-shape thunder on 2 pairs of flat handles.	48	27	麻江型 Majiang Type	
67	族鼓 0068 人物走兽纹铜鼓 ZG No.0068 Bronze Drum with man and beast patterns	广西民族博物馆 Anthropology Museum of Guangxi	1973 年收购于河池废品公司 Collected at Hechi Waste Recycle Company in 1973	鼓面：太阳纹（12 芒）、酉字纹、回形雷纹、乳钉纹、人物动物纹（人、双龙戏珠、牛、猪、狗、鹿、鹤）、花卉纹； 鼓身：梅花状乳钉纹、回形雷纹、云纹、酉字纹、复线三角纹；扁耳两对饰辫纹 Drum face: patterns of sun(12rays), 西-character, 回-shape thunder, nipple protrusion, men and animals(including men, 2 dragons play with a pearl, cattle, pig, dog, deer, crane), flower; Drum body: patterns of nipple protrusion in plum blossom shape, 回-shape thunder, cloud, 西-character, double line triangle; Braids on 2 pairs of flat handles.	44.5	25	麻江型 Majiang Type	
68	族鼓 0069 游旗纹铜鼓 ZG No.0069 Bronze Drum with flying flag patterns	广西民族博物馆 Anthropology Museum of Guangxi	1973 年收购于河池废品公司 Collected at Hechi Waste Recycle Company in 1973	鼓面：太阳纹（12 芒）、酉字纹、S 云纹、乳钉纹、游旗纹、栉纹、云纹； 鼓身：乳钉纹、如意云纹、回形雷纹、云纹、栉纹、复线三角纹；扁耳两对饰辫纹 Drum face: patterns of sun(12rays), 西-character, S-shape cloud, nipple protrusion, flying flag, comb line, cloud; Drum body: patterns of nipple protrusion, Ruyi-shape cloud, 回-shape thunder, cloud, comb line, double line triangle; Braid and strings on 2 pairs of flat handles.	47.4	26	麻江型 Majiang Type	

序号 N0.	原编号及鼓名 Stock Number & Name	收藏单位 Museum	出土（征集） 时间、地点 Time & Spot for discovered or collected	主要装饰 Main Decorations	尺寸（厘米） Size(cm)		类型 Type	图片 Picture
					面径 Face Diameter	身高 Height		
69	族鼓 0070 符箓纹铜鼓 ZG No.0070 Bronze Drum with Ofuda patterns	广西民族博物馆 Anthropology Museum of Guangxi	1973 年收购于河池废品公司 Collected at Hechi Waste Recycle Company in 1973	鼓面：太阳纹（12 芒）、水滴纹、云纹、乳钉纹、符箓纹、回形雷纹； 鼓身：乳钉纹、云纹、半同心圆纹、图案三角纹；扁耳两对饰辫纹 Drum face: patterns of sun(12rays), water drop, cloud, nipple protrusion, Ofuda, 回 -shape thunder; Drum body: patterns of nipple protrusion, cloud, semi-concentric circle, double line triangle with motif inside; Braid on 2 pairs of flat handles.	45.2–45.7	26.5	麻江型 Majiang Type	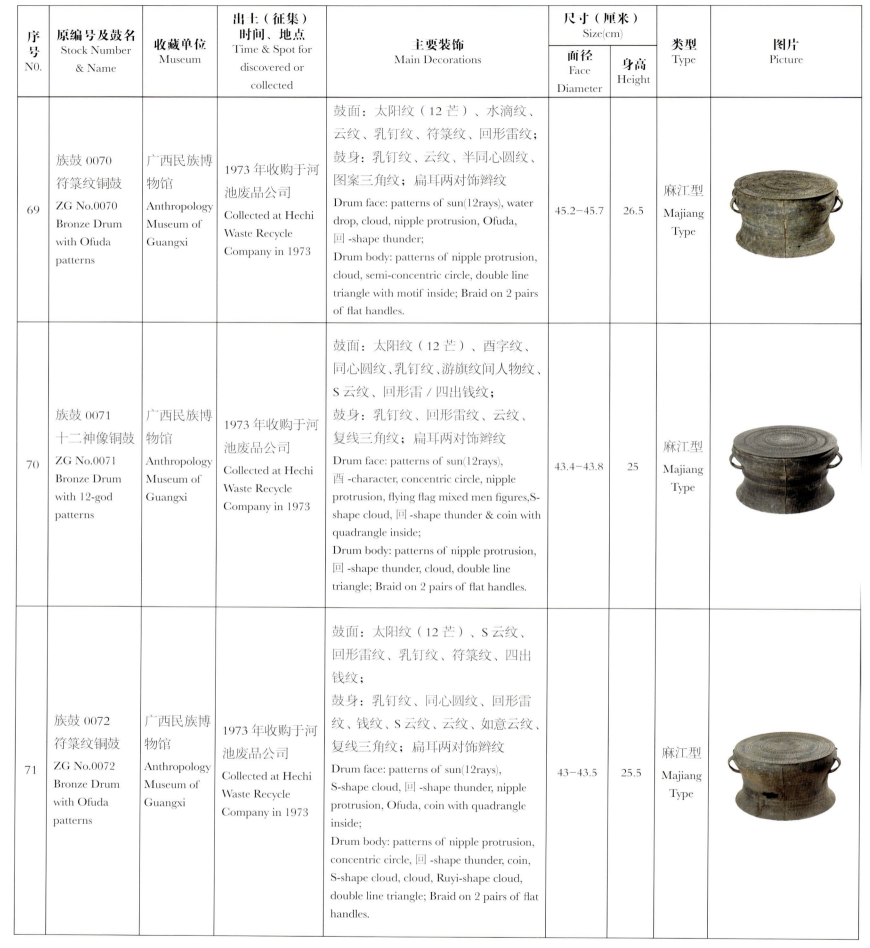
70	族鼓 0071 十二.神像铜鼓 ZG No.0071 Bronze Drum with 12-god patterns	广西民族博物馆 Anthropology Museum of Guangxi	1973 年收购于河池废品公司 Collected at Hechi Waste Recycle Company in 1973	鼓面：太阳纹（12 芒）、酉字纹、同心圆纹、乳钉纹、游旗纹间人物纹、S 云纹、回形雷 / 四出钱纹； 鼓身：乳钉纹、回形雷纹、云纹、复线三角纹；扁耳两对饰辫纹 Drum face: patterns of sun(12rays), 酉 -character, concentric circle, nipple protrusion, flying flag mixed men figures,S-shape cloud, 回 -shape thunder & coin with quadrangle inside; Drum body: patterns of nipple protrusion, 回 -shape thunder, cloud, double line triangle; Braid on 2 pairs of flat handles.	43.4–43.8	25	麻江型 Majiang Type	
71	族鼓 0072 符箓纹铜鼓 ZG No.0072 Bronze Drum with Ofuda patterns	广西民族博物馆 Anthropology Museum of Guangxi	1973 年收购于河池废品公司 Collected at Hechi Waste Recycle Company in 1973	鼓面：太阳纹（12 芒）、S 云纹、回形雷纹、乳钉纹、符箓纹、四出钱纹； 鼓身：乳钉纹、同心圆纹、回形雷纹、钱纹、S 云纹、云纹、如意云纹、复线三角纹；扁耳两对饰辫纹 Drum face: patterns of sun(12rays), S-shape cloud, 回 -shape thunder, nipple protrusion, Ofuda, coin with quadrangle inside; Drum body: patterns of nipple protrusion, concentric circle, 回 -shape thunder, coin, S-shape cloud, cloud, Ruyi-shape cloud, double line triangle; Braid on 2 pairs of flat handles.	43–43.5	25.5	麻江型 Majiang Type	

序号 NO.	原编号及鼓名 Stock Number & Name	收藏单位 Museum	出土（征集） 时间、地点 Time & Spot for discovered or collected	主要装饰 Main Decorations	尺寸（厘米） Size(cm)		类型 Type	图片 Picture
					面径 Face Diameter	身高 Height		
72	族鼓 0073 符箓纹铜鼓 ZG No.0073 Bronze Drum with Ofuda patterns	广西民族博物馆 Anthropology Museum of Guangxi	1973 年收购于河池废品公司 Collected at Hechi Waste Recycle Company in 1973	鼓面：太阳纹（12 芒）、西字纹、回形雷纹、乳钉纹、游旗纹、同心圆纹、云纹、卦纹； 鼓身：乳钉纹、云纹、雷纹、S 云纹、回形雷纹、复线三角纹；扁耳两对饰辫纹 Drum face: patterns of sun(12rays), 西 -character, 回 -shape thunder, nipple protrusion, flying flag, concentric circle, cloud, divinatory symbol; Drum body: patterns of nipple protrusion, cloud, thunder, S-shape cloud, 回 -shape thunder, double line triangle; Braid and strings on 2 pairs of flat handles.	51.8–52	25.3	麻江型 Majiang Type	
73	族鼓 0074 符箓纹铜鼓 ZG No.0074 Bronze Drum with Ofuda patterns	广西民族博物馆 Anthropology Museum of Guangxi	1973 年收购于河池废品公司 Collected at Hechi Waste Recycle Company in 1973	鼓面：太阳纹（12 芒）、S 云纹、四出钱纹、乳钉纹、符箓纹、回形雷纹、同心圆纹 / 回形雷纹； 鼓身：乳钉纹、同心圆纹、云纹、复线三角纹；扁耳两对饰辫纹 Drum face: patterns of sun(12rays), S-shape cloud, coin with quadrangle insid, nipple protrusion, Ofuda, 回 -shape thunder, concentric circle & 回 -shape thunder; Drum body: patterns of nipple protrusion, concentric circle, cloud, double line triangle; Braid pattern on 2 pairs of flat handles.	46.9–47.2	27.5	麻江型 Majiang Type	
74	族鼓 0075 符箓纹铜鼓 ZG No.0075 Bronze Drum with Ofuda patterns	广西民族博物馆 Anthropology Museum of Guangxi	1973 年收购于河池废品公司 Collected at Hechi Waste Recycle Company in 1973	鼓面：太阳纹（12 芒）、同心圆纹、钱纹、乳钉纹、符箓纹、如意云纹、云纹； 鼓身：乳钉纹、如意云纹、钱纹、云纹、复线三角纹；扁耳两对饰辫纹 Drum face: patterns of sun(12rays), concentric circle, coin, nipple protrusion, Ofuda, Ruyi-shape cloud, cloud; Drum body: patterns of nipple protrusion, Ruyi-shape cloud, coin, cloud, double line triangle; Braid patterns on 2 pairs of flat handles.	42.8–43	26	麻江型 Majiang Type	

序号 N0.	原编号及鼓名 Stock Number & Name	收藏单位 Museum	出土（征集）时间、地点 Time & Spot for discovered or collected	主要装饰 Main Decorations	尺寸（厘米）Size(cm)		类型 Type	图片 Picture
					面径 Face Diameter	身高 Height		
75	族鼓 0076 双花人物铜鼓 ZG No.0076 Bronze Drum with 2 flowers and person patterns	广西民族博物馆 Anthropology Museum of Guangxi	1973 年收购于河池废品公司 Collected at Hechi Waste Recycle Company in 1973	鼓面：太阳纹（12 芒）、同心圆纹、回形雷纹、乳钉纹、荷耙人纹、圆形雷纹、团花纹、菱形雷纹、叶纹、菱形四瓣花纹；鼓身：可辨乳钉纹、如意云纹、复线三角纹、其余磨蚀；扁耳两对饰辫纹 Drum face: patterns of sun(12rays), concentric circle, 回 -shape thunder, nipple protrusion, pattern group of hoer, round thunder and flower cluster, diamond-shape thunder, leaf, diamond-shape quatrefoil; Drum body: patterns of nipple protrusion, Ruyi-shape cloud, double line triangle; the other patterns are obscure; Braid patterns on 2 pairs of flat handles.	47~47.3	27	麻江型 Majiang Type	
76	族鼓 0077 人物动物图案纹铜鼓 ZG No.0077 Bronze Drum with man and animal patterns	广西民族博物馆 Anthropology Museum of Guangxi	1973 年收购于河池废品公司 Collected at Hechi Waste Recycle Company in 1973	鼓面：太阳纹（12 芒）、同心圆纹、回形雷纹、乳钉纹、人物纹、动物纹、窗花纹间同心圆纹；鼓身：梅花状乳钉纹、如意云纹、云纹、回形雷纹、同心圆纹、复线三角纹；扁耳两对饰辫纹 Drum face: patterns of sun(12rays), concentric circle, 回 -shape thunder, nipple protrusion, men & animal, widow lattices mixed concentric circle; Drum body: patterns of nipple protrusion in plum-blossom shape, Ruyi-shape cloud, cloud, 回 -shape thunder, concentric circle, double line triangle; Braid patterns on 2 pairs of flat handles.	44.1~44.9	25.5	麻江型 Majiang Type	
77	族鼓 0078 孔明将军出行图铜鼓 ZG No.0078 Bronze Drum with Genaral kongming parading patterns	广西民族博物馆 Anthropology Museum of Guangxi	1973 年收购于河池废品公司 Collected at Hechi Waste Recycle Company in 1973	鼓面：太阳纹（12 芒）、乳钉纹、人物纹、云纹、对称同心圆纹；鼓身：梅花状乳钉纹、圆圈纹、复线三角纹；扁耳两对饰辫纹 Drum face: patterns of sun(12rays), nipple protrusion, men, cloud, symmetrical concentric circle; Drum body: patterns of nipple protrusion in plum-blossom shape, circle, double line triangle; Braid patterns on 2 pairs of flat handles.	47~47.3	26.8	麻江型 Majiang Type	

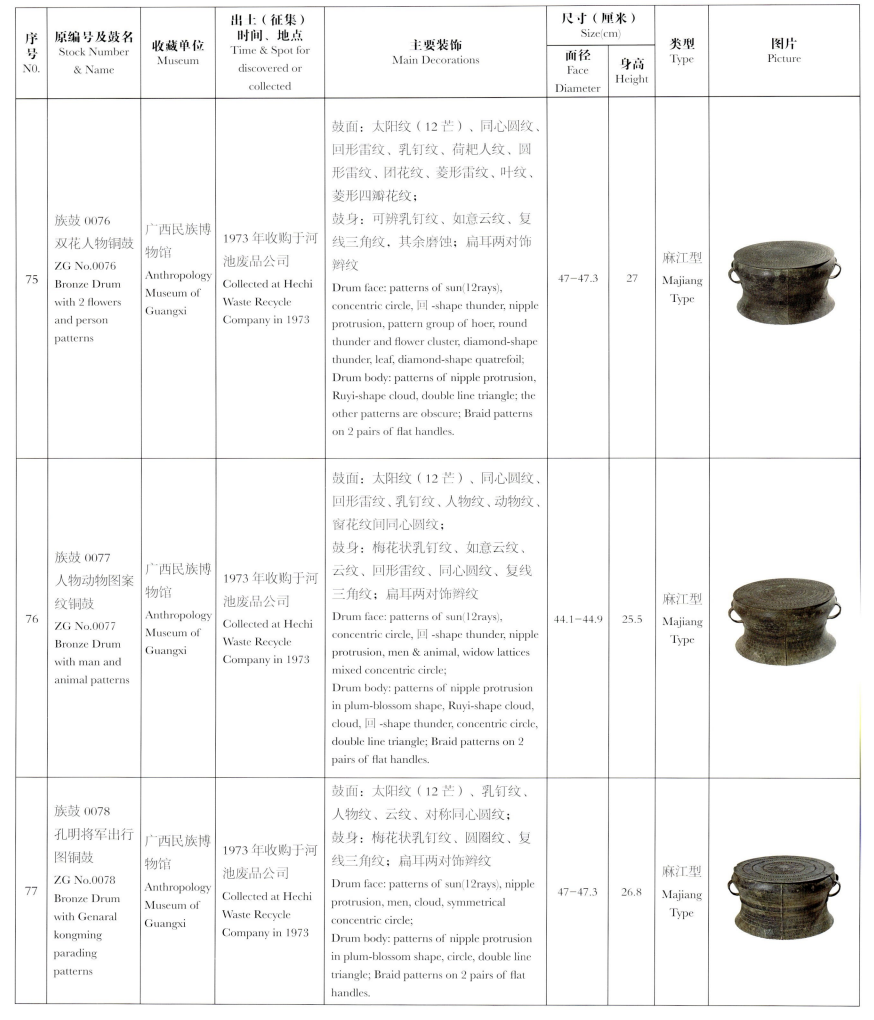

序号 NO.	原编号及鼓名 Stock Number & Name	收藏单位 Museum	出土（征集）时间、地点 Time & Spot for discovered or collected	主要装饰 Main Decorations	尺寸（厘米）Size(cm)		类型 Type	图片 Picture
					面径 Face Diameter	身高 Height		
78	族鼓 0079 人物符箓纹铜鼓 ZG No.0079 Bronze Drum with man&Ofuda patterns	广西民族博物馆 Anthropology Museum of Guangxi	来源不详，原存广西壮自治区博物馆 Original source unknown, preserved previously in Museum of Guangxi Zhuang Autonomous Region	鼓面：太阳纹（12 芒）、同心圆纹、回形雷纹、乳钉纹、符箓纹、荷耙人纹、花纹； 鼓身：乳钉纹、同心圆纹、如意云纹、回形雷纹、云纹、复线三角纹；扁耳两对饰辫纹 Drum face: patterns of sun(12rays), concentric circle, 回 -shape thunder, nipple protrusion, men &Ofuda, flowers; Drum body: patterns of nipple protrusion,concentric circle,Ruyi-shape cloud, 回 -shape thunder, cloud, double line triangle; Braid patterns on 2 pairs of flat handles.	47.3～47.5	27	麻江型 Majiang Type	
79	族鼓 0080 人物纹鱼纹铜鼓 ZG No.0080 Bronze Drum with man&fish patterns	广西民族博物馆 Anthropology Museum of Guangxi	来源不详，原存广西壮自治区博物馆 Original source unknown, preserved previously in Museum of Guangxi Zhuang Autonomous Region	鼓面：太阳纹（12 芒）、同心圆纹、回形雷纹、乳钉纹、双鱼戏珠纹、人物纹、云纹、兽形云纹、同心圆纹、回形雷纹； 鼓身：乳钉纹、云纹、复线三角纹；扁耳两对饰辫纹 Drum face: patterns of sun(12rays), concentric circle, 回 -shape thunder, nipple protrusion, men & 2 fishes playing pearl, cloud, beast-shape cloud, concentric circle & 回 -shape thunder; Drum body: patterns of nipple protrusion, cloud, double line triangle; Braid patterns on 2 pairs of flat handles.	45.5～45.9	27.5	麻江型 Majiang Type	
80	族鼓 0081 团花纹铜鼓 ZG No.0081 Bronze Drum with flower cluster patterns	广西民族博物馆 Anthropology Museum of Guangxi	来源不详，原存广西壮自治区博物馆 Original source unknown, preserved previously in Museum of Guangxi Zhuang Autonomous Region	鼓面：太阳纹（12 芒）、同心圆纹、回形雷纹、乳钉纹、团花纹、如意云纹、云纹； 鼓身：乳钉纹、如意云纹、复线三角纹；扁耳两对饰辫纹 Drum face: patterns of sun(12rays), concentric circle, 回 -shape thunder, nipple protrusion, flower cluster, Ruyi-shape cloud, cloud; Drum body: patterns of nipple protrusion, Ruyi-shape cloud, double line triangle; Braid patterns on 2 pairs of flat handles.	44.3～44.6	25.8	麻江型 Majiang Type	

续表

序号 N0.	原编号及鼓名 Stock Number & Name	收藏单位 Museum	出土（征集）时间、地点 Time & Spot for discovered or collected	主要装饰 Main Decorations	尺寸（厘米）Size(cm)		类型 Type	图片 Picture
					面径 Face Diameter	身高 Height		
81	族鼓 0082 人物纹鱼纹铜鼓 ZG No.0082 Bronze Drum with man&fish patterns	广西民族博物馆 Anthropology Museum of Guangxi	1973 年收购于河池废品公司 Collected at Hechi Waste Recycle Company in 1973	鼓面：太阳纹（12 芒）、同心圆纹、乳钉纹、桂鱼戏珠纹、人物纹、回形雷纹、同心圆纹；鼓身：乳钉纹，其余磨蚀；扁耳两对饰辫纹 Drum face: patterns of sun(12rays), concentric circle, nipple protrusion, mandarin fish playing pearl & men, concentric circle & 回 -shape thunder; Drum body: patterns of nipple protrusion, the other patterns are obscure; Braid patterns on 2 pairs of flat handles.	45.5	27.5	麻江型 Majiang Type	
82	族鼓 0083 八人符箓纹铜鼓 ZG No.0083 Bronze Drum with 8 men and Ofuda patterns	广西民族博物馆 Anthropology Museum of Guangxi	1973 年收购于河池废品公司 Collected at Hechi Waste Recycle Company in 1973	鼓面：太阳纹（12 芒）、S 云纹、同心圆纹、乳钉纹、荷耙人、符箓纹、钱纹、雷纹、蒲叶纹；鼓身：乳钉纹、S 云纹、如意云纹、云纹、同心圆纹、蒲叶纹、复线三角纹；扁耳两对饰辫纹 Drum face: patterns of sun(12rays), S-shape cloud, concentric circle, nipple protrusion, pattern group of hoer, Ofuda, coin, thunder and cattail; Drum body: patterns of nipple protrusion, S-shape cloud, Ruyi-shape cloud, cloud, concentric circle, cattail, double line triangle; Braid patterns on 2 pairs of flat handles.	45	27	麻江型 Majiang Type	
83	族鼓 0084 人物纹鱼纹铜鼓 ZG No.0084 Bronze Drum with man&fish patterns	广西民族博物馆 Anthropology Museum of Guangxi	1973 年收购于河池废品公司 Collected at Hechi Waste Recycle Company in 1973	鼓面：太阳纹（12 芒）、同心圆纹、回形雷纹、乳钉纹、桂鱼人物纹、双龙戏珠纹；鼓身：梅花状乳钉纹、同心圆纹、复线三角纹，其余磨蚀；扁耳两对饰辫纹 Drum face: patterns of sun(12rays), concentric circle, 回 -shape thunder, nipple protrusion, pattern group of mandarin fish, men and 2 dragons playing pearl; Drum body: patterns of nipple protrusion in plum-blossom shape, concentric circle, double line triangle;the other patterns are obscure; Braid patterns on 2 pairs of flat handles.	45.5-45.9	27.5	麻江型 Majiang Type	

续表

序号 NO.	原编号及鼓名 Stock Number & Name	收藏单位 Museum	出土（征集）时间、地点 Time & Spot for discovered or collected	主要装饰 Main Decorations	尺寸（厘米）Size(cm)		类型 Type	图片 Picture
					面径 Face Diameter	身高 Height		
84	族鼓 0085 双龙戏游旗纹铜鼓 ZG No.0085 Bronze Drum with 2 dragons flying flag patterns	广西民族博物馆 Anthropology Museum of Guangxi	来源不详，原存广西壮自治区博物馆 Original source unknown, preserved previously in Museum of Guangxi Zhuang Autonomous Region	鼓面：太阳纹（12芒）、西字纹、云纹、乳钉纹、双龙戏游旗纹、双兽纹； 鼓身：乳钉纹、回形雷纹、云纹、复线三角纹；扁耳两对饰回形纹 Drum face: patterns of sun(12rays), 西-character, cloud, nipple protrusion, 2 dragons playing fly-flag, 2 beasts; Drum body: patterns of nipple protrusion, 回-shape thunder, cloud, double line triangle; 回-shape motif on 2 pairs of flat handles.	49–49.2	26.5	麻江型 Majiang Type	
85	族鼓 0086 游旗纹铜鼓 ZG No.0086 Bronze Drum with flying flag patterns	广西民族博物馆 Anthropology Museum of Guangxi	1973年收购于河池废品公司 Collected at Hechi Waste Recycle Company in 1973	鼓面：太阳纹（12芒）、西字纹、梳纹、乳钉纹、菱形填四瓣花纹、雷纹、定胜、游旗纹、兽形云纹； 鼓身：乳钉纹、雷纹、图案三角纹；扁耳两对饰辫纹 Drum face: patterns of sun(12rays), 西-character, comb line, nipple protrusion, pattern group of diamond-shape quatrefoil, thunder and Dingsheng, flying flag, beast-shape cloud; Drum body: patterns of nipple protrusion, thunder, double line triangle with motif inside; Braid patterns on 2 pairs of flat handles.	46.5	25.2	麻江型 Majiang Type	
86	族鼓 0087 游旗纹铜鼓 ZG No.0087 Bronze Drum with flying flag patterns	广西民族博物馆 Anthropology Museum of Guangxi	1973年收购于河池废品公司 Collected at Hechi Waste Recycle Company in 1973	鼓面：太阳纹（14芒）、西字纹、S云纹、蔓草纹、乳钉纹、窗花纹、回形雷纹、云纹； 鼓身：梅花状乳钉纹、缠枝纹、云纹、云纹、蔓草纹、蔓草纹、回形雷纹、复线三角纹；扁耳两对饰辫纹 Drum face: patterns of sun(14rays), 西-character, S-shape cloud & liana, nipple protrusion, window lattices, 回-shape thunder, cloud; Drum body: patterns of nipple protrusion in plum blossom shape, twisted branches, cloud, liana, 回-shape thunder, double line triangle; Braid patterns on 2 pairs of flat handles.	48.2–48.4	27.3	麻江型 Majiang Type	

序号 N0.	原编号及鼓名 Stock Number & Name	收藏单位 Museum	出土（征集）时间、地点 Time & Spot for discovered or collected	主要装饰 Main Decorations	尺寸（厘米） Size(cm)		类型 Type	图片 Picture
					面径 Face Diameter	身高 Height		
87	族鼓 0088 游旗纹铜鼓 ZG No.0088 Bronze Drum with flying flag patterns	广西民族博物馆 Anthropology Museum of Guangxi	1973 年收购于河池废品公司 Collected at Hechi Waste Recycle Company in 1973	鼓面：太阳纹（12 芒）、同心圆纹、S 云纹、乳钉纹、游旗纹、栉纹、兽形云纹； 鼓身：乳钉纹、如意云纹、回形雷纹、栉纹、云纹、复线三角纹；扁耳两对饰辫纹 Drum face: patterns of sun(12rays), concentric circle, S-shape cloud, nipple protrusion, flying flag, comb line, beast-shape cloud; Drum body: patterns of nipple protrusion, Ruyi-shape cloud, 回 -shape thunder, comb line, cloud, double line triangle; Braid pattern on 2 pairs of flat handles.	47—47.5	26.5	麻江型 Majiang Type	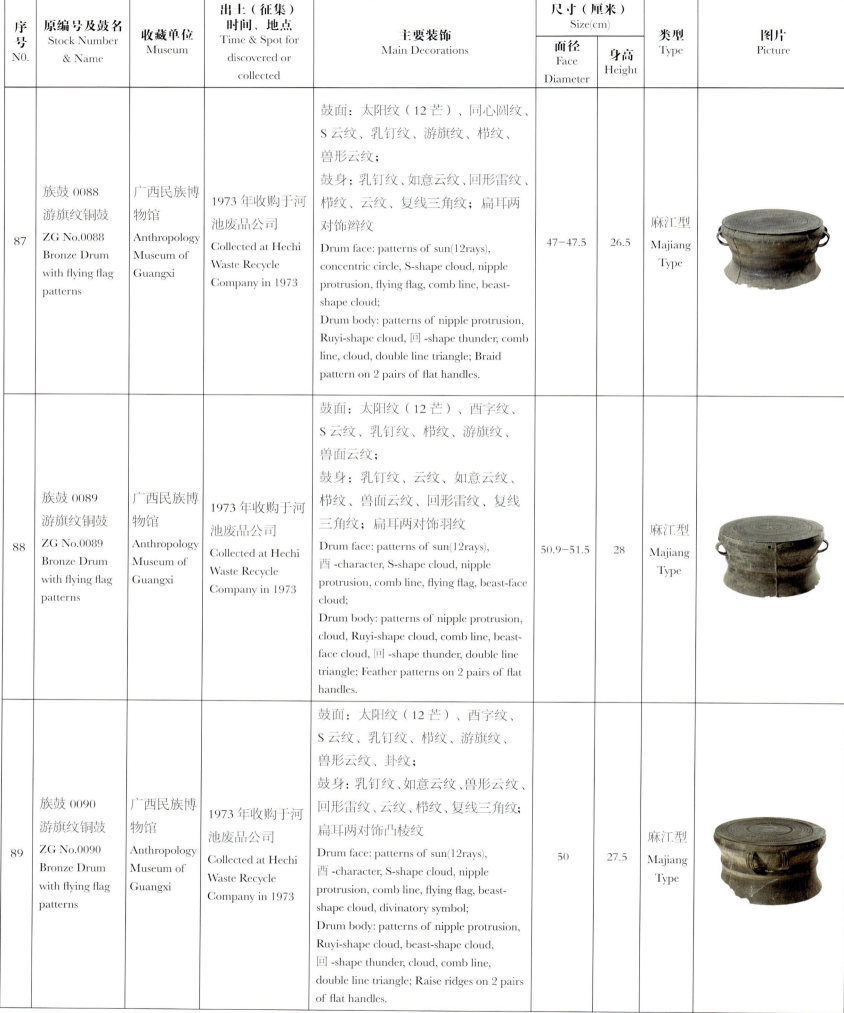
88	族鼓 0089 游旗纹铜鼓 ZG No.0089 Bronze Drum with flying flag patterns	广西民族博物馆 Anthropology Museum of Guangxi	1973 年收购于河池废品公司 Collected at Hechi Waste Recycle Company in 1973	鼓面：太阳纹（12 芒）、酉字纹、S 云纹、乳钉纹、栉纹、游旗纹、兽面云纹； 鼓身：乳钉纹、云纹、如意云纹、栉纹、兽面云纹、回形雷纹、复线三角纹；扁耳两对饰羽纹 Drum face: patterns of sun(12rays), 酉 -character, S-shape cloud, nipple protrusion, comb line, flying flag, beast-face cloud; Drum body: patterns of nipple protrusion, cloud, Ruyi-shape cloud, comb line, beast-face cloud, 回 -shape thunder, double line triangle; Feather patterns on 2 pairs of flat handles.	50.9—51.5	28	麻江型 Majiang Type	
89	族鼓 0090 游旗纹铜鼓 ZG No.0090 Bronze Drum with flying flag patterns	广西民族博物馆 Anthropology Museum of Guangxi	1973 年收购于河池废品公司 Collected at Hechi Waste Recycle Company in 1973	鼓面：太阳纹（12 芒）、酉字纹、S 云纹、乳钉纹、栉纹、游旗纹、兽形云纹、卦纹； 鼓身：乳钉纹、如意云纹、兽形云纹、回形雷纹、云纹、栉纹、复线三角纹；扁耳两对饰凸棱纹 Drum face: patterns of sun(12rays), 酉 -character, S-shape cloud, nipple protrusion, comb line, flying flag, beast-shape cloud, divinatory symbol; Drum body: patterns of nipple protrusion, Ruyi-shape cloud, beast-shape cloud, 回 -shape thunder, cloud, comb line, double line triangle; Raise ridges on 2 pairs of flat handles.	50	27.5	麻江型 Majiang Type	

续表

序号 NO.	原编号及鼓名 Stock Number & Name	收藏单位 Museum	出土（征集） 时间、地点 Time & Spot for discovered or collected	主要装饰 Main Decorations	尺寸（厘米） Size(cm)		类型 Type	图片 Picture
					面径 Face Diameter	身高 Height		
90	族鼓 0091 游旗纹铜鼓 ZG No.0091 Bronze Drum with flying flag patterns	广西民族博物馆 Anthropology Museum of Guangxi	1973 年收购于河池废品公司 Collected at Hechi Waste Recycle Company in 1973	鼓面：太阳纹（12 芒）、酉字纹、S 云纹、乳钉纹、游旗纹、栉纹、兽形云纹； 鼓身：乳钉纹、如意云纹、回形雷纹、栉纹、云纹、复线三角纹；扁耳两对饰凸棱纹 Drum face: patterns of sun(12rays), 酉-character, S-shape cloud, nipple protrusion, flying flag, comb line, beast-shape cloud; Drum body: patterns of nipple protrusion, Ruyi-shape cloud, 回-shape thunder, comb line, cloud, double line triangle; Raise ridges on 2 pairs of flat handles.	47	26	麻江型 Majiang Type	
91	族鼓 0092 游旗纹铜鼓 ZG No.0092 Bronze Drum with flying flag patterns	广西民族博物馆 Anthropology Museum of Guangxi	1973 年收购于河池废品公司 Collected at Hechi Waste Recycle Company in 1973	鼓面：太阳纹（12 芒）、酉字纹、S 云纹、乳钉纹、栉纹、游旗纹、兽形纹； 鼓身：乳钉纹、云纹、如意云纹、栉纹、回形雷纹、复线三角纹；扁耳两对饰辫纹 Drum face: patterns of sun(12rays), 酉-character, S-shape cloud, nipple protrusion, comb line, flying flag, beast-shape cloud; Drum body: patterns of nipple protrusion, cloud, Ruyi-shape cloud, comb line, 回-shape thunder, double line triangle; Braid patterns on 2 pairs of flat handles.	48.5－49	29	麻江型 Majiang Type	
92	族鼓 0093 游旗纹铜鼓 ZG No.0093 Bronze Drum with flying flag patterns	广西民族博物馆 Anthropology Museum of Guangxi	1973 年收购于河池废品公司 Collected at Hechi Waste Recycle Company in 1973	鼓面：太阳纹（12 芒）、回形雷纹、钱纹、乳钉纹、双龙团寿纹／禽兽（鹤、牛）纹、游旗纹、羽纹、同心圆纹； 鼓身：梅花状乳钉纹、如意云纹、回形雷纹、花纹、图案三角纹；扁耳两对饰辫纹 Drum face: patterns of sun(12rays), 回-shape thunder, coin, nipple protrusion, pattern group of 2 dragons and round " 寿 "-character, animal(crane, ox), flying flag, feather, concentric circle; Drum body: patterns of nipple protrusion in plum-blossom shape, Ruyi-shape cloud, 回-shape thunder, flower, double line triangle with motif; Braid patterns on 2 pairs of flat handles.	45.2－45.5	25.5	麻江型 Majiang Type	

序号 N0.	原编号及鼓名 Stock Number & Name	收藏单位 Museum	出土（征集） 时间、地点 Time & Spot for discovered or collected	主要装饰 Main Decorations	尺寸（厘米） Size(cm)		类型 Type	图片 Picture
					面径 Face Diameter	身高 Height		
93	族鼓 0094 游旗纹铜鼓 ZG No.0094 Bronze Drum with flying flag patterns	广西民族博物馆 Anthropology Museum of Guangxi	1973 年收购于河池废品公司 Collected at Hechi Waste Recycle Company in 1973	鼓面：太阳纹（12 芒）、酉字纹、S 云纹、乳钉纹、游旗纹、栉纹、兽形云纹； 鼓身：乳钉纹、如意云纹、回形雷纹、云纹、栉纹、复线三角纹；扁耳两对饰辫纹 Drum face: patterns of sun(12rays), 酉 -character, S-shape cloud, nipple protrusion, flying flag, comb line, beast-shape cloud; Drum body: patterns of nipple protrusion, Ruyi-shape cloud, 回 -shape thunder, cloud, comb line, double line triangle; Braid patterns on 2 pairs of flat handles.	47.5	26	麻江型 Majiang Type	
94	族鼓 0096 游旗纹铜鼓 ZG No.0096 Bronze Drum with flying flag patterns	广西民族博物馆 Anthropology Museum of Guangxi	1973 年收购于河池废品公司 Collected at Hechi Waste Recycle Company in 1973	鼓面：太阳纹（12 芒）、酉字纹、云纹、乳钉纹、游旗纹、栉纹； 鼓身：乳钉纹、云纹、回形雷纹、栉纹、复线三角纹；扁耳两对饰辫纹 Drum face: patterns of sun(12rays), 酉 -character, cloud, nipple protrusion, flying flag, comb line; Drum body: patterns of nipple protrusion, cloud, 回 -shape thunder, comb line, double line triangle; Braid patterns on 2 pairs of flat handles.	45.5－45.9	25.5	麻江型 Majiang Type	
95	族鼓 0097 游旗纹铜鼓 ZG No.0097 Bronze Drum with flying flag patterns	广西民族博物馆 Anthropology Museum of Guangxi	1973 年收购于河池废品公司 Collected at Hechi Waste Recycle Company in 1973	鼓面：太阳纹（12 芒）、酉字纹、S 云纹、乳钉纹、游旗纹、栉纹、兽形云纹、卦纹； 鼓身：梅花状乳钉纹、回形雷纹、如意云纹、栉纹、兽面云纹、复线三角纹；扁耳两对饰辫纹、回形雷纹 Drum face: patterns of sun(12rays), 酉 -character, S-shape cloud, nipple protrusion, flying flag, comb line, beast-shape cloud, divinatory symbol; Drum body: patterns of nipple protrusion in plum blossom shape, 回 -shape thunder, Ruyi-shape cloud, comb line, beast-face cloud, double line triangle; Braid and 回 -shape thunder patterns on 2 pairs of flat handles.	48.5	28	麻江型 Majiang Type	

序号 NO.	原编号及鼓名 Stock Number & Name	收藏单位 Museum	出土（征集）时间、地点 Time & Spot for discovered or collected	主要装饰 Main Decorations	尺寸（厘米） Size(cm)		类型 Type	图片 Picture
					面径 Face Diameter	身高 Height		
96	族鼓 0098 游旗纹铜鼓 ZG No.0098 Bronze Drum with flying flag patterns	广西民族博物馆 Anthropology Museum of Guangxi	1973 年收购于河池废品公司 Collected at Hechi Waste Recycle Company in 1973	鼓面：太阳纹（12 芒）、酉字纹、乳钉纹、游旗纹、栉纹、云纹、兽形云纹； 鼓身：乳钉纹、如意云纹、回形雷纹；扁耳两对饰辫纹、回形雷纹 Drum face: patterns of sun(12rays), 西 -character, nipple protrusion, flying flag, comb line, beast-shape cloud; Drum body: patterns of nipple protrusion, Ruyi-shape cloud, 回 -shape thunder; Braid and 回 -shape thunder patterns on 2 pairs of flat handles.	47	17.5（残）Incomplete	麻江型 Majiang Type	
97	族鼓 0099 九塘铜鼓 ZG No.0099 Bronze Drum Jiutang	广西民族博物馆 Anthropology Museum of Guangxi	1979 年 10 月 19 日出土于邕宁县九塘公社九塘大队十八队 Unearthed at Jiutang Team 18, Jiutang Community, Yongning county on October 19th, 1979	鼓面：太阳纹（12 芒）、羽纹、栉纹、切线同心圆纹、复线交叉纹、变形羽人纹、变形翔鹭纹间定胜纹，鼓面边缘饰四只逆时针四足素面立体青蛙； 鼓身：羽纹、栉纹、切线同心圆纹、羽纹栉纹切线同心圆垂直纹带、圆心三角垂叶纹；扁耳两对饰辫纹 Drum face: patterns of sun(12rays), feather, comb line, tangent concentric circles, crossed double lines, transformed feathermen, transformed flying heron mixed Dingsheng; 4 frog statues of 4 feet and blank back anticlockwise stand on the edge of drum face; Drum body: patterns of feather, comb line, tangent concentric circles, vertical ribbon of feather, straight line and tangent concentric circle, leaf-shape triangle with circle in the middle; Braid patterns on 2 pairs of flat handles.	74.5~75.3	42.8（残）Incomplete	冷水冲型 Lengshui-chong Type	

序号 N0.	原编号及鼓名 Stock Number & Name	收藏单位 Museum	出土（征集） 时间、地点 Time & Spot for discovered or collected	主要装饰 Main Decorations	尺寸（厘米） Size(cm)		类型 Type	图片 Picture
					面径 Face Diameter	身高 Height		
98	族鼓 0100 乘骑饰变形羽 人纹铜鼓 ZG No.0100 Bronze Drum with horse- ride statue and transformed feathermen patterns	广西民族博 物馆 Anthropology Museum of Guangxi	1975 年出土于梧 州市藤县蒙江镇 横村冷水冲 Unearthed at Lengshuichong, Heng Village, Mengjiang Town, Wuzhou City in 1975	鼓面：太阳纹（12 芒）、水波纹、 同心圆纹、栉纹、复线交叉纹、羽纹、 变形羽人纹、变形翔鹭纹、眼纹， 鼓面边缘饰四只逆时针四足谷穗纹 立体青蛙，蛙间饰乘骑立饰； 鼓身：水波纹、同心圆纹、栉纹、 船纹、羽纹、变形羽人纹、网纹、 圆心三角垂叶间半太阳纹、眼纹； 扁耳两对饰辫纹，附耳环形饰谷穗 纹、波浪纹 Drum face: patterns of sun(12rays), water wave, concentric circles, comb line, crossed double lines, feather, transformed feathermen, transformed flying heron, diamond-shape eye; 4 frog statues of 4 feet and rice ears on back anticlockwise stand on the edge of drum face; horse-rider statues between the frogs; Drum body: patterns of water wave, concentric circles, comb line, boat, feather, transformed feathermen, net, leaf-shape triangle with circle in the middle mixed sun, diamond-shape eye; Braid patterns on 2 pairs of flat handles, rice ear and water wave patterns on the attached handles.	83−83.6	60.3	冷水冲 型 Lengshui- chong Type	
99	族鼓 0101 云雷纹大铜鼓 ZG No.0101 Bronze Drum with cloud & thunder patterns	广西民族博 物馆 Anthropology Museum of Guangxi	来源不详，原存 广西壮自治区博 物馆 Original source unknown, preserved previously in Museum of Guangxi Zhuang Autonomous Region	鼓面：太阳纹（8 芒）、云纹、雷纹； 鼓身：云纹、雷纹；环耳两对饰缠 丝纹 Drum face: patterns of sun(8rays),cloud, thunder; Drum body: patterns of cloud, thunder; Silk- like patterns on 2 pairs of blank ring handles.	163.5− 164.8	63.5 （残） Incom- plete	北流型 Beiliu Type	

序号 NO.	原编号及鼓名 Stock Number & Name	收藏单位 Museum	出土（征集）时间、地点 Time & Spot for discovered or collected	主要装饰 Main Decorations	尺寸（厘米） Size(cm)		类型 Type	图片 Picture
					面径 Face Diameter	身高 Height		
100	族鼓 0102 乘骑水鸟饰变形羽人纹铜鼓 ZG No.0102 Bronze Drum with horse-ride, waterfowl statues and transformed feathermen patterns	广西民族博物馆 Anthropology Museum of Guangxi	20 世纪 50 年代出土于梧州市藤县古竹乡 Unearthed at Guzhu, Teng County, Wuzhou City in 1950s'	鼓面：太阳纹（12 芒）、羽纹、栉纹、同心圆纹、复线交叉纹、变形羽人纹、变形翔鹭纹、眼纹，鼓面边缘饰四只逆时针四足谷穗纹立体青蛙，蛙间饰乘骑、水鸟； 鼓身：羽纹、栉纹、同心圆纹、船纹、变形羽人纹、网纹、水波纹、圆心三角垂叶纹／水波纹、眼纹；扁耳两对饰辫纹，附耳一对饰辫纹 Drum face: patterns of sun(12rays), feather, comb line, concentric circles, crossed double lines, transformed feathermen, transformed flying heron, diamomd-shape eye; 4 frog statues of 4 feet and rice ear on back stand anticlockwise on the edge of drum face; a horse-rider and a bird statues between the frogs; Drum body: patterns of feather, comb line, concentric circles, boat, transformed feathermen, net, water wave, leaf-shape triangle with concentric circle in the middle, water wave and diamond-shape eye; Braid patterns on 2 pairs of flat handles and a pair of attached handles.	87.8−89	66.5	冷水冲型 Lengshui-chong Type	
101	族鼓 0103 牛拉橇变形羽人纹铜鼓 ZG No.0103 Bronze Drum with cart-dragging ox statues and transformed feathermen patterns	广西民族博物馆 Anthropology Museum of Guangxi	1954 年征集于桂平县（现桂平市） Collected in Guiping County in 1954	鼓面：太阳纹（12 芒）、水波纹、同心圆纹、栉纹、复线交叉纹、羽纹、变形羽人纹、变形翔鹭纹、眼纹，鼓面边缘饰四只逆时针四足谷穗纹立体青蛙，蛙间饰牛拉橇立饰，牛背有两只小鸟； 鼓身：水波纹、同心圆纹、栉纹、船纹、羽纹、变形羽人纹栉纹切线同心圆纹垂直纹带、网纹、眼纹、圆心三角垂叶纹；扁耳两对饰辫纹，环形附耳一对饰几何纹 Drum face: patterns of sun(12rays), water wave, concentric circles, comb line, crossed double lines, feather, transformed feathermen, transformed flying heron, diamomd-shape eye; 4 frog statues of 4 feet and rice ear on back stand anticlockwise on the edge of drum face; a cart-dragging ox statue with 2 birds on its' back between the frogs; Drum body: patterns of water wave, concentric circles, comb line, boat, feather, vertical ribbon of transformed feathermen, straight line and tangent concentric circle, net, diamomd-shape eye, leaf-shape triangle with concentric circle in the middle; Braid patterns on 2 pairs of flat handles, geometry patterns on a pair of attached ring handles.	82−82.7	59.5	冷水冲型 Lengshui-chong Type	

序号 N0.	原编号及鼓名 Stock Number & Name	收藏单位 Museum	出土（征集）时间、地点 Time & Spot for discovered or collected	主要装饰 Main Decorations	尺寸（厘米）Size(cm)		类型 Type	图片 Picture
					面径 Face Diameter	身高 Height		
102	族鼓 0104 变形羽人纹四出钱纹铜鼓 ZG No.0104 Bronze Drum with transformed feathermen and coin with quadrangle inside patterns	广西民族博物馆 Anthropology Museum of Guangxi	1962 年出土于南宁市心圩 Unearthed at Xinxu, Nanning in 1962	鼓面：太阳纹（10 芒）、蝉纹、四瓣花纹、四出钱纹、鸟纹、连钱纹、变形羽人纹、席纹，鼓面边缘饰六组逆时针三足螺旋纹立体青蛙，其中三组为累蹲蛙； 鼓身：蝉纹、连钱纹、四出钱纹、兽面纹、虫形纹、席纹、鸟纹、四瓣花纹；扁耳两对饰羽纹 Drum face: patterns of sun(10rays), cicada, quatrefoil, coin with quadrangle inside, bird, coins part of overlap, transformed feathermen, woven mat; 6 frogs with 3 feet and spiracles on back anticlockwise stand on the edge, three of them are overlap; Drum body: patterns of cicada, coins part of overlap, coin with quadrangle inside, beast face, insect, woven mat, bird, quatrefoil;Feather patterns on 2 pairs of flat handles.	69.4−69.5	41	灵山型 Lingshan Type	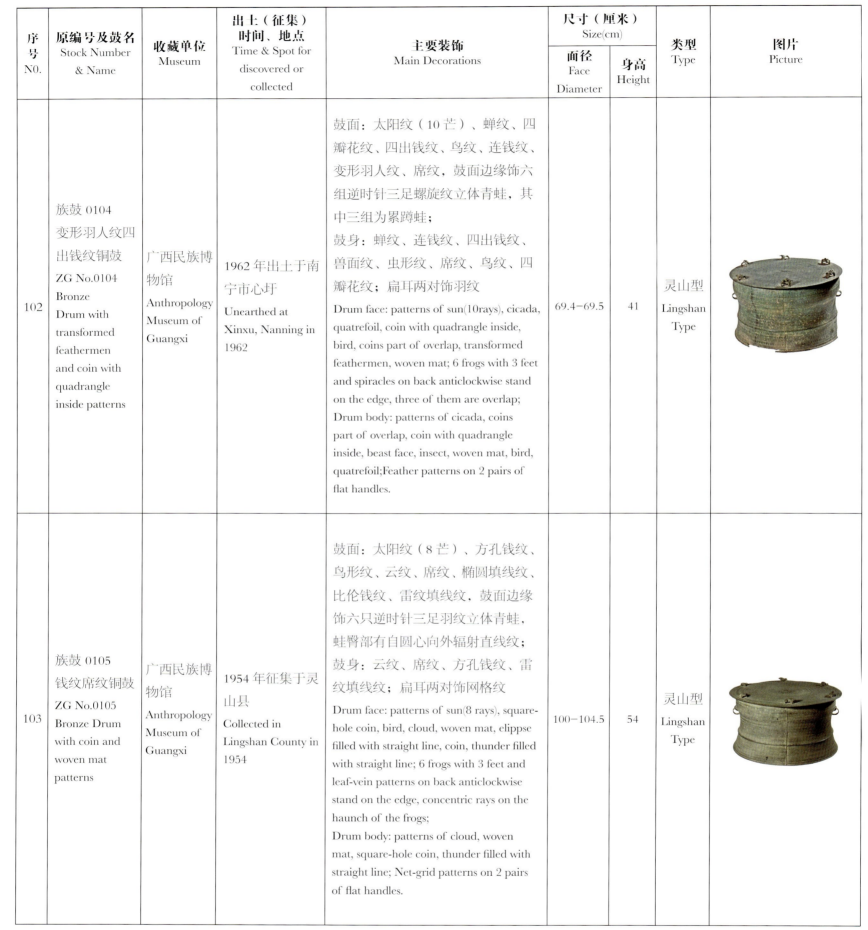
103	族鼓 0105 钱纹席纹铜鼓 ZG No.0105 Bronze Drum with coin and woven mat patterns	广西民族博物馆 Anthropology Museum of Guangxi	1954 年征集于灵山县 Collected in Lingshan County in 1954	鼓面：太阳纹（8 芒）、方孔钱纹、鸟形纹、云纹、席纹、椭圆填线纹、比伦钱纹、雷纹填线纹，鼓面边缘饰六只逆时针三足羽纹立体青蛙，蛙臀部有自圆心向外辐射直线纹； 鼓身：云纹、席纹、方孔钱纹、雷纹填线纹；扁耳两对饰网格纹 Drum face: patterns of sun(8 rays), square-hole coin, bird, cloud, woven mat, ellippse filled with straight line, coin, thunder filled with straight line; 6 frogs with 3 feet and leaf-vein patterns on back anticlockwise stand on the edge, concentric rays on the haunch of the frogs; Drum body: patterns of cloud, woven mat, square-hole coin, thunder filled with straight line; Net-grid patterns on 2 pairs of flat handles.	100−104.5	54	灵山型 Lingshan Type	

续表

序号 NO.	原编号及鼓名 Stock Number & Name	收藏单位 Museum	出土（征集）时间、地点 Time & Spot for discovered or collected	主要装饰 Main Decorations	尺寸（厘米） Size(cm)		类型 Type	图片 Picture
					面径 Face Diameter	身高 Height		
104	族鼓 0106 变形羽人纹铜鼓 ZG No.0106 Bronze Drum with transformed feathermen patterns	广西民族博物馆 Anthropology Museum of Guangxi	广西文化局拨交，原存广西壮族自治区博物馆 Allocated by Guangxi Cultural Bureau, preserved previously in Museum of Guangxi Zhuang Autonomous Region	鼓面：太阳纹（12 芒）、蝉纹、四出钱纹、鸟纹、连钱纹、变形羽人纹、四瓣花纹、鼓面边缘饰六组逆时针三足螺旋纹立体青蛙其中三组为累蹲蛙； 鼓身：蝉纹、连钱纹、四出钱纹、鸟纹、席纹、雷纹填线纹、变形羽人纹、四瓣花填线纹、虫形纹；扁耳两对饰叶脉纹 Drum face: patterns of sun(12rays), cicada, coin with quadrangle inside, bird, coins part of overlap, transformed feathermen, quatrefoil; 6 frogs with 3 feet and spiracles on back anticlockwise stand on the edge, three of them are overlap; Drum body: patterns of cicada, coins part of overlap, bird, woven mat, thunder filled with straight line, transformed feathermen, quatrefoil filled with straight line, insect; Leaf-vein patterns on 2 pairs of flat handles.	70~70.5	41.4	灵山型 Lingshan Type	
105	族鼓 0107 雷纹铜鼓 ZG No.0107 Bronze Drum with thunder patterns	广西民族博物馆 Anthropology Museum of Guangxi	1952 年出土于桂平县（现桂平市）麻洞村 Unearthed at Madong Village, Guiping county in 1952	鼓面：太阳纹 (12 芒)、连钱纹、雷纹交替，鼓面边缘饰六只逆时针四足螺旋纹立体青蛙； 鼓身：雷纹、席纹、蝉纹；环耳两对、环形附耳一对 Drum face: patterns of sun(12 rays), coins part of overlap and thunder in turn; 6 frogs with 4 feet and spiracles on back anticlockwise stand on the edge; Drum body: patterns of thunder, woven mat, cicada; 2 pairs of ring handles and a pair of attached ring handles.	134.5~138	72.5	北流型 Beiliu Type	
106	族鼓 0108 雷纹填线纹铜鼓 ZG No.0108 Bronze Drum with straight-line-filled thunder patterns	广西民族博物馆 Anthropology Museum of Guangxi	新中国成立初征集于合浦 Collected in Hepu county at the beginning of People's Republic of China	鼓面：太阳纹（8 芒）、雷纹填线纹，鼓面边缘饰六只顺时针四足立体青蛙； 鼓身：雷纹填线纹、半云填线纹；环耳两对饰缠丝纹 Drum face: patterns of sun(8rays), thunder filled with straight line; 6 frogs with 4 feet clockwisely stand on the edge; Drum body: patterns of thunder filled with straight line, semicloud straight line; Silk-like patterns on 2 pairs of ring handles.	90.2	49.5	北流型 Beiliu Type	

序号 N0.	原编号及鼓名 Stock Number & Name	收藏单位 Museum	出土（征集） 时间、地点 Time & Spot for discovered or collected	主要装饰 Main Decorations	尺寸（厘米） Size(cm)		类型 Type	图片 Picture
					面径 Face Diameter	身高 Height		
107	族鼓 0109 变形羽人纹鸟纹铜鼓 ZG No.0109 Bronze Drum with transformed feathermen & bird patterns	广西民族博物馆 Anthropology Museum of Guangxi	20 世纪 50 年代征集于横县 Collected at Hengxian County in 1950s'	鼓面：太阳纹（10 芒）、四瓣花纹、虫形纹、席纹、四出钱纹、鸟纹、连钱纹、变形羽人纹、蝉纹，鼓面边缘饰六只逆时针三足螺旋纹立体青蛙； 鼓身：蝉纹、虫形纹、席纹、四出钱纹、四瓣花纹、连钱纹、变形羽人纹、鸟纹；扁耳两对饰羽纹 Drum face: patterns of sun(10rays), quatrefoil, insect, woven mat, coin with quadrangle inside, bird, coins part of overlap, transformed feathermen, cicada; 6 frogs with 3 feet and spiracles on back anticlockwise stand on the edge; Drum body: patterns of cicada, insect, woven mat, coin with quadrangle inside, quatrefoil, coins part of overlap, transformed feathermen, bird; Feather patterns on 2 pairs of flat handles.	81.1–81.7	49.5	灵山型 Lingshan Type	
108	族鼓 0110 乘骑饰变形羽人纹铜鼓 ZG No.0110 Bronze Drum with horse-ride statue and transformed feathermen patterns	广西民族博物馆 Anthropology Museum of Guangxi	1956 年出土于金秀瑶族自治县平道乡 Unearthed at Pingdao, Jinxiu Yao Autonomous County in 1956	鼓面：太阳纹 (12 芒)、水波纹、同心圆纹、栉纹、复线交叉纹、变形羽人纹、变形翔鹭纹、眼纹，鼓面边缘饰四只逆时针四足谷穗纹立体青蛙，蛙间饰乘骑立饰； 鼓身：水波纹、同心圆纹、船纹、变形羽人纹、网纹、圆心三角垂叶纹、眼纹；扁耳两对饰辫纹 Drum face: patterns of sun(12rays), water wave, concentric circles, comb line, crossed double lines, transformed feathermen, transformed flying heron, diamond-shape eye; 4 frog statues of 4 feet and rice ear on back anticlockwise stand on the edge of drum face; horse-rider statue between the frogs; Drum body: patterns of water wave, concentric circles, boat, transformed feathermen, net, leaf-shape triangle with concentric circle in the middle, diamond-shape eye; Braid patterns on 2 pairs of flat handles.	62.2–63.5	41.8	冷水冲型 Lengshui-chong Type	

续表

序号 N0.	原编号及鼓名 Stock Number & Name	收藏单位 Museum	出土（征集） 时间、地点 Time & Spot for discovered or collected	主要装饰 Main Decorations	尺寸（厘米） Size(cm)		类型 Type	图片 Picture
					面径 Face Diameter	身高 Height		
109	族鼓 0111 鸟饰变形羽人纹铜鼓 ZG No.0111 Bronze Drum with bird statue and transformed feathermen patterns	广西民族博物馆 Anthropology Museum of Guangxi	20 世纪 50 年代出土于藤县和平区 Unearthed at Heping District, Teng County in 1950s'	鼓面：太阳纹（12 芒）、水波纹、同心圆纹、栉纹、复线交叉纹、羽纹、变形羽人纹、变形翔鹭纹、眼纹，鼓面边缘饰四只逆时针四足谷穗纹立体青蛙，蛙间饰单鸟、双鸟、人骑牛立饰； 鼓身：水波纹、栉纹、同心圆纹、船纹、变形羽人纹、羽纹、网纹、圆心三角垂叶纹、眼纹；扁耳两对饰辫纹、环形附耳一对 Drum face: patterns of sun(12rays), water wave, concentric circles, comb line, crossed double lines, feather, transformed feathermen, transformed flying heron, diamond-shape eye; 4 frog statues of 4 feet and rice ear on back anticlockwise stand on the edge of drum face; birds and ox-rider statues between the frogs. Drum body: patterns of water wave, comb line, concentric circles, boat, transformed feathermen, feather, net, leaf-shape triangle with concentric circle in the middle, diamond-shape eye; Braid patterns on 2 pairs of flat handles, a pair of attached ring handles.	80–80.5	55.2	冷水冲型 Lengshui-chong Type	
110	族鼓 0112 双龙纹铜鼓 ZG No.0112 Bronze Drum with 2 dragons pattern	广西民族博物馆 Anthropology Museum of Guangxi	1964 年采集于柳州二级站 Collected at Liuzhou Secondary Waste Recycle Station in 1964	鼓面：太阳纹（12 芒）、酉字纹、云纹、乳钉纹、双龙纹、"福如东海、寿比南山、永世家财、万代进宝"铭文、回形雷纹； 鼓身：乳钉纹、回形雷纹、云纹、如意云纹／回形雷纹、复线三角纹；扁耳两对饰辫纹、回纹 Drum face: patterns of sun(12rays), 酉 -character, cloud, nipple protrusion, complex patterns of 2 dragons and "福如东海、寿比南山、永世家财、万代进宝"-character, 回 -shape thunder; Drum body: patterns of nipple protrusion, 回 -shape thunder, cloud, complex patterns of Ruyi-shape cloud and 回 -shape thunder, double line triangle; Braid and 回 patterns on 2 pairs of flat handles.	48.3	27	麻江型 Majiang Type	

序号 N0.	原编号及鼓名 Stock Number & Name	收藏单位 Museum	出土（征集）时间、地点 Time & Spot for discovered or collected	主要装饰 Main Decorations	尺寸（厘米）Size(cm) 面径 Face Diameter	身高 Height	类型 Type	图片 Picture
111	族鼓 0113 双龙团寿纹铜鼓 ZG No.0113 Bronze Drum with 4 dragons flying pearl patterns	广西民族博物馆 Anthropology Museum of Guangxi	1964 年采集于柳州二级站 Collected at Liuzhou Secondary Waste Recycle Station in 1964	鼓面：太阳纹（12 芒）、酉字纹、S 云纹、乳钉纹、双龙团寿纹、"万代进宝、永世家财"铭文、云纹、水波纹、雷纹；鼓身：梅花状乳钉纹、回形雷纹、雷纹、复线三角纹；扁耳两对饰凸棱纹 Drum face: patterns of sun(12rays), 酉-character, S-shape cloud nipple protrusion, complex patterns of 2 dragons mixed round 寿-character and"万代进宝、永世家财"-character, cloud, water wave, thunder; Drum body: patterns of nipple protrusion in plum-blossom shape, 回-shape thunder, thunder, double line triangle; Raise ridges on 2 pairs of flat handles.	47.6−47.8	26.5	麻江型 Majiang Type	
112	族鼓 0115 雷纹铜鼓 ZG No.0115 Bronze Drum with thunder patterns	广西民族博物馆 Anthropology Museum of Guangxi	采集于灵山县 Collected in Lingshan County	鼓面：太阳纹（6 芒）、半雷纹填线纹、雷纹，鼓面边缘饰四只四足立体青蛙；鼓身：雷纹、半雷纹填线纹；环耳两对饰缠丝纹 Drum face: patterns of sun(6 rays), thunder and semithunder filled with straight line, thunder; 4 frogs with 4 feet stand on the edge; Drum body: patterns of thunder, semithunder filled with straight line; Silk-like patterns on 2 pairs of ring handles.	88.5−89	55	北流型 Beiliu Type	
113	族鼓 0116 牛岑铜鼓 ZG No.0116 Bronze Drum Niucen	广西民族博物馆 Anthropology Museum of Guangxi	1965 年 7 月收购于北流县（现北流市）物资局，出土于北流县平政区六沙公社牛岑 Collected at Beiliu County Material Bureau in July, 1965; unearthed at Niucen, Liusha Community, Pingzheng District, Beiliu County.	鼓面：太阳纹 (8 芒)、雷纹，鼓面边缘饰四只逆时针四足素面立体青蛙；鼓身：云纹、雷纹；环耳两对饰缠丝纹 Drum face: patterns of sun(8 rays), thunder; 4 frogs with 4 feet and blank back stand anticlockwise on the edge; Drum body: patterns of cloud and thunder; Silk-like patterns on 2 pairs of ring handles.	68.3−69	37.8	北流型 Beiliu Type	

续表

序号 NO.	原编号及鼓名 Stock Number & Name	收藏单位 Museum	出土（征集） 时间、地点 Time & Spot for discovered or collected	主要装饰 Main Decorations	尺寸（厘米） Size(cm)		类型 Type	图片 Picture
					面径 Face Diameter	身高 Height		
114	族鼓 0117 乘骑饰变形羽人纹 ZG No.0117 Bronze Drum with horse-ride statue and transformed feathermen patterns	广西民族博物馆 Anthropology Museum of Guangxi	来源不详，原存广西壮族自治区博物馆 Original source unknown; preserved previously in Museum of Guangxi Zhuang Autonomous Region	鼓面：太阳纹（12 芒）、水波纹、栉纹、同心圆纹、复线交叉纹、变形羽人纹、羽纹、变形翔鹭纹、眼纹，鼓面边缘饰四只逆时针四足谷穗纹立体青蛙，蛙间饰乘骑； 鼓身：栉纹、同心圆纹、船纹、水波纹、变形羽人纹、羽纹、网纹、圆心三角垂叶纹间半太阳纹、眼纹；扁耳两对饰辫纹，环形附耳一对饰缠丝纹 Drum face: patterns of sun(12rays), water wave, comb line, concentric circles, crossed double lines, transformed feathermen, feather, transformed flying heron, diamond-shape eye; 4 frog statues of 4 feet and rice ears on back anticlockwise stand on the edge of drum face; horse-rider statue between the frogs; Drum body: patterns of comb line, concentric circles, boat, water wave, transformed feathermen, feather, net, leaf-shape triangle with circle in the middle mixed semi-sun, diamond-shape eye; Braid patterns on 2 pairs of flat handles, silk-like patterns on a pair of attached ring handles.	72.5～73.3	51	冷水冲型 Lengshui-chong Type	
115	族鼓 0118 ZG No.0118 雷纹铜鼓 Bronze Drum with thunder patterns	广西民族博物馆 Anthropology Museum of Guangxi	来源不详，原存广西壮族自治区博物馆 Original source unknown; preserved previously in Museum of Guangxi Zhuang Autonomous Region	鼓面：太阳纹（8 芒）、雷纹，鼓面边缘饰四只顺时针四足蛙； 鼓身：雷纹，环耳两对饰缠丝纹 Drum face: patterns of sun(8 rays), thunder; 4 frogs with 4 feet and blank back stand clockwisly on the edge; Drum body: patterns of thunder; Silk-like patterns on 2 pairs of ring handles.	85.8	50	北流型 Beiliu Type	

序号 N0.	原编号及鼓名 Stock Number & Name	收藏单位 Museum	出土（征集） 时间、地点 Time & Spot for discovered or collected	主要装饰 Main Decorations	尺寸（厘米） Size(cm)		类型 Type	图片 Picture
					面径 Face Diameter	身高 Height		
116	族鼓 0119 大新铜鼓 ZG No.0119 Bronze Drum Daxin	广西民族博物馆 Anthropology Museum of Guangxi	1958 年出土于贵港市平南县大新区铜鼓山 Unearthed at Tonggu Hill, Daxin District, Pingnan County, Guigang City in 1958	鼓面：太阳纹（13 芒）、栉纹、同心圆纹、复线交叉纹、变形羽人纹变形、变形翔鹭纹间定胜纹，鼓面边缘饰四只逆时针四足素面立体青蛙； 鼓身：栉纹、同心圆纹、素纹栉纹同心圆纹垂直纹带、圆心三角垂叶纹、扁耳两对饰辫纹 Drum face: patterns of sun(13rays), comb line, concentric circles, crossed double lines, transformed feathermen, transformed flying heron mixed Dingsheng; 4 frog statues of 4 feet and blank back anticlockwise stand on the edge of drum face; Drum body: patterns of comb line, concentric circles, vertical ribbon of blank, straight line and concentric circle, leaf-shape triangle with circle in the middle; Braid patterns on 2 pairs of flat handles.	69–70	47.4	冷水冲型 Lengshui-chong Type	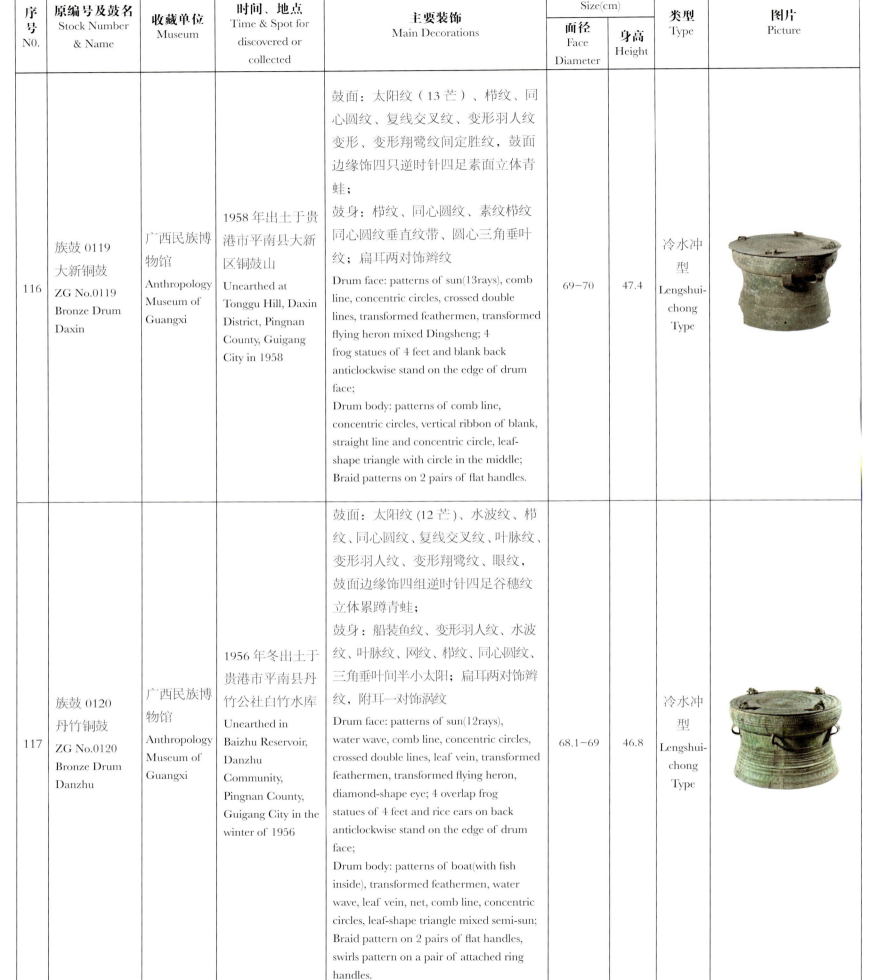
117	族鼓 0120 丹竹铜鼓 ZG No.0120 Bronze Drum Danzhu	广西民族博物馆 Anthropology Museum of Guangxi	1956 年冬出土于贵港市平南县丹竹公社白竹水库 Unearthed in Baizhu Reservoir, Danzhu Community, Pingnan County, Guigang City in the winter of 1956	鼓面：太阳纹(12 芒)、水波纹、栉纹、同心圆纹、复线交叉纹、叶脉纹、变形羽人纹、变形翔鹭纹、眼纹，鼓面边缘饰四组逆时针四足谷穗纹立体累蹲青蛙； 鼓身：船装鱼纹、变形羽人纹、水波纹、叶脉纹、网纹、栉纹、同心圆纹、三角垂叶间半小太阳；扁耳两对饰辫纹，附耳一对饰涡纹 Drum face: patterns of sun(12rays), water wave, comb line, concentric circles, crossed double lines, leaf vein, transformed feathermen, transformed flying heron, diamond-shape eye; 4 overlap frog statues of 4 feet and rice ears on back anticlockwise stand on the edge of drum face; Drum body: patterns of boat(with fish inside), transformed feathermen, water wave, leaf vein, net, comb line, concentric circles, leaf-shape triangle mixed semi-sun; Braid pattern on 2 pairs of flat handles, swirls pattern on a pair of attached ring handles.	68.1–69	46.8	冷水冲型 Lengshui-chong Type	

续表

序号 NO.	原编号及鼓名 Stock Number & Name	收藏单位 Museum	出土（征集）时间、地点 Time & Spot for discovered or collected	主要装饰 Main Decorations	尺寸（厘米） Size(cm)		类型 Type	图片 Picture
					面径 Face Diameter	身高 Height		
118	族鼓 0121 翔鹭纹骑士纹铜鼓 ZG No.0121 Bronze Drum with flying heron and rider patterns	广西民族博物馆 Anthropology Museum of Guangxi	1964 年出土于梧州市藤县古龙公社 Unearthed at Gulong Community, Teng County, Wuzhou in 1964	鼓面：太阳纹（12 芒）、水波纹、同心圆纹、席纹、复线交叉纹、羽纹、变形羽人纹、变形翔鹭间双鸟纹、骑士纹、眼纹，鼓面边缘饰四只逆时针四足谷穗纹立体青蛙（两蛙已失），蛙间有立饰痕迹； 鼓身：水波纹、席纹、同心圆纹、船纹、变形羽人纹、羽纹、网纹、圆心三角垂叶纹间半同心圆纹、眼纹；扁耳两对饰辫纹，环形附耳一对饰羽纹 Drum face: patterns of sun(12rays), water wave, concentric circles, woven mat, crossed double lines, feather, transformed feathermen, transformed flying heron mixed 2 birds, rider, diamond-shape eye; 4 frog statues of 4 feet and rice ears on back anticlockwise stand on the edge of drum face(two lost); marks of statues between the frogs; Drum body: patterns of water wave, woven mat, concentric circles, boat, transformed feathermen, feather, net, leaf-shape triangle with concentric circle inside mixed semi-concentric circle, diamond-shape eye; Braid patterns on 2 pairs of flat handles, feather pattern on a pair of attached ring handles.	82-84.5	61.3	冷水冲型 Lengshui-chong Type	
119	族鼓 0122 变形羽人纹铜鼓 ZG No.0122 Bronze Drum with transformed feather patterns	广西民族博物馆 Anthropology Museum of Guangxi	1954 年采集于合浦县 Collected in Hepu County in 1954	鼓面：太阳纹（8 芒）、虫形纹、云纹、四瓣花填线纹、兽形纹、半同心圆羽纹、席纹、蝉纹，鼓面边缘饰六只逆时针三足羽纹立体青蛙； 鼓身：同心圆纹、席纹、云纹、半同心圆羽纹、四瓣花填线纹、兽形纹、蝉纹；扁耳两对饰羽纹 Drum face: patterns of sun(8rays), insect, cloud, quatrefoil filled with straight lines, beast-shape motif, semi-concentric circle mixed feather, woven mat, cicada; 6 frogs with 3 feet and feather patterns on back anticlockwise stand on the edge; Drum body: patterns of concentric circle, woven mat, cloud, semi-concentric circle mixed feather, quatrefoil filled with straight lines, beast-shape motif, cicada; feather patterns on 2 pairs of flat handles.	75.4-75.7	46.5	灵山型 Lingshan Type	

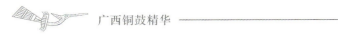

序号 N0.	原编号及鼓名 Stock Number & Name	收藏单位 Museum	出土（征集）时间、地点 Time & Spot for discovered or collected	主要装饰 Main Decorations	尺寸（厘米）Size(cm)		类型 Type	图片 Picture
					面径 Face Diameter	身高 Height		
120	族鼓 0123 下渡铜鼓 ZG No.0123 Bronze Drum Xiadu	广西民族博物馆 Anthropology Museum of Guangxi	1958 年出土于贵港市平南县上渡公社下渡水闸 Unearthed at Xiadu Watergate, Shangdu Community, Pingnan County, Guigang City in 1958	鼓面：太阳纹（12 芒）、水波纹、栉纹、同心圆纹、复线交叉纹、羽纹、变形羽人纹、变形翔鹭纹、眼纹、斜线纹，鼓面边缘饰四只逆时针四足谷穗纹立体青蛙（一蛙已失），两蛙间分饰三组累蹲蛙；鼓身：羽纹、栉纹、同心圆纹、水波纹、船纹、变形羽人纹、网纹、圆心三角垂叶间半同心圆纹、眼纹；扁耳两对饰辫纹；环形附耳饰谷穗纹；鼓内胸、足各对称两对附耳 Drum face: patterns of sun(12rays), water wave, comb line, concentric circles, crossed double lines, feather, transformed feathermen, transfored flying heron, diamond-shape eye, oblique line; 4 frog statues of 4 feet and rice ears on back anticlockwise stand on the edge of drum face; 3(one lost) groups of overlap frog statues between the frogs; Drum body: patterns of feather, comb line, concentric circles, water wave, boat, transformed feathermen, net, leaf-shape triangle with circle in the middle mixed semi-concentric circle, diamond-shape eye; Braid patterns on 2 pairs of flat handles; rice ear patterns on a pair of attached ring handles inside the drum, 2 pairs of ring handles separately on the chest and the foot.	76—77	52.5	冷水冲型 Lengshui-chong Type	
121	族鼓 0124 下陶村铜鼓 ZG No.0124 Bronze Drum Xiatao Cun	广西民族博物馆 Anthropology Museum of Guangxi	1962 年出土于贵港市平南县思旺区三江乡下陶村 Unearthed at Xiatao Village, Sanjiang, Siwang District, Pingnan County, Guigang City in 1962	鼓面：太阳纹（12 芒）、水波纹、栉纹、同心圆纹、复线交叉纹、变形羽人、变形翔鹭纹、眼纹，鼓面边缘饰四只逆时针四足谷穗纹立体青蛙；鼓身：羽纹、栉纹、同心圆纹、船纹、变形羽人纹、网纹、圆心三角垂叶纹；扁耳两对饰羽纹 Drum face: patterns of sun(12rays), water wave, comb line, concentric circles, crossed double lines, transformed feathermen, transformed flying heron, diamond-shape eye; 4 frog statues of 4 feet and rice ears on back anticlockwise stand on the edge of drum face; Drum body: patterns of feather, comb line, concentric circles, boat, transformed feathermen, net, leaf-shape triangle with circle in the middle; feather patterns on 2 pairs of flat handles.	56.8—57.3	38	冷水冲型 Lengshui-chong Type	

续表

序号 NO.	原编号及鼓名 Stock Number & Name	收藏单位 Museum	出土（征集）时间、地点 Time & Spot for discovered or collected	主要装饰 Main Decorations	尺寸（厘米）Size(cm)		类型 Type	图片 Picture
					面径 Face Diameter	身高 Height		
122	族鼓 0125 花鸟雷纹铜鼓 ZG No.0125 Bronze Drum with flower, bird and thunder patterns	广西民族博物馆 Anthropology Museum of Guangxi	来源不详，原存广西壮族自治区博物馆 Original source unknown; preserved previously in Museum of Guangxi Zhuang Autonomous Region	鼓面：太阳纹（10芒）、蝉纹、雷纹、四瓣花填线纹、鸟纹、云纹、虫形纹、席纹、兽形纹、半同心圆纹，鼓面边缘饰四只逆时针三足素面立体青蛙（两蛙已失）； 鼓身：四瓣花填线纹、云纹、兽面纹、席纹、蝉纹、雷纹填线纹、虫形纹、雷纹、鸟纹、半同心圆纹；扁耳两对饰辫纹 Drum face: patterns of sun(10rays), cicada, thunder, quatrefoil filled with straight lines, bird, cloud, insect, woven mat, beast-shape motif, semi-concentric circle; 4 frogs with 3 feet and blank back anticlockwise stand on the edge(two lost); Drum body: patterns of quatrefoil filled with straight lines, cloud, beast face, woven mat, cicada, thunder filled with straight lines, insect, thunder, bird, semi-concentric circle; Braid patterns on 2 pairs of flat handles.	77.7–78	49.5	灵山型 Lingshan Type	
123	族鼓 0126 雷纹铜鼓 ZG No.0126 Bronze Drum with thunder patterns	广西民族博物馆 Anthropology Museum of Guangxi	收购于梧州市藤县濛江区供销社 Collected at mengjiang District Supply& Marketing Cooperative, Teng County, Wuzhou City	鼓面：太阳纹（9芒）、变形羽人纹、雷纹，鼓面边缘饰四只逆时针四只素面立体青蛙； 鼓身：雷纹填线纹、半圆填线纹、复线角形纹、半同心圆填线纹、变形羽人纹、半雷纹填线纹；扁耳两对饰羽纹 Drum face: patterns of sun(9rays), transformed feathermen, thunder; 4 frog statues of 4 feet and blank back anticlockwise stand on the edge of drum face; Drum body: patterns of thunder filled with straight line & semicircle filled with straight line, double line triangle, transformed feathermen, semi-thunder filled with straight line; Feather patterns on 2 pairs of flat handle.	68–69.3	44	冷水冲型 Lengshuichong Type	

279

序号 N0.	原编号及鼓名 Stock Number & Name	收藏单位 Museum	出土（征集） 时间、地点 Time & Spot for discovered or collected	主要装饰 Main Decorations	尺寸（厘米） Size(cm)		类型 Type	图片 Picture
					面径 Face Diameter	身高 Height		
124	族鼓 0128 安矿村铜鼓 ZG No.0128 Bronze Drum Ankuang Cun	广西民族博物馆 Anthropology Museum of Guangxi	1966 年 1 月 31 日出土于玉林市陆川县平东八晋安矿村 Unearthed at Ankuang Village, Bajin, Pingdong, Luchuan County, Yulin City on January 31st, 1966	鼓面：太阳纹（10 芒）、雷纹、四出钱纹、云纹、雷纹填线纹、虫形纹、鼓面边缘饰六组顺时针三足羽纹立体累蹲青蛙（两组已失）； 鼓身：云纹、雷纹、虫形纹、四出钱纹、席纹；扁耳两对饰羽纹、乳钉纹、环形附耳一对饰缠丝纹 Drum face: patterns of sun(10rays), thunder, coins with quadrangle inside, cloud, thunder filled with straight line, insect; 6 overlap frogs with 3 feet and feather patterns on back clockwise stand on the edge(two lost); Drum body: patterns of cloud, thunder, insect, coins with quadrangle inside, woven mat; Feather and nipple protrusion patterns on 2 pairs of flat handles, silk-like patterns on a pair of attached ring handles.	93.5~95	52 （残） Incomplete	灵山型 Lingshan Type	
125	族鼓 0129 云雷纹铜鼓 ZG No.0129 Bronze Drum with cloud & thunder patterns	广西民族博物馆 Anthropology Museum of Guangxi	南宁市出土 Unearthed in Nanning City	鼓面：太阳纹（8 芒）、雷纹、半同心圆填线纹交替，鼓面边缘饰六只顺时针四足素面立体青蛙； 鼓身：半同心圆填线纹、雷纹填线纹；扁耳两对饰辫纹、网格纹 Drum face: patterns of sun(8 rays), thunder and semi-concentric circle filled with straight line arrayed in turn; 6 frogs with 4 feet and plain back clockwise stand on the edge; Drum body: patterns of semi-concentric circle filled with straight line, thunder filled with straight line; Braid and grid patterns on 2 pairs of flat handles.	97.5~100.3	53.6	北流型 Beiliu Type	
126	族鼓 0130 变形羽人纹铜鼓 ZG No.0130 Bronze Drum with transformed feathermen patterns	广西民族博物馆 Anthropology Museum of Guangxi	1963 年 11 月收购于梧州市废品收购站 Collected at Wuzhou City Waste Recycle Station in November, 1963	鼓面：太阳纹（12 芒）、栉纹、同心圆纹、复线交叉纹、变形羽人纹、变形翔鹭间定胜纹； 鼓身：栉纹、同心圆纹、素纹、栉纹、同心圆垂直纹带、圆心三角垂叶纹；扁耳两对饰羽纹。 Drum face: patterns of sun(12rays), comb line, concentric circle, crossed double lines, transformed feathermen, transformed flying heron mixed Disheng; Drum body: patterns of comb line, concentric circle, vertical ribbon of blank and concentric circle, leaf-shape triangle with circle in the middle; Feather patterns on 2 pairs of flat handle.	82~83	55 （残） Incomplete	冷水冲型 Lengshuichong Type	

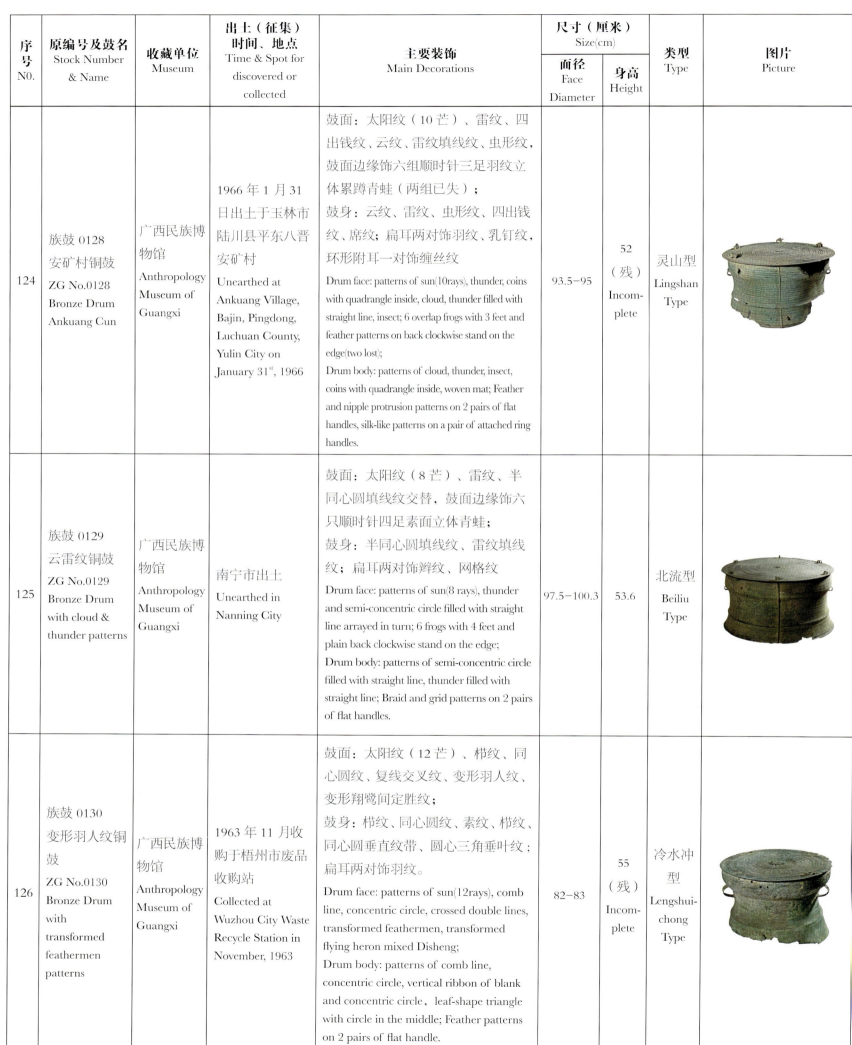

序号 N0.	原编号及鼓名 Stock Number & Name	收藏单位 Museum	出土（征集） 时间、地点 Time & Spot for discovered or collected	主要装饰 Main Decorations	尺寸（厘米） Size(cm)		类型 Type	图片 Picture
					面径 Face Diameter	身高 Height		
127	族鼓 0131 变形羽人纹铜鼓 ZG No.0131 Bronze Drum With transformed feathermen patterns	广西民族博物馆 Anthropology Museum of Guangxi	来源不详，原存广西壮族自治区博物馆 Original source unknown; preserved previously in Museum of Guangxi Zhuang Autonomous Region	鼓面：太阳纹（12 芒）、水波纹、同心圆纹、栉纹、复线交叉纹、变形羽人纹、变形翔鹭纹、切线同心圆纹、羽纹，鼓面边缘饰四只逆时针四足 立体青蛙； 鼓身：栉纹、同心圆纹、船纹、变形羽人纹、水波纹、圆心三角垂叶纹、羽纹、眼纹；扁耳两对饰羽纹 Drum face: patterns of sun(12rays), water wave, concentric circles, comb line, crossed double lines, transformed feathermen, transformed flying heron, tangent concentric circles, feather; 4 frog statues of 4 feet anticlockwise stand on the edge of drum face; Drum body: patterns of comb line, concentric circles, boat, ransformed feathermen, water wave, leaf-shape triangle with concentric circle in the middle, feather, diamod-shape eye; feather patterns on 2 pairs of flat handles.	76~77.5	52.4	冷水冲型 Lengshui-chong Type	
128	族鼓 0132 变形羽人纹铜鼓 ZG No.0132 Bronze Drum With transformed feathermen patterns	广西民族博物馆 Anthropology Museum of Guangxi	来源不详，原存广西壮族自治区博物馆 Original source unknown; preserved previously in Museum of Guangxi Zhuang Autonomous Region	鼓面：太阳纹（8 芒）、四出钱纹、四瓣花纹、席纹、虫形纹、四瓣花填线纹、兽面纹、比伦钱纹、连钱纹、骑兽纹、雷纹填线纹、鸟形纹、蝉纹，鼓面边缘饰六只逆时针三足栉纹、羽纹立体青蛙（一只已失）； 鼓身：蝉纹、四出钱纹、四瓣花纹、兽面纹、虫形纹、四瓣花填线纹、席纹、比伦钱纹、骑兽纹、连钱纹、雷纹填线纹、鸟纹；扁耳两对饰辫纹 Drum face: patterns of sun(8rays), coins with quadrangle inside,quatrefoil, woven mat, insect−shape motif, quatrefoil filled with straight line, beast face, Bilun Coin, coins part of overlap, beastback−rider, thunder filled with straight line, bird, cicada; 6 frogs with 3 feet and straight line & feather patterns on back anticlockwise stand on the edge(one lost); Drum body: patterns of cicada, coins with quadrangle inside, quatrefoil, beast face, insect-shape motif, quatrefoil filled with straight line, woven mat, Bilun Coin, beastback-rider, coins part of overlap, thunder filled with straight line, bird; Braid patterns on 2 pairs of flat handles.	90.4~91.5	50 （残） Incom-plete	灵山型 Lingshan Type	

序号 N0.	原编号及鼓名 Stock Number & Name	收藏单位 Museum	出土（征集）时间、地点 Time & Spot for discovered or collected	主要装饰 Main Decorations	尺寸（厘米）Size(cm)		类型 Type	图片 Picture
					面径 Face Diameter	身高 Height		
129	族鼓 0134 变形羽人纹铜鼓 ZG No.0134 Bronze Drum with transformed feathermen patterns	广西民族博物馆 Anthropology Museum of Guangxi	前广西文教厅拨交，原存广西壮族自治区博物馆 Allocated by Guangxi Cultural and Educational Bureau(Previous Name); Preserved previously in Museum of Guangxi Zhuang Autonomous Region	鼓面：太阳纹（12 芒）、羽纹、栉纹、切线同心圆纹、复线交叉纹、变形羽人纹、变形翔鹭间定胜纹、鼓面边缘饰四只逆时针四足素面立体青蛙；鼓身：栉纹、切线同心圆纹、羽纹、素 / 栉纹 / 切线同心圆纹垂直纹带、圆心三角垂叶间同心圆纹；扁耳两对饰辫纹 Drum face: patterns of sun(12rays), feather, comb line, tangent concentric circles, crossed double lines, transformed feathermen, transformed flying heron mixed Dingsheng; 4 frog statues of 4 feet and blank back anticlockwise stand on the edge of drum face; Drum body: patterns of comb line, tangent concentric circles, feather, vertical ribbon of blank, straight line and tangent concentric circles, leaf-shape triangle with concentric circle in the middle; Braid patterns on 2 pairs of flat handles.	66.3~67	44	冷水冲型 Lengshui-chong Type	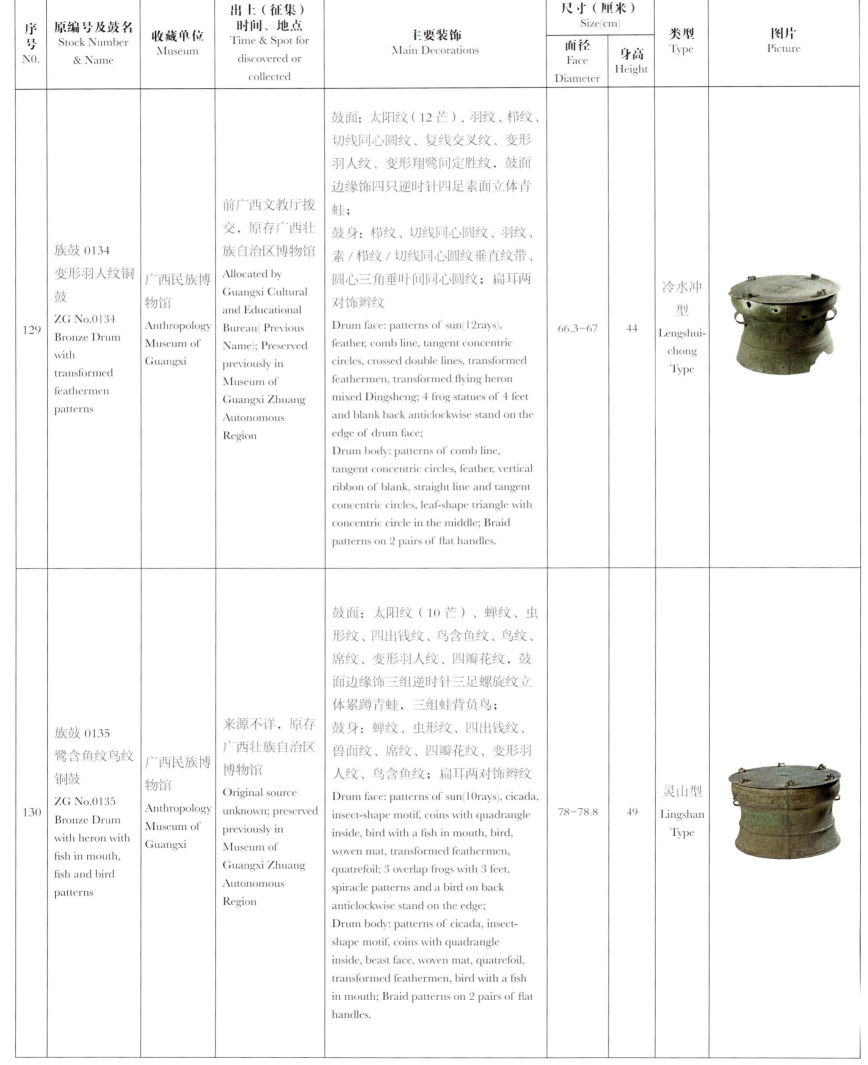
130	族鼓 0135 鹭含鱼纹鸟纹铜鼓 ZG No.0135 Bronze Drum with heron with fish in mouth, fish and bird patterns	广西民族博物馆 Anthropology Museum of Guangxi	来源不详，原存广西壮族自治区博物馆 Original source unknown; preserved previously in Museum of Guangxi Zhuang Autonomous Region	鼓面：太阳纹（10 芒）、蝉纹、虫形纹、四出钱纹、鸟含鱼纹、鸟纹、席纹、变形羽人纹、四瓣花纹、鼓面边缘饰三组逆时针三足螺旋纹立体累蹲青蛙，三组蛙背负鸟；鼓身：蝉纹、虫形纹、四出钱纹、兽面纹、席纹、四瓣花纹、变形羽人纹、鸟含鱼纹；扁耳两对饰辫纹 Drum face: patterns of sun(10rays), cicada, insect-shape motif, coins with quadrangle inside, bird with a fish in mouth, bird, woven mat, transformed feathermen, quatrefoil; 3 overlap frogs with 3 feet, spiracle patterns and a bird on back anticlockwise stand on the edge; Drum body: patterns of cicada, insect-shape motif, coins with quadrangle inside, beast face, woven mat, quatrefoil, transformed feathermen, bird with a fish in mouth; Braid patterns on 2 pairs of flat handles.	78~78.8	49	灵山型 Lingshan Type	

序号 NO.	原编号及鼓名 Stock Number & Name	收藏单位 Museum	出土（征集） 时间、地点 Time & Spot for discovered or collected	主要装饰 Main Decorations	尺寸（厘米） Size(cm)		类型 Type	图片 Picture
					面径 Face Diameter	身高 Height		
131	族鼓 0136 变形羽人纹铜鼓 ZG No.0136 Bronze Drum with transformed feathermen patterns	广西民族博物馆 Anthropology Museum of Guangxi	1954 年征集于横县第一区 Collected at the first district of Hengxian County in 1954	鼓面：太阳纹（12 芒）、席纹、栉纹间勾连同心圆纹、复线交叉纹、变形羽人纹、变形翔鹭纹间定胜纹、压胜钱纹，鼓面饰四只逆时针四足立体青蛙； 鼓身：栉纹间勾连同心圆纹、变形划船纹、变形羽人纹；扁耳两对饰辫纹 Drum face: patterns of sun(12rays), woven mat, straight line& tangent concentric circles, crossed double lines, transformed feathermen, transformed flying heron mixed Dingsheng, Yasheng Coin; 4 frog statues of 4 feet anticlockwise stand on the edge of drum face; Drum body: patterns of straight line&tangent concentric circles, transformed boat, transformed feathermen; Braid patterns on 2 pairs of flat handles.	75.2	49.1	冷水冲型 Lengshui-chong Type	
132	族鼓 0137 云雷纹铜鼓 ZG No.0137 Bronze Drum with cloud & thunder patterns	广西民族博物馆 Anthropology Museum of Guangxi	1954 年征集于梧州市岑溪县 Collected in Cenxi County, Wuzhou City in 1954	鼓面：太阳纹（8 芒）、云纹，鼓面边缘饰四只两两相对四足素面立体青蛙； 鼓身：云纹、雷纹填线纹；环耳两对饰缠丝纹 Drum face: patterns of sun(8 rays), cloud, 4 frogs with 4 feet and plain back stand on the edge, face to each other in pairs; Drum body: patterns of cloud, thunder filled with straight line; silk-like patterns on 2 pairs of ring handles.	93~94.4	53.8	北流型 Beiliu Type	
133	族鼓 0138 云雷纹铜鼓 ZG No.0138 Bronze Drum with transformed feathermen patterns	广西民族博物馆 Anthropology Museum of Guangxi	采集于容县 Collected in Rongxian County	鼓面：太阳纹（10 芒）、云纹、席纹，鼓面边缘饰六只顺时针四足素面立体青蛙； 鼓身：云纹、席纹；扁耳两对 Drum face: patterns of sun(10 rays), cloud, woven mat; 6 frogs with 4 feet and blank back clockwise stand on the edge; Drum body: patterns of cloud, woven mat; 2 pairs of flat handles.	83.6~84	50.3	北流型 Beiliu Type	

序号 N0.	原编号及鼓名 Stock Number & Name	收藏单位 Museum	出土（征集） 时间、地点 Time & Spot for discovered or collected	主要装饰 Main Decorations	尺寸（厘米） Size(cm)		类型 Type	图片 Picture
					面径 Face Diameter	身高 Height		
134	族鼓 0139 云雷纹铜鼓 ZG No.0139 Bronze Drum with cloud& thunder patterns	广西民族博物馆 Anthropology Museum of Guangxi	采集于北流县 （现北流市）第 十一区 Collected at District 11, Beiliu County	鼓面：太阳纹（8芒）、云纹、雷纹，鼓面边缘饰四只顺时针四足素面立体青蛙； 鼓身：雷纹、云纹；环耳两对饰缠丝纹 Drum face: patterns of sun(8 rays), cloud, thunder; 4 frogs with 4 feet and blank back clockwise stand on the edge; Drum body: patterns of cloud, thunder; Silk-like patterns on 2 pairs of ring handles.	123-124	65.5	北流型 Beiliu Type	
135	族鼓 0140 云雷纹铜鼓 ZG No.0140 Bronze Drum with cloud& thunder patterns	广西民族博物馆 Anthropology Museum of Guangxi	采集于玉林市博白县 Collected in Bobai County, Yulin City	鼓面：太阳纹（8芒）、可辨雷纹，其余磨蚀，鼓面边缘饰六只顺时针四足素面立体青蛙； 鼓身：可辨雷纹、半同心圆纹、水波纹、席纹、钱纹，其余磨蚀；环耳两对，一侧环耳上各对应一对小蛙立饰 Drum face: patterns of sun(8 rays), thunder, the other patterns are obscure; 6 frogs with 4 feet and blank back clockwisly stand on the edge; Drum body: patterns of thunder, semi-concentric circle, water wave, woven mat, coin, the other patterns are obscure; 2 pairs of ring handles; a pair of little frog-statues on the chest beyond 2 of the handles.	114.5-115.3	63.5	北流型 Beiliu Type	

续表

序号 NO.	原编号及鼓名 Stock Number & Name	收藏单位 Museum	出土（征集）时间、地点 Time & Spot for discovered or collected	主要装饰 Main Decorations	尺寸（厘米）Size(cm)		类型 Type	图片 Picture
					面径 Face Diameter	身高 Height		
136	族鼓 0141 骑上纹铜鼓 ZG No.0141 Bronze Drum with rider patterns	广西民族博物馆 Anthropology Museum of Guangxi	来源不详，原存广西壮族自治区博物馆 Original source unknown; preserved previously in Museum of Guangxi Zhuang Autonomous Region	鼓面：太阳纹（10 芒）、五字钱纹、席纹、四出钱纹、兽面纹、虫形纹、比伦钱纹、兽形纹、雷纹、鸟纹、四瓣花纹、蝉纹，鼓面边缘饰六组逆时针三足谷穗纹涡纹立体青蛙（其中三组为累蹲蛙）； 鼓身：虫形纹、半同心圆填线纹、四出钱纹、兽面纹、鸟纹、比伦钱纹、雷纹、四瓣花纹、席纹、五字钱纹、兽形纹、蝉纹；扁耳两对饰羽纹、谷穗纹 Drum face: patterns of sun(10rays), 五-character coin, woven mat, coins with quadrangle inside, beast face, insect-shape motif, Bilun Coin, beast, thunder, bird, quatrefoil, cicada; 6 frogs with 3 feet and rice ear, swirls patterns on back anticlockwise stand on the edge(three of them are overlap); Drum body: patterns of insect-shape motif, semi-concentric circle filled with straight line, coins with quadrangle inside, beast face, bird, Bilun Coin, thunder, quatrefoil, woven mat, 五-character coin, beast, cicada; Feather and rice ear patterns on 2 pairs of flat handles.	85.2—86	50.8	灵山型 Lingshan Type	
137	族鼓 0142 四出钱纹铜鼓 ZG No.0142 Bronze Drum with coin with quadrangle inside patterns	广西民族博物馆 Anthropology Museum of Guangxi	采集于南宁市横县 Collected in Hengxian County, Nanning	鼓面：太阳纹（12 芒）、连钱纹、席纹、四出钱纹、鸟纹、四瓣花填线纹、虫形纹、雷纹填线纹、兽形纹、蝉纹，鼓面边缘饰六只逆时针三足立体青蛙（已失）； 鼓身：蝉纹、连钱纹、四出钱纹、鸟纹、虫形纹、雷纹填线纹、席纹、兽形纹；扁耳两对饰羽纹，一侧鼓耳下有一穿山甲立饰 Drum face: patterns of sun(12rays), coins part of overlap, woven mat, coins with quadrangle inside, bird, quatrefoil filled with straight line, insect-shape motif, thunder filled with straight line, beast, cicada; 6 frogs with 3 feet anticlockwise stand on the edge(lost); Drum body: patterns of cicada, coins part of overlap, coins with quadrangle inside, bird, insect-shape motif, thunder filled with straight line, woven mat, beast; Feather patterns on 2 pairs of flat handles; A pangolin statue under one of the handle.	92—93	55.5 （残） Incomplete	灵山型 Lingshan Type	

序号 N0.	原编号及鼓名 Stock Number & Name	收藏单位 Museum	出土（征集） 时间、地点 Time & Spot for discovered or collected	主要装饰 Main Decorations	尺寸（厘米） Size(cm)		类型 Type	图片 Picture
					面径 Face Diameter	身高 Height		
138	族鼓 0143 云雷纹水波纹 铜鼓 ZG No.0143 Bronze Drum with cloud, thunder and water wave patterns	广西民族博物馆 Anthropology Museum of Guangxi	1954 年征集于贵港市平南县 Collected in Pingnan County, Guigang City in 1954	鼓面：太阳纹（12 芒）、云纹、雷纹交替，鼓面边缘饰六只逆时针四足立体青蛙，蛙间有一四足立饰痕迹； 鼓身：水波纹、云纹、雷纹；环耳两对饰凸棱纹 Drum face: patterns of sun(12 rays), cloud and thunder arrayed in turn; 6 frogs with 4 feet anticlockwise stand on the edge, mark of a 4-feet statue between the frogs; Drum body: patterns of water wave, cloud, thunder; Raise ridges on 2 pairs of ring handles.	122−122.5	68.4	北流型 Beiliu Type	
139	族鼓 0144 鸟纹铜鼓 ZG No.0144 Bronze Drum with bird patterns	广西民族博物馆 Anthropology Museum of Guangxi	1954 年采集于贵县（现贵港市） Collected in Guixian County(Now Guigang City) in 1954	鼓面：太阳纹（9 芒）、席纹、比伦钱纹、兽面纹、四出钱纹、连钱纹、鸟纹、虫形纹、四瓣花纹、蝉纹，鼓面边缘饰六只逆时针三足素面立体青蛙（五只已失）； 鼓身：四出钱纹、虫形纹、比伦钱纹、席纹、四瓣花纹、兽面纹、连钱纹、鸟纹、蝉纹；扁耳两对饰羽纹 Drum face: patterns of sun(9rays), woven mat, Bilun Coin, beast face, coins with quadrangle inside, coins part of overlap, bird, insect-shape motif, quatrefoil, cicada; 6 frogs with 3 feet and blank back anticlockwise stand on the edge(five lost); Drum body: patterns of coins with quadrangle inside, insect-shape motif, Bilun Coin, woven mat, quatrefoil; beast face, coins part of overlap, bird,cicada; Feather patterns on 2 pairs of flat handles.	95.8−97.5	55.3	灵山型 Lingshan Type	
140	族鼓 0146 云纹铜鼓 ZG No.0146 Bronze Drum with cloud patterns	广西民族博物馆 Anthropology Museum of Guangxi	采集于梧州市岑溪县 Collected in Cenxi County, Wuzhou	鼓面：太阳纹（9 芒）、云纹，鼓面边缘饰四只顺时针四足羽纹立体青蛙； 鼓身：雷纹填线纹、云纹、水波纹；扁耳两对饰羽纹 Drum face: patterns of sun(9rays), cloud; 4 frogs with 4 feet clockwise stand on the edge; Drum body: patterns of thunder filled with straight line, cloud, water wave; Feather patterns on 2 pairs of flat handles.	92.8−94	54.3	北流型 Beiliu Type	

序号 NO.	原编号及鼓名 Stock Number & Name	收藏单位 Museum	出土（征集） 时间、地点 Time & Spot for discovered or collected	主要装饰 Main Decorations	尺寸（厘米） Size(cm)		类型 Type	图片 Picture
					面径 Face Diameter	身高 Height		
141	族鼓 0147 四出钱纹铜鼓 ZG No.0147 Bronze Drum with coin with quad rangle inside patterns	广西民族博物馆 Anthropology Museum of Guangxi	采集于玉林县（现玉林市）第十一区 Collected in District 11, Yulin City	鼓面：太阳纹（10 芒）、蝉纹、兽形纹、连钱纹、四出钱纹、鸟纹、虫形纹、四瓣花填线纹、席纹、变形羽人纹，鼓面边缘饰六只逆时针三足立体青蛙（已失）； 鼓身：蝉纹、席纹、虫形纹、四出钱纹、鸟纹、连钱纹、四瓣花填线纹、兽形纹、变形羽人纹、雷纹填线纹；扁耳两对饰辫纹 Drum face: patterns of sun(10rays), cicada, beast, coins part of overlap, coins with quadrangle inside, bird, insect-shape motif, quatrefoil filled with straight line, woven mat, transformed feathermen; 6 frogs with 3 feet anticlockwise stand on the edge(lost); Drum body: patterns of cicada, woven mat, insect-shape motif, coins with quadrangle inside, bird, coins part of overlap, quatrefoil filled with straight line, beast, transformed feathermen, thunder filled with straight line; Braid patterns on 2 pairs of flat handles.	103.5－104	59	灵山型 Lingshan Type	
142	族鼓 0149 变形羽人纹铜鼓 ZG No.0149 Bronze Drum with transformed feathermen patterns	广西民族博物馆 Anthropology Museum of Guangxi	征购于南宁市宾阳县 Collected in Binyang County, Nanning City	鼓面：太阳纹（12 芒）、羽纹、栉纹、同心圆纹、复线交叉纹、变形羽人纹、变形翔鹭间定胜纹，鼓面边缘饰四只逆时针四足素面立体青蛙； 鼓身：羽纹、栉纹、同心圆纹、羽纹栉纹同心圆纹垂直纹带、三角垂叶纹；扁耳两对饰叶脉纹 Drum face: patterns of sun(12rays), feather, comb line, concentric circles, crossed double lines, transformed feathermen, transformed flying heron mixed Dingsheng; 4 frog statues of 4 feet and blank back anticlockwise stand on the edge of drum face; Drum body: patterns of feather, comb line, concentric circles, vertical ribbon of feather, straight line and tangent concentric circles, leaf-shape triangle; leaf vein patterns on 2 pairs of flat handles.	66.3－66.7	45.5	冷水冲型 Lengshui-chong Type	

序号 N0.	原编号及鼓名 Stock Number & Name	收藏单位 Museum	出土（征集）时间、地点 Time & Spot for discovered or collected	主要装饰 Main Decorations	尺寸（厘米） Size(cm)		类型 Type	图片 Picture
					面径 Face Diameter	身高 Height		
143	族鼓 0150 云纹铜鼓 ZG No.0150 Bronze Drum with cloud patterns	广西民族博物馆 Anthropology Museum of Guangxi	来源不详，原存广西壮族自治区博物馆 Original source unknown; preserved previously in Museum of Guangxi Zhuang Autonomous Region	鼓面：太阳纹（8芒）、虫形纹、云纹、花纹、云纹、水波纹、半同心圆羽纹，鼓面边缘饰六只顺时针四足素面立体青蛙； 鼓身：云纹、花纹、半同心圆纹填线纹、水波纹；扁耳两对 Drum face: patterns of sun(8rays), insect-shape motif, cloud, flower, cloud & water wave, semi-concentric circle in feather; 6 frogs with 4 feet and blank back clockwise stand on the edge; Drum body: patterns of cloud, flower, semi-concentric circle filled with straight line, water wave; 2 pairs of flat handles.	71—71.5	34.5 （残） Incom-plete	灵山型 Lingshan Type	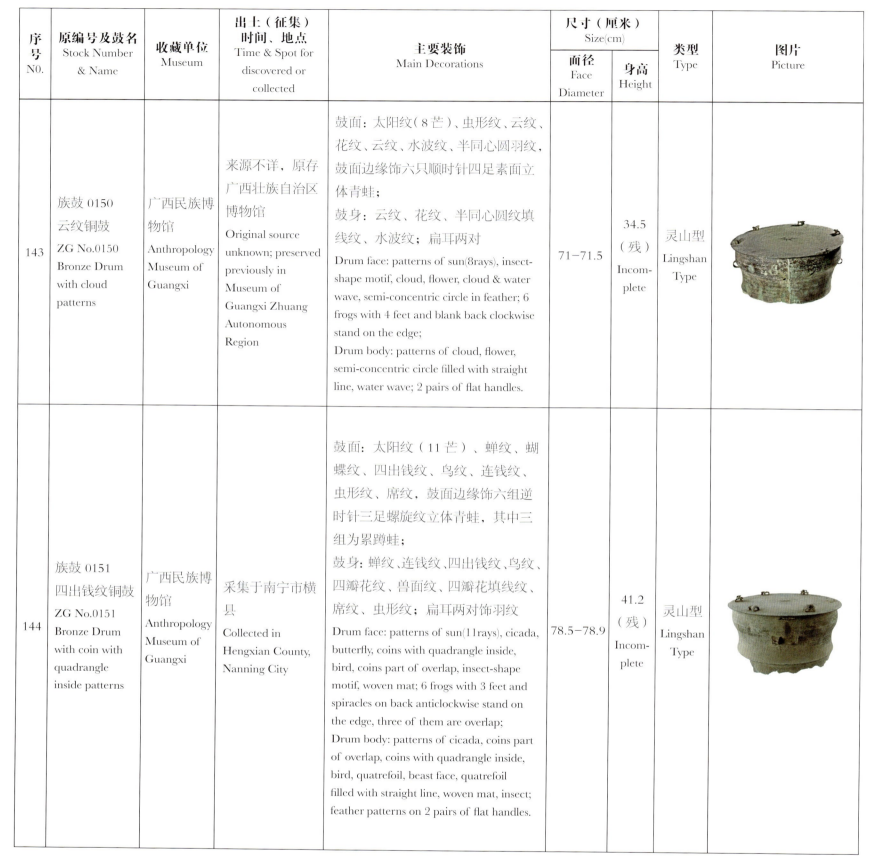
144	族鼓 0151 四出钱纹铜鼓 ZG No.0151 Bronze Drum with coin with quadrangle inside patterns	广西民族博物馆 Anthropology Museum of Guangxi	采集于南宁市横县 Collected in Hengxian County, Nanning City	鼓面：太阳纹（11芒）、蝉纹、蝴蝶纹、四出钱纹、鸟纹、连钱纹、虫形纹、席纹，鼓面边缘饰六组逆时针三足螺旋纹立体青蛙，其中三组为累蹲蛙； 鼓身：蝉纹、连钱纹、四出钱纹、鸟纹、四瓣花纹、兽面纹、四瓣花填线纹、席纹、虫形纹；扁耳两对饰羽纹 Drum face: patterns of sun(11rays), cicada, butterfly, coins with quadrangle inside, bird, coins part of overlap, insect-shape motif, woven mat; 6 frogs with 3 feet and spiracles on back anticlockwise stand on the edge, three of them are overlap; Drum body: patterns of cicada, coins part of overlap, coins with quadrangle inside, bird, quatrefoil, beast face, quatrefoil filled with straight line, woven mat, insect; feather patterns on 2 pairs of flat handles.	78.5—78.9	41.2 （残） Incom-plete	灵山型 Lingshan Type	

续表

序号 NO.	原编号及鼓名 Stock Number & Name	收藏单位 Museum	出土（征集） 时间、地点 Time & Spot for discovered or collected	主要装饰 Main Decorations	尺寸（厘米） Size(cm)		类型 Type	图片 Picture
					面径 Face Diameter	身高 Height		
145	族鼓 0152 变形羽人纹铜鼓 ZG No.0152 Bronze Drum with transformed feather patterns	广西民族博物馆 Anthropology Museum of Guangxi	来源不详，原存广西壮族自治区博物馆 Original source unknown; preserved previously in Museum of Guangxi Zhuang Autonomous Region	鼓面：太阳纹（12 芒）、栉纹、同心圆纹、复线交叉纹、变形羽人纹、变形翔鹭间定胜纹，鼓面边缘饰四只逆时针四足素面立体青蛙； 鼓身：栉纹、同心圆纹、栉纹素纹同心圆纹垂直纹带；扁耳两对饰辫纹 Drum face: patterns of sun(12rays), comb line, concentric circles, crossed double lines, transformed feathermen, transformed flying heron mixed Dingsheng; 4 frog statues of 4 feet and blank back anticlockwise stand on the edge of drum face; Drum body: patterns of comb line, concentric circles, vertical ribbon of blank, straight line and concentric circles; Braid patterns on 2 pairs of flat handles.	67.7-68.3	37.5 （残，连底座） Incomplete, with a base	冷水冲型 Lengshui-chong Type	
146	族鼓 0153 云纹铜鼓 ZG No.0153 Bronze Drum with cloud patterns	广西民族博物馆 Anthropology Museum of Guangxi	采集于玉林市容县 Collected in Rongxian County, Yulin City	鼓面：太阳纹（8 芒）、纹饰磨蚀，可辨云纹，鼓面边缘饰六只顺时针三足羽纹立体青蛙（三只已失）； 鼓身：纹饰磨蚀；扁耳两对饰羽纹、乳钉纹 Drum face: patterns of sun(8rays), cloud, all patterns are obscure; 6 frogs with 3 feet and feather on back clockwise stand on the edge(three lost); Drum body: all patterns are obscure; Feather and nipple protrusion patterns on 2 pairs of flat handles.	81-84	42 （残） Incomplete	灵山型 Lingshan Type	

序号 N0.	原编号及鼓名 Stock Number & Name	收藏单位 Museum	出土（征集）时间、地点 Time & Spot for discovered or collected	主要装饰 Main Decorations	尺寸（厘米） Size(cm)		类型 Type	图片 Picture
					面径 Face Diameter	身高 Height		
147	族鼓 0154 变形羽人纹铜鼓 ZG No.0154 Bronze Drum with transformed feather patterns	广西民族博物馆 Anthropology Museum of Guangxi	采集于玉林市容县 Collected in Rongxian County, Yulin City	鼓面：太阳纹（12 芒）、羽纹、栉纹、切线同心圆纹、复线交叉纹、变形羽人纹、变形翔鹭间定胜纹，鼓面边缘饰四只逆时针四足素面立体青蛙； 鼓身：羽纹、栉纹、切线同心圆纹、栉纹同心圆纹垂直纹带、圆心三角垂叶纹、扁耳两对饰辫纹 Drum face: patterns of sun(12rays), feather, comb line, tangent concentric circles, crossed double lines, transformed feathermen, transformed flying heron mixed Dingsheng; 4 frog statues of 4 feet and blank back anticlockwise stand on the edge of drum face; Drum body: patterns of feather, comb line, tangent concentric circles, vertical ribbon of straight line and concentric circles, leaf-shape triangle with circle in the middle; Braid patterns on 2 pairs of flat handles.	72.5－74.5	49.5	冷水冲型 Lengshui-chong Type	
148	族鼓 0155 铜鼓 ZG No.0155 Bronze Drum	广西民族博物馆 Anthropology Museum of Guangxi	来源不详，原存广西壮族自治区博物馆 Original source unknown; preserved previously in Museum of Guangxi Zhuang Autonomous Region	鼓面：太阳纹（12 芒）、栉纹、同心圆纹、其余磨蚀； 鼓身：栉纹、同心圆纹、栉纹同心圆纹垂直纹带、复线三角纹；扁耳两对饰辫纹 Drum face: patterns of sun(12rays), comb line, concentric circles, the other patterns are obscure; Drum body: patterns of comb line, concentric circles, vertical ribbon of straight line and concentric circles, double line triangle; Braid patterns on 2 pairs of flat handles.	55.8－56	35.8	遵义型 Zunyi Type	
149	族鼓 0156 云雷纹铜鼓 ZG No.0156 Bronze Drum with cloud & thunder patterns	广西民族博物馆 Anthropology Museum of Guangxi	采集于玉林市北流县 Collected in Beiliu County, Yulin City	鼓面：太阳纹（8 芒）、云纹，鼓面边缘饰四只逆时针四足素面立体青蛙； 鼓身：云纹、雷纹填线纹；环耳两对饰缠丝纹 Drum face: patterns of sun(8rays), cloud; 4 frog statues of 4 feet and blank back anticlockwise stand on the edge of drum face; Drum body: patterns of cloud, thunder filled with straight line; Silk-like patterns on 2 pairs of ring handles.	82.5－83.5	48.5（残） Incomplete	北流型 Beiliu Type	

续表

序号 N0.	原编号及鼓名 Stock Number & Name	收藏单位 Museum	出土（征集）时间、地点 Time & Spot for discovered or collected	主要装饰 Main Decorations	尺寸（厘米）Size(cm)		类型 Type	图片 Picture
					面径 Face Diameter	身高 Height		
150	族鼓 0157 雷纹铜鼓 ZG No.0157 Bronze Drum with thunder patterns	广西民族博物馆 Anthropology Museum of Guangxi	采集于梧州市岑溪县南渡区 Collected at Nandu District, Cenxi County, Wuzhou City	鼓面：太阳纹（8芒）、云纹、雷纹，鼓面边缘饰四只四足立体青蛙；鼓身：雷纹、云纹；环耳两对饰缠丝纹 Drum face: patterns of sun(8rays), cloud, thunder; 4 frog statues of 4 feet stand on the edge of drum face; Drum body: patterns of cloud, thunder; Silk-like patterns on 2 pairs of ring handles.	90.5～92	51.7	北流型 Beiliu Type	
151	族鼓 0158 变形羽人纹铜鼓 ZG No.0158 Bronze Drum with transformed feather patterns	广西民族博物馆 Anthropology Museum of Guangxi	崇左市大新县文化馆移交 Transferred by Daxin County Cultural House Chongzuo City	鼓面：太阳纹（12芒）、栉纹、同心圆纹、复线交叉纹、变形羽人纹、变形翔鹭纹间定胜纹，鼓面边缘饰四只逆时针四只素面立体青蛙；鼓身：栉纹、同心圆纹、素纹栉纹同心圆纹垂直纹带、圆心三角垂叶纹；扁耳两对饰辫纹 Drum face: patterns of sun(12rays), comb line, concentric circles, crossed double lines, transformed feathermen, transformed flying heron mixed Dingsheng; 4 frog statues of 4 feet and blank back anticlockwise stand on the edge of drum face; Drum body: patterns of comb line, concentric circles, vertical ribbon of blank, straight line and concentric circles, leaf-shape triangle with circle in the middle; Braid patterns on 2 pairs of flat handles.	66～67.2	42.5	冷水冲型 Lengshuichong Type	
152	族鼓 0159 云雷纹铜鼓 ZG No.0159 Bronze Drum with cloud & thunder patterns	广西民族博物馆 Anthropology Museum of Guangxi	来源不详，原存广西壮族自治区博物馆 Original source unknown; preserved previously in Museum of Guangxi Zhuang Autonomous Region	鼓面：太阳纹（12芒）、云纹、雷纹，鼓面边缘饰四只两两相对四足素面立体青蛙；鼓身：雷纹；环耳两对饰缠丝纹 Drum face: patterns of sun(12rays), cloud, thunder; 4 frog statues of 4 feet stand on the edge of drum face, face to each other in pairs; Drum body: patterns of thunder; Silk-like patterns on 2 pairs of ring handles.	75.5～76.6	42.5	北流型 Beiliu Type	

序号 NO.	原编号及鼓名 Stock Number & Name	收藏单位 Museum	出土（征集）时间、地点 Time & Spot for discovered or collected	主要装饰 Main Decorations	尺寸（厘米）Size(cm)		类型 Type	图片 Picture
					面径 Face Diameter	身高 Height		
153	族鼓 0161 雷纹铜鼓 ZG No.0161 Bronze Drum with thunder patterns	广西民族博物馆 Anthropology Museum of Guangxi	采集于北流县（现北流市）第十一区 Collected at District 11, Beiliu County(Now Beiliu City)	鼓面：太阳纹（8芒）、通面雷纹，鼓面边缘饰四只逆时针四足素面立体青蛙；鼓身：雷纹、雷纹填线纹；环耳两对饰缠丝纹 Drum face: patterns of sun(8rays), thunder; 4 frog statues of 4 feet and blank back stand on the edge of drum face; Drum body: patterns of thunder, thunder filled with straight lilne; Silk-like patterns on 2 pairs of ring handles.	76-76.5	44.4（残）Incomplete	北流型 Beiliu Type	
154	族鼓 0162 钱纹铜鼓 ZG No.0162 Bronze Drum with coin patterns	广西民族博物馆 Anthropology Museum of Guangxi	收购于南宁市二级站 Collected at Nanning Secondary Waste	鼓面：太阳纹（10芒）、蝉纹、四出钱纹、鸟纹、四瓣花纹、连钱纹，鼓面边缘饰六只逆时针三足立体青蛙（已失）；鼓身：蝉纹、四出钱纹、鸟纹、四瓣花纹、虫形纹；扁耳两对 Drum face: patterns of sun(10rays), cicada, coins with quadrangle inside, bird, quatrefoil, coins part of overlap; 6 frogs with 3 feet anticlockwise stand on the edge(lost); Drum body: patterns of cicada, coins with quadrangle inside, bird, quatrefoil, insect; 2 pairs of flat handles.	58.7-59.3	11.5-19.5（残）Incomplete	灵山型 Lingshan Type	
155	族鼓 0163 山口村铜鼓 ZG No.0163 Bronze Drum Shankou Cun	广西民族博物馆 Anthropology Museum of Guangxi	出土于南宁市横县南乡合山公社山口村 Unearthed at Shankou Village, Heshan Community, Nanxiang, Hengxian County, Nanning City	鼓面：太阳纹（10芒）、云纹，鼓面边缘饰四只逆时针四足素面立体青蛙；鼓身：云纹、雷纹填线纹；扁耳两对 Drum face: patterns of sun(10rays), cloud; 4 frog statues of 4 feet and blank back stand anticlockwise on the edge of drum face; Drum body: patterns of cloud, thunder filled with straight lines; 2 pairs of flat handles.	67.8-69.5	22（残）Incomplete	北流型 Lingshan Type	

序号 NO.	原编号及鼓名 Stock Number & Name	收藏单位 Museum	出土（征集）时间、地点 Time & Spot for discovered or collected	主要装饰 Main Decorations	尺寸（厘米）Size(cm)		类型 Type	图片 Picture
					面径 Face Diameter	身高 Height		
156	族鼓 0164 变形羽人纹铜鼓 ZG No.0164 Bronze Drum with transformed feather patterns	广西民族博物馆 Anthropology Museum of Guangxi	采集于玉林县（今玉林市）第二区 Collected at the second District, Yulin County(Now Yulin City)	鼓面：太阳纹（12芒）、同心圆纹、栉纹、切线同心圆纹、复线交叉纹、变形羽人纹、翔鹭纹，鼓面边缘饰四蛙趾； 鼓身：同心圆纹、栉纹、切线同心圆纹素纹垂直方格纹带、图案三角纹；扁耳两对饰辫纹 Drum face: patterns of sun(12rays), concentric circles, comb line, tangent concentric circles, crossed double lines, transformed feathermen, flying heron; toes of 4 frog-statues on the edge of drum face; Drum body: patterns of concentric circles, comb line, vertical ribbon of tangent concentric circles, blank, and grids, motif triangle; Braid patterns on 2 pairs of flat handles.	60.7~60.9	38.7	遵义型 Zunyi Type	
157	族鼓 0165 变形羽人纹铜鼓 ZG No.0165 Bronze Drum with transformed feathermen patterns	广西民族博物馆 Anthropology Museum of Guangxi	收购于南宁市宾阳县 Collected in Binyang County, Nanning City	鼓面：太阳纹（12芒）、栉纹、同心圆纹、复线交叉纹、变形羽人纹、变形翔鹭纹间定胜纹，鼓面边缘饰四只逆时针四足素面立体青蛙； 鼓身：栉纹、同心圆纹、素纹栉纹同心圆纹垂直纹带；扁耳两对饰辫纹 Drum face: patterns of sun(12rays), comb line, concentric circles, crossed double lines, transformed feathermen, transformed flying heron mixed Dingsheng; 4 frog statues of 4 feet and blank back anticlockwise stand on the edge of drum face; Drum body: patterns of comb line, concentric circles, vertical ribbon of blank, straight line and concentric circles; Braid patterns on 2 pairs of flat handles.	68.7~69.5	31.2（残）Incomplete	冷水冲型 Lengshuichong Type	

序号 N0.	原编号及鼓名 Stock Number & Name	收藏单位 Museum	出土（征集）时间、地点 Time & Spot for discovered or collected	主要装饰 Main Decorations	尺寸（厘米）Size(cm)		类型 Type	图片 Picture
					面径 Face Diameter	身高 Height		
158	族鼓 0166 变形羽人纹铜鼓 ZG No.0166 Bronze Drum with transformed feathermen patterns	广西民族博物馆 Anthropology Museum of Guangxi	1957 年征集于南宁市横县陶圩乡大塘村 Collected at Datang Village, Taoxu, Hengxian County, Nanning City in 1957	鼓面：太阳纹（12 芒）、水波纹、同心圆纹、栉纹、复线交叉纹、变形羽人纹、变形翔鹭纹、眼纹、鼓面边缘饰四只逆时针四足谷穗纹立体青蛙；鼓身：栉纹、同心圆纹、船纹、变形羽人纹、网纹、水波纹、圆心三角垂叶纹、羽纹、眼纹；扁耳两对饰辫纹，鼓内胸、足各对称两对附耳 Drum face: patterns of sun(12rays), water wave, concentric circles, comb line, crossed double lines, transformed feathermen, transformed flying heron, diamond-shape eye; 4 frog statues of 4 feet and rice ear on back anticlockwise stand on the edge of drum face; Drum body: patterns of comb line, concentric circles, boat, transformed feathermen, net, water wave, leaf-shape triangle with circle in the middle,feather, diamond-shape eye; Braid patterns on 2 pairs of flat handles; 2 pairs of attached ring handles separately on the chest and the foot in the drum body.	72.5~73.5	52	冷水冲型 Lengshui-chong Type	
159	族鼓 0167 云雷纹铜鼓 ZG No.0167 Bronze Drum with cloud & thunder patterns	广西民族博物馆 Anthropology Museum of Guangxi	来源不详，原存广西壮族自治区博物馆 Original source unknown; preserved previously in Museum of Guangxi Zhuang Autonomous Region	鼓面：太阳纹（8 芒）、雷纹，鼓面边缘饰四只顺时针四足素面立体青蛙；鼓身：雷纹、云纹；环耳两对饰缠丝纹 Drum face: patterns of sun(8rays), thunder; 4 frog statues of 4 feet and blank back stand clockwisly on the edge of drum face; Drum body: patterns of cloud, thunder; Silk-like patterns on 2 pairs of ring handles.	90.5~91.5	51.9	北流型 Beiliu Type	

序号 NO.	原编号及鼓名 Stock Number & Name	收藏单位 Museum	出土（征集） 时间、地点 Time & Spot for discovered or collected	主要装饰 Main Decorations	尺寸（厘米） Size(cm)		类型 Type	图片 Picture
					面径 Face Diameter	身高 Height		
160	族鼓 0169 变形羽人纹铜鼓 ZG No.0169 Bronze Drum with transformed feathermen patterns	广西民族博物馆 Anthropology Museum of Guangxi	来源不详，原存广西壮族自治区博物馆 Original source unknown; preserved previously in Museum of Guangxi Zhuang Autonomous Region	鼓面：太阳纹（12 芒）、栉纹、同心圆纹、复线交叉纹、变形羽人纹、变形翔鹭纹间定胜纹，鼓面边缘饰四只逆时针四足素面立体青蛙； 鼓身：栉纹、同心圆纹、素纹栉纹同心圆纹垂直纹带、圆心三角垂叶纹；扁耳两对饰辫纹 Drum face: patterns of sun(12rays), comb line, concentric circles, crossed double lines, transformed feathermen, transformed flying heron mixed Dingsheng; 4 frog statues of 4 feet and blank back anticlockwise stand on the edge of drum face; Drum body: patterns of comb line, concentric circles, vertical ribbon of blank, straight line and concentric circles, leaf-shape triangle with circle in the middle; Braid patterns on 2 pairs of flat handles.	60.8~63.2	37.3	冷水冲型 Lengshui-chong Type	
161	族鼓 0170 变形游旗纹铜鼓 ZG No.0170 Bronze Drum with transformed flying flag patterns	广西民族博物馆 Anthropology Museum of Guangxi	1958 年征购于柳州收购站 Collected at Liuzhou Waste Recycle Station in 1958	鼓面：太阳纹（12 芒）、S 云纹、乳钉纹、变形游旗纹、栉纹、回形雷纹、同心圆纹； 鼓身：乳钉纹、四出钱纹、S 云纹、蒲叶纹、回形雷纹、复线三角纹；扁耳两对饰凸棱纹 Drum face: patterns of sun(12rays), S-shape cloud, nipple protrusion, transformed flying flag, comb line, 回 -shape thunder, concentric circle; Drum body: patterns of nipple protrusion, coins with quadrangle inside, S-shape cloud, cattail, 回 -shape thunder, double line triangle; Raise ridges on 2 pairs of flat handles.	46	26.5	麻江型 Majiang Type	

序号 N0.	原编号及鼓名 Stock Number & Name	收藏单位 Museum	出土（征集）时间、地点 Time & Spot for discovered or collected	主要装饰 Main Decorations	尺寸（厘米）Size(cm)		类型 Type	图片 Picture
					面径 Face Diameter	身高 Height		
162	族鼓 0171 游旗纹铜鼓 ZG No.0171 Bronze Drum with flying flag patterns	广西民族博物馆 Anthropology Museum of Guangxi	1962 年征购于柳州市 Collected in Liuzhou City in 1962	鼓面：太阳纹（12 芒）、酉字纹、S 云纹、乳钉纹、栉纹、游旗纹、云纹；鼓身：云纹、如意云纹、栉纹、缠枝纹、兽形云纹、回形雷纹、复线三角纹；扁耳两对饰辫纹 Drum face: patterns of sun(12rays), 酉 -character, S-shape cloud, nipple protrusion, comb line, flying flag, cloud; Drum body: patterns of cloud, Ruyi-shape cloud, comb line, twisted branches, beast-shape cloud, 回 -shape thunder, double line triangle; Braid patterns on 2 pairs of flat handles.	51.6–51.8	28	麻江型 Majiang Type	
163	族鼓 0172 游旗纹铜鼓 ZG No.0172 Bronze Drum with flying flag patterns	广西民族博物馆 Anthropology Museum of Guangxi	1962 年收购于柳州 Collected in Liuzhou City in 1962	鼓面：太阳纹（12 芒）、酉字纹、S 云纹、乳钉纹、栉纹、游旗纹、兽面云纹；鼓身：乳钉纹、兽面云纹、栉纹、回形雷纹、云纹、复线三角纹；扁耳两对饰辫纹、回形纹 Drum face: patterns of sun(12rays), 酉 -character, S-shape cloud, nipple protrusion, comb line, flying flag, beast-face cloud; Drum body: patterns of nipple protrusion, beast-face cloud, comb line, 回 -shape thunder, cloud, double line triangle; braid & dual-rectangle patterns on 2 pairs of flat handles.	49.3–49.7	26.7	麻江型 Majiang Type	
164	族鼓 0173 游旗纹铜鼓 ZG No.0173 Bronze Drum with flying flag patterns	广西民族博物馆 Anthropology Museum of Guangxi	征购于桂林市临桂县（现临桂区）Collected in Lingui County(Now Lingui District), Guilin City	鼓面：太阳纹(12 芒）、复线酉字纹、S 云纹、乳钉纹、栉纹、游旗纹、云纹；鼓身：乳钉纹、云纹、回形雷纹、水滴纹、栉纹、复线三角纹；扁耳两对饰辫纹 Drum face: patterns of sun(12rays), double line 酉 -character, S-shape cloud, nipple protrusion, comb line, flying flag, cloud; Drum body: patterns of nipple protrusion, cloud, 回 -shape thunder, water drop, comb line, double line triangle; Braid patterns on 2 pairs of flat handles.	47.3	27.3	麻江型 Majiang Type	

续表

序号 NO.	原编号及鼓名 Stock Number & Name	收藏单位 Museum	出土（征集）时间、地点 Time & Spot for discovered or collected	主要装饰 Main Decorations	尺寸（厘米） Size(cm)		类型 Type	图片 Picture
					面径 Face Diameter	身高 Height		
165	族鼓 0174 游旗纹铜鼓 ZG No.0174 Bronze Drum with flying flag patterns	广西民族博物馆 Anthropology Museum of Guangxi	征购于柳州市 Collected in Liuzhou City	鼓面：太阳纹（12 芒）、西字纹、S 云纹、乳钉纹、游旗纹、栉纹；鼓身：乳钉纹、云纹、回形雷纹、栉纹、复线三角纹；扁耳两对饰辫纹 Drum face: patterns of sun(12rays), 西-character, S-shape cloud, nipple protrusion, flying flag, comb line; Drum body: patterns of nipple protrusion, cloud, 回-shape thunder, comb line, double line triangle; Braid patterns on 2 pairs of flat handles.	47.5-47.8	26	麻江型 Majiang Type	
166	族鼓 0175 游旗纹铜鼓 ZG No.0175 Bronze Drum with flying flag patterns	广西民族博物馆 Anthropology Museum of Guangxi	征购于柳州市 Collected in Liuzhou City	鼓面：太阳纹（12 芒）、西字纹、S 云纹、乳钉纹、游旗纹、栉纹、兽形云纹；鼓身：乳钉纹、如意云纹、回形雷纹、栉纹、云纹、复线三角纹；扁耳两对饰辫纹、回形雷纹 Drum face: patterns of sun(12rays), 西-character, S-shape cloud, nipple protrusion, flying flag, comb line, beast-shape cloud; Drum body: patterns of nipple protrusion, Ruyi-shape cloud, 回-shape thunder, comb line, cloud, double line triangle; Braid & 回-shape thunder patterns on 2 pairs of flat handles.	47	26	麻江型 Majiang Type	
167	族鼓 0176 莲花纹铜鼓 ZG No.0176 Bronze Drum with lotus patterns	广西民族博物馆 Anthropology Museum of Guangxi	征购于柳州市 Collected in Liuzhou City	鼓面：太阳纹（12 芒）、四瓣花纹、乳钉纹、莲花纹、波浪纹、雷纹、西字纹、菱形填四瓣花纹；鼓身：乳钉纹、S 云纹、波浪纹、菱形填四瓣花纹、云幔纹；扁耳两对饰凸棱纹 Drum face: patterns of sun(12rays), quatrefoil, nipple protrusion, lotus, water wave, thunder, 西-character, diamond filled with quatrefoils; Drum body: patterns of nipple protrusion, S-shape cloud, water wave, diamond filled with quatrefoils, cloud ribbon; raise ridges on 2 pairs of flat handles.	46.4	26.5	麻江型 Majiang Type	

序号 N0.	原编号及鼓名 Stock Number & Name	收藏单位 Museum	出土（征集）时间、地点 Time & Spot for discovered or collected	主要装饰 Main Decorations	尺寸（厘米）Size(cm)		类型 Type	图片 Picture
					面径 Face Diameter	身高 Height		
168	族鼓 0177 游旗纹铜鼓 ZG No.0177 Bronze Drum with flying flag patterns	广西民族博物馆 Anthropology Museum of Guangxi	解放初征购于北流县（现北流市） Collected at Beiliu County(Now Beiliu City) at the beginning of the establishment of PRC	鼓面：太阳纹（12芒）、酉字纹、S云纹、乳钉纹、游旗纹、栉纹、兽形云纹、卦纹；鼓身：乳钉纹、回形雷纹、如意云纹、栉纹、云纹、复线三角纹；扁耳两对饰辫纹、回形雷纹 Drum face: patterns of sun(12rays), 酉-character, S-shape cloud, nipple protrusion, flying flag, comb line, beast-shape cloud, divinatory symbol; Drum body: patterns of nipple protrusion, 回-shape thunder, Ruyi-shape cloud, comb line, cloud, double line triangle; Braid & 回-shape thunder patterns on 2 pairs of flat handles.	47.5–47.8	26	麻江型 Majiang Type	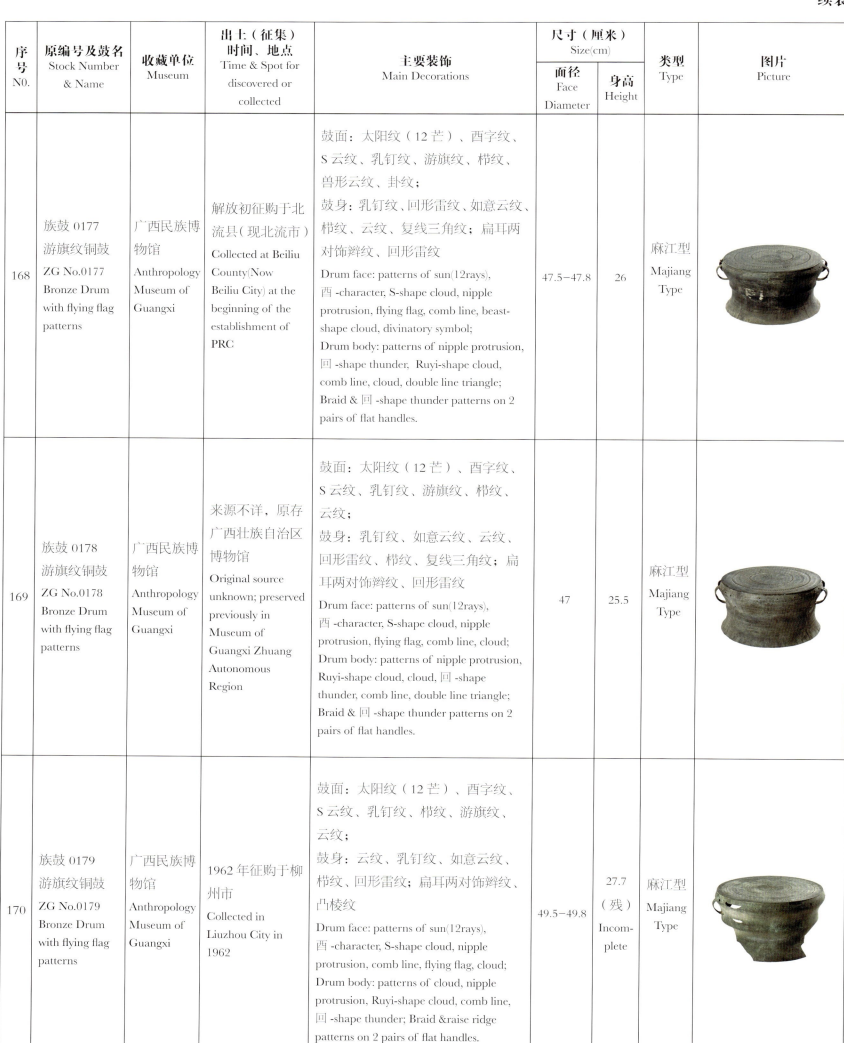
169	族鼓 0178 游旗纹铜鼓 ZG No.0178 Bronze Drum with flying flag patterns	广西民族博物馆 Anthropology Museum of Guangxi	来源不详，原存广西壮族自治区博物馆 Original source unknown; preserved previously in Museum of Guangxi Zhuang Autonomous Region	鼓面：太阳纹（12芒）、酉字纹、S云纹、乳钉纹、游旗纹、栉纹、云纹；鼓身：乳钉纹、如意云纹、云纹、回形雷纹、栉纹、复线三角纹；扁耳两对饰辫纹、回形雷纹 Drum face: patterns of sun(12rays), 酉-character, S-shape cloud, nipple protrusion, flying flag, comb line, cloud; Drum body: patterns of nipple protrusion, Ruyi-shape cloud, cloud, 回-shape thunder, comb line, double line triangle; Braid & 回-shape thunder patterns on 2 pairs of flat handles.	47	25.5	麻江型 Majiang Type	
170	族鼓 0179 游旗纹铜鼓 ZG No.0179 Bronze Drum with flying flag patterns	广西民族博物馆 Anthropology Museum of Guangxi	1962年征购于柳州市 Collected in Liuzhou City in 1962	鼓面：太阳纹（12芒）、酉字纹、S云纹、乳钉纹、栉纹、游旗纹、云纹；鼓身：云纹、乳钉纹、如意云纹、栉纹、回形雷纹；扁耳两对饰辫纹、凸棱纹 Drum face: patterns of sun(12rays), 酉-character, S-shape cloud, nipple protrusion, comb line, flying flag, cloud; Drum body: patterns of cloud, nipple protrusion, Ruyi-shape cloud, comb line, 回-shape thunder; Braid &raise ridge patterns on 2 pairs of flat handles.	49.5–49.8	27.7（残）Incomplete	麻江型 Majiang Type	

续表

序号 NO.	原编号及鼓名 Stock Number & Name	收藏单位 Museum	出土（征集） 时间、地点 Time & Spot for discovered or collected	主要装饰 Main Decorations	尺寸（厘米） Size(cm)		类型 Type	图片 Picture
					面径 Face Diameter	身高 Height		
171	族鼓 0180 游旗纹铜鼓 ZG No.0180 Bronze Drum with flying flag patterns	广西民族博物馆 Anthropology Museum of Guangxi	1955 年征购于南宁 Collected in Nanning City in 1955	鼓面：太阳纹（12 芒）、四出钱纹、S 云纹、乳钉纹、游旗纹、栉纹、兽形云纹； 鼓身：乳钉纹、如意云纹、回形雷纹、栉纹、四出钱纹、复线三角纹；扁耳两对饰凸棱纹 Drum face: patterns of sun(12rays), coins with quadrangle inside, S-shape cloud, nipple protrusion, flying flag, comb line, beast-shape cloud; Drum body: patterns of nipple protrusion, Ruyi-shape cloud, comb line, coins with quadrangle inside, double line triangle; Raise ridges on 2 pairs of flat handles.	47.5	26.5	麻江型 Majiang Type	
172	族鼓 0181 游旗纹铜鼓 ZG No.0181 Bronze Drum with flying flag patterns	广西民族博物馆 Anthropology Museum of Guangxi	1958 年征购于柳州市 Collected in Liuzhou City in 1958	鼓面：太阳纹（12 芒）、西字纹、S 云纹、乳钉纹、游旗纹、栉纹、兽形云纹、卦纹； 鼓身：乳钉纹、回形雷纹、如意云纹、栉纹、兽面云纹、复线三角纹；扁耳两对饰辫纹、回形雷纹 Drum face: patterns of sun(12rays), 西 -character, S-shape cloud, nipple protrusion, flying flag, comb line, beast-shape cloud, divinatory symbol; Drum body: patterns of nipple protrusion, 回 -shape thunder, Ruyi-shape cloud, comb line, beast-face cloud, double line triangle; Braid & 回 -shape thunder patterns on 2 pairs of flat handles.	47.5–48	26.5	麻江型 Majiang Type	
173	族鼓 0182 游旗纹铜鼓 ZG No.0182 Bronze Drum with flying flag patterns	广西民族博物馆 Anthropology Museum of Guangxi	1958 年征购于柳州市 Collected in Liuzhou City in 1958	鼓面：太阳纹（12 芒）、西字纹、S 云纹、游旗纹、乳钉纹、云纹、回形雷纹； 鼓身：乳钉纹、回形雷纹、云纹、复线三角纹；扁耳两对饰辫纹、回形雷纹 Drum face: patterns of sun(12rays), 西 -character, S-shape cloud, flying flag, nipple protrusion, cloud, 回 -shape thunder; Drum body: patterns of nipple protrusion, 回 -shape thunder, cloud, double line triangle; Braid & 回 -shape thunder patterns on 2 pairs of flat handles.	48–49	25.5	麻江型 Majiang Type	

序号 N0.	原编号及鼓名 Stock Number & Name	收藏单位 Museum	出土（征集） 时间、地点 Time & Spot for discovered or collected	主要装饰 Main Decorations	尺寸（厘米） Size(cm)		类型 Type	图片 Picture
					面径 Face Diameter	身高 Height		
174	族鼓 0183 游旗纹铜鼓 ZG No.0183 Bronze Drum with flying flag patterns	广西民族博 物馆 Anthropology Museum of Guangxi	1974 年收购于柳 州二级站 Collected in Liuzhou City Waste Recycle Station in 1974	鼓面：太阳纹（12 芒）、西字纹、 S 云纹、乳钉纹、栉纹、游旗纹、 云纹； 鼓身：乳钉纹、如意云纹、回形雷 纹、栉纹、云纹、复线三角纹；扁 耳两对饰辫纹 Drum face: patterns of sun(12rays), 西 -character, S-shape cloud, nipple protrusion, comb line, flying flag, cloud; Drum body: patterns of nipple protrusion, Ruyi-shape cloud, 回 -shape thunder, comb line, cloud, double line triangle; Braid patterns on 2 pairs of flat handles.	47.5	27 （残） Incom- plete	麻江型 Majiang Type	
175	族鼓 0184 游旗纹铜鼓 ZG No.0184 Bronze Drum with flying flag patterns	广西民族博 物馆 Anthropology Museum of Guangxi	征集于柳州市 Collected in Liuzhou City	鼓面：太阳纹（12 芒）、西字纹、 S 云纹、乳钉纹、游旗纹、栉纹、 兽形云纹； 鼓身：乳钉纹、如意云纹、兽形云 纹、回形雷纹、栉纹、复线三角纹； 扁耳两对饰绳纹 Drum face: patterns of sun(12rays), 酉 -character, S-shape cloud, nipple protrusion, flying flag, comb line, beast- shape cloud; Drum body: patterns of nipple protrusion, Ruyi-shape cloud, beast-shape cloud, 回 -shape thunder, comb line, double line triangle; Rope patterns on 2 pairs of flat handles.	47－47.3	26	麻江型 Majiang Type	
176	族鼓 0185 游旗纹铜鼓 ZG No.0185 Bronze Drum with flying flag patterns	广西民族博 物馆 Anthropology Museum of Guangxi	采集于玉林市容 县 Collected in Rongxian County, Yulin City	鼓面：太阳纹（12 芒）、西字纹、 S 云纹、乳钉纹、游旗纹、栉纹、 兽形云纹、卦纹； 鼓身：乳钉纹、回形雷纹、如意云 纹、栉纹、兽面云纹、复线三角纹； 扁耳两对饰辫纹、回形雷纹 Drum face: patterns of sun(12rays), 西 -character, S-shape cloud, nipple protrusion, flying flag, comb line, beast- shape cloud, divinatory symbol; Drum body: patterns of nipple protrusion, 回 -shape thunder, Ruyi-shape cloud, comb line, beast-face cloud, double line triangle; braid & 回 -shape thunder patterns on 2 pairs of flat handles.	47	25.5	麻江型 Majiang Type	

续表

序号 NO.	原编号及鼓名 Stock Number & Name	收藏单位 Museum	出土（征集）时间、地点 Time & Spot for discovered or collected	主要装饰 Main Decorations	尺寸（厘米）Size(cm)		类型 Type	图片 Picture
					面径 Face Diameter	身高 Height		
177	族鼓 0186 蛙趾纹变形羽人纹铜鼓 ZG No.0186 Bronze Drum with frog toe and flying flag patterns	广西民族博物馆 Anthropology Museum of Guangxi	20 世纪 50 年代征集于容县城厢镇 Collected in Chengxiang Town, Rongxian County in 1950s'	鼓面：太阳纹 (12 芒)、栉纹、同心圆纹、复线交叉纹、变形羽人纹、变形翔鹭纹，鼓面边缘饰四组顺时针蛙趾；鼓身：栉纹、同心圆纹、栉纹；扁耳两对饰辫纹 Drum face: patterns of sun(12rays), comb line, concentric circles, crossed double lines, transformed feathermen, transformed flying heron; toes of 4 frog-statues clockwisely arrayed on the edge of drum face ; Drum body: patterns of comb line, concentric circles, grids; Braid patterns on 2 pairs of flat handles.	61.3	28	遵义型 Zunyi Type	
178	族鼓 0187 游旗纹铜鼓 ZG No.0187 Bronze Drum with flying flag patterns	广西民族博物馆 Anthropology Museum of Guangxi	来源不详，原存广西壮族自治区博物馆 Original source unknown; preserved previously in Museum of Guangxi Zhuang Autonomous Region	鼓面：太阳纹（12 芒）、西字纹、S 云纹、乳钉纹、游旗纹、栉纹、兽形云纹、卦纹；鼓身：乳钉纹、回形雷纹、如意纹、栉纹、兽面云纹、复线三角纹；扁耳两对饰辫纹、回形雷纹 Drum face: patterns of sun(12rays), 酉 -character, S-shape cloud, nipple protrusion, flying flag, comb line, beast-shape cloud, divinatory symbol; Drum body: patterns of nipple protrusion, 回 -shape thunder, Ruyi-shape cloud, comb line, beast-face cloud, double line triangle; Braid & 回 -shape thunder patterns on 2 pairs of flat handles.	46.5	26	麻江型 Majiang Type	
179	族鼓 0191 团花纹铜鼓 ZG No.0191 Bronze Drum with flower cluster patterns	广西民族博物馆 Anthropology Museum of Guangxi	1964 年征集于柳州二级站 Collected in Liuzhou City Waste Recycle Station in 1964	鼓面：太阳纹（12 芒）、回形雷纹、雷纹、乳钉纹、团花纹、菱形填四瓣花纹、双鱼戏珠纹；鼓身：梅花状乳钉纹、S 云纹、团花纹、菱形填四瓣花纹、同心圆纹、方格云纹、梅花纹、复线三角纹；扁耳两对饰辫纹 Drum face: patterns of sun(12rays), 回 -shape thunder, thunder, nipple protrusion, flower cluster, diamond filled with quatrefoils, 2 fishes playing pearl; Drum body: patterns of nipple protrusion in plum blossom shape, S-shape cloud, flower cluster, diamond filled with quatrefoils, concentric circle, cloud grid, flower grid, double line triangle; Braid patterns on 2 pairs of flat handles.	44.4~44.8	25.5 （残） Incomplete	麻江型 Majiang Type	

序号 N0.	原编号及鼓名 Stock Number & Name	收藏单位 Museum	出土（征集）时间、地点 Time & Spot for discovered or collected	主要装饰 Main Decorations	尺寸（厘米）Size(cm)		类型 Type	图片 Picture
					面径 Face Diameter	身高 Height		
180	族鼓 0192 双龙团寿纹铜鼓 ZG No.0192 Bronze Drum with 2 dragons playing round "寿"-character patterns	广西民族博物馆 Anthropology Museum of Guangxi	来源不详，原存广西壮族自治区博物馆 Original source unknown; preserved previously in Museum of Guangxi Zhuang Autonomous Region	鼓面：太阳纹（12芒）、酉字纹、乳钉纹、双龙团寿纹、"永世家财、万世进宝"铭文、云纹、回形雷纹；鼓身：乳钉纹、云纹、回形雷纹、复线三角纹；扁耳两对饰辫纹、回形雷纹 Drum face: patterns of sun(12rays), 酉-character, nipple protrusion, complex patterns of 2 dragons with round "寿"-character, "永世家财、万世进宝"-character, cloud, 回-shape thunder; Drum body: patterns of nipple protrusion, cloud, 回-shape thunder, double line triangle; Braid & 回-shape thunder patterns on 2 pairs of flat handles.	47-47.5	27	麻江型 Majiang Type	
181	族鼓 0193 游旗纹铜鼓 ZG No.0193 Bronze Drum with flying flag patterns	广西民族博物馆 Anthropology Museum of Guangxi	1962年收购于柳州市 Collected in Liuzhou City in 1962	鼓面：太阳纹（12芒）、酉字纹、乳钉纹、羽纹、四出钱纹、绹纹、五瓣花纹、游旗纹、S云纹、如意云纹；鼓身：栉纹、乳钉纹、回形雷纹、如意云纹、复线三角纹；扁耳两对饰凸棱纹 Drum face: patterns of sun(12rays), 酉-character, nipple protrusion, feather, coins with quadrangle inside, twisted rope, cinquefoil, flying flag, S-shape cloud, Ruyi-shape cloud; Drum body: patterns of comb line, nipple protrusion, 回-shape thunder, Ruyi-shape cloud, double line triangle; Raise ridges on 2 pairs of flat handles.	47.5	29.3（残）Incomplete	麻江型 Majiang Type	
182	族鼓 0194 寿字纹铜鼓 ZG No.0194 Bronze Drum with "寿"-character patterns	广西民族博物馆 Anthropology Museum of Guangxi	1964年征集于柳州市二级站 Collected in Liuzhou City Waste Recycle Station in 1964	鼓面：太阳纹（12芒）、同心圆纹、回形雷纹、乳钉纹、符箓纹、团寿纹、云纹；鼓身：乳钉纹、云纹、复线三角纹；扁耳两对饰辫纹 Drum face: patterns of sun(12rays), concentric circle, 回-shape thunder, nipple protrusion, Ofuda, round 寿-character, cloud; Drum body: patterns of nipple protrusion, cloud, double line triangle; Braid patterns on 2 pairs of flat handles.	47.5	26.5	麻江型 Majiang Type	

序号 NO.	原编号及鼓名 Stock Number & Name	收藏单位 Museum	出土（征集）时间、地点 Time & Spot for discovered or collected	主要装饰 Main Decorations	尺寸（厘米） Size(cm) 面径 Face Diameter	身高 Height	类型 Type	图片 Picture
183	族鼓 0195 游旗纹铜鼓 ZG No.0195 Bronze Drum with flying flag patterns	广西民族博物馆 Anthropology Museum of Guangxi	来源不详，原存广西壮族自治区博物馆 Original source unknown; preserved previously in Museum of Guangxi Zhuang Autonomous Region	鼓面：太阳纹（12 芒）、西字纹、S 云纹、乳钉纹、游旗纹、栉纹、云纹、卦纹； 鼓身：乳钉纹、如意云纹、回形雷纹、栉纹、复线三角纹；扁耳两对饰辫纹 Drum face: patterns of sun(12rays), 西-character, S-shape cloud, nipple protrusion, flying flag, comb line, cloud, divinatory symbol; Drum body: patterns of nipple protrusion, Ruyi-shape cloud, 回-shape thunder, comb line, double line triangle; Braid patterns on 2 pairs of flat handles.	47	26	麻江型 Majiang Type	
184	族鼓 0196 游旗纹铜鼓 ZG No.0196 Bronze Drum with flying flag patterns	广西民族博物馆 Anthropology Museum of Guangxi	收购于柳州市 Collected in Liuzhou City	鼓面：太阳纹（12 芒）、西字纹、S 云纹、乳钉纹、游旗纹、栉纹、兽面云纹； 鼓身：乳钉纹、回形雷纹、如意云纹、栉纹、复线三角纹；扁耳两对饰辫纹、回形雷纹 Drum face: patterns of sun(12rays), 西-character, S-shape cloud, nipple protrusion, flying flag, comb line,beast-face cloud; Drum body: patterns of nipple protrusion, 回-shape thunder, Ruyi-shape cloud, comb line, double line triangle; Braid& 回-shape thunder patterns on 2 pairs of flat handles.	47	27	麻江型 Majiang Type	
185	族鼓 0197 游旗纹铜鼓 ZG No.0197 Bronze Drum with flying flag patterns	广西民族博物馆 Anthropology Museum of Guangxi	1962 年征集于柳州市 Collected in Liuzhou City in 1962	鼓面：太阳纹（12 芒）、西字纹、S 云纹、乳钉纹、栉纹、游旗纹、兽面云纹； 鼓身：乳钉纹、栉纹；扁耳两对饰辫纹、回形雷纹 Drum face: patterns of sun(12rays), 西-character, S-shape cloud, nipple protrusion, comb line, flying flag, beast-face cloud; Drum body: patterns of nipple protrusion, comb line; Braid & 回-shape thunder patterns on 2 pairs of flat handles.	49	18.5 （残） Incomplete	麻江型 Majiang Type	

续表

序号 N0.	原编号及鼓名 Stock Number & Name	收藏单位 Museum	出土（征集）时间、地点 Time & Spot for discovered or collected	主要装饰 Main Decorations	尺寸（厘米）Size(cm)		类型 Type	图片 Picture
					面径 Face Diameter	身高 Height		
186	族鼓 0198 游旗纹铜鼓 ZG No.0198 Bronze Drum with flying flag patterns	广西民族博物馆 Anthropology Museum of Guangxi	1962 年征集于柳州市 Collected in Liuzhou City in 1962	鼓面：太阳纹（12 芒）、西字纹、S 云纹、乳钉纹、游旗纹、栉纹、兽面云纹、卦纹；鼓身：乳钉纹、回形雷纹、如意云纹、栉纹、云纹、复线三角纹；扁耳两对饰辫纹、回形雷纹 Drum face: patterns of sun(12rays), 西 -character, S-shape cloud, nipple protrusion, flying flag, comb line, beast-face cloud, divinatory symbol; Drum body: patterns of nipple protrusion, 回 -shape thunder, Ruyi-shape cloud, comb line, cloud, double line triangle; Braid & 回 -shape thunder patterns on 2 pairs of flat handles.	47	27.5（残）Incom-plete	麻江型 Majiang Type	
187	族鼓 0199 游旗纹铜鼓 ZG No.0199 Bronze Drum with flying flag patterns	广西民族博物馆 Anthropology Museum of Guangxi	1958 年征集于柳州市收购站 Collected in Liuzhou City Waste Recycle Station in 1958	鼓面：太阳纹（12 芒）、西字纹、S 云纹、乳钉纹、游旗纹、栉纹、兽面云纹、卦纹；鼓身：乳钉纹、回形雷纹、如意云纹、回纹、栉纹、云纹、复线三角纹；扁耳两对饰辫纹、回形雷纹 Drum face: patterns of sun(12rays), 西 -character, S-shape cloud, nipple protrusion, flying flag, comb line, beast-face cloud, divinatory symbol; Drum body: patterns of nipple protrusion, 回 -shape thunder, Ruyi-shape cloud, comb line, cloud, double line triangle; Braid & 回 -shape thunder patterns on 2 pairs of flat handles.	47－47.5	27.5	麻江型 Majiang Type	
188	族鼓 0200 游旗纹铜鼓 ZG No.0200 Bronze Drum with flying flag patterns	广西民族博物馆 Anthropology Museum of Guangxi	征集于柳州市 Collected in Liuzhou City	鼓面：太阳纹（12 芒）、西字纹、S 云纹、乳钉纹、栉纹、游旗纹、云纹；鼓身：乳钉纹、云纹、如意云纹、栉纹、回形雷纹、复线三角纹；扁耳两对饰羽纹 Drum face: patterns of sun(12rays), 酉 -character, S-shape cloud, nipple protrusion, comb line, flying flag, cloud; Drum body: patterns of nipple protrusion, cloud, Ruyi-shape cloud, comb line, 回 -shape thunder, double line triangle; Feather patterns on 2 pairs of flat handles.	50.8－51.3	27.3	麻江型 Majiang Type	

序号 NO.	原编号及鼓名 Stock Number & Name	收藏单位 Museum	出土（征集）时间、地点 Time & Spot for discovered or collected	主要装饰 Main Decorations	尺寸（厘米）Size(cm)		类型 Type	图片 Picture
					面径 Face Diameter	身高 Height		
189	族鼓 0201 十二生肖纹铜鼓 ZG No.0201 Bronze Drum with zodiac patterns	广西民族博物馆 Anthropology Museum of Guangxi	征集于柳州市 Collected in Liuzhou City	鼓面：太阳纹（12 芒）、酉字纹、乳钉纹、栉纹、游旗纹、十二生肖纹、蔓草纹、云纹；鼓身：乳钉纹、栉纹、云纹、回形雷纹、复线三角纹；扁耳两对饰凸棱纹 Drum face: patterns of sun(12rays), 酉 -character, nipple protrusion, comb line, flying flag,zodiac, liana, cloud; Drum body: patterns of nipple protrusion, comb line, cloud, 回 -shape thunder, double line triangle; Raise ridges on 2 pairs of flat handles.	50	28.6	麻江型 Majiang Type	
190	族鼓 0202 游旗纹铜鼓 ZG No.0202 Bronze Drum with flying flag patterns	广西民族博物馆 Anthropology Museum of Guangxi	1964 年收购于柳州二级站 Collected in Liuzhou City Waste Recycle Station in 1964	鼓面：太阳纹（12 芒）、酉字纹、同心圆纹、乳钉纹、如意云组合图案纹、游旗纹；鼓身：乳钉纹、雷纹、复线三角图案纹；扁耳两对饰辫纹 Drum face: patterns of sun(12rays), 酉 -character, concentric circle, nipple protrusion, complex group of Ruyi-shape cloud, flying flag; Drum body: patterns of nipple protrusion, thunder, double line triangle; Braid patterns on 2 pairs of flat handles.	45	26	麻江型 Majiang Type	
191	族鼓 0203 游旗纹铜鼓 ZG No.0203 Bronze Drum with flying flag patterns	广西民族博物馆 Anthropology Museum of Guangxi	1962 年征集于柳州 Collected in Liuzhou City in 1962	鼓面：太阳纹（12 芒）、酉字纹、S 云纹、乳钉纹、栉纹、游旗纹、云纹；鼓身：乳钉纹、如意云纹、回形雷纹、兽面云纹、栉纹、复线三角纹；扁耳两对饰辫纹、回形雷纹 Drum face: patterns of sun(12rays), 酉 -character, S-shape cloud, nipple protrusion, comb line, flying flag, cloud; Drum body: patterns of nipple protrusion, Ruyi-shape cloud, 回 -shape thunder, beast-face cloud, comb line, double line triangle; Braid & 回 -shape thunder patterns on 2 pairs of flat handles.	47—48.3	26	麻江型 Majiang Type	

序号 NO.	原编号及鼓名 Stock Number & Name	收藏单位 Museum	出土（征集） 时间、地点 Time & Spot for discovered or collected	主要装饰 Main Decorations	尺寸（厘米） Size(cm)		类型 Type	图片 Picture
					面径 Face Diameter	身高 Height		
192	族鼓 0204 游旗纹铜鼓 ZG No.0204 Bronze Drum with flying flag patterns	广西民族博 物馆 Anthropology Museum of Guangxi	征集于柳州市收 购站 Collected in Liuzhou City Waste Recycle Station	鼓面：太阳纹（12 芒）、复线西字 纹、S 云纹、乳钉纹、游旗纹、栉纹、 兽形云纹、卦纹； 鼓身：乳钉纹、如意云纹、回形雷 纹、栉纹、云纹、复线三角纹；扁 耳两对饰凸棱纹 Drum face: patterns of sun(12rays), double line 西 -character, S-shape cloud, nipple protrusion, flying flag, comb line, beast- shape cloud, divinatory symbol; Drum body: patterns of nipple protrusion, Ruyi-shape cloud, 回 -shape thunder, comb line, cloud, double line triangle; Raise ridges on 2 pairs of flat handles.	47-47.5	27	麻江型 Majiang Type	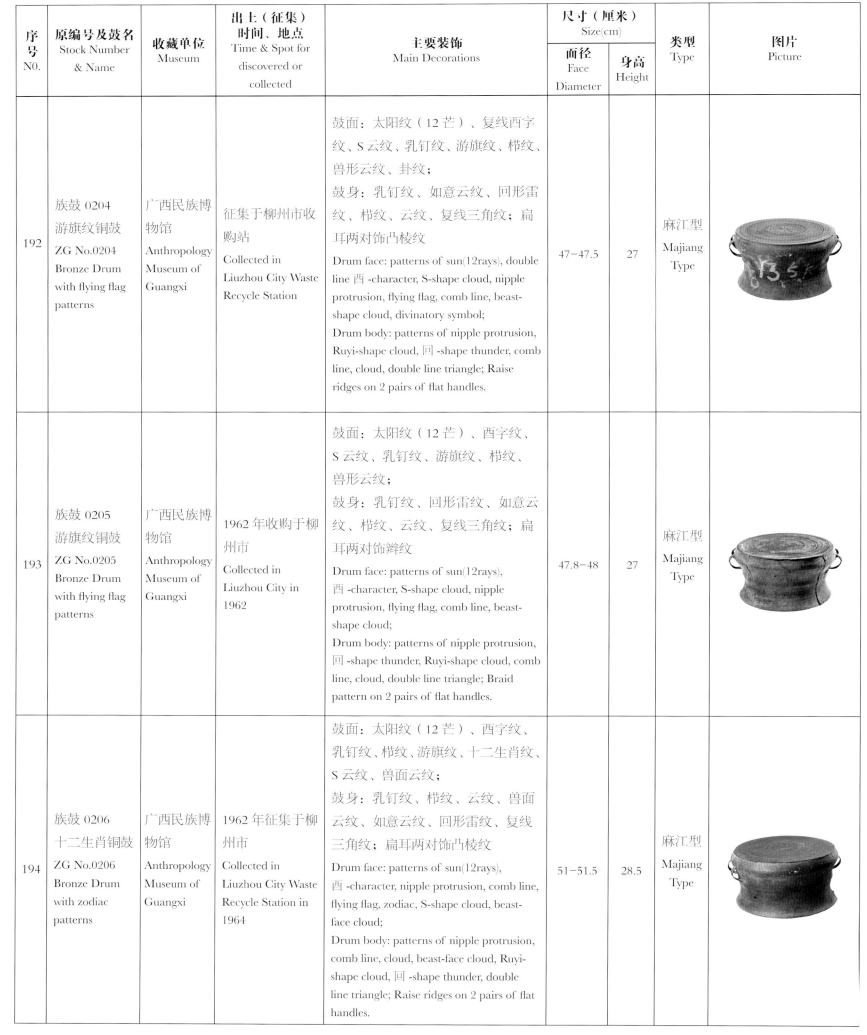
193	族鼓 0205 游旗纹铜鼓 ZG No.0205 Bronze Drum with flying flag patterns	广西民族博 物馆 Anthropology Museum of Guangxi	1962 年收购于柳 州市 Collected in Liuzhou City in 1962	鼓面：太阳纹（12 芒）、西字纹、 S 云纹、乳钉纹、游旗纹、栉纹、 兽形云纹； 鼓身：乳钉纹、回形雷纹、如意云 纹、栉纹、云纹、复线三角纹；扁 耳两对饰辫纹 Drum face: patterns of sun(12rays), 西 -character, S-shape cloud, nipple protrusion, flying flag, comb line, beast- shape cloud; Drum body: patterns of nipple protrusion, 回 -shape thunder, Ruyi-shape cloud, comb line, cloud, double line triangle; Braid pattern on 2 pairs of flat handles.	47.8-48	27	麻江型 Majiang Type	
194	族鼓 0206 十二生肖铜鼓 ZG No.0206 Bronze Drum with zodiac patterns	广西民族博 物馆 Anthropology Museum of Guangxi	1962 年征集于柳 州市 Collected in Liuzhou City Waste Recycle Station in 1964	鼓面：太阳纹（12 芒）、西字纹、 乳钉纹、栉纹、游旗纹、十二生肖纹、 S 云纹、兽面云纹； 鼓身：乳钉纹、栉纹、云纹、兽面 云纹、如意云纹、回形雷纹、复线 三角纹；扁耳两对饰凸棱纹 Drum face: patterns of sun(12rays), 酉 -character, nipple protrusion, comb line, flying flag, zodiac, S-shape cloud, beast- face cloud; Drum body: patterns of nipple protrusion, comb line, cloud, beast-face cloud, Ruyi- shape cloud, 回 -shape thunder, double line triangle; Raise ridges on 2 pairs of flat handles.	51-51.5	28.5	麻江型 Majiang Type	

序号 N0.	原编号及鼓名 Stock Number & Name	收藏单位 Museum	出土（征集） 时间、地点 Time & Spot for discovered or collected	主要装饰 Main Decorations	尺寸（厘米） Size(cm)		类型 Type	图片 Picture
					面径 Face Diameter	身高 Height		
195	族鼓 0207 游旗纹铜鼓 ZG No.0207 Bronze Drum with flying flag patterns	广西民族博物馆 Anthropology Museum of Guangxi	1962 年征集于柳州 Collected in Liuzhou City in 1962	鼓面：太阳纹（12 芒）、酉字纹、云纹、乳钉纹、栉纹、游旗纹、卦纹； 鼓身：乳钉纹、如意云纹、回形雷纹、栉纹、云纹、复线三角纹；扁耳两对饰辫纹 Drum face: patterns of sun(12rays), 酉 -character, cloud, nipple protrusion, comb line, flying flag, divinatory symbol; Drum body: patterns of nipple protrusion, Ruyi-shape cloud, 回 -shape thunder, comb line, cloud, double line triangle; Braid patterns on 2 pairs of flat handles.	49.7–50	28	麻江型 Majiang Type	
196	族鼓 0208 游旗纹铜鼓 ZG No.0208 Bronze Drum with flying flag patterns	广西民族博物馆 Anthropology Museum of Guangxi	1962 年征集于柳州市 Collected in Liuzhou City in 1962	鼓面：太阳纹（12 芒）、酉字纹、S 云纹、乳钉纹、游旗纹、栉纹、兽形云纹、卦纹； 鼓身：乳钉纹、回形雷纹、如意云纹、栉纹、兽面云纹、复线三角纹；扁耳两对饰辫纹、回形雷纹 Drum face: patterns of sun(12rays), 酉 -character, S-shape cloud, nipple protrusion, flying flag, comb line, beast-shape cloud, divinatory symbol; Drum body: patterns of nipple protrusion, 回 -shape thunder, Ruyi-shape cloud, comb line, beast-face cloud, double line triangle; Braid & 回 -shape thunder patterns on 2 pairs of flat handles.	47.8–48.3	25(残) Incomplete	麻江型 Majiang Type	
197	族鼓 0209 游旗纹铜鼓 ZG No.0209 Bronze Drum with flying flag patterns	广西民族博物馆 Anthropology Museum of Guangxi	来源不详，原存广西壮族白治区博物馆 Original source unknown; preserved previously in Museum of Guangxi Zhuang Autonomous Region	鼓面：太阳纹（12 芒）、酉字纹、S 云纹、乳钉纹、游旗纹、栉纹、兽形云纹、卦纹； 鼓身：乳钉纹、回形雷纹、如意纹、栉纹、云纹、复线三角纹；扁耳两对饰辫纹、回形雷纹 Drum face: patterns of sun(12rays), 酉 -character, S-shape cloud, nipple protrusion, flying flag, comb line, beast-shape cloud, divinatory symbol; Drum body: patterns of nipple protrusion, 回 -shape thunder, Ruyi-shape cloud, comb line, cloud, double line triangle; Braid & 回 -shape thunder patterns on 2 pairs of flat handles.	47–47.2	26.5	麻江型 Majiang Type	

序号 N0.	原编号及鼓名 Stock Number & Name	收藏单位 Museum	出土（征集）时间、地点 Time & Spot for discovered or collected	主要装饰 Main Decorations	尺寸（厘米）Size(cm)		类型 Type	图片 Picture
					面径 Face Diameter	身高 Height		
198	族鼓 0210 游旗纹铜鼓 ZG No.0210 Bronze Drum with flying flag patterns	广西民族博物馆 Anthropology Museum of Guangxi	1962 年征集于柳州市 Collected in Liuzhou City in 1962	鼓面：太阳纹（12 芒）、西字纹、S 云纹、乳钉纹、栉纹、游旗纹、兽形云纹；鼓身：乳钉纹、如意云纹、栉纹、兽形云纹、回形雷纹、复线三角纹；扁耳两对饰辫纹 Drum face: patterns of sun(12rays), 西 -character, S-shape cloud, nipple protrusion, comb line, flying flag, beast-shape cloud; Drum body: patterns of nipple protrusion, Ruyi-shape cloud, comb line, beast-shape cloud, 回 -shape thunder, double line triangle; Braid patterns on 2 pairs of flat handles.	49.8-50.3	28.5	麻江型 Majiang Type	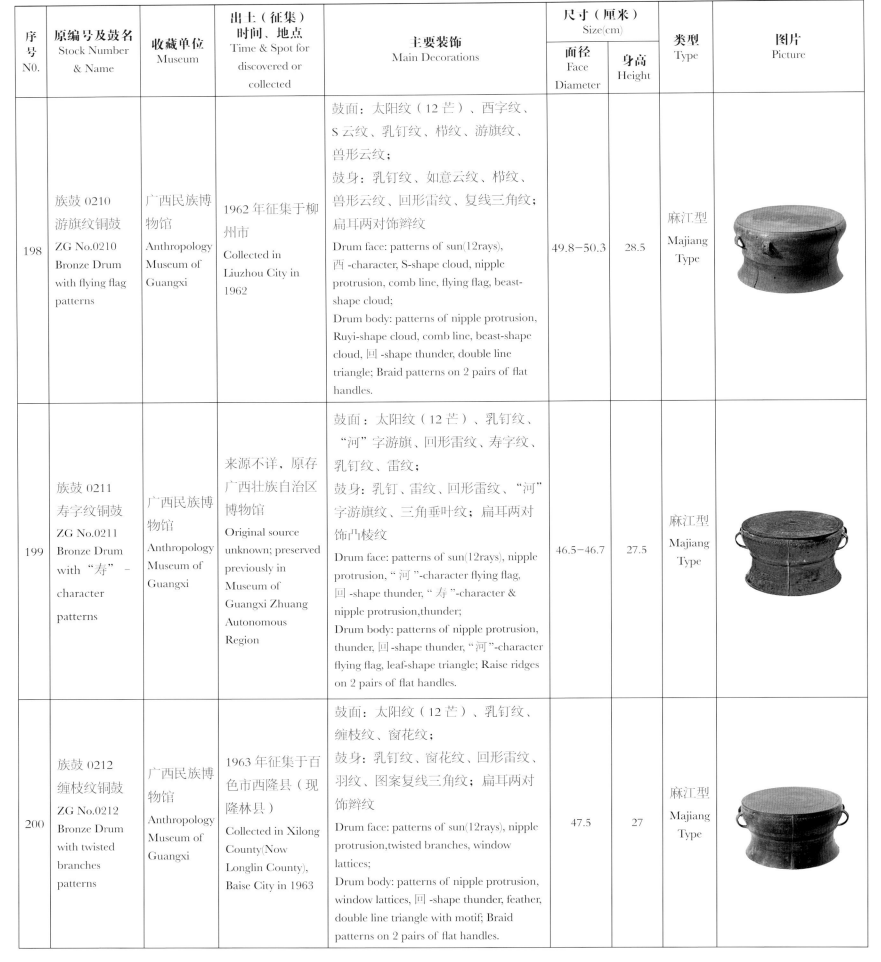
199	族鼓 0211 寿字纹铜鼓 ZG No.0211 Bronze Drum with "寿" -character patterns	广西民族博物馆 Anthropology Museum of Guangxi	来源不详，原存广西壮族自治区博物馆 Original source unknown; preserved previously in Museum of Guangxi Zhuang Autonomous Region	鼓面：太阳纹（12 芒）、乳钉纹、"河"字游旗、回形雷纹、寿字纹、乳钉纹、雷纹；鼓身：乳钉、雷纹、回形雷纹、"河"字游旗纹、三角垂叶纹；扁耳两对饰凸棱纹 Drum face: patterns of sun(12rays), nipple protrusion, " 河 "-character flying flag, 回 -shape thunder, " 寿 "-character & nipple protrusion,thunder; Drum body: patterns of nipple protrusion, thunder, 回 -shape thunder, " 河 "-character flying flag, leaf-shape triangle; Raise ridges on 2 pairs of flat handles.	46.5-46.7	27.5	麻江型 Majiang Type	
200	族鼓 0212 缠枝纹铜鼓 ZG No.0212 Bronze Drum with twisted branches patterns	广西民族博物馆 Anthropology Museum of Guangxi	1963 年征集于百色市西隆县（现隆林县）Collected in Xilong County(Now Longlin County), Baise City in 1963	鼓面：太阳纹（12 芒）、乳钉纹、缠枝纹、窗花纹；鼓身：乳钉纹、窗花纹、回形雷纹、羽纹、图案复线三角纹；扁耳两对饰辫纹 Drum face: patterns of sun(12rays), nipple protrusion,twisted branches, window lattices; Drum body: patterns of nipple protrusion, window lattices, 回 -shape thunder, feather, double line triangle with motif; Braid patterns on 2 pairs of flat handles.	47.5	27	麻江型 Majiang Type	

序号 N0.	原编号及鼓名 Stock Number & Name	收藏单位 Museum	出土（征集） 时间、地点 Time & Spot for discovered or collected	主要装饰 Main Decorations	尺寸（厘米） Size(cm)		类型 Type	图片 Picture
					面径 Face Diameter	身高 Height		
201	族鼓 0213 十二生肖纹铜鼓 ZG No.0213 Bronze Drum with zodiac patterns	广西民族博物馆 Anthropology Museum of Guangxi	1962 年收购于柳州市收购站 Collected in Liuzhou City Waste Recycle Station in 1964	鼓面：太阳纹（12 芒）、西字纹、S 云纹、乳钉纹、栉纹、游旗纹、十二生肖纹、兽形云纹、卦纹； 鼓身：乳钉纹、如意纹、如意云纹、回形雷纹、云纹、栉纹、复线三角纹；扁耳两对饰辫纹 Drum face: patterns of sun(12rays), 西-character, S-shape cloud, nipple protrusion, comb line, flying flag & zodiac, beast-shape cloud, divinatory symbol; Drum body: patterns of nipple protrusion, Ruyi, Ruyi-shape cloud, 回-shape thunder, cloud, comb line, double line triangle; Braid patterns on 2 pairs of flat handles.	50	28	麻江型 Majiang Type	
202	族鼓 0214 ZG No.0214 缠枝纹铜鼓 Bronze Drum with twisted branches pattern	广西民族博物馆 Anthropology Museum of Guangxi	1954 年征集于横县 Collected in Hengxian County in 1954	鼓面：太阳纹（12 芒）、乳钉纹、复线角形纹、缠枝纹； 鼓身：鼓腰处三道突棱，鼓足处三道弦纹；扁耳两对 Drum face: patterns of sun(12rays), nipple protrusion, double line triangle, twisted branches; Drum body: 3 raise ridges on drum waist, 3 strings on the foot; 2 pairs of flat handles.	47.5	27	麻江型 Majiang Type	
203	族鼓 0215 游旗纹铜鼓 ZG No.0215 Bronze Drum with flying flag patterns	广西民族博物馆 Anthropology Museum of Guangxi	来源不详，原存广西壮族自治区博物馆 Original source unknown; preserved previously in Museum of Guangxi Zhuang Autonomous Region	鼓面：太阳纹（12 芒）、乳钉纹、缠枝花纹、游旗纹、窗花纹； 鼓身：乳钉纹、菱形填四瓣花纹、回形雷纹、雷纹、游旗纹、图案复线三角纹；扁耳两对饰辫纹 Drum face: patterns of sun(12rays), nipple protrusion, twisted branches, flying flag, window lattices; Drum body: patterns of nipple protrusion, diamond filled with quatrefoils, 回-shape thunder, thunder, flying flag, motif triangle; Braid patterns on 2 pairs of flat handles.	47－47.5	27	麻江型 Majiang Type	

序号 NO.	原编号及鼓名 Stock Number & Name	收藏单位 Museum	出土（征集） 时间、地点 Time & Spot for discovered or collected	主要装饰 Main Decorations	尺寸（厘米） Size(cm)		类型 Type	图片 Picture
					面径 Face Diameter	身高 Height		
204	族鼓 0216 缠枝纹铜鼓 ZG No.0216 Bronze Drum with twisted branches pattern	广西民族博物馆 Anthropology Museum of Guangxi	征集于南宁市 Collected in Nanning City	鼓面：太阳纹（12 芒）、乳钉纹、菱形填四瓣花纹、缠枝纹、梅花图案纹； 鼓身：乳钉纹、席纹、雷纹、回形雷纹、缠枝纹、三角垂叶纹；扁耳两对饰辫纹 Drum face: patterns of sun(12rays), nipple protrusion,diamond filled with quatrefoils, twisted branches, plum blossom; Drum body: patterns of nipple protrusion, woven mat, thunder, 回 -shape thunder, twisted branches, leaf-shape triangle; Braid patterns on 2 pairs of flat handles.	47.2–47.4	26.8	麻江型 Majiang Type	
205	族鼓 0217 游旗纹铜鼓 ZG No.0217 Bronze Drum with flying flag patterns	广西民族博物馆 Anthropology Museum of Guangxi	征集于柳州市收购站 Collected in Liuzhou City Waste Recycle Station	鼓面：太阳纹（12 芒）、酉字纹、S 云纹、乳钉纹、游旗纹、栉纹、兽形云纹、卦纹； 鼓身：回形雷纹、如意云纹、栉纹、云纹、复线三角纹；扁耳两对饰辫纹、回形雷纹 Drum face: patterns of sun(12rays), 酉 -character, S-shape cloud, nipple protrusion, flying flag, comb line, beast-shape cloud, divinatory symbol; Drum body: patterns of 回 -shape thunder, Ruyi-shape cloud, comb line, cloud, double line triangle; Braid & 回 -shape thunder patterns on 2 pairs of flat handles.	47	27	麻江型 Majiang Type	
206	族鼓 0218 十二生肖铜鼓 ZG No.0218 Bronze Drum with zodiac patterns	广西民族博物馆 Anthropology Museum of Guangxi	征集于柳州市收购站 Collected in Liuzhou City Waste Recycle Station	鼓面：太阳纹（12 芒）、酉字纹、S 云纹、乳钉纹、栉纹、游旗纹、十二生肖纹、如意云纹； 鼓身：如意云纹、乳钉纹、栉纹、八宝结纹、云纹、回形雷纹、复线三角纹；扁耳两对饰辫纹 Drum face: patterns of sun(12rays), 酉 -character, S-shape cloud, nipple protrusion, comb line, flying flag, zodiac, Ruyi-shape cloud; Drum body: patterns of Ruyi-shape cloud, nipple protrusion, comb line, Buddhist 8 treasures, cloud, 回 -shape thunder, double line triangle; Braid patterns on 2 pairs of flat handles.	52–52.4	28.5	麻江型 Majiang Type	

序号 NO.	原编号及鼓名 Stock Number & Name	收藏单位 Museum	出土（征集） 时间、地点 Time & Spot for discovered or collected	主要装饰 Main Decorations	尺寸（厘米） Size(cm)		类型 Type	图片 Picture
					面径 Face Diameter	身高 Height		
207	族鼓 0219 鸟兽纹铜鼓 ZG No.0219 Bronze Drum with bird and beast patterns	广西民族博物馆 Anthropology Museum of Guangxi	1962 年征集于柳州市 Collected in Liuzhou City in 1962	鼓面：太阳纹（12 芒）、西字纹、栉纹、乳钉纹、动物（龙、牛、鱼）纹、回形雷纹； 鼓身：乳钉纹、云纹、钱纹、回形雷纹、S 云纹、复线三角纹；扁耳两对饰辫纹 Drum face: patterns of sun(12rays), 西 -character, comb line, nipple protrusion, animals(including dragon, ox,fish), 回 -shape thunder; Drum body: patterns of nipple protrusion, cloud, coin, 回 -shape thunder, S-shape cloud, double line triangle; Braid patterns on 2 pairs of flat handles.	44.5	25	麻江型 Majiang Type	
208	族鼓 0220 二龙戏珠纹铜鼓 ZG No.0220 Bronze Drum with 2 dragons playing pearl patterns	广西民族博物馆 Anthropology Museum of Guangxi	1962 年征集于柳州 Collected in Liuzhou City in 1962	鼓面：太阳纹（12 芒）、西字纹、S 云纹、乳钉纹、栉纹、游旗纹、兽形云纹、双龙戏珠间扑纹； 鼓身：乳钉纹、如意云纹、兽形云纹、回形雷纹、栉纹、复线三角纹；扁耳两对饰辫纹 Drum face: patterns of sun(12rays), 西 -character, S-shape cloud, nipple protrusion, comb line, flying flag, beast-shape cloud, 2 dragons playing pearl mixed divinatory symbol; Drum body: patterns of nipple protrusion, Ruyi-shape cloud, beast-shape cloud, 回 -shape thunder, comb line, double line triangle; Braid patterns on 2 pairs of flat handles.	55–57	28	麻江型 Majiang Type	
209	族鼓 0221 梿花纹铜鼓 ZG No.0221 Bronze Drum with window lattices patterns	广西民族博物馆 Anthropology Museum of Guangxi	征集于柳州市收购站 Collected in Liuzhou City Waste Recycle Station	鼓面：太阳纹（12 芒）、西字纹、S 云纹、乳钉纹、梿花纹、云纹、回形雷纹； 鼓身：梅花状乳钉纹、如意纹、回形雷纹、云纹、复线三角纹；扁耳两对饰辫纹、回形雷纹 Drum face: patterns of sun(12rays), 西 -character, S-shape cloud, nipple protrusion, window lattices, cloud, 回 -shape thunder; Drum body: patterns of nipple protrusion array in plum blossom shape, Ruyi-shape cloud, 回 -shape thunder, cloud, double line triangle; Braid & 回 -shape thunder patterns on 2 pairs of flat handles.	47.3–47.5	27.5	麻江型 Majiang Type	

序号 N0.	原编号及鼓名 Stock Number & Name	收藏单位 Museum	出土（征集） 时间、地点 Time & Spot for discovered or collected	主要装饰 Main Decorations	尺寸（厘米） Size(cm)		类型 Type	图片 Picture
					面径 Face Diameter	身高 Height		
210	族鼓 0222 变形游旗纹铜鼓 ZG No.0222 Bronze Drum with transformed flying flag patterns	广西民族博物馆 Anthropology Museum of Guangxi	1963 年征集于南宁市 Collected in Nanning City in 1963	鼓面：太阳纹（12 芒）、王字纹、同心圆纹、花纹、羽纹、缠枝纹、栉纹、乳钉纹、绚纹； 鼓身：素面；扁耳两对饰凹弦纹 Drum face: patterns of sun(12rays), " 王 "-character,concentric circle, flower, feather, twisted branches, comb line, nipple protrusion, twisted rope; Drum body: no patterns; Concave strings on 2 pairs of flat handles.	46.6－47	29	麻江型 Majiang Type	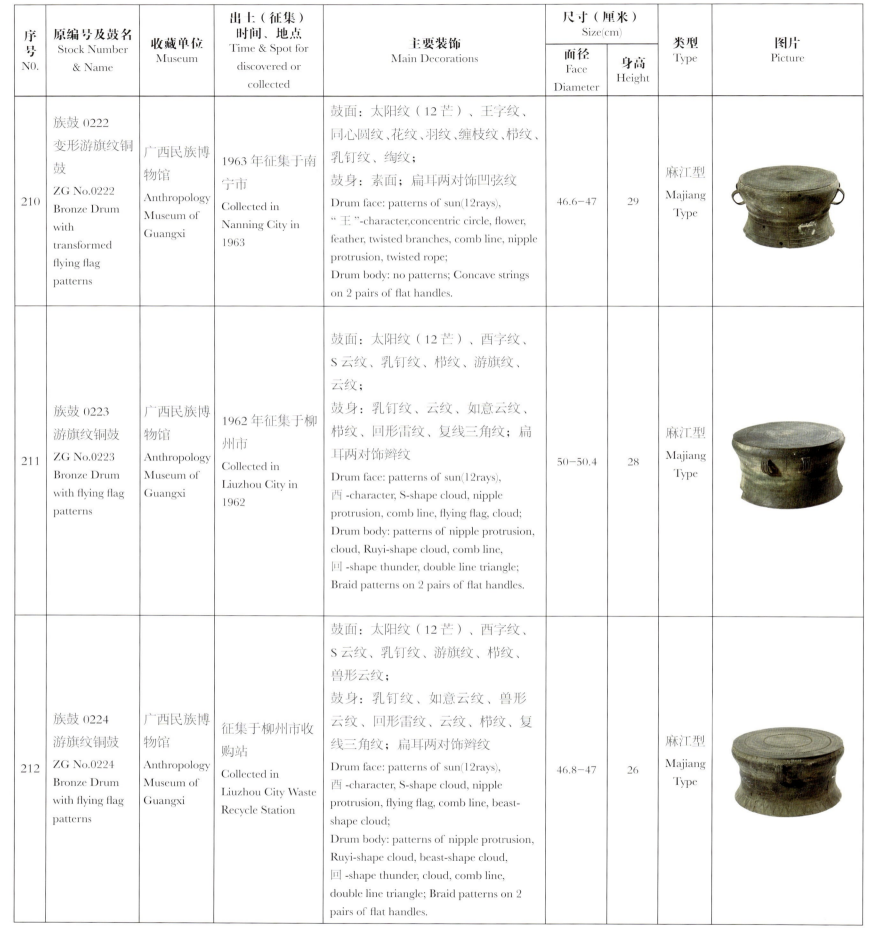
211	族鼓 0223 游旗纹铜鼓 ZG No.0223 Bronze Drum with flying flag patterns	广西民族博物馆 Anthropology Museum of Guangxi	1962 年征集于柳州市 Collected in Liuzhou City in 1962	鼓面：太阳纹（12 芒）、酉字纹、S 云纹、乳钉纹、栉纹、游旗纹、云纹； 鼓身：乳钉纹、云纹、如意云纹、栉纹、回形雷纹、复线三角纹；扁耳两对饰辫纹 Drum face: patterns of sun(12rays), 酉 -character, S-shape cloud, nipple protrusion, comb line, flying flag, cloud; Drum body: patterns of nipple protrusion, cloud, Ruyi-shape cloud, comb line, 回 -shape thunder, double line triangle; Braid patterns on 2 pairs of flat handles.	50－50.4	28	麻江型 Majiang Type	
212	族鼓 0224 游旗纹铜鼓 ZG No.0224 Bronze Drum with flying flag patterns	广西民族博物馆 Anthropology Museum of Guangxi	征集于柳州市收购站 Collected in Liuzhou City Waste Recycle Station	鼓面：太阳纹（12 芒）、酉字纹、S 云纹、乳钉纹、游旗纹、栉纹、兽形云纹； 鼓身：乳钉纹、如意云纹、兽形云纹、回形雷纹、云纹、栉纹、复线三角纹；扁耳两对饰辫纹 Drum face: patterns of sun(12rays), 酉 -character, S-shape cloud, nipple protrusion, flying flag, comb line, beast-shape cloud; Drum body: patterns of nipple protrusion, Ruyi-shape cloud, beast-shape cloud, 回 -shape thunder, cloud, comb line, double line triangle; Braid patterns on 2 pairs of flat handles.	46.8－47	26	麻江型 Majiang Type	

续表

序号 NO.	原编号及鼓名 Stock Number & Name	收藏单位 Museum	出土（征集）时间、地点 Time & Spot for discovered or collected	主要装饰 Main Decorations	尺寸（厘米） Size(cm)		类型 Type	图片 Picture
					面径 Face Diameter	身高 Height		
213	族鼓 0225 游旗纹铜鼓 ZG No.0225 Bronze Drum with flying flag patterns	广西民族博物馆 Anthropology Museum of Guangxi	收购于柳州市 Collected in Liuzhou City	鼓面：太阳纹（12 芒）、酉字纹、S 云纹、乳钉纹、游旗纹、栉纹、云纹： 鼓身：乳钉纹、如意云纹、回形雷纹、栉纹、复线三角纹；扁耳两对 Drum face: patterns of sun(12rays), 西-character, S-shape cloud, nipple protrusion, flying flag, comb line, cloud; Drum body: patterns of nipple protrusion, Ruyi-shape cloud, 回-shape thunder, comb line, double line triangle; 2 pairs of flat handles.	46.7	26.3	麻江型 Majiang Type	
214	族鼓 0226 游旗纹铜鼓 ZG No.0226 Bronze Drum with flying flag patterns	广西民族博物馆 Anthropology Museum of Guangxi	1962 年征集于柳州市 Collected in Liuzhou City in 1962	鼓面：太阳纹（12 芒）、西字纹、乳钉纹、游旗纹、回形雷纹、栉纹、如意云纹； 鼓身：乳钉纹、云纹、回形雷纹、雷纹、复线三角纹；扁耳两对饰辫纹 Drum face: patterns of sun(12rays), 西-character, nipple protrusion, flying flag, 回-shape thunder, comb line, Ruyi-shape cloud; Drum body: patterns of nipple protrusion, cloud, 回-shape thunder, thunder, double line triangle; Braid patterns on 2 pairs of flat handles.	49.2	27.5	麻江型 Majiang Type	
215	族鼓 0227 鱼纹铜鼓 ZG No.0227 Bronze Drum with fish patterns	广西民族博物馆 Anthropology Museum of Guangxi	1962 年征集于柳州市 Collected in Liuzhou City in 1962	鼓面：太阳纹（12 芒）、同心圆纹、乳钉纹、桂鱼戏珠纹、三角乳钉纹、兽面云纹、回形雷纹； 鼓身：可辨乳钉纹、回形雷纹、云纹，其余磨蚀；扁耳两对饰辫纹 Drum face: patterns of sun(12rays), concentric circle, nipple protrusion, mandarin fish playing pearl, triangle nipple protrusion, beast-face cloud, 回-shape thunder; Drum body: patterns of nipple protrusion, 回-shape thunder, cloud, the other patterns are obscure; Braid patterns on 2 pairs of flat handles.	44.5	25.8	麻江型 Majiang Type	

序号 N0.	原编号及鼓名 Stock Number & Name	收藏单位 Museum	出土（征集）时间、地点 Time & Spot for discovered or collected	主要装饰 Main Decorations	尺寸（厘米） Size(cm)		类型 Type	图片 Picture
					面径 Face Diameter	身高 Height		
216	族鼓 0228 游旗纹铜鼓 ZG No.0228 Bronze Drum with flying flag patterns	广西民族博物馆 Anthropology Museum of Guangxi	征集于柳州市收购站 Collected in Liuzhou City Waste Recycle Station	鼓面：太阳纹（12 芒）、酉字纹、S 云纹、乳钉纹、游旗纹、栉纹、兽形云纹； 鼓身：乳钉纹、回形雷纹、如意云纹、栉纹、兽面云纹、复线三角纹；扁耳两对饰辫纹 Drum face: patterns of sun(12rays), 酉 -character, S-shape cloud, nipple protrusion, flying flag, comb line, beast-shape cloud; Drum body: patterns of nipple protrusion, 回 -shape thunder, Ruyi-shape cloud, comb line, beast-face cloud, double line triangle; Braid patterns on 2 pairs of flat handles.	46.5－47	26.5	麻江型 Majiang Type	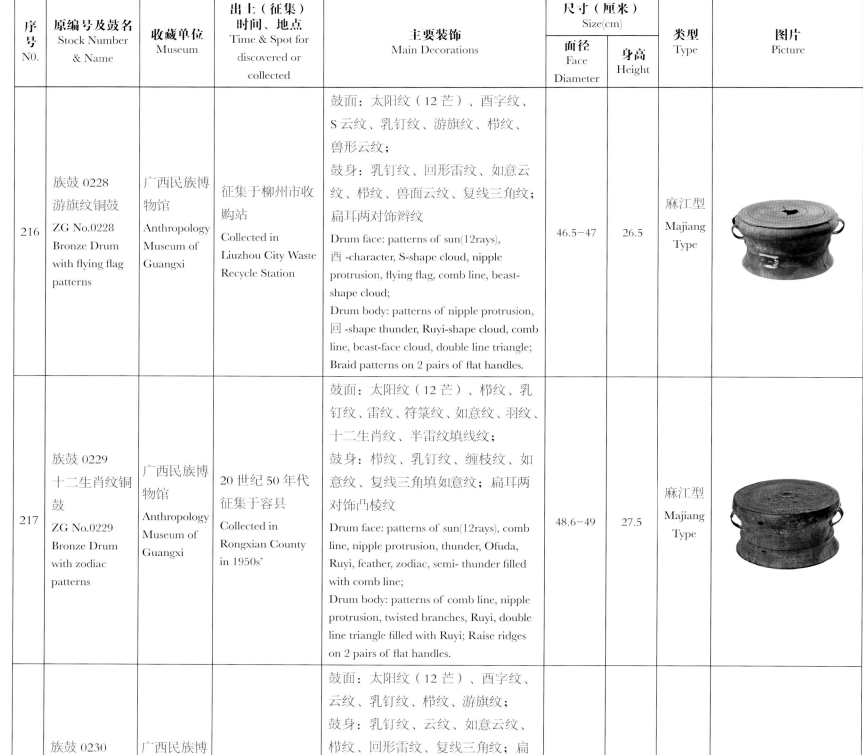
217	族鼓 0229 十二生肖纹铜鼓 ZG No.0229 Bronze Drum with zodiac patterns	广西民族博物馆 Anthropology Museum of Guangxi	20 世纪 50 年代征集于容县 Collected in Rongxian County in 1950s'	鼓面：太阳纹（12 芒）、栉纹、乳钉纹、雷纹、符箓纹、如意纹、羽纹、十二生肖纹、半雷纹填线纹； 鼓身：栉纹、乳钉纹、缠枝纹、如意纹、复线三角填如意纹；扁耳两对饰凸棱纹 Drum face: patterns of sun(12rays), comb line, nipple protrusion, thunder, Ofuda, Ruyi, feather, zodiac, semi- thunder filled with comb line; Drum body: patterns of comb line, nipple protrusion, twisted branches, Ruyi, double line triangle filled with Ruyi; Raise ridges on 2 pairs of flat handles.	48.6－49	27.5	麻江型 Majiang Type	
218	族鼓 0230 游旗纹铜鼓 ZG No.0230 Bronze Drum with flying flag patterns	广西民族博物馆 Anthropology Museum of Guangxi	征集于柳州市 Collected in Liuzhou City	鼓面：太阳纹（12 芒）、酉字纹、云纹、乳钉纹、栉纹、游旗纹； 鼓身：乳钉纹、云纹、如意云纹、栉纹、回形雷纹、复线三角纹；扁耳两对饰辫纹、回形雷纹 Drum face: patterns of sun(12rays), 酉 -character, cloud, nipple protrusion, comb line, flying flag; Drum body: patterns of nipple protrusion, cloud, Ruyi-shape cloud, comb line, 回 -shape thunder, double line triangle; Braid & 回 -shape thunder patterns on 2 pairs of flat handles.	52.5－52.7	30.3	麻江型 Majiang Type	

续表

序号 NO.	原编号及鼓名 Stock Number & Name	收藏单位 Museum	出土（征集） 时间、地点 Time & Spot for discovered or collected	主要装饰 Main Decorations	尺寸（厘米） Size(cm)		类型 Type	图片 Picture
					面径 Face Diameter	身高 Height		
219	族鼓 0231 回形雷纹云纹铜鼓 ZG No.0231 Bronze Drum with 回－shape thunder& cloud patterns	广西民族博物馆 Anthropology Museum of Guangxi	1963 年征集于西隆县（现隆林县） Collected in Xilong County(Now Longlin County) in 1963	鼓面：太阳纹（芒磨蚀）、乳钉纹、云纹、缠枝纹、回形雷纹； 鼓身：乳钉纹、云纹、回形雷纹、复线三角纹；扁耳两对饰凸棱纹 Drum face: patterns of sun(rays obscure), nipple protrusion, cloud, twisted branches, 回 -shape thunder; Drum body: patterns of nipple protrusion, cloud, 回 -shape thunder, double line triangle; Raise ridges on 2 pairs of flat handles.	45.5－45.7	27.5	麻江型 Majiang Type	
220	族鼓 0232 游旗纹铜鼓 ZG No.0232 Bronze Drum with flying flag patterns	广西民族博物馆 Anthropology Museum of Guangxi	1962 年征集于柳州 Collected in Liuzhou City in 1962	鼓面：太阳纹（12 芒）、酉字纹、S 云纹、乳钉纹、游旗纹、栉纹、兽面云纹、卦纹； 鼓身：乳钉纹、回形雷纹、如意云纹、栉纹、云纹、复线三角纹；扁耳两对饰辫纹、回形雷纹 Drum face: patterns of sun(12rays), 酉 -character, S-shape cloud, nipple protrusion, flying flag, comb line, beast-face cloud, divinatory symbol; Drum body: patterns of nipple protrusion, 回 -shape thunder, Ruyi-shape cloud, comb line, cloud, double line triangle; Braid & 回 -shape thunder patterns on 2 pairs of flat handles.	47－47.5	27	麻江型 Majiang Type	
221	族鼓 0233 奔马寿字纹铜鼓 ZG No.0233 Bronze Drum with galloping horse and 寿－character patterns	广西民族博物馆 Anthropology Museum of Guangxi	来源不详，原存广西壮族自治区博物馆 Original source unknown; preserved previously in Museum of Guangxi Zhuang Autonomous Region	鼓面：太阳纹（12 芒）、栉纹、同心圆纹、乳钉纹、符箓纹、团寿纹、马纹、品字乳钉纹、云纹； 鼓身：梅花状乳钉纹、同心圆纹、回形雷纹、云纹、复线三角纹；扁耳两对饰辫纹 Drum face: patterns of sun(12rays), comb line, concentric circle, nipple protrusion, complex patterns of Ofuda, round 寿 -character and horse, nipple protrusion array in 品 -shape, cloud; Drum body: patterns of nipple protrusion array in plum blossom shape, concentric circle, 回 -shape thunder, cloud, double line triangle; Braid patterns on 2 pairs of flat handles.	44.7－45.4	26	麻江型 Majiang Type	

315

序号 NO.	原编号及鼓名 Stock Number & Name	收藏单位 Museum	出土（征集） 时间、地点 Time & Spot for discovered or collected	主要装饰 Main Decorations	尺寸（厘米） Size(cm)		类型 Type	图片 Picture
					面径 Face Diameter	身高 Height		
222	族鼓 0234 钱纹铜鼓 ZG No.0234 Bronze Drum with coin patterns	广西民族博物馆 Anthropology Museum of Guangxi	征集于柳州市收购站 Collected in Liuzhou City Waste Recycle Station	鼓面：太阳纹（12芒）、乳钉纹、S勾纹、同心圆纹、回形雷纹、钱纹间螃蟹纹、兽面云纹、绚纹； 鼓身：乳钉纹、兽面云纹、如意云纹、回形雷纹、缠枝花纹、复线三角纹；扁耳两对饰辫纹 Drum face: patterns of sun(12rays), nipple protrusion, S-hook, concentric circle, 回-shape thunder, coins mixed crab, beast-face cloud, twisted rope; Drum body: patterns of nipple protrusion, beast-face cloud, Ruyi-shape cloud, 回-shape thunder, twisted branches, double line triangle; Braid patterns on 2 pairs of flat handles.	48.5	26	麻江型 Majiang Type	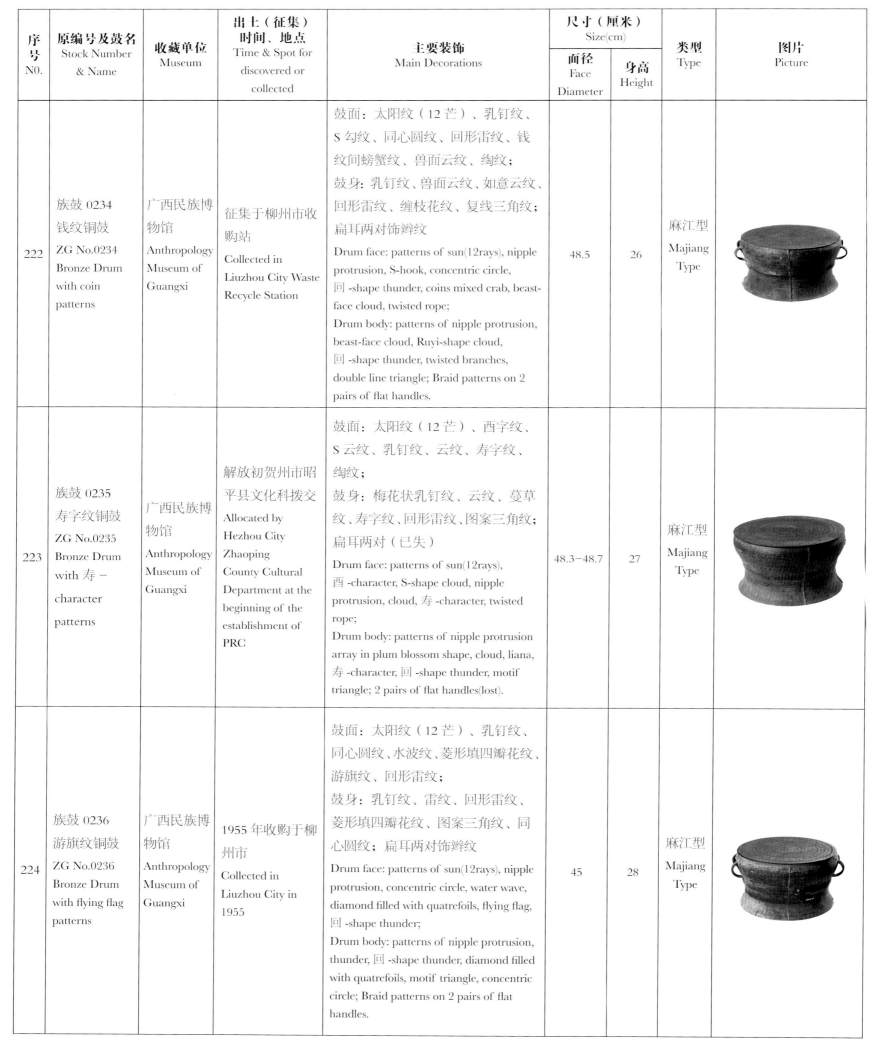
223	族鼓 0235 寿字纹铜鼓 ZG No.0235 Bronze Drum with 寿－character patterns	广西民族博物馆 Anthropology Museum of Guangxi	解放初贺州市昭平县文化科拨交 Allocated by Hezhou City Zhaoping County Cultural Department at the beginning of the establishment of PRC	鼓面：太阳纹（12芒）、西字纹、S云纹、乳钉纹、云纹、寿字纹、绚纹； 鼓身：梅花状乳钉纹、云纹、蔓草纹、寿字纹、回形雷纹、图案三角纹；扁耳两对（已失） Drum face: patterns of sun(12rays), 西-character, S-shape cloud, nipple protrusion, cloud, 寿-character, twisted rope; Drum body: patterns of nipple protrusion array in plum blossom shape, cloud, liana, 寿-character, 回-shape thunder, motif triangle; 2 pairs of flat handles(lost).	48.3-48.7	27	麻江型 Majiang Type	
224	族鼓 0236 游旗纹铜鼓 ZG No.0236 Bronze Drum with flying flag patterns	广西民族博物馆 Anthropology Museum of Guangxi	1955年收购于柳州市 Collected in Liuzhou City in 1955	鼓面：太阳纹（12芒）、乳钉纹、同心圆纹、水波纹、菱形填四瓣花纹、游旗纹、回形雷纹； 鼓身：乳钉纹、雷纹、回形雷纹、菱形填四瓣花纹、图案三角纹、同心圆纹；扁耳两对饰辫纹 Drum face: patterns of sun(12rays), nipple protrusion, concentric circle, water wave, diamond filled with quatrefoils, flying flag, 回-shape thunder; Drum body: patterns of nipple protrusion, thunder, 回-shape thunder, diamond filled with quatrefoils, motif triangle, concentric circle; Braid patterns on 2 pairs of flat handles.	45	28	麻江型 Majiang Type	

续表

序号 N0.	原编号及鼓名 Stock Number & Name	收藏单位 Museum	出土（征集）时间、地点 Time & Spot for discovered or collected	主要装饰 Main Decorations	尺寸（厘米）Size(cm)		类型 Type	图片 Picture
					面径 Face Diameter	身高 Height		
225	族鼓 0237 人物游旗纹铜鼓 ZG No.0237 Bronze Drum with man and flying flag patterns	广西民族博物馆 Anthropology Museum of Guangxi	1958 年征集于柳州市收购站 Collected in Liuzhou City Waste Recycle Station in 1958	鼓面：太阳纹（12 芒）、酉字纹、S 云纹、乳钉纹、人物游旗纹、绚纹、莲花纹、钱纹、回形雷纹；鼓身：梅花状乳钉纹、钱纹、回形雷纹、云纹、S 云纹、复线三角纹；扁耳两对饰辫纹 Drum face: patterns of sun(12rays), 酉 -character, S-shape cloud, nipple protrusion, men & flying flag, twisted rope, lotus, coin, 回 -shape thunder; Drum body: patterns of nipple protrusion array in plum blossom shape, coin, 回 -shape thunder, cloud, S-shape cloud, double line triangle; Braid patterns on 2 pairs of flat handles.	44.6－45	25	麻江型 Majiang Type	
226	族鼓 0238 游旗纹铜鼓 ZG No.0238 Bronze Drum with flying flag patterns	广西民族博物馆 Anthropology Museum of Guangxi	1958 年收购于柳州市收购站 Collected in Liuzhou City Waste Recycle Station in 1958	鼓面：太阳纹（12 芒）、酉字纹、S 云纹、乳钉纹、游旗纹、栉纹、兽形云纹；鼓身：乳钉纹、如意纹、回形雷纹、栉纹、云纹、复线三角纹；扁耳两对（已失） Drum face: patterns of sun(12rays), 酉 -character, S-shape cloud, nipple protrusion, flying flag, comb line, beast; Drum body: patterns of nipple protrusion, Ruyi, 回 -shape thunder, comb line, cloud, double line triangle; 2 pairs of flat handles(lost).	45.5－45.8	26	麻江型 Majiang Type	
227	族鼓 0239 符箓纹铜鼓 ZG No.0239 Bronze Drum with Ofuda patterns	广西民族博物馆 Anthropology Museum of Guangxi	来源不详，原存广西壮族自治区博物馆 Original source unknown; preserved previously in Museum of Guangxi Zhuang Autonomous Region	鼓面：太阳纹（12 芒）、S 云纹、如意纹、乳钉纹、符箓纹、兽面云纹、动物纹；鼓身：乳钉纹、如意纹、云纹、复线三角纹；扁耳两对饰凸棱纹 Drum face: patterns of sun(12rays), S-shape cloud, Ruyi, nipple protrusion, Ofuda, beast-face cloud, animal figure; Drum body: patterns of nipple protrusion, Ruyi, cloud, double line triangle; Raise ridges on 2 pairs of flat handles.	46－46.4	27	麻江型 Majiang Type	

序号 NO.	原编号及鼓名 Stock Number & Name	收藏单位 Museum	出土（征集） 时间、地点 Time & Spot for discovered or collected	主要装饰 Main Decorations	尺寸（厘米） Size(cm)		类型 Type	图片 Picture
					面径 Face Diameter	身高 Height		
228	族鼓 0240 游旗纹铜鼓 ZG No.0240 Bronze Drum with flying flag patterns	广西民族博物馆 Anthropology Museum of Guangxi	收购于柳州市收购站 Collected in Liuzhou City Waste Recycle Station	鼓面：太阳纹（12 芒）、酉字纹、S 云纹、乳钉纹、游旗纹、栉纹、兽形云纹、卦纹； 鼓身：乳钉纹、回形雷纹、如意云纹、栉纹、兽面云纹、复线三角纹；扁耳两对饰凸棱纹 Drum face: patterns of sun(12rays), 酉-character, S-shape cloud, nipple protrusion, flying flag, beast-shape cloud, divinatory symbol; Drum body: patterns of nipple protrusion, 回-shape thunder, Ruyi-shape cloud, comb line, beast-face cloud, double line triangle; Raise ridges on 2 pairs of flat handles.	46	27	麻江型 Majiang Type	
229	族鼓 0241 游旗纹铜鼓 ZG No.0241 Bronze Drum with flying flag patterns	广西民族博物馆 Anthropology Museum of Guangxi	采集于柳州市 Collected in Liuzhou City	鼓面：太阳纹（12 芒）、酉字纹、S 云纹、乳钉纹、游旗纹、栉纹、兽形云纹、卦纹； 鼓身：乳钉纹、如意云纹、回形雷纹、云纹、栉纹、复线三角纹；扁耳两对饰辫纹、回形雷纹 Drum face: patterns of sun(12rays), 酉-character, S-shape cloud, nipple protrusion, flying flag, comb line, beast-shape cloud, divinatory symbol; Drum body: patterns of nipple protrusion, Ruyi-shape cloud, 回-shape thunder, cloud, comb line, double line triangle; Braid & 回-shape thunder on 2 pairs of flat handles.	47.6	26.5	麻江型 Majiang Type	
230	族鼓 0242 游旗纹铜鼓 ZG No.0242 Bronze Drum with flying flag patterns	广西民族博物馆 Anthropology Museum of Guangxi	收购于柳州市收购站 Collected in Liuzhou City Waste Recycle Station	鼓面：太阳纹（12 芒）、酉字纹、云纹、乳钉纹、栉纹、游旗纹、兽形云纹； 鼓身：乳钉纹、蔓草纹、如意云纹、栉纹、云纹、回形雷纹、复线三角纹；扁耳两对饰辫纹 Drum face: patterns of sun(12rays), 酉-character, cloud, nipple protrusion, comb line, flying flag, beast-shape cloud; Drum body: patterns of nipple protrusion, liana, Ruyi-shape cloud, comb line, cloud, 回-shape thunder, double line triangle; Braid patterns on 2 pairs of flat handles.	50—51	28 （残） Incomplete	麻江型 Majiang Type	

续表

序号 NO.	原编号及鼓名 Stock Number & Name	收藏单位 Museum	出土（征集）时间、地点 Time & Spot for discovered or collected	主要装饰 Main Decorations	尺寸（厘米）Size(cm)		类型 Type	图片 Picture
					面径 Face Diameter	身高 Height		
231	族鼓 0243 游旗纹铜鼓 ZG No.0243 Bronze Drum with flying flag patterns	广西民族博物馆 Anthropology Museum of Guangxi	收购于柳州市收购站 Collected in Liuzhou City Waste Recycle Station	鼓面：太阳纹（12 芒）、西字纹、乳钉纹、栉纹、梅花纹、游旗纹、S 云纹、兽面云纹；鼓身：栉纹、乳钉纹、云纹、回形雷纹、复线三角纹；扁耳两对饰凸棱纹 Drum face: patterns of sun(12rays), 西 -character, nipple protrusion, comb line , plum blossom, flying flag, S-shape cloud, cloud; Drum body: patterns of comb line, nipple protrusion, cloud, 回 -shape thunder, double line triangle; Raise ridges on 2 pairs of flat handles.	47.2~47.5	29	麻江型 Majiang Type	
232	族鼓 0244 游旗纹铜鼓 ZG No.0244 Bronze Drum with flying flag patterns	广西民族博物馆 Anthropology Museum of Guangxi	解放初征集于北流县（现北流市）Collected in Beiliu County(Now Beiliu City) at the beginning of the establishment of PRC	鼓面：太阳纹（12 芒）、西字纹、S 云纹、乳钉纹、游旗纹、栉纹、如意云纹；鼓身：乳钉纹、如意云纹、回形雷纹、栉纹、云纹、复线三角纹；扁耳两对饰凸棱纹 Drum face: patterns of sun(12rays), 西 -character, S-shape cloud, nipple protrusion, flying flag, comb line , Ruyi-shape cloud; Drum body: patterns of nipple protrusion, Ruyi-shape cloud, 回 -shape thunder, comb line, cloud, double line triangle; Raise ridges on 2 pairs of flat handles.	47	26	麻江型 Majiang Type	
233	族鼓 0245 游旗纹铜鼓 ZG No.0245 Bronze Drum with flying flag patterns	广西民族博物馆 Anthropology Museum of Guangxi	1958 年征集于柳州市收购站 Collected in Liuzhou City Waste Recycle Station in 1958	鼓面：太阳纹（12 芒）、西字纹、乳钉纹、栉纹、游旗纹、缠枝花纹；鼓身：栉纹、乳钉纹、云纹、缠枝花纹、回形雷纹、复线三角纹；扁耳两对饰羽纹 Drum face: patterns of sun(12rays), 西 -character, nipple protrusion, comb line , flying flag, twisted branches; Drum body: patterns of comb line, nipple protrusion, cloud, twisted branches, 回 -shape thunder, double line triangle; Feather patterns on 2 pairs of flat handles.	48	29	麻江型 Majiang Type	

序号 N0.	原编号及鼓名 Stock Number & Name	收藏单位 Museum	出土（征集）时间、地点 Time & Spot for discovered or collected	主要装饰 Main Decorations	尺寸（厘米） Size(cm)		类型 Type	图片 Picture
					面径 Face Diameter	身高 Height		
234	族鼓 0246 游旗纹铜鼓 ZG No.0246 Bronze Drum with flying flag patterns	广西民族博物馆 Anthropology Museum of Guangxi	来源不详，原存广西壮族自治区博物馆 Original source unknown; preserved previously in Museum of Guangxi Zhuang Autonomous Region	鼓面：太阳纹（12 芒）、西字纹、云纹、乳钉纹、游旗纹、栉纹、兽形云纹、卦纹； 鼓身：乳钉纹、回形雷纹、如意云纹、栉纹、云纹、复线三角纹；扁耳两对饰辫纹、回形雷纹 Drum face: patterns of sun(12rays), 西 -character, cloud, nipple protrusion, flying flag, comb line , beast-shape cloud, divinatory symbol; Drum body: patterns of nipple protrusion, 回 -shape thunder, Ruyi-shape cloud, comb line, cloud, double line triangle; Braid & 回 -shape thunder patterns on 2 pairs of flat handles.	46.9	27	麻江型 Majiang Type	
235	族鼓 0247 游旗纹铜鼓 ZG No.0247 Bronze Drum with flying flag patterns	广西民族博物馆 Anthropology Museum of Guangxi	1962 年收购于柳州市收购站 Collected in Liuzhou City Waste Recycle Station in 1962	鼓面：太阳纹（12 芒）、西字纹、S 云纹、乳钉纹、栉纹、游旗纹、羽纹、卦纹； 鼓身：乳钉纹、云纹、回形雷纹、栉纹、复线三角纹；扁耳两对饰辫纹 Drum face: patterns of sun(12rays), 西 -character, S-shape cloud, nipple protrusion, comb line , flying flag, feather, divinatory symbol; Drum body: patterns of nipple protrusion, cloud, 回 -shape thunder, comb line, double line triangle; Braid patterns on 2 pairs of flat handles.	50.5	29 （残） Incomplete	麻江型 Majiang Type	
236	族鼓 0248 游旗纹铜鼓 ZG No.0248 Bronze Drum with flying flag patterns	广西民族博物馆 Anthropology Museum of Guangxi	来源不详，原存广西壮族自治区博物馆 Original source unknown; preserved previously in Museum of Guangxi Zhuang Autonomous Region	鼓面：太阳纹（12 芒）、乳钉纹、西字纹、栉纹、游旗纹、四瓣花纹、窗花纹、雷纹、回形雷纹； 鼓身：乳钉纹、羽纹、雷纹、水波纹、四瓣花纹、复线三角纹；扁耳两对饰凸棱纹 Drum face: patterns of sun(12rays), nipple protrusion, 西 -character, comb line , flying flag, quatrefoil, window lattices, thunder, 回 -shape thunder; Drum body: patterns of nipple protrusion, feather, thunder, water wave, quatrefoil, double line triangle; Raise ridges on 2 pairs of flat handles.	48	27	麻江型 Majiang Type	

序号 N0.	原编号及鼓名 Stock Number & Name	收藏单位 Museum	出土（征集）时间、地点 Time & Spot for discovered or collected	主要装饰 Main Decorations	尺寸（厘米） Size(cm)		类型 Type	图片 Picture
					面径 Face Diameter	身高 Height		
237	族鼓 0249 游旗纹铜鼓 ZG No.0249 Bronze Drum with flying flag patterns	广西民族博物馆 Anthropology Museum of Guangxi	1958 年征集于柳州市收购站 Collected in Liuzhou City Waste Recycle Station in 1958	鼓面：太阳纹（12 芒）、西字纹、S 云纹、乳钉纹、游旗纹、栉纹、兽面云纹； 鼓身：乳钉纹间回形雷纹、回形雷纹、如意云纹、栉纹、云纹、复线三角纹；扁耳两对饰辫纹、回形雷纹（一对已失） Drum face: patterns of sun(12rays), 酉 -character, S-shape cloud, nipple protrusion, flying flag, comb line, beast-face cloud; Drum body: patterns of nipple protrusion mixed 回 -shape thunder, 回 -shape thunder, Ruyi-shape cloud, comb line, cloud, double line triangle; Braid & 回 -shape thunder on 2 pairs of flat handles(one pair lost).	47	26.6	麻江型 Majiang Type	
238	族鼓 0250 动物纹铜鼓 ZG No.0250 Bronze Drum with animal figure	广西民族博物馆 Anthropology Museum of Guangxi	1958 年征集于柳州市收购站 Collected in Liuzhou City Waste Recycle Station in 1958	鼓面：太阳纹（12 芒）、圆圈纹、水波纹、动物纹； 鼓身：乳钉纹；扁耳两对饰凸棱纹 Drum face: patterns of sun(12rays), circle, water wave, animal figure; Drum body: patterns of nipple protrusion; Raise ridges on 2 pairs of flat handles.	46	27.3	麻江型 Majiang Type	
239	族鼓 0251 游旗纹铜鼓 ZG No.0251 Bronze Drum with flying flag patterns	广西民族博物馆 Anthropology Museum of Guangxi	1962 年收购于柳州市 Collected in Liuzhou City in 1962	鼓面：太阳纹（12 芒）、西字纹、云纹、乳钉纹、栉纹、游旗纹、云纹； 鼓身：乳钉纹、云纹、栉纹、回形雷纹、复线三角纹；扁耳两对饰辫纹、回形雷纹 Drum face: patterns of sun(12rays), 酉 -character, cloud, nipple protrusion, comb line, flying flag, cloud; Drum body: patterns of nipple protrusion, cloud, comb line, 回 -shape thunder, double line triangle; Braid & 回 -shape thunder on 2 pairs of flat handles.	49.7—50	28	麻江型 Majiang Type	

序号 NO.	原编号及鼓名 Stock Number & Name	收藏单位 Museum	出土（征集） 时间、地点 Time & Spot for discovered or collected	主要装饰 Main Decorations	尺寸（厘米） Size(cm)		类型 Type	图片 Picture
					面径 Face Diameter	身高 Height		
240	族鼓 0252 游旗纹铜鼓 ZG No.0252 Bronze Drum with flying flag patterns	广西民族博物馆 Anthropology Museum of Guangxi	1955 年征集于南宁市供销社 Collected at Nanning City Supply & Marketing Cooperative in 1955	鼓面：太阳纹（12 芒）、酉字纹、S 云纹、乳钉纹、游旗纹、栉纹、兽形云纹； 鼓身：乳钉纹、如意云纹、兽面云纹、回形雷纹、栉纹、复线三角纹；扁耳两对饰辫纹、雷纹 Drum face: patterns of sun(12rays), 酉 -character, S-shape cloud, nipple protrusion, flying flag, comb line, beast-shape cloud; Drum body: patterns of nipple protrusion, Ruyi-shape cloud, beast-face cloud, 回 -shape thunder, comb line, double line triangle; Braid & 回 -shape thunder on 2 pairs of flat handles.	47	26	麻江型 Majiang Type	
241	族鼓 0253 波浪纹回形纹铜鼓 ZG No.0253 Bronze Drum with water wave& 回 −shape patterns	广西民族博物馆 Anthropology Museum of Guangxi	1958 年征集于柳州市 Collected in Liuzhou City in 1958	鼓面：太阳纹（12 芒）、乳钉纹、波浪纹、雷纹、回形雷纹、波浪纹、缠枝纹； 鼓身：乳钉纹、复线三角纹、缠枝纹、波浪纹、复线三角纹；扁耳两对饰凸棱纹 Drum face: patterns of sun(12rays), nipple protrusion, water wave, thunder, 回 -shape thunder & water wave, twisted branches; Drum body: patterns of nipple protrusion, double line triangle, twisted branches, water wave, double line triangle; Raise ridges on 2 pairs of flat handles.	47.8	27.2	麻江型 Majiang Type	
242	族鼓 0254 游旗纹铜鼓 ZG No.0254 Bronze Drum with flying flag patterns	广西民族博物馆 Anthropology Museum of Guangxi	20 世纪 50 年代征集于梧州市 Collected in Wuzhou City in 1950s'	鼓面：太阳纹（12 芒）、酉字纹、S 云纹、乳钉纹、栉纹、游旗纹、兽面云纹； 鼓身：乳钉纹、兽面云纹、如意云纹、栉纹、云纹、回形雷纹、复线三角纹；扁耳两对饰辫纹 Drum face: patterns of sun(12rays), 酉 -character, S-shape cloud, nipple protrusion, comb line, flying flag, beast-face cloud; Drum body: patterns of nipple protrusion, beast-face cloud, Ruyi-shape cloud, comb line, cloud, 回 -shape thunder, double line triangle; Braid patterns on 2 pairs of flat handles.	51−51.5	28.3	麻江型 Majiang Type	

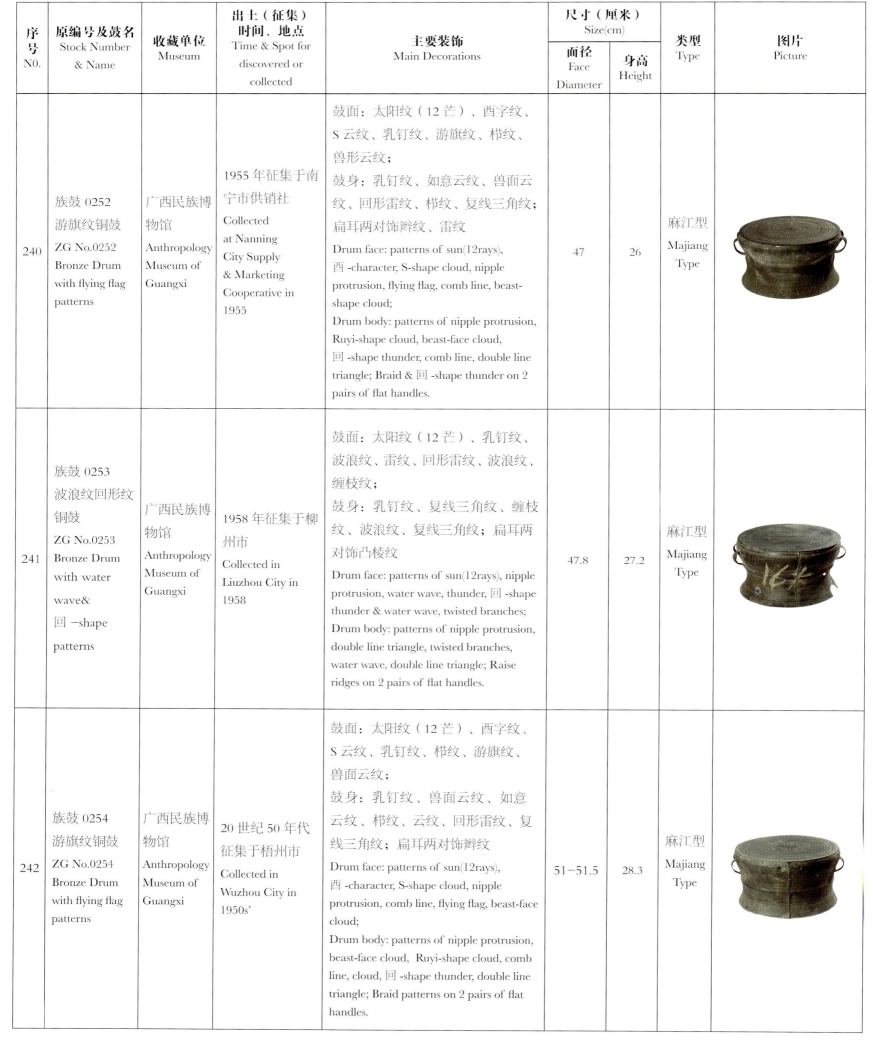

序号 NO.	原编号及鼓名 Stock Number & Name	收藏单位 Museum	出土（征集） 时间、地点 Time & Spot for discovered or collected	主要装饰 Main Decorations	尺寸（厘米） Size(cm)		类型 Type	图片 Picture
					面径 Face Diameter	身高 Height		
243	族鼓 0255 回形纹铜鼓 ZG No.0255 Bronze Drum with 回 –shape patterns	广西民族博物馆 Anthropology Museum of Guangxi	1964 年征集于柳州市二级站 Collected in Liuzhou City Waste Recycle Station in 1964	鼓面：太阳纹（13 芒）、回形雷纹、波浪纹、窗花纹、乳钉纹、回形纹、波浪纹／乳钉纹； 鼓身：乳钉纹、符箓纹、窗花纹、图案三角纹；扁耳两对（已失） Drum face: patterns of sun(13rays), 回 -shape thunder, water wave, window lattices, nipple protrusion, dual-rectangle, water wave & nipple protrusion; Drum body: patterns of nipple protrusion, Ofuda, window lattices,motif triangle; 2 pairs of flat handles(lost).	46.8	26.6	麻江型 Majiang Type	
244	族鼓 0256 游旗纹铜鼓 ZG No.0256 Bronze Drum with flying flag patterns	广西民族博物馆 Anthropology Museum of Guangxi	1962 年征集于柳州市 Collected in Liuzhou City in 1962	鼓面：太阳纹（12 芒）、酉字纹、S 云纹、乳钉纹、栉纹、游旗纹、兽形云纹； 鼓身：乳钉纹、兽形云纹、如意云纹、栉纹、图案花纹、云纹、回形雷纹、复线三角纹；扁耳两对饰辫纹、回形雷纹 Drum face: patterns of sun(12rays), 酉 -character, S-shape cloud, nipple protrusion, comb line, flying flag, beast-shape cloud; Drum body: patterns of nipple protrusion, beast-shape cloud, Ruyi-shape cloud, comb line, flower, cloud, 回 -shape thunder, double line triangle; Braid & 回 -shape thunder patterns on 2 pairs of flat handles.	49—49.4	27	麻江型 Majiang Type	
245	族鼓 0257 复线角形纹马纹铜鼓 ZG No.0257 Bronze Drum with double line triangle ahd horse patterns	广西民族博物馆 Anthropology Museum of Guangxi	来源不详，原存广西壮族自治区博物馆 Original source unknown; preserved previously in Museum of Guangxi Zhuang Autonomous Region	鼓面：太阳纹（12 芒）、乳钉纹、酉字纹、勾连雷纹、栉纹、缠枝纹、复线角形纹； 鼓身：花卉纹、马纹、缠枝纹、云纹、复线三角纹；扁耳两对饰凸棱纹 Drum face: patterns of sun(12rays), nipple protrusion, 酉 -character, hooked thunder, comb line, twisted branches, double line triangle; Drum body: patterns of flower & horse, twisted branches, cloud, double line triangle; Raise ridges on 2 pairs of flat handles.	48.7	27	麻江型 Majiang Type	

序号 N0.	原编号及鼓名 Stock Number & Name	收藏单位 Museum	出土（征集）时间、地点 Time & Spot for discovered or collected	主要装饰 Main Decorations	尺寸（厘米）Size(cm)		类型 Type	图片 Picture
					面径 Face Diameter	身高 Height		
246	族鼓 0258 游旗纹铜鼓 ZG No.0258 Bronze Drum with flying flag patterns	广西民族博物馆 Anthropology Museum of Guangxi	1958 年征集于柳州市收购站 Collected in Liuzhou City Waste Recycle Station in 1958	鼓面：太阳纹（12 芒）、同心圆纹、栉纹、乳钉纹、游旗纹、羽纹、绚纹；鼓身：乳钉纹、绚纹、复线三角纹；扁耳两对饰辫纹 Drum face: patterns of sun(12rays), concentric circle, comb line, nipple protrusion, flying flag, feather, twisted rope; Drum body: patterns of nipple protrusion, twisted rope, double line triangle; Braid patterns on 2 pairs of flat handles.	48.6-48.8	28	麻江型 Majiang Type	
247	族鼓 0259 符箓纹铜鼓 ZG No.0259 Bronze Drum with Ofuda patterns	广西民族博物馆 Anthropology Museum of Guangxi	1956 年征集于柳州市 Collected in Liuzhou City in 1956	鼓面：太阳纹（12 芒）、如意云纹、四出钱纹、乳钉纹、符箓纹、云纹；鼓身：乳钉纹、云纹、兽面云纹、复线三角纹；扁耳两对饰凸棱纹 Drum face: patterns of sun(12rays), Ruyi-shape, coins with quadrangle inside, nipple protrusion, Ofuda, cloud; Drum body: patterns of nipple protrusion, cloud, beast-face cloud, double line triangle; Raise ridges on 2 pairs of flat handles.	43.5-44	26	麻江型 Majiang Type	
248	族鼓 0260 变形游旗纹铜鼓 ZG No.0260 Bronze Drum with transformed flying flag patterns	广西民族博物馆 Anthropology Museum of Guangxi	1955 年收购于柳州市供销社 Collected at Liuzhou City Supply & Marketing Cooperative in 1955	鼓面：太阳纹（12 芒）、酉字纹、云纹、乳钉纹、变形游旗纹；鼓身：乳钉纹、如意纹、云纹、回形雷纹、复线三角纹；扁耳两对饰辫纹、回纹、卍字纹、铭文（磨蚀）Drum face: patterns of sun(12rays), 酉-character, cloud, nipple protrusion, transformed flying flag; Drum body: patterns of nipple protrusion, Ruyi, cloud, 回-shape thunder, double line triangle; Braid, dual-rectangle, 卍 and some characters(obscure) on 2 pairs of flat handles.	47.5	27.5	麻江型 Majiang Type	

续表

序号 NO.	原编号及鼓名 Stock Number & Name	收藏单位 Museum	出土（征集） 时间、地点 Time & Spot for discovered or collected	主要装饰 Main Decorations	尺寸（厘米） Size(cm)		类型 Type	图片 Picture
					面径 Face Diameter	身高 Height		
249	族鼓 0261 游旗纹铜鼓 ZG No.0261 Bronze Drum with flying flag patterns	广西民族博物馆 Anthropology Museum of Guangxi	来源不详，原存广西壮族自治区博物馆 Original source unknown; preserved previously in Museum of Guangxi Zhuang Autonomous Region	鼓面：太阳纹（12 芒）、西字纹、云纹、乳钉纹、栉纹、游旗纹、龙纹／回形雷纹； 鼓身：如意云纹、回形雷纹、云纹、栉纹、复线三角纹；扁耳两对饰辫纹 Drum face: patterns of sun(12rays), 西-character, cloud, nipple protrusion, comb line, flying flag, dragon & 回-shape thunder; Drum body: patterns of Ruyi-shape cloud, 回-shape thunder, cloud, comb line, double line triangle; Braid patterns on 2 pairs of flat handles.	50	28	麻江型 Majiang Type	
250	族鼓 0262 十二生肖纹铜鼓 ZG No.0262 Bronze Drum with zodiac patterns	广西民族博物馆 Anthropology Museum of Guangxi	1963 年征集于河池市都安县 Collected in Du'an County, Hechi City in 1963	鼓面：太阳纹（12 芒）、S 云纹、同心圆纹、羽纹、游旗纹、兽纹、云纹、卦纹； 鼓身：乳钉纹、云纹、栉纹、缠枝纹、回形雷纹、复线三角纹；扁耳两对饰辫纹 Drum face: patterns of sun(12rays), S-shape cloud, concentric circle, feather, flying flag, beast, cloud, divinatory symbol; Drum body: patterns of nipple protrusion, cloud, comb line, twisted branches, 回-shape thunder, double line triangle; Braid patterns on 2 pairs of flat handles.	48.5~48.8	29.8	麻江型 Majiang Type	
251	族鼓 0263 人物禽兽纹铜鼓 ZG No.0263 Bronze Drum with man and beast patterns	广西民族博物馆 Anthropology Museum of Guangxi	1964 年征集于柳州市二级站 Collected in Liuzhou City Waste Recycle Station in 1964	鼓面：太阳纹（12 芒）、S 云纹、回形雷纹、乳钉纹、荷耙人纹、鹤纹、牛纹、符箓纹； 鼓身：梅花状乳钉纹、云纹、回形雷纹、如意云纹、复线三角纹；扁耳两对饰辫纹 Drum face: patterns of sun(12rays), S-shape cloud, 回-shape thunder, nipple protrusion, complex patterns(including hoer, crane, ox, Ofuda); Drum body: patterns of nipple protrusion array in plum blossom shape, cloud, 回-shape thunder, Ruyi-shape cloud, double line triangle; Braid patterns on 2 pairs of flat handles.	44.5~44.8	25	麻江型 Majiang Type	

序号 N0.	原编号及鼓名 Stock Number & Name	收藏单位 Museum	出土（征集）时间、地点 Time & Spot for discovered or collected	主要装饰 Main Decorations	尺寸（厘米） Size(cm)		类型 Type	图片 Picture
					面径 Face Diameter	身高 Height		
252	族鼓 0264 游旗纹铜鼓 ZG No.0264 Bronze Drum with flying flag patterns	广西民族博物馆 Anthropology Museum of Guangxi	1965 年收购于南宁市 Collected in Nanning City in 1965	鼓面：太阳纹（12 芒）、酉字纹、S 云纹、乳钉纹、游旗纹、栉纹、兽形云纹； 鼓身：乳钉纹、如意纹、回形雷纹、栉纹、兽面云纹、复线三角纹；扁耳两对饰辫纹 Drum face: patterns of sun(12rays), 酉-character, S-shape cloud, nipple protrusion, flying flag, comb line, beast-shape cloud; Drum body: patterns of nipple protrusion, Ruyi-shape cloud, 回-shape thunder, comb line, beast-face cloud , double line triangle; Braid patterns on 2 pairs of flat handles.	45.7-46	26	麻江型 Majiang Type	
253	族鼓 0265 素纹铜鼓 ZG No.0265 Bronze Drum with no pattern	广西民族博物馆 Anthropology Museum of Guangxi	1955 年征集于南宁市供销社 Collected at Nanning City Supply & Marketing Cooperative in 1955	鼓面：太阳纹（12 芒）、素面； 鼓身：素面；扁耳两对饰图案花瓶纹 Drum face: patterns of sun(12rays), the other rings are blank; Drum body: no patterns; vase patterns on 2 pairs of flat handles.	50-50.4	28.5	麻江型 Majiang Type	
254	族鼓 0266 乳钉纹铜鼓 ZG No.0266 Bronze Drum with nipple protrusion patterns	广西民族博物馆 Anthropology Museum of Guangxi	征集于南宁市 Collected in Nanning City	鼓面：太阳纹（12 芒）、乳钉纹； 鼓身：乳钉纹；扁耳两对饰凸棱纹 Drum face: patterns of sun(12rays), nipple protrusion; Drum body: nipple protrusion; Raise ridges on 2 pairs of flat handles.	48.5	28	麻江型 Majiang Type	
255	族鼓 0267 缠枝纹铜鼓 ZG No.0267 Bronze Drum with twisted branches pattern	广西民族博物馆 Anthropology Museum of Guangxi	来源不详，原存广西壮族自治区博物馆 Original source unknown; preserved previously in Museum of Guangxi Zhuang Autonomous Region	鼓面：太阳纹（12 芒）、乳钉纹、菱形填四瓣花纹、缠枝花纹、窗花纹、乳钉纹； 鼓身：乳钉纹、水波纹、雷纹、回形雷纹、缠枝纹、图案复线三角纹；扁耳两对饰辫纹 Drum face: patterns of sun(12rays), nipple protrusion, diamond filled with quatrefoils, twisted branches, window lattices & nipple protrusion; Drum body: patterns of nipple protrusion, water wave, thunder, 回-shape thunder, twisted branches, double line triangle with motif inside; Braid patterns on 2 pairs of flat handles.	47	27	麻江型 Majiang Type	

续表

序号 No.	原编号及鼓名 Stock Number & Name	收藏单位 Museum	出土（征集）时间、地点 Time & Spot for discovered or collected	主要装饰 Main Decorations	尺寸（厘米）Size(cm)		类型 Type	图片 Picture
					面径 Face Diameter	身高 Height		
256	族鼓 0268 回形纹铜鼓 ZG No.0268 Bronze Drum with 回-shape pattern	广西民族博物馆 Anthropology Museum of Guangxi	1955 年征集于南宁市供销社 Collected at Nanning City Supply & Marketing Cooperative in 1955	鼓面：太阳纹（12 芒）、乳钉纹、回形雷纹、工字纹、羽纹、缠枝纹；鼓身：乳钉纹、龙戏四出钱纹；扁耳两对饰凸棱纹 Drum face: patterns of sun(12rays), nipple protrusion, 回-shape thunder, 工-character, feather, twisted branches; Drum body: patterns of nipple protrusion, dragons and coin with quadrangle inside; Raise ridges on 2 pairs of flat handles.	46.5～47	27	麻江型 Majiang Type	
257	族鼓 0270 符箓纹铜鼓 ZG No.0270 Bronze Drum with Ofuda patterns	广西民族博物馆 Anthropology Museum of Guangxi	来源不详，原存广西壮族自治区博物馆 Original source unknown; preserved previously in Museum of Guangxi Zhuang Autonomous Region	鼓面：太阳纹（12 芒）、同心圆纹、回形雷纹、乳钉纹、符箓纹、S 云纹；鼓身：梅花状乳钉纹间乳钉纹、回形雷纹、云纹、如意云纹、同心圆纹、图案三角纹；扁耳两对饰辫纹 Drum face: patterns of sun(12rays), concentric circle, 回-shape thunder, nipple protrusion in plum blossom shape, Ofuda, S-shape cloud; Drum body: patterns of nipple protrusion in plum blossom shape, 回-shape thunder, cloud, Ruyi-shape cloud, concentric circle, motif triangle; Braid patterns on 2 pairs of flat handles.	44～44.5	25.5	麻江型 Majiang Type	
258	族鼓 0271 符箓纹铜鼓 ZG No.0271 Bronze Drum with Ofuda pattern	广西民族博物馆 Anthropology Museum of Guangxi	1958 年征集于柳州市收购站 Collected in Liuzhou City Waste Recycle Station in 1958	鼓面：太阳纹（12 芒）、乳钉纹、云纹、栉纹、符箓纹、回形雷纹、绹纹；鼓身：乳钉纹、栉纹、如意云纹、回形雷纹、S 云纹、复线三角纹；扁耳两对饰羽纹 Drum face: patterns of sun(12rays), nipple protrusion, cloud, comb line, Ofuda, 回-shape thunder, twisted rope; Drum body: patterns of nipple protrusion, comb line, Ruyi-shape cloud, 回-shape thunder, S-shape cloud, double line triangle; Feather patterns on 2 pairs of flat handles.	48.5	27	麻江型 Majiang Type	

序号 N0.	原编号及鼓名 Stock Number & Name	收藏单位 Museum	出土（征集）时间、地点 Time & Spot for discovered or collected	主要装饰 Main Decorations	尺寸（厘米） Size(cm)		类型 Type	图片 Picture
					面径 Face Diameter	身高 Height		
259	族鼓 0272 荷耙人纹符箓纹铜鼓 ZG No.0272 Bronze Drum with hoer and Ofuda patterns	广西民族博物馆 Anthropology Museum of Guangxi	1965 年征集于南宁市二级站 Collected in Nanning City Secondary Waste Recycle Station in 1965	鼓面：太阳纹（12 芒）、同心圆纹、回形雷纹、乳钉纹，荷耙人纹、牛纹、羊纹、猪纹、团寿纹、符箓纹组合图案、窗花纹、四出钱纹； 鼓身：乳钉纹、云纹、复线三角纹；扁耳两对饰辫纹 Drum face: patterns of sun(12rays), concentric circle, 回 -shape thunder, nipple protrusion, complex patterns(including hoer, ox, goat, pig, round 寿 -character, Ofuda), window latticees, coin with quadrangle inside； Drum body: patterns of nipple protrusion, cloud, double line triangle; Braid patterns on 2 pairs of flat handles.	44.9	27	麻江型 Majiang Type	
260	族鼓 0273 缠枝纹铜鼓 ZG No.0273 Bronze Drum with twisted branches pattern	广西民族博物馆 Anthropology Museum of Guangxi	1958 年集于柳州市收购站 Collected in Liuzhou City Waste Recycle Station in 1958	鼓面：太阳纹、圆圈纹、四瓣花纹、乳钉纹； 鼓身：素面；扁耳两对饰凸棱纹 Drum face: patterns of sun(12rays), circle, quatrefoil, nipple protrusion； Drum body: no patterns; Raise ridges on 2 pairs of flat handles.	48.5	29	麻江型 Majiang Type	
261	族鼓 0274 游旗纹铜鼓 ZG No.0274 Bronze Drum with flying flag patterns	广西民族博物馆 Anthropology Museum of Guangxi	1962 年征集于柳州市 Collected in Liuzhou City in 1962	鼓面：太阳纹（12 芒）、酉字纹、S 云纹、乳钉纹、栉纹、游旗纹、兽面云纹； 鼓身：乳钉纹、兽面云纹、栉纹、云纹、回形雷纹、缠枝花纹、复线三角纹；扁耳两对饰辫纹 Drum face: patterns of sun(12rays), 酉 -character, S-shape cloud, nipple protrusion, flying flag, comb line, beast-face cloud； Drum body: patterns of nipple protrusion, Ruyi-face cloud, comb line, cloud, 回 -shape thunder, twisted braches, double line triangle; Braid patterns on 2 pairs of flat handles.	52—52.5	27.5	麻江型 Majiang Type	
262	族鼓 0275 缠枝纹铜鼓 ZG No.0275 Bronze Drum with twisted branches pattern	广西民族博物馆 Anthropology Museum of Guangxi	20 世纪 50 年代征集于梧州市 Collected in Wuzhou City in 1950s'	鼓面：太阳纹（12 芒）、乳钉纹、变形游旗纹、缠枝纹； 鼓身：素面；扁耳两对饰凸棱纹 Drum face: patterns of sun(12rays), nipple protrusion, transformed flying flag, twisted branches； Drum body: no patterns; Raise ridges on 2 pairs of flat handles.	46.9—48	27.8	麻江型 Majiang Type	

续表

序号 N0.	原编号及鼓名 Stock Number & Name	收藏单位 Museum	出土（征集） 时间、地点 Time & Spot for discovered or collected	主要装饰 Main Decorations	尺寸（厘米） Size(cm)		类型 Type	图片 Picture
					面径 Face Diameter	身高 Height		
263	族鼓 0276 符箓纹铜鼓 ZG No.0276 Bronze Drum with Ofuda patterns	广西民族博物馆 Anthropology Museum of Guangxi	来源不详，原存广西壮族自治区博物馆 Original source unknown; preserved previously in Museum of Guangxi Zhuang Autonomous Region	鼓面：太阳纹（14 芒）、酉字纹、云纹、乳钉纹、游旗纹、回形雷纹； 鼓身：乳钉纹、同心圆纹、回形雷纹、S 云纹、花纹、复线三角纹；扁耳两对饰辫纹 Drum face: patterns of sun(14rays), 酉 -character, cloud, nipple protrusion, flying flag, 回 -shape thunder; Drum body: patterns of nipple protrusion, concentric circle, 回 -shape thunder, S-shape cloud, flower, double line triangle; Braid patterns on 2 pairs of flat handles.	44.6-44.8	25	麻江型 Majiang Type	
264	族鼓 0277 游旗纹铜鼓 ZG No.0277 Bronze Drum with flying flag patterns	广西民族博物馆 Anthropology Museum of Guangxi	1958 年征集于柳州市 Collected in Liuzhou City in 1958	鼓面：太阳纹（12 芒）、酉字纹、S 云纹、乳钉纹、游旗纹、云纹、回形雷纹、缠枝纹； 鼓身：乳钉纹、雷纹、回形雷纹、复线三角纹；扁耳两对 Drum face: patterns of sun(12rays), 酉 -character, S-shape cloud, nipple protrusion, flying flag cloud, 回 -shape thunder, twisted braches; Drum body: patterns of nipple protrusion, thunder, 回 -shape thunder, double line triangle; 2 pairs of flat handles.	46.5-46.7	26.8	麻江型 Majiang Type	
265	族鼓 0278 凤字形符箓纹铜鼓 ZG No.0278 Bronze Drum with 凤 -shape Ofuda patterns	广西民族博物馆 Anthropology Museum of Guangxi	1958 年收购于柳州市收购站 Collected in Liuzhou City Waste Recycle Station in 1958	鼓面：太阳纹（12 芒）、S 云纹、乳钉纹、凤字符箓纹、栉纹、同心圆纹、云纹、四瓣花纹、绹纹、如意云纹； 鼓身：如意云纹、云纹、栉纹、回形雷纹、复线三角纹；扁耳两对饰辫纹 Drum face: patterns of sun(12rays), S-shape cloud, nipple protrusion, 凤 -shape Ofuda, comb line, concentric circle, cloud, quatrefoil, twisted rope, Ruyi-shape cloud; Drum body: patterns of Ruyi-shape cloud, cloud, comb line, 回 -shape thunder, double line triangle; Braid patterns 2 pairs of flat handles.	50-51	23.5 （残） Incomplete	麻江型 Majiang Type	

序号 N0.	原编号及鼓名 Stock Number & Name	收藏单位 Museum	出土（征集）时间、地点 Time & Spot for discovered or collected	主要装饰 Main Decorations	尺寸（厘米） Size(cm)		类型 Type	图片 Picture
					面径 Face Diameter	身高 Height		
266	族鼓 0279 寿字纹铜鼓 ZG No.0279 Bronze Drum with 寿 – character patterns	广西民族博物馆 Anthropology Museum of Guangxi	1955 年征集于南宁市供销社 Collected at Nanning City Supply & Marketing Cooperative in 1955	鼓面：太阳纹（12 芒）、乳钉纹、游旗纹、符箓纹、水波纹； 鼓身：羽纹、虫形纹、回形雷纹、水波纹、雷纹、图案复线三角纹；扁耳两对饰羽纹、乳钉纹 Drum face: patterns of sun(12rays), nipple protrusion, flying flag, Ofuda, water wave; Drum body: patterns of feather, insect thunder, water wave, 回 -shape thunder, double line triangle with motifs inside; Feather & nipple protrusion on 2 pairs of flat handles.	46.5	27	麻江型 Majiang Type	
267	族鼓 0280 凤字纹铜鼓 ZG No.0280 Bronze Drum with 凤 – character patterns	广西民族博物馆 Anthropology Museum of Guangxi	1964 年征集于柳州市二级站 Collected in Liuzhou City Secondary Waste Recycle Station in 1964	鼓面：太阳纹（12 芒）、栉纹、乳钉纹、同心圆纹、符箓纹、如意云纹、回形雷纹、绚纹； 鼓身：乳钉纹、单线波浪间 S 勾纹、复线三角纹；扁耳两对饰羽纹 Drum face: patterns of sun(12rays), comb line, nipple protrusion, concentric circle, Ofuda, Ruyi-shape cloud, 回 -shape thunder, twisted rope; Drum body: patterns of nipple protrusion, water wave mixed S-hook,double line triangle; Feather patterns on 2 pairs of flat handles.	48—48.4	27	麻江型 Majiang Type	
268	族鼓 0281 游旗纹铜鼓 ZG No.0281 Bronze Drum with flying flag patterns	广西民族博物馆 Anthropology Museum of Guangxi	来源不详，原存广西壮族自治区博物馆 Original source unknown; preserved previously in Museum of Guangxi Zhuang Autonomous Region	鼓面：太阳纹（12 芒）、酉字纹、S 云纹、乳钉纹、栉纹、游旗纹、云纹； 鼓身：云纹、如意纹、栉纹、回形雷纹、复线三角纹；扁耳两对饰辫纹、回形雷纹 Drum face: patterns of sun(12rays), 酉 -character, S-shape cloud, nipple protrusion, comb line, flying flag, cloud; Drum body: patterns of cloud, Ruyi-shape cloud, comb line, 回 -shape thunder, double line triangle; Braid & 回 -shape thunder patterns on 2 pairs of flat handles.	51.5—52.5	27.5	麻江型 Majiang Type	

序号 NO.	原编号及鼓名 Stock Number & Name	收藏单位 Museum	出土（征集） 时间、地点 Time & Spot for discovered or collected	主要装饰 Main Decorations	尺寸（厘米） Size(cm)		类型 Type	图片 Picture
					面径 Face Diameter	身高 Height		
269	族鼓 0282 游旗纹铜鼓 ZG No.0282 Bronze Drum with flying flag patterns	广西民族博物馆 Anthropology Museum of Guangxi	解放初广西土改委员会拨交 Allocated by Guangxi Earth Revolutionary Committee at the beginning of the establishment of PRC	鼓面：太阳纹（12 芒）、酉字纹、S 云纹、乳钉纹、游旗纹、栉纹、兽形云纹、卦纹； 鼓身：乳钉纹、回形雷纹、云纹、栉纹、复线三角纹；扁耳两对饰辫纹、回形雷纹 Drum face: patterns of sun(12rays), 酉-character, S-shape cloud, nipple protrusion, flying flag, comb line, beast-shape cloud, divinatory symbol; Drum body: patterns of nipple protrusion, cloud, comb line, 回-shape thunder, double line triangle; Braid & 回-shape thunder patterns on 2 pairs of flat handles.	47.5	26.5	麻江型 Majiang Type	
270	族鼓 0283 十二生肖纹铜鼓 ZG No.0283 Bronze Drum with zodiac patterns	广西民族博物馆 Anthropology Museum of Guangxi	来源不详，原存广西壮族自治区博物馆 Original source unknown; preserved previously in Museum of Guangxi Zhuang Autonomous Region	鼓面：太阳纹（12 芒）、酉字纹、S 云纹、乳钉纹、栉纹、游旗纹、十二生肖纹、如意云纹； 鼓身：乳钉纹、如意云纹、栉纹、S 勾纹、回形雷纹、复线三角纹；扁耳两对饰辫纹 Drum face: patterns of sun(12rays), 酉-character, S-shape cloud, nipple protrusion, comb line, flying flag, zodiac, Ruyi-shape cloud; Drum body: patterns of nipple protrusion, Ruyi-shape cloud, comb line, S-shape hook, 回-shape thunder, double line triangle; Braid patterns on 2 pairs of flat handles.	50.5–51	28	麻江型 Majiang Type	
271	族鼓 0284 游旗纹铜鼓 ZG No.0284 Bronze Drum with flying flag patterns	广西民族博物馆 Anthropology Museum of Guangxi	1958 年征集于柳州市收购站 Collected in Liuzhou City in 1958	鼓面：太阳纹（12 芒）、酉字纹、云纹、乳钉纹、回形雷纹、游旗纹、缠枝纹、兽形云纹、卦纹； 鼓身：云纹、乳钉纹、如意云纹、回形雷纹、缠枝纹、兽形云纹、图案三角纹；扁耳两对饰辫纹、雷纹、菱形纹 Drum face: patterns of sun(12rays), 酉-character, cloud, nipple protrusion, 回-shape thunder, flying flag, twisted branches, beast-shape cloud, divinatory symbol; Drum body: patterns of cloud, nipple protrusion, Ruyi-shape cloud, 回-shape thunder, twisted branches, beast-shape cloud, motif triangle; Braid, thunder and diamond patterns on 2 pairs of flat handles.	48.3–48.5	27.7	麻江型 Majiang Type	

序号 N0.	原编号及鼓名 Stock Number & Name	收藏单位 Museum	出土（征集） 时间、地点 Time & Spot for discovered or collected	主要装饰 Main Decorations	尺寸（厘米） Size(cm)		类型 Type	图片 Picture
					面径 Face Diameter	身高 Height		
272	族鼓 0285 游旗纹铜鼓 ZG No.0285 Bronze Drum with flying flag patterns	广西民族博物馆 Anthropology Museum of Guangxi	1962 年征集于柳州市收购站 Collected in Liuzhou City Waste Recycle Station in 1962	鼓面：太阳纹（12 芒）、复线西字纹、S 云纹、乳钉纹、栉纹、游旗纹、云纹、卦纹；鼓身：乳钉纹、如意云纹、云纹、回形雷纹、栉纹、复线三角纹；扁耳两对饰辫纹、回形雷纹 Drum face: patterns of sun(12rays), double line 西 -character, S-shape cloud, nipple protrusion, comb line, flying flag, cloud, divinatory symbol; Drum body: patterns of nipple protrusion, Ruyi-shape cloud, cloud, 回 -shape thunder, comb line, double line triangle; Braid & 回 -shape thunder patterns on 2 pairs of flat handles.	50－50.3	29.3	麻江型 Majiang Type	
273	族鼓 0286 游旗纹铜鼓 ZG No.0286 Bronze Drum with flying flag patterns	广西民族博物馆 Anthropology Museum of Guangxi	1955 年征集自南宁市 Collected in Nanning City in 1955	鼓面：太阳纹（12 芒）、西字纹、S 云纹、乳钉纹、游旗纹、栉纹、兽形云纹、回形雷纹；鼓身：乳钉纹、如意云纹、回形雷纹、栉纹、云纹、复线三角纹；扁耳两对饰辫纹、回形雷纹 Drum face: patterns of sun(12rays), 西 -character, S-shape cloud, nipple protrusion, flying flag, comb line, beast-shape cloud, 回 -shape thunder; Drum body: patterns of nipple protrusion, Ruyi-shape cloud, 回 -shape thunder, comb line, cloud, double line triangle; Braid & 回 -shape thunder patterns on 2 pairs of flat handles.	47.5	26.5	麻江型 Majiang Type	
274	族鼓 0287 游旗纹铜鼓 ZG No.0287 Bronze Drum with flying flag patterns	广西民族博物馆 Anthropology Museum of Guangxi	1958 年征集于柳州市收购站 Collected in Liuzhou City Waste Recycle Station in 1958	鼓面：太阳纹（12 芒）、西字纹、S 云纹、乳钉纹、栉纹、游旗纹、兽面云纹、卦纹；鼓身：乳钉纹、兽面云纹、如意云纹、回形雷纹、栉纹、复线三角纹；扁耳两对饰辫纹 Drum face: patterns of sun(12rays), 西 -character, S-shape cloud, nipple protrusion, comb line, flying flag, beast-face cloud, divinatory symbol; Drum body: patterns of nipple protrusion, beast-face cloud, Ruyi-shape cloud, 回 -shape thunder, comb line, double line triangle; Braid patterns on 2 pairs of flat handles.	50	27.5	麻江型 Majiang Type	

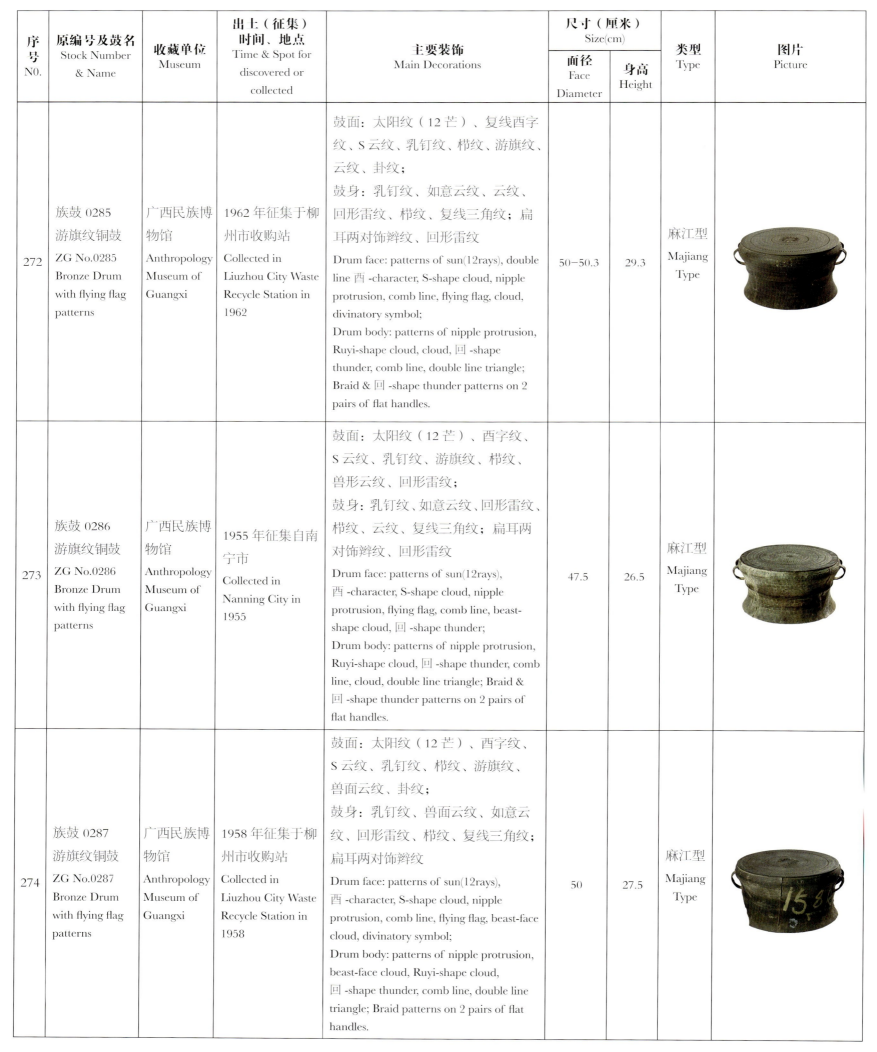

续表

序号 NO.	原编号及鼓名 Stock Number & Name	收藏单位 Museum	出土（征集）时间、地点 Time & Spot for discovered or collected	主要装饰 Main Decorations	尺寸（厘米）Size(cm)		类型 Type	图片 Picture
					面径 Face Diameter	身高 Height		
275	族鼓 0288 游旗纹铜鼓 ZG No.0288 Bronze Drum with flying flag patterns	广西民族博物馆 Anthropology Museum of Guangxi	1964 年征集于柳州市二级站 Collected in Liuzhou City Secondary Waste Recycle Station in 1964	鼓面：太阳纹（12 芒）、酉字纹、S 云纹、乳钉纹、栉纹、游旗纹、云纹；鼓身：乳钉纹、云纹、回形雷纹、栉纹、如意云纹；扁耳两对（已失）Drum face: patterns of sun(12rays), 酉 -character, S-shape cloud, nipple protrusion, comb line, flying flag, cloud; Drum body: patterns of nipple protrusion, cloud, 回 -shape thunder, comb line, Ruyi-shape cloud; 2 pairs of flat handles(lost).	50−50.8	24.7 （残）Incomplete	麻江型 Majiang Type	
276	族鼓 0289 变形游旗纹铜鼓 ZG No.0289 Bronze Drum with transformed flying flag patterns	广西民族博物馆 Anthropology Museum of Guangxi	1964 年征集于柳州市二级站 Collected in Liuzhou City Secondary Waste Recycle Station in 1964	鼓面：太阳纹（12 芒）、酉字纹、S 云纹、乳钉纹、变形游旗纹、云纹；鼓身：梅花状乳钉纹间单乳钉纹、如意云纹、云纹、回形雷纹、复线三角纹；扁耳两对饰辫纹、回形雷纹 Drum face: patterns of sun(12rays), 酉 -character, S-shape cloud, nipple protrusion, transformed flying flag, cloud; Drum body: patterns of nipple protrusion, Ruyi-shape cloud, cloud, 回 -shape thunder, double line triangle; Braid & 回 -shape thunder patterns on 2 pairs of flat handles.	47	27.5	麻江型 Majiang Type	
277	族鼓 0290 人物、鸟纹铜鼓 ZG No.0290 Bronze Drum with man and bird patterns	广西民族博物馆 Anthropology Museum of Guangxi	1954 年征集于柳州市 Collected in Liuzhou City in 1954	鼓面：太阳纹（12 芒）、同心圆纹、回形雷纹、乳钉纹，荷耙人纹、符箓纹、鹤纹、交叉同心圆纹组合图案、云纹；鼓身：梅花状乳钉纹、同心圆纹、如意云纹、回形雷纹、云纹、复线三角纹；扁耳两对饰辫纹 Drum face: patterns of sun(12rays), concentric circle, 回 -shape thunder, nipple protrusion, complex patterns(including hoer, Ofuda, crane, circle-cross), cloud; Drum body: patterns of nipple protrusion, concentric circle, Ruyi-shape cloud, 回 -shape thunder, cloud, double line triangle; Braid patterns on 2 pairs of flat handles.	42.8−43.3	25.5	麻江型 Majiang Type	

序号 N0.	原编号及鼓名 Stock Number & Name	收藏单位 Museum	出土（征集）时间、地点 Time & Spot for discovered or collected	主要装饰 Main Decorations	尺寸（厘米）Size(cm)		类型 Type	图片 Picture
					面径 Face Diameter	身高 Height		
278	族鼓 0291 动物纹铜鼓 ZG No.0291 Bronze Drum with animal patterns	广西民族博物馆 Anthropology Museum of Guangxi	1965 年征集于南宁市二级站 Collected in Nanning City Secondary Waste Recycle Station in 1965	鼓面：太阳纹（12 芒）、云纹、S 勾纹、符箓纹、同心圆纹、回形雷纹、动物纹、乳钉纹、绚纹；鼓身：乳钉纹、弦纹；扁耳两对饰辫纹、凸棱纹 Drum face: patterns of sun(12rays), cloud, S-shape hook, Ofuda, concentric circle, 回 -shape thunder, animal, nipple protrusion, twisted rope; Drum body: patterns of nipple protrusion, strings; Braid &raise ridges on 2 pairs of flat handles.	49.8	26	麻江型 Majiang Type	
279	族鼓 0292 人物纹铜鼓 ZG No.0292 Bronze Drum with man patterns	广西民族博物馆 Anthropology Museum of Guangxi	1964 年征集于柳州市二级站 Collected in Liuzhou City Secondary Waste Recycle Station in 1964	鼓面：太阳纹（12 芒）、同心圆纹、回形雷纹、乳钉纹、桂鱼戏珠纹间人物纹、云纹、人物纹、同心圆纹、回形雷纹；鼓身：乳钉纹、同心圆纹、回形雷纹、如意云纹、云纹、复线三角纹；扁耳两对饰辫纹 Drum face: patterns of sun(12rays), concentric circle, 回 -shape thunder, nipple protrusion, mandarin fish playing pearl & man, cloud, Complex patterns(including man, concentric circle and 回 -shape thunder); Drum body: patterns of nipple protrusion, concentric circle, 回 -shape thunder, Ruyi-shape cloud, cloud, double line triangle; Braid patterns on 2 pairs of flat handles.	45.5−46	27.5	麻江型 Majiang Type	
280	族鼓 0293 缠枝纹铜鼓 ZG No.0293 Bronze Drum with twisted branch patterns	广西民族博物馆 Anthropology Museum of Guangxi	来源不详，原存广西壮族自治区博物馆 Original source unknown; preserved previously in Museum of Guangxi Zhuang Autonomous Region	鼓面：太阳纹（12 芒）、同心圆纹、羽纹、缠枝花纹、回形雷纹、乳钉纹、绚纹；鼓身：乳钉纹；扁耳两对饰羽纹 Drum face: patterns of sun(12rays), concentric circle, feather, twisted branches, 回 -shape thunder, nipple protrusion, twisted rope; Drum body: patterns of nipple protrusion; Feather patterns on 2 pairs of flat handles.	48.5	29	麻江型 Majiang Type	

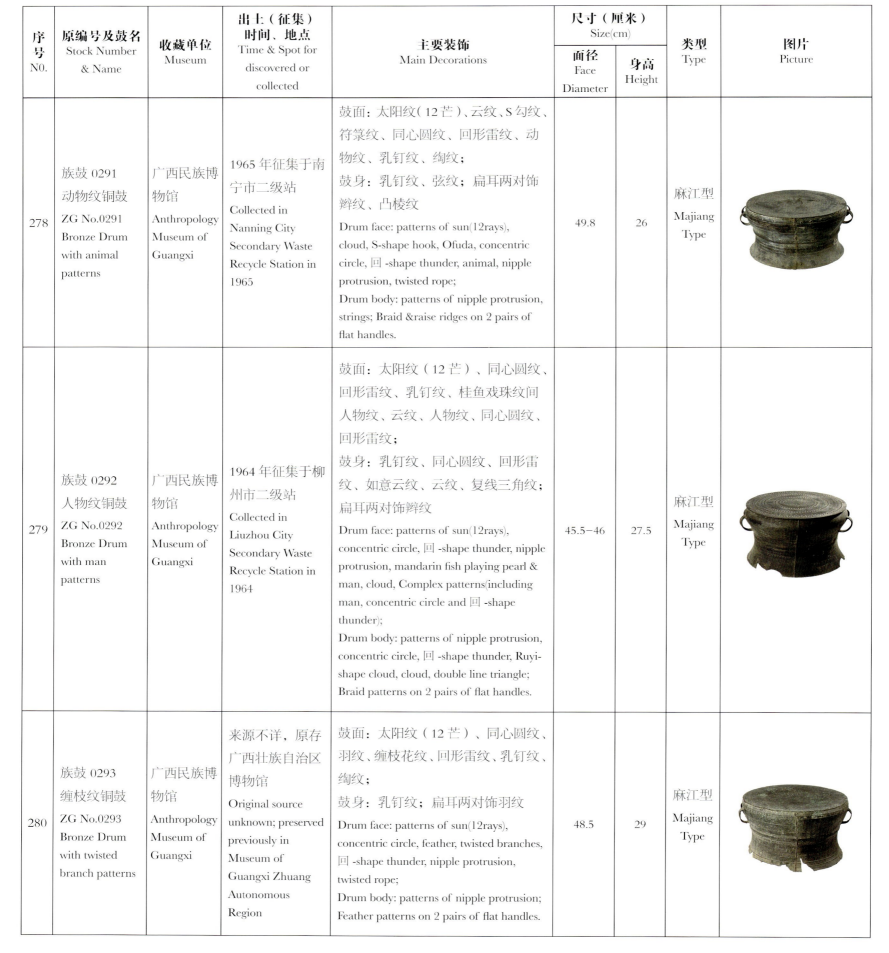

序号 NO.	原编号及鼓名 Stock Number & Name	收藏单位 Museum	出土（征集）时间、地点 Time & Spot for discovered or collected	主要装饰 Main Decorations	尺寸（厘米）Size(cm)		类型 Type	图片 Picture
					面径 Face Diameter	身高 Height		
281	族鼓 0294 风字形符箓纹铜鼓 ZG No.0294 Bronze Drum with 风-shape Ofuda patterns	广西民族博物馆 Anthropology Museum of Guangxi	1958 年征集于柳州市收购站 Collected in Liuzhou City Waste Recycle Station in 1958	鼓面：太阳纹（12 芒）、火焰纹、乳钉纹、风字符箓纹、同心圆纹、栉纹、回形雷纹；鼓身：乳钉纹、弦纹、缠枝纹、复线三角纹；扁耳两对饰羽纹 Drum face: patterns of sun(12rays), flame, nipple protrusion, 风-shape Ofuda, concentric circle, comb line, 回-shape thunder; Drum body: patterns of nipple protrusion, string, twisted branches, double line triangle; Feather patterns on 2 pairs of flat handles.	49.5—50	26.5	麻江型 Majiang Type	
282	族鼓 0295 游旗纹铜鼓 ZG No.0295 Bronze Drum with flying flag patterns	广西民族博物馆 Anthropology Museum of Guangxi	20 世纪 50 年代征集于北流县（现北流市）Collected in Beiliu County(Now Beiliu City) in 1950s'	鼓面：太阳纹（12 芒）、栉纹、游旗纹、同心圆纹、其余磨蚀；鼓身：栉纹、同心圆纹、酉字纹、复线三角纹；扁耳两对饰辫纹 Drum face: patterns of sun(12rays), comb line, flying flag, concentric circle, the other patterns are obscure; Drum body: patterns of comb line, concentric circle, 酉-character, double line triangle; Braid patterns on 2 pairs of flat handles.	37—37.7	23.8	遵义型 Zunyi Type	
283	族鼓 0296 寿字纹铜鼓 ZG No.0294 Bronze Drum with 寿-character patterns	广西民族博物馆 Anthropology Museum of Guangxi	1958 年征集于柳州市收购站 Collected in Liuzhou City Waste Recycle Station in 1958	鼓面：太阳纹（12 芒）、酉字纹、S 云纹、乳钉纹、团寿纹、窗花纹、云纹、回形雷纹；鼓身：梅花状乳钉纹、如意云纹、云纹、回形雷纹、图案三角纹；扁耳两对饰辫纹、回形雷纹 Drum face: patterns of sun(12rays), 酉-character, S-shape cloud, nipple protrusion, complex patterns(including round 寿-character, window lattices), cloud and 回-shape thunder; Drum body: patterns of nipple protrusion, Ruyi-shape cloud, cloud, 回-shape thunder, motif triangle; Braid & 回-shape thunder patterns on 2 pairs of flat handles.	47.3	27.3	麻江型 Majiang Type	

序号 N0.	原编号及鼓名 Stock Number & Name	收藏单位 Museum	出土（征集） 时间、地点 Time & Spot for discovered or collected	主要装饰 Main Decorations	尺寸（厘米） Size(cm)		类型 Type	图片 Picture
					面径 Face Diameter	身高 Height		
284	族鼓 0297 游旗纹铜鼓 ZG No.0297 Bronze Drum with flying flag patterns	广西民族博物馆 Anthropology Museum of Guangxi	1962 年征集于柳州市二级站 Collected in Liuzhou City Secondary Waste Recycle Station in 1962	鼓面：太阳纹（12 芒）、酉字纹、S 云纹、乳钉纹、游旗纹、栉纹、兽形云纹、卦纹； 鼓身：乳钉纹、如意云纹、回形雷纹、栉纹、云纹、复线三角纹；扁耳两对饰辫纹、回形雷纹 Drum face: patterns of sun(12rays), 酉-character, S-shape cloud, nipple protrusion, flying flag, comb line, beast-shape cloud, divinatory symbol; Drum body: patterns of nipple protrusion, Ruyi-shape cloud, 回-shape thunder, comb line, cloud, double line triangle; Braid & 回-shape thunder patterns on 2 pairs of flat handles.	47	26	麻江型 Majiang Type	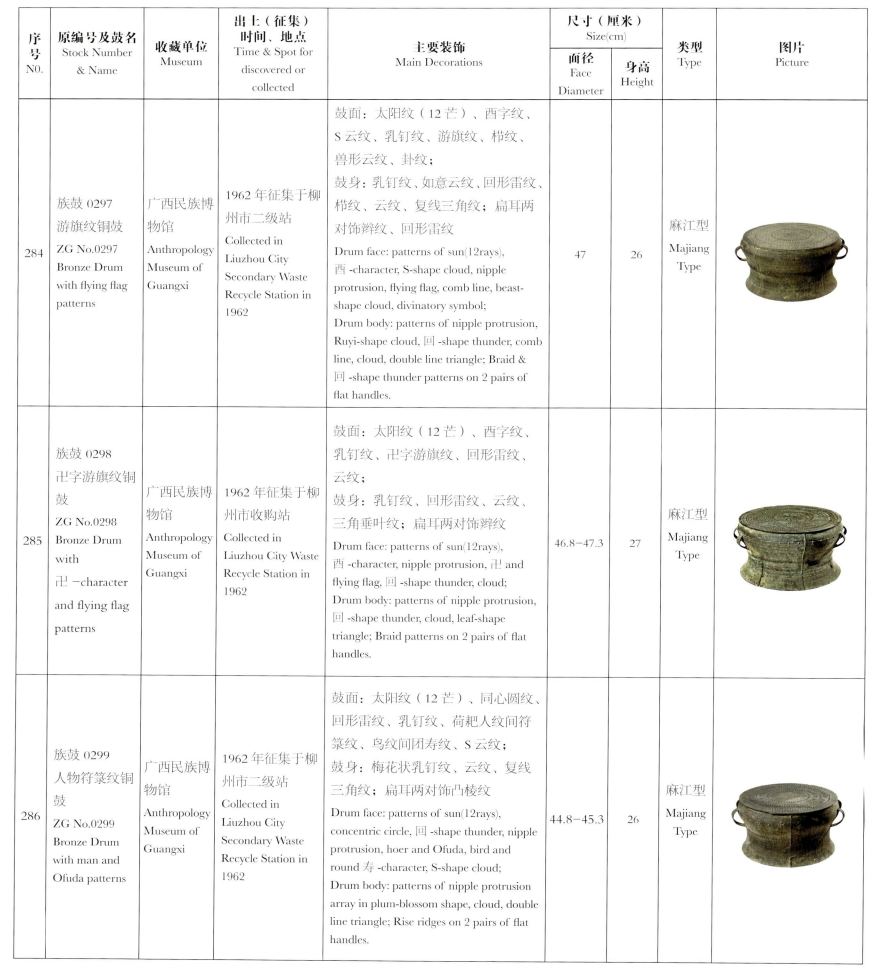
285	族鼓 0298 卐字游旗纹铜鼓 ZG No.0298 Bronze Drum with 卐-character and flying flag patterns	广西民族博物馆 Anthropology Museum of Guangxi	1962 年征集于柳州市收购站 Collected in Liuzhou City Waste Recycle Station in 1962	鼓面：太阳纹（12 芒）、酉字纹、乳钉纹、卐字游旗纹、回形雷纹、云纹； 鼓身：乳钉纹、回形雷纹、云纹、三角垂叶纹；扁耳两对饰辫纹 Drum face: patterns of sun(12rays), 酉-character, nipple protrusion, 卐 and flying flag, 回-shape thunder, cloud; Drum body: patterns of nipple protrusion, 回-shape thunder, cloud, leaf-shape triangle; Braid patterns on 2 pairs of flat handles.	46.8－47.3	27	麻江型 Majiang Type	
286	族鼓 0299 人物符箓纹铜鼓 ZG No.0299 Bronze Drum with man and Ofuda patterns	广西民族博物馆 Anthropology Museum of Guangxi	1962 年征集于柳州市二级站 Collected in Liuzhou City Secondary Waste Recycle Station in 1962	鼓面：太阳纹（12 芒）、同心圆纹、回形雷纹、乳钉纹、荷耙人纹间符箓纹、鸟纹间团寿纹、S 云纹； 鼓身：梅花状乳钉纹、云纹、复线三角纹；扁耳两对饰凸棱纹 Drum face: patterns of sun(12rays), concentric circle, 回-shape thunder, nipple protrusion, hoer and Ofuda, bird and round 寿-character, S-shape cloud; Drum body: patterns of nipple protrusion array in plum-blossom shape, cloud, double line triangle; Rise ridges on 2 pairs of flat handles.	44.8－45.3	26	麻江型 Majiang Type	

续表

序号 N0.	原编号及鼓名 Stock Number & Name	收藏单位 Museum	出土（征集） 时间、地点 Time & Spot for discovered or collected	主要装饰 Main Decorations	尺寸（厘米） Size(cm)		类型 Type	图片 Picture
					面径 Face Diameter	身高 Height		
287	族鼓 0300 游旗纹铜鼓 ZG No.0300 Bronze Drum with flying flag patterns	广西民族博物馆 Anthropology Museum of Guangxi	1962 年征集于柳州市 Collected in Liuzhou City in 1962	鼓面：太阳纹（12 芒）、酉字纹、S 云纹、乳钉纹、游旗纹、栉纹、兽面纹； 鼓身：乳钉纹、如意云纹、回形雷纹、栉纹、兽面云纹、复线三角纹；扁耳两对饰辫纹 Drum face: patterns of sun(12rays), 酉-character, S-shape cloud, nipple protrusion, flying flag, comb line, beast-face cloud; Drum body: patterns of nipple protrusion, Ruyi-shape cloud, 回 -shape thunder, comb line, beast-face cloud, double line triangle; Braid patterns on 2 pairs of flat handles.	48.9~49.4	26	麻江型 Majiang Type	
288	族鼓 0301 莲花纹小铜鼓 ZG No.0301 Bronze Drum with lotus patterns	广西民族博物馆 Anthropology Museum of Guangxi	来源不详，原存广西壮族自治区博物馆 Original source unknown; preserved previously in Museum of Guangxi Zhuang Autonomous Region	鼓面：太阳纹（11 芒）、乳钉纹、舌形花瓣纹、风火轮纹间钱纹、同心椭圆纹、五字纹间椭圆纹、鼓面四只逆时针四足弦线纹立体青蛙； 鼓身：乳钉纹、兽面纹、缠枝花纹、工字纹、图案倒三角垂叶纹；扁耳两对饰凹弦纹 Drum face: patterns of sun(11rays), nipple protrusion, flower petal, wind & flame wheel mixed coins, concentric ellipse, 五 -character mixed ellipse; 4 frogs of 4 feet and string patterns on back stand anticlockwise on the edge of the drum face; Drum body: patterns of nipple protrusion, beast-face cloud, twisted branches, 工 -character, reverse motif triangle; Carve strings on 2 pairs of flat handles.	24	13.2	异型 Abnormal	
289	族鼓 0302 游旗纹铜鼓 ZG No.0302 Bronze Drum with flying flag patterns	广西民族博物馆 Anthropology Museum of Guangxi	解放初征集于桂平市 Collected in Guiping City at the beginning of the establishment of PRC	鼓面：太阳纹（12 芒）、酉字纹、S 云纹、乳钉纹、栉纹、游旗纹、兽形云纹； 鼓身：乳钉纹、如意云纹、回形雷纹、云纹、栉纹、复线三角纹；扁耳两对饰辫纹 Drum face: patterns of sun(12rays), 酉 -character, S-shape cloud, nipple protrusion, comb line, flying flag, beast-shape cloud; Drum body: patterns of nipple protrusion, Ruyi-shape cloud, 回 -shape thunder, cloud, comb line, double line triangle; Braid patterns on 2 pairs of flat handles.	47~47.2	25.7	麻江型 Majiang Type	

序号 NO.	原编号及鼓名 Stock Number & Name	收藏单位 Museum	出土（征集）时间、地点 Time & Spot for discovered or collected	主要装饰 Main Decorations	尺寸（厘米）Size(cm)		类型 Type	图片 Picture
					面径 Face Diameter	身高 Height		
290	族鼓 0303 十二生肖纹铜鼓 ZG No.0303 Bronze Drum with zodiac patterns	广西民族博物馆 Anthropology Museum of Guangxi	1972 年征购于南宁市废品仓库 Collected at Nanning Waste Storage in 1972	鼓面：太阳纹（12 芒）、酉字纹、S 云纹、乳钉纹、栉纹、游旗纹、动物纹、兽面云纹、卦纹；鼓身：乳钉纹、兽面云纹、如意云纹、栉纹、"ȝ1ε"纹、回形雷纹、云纹、复线三角纹；扁耳两对饰辫纹、回形雷纹 Drum face: patterns of sun(12rays), 酉 -character, S-shape cloud, nipple protrusion, comb line, flying flag, animal, beast-face cloud, divinatory symbol; Drum body: patterns of nipple protrusion, beast-face cloud, Ruyi-shape cloud, comb line, "ȝ1ε" motif, 回 -shape thunder, cloud, double line triangle; Braid & 回 -shape thunder patterns on 2 pairs of flat handles.	49.5	28.5	麻江型 Majiang Type	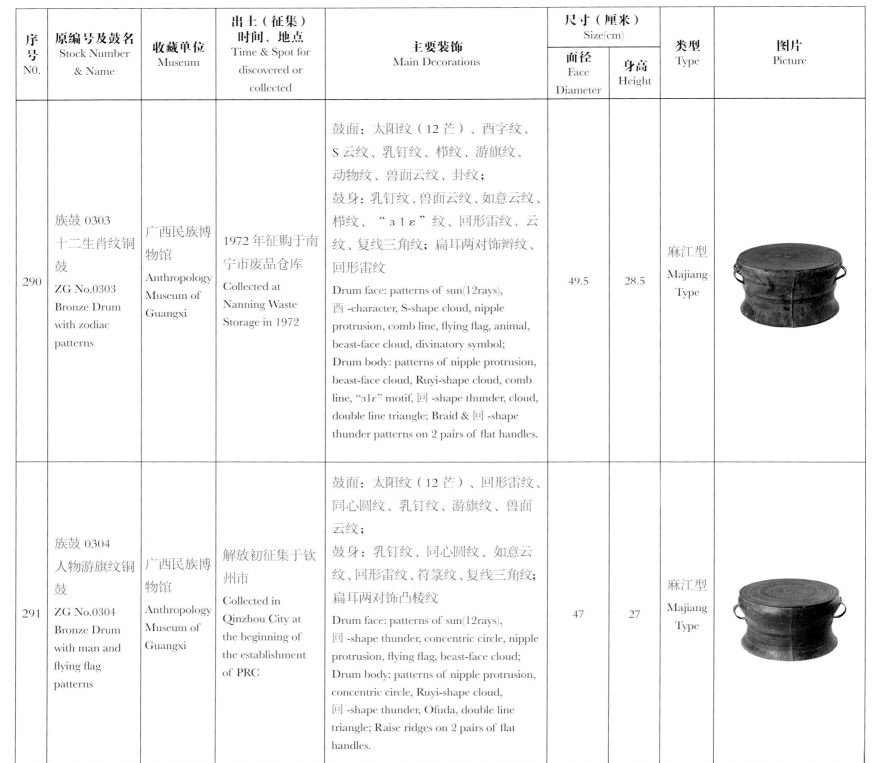
291	族鼓 0304 人物游旗纹铜鼓 ZG No.0304 Bronze Drum with man and flying flag patterns	广西民族博物馆 Anthropology Museum of Guangxi	解放初征集于钦州市 Collected in Qinzhou City at the beginning of the establishment of PRC	鼓面：太阳纹（12 芒）、回形雷纹、同心圆纹、乳钉纹、游旗纹、兽面云纹；鼓身：乳钉纹、同心圆纹、如意云纹、回形雷纹、符箓纹、复线三角纹；扁耳两对饰凸棱纹 Drum face: patterns of sun(12rays), 回 -shape thunder, concentric circle, nipple protrusion, flying flag, beast-face cloud; Drum body: patterns of nipple protrusion, concentric circle, Ruyi-shape cloud, 回 -shape thunder, Ofuda, double line triangle; Raise ridges on 2 pairs of flat handles.	47	27	麻江型 Majiang Type	

序号 NO.	原编号及鼓名 Stock Number & Name	收藏单位 Museum	出土（征集） 时间、地点 Time & Spot for discovered or collected	主要装饰 Main Decorations	尺寸（厘米） Size(cm)		类型 Type	图片 Picture
					面径 Face Diameter	身高 Height		
292	族鼓 0305 变形羽人纹铜鼓 ZG No.0305 Bronze Drum with transformed feathermen patterns	广西民族博物馆 Anthropology Museum of Guangxi	1957 年出土于南宁市邕宁县六增村六鸣山 Unearthed at Liuming Hill, Liuzeng Village, Yongning County, Nanning City in 1957	鼓面：太阳纹（12 芒）、羽纹、栉纹、切线同心圆纹、复线交叉纹、变形羽人纹、变形翔鹭纹间定胜纹、鼓面边缘饰四只逆时针四足素面立体青蛙；鼓身：羽纹、栉纹、切线同心圆纹、羽纹栉纹切线同心圆纹垂直纹带、同心圆纹、圆心三角垂叶纹；扁耳两对饰辫纹 Drum face: patterns of sun(12rays), feather, comb line, tangent concentric circles, crossed double lines, transformed feathermen, transformed flying heron mixed Dingsheng;4 frog statues of 4 feet and blank back anticlockwise stand on the edge of drum face; Drum body: patterns of feather, comb line, tangent concentric circles, vertical ribbon of feather, straight line and tangent concentric circles, concentric circles, leaf-shape triangle with concentric circles in the middle; Braids pattern on 2 pairs of flat handles.	67－68	47.5	冷水冲型 Lengshui-chong Type	
293	族鼓 0306 鸟纹钱纹铜鼓 ZG No.0306 Bronze Drum with bird and coin patterns	广西民族博物馆 Anthropology Museum of Guangxi	1964 年出土于南宁市横县 Unearted at Hengxian County, Nanning in 1964	鼓面：太阳纹（10 芒）、虫形纹、鸟纹、四出钱纹、连钱纹、席纹、兽面纹、蝉纹、鼓面边缘饰六组逆时针三足螺旋纹立体青蛙其中三组为累蹲蛙；鼓身：蝉纹、四出钱纹、鸟纹、连钱纹、四瓣花纹、兽面纹、虫形纹、变形羽人纹、席纹、蝉纹；扁耳两对饰辫纹 Drum face: patterns of sun(10 rays), insect, bird, coin with quadrangle inside, coins part of overlap, woven mat, beast face, cicada; 6 frogs with 3 feet and spiracle on their backs anticlockwise stand on the edge, three of them are overlap; Drum body: patterns of cicada, coin with quadrangle inside, bird, coins part of overlap, quatrefoil, beast face, insect-shape motif, transformed feathermen, woven mat, cicada; Braid patterns on 2 pairs of flat handles.	79.6－80	46.8	灵山型 Lingshan Type	

序号 N0.	原编号及鼓名 Stock Number & Name	收藏单位 Museum	出土（征集）时间、地点 Time & Spot for discovered or collected	主要装饰 Main Decorations	尺寸（厘米）Size(cm)		类型 Type	图片 Picture
					面径 Face Diameter	身高 Height		
294	族鼓 0307 变形羽人纹铜鼓 ZG No.0307 Bronze Drum with transformed feathermen patterns	广西民族博物馆 Anthropology Museum of Guangxi	1963 年收购于南宁市宾阳县邹圩公社长村 Unearthed at Chang Village, Zouxu Community, Binyang County, Nanning City in 1963	鼓面：太阳纹（12 芒）、羽纹、栉纹、切线同心圆纹、复线交叉纹、变形羽人纹、变形翔鹭纹间定胜纹，鼓面边缘饰四只逆时针四足立体青蛙；鼓身：羽纹、栉纹、切线同心圆纹、羽纹栉纹切线同心圆纹垂直纹带、圆心三角垂叶纹；扁耳两对饰辫纹 Drum face: patterns of sun(12rays), feather, comb line, tangent concentric circles, crossed double lines, transformed feathermen, transformed flying heron mixed Dingsheng;4 frog statues of 4 feet anticlockwise stand on the edge of drum face; Drum body: patterns of feather, comb line, tangent concentric circles, vertical ribbon of feather, straight line and tangent concentric circles, leaf-shape triangle with concentric circles in the middle; Braids pattern on 2 pairs of flat handles.	66.3~67.3	46.9	冷水冲型 Lengshui-chong Type	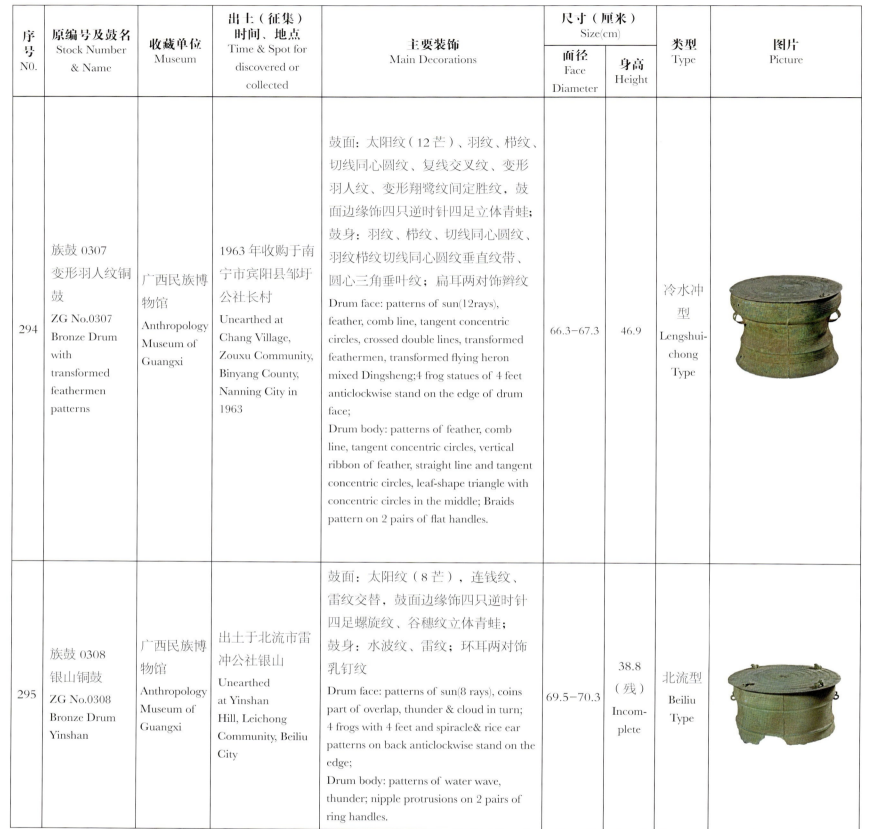
295	族鼓 0308 银山铜鼓 ZG No.0308 Bronze Drum Yinshan	广西民族博物馆 Anthropology Museum of Guangxi	出土于北流市雷冲公社银山 Unearthed at Yinshan Hill, Leichong Community, Beiliu City	鼓面：太阳纹（8 芒），连钱纹、雷纹交替，鼓面边缘饰四只逆时针四足螺旋纹、谷穗纹立体青蛙；鼓身：水波纹、雷纹；环耳两对饰乳钉纹 Drum face: patterns of sun(8 rays), coins part of overlap, thunder & cloud in turn; 4 frogs with 4 feet and spiracle& rice ear patterns on back anticlockwise stand on the edge; Drum body: patterns of water wave, thunder; nipple protrusions on 2 pairs of ring handles.	69.5~70.3	38.8（残）Incomplete	北流型 Beiliu Type	

序号 NO.	原编号及鼓名 Stock Number & Name	收藏单位 Museum	出土（征集） 时间、地点 Time & Spot for discovered or collected	主要装饰 Main Decorations	尺寸（厘米） Size(cm)		类型 Type	图片 Picture
					面径 Face Diameter	身高 Height		
296	族鼓 0309 橄材村铜鼓 ZG No.0309 Bronze Drum Gancai	广西民族博物馆 Anthropology Museum of Guangxi	1976 年出土于南宁市邕宁县五塘公社英广大队橄材村青山 Unearthed at Qing Hill, Gancai Village, Yingguang Team, Wutang Community, Yongning County, Nanning City in 1976	鼓面：太阳纹（12 芒）、栉纹、同心圆纹、复线交叉纹、变形羽人纹、变形翔鹭纹间定胜纹，鼓面边缘饰四只逆时针四足 素面立体青蛙； 鼓身：栉纹、同心圆纹、素纹栉纹同心圆纹垂直纹带、圆心三角垂叶纹；扁耳两对饰辫纹 Drum face: patterns of sun(12rays), comb line, concentric circles, crossed double lines, transformed feathermen, transformed flying heron mixed Dingsheng;4 frog statues of 4 feet and blank back anticlockwise stand on the edge of drum face; Drum body: patterns of comb line, concentric circles, vertical ribbon of blank, straight line and concentric circles, leaf-shape triangle with concentric circles in the middle; Braids pattern on 2 pairs of flat handles.	66–67.4	45 （残） Incomplete	冷水冲型 Lengshui-chong Type	
297	族鼓 0310 龙纹鱼纹铜鼓 ZG No.0310 Bronze Drum with dragon and fish patterns	广西民族博物馆 Anthropology Museum of Guangxi	1977 年征集于河池市东兰县 Collected in Donglan County, Hechi City in 1977	鼓面：太阳纹（12 芒）、四出钱纹、酉字纹、乳钉纹、波浪纹、同心圆纹、龙纹、鱼纹、波浪纹、四出钱纹； 鼓身：如意云纹、波浪纹、S 云纹、复线三角填 S 云纹；扁耳两对饰辫纹、回形雷纹 Drum face: patterns of sun(12rays), coin with quadrangle inside & 酉 -character, nipple protrusion, water wave, concentric circle, complex patterns(including dragon, fish, water wave and coin with quadrangle inside); Drum body: patterns of Ruyi-shape cloud, water wave, S-shape cloud, double line triangle filled with S-shape cloud; Braid & 回 -shape thunder patterns on 2 pairs of flat handles.	48.3	27.2 （残） Incomplete	麻江型 Majiang Type	

序号 N0.	原编号及鼓名 Stock Number & Name	收藏单位 Museum	出土（征集）时间、地点 Time & Spot for discovered or collected	主要装饰 Main Decorations	尺寸（厘米）Size(cm)		类型 Type	图片 Picture
					面径 Face Diameter	身高 Height		
298	族鼓 0311 游旗纹铜鼓 ZG No.0311 Bronze Drum with flying flag patterns	广西民族博物馆 Anthropology Museum of Guangxi	1977 年征集于南宁市金属制品厂（原自东兰钢筋厂送南宁加工） Collected at Nanning City Metal Product Plant (transferred for process from Donglan Rebar Plant to Nanning) in 1977	鼓面：太阳纹（12 芒）、酉字纹、花卉图案纹、乳钉纹、游旗纹、兽面云纹、窗花纹； 鼓身：乳钉纹、如意云纹、回形雷纹、兽面云纹、菱形填四瓣花纹、复线三角纹；扁耳两对饰辫纹、回形雷纹 Drum face: patterns of sun(12rays), 酉-character, flower, nipple protrusion, flying flag, beast-face cloud, window lattices; Drum body: patterns of nipple protrusion, Ruyi-shape cloud, 回-shape thunder, beast-face cloud, diamond filled with quatrefoils, double line triangle; Braid & 回-shape thunder patterns on 2 pairs of flat handles.	48.5	26	麻江型 Majiang Type	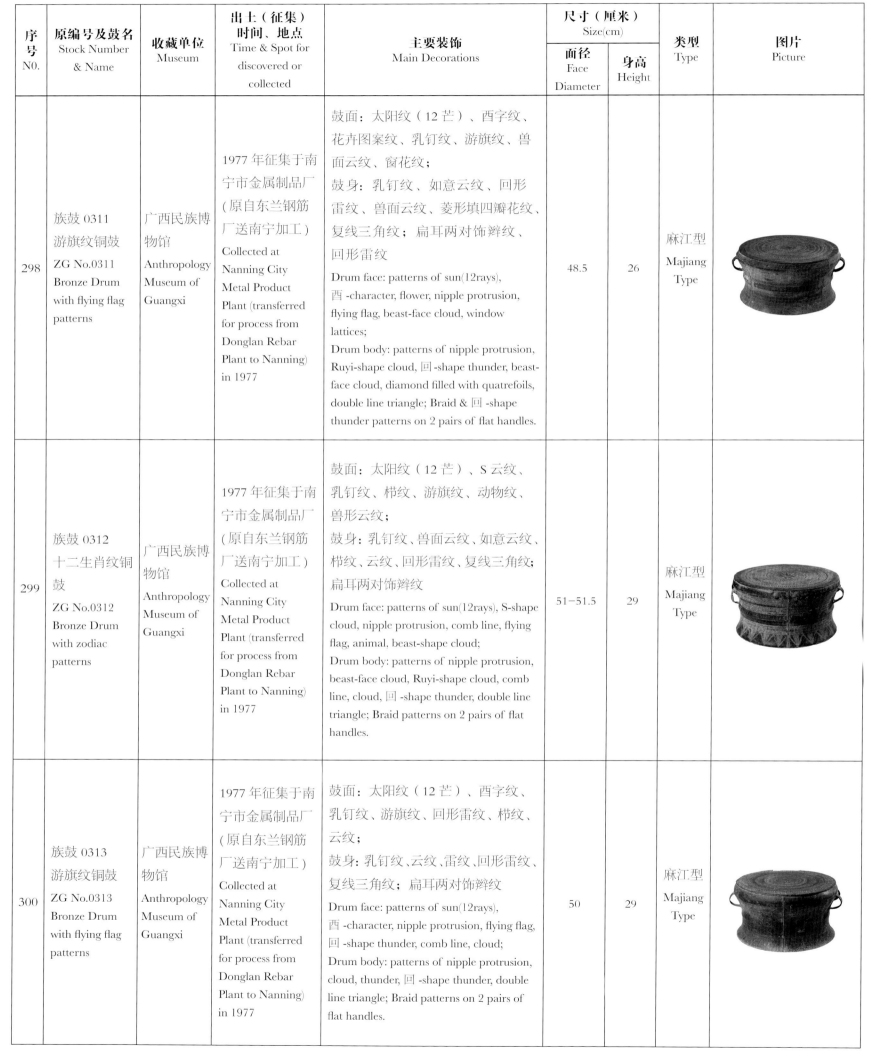
299	族鼓 0312 十二生肖纹铜鼓 ZG No.0312 Bronze Drum with zodiac patterns	广西民族博物馆 Anthropology Museum of Guangxi	1977 年征集于南宁市金属制品厂（原自东兰钢筋厂送南宁加工） Collected at Nanning City Metal Product Plant (transferred for process from Donglan Rebar Plant to Nanning) in 1977	鼓面：太阳纹（12 芒）、S 云纹、乳钉纹、栉纹、游旗纹、动物纹、兽形云纹； 鼓身：乳钉纹、兽面云纹、如意云纹、栉纹、云纹、回形雷纹、复线三角纹；扁耳两对饰辫纹 Drum face: patterns of sun(12rays), S-shape cloud, nipple protrusion, comb line, flying flag, animal, beast-shape cloud; Drum body: patterns of nipple protrusion, beast-face cloud, Ruyi-shape cloud, comb line, cloud, 回-shape thunder, double line triangle; Braid patterns on 2 pairs of flat handles.	51－51.5	29	麻江型 Majiang Type	
300	族鼓 0313 游旗纹铜鼓 ZG No.0313 Bronze Drum with flying flag patterns	广西民族博物馆 Anthropology Museum of Guangxi	1977 年征集于南宁市金属制品厂（原自东兰钢筋厂送南宁加工） Collected at Nanning City Metal Product Plant (transferred for process from Donglan Rebar Plant to Nanning) in 1977	鼓面：太阳纹（12 芒）、酉字纹、乳钉纹、游旗纹、回形雷纹、栉纹、云纹； 鼓身：乳钉纹、云纹、雷纹、回形雷纹、复线三角纹；扁耳两对饰辫纹 Drum face: patterns of sun(12rays), 酉-character, nipple protrusion, flying flag, 回-shape thunder, comb line, cloud; Drum body: patterns of nipple protrusion, cloud, thunder, 回-shape thunder, double line triangle; Braid patterns on 2 pairs of flat handles.	50	29	麻江型 Majiang Type	

续表

序号 NO.	原编号及鼓名 Stock Number & Name	收藏单位 Museum	出土（征集） 时间、地点 Time & Spot for discovered or collected	主要装饰 Main Decorations	尺寸（厘米） Size(cm)		类型 Type	图片 Picture
					面径 Face Diameter	身高 Height		
301	族鼓 0314 新坡铜鼓 ZG No.0314 Bronze Drum Xinpo	广西民族博物馆 Anthropology Museum of Guangxi	1976 年出土于南宁市邕宁县良庆公社那黄大队新坡村 Unearthed at Xinpo Village, Nahuang Team, Liangqing Community, Yongning County, Nanning City in 1976	鼓面：太阳纹（11 芒）、栉纹、复线三角纹、S 勾纹、复线交叉纹、变形羽人纹、变形翔鹭纹、鼓面边缘饰四只逆时针三足素面立体青蛙； 鼓身：栉纹、复线三角纹、S 勾纹 Drum face: patterns of sun(11rays), comb line, double line triangle, S-hook, crossed double lines, transformed feathermen, transformed flying heron;4 frog statues of 3 feet and blank back anticlockwise stand on the edge of drum face; Drum body: patterns of comb line, double line triangle, S-hook.	94.5~95.5	28 （残） Incomplete	冷水冲型 Lengshui-chong Type	
302	族鼓 0315 云雷纹鱼鸟混合纹铜鼓 ZG No.0315 Bronze Drum With cloud, thunder, fish and bird patterns	广西民族博物馆 Anthropology Museum of Guangxi	1970 年出土于北流县荔枝场果园 Unearthed at a Lizhi Orchard of Beiliu County in 1970	鼓面：太阳纹（8 芒）、云纹、雷纹、雷纹填线纹、连钱纹、鸟鱼混合纹、变形羽人纹、鼓面边缘饰六只逆时针四足素面立体青蛙； 鼓身：雷纹、连钱纹、云纹、雷纹填线纹、四瓣花纹；环耳两对饰缠丝纹 Drum face: patterns of sun(8 rays), cloud, thunder, thunder filled with straight line, coins part of overlap, fish and bird, transformed feathermen; 6 frogs with 4 feet and blank back anticlockwise stand on the edge; Drum body: patterns of thunder, coins part of overlap, cloud, thunder filled with straight line, quatrefoil; Silk-like patterns on 2 pairs of ring handles.	98.5~99.8	55	北流型 Beiliu Type	
303	族鼓 0316 人形图案云雷纹铜鼓 ZG No.0316 Bronze Drum with man, thunder and cloud patterns	广西民族博物馆 Anthropology Museum of Guangxi	1976 年出土于玉林市陆川县何莫村 Unearthed at Hemo Village, Luchuan County, Yulin City in 1976	鼓面：太阳纹（8 芒）、云纹、雷纹、人形图案，鼓面边缘饰六只逆时针四只立体青蛙； 鼓身：雷纹、云纹；环耳两对饰凸棱纹 Drum face: patterns of sun(8 rays), cloud, thunder, man; 6 frogs with 4 feet anticlockwise stand on the edge; Drum body: patterns of thunder, cloud; raise ridges on 2 pairs of ring handles.	104.2~106	55.5	北流型 Beiliu Type	

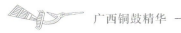

序号 N0.	原编号及鼓名 Stock Number & Name	收藏单位 Museum	出土（征集） 时间、地点 Time & Spot for discovered or collected	主要装饰 Main Decorations	尺寸（厘米） Size(cm)		类型 Type	图片 Picture
					面径 Face Diameter	身高 Height		
304	族鼓 0317 那团铜鼓 ZG No.0317 Bronze Drum Natuan	广西民族博物馆 Anthropology Museum of Guangxi	来源不详，原存广西壮族自治区博物馆 Original source unknown; preserved previously in Museum of Guangxi Zhuang Autonomous Region	鼓面：太阳纹（8芒）、雷纹填线纹，鼓面边缘饰四只两两相对四足素面立体青蛙； 鼓身：云纹；环耳两对饰缠丝纹 Drum face: patterns of sun(8 rays), thunder filled with straight line; 4 frogs with 4 feet and blank back stand on the edge, face to each other in pairs; Drum body: patterns of cloud; Silk-like patterns on 2 pairs of ring handles.	97.4–98.3	58.5	北流型 Beiliu Type	
305	族鼓 0318 图案化羽人纹铜鼓 ZG No.0318 Bronze Drum with patterning feathermen patterns	广西民族博物馆 Anthropology Museum of Guangxi	1982年元旦出土于百色市靖西县胡润公社华利大队亳山 Unearthed at Haoshan Hill, Huali Team, Hurun Community, Jingxi County, Baise City on New Year's Day of 1982	鼓面：太阳纹残缺，栉纹、雷纹填线纹、同心圆、变形羽人纹、鸟纹、雷纹、图案花纹，鼓面边缘饰四只立体青蛙； 鼓身：栉纹、同心圆纹 Drum face: the central part is lost, the other patterns are comb line, thunder fill with straight line, concentric circle, transformed feathermen, bird, complex patterns(including bird, thunder and flower); 4 frogs stand on the edge of the drum face; Drum body: patterns of comb line, concentric circle.	45.2–45.5	7.4 （残） Incomplete	西盟型 Ximeng Type	
306	族鼓 0319 罗算铜鼓 ZG No.0319 Bronze Drum Luosuan	广西民族博物馆 Anthropology Museum of Guangxi	1982年9月14日出土于梧州市藤县岭景公社罗算大队 Unearthed at Luosuan Team, Lingjing Community, Teng County, Wuzhou City on September 14th, 1982	鼓面：太阳纹（12芒）、云纹、雷纹，鼓面边缘饰六只逆时针四足素面立体青蛙； 鼓身：雷纹填线纹、云纹；扁耳两对 Drum face: patterns of sun(12 rays), cloud, thunder; 6 frogs with 4 feet and blank back stand on the edge; Drum body: patterns of thunder filled with straight line, cloud; 2 pairs of flat handles.	81.8–82	44 （残） Incomplete	北流型 Beiliu Type	

续表

序号 N0.	原编号及鼓名 Stock Number & Name	收藏单位 Museum	出土（征集） 时间、地点 Time & Spot for discovered or collected	主要装饰 Main Decorations	尺寸（厘米） Size(cm)		类型 Type	图片 Picture
					面径 Face Diameter	身高 Height		
307	族鼓 0320 覃村铜鼓 ZG No.0320 Bronze Drum Qincun	广西民族博物馆 Anthropology Museum of Guangxi	1974 年出土于南宁市宾阳县芦圩公社覃村二队水瓶 Unearthed at Shuizeng, Qincun Team 2, Luxu Community, Binyang County, Nanning City in 1974	鼓面：太阳纹（13 芒）、羽纹、同心圆纹、斜线纹、栉纹、复线纹、变形羽人纹、变形翔鹭纹，鼓面边缘饰四只逆时针四足素面立体青蛙； 鼓身：斜线纹、栉纹、同心圆纹、羽纹、船纹、变形羽人纹、圆心三角垂叶纹；扁耳两对饰辫纹 Drum face: patterns of sun(13rays), feather, concentric circle, oblique line, comb line, crossed double lines, transformed feathermen, transformed flying heron; 4 frog statues of 4 feet and blank back anticlockwise stand on the edge of drum face; Drum body: patterns of oblique line, comb line, concentric circle, feather, boat, transformed feathermen, leaf-shape triangle with circle in the middle; Braid patterns on 2 pairs of flat handles.	81－82.5	58.5	冷水冲型 Lengshui-chong Type	
308	族鼓 0321 变形羽人纹铜鼓 ZG No.0321 Bronze Drum with transformed feathermen patterns	广西民族博物馆 Anthropology Museum of Guangxi	出土于南宁市宾阳县，1983 年 7 月征集 Unearthed in Binyang County, Nanning City; Collected in July, 1983	鼓面：太阳纹（15 芒）、羽纹、栉纹、同心圆纹、复线交叉纹、变形羽人纹、变形翔鹭纹，鼓面边缘饰四只逆时针四足叶脉纹立体青蛙； 鼓身：羽纹、栉纹、切线同心圆纹、变形羽人纹、斜线纹、圆心三角垂叶纹；扁耳两对饰辫纹 Drum face: patterns of sun(15rays), feather, comb line, concentric circle, crossed double lines, transformed feathermen, transformed flying heron; 4 frog statues of 4 feet and leaf vein on back anticlockwise stand on the edge of drum face; Drum body: patterns of feather, comb line, tangent concentric circle, transformed feathermen, blank & oblique line, leaf-shape triangle with circle in the middle; Braid patterns on 2 pairs of flat handles.	89.5－91.5	55（残） Incomplete	冷水冲型 Lengshui-chong Type	

序号 NO.	原编号及鼓名 Stock Number & Name	收藏单位 Museum	出土（征集） 时间、地点 Time & Spot for discovered or collected	主要装饰 Main Decorations	尺寸（厘米） Size(cm)		类型 Type	图片 Picture
					面径 Face Diameter	身高 Height		
309	族鼓 0322 林村铜鼓 ZG No.0322 Bronze Drum Lincun	广西民族博物馆 Anthropology Museum of Guangxi	1975 年出土于南宁市宾阳县黎塘公社林村荒茅头 Unearthed at Huangmaotou, Lin Village, Litang Community, Binyang County, Nanning City in 1975	鼓面：太阳纹（12 芒）、栉纹、同心圆纹、谷穗交叉纹、变形羽人纹、变形翔鹭纹间定胜纹，鼓面边缘饰四只逆时针四足素面立体青蛙； 鼓身：栉纹、同心圆纹、素纹栉纹同心圆纹垂直纹带、圆心三角垂叶纹；扁耳两对饰辫纹 Drum face: patterns of sun(12rays), comb line, concentric circle, crossed double lines of rice ears, transformed feathermen, transformed flying heron mixed Dingsheng; 4 frog statues of 4 feet and blank back anticlockwise stand on the edge of drum face; Drum body: patterns of comb line, concentric circle, vertical ribbon of blank, straight line and concentric circle, leaf-shape triangle with circle in the middle; Braid patterns on 2 pairs of flat handles.	65.5-66	45.5 （残） Incomplete	冷水冲型 Lengshui-chong Type	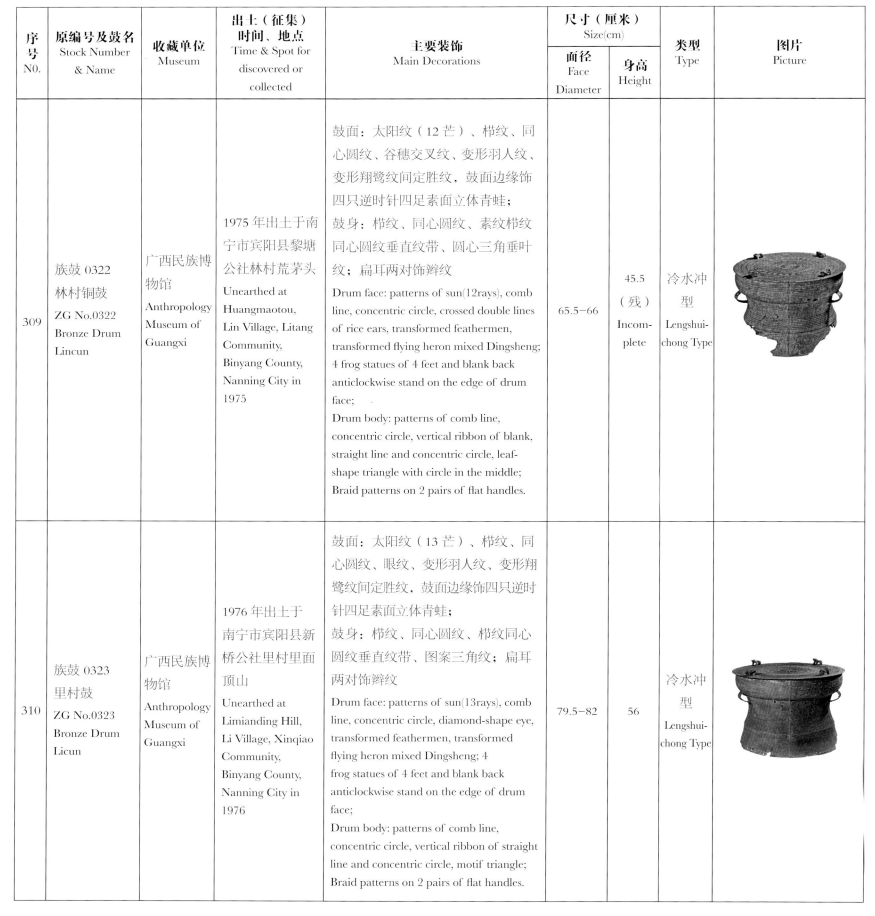
310	族鼓 0323 里村鼓 ZG No.0323 Bronze Drum Licun	广西民族博物馆 Anthropology Museum of Guangxi	1976 年出土于南宁市宾阳县新桥公社里村里面顶山 Unearthed at Limianding Hill, Li Village, Xinqiao Community, Binyang County, Nanning City in 1976	鼓面：太阳纹（13 芒）、栉纹、同心圆纹、眼纹、变形羽人纹、变形翔鹭纹间定胜纹，鼓面边缘饰四只逆时针四足素面立体青蛙； 鼓身：栉纹、同心圆纹、栉纹同心圆纹垂直纹带、图案三角纹；扁耳两对饰辫纹 Drum face: patterns of sun(13rays), comb line, concentric circle, diamond-shape eye, transformed feathermen, transformed flying heron mixed Dingsheng; 4 frog statues of 4 feet and blank back anticlockwise stand on the edge of drum face; Drum body: patterns of comb line, concentric circle, vertical ribbon of straight line and concentric circle, motif triangle; Braid patterns on 2 pairs of flat handles.	79.5-82	56	冷水冲型 Lengshui-chong Type	

序号 NO.	原编号及鼓名 Stock Number & Name	收藏单位 Museum	出土（征集） 时间、地点 Time & Spot for discovered or collected	主要装饰 Main Decorations	尺寸（厘米） Size(cm)		类型 Type	图片 Picture
					面径 Face Diameter	身高 Height		
311	族鼓 0324 变形羽人纹铜鼓 ZG No.0324 Bronze Drum with transformed feathermen patterns	广西民族博物馆 Anthropology Museum of Guangxi	出土于南宁市宾阳县，1983 年 7 月征集 Unearthed in Binyang County, Nanning City; Collected in July, 1983	鼓面：太阳纹（12 芒）、栉纹、切线同心圆纹、复线交叉纹、变形羽人纹、变形翔鹭纹间定胜纹，鼓面边缘饰四只逆时针四足素面立体青蛙； 鼓身：栉纹、切线同心圆纹、栉纹素纹同心圆纹垂直纹带、圆心三角垂叶纹；扁耳两对饰辫纹 Drum face: patterns of sun(12rays), comb line, tangent concentric circle, crossed double lines, transformed feathermen, transformed flying heron mixed Dingsheng; 4 frog statues of 4 feet and blank back anticlockwise stand on the edge of drum face; Drum body: patterns of comb line, tangent concentric circle, vertical ribbon of straight line, blank and concentric circle, leaf-shape triangle with circle in the middle; Braid patterns on 2 pairs of flat handles.	70.5	46.8 （残） Incom-plete	冷水冲型 Lengshui-chong Type	
312	族鼓 0325 变形羽人纹铜鼓 ZG No.0325 Bronze Drum with transformed feathermen patterns	广西民族博物馆 Anthropology Museum of Guangxi	1983 年征集于南宁市宾阳县 Collected at Binyang County, Nanning City in July, 1983	鼓面：太阳纹（12 芒）、栉纹、切线同心圆纹、羽纹、复线交叉纹、变形羽人纹、变形翔鹭夹定胜纹，鼓面边缘饰四只逆时针四足素面立体青蛙； 鼓身：羽纹、栉纹、同心圆纹、素纹栉纹切线同心圆纹垂直纹带、切线同心圆纹、圆心三角垂叶纹；扁耳两对饰辫纹 Drum face: patterns of sun(12rays), comb line, tangent concentric circle, feather, crossed double lines, transformed feathermen, transformed flying heron mixed Dingsheng; 4 frog statues of 4 feet and blank back anticlockwise stand on the edge of drum face; Drum body: patterns of feather, comb line, concentric circle, vertical ribbon of blank, straight line and tangent concentric circle, tangent concentric circle, leaf-shape triangle with circle in the middle; Biaid pattern on 2 pairs of flat handles.	67—68	47 （残） Incom-plete	冷水冲型 Lengshui-chong Type	

序号 N0.	原编号及鼓名 Stock Number & Name	收藏单位 Museum	出土（征集） 时间、地点 Time & Spot for discovered or collected	主要装饰 Main Decorations	尺寸（厘米） Size(cm)		类型 Type	图片 Picture
					面径 Face Diameter	身高 Height		
313	族鼓 0326 四出钱纹铜鼓 ZG No.0326 Bronze Drum with coin with quadrangle inside patterns	广西民族博物馆 Anthropology Museum of Guangxi	1982 年出土于钦州市灵山县石塘东采村 Unearthed at Dongcai Village, Shitang, Lingshan County, Qinzhou City in 1982	鼓面：太阳纹（12 芒）、蝉纹、虫形纹、连钱纹、四出钱纹、鸟纹、雷纹填线纹、变形羽人纹、四瓣花纹，鼓面边缘饰六组逆时针三足螺旋纹立体青蛙其中三组为累蹲蛙； 鼓身：蝉纹、四瓣花填线纹、连钱纹、四出钱纹、鸟纹、虫形纹、席纹、雷纹填线纹、变形羽人纹、四瓣花纹；扁耳两对饰辫纹，一侧耳下足部饰一只立体鸟，一侧胸、足对称三只附耳，鼓胸内壁饰一只立体牛 Drum face: patterns of sun(12 rays), cicada, insect-shape motif, coins part of overlap, coins with quadrangle inside, bird, thunder filled with straight line, transformed feathermen, quatrefoil; 6 overlap frogs with 3 feet and spiracle patterns on back anticlockwise stand on the edge three of them are overlap; Drum body: patterns of cicada, quatrefoil filled with straight line, coins part of overlap, coins with quadrangle inside, bird, insect, woven mat, thunder filled with straight line, transformed feathermen,quatrefoil; a bird statue stands under one of the handle on the drum foot, and an ox statue stands inside the chest; 3 attached ring handles on the chest and foot symmetrically; Braid patterns on 2 pairs of flat handles.	87.5－87.8	52.3	灵山型 Lingshan Type	
314	族鼓 0327 牛南铜鼓 ZG No.0327 Bronze Drum Niunan	广西民族博物馆 Anthropology Museum of Guangxi	1983 年 4 月出土于玉林市陆川县米场公社东平大队牛南 Unearthed at Niunan, Dongping Team, Michang Community, Luchuan County, Yulin City in April, 1983	鼓面：太阳纹（8 芒）、圆雷纹，鼓面边缘饰四只立体青蛙（已失）； 鼓身：雷纹；环耳两对饰缠丝纹 Drum face: patterns of sun(8 rays) and round cloud; 4 frogs stand on the edge(lost); Drum body: patterns of thunder;Silk-like pattern on 2 pairs of ring handles.	69.7－71	25.5 （残） Incomplete	北流型 Beiliu Type	

续表

序号 NO.	原编号及鼓名 Stock Number & Name	收藏单位 Museum	出土（征集）时间、地点 Time & Spot for discovered or collected	主要装饰 Main Decorations	尺寸（厘米） Size(cm)		类型 Type	图片 Picture
					面径 Face Diameter	身高 Height		
315	族鼓 0328 新安铜鼓 ZG No.0328 Bronze Drum Xin'an	广西民族博物馆 Anthropology Museum of Guangxi	1984 年 1 月 18 日出土于南宁市宾阳县思陇公社太平大队新安十六队 Unearthed at Xin'an Team 16, Taiping Team, Silong Community, Binyang County, Nanning City on January 18th, 1984	鼓面：太阳纹（11 芒）、羽纹、栉纹、同心圆纹、复线交叉纹、变形羽人纹、变形翔鹭纹间同心圆纹，鼓面边缘饰四只逆时针四足素面立体青蛙； 鼓身：栉纹、同心圆纹、羽纹、变形羽人纹、圆心三角垂叶纹；扁耳两对饰辫纹 Drum face: patterns of sun(11rays), feather, comb line, concentric circles, crossed double lines, transformed feathermen, transformed flying heron mixed concentric circle; 4 frog statues of 4 feet and blank back anticlockwise stand on the edge of drum face; Drum body: patterns of comb line, concentric circles, feather, transformed feathermen, leaf-shape triangle with circle in the middle; Braids pattern on 2 pairs of flat handles.	68-68.8	46	冷水冲型 Lengshui-chong Type	
316	族鼓 0329 羽人纹铜鼓 ZG No.0329 Bronze Drum with feathermen patterns	广西民族博物馆 Anthropology Museum of Guangxi	1983 年 12 月征购于南宁土产公司 Unearthed at Nanning Native Products Cooperative in December, 1983	鼓面：太阳纹（12 芒）、羽纹、栉纹、同心圆纹、复线交叉纹、变形羽人纹、变形翔鹭纹间定胜纹，鼓面边缘饰四只逆时针四足立体青蛙；鼓身缺失 Drum face: patterns of sun(12rays), feather, comb line, concentric circles, crossed double lines, transformed feathermen, transformed flying heron mixed Dingsheng; 4 frog statues of 4 feet anticlockwise stand on the edge of drum face; the drum body was lost.	72.5	（残） Incomplete	冷水冲型 Lengshui-chong Type	
317	族鼓 0330 羽人纹铜鼓 ZG No.0330 Bronze Drum with feathermen patterns	广西民族博物馆 Anthropology Museum of Guangxi	1983 年 12 月征购于南宁土产公司 Unearthed at Nanning Native Products Cooperative in December, 1983	鼓面：太阳纹（12 芒）、羽纹、栉纹、切线同心圆纹、复线交叉纹、变形羽人纹、变形翔鹭夹定胜纹，鼓面边缘饰四只逆时针四足立体青蛙；鼓身缺失 Drum face: patterns of sun(12rays), feather, comb line, tangent concentric circles, crossed double lines, transformed feathermen, transformed flying heron mixed Dingsheng; 4 frog statues of 4 feet anticlockwise stand on the edge of drum face; the drum body was lost.	63-63.5	（残） Incomplete	冷水冲型 Lengshui-chong Type	

序号 N0.	原编号及鼓名 Stock Number & Name	收藏单位 Museum	出土（征集） 时间、地点 Time & Spot for discovered or collected	主要装饰 Main Decorations	尺寸（厘米） Size(cm)		类型 Type	图片 Picture
					面径 Face Diameter	身高 Height		
318	族鼓 0331 素纹铜鼓 ZG No.0331 Bronze Drum with no pattern	广西民族博物馆 Anthropology Museum of Guangxi	出土于云南西部地区，1984 年云南省博物馆移交 Unearthed in the western area of Yunnan Province; transfered by Yunnan Museum in 1984	通体素面，无耳 The whole drum is blank; no handles.	36–37	31.8	万家坝型 Wanjiaba Type	
319	族鼓 0332 鱼纹鸟纹菊花纹铜鼓 ZG No.0332 Bronze Drum with fish, bird and chrysanthemum patterns	广西民族博物馆 Anthropology Museum of Guangxi	出土于云南西部地区，1984 年云南省博物馆移交 Unearthed in the western area of Yunnan Province; transfered by Yunnan Museum in 1984	鼓面：太阳纹（8 芒）、小比伦钱纹、栉纹、绹纹、同心圆纹、双绹纹、鸟纹、变形羽人纹、鱼纹、花纹、鸟纹，鼓面边缘饰四只逆时针四足素面立体青蛙； 鼓身：双绹纹、栉纹、绹纹、同心圆纹、鱼骨纹；扁耳两对饰辫纹、凹弦纹 Drum face: patterns of sun(8rays), small Bilun Coin, comb line, twisted rope, concentric circles, double twisted ropes, bird, transformed feathermen, complex patterns of fish, flower and bird; 4 frog statues of 4 feet and blank back anticlockwise stand on the edge of drum face; Drum body: patterns of double twisted ropes, comb line, twisted rope, concentric circle, fishbone; Braid & carve strings on 2 pairs of flat handles.	53.4	41	西盟型 Ximeng Type	
320	族鼓 0333 大合村铜鼓 ZG No.0333 Bronze Drum Dahecun	广西民族博物馆 Anthropology Museum of Guangxi	1970 年出土于南宁市横县云表公社六合大队大合村山坡 Unearthed at the hillside of Dahe Village, Liuhe Team, Yunbiao Community, Heng County, Nanning City in 1970	鼓面：太阳纹（8 芒）、四瓣花纹、四出钱纹、云纹、雷纹、席纹、雷纹填线纹，鼓面边缘饰六组顺时针三足素面立体青蛙（一组已失，两组为累蹲蛙）； 鼓身：四瓣花纹、半同心圆纹、四出钱纹、雷纹、云纹、席纹；扁耳两对 Drum face: patterns of sun(8 rays), quatrefoil, coins with quadrangle inside, cloud, thunder, woven mat, thunder filled with straight line;6 frogs with 3 feet and blank back clockwise stand on the edge(one lost, two of them are overlap); Drum body: patterns of quatrefoil, semi-concentric circle, coin with quadrangle inside, cloud, thunder, 2 pairs of flat handles.	65.2–66.5	33.5 （残） Incom- plete	灵山型 Lingshan Type	

续表

序号 NO.	原编号及鼓名 Stock Number & Name	收藏单位 Museum	出土（征集）时间、地点 Time & Spot for discovered or collected	主要装饰 Main Decorations	尺寸（厘米） Size(cm)		类型 Type	图片 Picture
					面径 Face Diameter	身高 Height		
321	族鼓 0334 大塘铜鼓 ZG No.0334 Bronze Drum Datang	广西民族博物馆 Anthropology Museum of Guangxi	1973 年出土于南宁市横县马山公社大塘 Unearthed at Datang, Mashan Community, Heng County, Nanning City in 1973	鼓面：太阳纹（8 芒）、四出钱纹、云纹、半同心圆羽纹、连钱纹、席纹、虫形纹，鼓面边缘饰六组顺时针三足立体青蛙其中三组为累蹲蛙； 鼓身：四出钱纹、连钱纹、云纹、雷纹填线纹、半同心圆填线纹、席纹、四瓣花纹；扁耳两对饰羽纹、乳钉纹 Drum face: patterns of sun(8 rays), coins with quadrangle inside, cloud, semi-concentric circle & feather, coins part of overlap, woven mat, insect; 6 frogs with 3 fee clockwise stand on the edge three of them are overlap; Drum body: patterns of coins with quadrangle inside, coins part of overlap, cloud, thunder filled with straight line & cloud, semi-concentric circle filled with straight lines, woven mat, quatrefoil; Feather & nipple prostrusion on 2 pairs of flat handles.	69.8~71.5	30（残）Incomplete	灵山型 Lingshan Type	
322	族鼓 0335 大浪铜鼓 ZG No.0335 Bronze Drum Dalang	广西民族博物馆 Anthropology Museum of Guangxi	1973 年出土于南宁市横县六景公社大浪大队 Unearthed at Dalang Team, Liujing Community, Hengxian County, Nanning City in 1973	鼓面：太阳纹（12 芒）、蝉纹、蝴蝶纹、四出钱纹、鸟纹、席纹、连钱纹、四瓣花填线纹，鼓面边缘饰六组逆时针三足螺旋纹立体青蛙，其中三组为累蹲蛙； 鼓身：蝉纹、蝴蝶纹、四出钱纹、鸟纹、连钱纹、兽面纹、席纹、虫形纹、四瓣花填线纹；扁耳两对饰羽纹、一侧耳下有一对鸟立饰，背饰羽纹 Drum face: patterns of sun(12 rays), cicada, butterfly, coins with quadrangle inside, bird, woven mat, coins part of overlap, quatrefoil filled with straight line; 6 overlap frogs with 3 feet and spiracle patterns on back anticlockwise stand on the edge, three of them are overlap; Drum body: patterns of cicada, butterfly, coins with quadrangle inside, bird, coins part of overlap, beast face, woven mat, insect, quatrefoil filled with straight line; A pair of bird statues stand under one of the handle on the drum foot, with feather patterns on back; Feather patterns on 2 pairs of flat handles.	78.7~78.9	47.2	灵山型 Lingshan Type	

序号 N0.	原编号及鼓名 Stock Number & Name	收藏单位 Museum	出土（征集）时间、地点 Time & Spot for discovered or collected	主要装饰 Main Decorations	尺寸（厘米）Size(cm)		类型 Type	图片 Picture
					面径 Face Diameter	身高 Height		
323	族鼓 0336 红宜村铜鼓 ZG No.0336 Bronze Drum Hongyicun	广西民族博物馆 Anthropology Museum of Guangxi	1973 年出土于南宁市横县南乡公社红宜村葫芦山 Unearthed at Hulu Hill, Hongyi Village, Nanxiang Community, Heng County, Nanning City in 1973	鼓面：太阳纹（10 芒）、四出钱纹、连钱纹、变形羽人纹，鼓面边缘饰六组顺时针三足席纹、羽纹立体青蛙其中三组为累蹲蛙；鼓身：连钱纹、四出钱纹；扁耳两对饰羽纹、乳钉纹，一侧耳下有四足立饰痕迹 Drum face: patterns of sun(10 rays), coins with quadrangle inside, coins part of overlap, transformed feathermen; 6 frogs of 3 feet with woven mat & feather patterns on back clockwise stand on the edge three of them are overlap; Drum body: patterns of coins part of overlap, coins with quadrangle inside; feather & nipple protrusion patterns on 2 pairs of flat handles; mark of a 4-feet statue under one of the handles.	77.2–81.2	45.3	灵山型 Lingshan Type	
324	族鼓 0337 水燕村铜鼓 ZG No.0337 Bronze Drum Shuiyancun	广西民族博物馆 Anthropology Museum of Guangxi	1974 年出土于南宁市横县石塘山公社水燕村山坡 Unearthed at hillside of Shuiyan Village, Shitangshan Community, Hengxian County, Nanning City in 1974	鼓面：太阳纹（12 芒）、栉纹、切线同心圆纹、复线交叉纹、变形羽人纹、变形翔鹭纹间定胜纹、蝉纹，鼓面边缘饰四只逆时针四足叶脉纹、方格纹立体青蛙；鼓身：栉纹、切线同心圆纹、竞渡纹、水鸟纹、复线菱形纹、变形羽人纹栉纹切线同心圆纹垂直纹带；扁耳两对饰羽纹 Drum face: patterns of sun(12rays), comb line, tangent concentric circles, crossed double lines, transformed feathermen, transformed flying heron mixed Dingsheng pattern, cicada;4 frog statues of 4 feet with leaf vein & grids on back anticlockwise stand on the edge of drum face; Drum body: patterns of comb line, tangent concentric circles, boat racing & waterfowl, double line diamond, vertical ribbon of transformed feathermen, straight line and tangent concentric circle; Feather patterns on 2 pairs of flat handles.	81.2–82.5	32.5（残）Incomplete	冷水冲型 Lengshuichong Type	

序号 N0.	原编号及鼓名 Stock Number & Name	收藏单位 Museum	出土（征集） 时间、地点 Time & Spot for discovered or collected	主要装饰 Main Decorations	尺寸（厘米） Size(cm)		类型 Type	图片 Picture
					面径 Face Diameter	身高 Height		
325	族鼓 0338 鸟纹变形羽人纹铜鼓 ZG No.0338 Bronze Drum with bird and transformed feathermen patterns	广西民族博物馆 Anthropology Museum of Guangxi	1976 年出土于南宁市横县良圻公社滕山村 Unearthed at TengshanVillage, Liangqi Community, Heng County, Nanning City in 1976	鼓面：太阳纹（10 芒）、蝉纹、虫形纹、四出钱纹、鸟纹、四瓣花纹、连钱纹、席纹、兽形纹、栉纹，鼓面边缘饰六组逆时针三足螺旋纹、辫纹立体青蛙（一组已失，三组为累蹲蛙）； 鼓身：蝉纹、虫形纹、四出钱纹、兽面纹、连钱纹、雷纹填线纹、兽形纹、席纹、四瓣花纹、鸟纹、四瓣花填线纹；扁耳两对饰辫纹、圆结纹，一侧耳下有一只鸟立饰，背饰复线纹 Drum face: patterns of sun(10 rays), cicada, insect-shape motif, coins with quadrangle inside, bird, quatrefoil, coins part of overlap, woven mat, beast-shape motif, comb line; 6 frogs of 3 feet with spiracle & braid patterns on back anticlockwise stand on the edge(one lost, three of them are overlap); Drum body: patterns of cicada, insect, coins with quadrangle inside, beast face, coins part of overlap, thunder filled with straight line, beast-shape motif, woven mat, quatrefoil, bird, quatrefoil filled with straight line; a bird statue stands under one of the handle on the drum foot, with lines on back; Braid & circle patterns on 2 pairs of flat handles.	95.5~95.8	56	灵山型 Lingshan Type	
326	族鼓 0339 大田村铜鼓 ZG No.0339 Bronze Drum Datiancun	广西民族博物馆 Anthropology Museum of Guangxi	1984 年出土于南宁市横县镇龙公社凤丹大队大田村 Unearthed at DatianVillage, Fengdan Team, Zhenlong Community, Hengxian County, Nanning City in 1984	鼓面：太阳纹（12 芒）、水波纹、切线同心圆纹、栉纹、复线交叉纹、变形羽人纹、变形翔鹭纹，鼓面边缘饰四只逆时针四足曲弦纹立体青蛙； 鼓身：水波纹、栉纹、切线同心圆纹、船纹、变形羽人纹、网纹、圆心三角垂叶纹、羽纹、眼纹；扁耳两对饰羽纹 Drum face: patterns of sun(12rays), water wave, tangent concentric circle, comb line, crossed double lines, transformed feathermen, flying heron; 4 frog statues of 4 feet with winding lines on back anticlockwise stand on the edge of drum face; Drum body: patterns of water wave, comb line, tangent concentric circle, boat, transformed feathermen, net, leaf-shape triangle with circle in the middle, feather, diamond-shape eye; feather patterns on 2 pairs of flat handles.	74.5~77.5	52.8 （残） Incomplete	冷水冲型 Lengshuichong Type	

序号 N0.	原编号及鼓名 Stock Number & Name	收藏单位 Museum	出土（征集）时间、地点 Time & Spot for discovered or collected	主要装饰 Main Decorations	尺寸（厘米） Size(cm)		类型 Type	图片 Picture
					面径 Face Diameter	身高 Height		
327	族鼓 0340 那阳铜鼓 ZG No.0340 Bronze Drum Nayang	广西民族博物馆 Anthropology Museum of Guangxi	1972 年出土于南宁市横县那阳公社 Unearthed at Nayang Community, Hengxian County, Nanning City in 1972	鼓面：太阳纹（12 芒）、蝉纹、蝴蝶纹、四出钱纹、鸟纹、连钱纹、席纹，鼓面边缘饰六组逆时针三足螺旋纹立体青蛙其中三组为累蹲蛙；鼓身：蝉纹、蝴蝶纹、四出钱纹、鸟纹、连钱纹、兽面纹、席纹、虫形纹、四瓣花填线纹；扁耳两对饰羽纹，一侧耳下有一只鸟立饰，背饰复线纹 Drum face: patterns of sun(12 rays), cicada, butterfly, coins with quadrangle inside, bird, coins part of overlap, woven mat; 6 frogs of 3 feet with spiracle on back anticlockwise stand on the edge three of them are overlap; Drum body: patterns of cicada, butterfly, coins with quadrangle inside, bird, coins part of overlap, beast face, woven mat, insect, quatrefoil filled with straight line; A bird statue stands under one of the handle, with lines on back; Feather patterns on 2 pairs of flat handles.	80~80.5	45.5 （残） Incomplete	灵山型 Lingshan Type	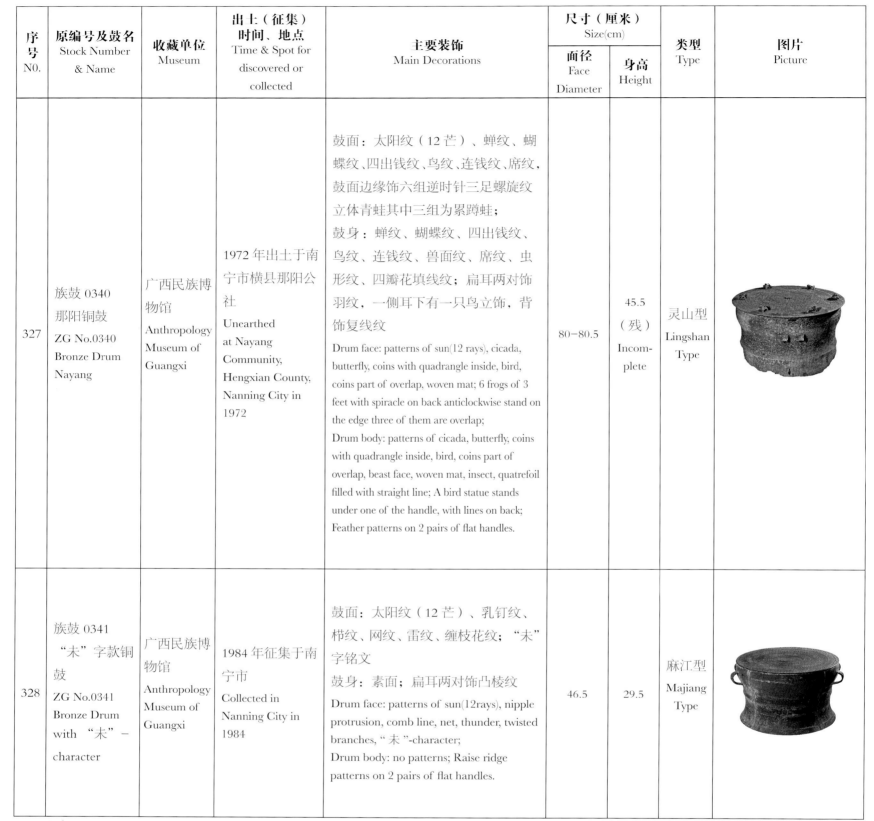
328	族鼓 0341 "未"字款铜鼓 ZG No.0341 Bronze Drum with "未"–character	广西民族博物馆 Anthropology Museum of Guangxi	1984 年征集于南宁市 Collected in Nanning City in 1984	鼓面：太阳纹（12 芒）、乳钉纹、栉纹、网纹、雷纹、缠枝花纹；"未"字铭文 鼓身：素面；扁耳两对饰凸棱纹 Drum face: patterns of sun(12rays), nipple protrusion, comb line, net, thunder, twisted branches, " 未 "-character; Drum body: no patterns; Raise ridge patterns on 2 pairs of flat handles.	46.5	29.5	麻江型 Majiang Type	

序号 NO.	原编号及鼓名 Stock Number & Name	收藏单位 Museum	出土（征集） 时间、地点 Time & Spot for discovered or collected	主要装饰 Main Decorations	尺寸（厘米）Size(cm)		类型 Type	图片 Picture
					面径 Face Diameter	身高 Height		
329	族鼓 0342 四合村铜鼓 ZG No.0342 Bronze Drum Sihecun Drum	广西民族博物馆 Anthropology Museum of Guangxi	1985 年出土于南宁市扶绥县昌平乡四合村恒平屯石标岭 Unearthed at Shibiao Ling, Hengping Tun, Sihe Village, Changping, Fusui County, Nanning in 1985	鼓面：太阳纹（12 芒）、栉纹、同心圆纹、复线交叉纹、变形羽人纹、变形翔鹭纹间定胜纹、羽纹、鼓面边缘饰四只逆时针四足素面立体青蛙；鼓身：栉纹、同心圆纹、素纹栉纹同心圆纹垂直纹带、圆心三角垂叶纹；扁耳两对饰辫纹 Drum face: patterns of sun(12rays), comb line, concentric circle, crossed double lines, transformed feathermen, transformed flying heron mixed Dingsheng, feather; 4 frog statues of 4 feet with blank back anticlockwise stand on the edge of drum face; Drum body: patterns of comb line, concentric circle. vertical ribbon of blank, straight line and concentric circles, leaf-shape triangle with circle in the middle; Braid patterns on 2 pairs of flat handles.	71.5~73.8	30~43（残） Incomplete	冷水冲型 Lengshui-chong Type	
330	族鼓 0344 骑兽纹"四出"钱纹铜鼓 ZG No.0344 Bronze Drum With beast-rider& coins with quadrangle inside patterns	广西民族博物馆 Anthropology Museum of Guangxi	1989 年征集于邕宁县吴圩镇敢绿村出土 Unearthed at Ganlv Village, Wuxu Town, Yongning County, Nanning City in 1989	鼓面：太阳纹（10 芒）、蝉纹、四瓣花纹、四出钱纹间鸟纹、连钱纹、鸟形纹、席纹、虫纹、骑兽纹，鼓面边缘饰六只逆时针三足立体青蛙；鼓身：四出钱纹间蝉纹、连钱纹、兽面纹、虫纹、四瓣花纹、席纹、骑兽纹，扁耳两对饰辫纹，一耳下方鼓腰处有一乘骑塑像。 Drum face: patterns of sun(10 rays), cicada, quatrefoil, coins with quadrangle inside& bird,coins part of overlap, bird, woven mat, insect, beast-rider, 6 frogs of 3 feet anticlockwise stand on the edge; Drum body: patterns of coins with quadrangle inside&cicada, coins part of overlap, beast face,insect, quatrefoil, woven mat, beast-rider; a horse-rider statue stands under one of the handle; Braid patterns on 2 pairs of flat handles.	91.5	55	灵山型 Lingshan Type	

序号 NO.	原编号及鼓名 Stock Number & Name	收藏单位 Museum	出土（征集） 时间、地点 Time & Spot for discovered or collected	主要装饰 Main Decorations	尺寸（厘米） Size(cm)		类型 Type	图片 Picture
					面径 Face Diameter	身高 Height		
331	族鼓 0345 那卜铜鼓 ZG No.0345 Bronze Drum Napu	广西民族博物馆 Anthropology Museum of Guangxi	1991 年出土于玉林市博白县那卜中学 Unearthed at , Napu Middle School Bobai County, Yulin City in 1991	鼓面：太阳纹（8 芒）、雷纹、云纹，鼓面边缘饰四只两两相对四足素面立体青蛙； 鼓身：雷纹、云纹；环耳两对 Drum face: patterns of sun(8rays), thunder, cloud; 4 frogs with 4 feet and blank back stand on the edge, face to each other in pairs; Drum body: patterns of thunder, cloud; 2 pairs of ring handles.	77.6－78	44.3	北流型 Beiliu Type	
332	017662 No.017662 游旗纹铜鼓 Bronze Drum with flying flag patterns	广西民族博物馆 Anthropology Museum of Guangxi	2014 年于百色市隆林县征购 Collected in Longlin County, Baise City in 2014	鼓面：太阳纹（12 芒）、西字纹、S 云纹、乳钉纹、绚纹、游旗纹、素纹两晕； 鼓身：乳钉纹、云纹、枋纹、回形雷纹、复线三角纹；扁耳两对饰辫纹 Drum face: patterns of sun(12rays), 酉 -character, S-shape cloud, nipple protrusion, twisted rope, flying flag, 2 blank loopes; Drum body: Pattern of nipple protrusion, cloud, comd line, 回 -shape thunder, double line triangle; Braid patterns on 2 pairs of flat handles.	51	28	麻江型 Majiang Type	
333	017663 No.017663 游旗纹铜鼓 Bronze Drum with flying flag patterns	广西民族博物馆 Anthropology Museum of Guangxi	2014 年于百色市隆林县征购 Collected in Longlin County, Baise City in 2014	鼓面：太阳纹（12 芒）、西字纹、云纹、乳钉纹、枋纹、游旗纹、雷纹； 鼓身：乳钉纹、如意云纹、回形雷纹、雷纹、复线三角纹；扁耳两对饰辫纹 Drum face: patterns of sun(12rays), 酉 -character, cloud, nipple protrusion,comb line, flying flag, thunder; Drum body: Pattern of nipple protrusion, Ruyi-shape cloud, 回 -shape thunder, thunder, double line triangle; Braid patterns on 2 pairs of flat handles.	51	29.5	麻江型 Majiang Type	

序号 NO.	原编号及鼓名 Stock Number & Name	收藏单位 Museum	出土（征集） 时间、地点 Time & Spot for discovered or collected	主要装饰 Main Decorations	尺寸（厘米） Size(cm)		类型 Type	图片 Picture
					面径 Face Diameter	身高 Height		
334	017664 游旗纹铜鼓 No.017664 Bronze Drum With flying flag patterns	广西民族博物馆 Anthropology Museum of Guangxi	2014 年于百色市隆林县征购 Collected in Longlin County, Baise City in 2014	鼓面：太阳纹（12 芒）、西字纹、乳钉纹、S 云纹、游旗纹、栉纹、回形雷纹； 鼓身：乳钉纹、回形雷纹、如意云纹、栉纹、复线三角纹；扁耳两对饰辫纹 Drum face: patterns of sun(12rays), 西 -character, nipple protrusion, S-shape cloud, flying flag, comb line, 回 -shape thunder; Drum body: Pattern of nipple protrusion, 回 -shape thunder, Ruyi-shape cloud, comb line, double line triangle; Braid patterns on 2 pairs of flat handles.	51.4	29	麻江型 Majiang Type	
335	017665 游旗纹铜鼓 No.017665 Bronze Drum With flying flag patterns	广西民族博物馆 Anthropology Museum of Guangxi	2014 年于百色市隆林县征购 Collected in Longlin County, Baise City in 2014	鼓面：太阳纹（12 芒）、西字纹、S 云纹、乳钉纹、绹纹、游旗纹、云纹、缠枝花纹 鼓身：乳钉纹、菱形填四瓣花纹、回形雷纹、栉纹、复线三角；扁耳两对饰辫纹 Drum face: patterns of sun(12rays), 西 -character, S-shape cloud, nipple protrusion, twisted rope, flying flag, cloud, twisted branches; Drum body: Pattern of nipple protrusion, diamond filled with quatrefoil, 回 -shape thunder, comb line, double line triangle; Braid patterns on 2 pairs of flat handles.	50.8	29	麻江型 Majiang Type	
336	参 000032 游旗纹铜鼓 C No.000032 Bronze Drum with flying flag patterns	广西民族博物馆 Anthropology Museum of Guangxi	2010 年于河池东兰县收购 Collected in Donglan County, Hechi City in 2010	鼓面：太阳纹（12 芒）、西字纹、S 云纹、乳钉纹、栉纹、兽形云纹； 鼓身：乳钉纹、如意云纹、回形雷纹、复线三角纹；扁耳两对饰辫纹 Drum face: patterns of sun(12rays), 西 -character, S-shape cloud, nipple protrusion, straight lilne, beast-shape cloud; Drum body: patterns of nipple protrusion, Ruyi-shape cloud, 回 -shape thunder, double line triangle; Braid patterns on 2 pairs of flat handles.	47.5－47.8	28	麻江型 Majiang Type	

序号 N0.	原编号及鼓名 Stock Number & Name	收藏单位 Museum	出土（征集）时间、地点 Time & Spot for discovered or collected	主要装饰 Main Decorations	尺寸（厘米）Size(cm)		类型 Type	图片 Picture
					面径 Face Diameter	身高 Height		
337	参 3－00001 游旗纹铜鼓 C3 No.00001 Bronze Drum with flying flag patterns	广西民族博物馆 Anthropology Museum of Guangxi	2010 年于隆林县者保乡上棒村那麻屯征集 Collected in Nama Tun, Shangbang Village, Zhebao, Longlin County, Baise City in 2010	鼓面：太阳纹（12 芒）、酉字纹、乳钉纹、栉纹、游旗纹、云纹、雷纹 鼓身：乳钉纹、雷纹、回形雷纹、栉纹、复线三角纹；扁耳两对饰辫纹 Drum face: patterns of sun(12rays), 酉 -character, nipple protrusion, comb line, flying flag, cloud, thunder; Drum body: Pattern of nipple protrusion, thunder, 回 -shape thunder, comb line, double line triangle; Braid patterns on 2 pairs of flat handles.	50	20	麻江型 Majiang Type	
338	参 3－00003 东山铜鼓 C3 No.00003 Dongson Bronze Drum	广西民族博物馆 Anthropology Museum of Guangxi	2012 年靖西县征集 Collected in Jingxi County, Baise City in 2012	鼓面：太阳纹（16 芒）、雷纹、栉纹、勾连云纹、复线菱形纹、羽人划船纹、翔鹭纹 鼓身：栉纹、勾连云纹、羽人划船纹、鸟纹、复线菱形纹；胸部以下残 Drum face: patterns of sun(16rays), thunder, comb line, hooked cloud, double line diamond, feathermen boating, flying heron; Drum body: patterns of comb line, hooked cloud, feathermen boating, bird, double line diamond; parts under drum chest was lost.	71	22（残） Incomplete	东山铜鼓 Dongson Type	
339	参 3－00004 云雷纹芒族铜鼓 C3 No.00004 Bronze Drum with cloud&thunder patterns of Mang People	广西民族博物馆 Anthropology Museum of Guangxi	2012 年靖西县征集 Collected in Jingxi County, Baise City in 2012	鼓面：太阳纹（6 芒）、四瓣花纹、雷纹、如意云纹、三叶纹，鼓面边缘饰四只逆时针列三足立体蛙 鼓身：弦纹，其余磨饰；扁耳两对 Drum face: patterns of sun(6rays), quatrefoil, thunder, Ruyi-shape cloud, clover; 4 frogs with 3 feet stand anticlockwisly on the edge of drum face. Drum body: patterns of strings, the other patterns are obseure; 2 pairs of flat handles	59	40.5	芒族铜鼓 Mang Type	
340	参 3－00005 游旗纹铜鼓 C3 No.00005 Bronze Drum with flying flag patterns	广西民族博物馆 Anthropology Museum of Guangxi	2012 年于贵州征集 Collected in Guizhou Province in 2012	鼓面：太阳纹（12 芒）、酉字纹、卷云纹、乳钉纹、游旗纹、菱纹 鼓身：乳钉纹、云纹、菱纹、回形纹；扁耳两对饰辫纹 Drum face: patterns of sun(12rays), 酉 -character, hooked cloud, nipple protrusion, flying flag diamond; Drum body: patterns of nipple protrusion, cloud,diamond, 回 -character; Braid patterns on 2 pairs of flat handles.	51	28.7	麻江型 Majiang Type	

续表

序号 N0.	原编号及鼓名 Stock Number & Name	收藏单位 Museum	出土（征集） 时间、地点 Time & Spot for discovered or collected	主要装饰 Main Decorations	尺寸（厘米） Size(cm)		类型 Type	图片 Picture
					面径 Face Diameter	身高 Height		
341	参 3-00006 游旗纹铜鼓 C3 No.00006 Bronze Drum with flying flag patterns	广西民族博物馆 Anthropology Museum of Guangxi	2012 年于贵州征集 Collected in Guizhou Province in 2012	鼓面：太阳纹（12 芒）、西字纹、卷云纹、乳钉纹、栉纹、游旗纹、菱纹、素纹 鼓身：乳钉纹、云纹、栉纹、菱纹、回形纹；扁耳两对饰辫纹 Drum face: patterns of sun(12rays), 西 -character, hooked cloud, nipple protrusion, comb line, flying flag, diamond; Drum body: patterns of nipple protrusion, cloud,comb line, diamond, 回 -character; Braid patterns on 2 pairs of flat handles.	50	30	麻江型 Majiang Type	
342	参 3-00007 游旗纹铜鼓 C3 No.00007 Bronze Drum with flying flag patterns	广西民族博物馆 Anthropology Museum of Guangxi	2012 年于田东县征集 Collected inTiandong County, Baise City in 2012	鼓面：太阳纹（12 芒）、游旗纹、花卉纹、钱纹、回形雷纹、乳钉纹、双龙团寿纹、牛纹、荷耙人纹 鼓身：乳钉纹、如意云纹、栉纹、回形雷纹、复线三角纹；扁耳两对饰辫纹 Drum face: patterns of sun(12rays), flying flag, flower, coin, 回 -shape thunder, nipple protrusion, 2 dragons&round " 寿 "-character, ox, hoers; Drum body: patterns of nipple protrusion, Ruyi-shape cloud, comb line, 回 -shape thunder, double line triangle; braid patterns on 2 pairs of flat handles.	50	20	麻江型 Majiang Type	
343	参 3-00008 变形羽人纹铜鼓 C3 No.00008 Bronze Drum with transformed feathermen patterns	广西民族博物馆 Anthropology Museum of Guangxi	2012 年于田东县征集 Collected inTiandong County, Baise City in 2012	鼓面：太阳纹（12 芒）、变形羽人纹、变形翔鹭纹间定胜纹、勾连云纹，鼓面边缘四蛙全失，断口处见蛙为三趾；鼓胸以下缺 Drum face: patterns of sun(12rays), transform feathermen, transformed flying heron with Dingsheng, hooked cloud; 4 frogs statue on the edge of drum face were all lost, and marks of 3 toes of them were saved; Parts under drum chest were lost.	50	20 （残） Incom-plete	冷水冲型 Lengshui-chong Type	

序号 N0.	原编号及鼓名 Stock Number & Name	收藏单位 Museum	出土（征集） 时间、地点 Time & Spot for discovered or collected	主要装饰 Main Decorations	尺寸（厘米） Size(cm)		类型 Type	图片 Picture
					面径 Face Diameter	身高 Height		
344	土 0280 西林 280 号鼓 Tu No.0280 Bronze Drum Xilin	广西壮族自治区博物馆 Museum of Guangxi Zhuang Autonomous Region	1972 年 7 月出土于百色市西林县普驮村铜鼓墓葬 Unearthed at Putuo Village, Xilin County, Baise City in July,1972	鼓面：太阳纹（16 芒），勾连云纹、翔鹭纹、锯齿纹、切线圆圈纹； 鼓身：羽人划船纹、鱼纹、鸟纹、羽人舞蹈纹、鹿纹；扁耳两对，已失 Drum face: patterns of sun(16rays), hooked cloud motifs, flying heron, saw tooth, tangent concentric circle; Drum body: patterns of feathermen boat racing, fish & bird, dancing feachermen and deer; 2 pairs of flat handles were lost.	77.5-78.2	49.5 （残） Incomplete	石寨山型 Shizhaishan Type	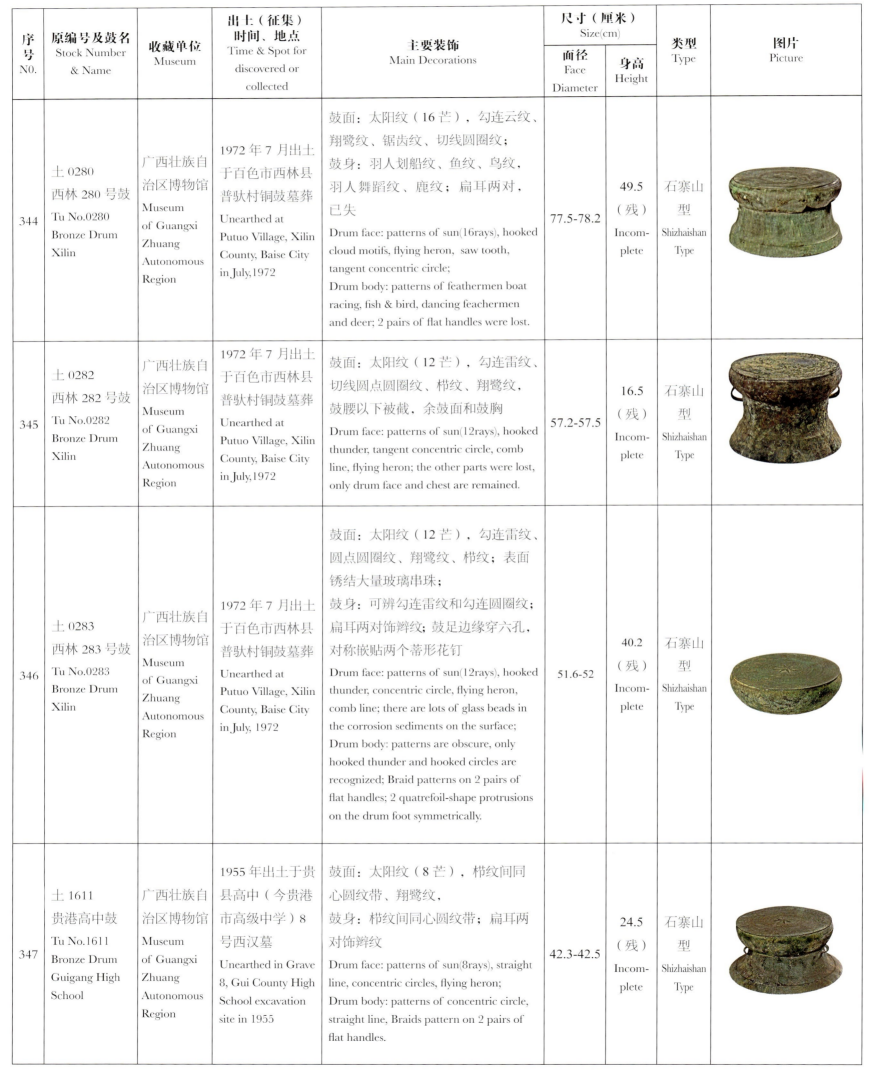
345	土 0282 西林 282 号鼓 Tu No.0282 Bronze Drum Xilin	广西壮族自治区博物馆 Museum of Guangxi Zhuang Autonomous Region	1972 年 7 月出土于百色市西林县普驮村铜鼓墓葬 Unearthed at Putuo Village, Xilin County, Baise City in July,1972	鼓面：太阳纹（12 芒），勾连雷纹、切线圆点圆圈纹、栉纹、翔鹭纹，鼓腰以下被截，余鼓面和鼓胸 Drum face: patterns of sun(12rays), hooked thunder, tangent concentric circle, comb line, flying heron; the other parts were lost, only drum face and chest are remained.	57.2-57.5	16.5 （残） Incomplete	石寨山型 Shizhaishan Type	
346	土 0283 西林 283 号鼓 Tu No.0283 Bronze Drum Xilin	广西壮族自治区博物馆 Museum of Guangxi Zhuang Autonomous Region	1972 年 7 月出土于百色市西林县普驮村铜鼓墓葬 Unearthed at Putuo Village, Xilin County, Baise City in July, 1972	鼓面：太阳纹（12 芒），勾连雷纹、圆点圆圈纹、翔鹭纹、栉纹；表面锈结大量玻璃串珠； 鼓身：可辨勾连雷纹和勾连圆圈纹；扁耳两对饰辫纹；鼓足边缘穿六孔，对称嵌贴两个蒂形花钉 Drum face: patterns of sun(12rays), hooked thunder, concentric circle, flying heron, comb line; there are lots of glass beads in the corrosion sediments on the surface; Drum body: patterns are obscure, only hooked thunder and hooked circles are recognized; Braid patterns on 2 pairs of flat handles; 2 quatrefoil-shape protrusions on the drum foot symmetrically.	51.6-52	40.2 （残） Incomplete	石寨山型 Shizhaishan Type	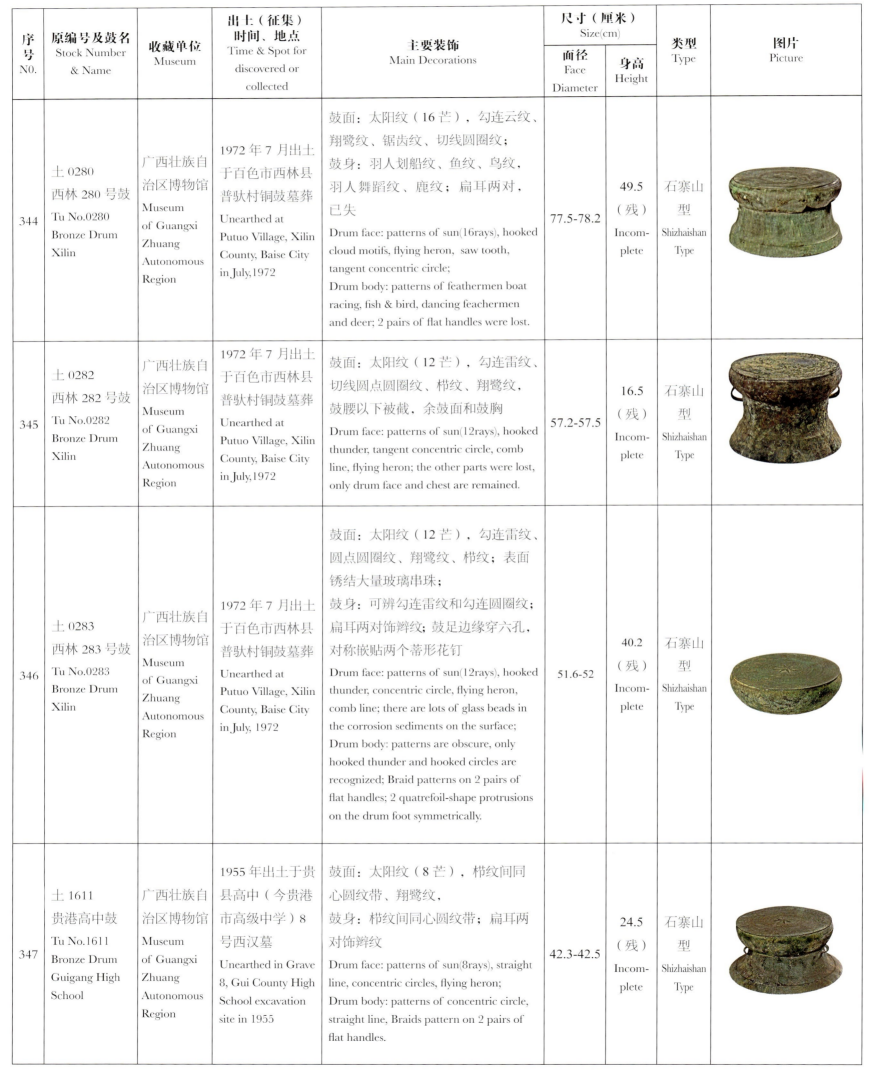
347	土 1611 贵港高中鼓 Tu No.1611 Bronze Drum Guigang High School	广西壮族自治区博物馆 Museum of Guangxi Zhuang Autonomous Region	1955 年出土于贵县高中（今贵港市高级中学）8 号西汉墓 Unearthed in Grave 8, Gui County High School excavation site in 1955	鼓面：太阳纹（8 芒），栉纹间同心圆纹带、翔鹭纹， 鼓身：栉纹间同心圆纹带；扁耳两对饰辫纹 Drum face: patterns of sun(8rays), straight line, concentric circles, flying heron; Drum body: patterns of concentric circle, straight line, Braids pattern on 2 pairs of flat handles.	42.3-42.5	24.5 （残） Incomplete	石寨山型 Shizhaishan Type	

续表

序号 NO.	原编号及鼓名 Stock Number & Name	收藏单位 Museum	出土（征集）时间、地点 Time & Spot for discovered or collected	主要装饰 Main Decorations	尺寸（厘米）Size(cm)		类型 Type	图片 Picture
					面径 Face Diameter	身高 Height		
348	土 3269 田东锅盖岭鼓 Tu No.3269 Bronze Drum Tiandong Guogailing	广西壮族自治区博物馆 Museum of Guangxi Zhuang Autonomous Region	1977 年 8 月出土于百色市田东县祥周公社（今祥周镇）甘蓬大队锅盖岭一号墓 Unearthed at Guogailing Grave I, Ganpeng Team, Xiangzhou Community, Tiandong County, Baise City in August, 1977	鼓面：太阳纹（8 芒）、翔鹭纹、圆点纹间锯齿纹带；鼓身：勾连雷纹、圆点纹、双弦纹；鼓腰以下残缺 Drum face: patterns of sun(8rays), flying heron, saw tooth, dots; Drum chest: hooked thunder, dots and bio-string patterns; the other parts were lost.	23.4	11.8（缺）Incom-plete	石寨山型 Shizhaishan Type	
349	土 10847 罗泊湾 M1：10 号鼓 Tu No.10847 Bronze Drum Luobowan M1:10	广西壮族自治区博物馆 Museum of Guangxi Zhuang Autonomous Region	1976 年出土于贵县（今贵港市）罗泊湾一号汉墓 Unearthed at Luobowan grave 1, Gui County(now the City area of Guigang City) in 1976	鼓面：太阳纹（12 芒）、斜线纹间同心圆纹带、勾连雷纹、翔鹭纹、锯齿纹间同心圆纹带；鼓身：锯齿纹间同心圆纹带、划船纹、羽人舞蹈纹、翔鹭纹、锯齿纹间同心圆纹带；扁耳两对饰辫纹 Drum face: patterns of sun(12rays), oblique line& concentric circles, hooked thunder, flying heron, saw tooth& concentric circles; Drum body: patterns of saw tooth& concentric circles, boat, dancing feathermen, flying heron, vertical ribbon of saw tooth and concentric circles; Braids pattern on 2 pairs of flat handles.	56.2-56.5	36.8	石寨山型 Shizhaishan Type	
350	土 10992 罗泊湾 M1：11 号鼓 Tu No.10992 Bronze Drum Luobowan M1:11	广西壮族自治区博物馆 Museum of Guangxi Zhuang Autonomous Region	1976 年出土于贵县（今贵港市）罗泊湾一号汉墓 Unearthed at Luobowan grave 1, Gui County(now the city area of Guigang City) in 1976	鼓面：太阳纹（10 芒）、点纹、点纹间锯齿纹带；鼓身：点纹间锯齿纹带、划船纹、点纹、锯齿纹、网纹；扁耳两对饰辫纹 Drum face: patterns of sun(10rays), dots, dots& saw tooth; Drum body: patterns of dots& saw tooth, boat dots, net; Braids pattern on 2 pairs of flat handles.	28.8-29.2	24.4	石寨山型 Shizhaishan Type	

序号 NO.	原编号及鼓名 Stock Number & Name	收藏单位 Museum	出土（征集）时间、地点 Time & Spot for discovered or collected	主要装饰 Main Decorations	尺寸（厘米） Size(cm)		类型 Type	图片 Picture
					面径 Face Diameter	身高 Height		
351	土 12275 菠萝岭鼓 Tu No.12275 Bronze Drum Boluo Ling	广西壮族自治区博物馆 Museum of Guangxi Zhuang Autonomous Region	2009 年 2 月出土于河池市环江县东头镇西菠萝岭 Unearthed at Boluo Ling, in the west of Dongtou Town, Huanjiang County, Hechi City in February, 2009	鼓面：太阳纹（12 芒），芒间饰翎眼纹，栉纹间切线同心圆纹带、羽纹、变形羽人纹、变形翔鹭纹间定胜纹，鼓面边缘饰四只逆时针四足素面立体青蛙； 鼓身：纹饰磨蚀；扁耳两对饰辫纹 Drum face: patterns of sun(12rays) with feather eye between the rays, tangent concentric circle& straight line, feather, transformed feathermen, transformed flying heron mixed Dingsheng; 4 frog statues of 4 feet and blank back anticlockwise stand on the edge of drum face; Drum body: patterns are obscure; Braids pattern on 2 pairs of flat handles.	51.2-51.5	32.5	冷水冲型 Lengshui-chong Type	
352	铜 216 号鼓 Bronze Drum Tong No.216	广西壮族自治区博物馆 Museum of Guangxi Zhuang Autonomous Region	2011 年 10 月广西文物商店代征集 Collected by Guangxi Cultural Relics Shop in October, 2011	鼓面：太阳纹（12 芒），纹饰磨蚀； 鼓身：乳钉纹、弦纹；扁耳两对饰凸棱纹 Drum face: sun(12rays), patterns were abraded; Drum body: patterns of nipple protrusion and string; Raise ridges on 2 pairs of flat handles.	47.5-47.8	29.3	麻江型 Majiang Type	
353	铜 217 号鼓 Bronze Drum Tong No.217	广西壮族自治区博物馆 Museum of Guangxi Zhuang Autonomous Region	2011 年征集 Collected in 2011	鼓面：太阳纹（12 芒），酉字纹、S 形云纹、乳钉纹、游旗纹、兽形云纹、卦纹； 鼓身：乳钉纹、云纹、回形雷纹、复线角形纹；扁耳两对饰辫纹间回形雷纹 Drum face: patterns of sun(12rays), 酉 -character, S-shape cloud, nipple protrusion, flying flag, beast, divinatory symbol; Drum body: patterns of nipple protrusion, cloud, 回 -shape thunder, double line triangle; Braid & 回 -shape thunder patterns on 2 pairs of flat handles.	50.1-50.3	30.5	麻江型 Majiang Type	

续表

序号 N0.	原编号及鼓名 Stock Number & Name	收藏单位 Museum	出土（征集） 时间、地点 Time & Spot for discovered or collected	主要装饰 Main Decorations	尺寸（厘米） Size(cm)		类型 Type	图片 Picture
					面径 Face Diameter	身高 Height		
354	铜 218 号鼓 Bronze Drum Tong No.218	广西壮族自治区博物馆 Museum of Guangxi Zhuang Autonomous Region	2011 年征集于河池市南丹县里湖乡怀里村 Collected at Huaili Village, Lihu, Nandan County, Hechi City in 2011	鼓面：太阳纹（12 芒），酉字纹、乳钉纹、栉纹、梅花纹、游旗纹、S 形云纹、云纹、辫纹、兽形云纹； 鼓身：栉纹、乳钉纹、回形雷纹、云纹、复线角形纹；扁耳两对饰辫纹 Drum face: patterns of sun(12rays), 酉 -character, nipple protrusion, comb line, plum blossom, flying flag, S-shape cloud, cloud, braid, beast-shape cloud; Drum body: patterns of comb line, nipple protrusion, 回 -shape thunder, cloud, double line triangle; Braid patterns on 2 pairs of flat handles.	47.2-47.7	29.8	麻江型 Majiang Type	
355	铜 219 号鼓 Bronze Drum Tong No.219	广西壮族自治区博物馆 Museum of Guangxi Zhuang Autonomous Region	2011 年征集于河池市南丹县里湖乡怀里村 Collected at Huaili Village, Lihu, Nandan County, Hechi City in 2011	鼓面：太阳纹（12 芒），酉字纹、兽形云纹、乳钉纹、栉纹、游旗纹； 鼓身：乳钉纹、兽形云纹、如意云纹、栉纹、云纹、回形雷纹、复线角形纹；扁耳两对饰辫纹间勾连纹、回形雷纹 Drum face: patterns of sun(12rays), 酉 -character, beast-shape cloud, nipple protrusion, comb line, flying flag; Drum body: patterns of nipple protrusion, beast-shape cloud, Ruyi-shape cloud, comb line, cloud, 回 -shape thunder, double line triangle; Braid, hooked motifs and thunder patterns on 2 pairs of flat handles.	49.2-49.5	29.5	麻江型 Majiang Type	
356	铜 221 号鼓 Bronze Drum Tong No.221	广西壮族自治区博物馆 Museum of Guangxi Zhuang Autonomous Region	2012 年 3 月广西文物商店代为征集 Collected by Guangxi Cultural Relics Shop in March, 2012	鼓面：太阳纹（12 芒），乳钉纹、缠枝纹、栉纹、符箓纹、如意云纹、回形雷纹、兽形云纹、绚纹； 鼓身：品字形乳钉纹、兽形云纹、如意云纹、栉纹、回形雷纹、缠枝纹、复线角形纹；扁耳两对饰羽纹 Drum face: patterns of sun(12rays), nipple protrusion, twisted branches, comb line, 凤 -shape Ofuda, Ruyi-shape cloud, 回 -shape thunder, beast-shape cloud, twisted rope; Drum body: patterns of nipple protrusion array in 品 -shape, beast-shape cloud, comb line, 回 -shape thunder, twist branches, double line triangle; Feather patterns on 2 pairs of flat handles.	48.7-49.2	26	麻江型 Majiang Type	

序号 N0.	原编号及鼓名 Stock Number & Name	收藏单位 Museum	出土（征集） 时间、地点 Time & Spot for discovered or collected	主要装饰 Main Decorations	尺寸（厘米） Size(cm)		类型 Type	图片 Picture
					面径 Face Diameter	身高 Height		
357	000421 号 蔓草纹铜鼓 No.000421 Bronze Drum with liana patterns	南宁市博物馆 Nanning City Museum	1982 年收购于废旧公司 Collected at waste recycle company in 1982	鼓面：太阳纹（12 芒），栉纹、同心圆纹、十二地支铭文、缠枝纹、栉纹间同心圆纹带；鼓身缺失 Drum face: patterns of sun(12rays), comb line, concentric circle, The twelve earthly branches characters, twisted branches,straight line& concentric circles; Drum body: lost.	56	5 （残） Incom-plete	遵义型 Zunyi Type	
358	000422 号 东汉四蛙饰变形羽人纹铜鼓 No.000422 East-Han Dynasty Bronze Drum with 4 frog statues and transformed feathermen patterns	南宁市博物馆 Nanning City Museum	1982 年收购于废旧公司 Collected at waste recycle company in 1982	鼓面：太阳纹（12 芒）、羽纹，水波纹、同心圆纹、栉纹、复线交叉纹、变形羽人纹、变形翔鹭纹、栉纹间同心圆纹带；鼓面边缘饰四只逆时针四足三趾立体青蛙，一只缺失，两蛙间饰一只立体乌龟； 鼓身：栉纹间同心圆纹带、变形划船纹，鼓腰以下缺失 Drum face: patterns of sun(12rays), feather, water wave, concentric circles, comb line, crossed double lines, transformed feathermen, transformed flying heron motif ribbon of straight line&. concentric circles; 4 frog statues with 4 feet and 3 toes counter-clockwise stand on the edge of the face, one of them was lost, and there is a tortoise statue between the frogs; Drum body: remained patterns of straight line&concentric circles, transformed boat; the part under the drum waist were lost.	76.5－77.6	15 （残） Incom-plete	冷水冲型 Lengshui-chong Type	
359	000423 号 清十二生肖纹铜鼓 No.000423 Qing Dynasty Bronze Drum with zodiac patterns	南宁市博物馆 Nanning City Museum	1991 年南宁市汽车总站派出所收缴 Took over by Police Substation of Nanning City Central Bus Station in 1991	鼓面：太阳纹（12 芒），乳钉纹、酉字纹、S 形云纹、十二生肖间回形雷纹、栉纹、如意云纹； 鼓身：乳钉纹、如意云纹、复线角形纹、扁耳两对饰辫纹 Drum face: patterns of sun(12rays), nipple protrusion, 酉 -character, S-shape cloud, zodiac& 回 -shape thunder, comb line, Ruyi-shape cloud; Drum body: patterns of nipple protrusion, Ruyi-shape cloud, double line triangle; Braid patterns on 2 pairs of flat handles.	47.5－47.8	28	麻江型 Majiang Type	

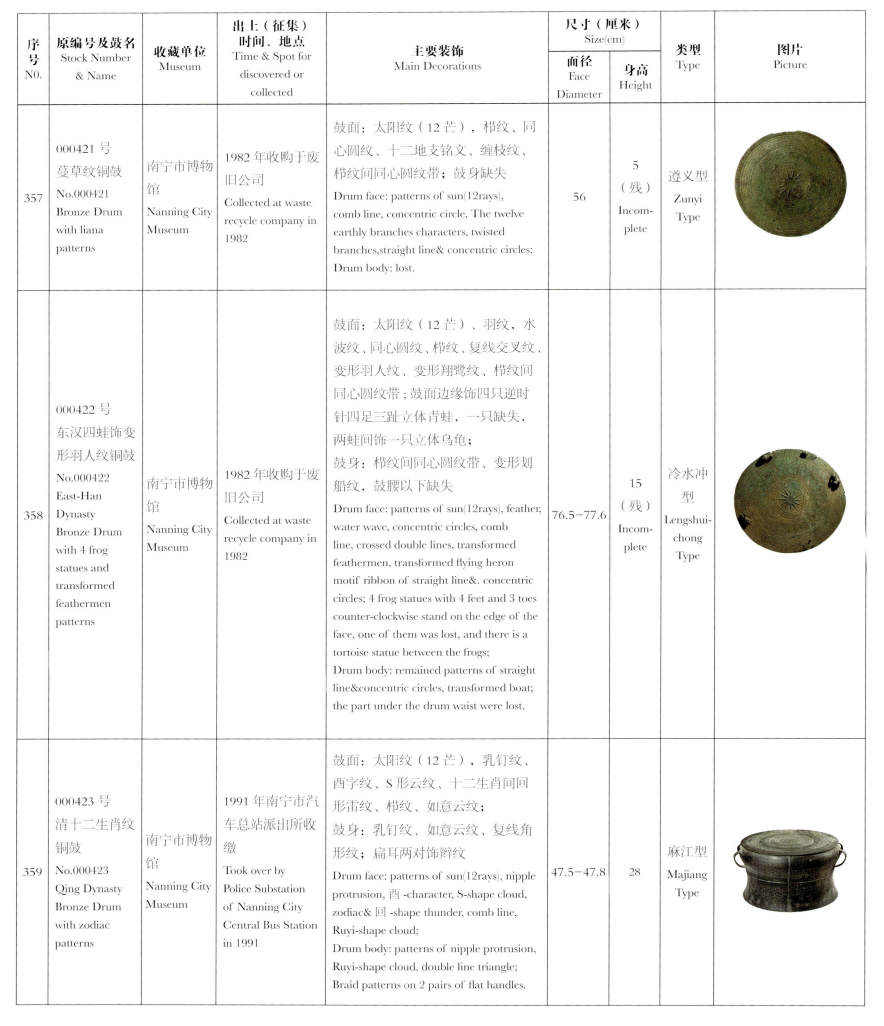

序号 NO.	原编号及鼓名 Stock Number & Name	收藏单位 Museum	出土（征集） 时间、地点 Time & Spot for discovered or collected	主要装饰 Main Decorations	尺寸（厘米） Size(cm)		类型 Type	图片 Picture
					面径 Face Diameter	身高 Height		
360	000017 号 清符箓纹绚 纹铜鼓 No.000017 Qing Dynasty Bronze Drum with Ofuda and twisted rope patterns	南宁市博物馆 Nanning City Museum	1982 年收购于废旧公司 Collected at waste recycle company in 1982	鼓面：太阳纹（12 芒），乳钉纹、S 勾形纹、同心圆纹、符箓纹、栉纹、回形雷纹、绚纹； 鼓身：乳钉纹、弦纹、回形雷纹、复线角形纹、扁耳两对饰羽纹 Drum face: patterns of sun(12rays), nipple protrusion, hook, concentric circle, Ofuda, comb line, 回 -shape thunder, twisted rope; Drum body: patterns of nipple protrusion, string, 回 -shape thunder, double line triangle; Feather patterns on 2 pairs of flat handles.	49–49.3	26.5	麻江型 Majiang Type	
361	000018 号 清游旗纹铜鼓 No.000018 Qing Dynasty Bronze Drum with flying flag patterns	南宁市博物馆 Nanning City Museum	1982 年收购于废旧公司 Collected at waste recycle company in 1982	鼓面：太阳纹（12 芒），酉字纹、S 形云纹、乳钉纹、游旗纹、栉纹、云纹、如意云纹； 鼓身：乳钉纹、如意云纹、回形雷纹、栉纹、云纹、复线角形纹；扁耳两对饰辫纹 Drum face: patterns of sun(12rays), 酉 -character, S-shape cloud, nipple protrusion, flying flag, comb line, cloud, Ruyi-shape cloud; Drum body: patterns of nipple protrusion, Ruyi-shape cloud, 回 -shape thunder, comb line, cloud, double line triangle; Braid patterns on 2 pairs of flat handles.	46.3–46.5	26.2	麻江型 Majiang Type	
362	000019 号 清游旗纹席纹铜鼓 No.000019 Qing Dynasty Bronze Drum with flying flag & woven mat patterns	南宁市博物馆 Nanning City Museum	1982 年收购于废旧公司 Collected at waste recycle company in 1982	鼓面：太阳纹（12 芒）、乳钉纹、雷纹、"東"字形纹、席纹、游旗纹； 鼓身：乳钉纹、西字纹、雷纹、回形雷纹、"寿"字形纹、图案三角形纹、席纹；扁耳两对、已失 Drum face: patterns of sun(12rays), nipple protrusion, thunder, " 東 "-character, woven mat, flying flag; Drum body: patterns of nipple protrusion, 西 -character, thunder, 回 -shape thunder, " 寿 "-character, double line triangle, woven mat; 2 pairs of flat handles were lost.	47	26.8	麻江型 Majiang Type	

序号 NO.	原编号及鼓名 Stock Number & Name	收藏单位 Museum	出土（征集）时间、地点 Time & Spot for discovered or collected	主要装饰 Main Decorations	尺寸（厘米）Size(cm)		类型 Type	图片 Picture
					面径 Face Diameter	身高 Height		
363	000020 号 清符篆纹铜鼓 No.000020 Qing Dynasty Bronze Drum with Ofuda patterns	南宁市博物馆 Nanning City Museum	1982 年收购于废旧公司 Collected at waste recycle company in 1982	鼓面：太阳纹（12 芒）、乳钉纹、缠枝纹、复线角形填线纹、符篆纹、栉纹、羽纹、回形雷纹、绹纹；鼓身：乳钉纹、四弦纹、如意云纹、同心圆纹、回形雷纹、花枝纹、复线角形纹、水波纹；扁耳两对饰羽纹 Drum face: patterns of sun(12rays), nipple protrusion, twisted branches, double line triangle filled with comb lines, Ofuda, comb line, feather, 回 -shape thunder, twisted rope; Drum body: patterns of nipple protrusion, 4 strings, Ruyi-shape cloud, concentric circle, 回 -shape thunder, twisted branches, double line triangle, water wave; Feather patterns on 2 pairs of flat handles.	48.8~49.4	26.5	麻江型 Majiang Type	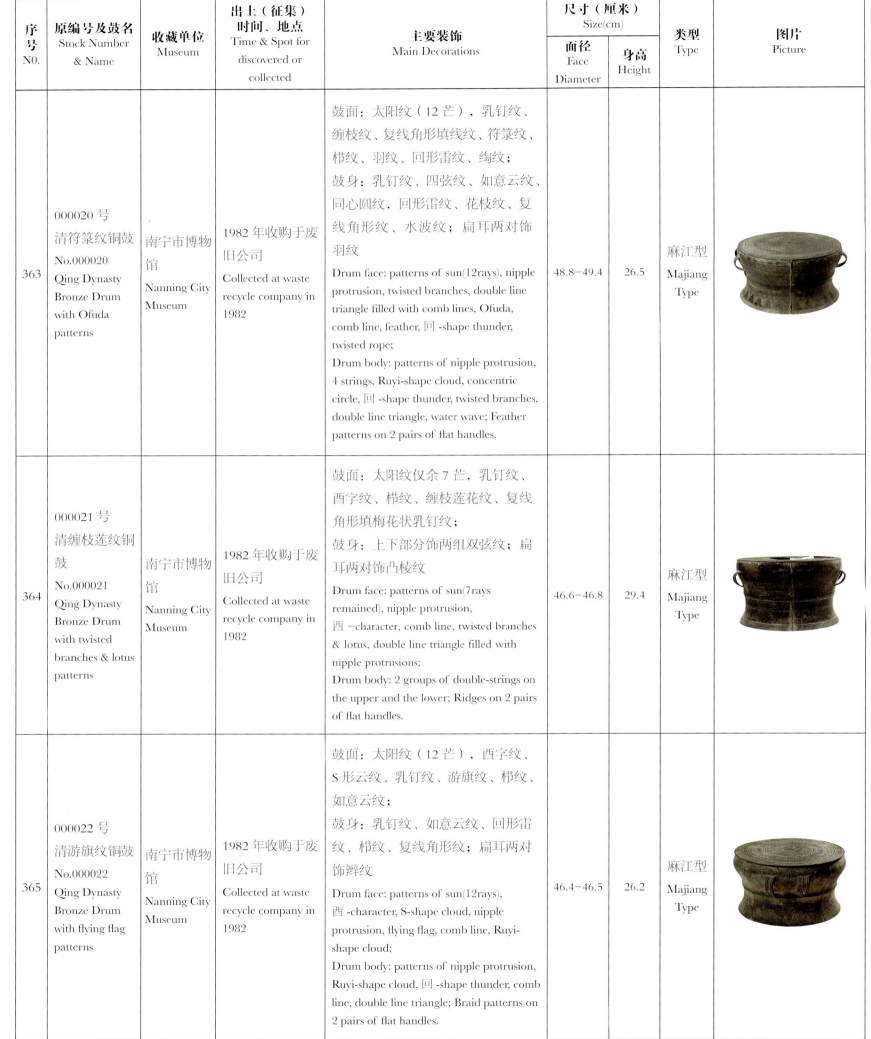
364	000021 号 清缠枝莲纹铜鼓 No.000021 Qing Dynasty Bronze Drum with twisted branches & lotus patterns	南宁市博物馆 Nanning City Museum	1982 年收购于废旧公司 Collected at waste recycle company in 1982	鼓面：太阳纹仅余 7 芒、乳钉纹、酉字纹、栉纹、缠枝莲花纹、复线角形填梅花状乳钉纹；鼓身：上下部分饰两组双弦纹；扁耳两对饰凸棱纹 Drum face: patterns of sun(7rays remained), nipple protrusion, 酉 -character, comb line, twisted branches & lotus, double line triangle filled with nipple protrusions; Drum body: 2 groups of double-strings on the upper and the lower; Ridges on 2 pairs of flat handles.	46.6~46.8	29.4	麻江型 Majiang Type	
365	000022 号 清游旗纹铜鼓 No.000022 Qing Dynasty Bronze Drum with flying flag patterns	南宁市博物馆 Nanning City Museum	1982 年收购于废旧公司 Collected at waste recycle company in 1982	鼓面：太阳纹（12 芒）、酉字纹、S 形云纹、乳钉纹、游旗纹、栉纹、如意云纹；鼓身：乳钉纹、如意云纹、回形雷纹、栉纹、复线角形纹；扁耳两对饰辫纹 Drum face: patterns of sun(12rays), 酉 -character, S-shape cloud, nipple protrusion, flying flag, comb line, Ruyi-shape cloud; Drum body: patterns of nipple protrusion, Ruyi-shape cloud, 回 -shape thunder, comb line, double line triangle; Braid patterns on 2 pairs of flat handles.	46.4~46.5	26.2	麻江型 Majiang Type	

续表

序号 N0.	原编号及鼓名 Stock Number & Name	收藏单位 Museum	出土（征集） 时间、地点 Time & Spot for discovered or collected	主要装饰 Main Decorations	尺寸（厘米） Size(cm)		类型 Type	图片 Picture
					面径 Face Diameter	身高 Height		
366	000023 号 清符箓纹铜鼓 No.000023 Qing Dynasty Bronze Drum with Ofuda patterns	南宁市博物馆 Nanning City Museum	1982 年收购于废旧公司 Collected at waste recycle company in 1982	鼓面：太阳纹（12 芒）、乳钉纹、回形雷纹、栉纹、符箓纹、如意云纹、同心圆纹、绹纹； 鼓身：乳钉纹、弦纹、回形雷纹、花枝纹、复线角形纹；扁耳两对饰羽纹 Drum face: patterns of sun(12rays), nipple protrusion, 回 -shape thunder, comb line, Ofuda, Ruyi-shape cloud, concentric circle, twisted ropes; Drum body: patterns of nipple protrusion, string, 回 -shape thunder, flowers& branches, double line triangle; Feather patterns on 2 pairs of flat handles.	48.5～48.8	25.8	麻江型 Majiang Type	
367	000024 号 清符箓纹铜鼓 No.000024 Qing Dynasty Bronze Drum with Ofuda patterns	南宁市博物馆 Nanning City Museum	1982 年收购于废旧公司 Collected at waste recycle company in 1982	鼓面：太阳纹（12 芒）、栉纹、乳钉纹、同形雷纹、符箓纹、如意云纹、同心圆纹、绹纹； 鼓身：弦纹、回形雷纹、花枝纹、复线角形纹；扁耳两对饰羽纹 Drum face: patterns of sun(12rays), comb line, nipple protrusion, 回 -shape thunder, Ofuda, Ruyi-shape cloud, concentric circle, twisted rope; Drum body: patterns of strings, 回 -shape thunder, plant branches, double line triangle; Feather patterns on 2 pairs of flat handles.	49～49.5	26.5	麻江型 Majiang Type	
368	000025 号 闭花纹卷云纹铜鼓 No.000025 Qing Dynasty Bronze Drum with begonia & cloud patterns	南宁市博物馆 Nanning City Museum	1982 年收购于废旧公司 Collected at waste recycle company in 1982	鼓面：太阳纹（12 芒）、同形雷纹、同心圆纹、乳钉纹、闭花纹、雷纹、如意云纹； 鼓身：乳钉纹、回形雷纹、如意云纹、复线角形纹；扁耳两对饰辫纹 Drum face: patterns of sun(12rays), 回 -shape thunder, Ruyi-shape cloud,concentric circle, nipple protrusion, begonia, thunder, Ruyi-shape cloud; Drum body: patterns of nipple protrusion, 回 -shape thunder, Ruyi-Shape cloud, double line triangle; Braid patterns on 2 pairs of flat handles.	44.5～44.8	26	麻江型 Majiang Type	

续表

序号 N0.	原编号及鼓名 Stock Number & Name	收藏单位 Museum	出土（征集）时间、地点 Time & Spot for discovered or collected	主要装饰 Main Decorations	尺寸（厘米）Size(cm)		类型 Type	图片 Picture
					面径 Face Diameter	身高 Height		
369	和同村鼓 Bronze Drum Hetong Cun	南宁市博物馆 Nanning City Museum	2003 年出土于南宁市江西镇和同村 Unearthed at Hetong Village, Jiangxi Town, Nanning City in 2003	鼓面：太阳纹（11 芒），变形羽人纹、雷纹、如意云组合花纹、云纹；鼓面边缘饰四只两两相对三足素面立体青蛙；鼓身：云纹、连钱纹；扁耳两对 Drum face: patterns of sun(11rays), transformed feathermen, thunder, Ruyi-shape cloud with motifs inside, cloud; 4 frog statues with 3 feet and blank back stand on the edge of drum face, face to face in pairs; Drum body: patterns of cloud, coins part of overlap; 2 pairs of flat handles.	93～94	54.9 （残）Incomplete	灵山型 Lingshan Type	
370	NK335 号 游旗纹铜鼓 No.NK335 Bronze Drum with flying flag patterns	南宁孔庙博物馆 Nanning Confucian Temple Museum	2006 年 10 月 10 日收购于河池市南丹县 Collected in Nandan County, Hechi City on October 10th, 2006	鼓面：太阳纹（12 芒），西字纹、S 形云纹、乳钉纹、游旗纹、栉纹、兽形云纹、卦纹；鼓身：乳钉纹、回形雷纹、如意云纹、栉纹、云纹、复线角形纹；扁耳两对饰辫纹 Drum face: patterns of sun(12rays), 西 -character, S-shape cloud, nipple protrusion, flying flag, comb line, beast-shape cloud, divinatory symbol; Drum body: patterns of nipple protrusion, 回 -shape thunder, Ruyi-shape cloud, comb line, cloud, double line triangle; Braid patterns on 2 pairs of flat handles.	47.5	28	麻江型 Majiang Type	
371	NK336 号 游旗纹铜鼓 No.NK336 Bronze Drum with flying flag patterns	南宁孔庙博物馆 Nanning Confucian Temple Museum	2006 年 7 月 30 日收购于河池市南丹县 Collected in Nandan County, Hechi City on July 30th, 2006	鼓面：太阳纹（12 芒），西字纹、S 形云纹、乳钉纹、栉纹、游旗纹、兽形云纹；鼓身：乳钉纹、如意云纹、回形雷纹、栉纹、兽形云纹、复线角形纹；扁耳两对饰辫纹 Drum face: patterns of sun(12rays), 西 -character, S-shape cloud, nipple protrusion, comb line, flying flag, beast-shape cloud; Drum body: patterns of nipple protrusion, Ruyi-shape cloud, 回 -shape thunder, comb line, beast-shape cloud, double line triangle; Braid patterns on 2 pairs of flat handles.	50.5	29	麻江型 Majiang Type	

序号 NO.	原编号及鼓名 Stock Number & Name	收藏单位 Museum	出土（征集）时间、地点 Time & Spot for discovered or collected	主要装饰 Main Decorations	尺寸（厘米）Size(cm)		类型 Type	图片 Picture
					面径 Face Diameter	身高 Height		
372	764 号游旗纹铜鼓 No.764 Bronze Drum with flying flag patterns	南宁孔庙博物馆 Nanning Confucian Temple Museum	2009 年 6 月 9 日征集于南宁市唐山路花鸟市场 Collected at Nanning Tangshan Bird & Flower Market on June 9th, 2009	鼓面：太阳纹（12 芒）、西字纹、S 形云纹、乳钉纹、栉纹、游旗纹、兽形云纹、卦纹； 鼓身：乳钉纹、如意云纹、云纹、回形雷纹、栉纹、复线角形纹；扁耳两对饰辫纹 Drum face: patterns of sun(12rays), 西 -character, S-shape cloud, nipple protrusion, comb line, flying flag, beast-shape cloud, divinatory symbol; Drum body: patterns of nipple protrusion, Ruyi-shape cloud, cloud, 回 -shape thunder, comb line, double line triangle; Braid patterns on 2 pairs of flat handles.	50-50.3	28.2	麻江型 Majiang Type	
373	子鹤山铜鼓 Bronze Drum Ziheshan	邕宁区文物管理所 Yongning County Cultural Relics Administration	1986 年 6 月出土于南宁市邕宁县（今南宁市邕宁区）吴圩镇那佳村子鹤山 Unearthed at Zihe Hill, Najia Village, Wuxu, Yongning County, Nanning City in June, 1986	鼓面：太阳纹（10 芒）、虫形纹、鸟形纹、四出钱纹、连钱纹、席纹、兽面纹、四瓣花纹、蝉纹，鼓面边缘饰六组逆时针三足螺旋纹立体青蛙，其中三组为累蹲蛙； 鼓身：复线角形纹、连钱纹、四出钱纹、鸟形纹、虫形纹、兽面纹、四瓣花纹、变形羽人纹、席纹、蝉纹；扁耳两对饰辫纹；鼓足饰一只立体鸟；鼓胸内壁饰一对划线纹立体青蛙 Drum face: patterns of sun(10 rays), insect, bird, coin with quadrangle inside, coins part of overlap, woven mat, beast face, cicada, quatrefoil; 6 frogs with 3 feet and spiracle on their backs anticlockwise stand on the edge, 3 of them are overlap; Drum body: patterns of leaf-shape triangle, coins part of overlap, coin with quadrangle inside, bird,insect, quatrefoil, beast face, transformed feathermen, woven mat, cicada; Braid patterns on 2 pairs of flat handles;A bird statue on the foot; A pair of frog statues on the chest inside the drum, with their heads towards to the drum foot.	81	48	灵山型 Lingshan Type	

序号 NO.	原编号及鼓名 Stock Number & Name	收藏单位 Museum	出土（征集）时间、地点 Time & Spot for discovered or collected	主要装饰 Main Decorations	尺寸（厘米） Size(cm)		类型 Type	图片 Picture
					面径 Face Diameter	身高 Height		
374	那口岭铜鼓 Bronze Drum Nakou Ling	邕宁区文物管理所 Yongning County Cultural Relics Administration	1989 年 5 月出土于南宁市邕宁县（今南宁市邕宁区）吴圩镇那德村那审坡那口岭北麓半山腰 Unearthed at the north hillside of Nakouling, Nashen Po, Nade Village, Wuxu, Yongning County, Nanning City in May, 1989	鼓面：太阳纹（8 芒）、连钱纹、比轮钱纹、四瓣花纹、虫形纹、四出钱纹、变形羽人纹、兽面纹、鸟形纹、半圆填线纹；鼓面边缘饰六只顺时针三足螺旋纹立体青蛙； 鼓身：兽面纹、四出钱纹、虫形纹、鸟形纹、雷纹、连钱纹、四瓣花纹、变形羽人纹、三角垂叶纹；扁耳两对饰辫纹；鼓足饰一只立体鸟 Drum face: patterns of sun(8rays), coin part of overlap, Bilun coin, quatrefoil, insect, coin with quadrangle inside, transformed feathermen, beast face, bird, semi-circle filled with straight lines; 6 frogs with 3 feet and spiracles on back clockwise stand on the edge; Drum body: patterns of beast face, coin with quadrangle inside, insect, bird, thunder, coins part of overlap, quatrefoil, thansformed feathermen, leaf-shape triangle; Braid patterns on 2 pairs of flat handles; A bird statue on the foot .	79	48	灵山型 Lingshan Type	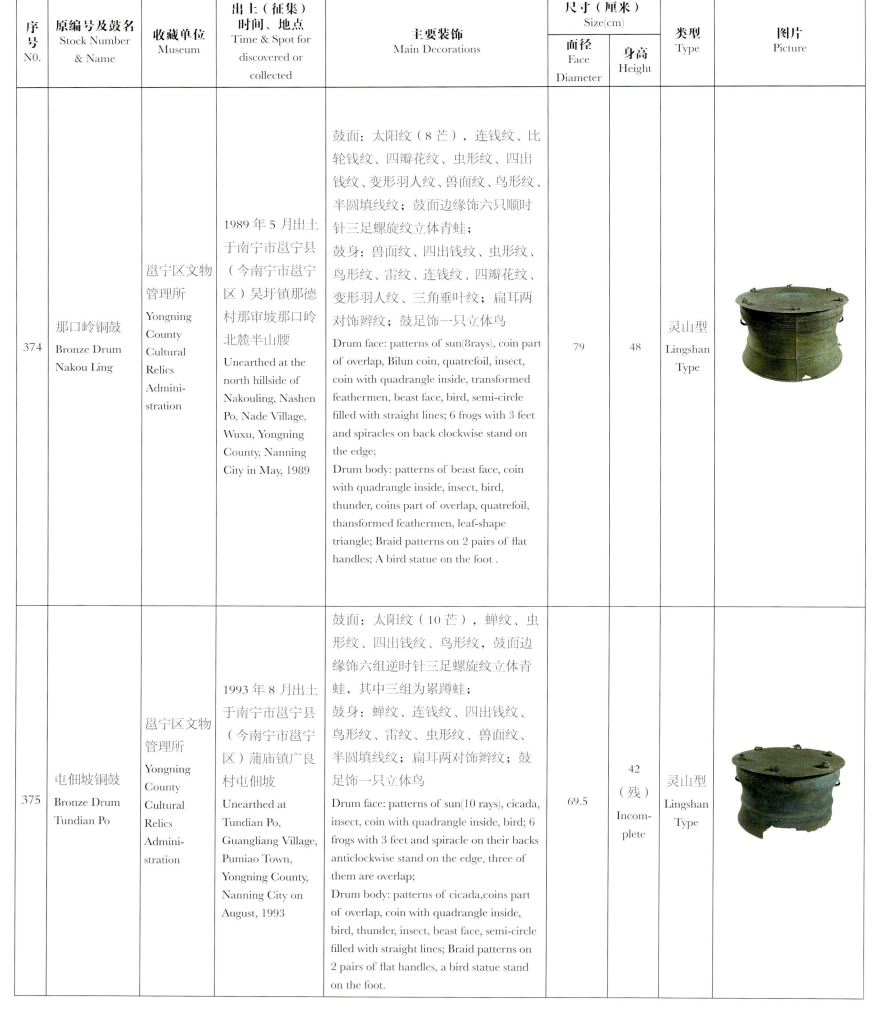
375	屯佃坡铜鼓 Bronze Drum Tundian Po	邕宁区文物管理所 Yongning County Cultural Relics Administration	1993 年 8 月出土于南宁市邕宁县（今南宁市邕宁区）蒲庙镇广良村屯佃坡 Unearthed at Tundian Po, Guangliang Village, Pumiao Town, Yongning County, Nanning City on August, 1993	鼓面：太阳纹（10 芒）、蝉纹、虫形纹、四出钱纹、鸟形纹，鼓面边缘饰六组逆时针三足螺旋纹立体青蛙，其中三组为累蹲蛙； 鼓身：蝉纹、连钱纹、四出钱纹、鸟形纹、雷纹、虫形纹、兽面纹、半圆填线纹；扁耳两对饰辫纹；鼓足饰一只立体鸟 Drum face: patterns of sun(10 rays), cicada, insect, coin with quadrangle inside, bird; 6 frogs with 3 feet and spiracle on their backs anticlockwise stand on the edge, three of them are overlap; Drum body: patterns of cicada,coins part of overlap, coin with quadrangle inside, bird, thunder, insect, beast face, semi-circle filled with straight lines; Braid patterns on 2 pairs of flat handles, a bird statue stand on the foot.	69.5	42 （残） Incomplete	灵山型 Lingshan Type	

序号 N0.	原编号及鼓名 Stock Number & Name	收藏单位 Museum	出土（征集）时间、地点 Time & Spot for discovered or collected	主要装饰 Main Decorations	尺寸（厘米）Size(cm)		类型 Type	图片 Picture
					面径 Face Diameter	身高 Height		
376	0058 号 崇丘铜鼓（原名武鸣 01 号鼓）No.0058 Bronze Drum Dongqiu (Former name: Wuming No.1)	武鸣区文物管理所 Wuming County Cultural Relics Administration	1975 年 5 月 22 日出土于南宁市武鸣县（今南宁市武鸣区）两江镇三联村那阮屯附近的崇丘坡 Unearthed at Dongqiu Po, Naruan Tun, Sanlian Village, Liangjiang Town, Wuming County, Nanning City on May 22nd, 1975	鼓面：太阳纹（12 芒），栉纹、切线同心圆纹、复线交叉纹、变形羽人纹、变形翔鹭纹间定胜纹，鼓面边缘饰四只逆时针四足素面三趾立体青蛙；鼓身：栉纹、切线同心圆纹、圆心垂叶纹；扁耳两对饰辫纹 Drum face: patterns of sun(12rays), comb line, tangent line& concentric circles, crossed double lines, transformed feathermen, transformed flying heron& Dingsheng;4 frog statues of 4 feet and blank back anticlockwise stand on the edge of drum face; Drum body: patterns of comb line, tangent line&concentric circles, leaf-shape triangle with concentric circle in the middle; Braids pattern on 2 pairs of flat handles.	70	46.5	冷水冲型 Lengshui-chong Type	
377	0059 号 牛角山铜鼓（原名武鸣 02 号鼓）No.0059 Bronze Drum Niujiaoshan (Former name: Wuming No.2)	武鸣区文物管理所 Wuming County Cultural Relics Administration	1979 年 3 月 7 日出土于南宁市武鸣县（今南宁市武鸣区）太平镇新联村牛角山 Unearthed at Niujiao Hill, Xinlian Village, Taiping Town, Wuming County, Nanning City on March 7th, 1979	鼓面：太阳纹（12 芒），栉纹、同心圆纹、复线交叉纹、变形羽人纹、变形翔鹭纹间定胜纹，鼓面边缘饰四只逆时针四足素面立体青蛙；鼓身：栉纹、同心圆纹、栉纹间同心圆垂直纹带、圆心垂叶纹；扁耳两对饰辫纹 Drum face: patterns of sun(12rays), comb line, concentric circles, crossed double lines, transformed feathermen, transformed flying heron mixed Dingsheng;4 frog statues of 4 feet and blank back anticlockwise stand on the edge of drum face; Drum body: patterns of comb line, concentric circles, vertical ribbon of straight line and concentric circles, leaf-shape triangle with concentric circles in the middle; Braids pattern on 2 pairs of flat handles.	72	51	冷水冲型 Lengshui-chong Type	

序号 N0.	原编号及鼓名 Stock Number & Name	收藏单位 Museum	出土（征集）时间、地点 Time & Spot for discovered or collected	主要装饰 Main Decorations	尺寸（厘米）Size(cm)		类型 Type	图片 Picture
					面径 Face Diameter	身高 Height		
378	0060号 那琅铜鼓 No.0060 Bronze Drum Nalang	武鸣区文物管理所 Wuming County Cultural Relics Administration	1983年2月8日出土于南宁市武鸣县（今南宁市武鸣区）府城镇那琅屯西北约500米崇床坡 Unearthed at Dongchuang Po, the northwest of 500m to Nalang Tun, Fucheng Town, Wuming County, Nanning City on February 8th, 1983	鼓面：太阳纹（11芒），水波纹、同心圆纹、栉纹、复线交叉眼纹、变形羽人纹、变形翔鹭纹间定胜纹，鼓面边缘饰四只逆时针四足素面立体青蛙；鼓身：栉纹、切线同心圆纹、变形羽人纹、圆心垂叶纹；扁耳两对饰辫纹 Drum face: patterns of sun(11rays), water wave, concentric circles, comb line, crossed double lines, transformed feathermen, transformed flying heron mixed Dingsheng;4 frog statues of 4 feet and blank back anticlockwise stand on the edge of drum face; Drum body: patterns of comb line, tangent line& concentric circles, transformed feathermen, leaf-shape triangle with concentric circle in the middle; Braids pattern on 2 pairs of flat handles.	76.6	52.5	冷水冲型 Lengshui-chong Type	
379	0061号 变形羽人纹铜鼓（原名武鸣72号鼓）No.0061 Bronze Drum with transformed feathermen patterns (Former name: Wuming No.72)	武鸣区文物管理所 Wuming County Cultural Relics Administration	1987年3月南宁市武鸣县（今南宁市武鸣区）法院移交 Transferred by Nanning City Wuming County Court in March, 1987(forfeit)	鼓面：太阳纹（12芒）、栉纹、同心圆纹、复线交叉填鱼纹、变形羽人纹、变形翔鹭纹间定胜纹，鼓面边缘饰四只逆时针四足素面立体青蛙；鼓身：栉纹、同心圆纹、栉纹同心圆纹垂直纹带，鼓足大部分缺失；扁耳两对饰辫纹 Drum face: patterns of sun(12rays), comb line, concentric circles, crossed double lines& fish, transformed feathermen, flying heron mixed Dingsheng;4 frog statues of 4 feet and blank back anticlockwise stand on the edge of drum face; Drum body: patterns of comb line, concentric circles, vertical ribbon of straight line and concentric circles; Braids pattern on 2 pairs of flat handles. Most of the foot was lost.	78	37.5	冷水冲型 Lengshui-chong Type	

续表

序号 NO.	原编号及鼓名 Stock Number & Name	收藏单位 Museum	出土（征集） 时间、地点 Time & Spot for discovered or collected	主要装饰 Main Decorations	尺寸（厘米） Size(cm)		类型 Type	图片 Picture
					面径 Face Diameter	身高 Height		
380	0070 号 乳钉纹铜鼓 No.0070 Bronze Drum with nipple protrusions	武鸣区文物 管理所 Wuming County Cultural Relics Admini- stration	1992 年 1 月南宁 市武鸣县公安局 破获文物走私案 后件移交 Transferred by Nanning City Wuming County Public Security Bereau in January, 1992	鼓面：太阳纹（12 芒）、乳钉纹、 雷纹、变形游旗纹、回形雷纹、同 心圆纹； 鼓身：乳钉纹、同心圆纹、回形雷纹、 雷纹、复线角形纹；扁耳两对饰⊓棱纹 Drum face: patterns of sun(12rays), nipple protrusion, thunder, flying flag, 回 -shape thunder, concentric circle; Drum body: patterns of nipple protrusion, concentric circle, 回 -shape thunder, thunder, leaf-shape triangle; Raise ridges on 2 pairs of flat handles.	45.7	22.5	麻江型 Majiang Type	
381	0104 号 西香铜鼓 No.0104 Bronze Drum Xixiang	武鸣区文物 管理所 Wuming County Cultural Relics Admini- stration	1995 年 2 月 20 日出土于南宁市 武鸣县（今南宁 市武鸣区）宁武 镇张朗村西香屯 武鸣河边 Unearthed beside Wuning River, Xixiang Tun, Zhanglang Village, Ningwu Town, Wuming County, Nanning City on February 20th, 1995	鼓面：太阳纹（12 芒）、栉纹、切 线圆圈纹、水波纹、变形羽人纹、 变形翔鹭纹，鼓面边缘饰四只逆时 针三足立体青蛙； 鼓身：栉纹、切线圆圈纹、变形划 船纹、水波纹、变形羽人纹；扁耳 两对饰辫纹 Drum face: patterns of sun(12rays), comb line, tangent circle, water wave, transformed feathermen, transformed flying heron;4 frog statues of 3 feet anticlockwise stand on the edge of drum face; Drum body: patterns of comb line, tangent circle, boat, water wave, transformed feathermen; Braids pattern on 2 pairs of flat handles.	81	58.5	冷水冲 型 Lengshui- chong Type	
382	凤林村铜鼓 Bronze Drum Fenglincun	武鸣区文物 管理所 Wuming County Cultural Relics Admini- stration	2014 年 6 月 1 日 出土于南宁市武 鸣县（今南宁市 武鸣区）罗波镇 凤林村 Unearthed at Fenglin Village, Luobo Town, Wuming County, Nanning City on June 1st, 2014	鼓面：太阳纹（12 芒）、栉纹、切 线同心圆纹、复线交叉纹、变形羽 人纹、变形翔鹭纹间定胜纹，鼓面 边缘饰三只逆时针一只顺时针四足 素面立体青蛙，其中一只蛙背上负 两只立体鸟； 鼓身：栉纹、切线同心圆纹、栉纹 切线同心圆纹垂直纹带、圆心垂叶 纹；扁耳两对饰辫纹 Drum face: patterns of sun(12rays), comb line, tangent concentric circles, crossed double lines, transformed feathermen, transformed flying heron mixed Dingsheng;3 frog statues of 4 feet and blank back anticlockwise(one clockwise) stand on the edge of drum face, one of them with 2 birds on the back; Drum body: patterns of comb line, tangent concentric circles, vertical ribbon of blank, straight line and tangent concentric circles, leaf- shape triangle with concentric circles in the middle; Braids pattern on 2 pairs of flat handles.	78.6–80	55	冷水冲 型 Lengshui- chong Type	

序号 N0.	原编号及鼓名 Stock Number & Name	收藏单位 Museum	出土（征集） 时间、地点 Time & Spot for discovered or collected	主要装饰 Main Decorations	尺寸（厘米） Size(cm)		类型 Type	图片 Picture
					面径 Face Diameter	身高 Height		
383	下康鼓 Bronze Drum Xiakang	马山县文物管理所 Mashan County Cultural Relics Administration	1993 年 9 月 2 日出土于南宁市马山县合群乡造华村下康屯村口水塘边 Unearthed next to the Pond, Xiakang Tun, Zaohua Village, Hequn, Mashan County, Nanning City on September 2nd, 1993	鼓面：太阳纹（12 芒），栉纹、同心圆纹、复线交叉纹、变形羽人纹、变形翔鹭间定胜纹，鼓面边缘饰四只逆时针四足素面立体青蛙； 鼓身：栉纹、同心圆纹、栉纹同心圆纹垂直纹带、圆心垂叶纹；扁耳两对饰辫纹 Drum face: patterns of sun(12rays), comb line, concentric circles, crossed double lines, transformed feathermen, transformed flying heron mixed Dingsheng;4 frog statues of 4 feet anticlockwise stand on the edge of drum face; Drum body: patterns of comb line, concentric circles, vertical ribbon of straight line and concentric circles, leaf-shape triangle with concentric circle in the middle; Braids pattern on 2 pairs of flat handles.	69.8~70.5	43	冷水冲型 Lengshui-chong Type	
384	0009 号附城鼓 No.0009 Bronze Drum Fucheng	横县博物馆 Heng County Museum	1989 年出土于南宁市横县附城镇清江河段 Unearthed in Qingjiang River, Fucheng Town, Heng County, Nanning City in 1989	鼓面：太阳纹（10 芒），方孔钱纹、雷纹填线纹、席纹、虫纹、云纹、雷纹、蝉纹，鼓面边缘饰六只逆时针三足斜线纹、半圆纹、螺旋纹立体青蛙； 鼓身：方孔钱纹、半圆填线纹、云纹、虫纹、席纹、四瓣花填线纹、雷纹、雷纹填线纹、蝉纹；扁耳两对饰辫纹 Drum face: patterns of sun(10 rays), square-hole coin, thunder filled with straight lines, woven mat, insect, cloud, thunder, cicada; 6 frogs of 3 feet with oblique lines, semi-circle and spiracle patterns on back anticlockwise stand on the edge; Drum body: patterns of square-hole coin, semi-circle filled with straight lines, cloud, insect, woven mat, quatrefoil filled with straight lines, thunder, thunder filled with straight lines, Cicadai; Braid patterns on 2 pairs of flat handles.	79.5	51	灵山型 Lingshan Type	

续表

序号 NO.	原编号及鼓名 Stock Number & Name	收藏单位 Museum	出土（征集）时间、地点 Time & Spot for discovered or collected	主要装饰 Main Decorations	尺寸（厘米）Size(cm) 面径 Face Diameter	尺寸（厘米）Size(cm) 身高 Height	类型 Type	图片 Picture
385	0147 号 清江河鼓 No.0147 Bronze Drum Qingjiang he	横县博物馆 Heng County Museum	1997 年 2 月出土于南宁市横县郁江清江河段 Unearthed in Qingjiang River, part of Yujiang River, Heng County, Nanning City in February, 1997	鼓面：太阳纹（12 芒）、水波纹、同心圆纹、栉纹、勾连雷纹、变形羽人纹、变形翔鹭纹间定胜纹，鼓面边缘饰四只逆时针四足辫纹、栉纹、螺旋纹立体青蛙；鼓身：栉纹、切线同心圆纹、栉纹切线同心圆纹垂直纹带、圆心垂叶纹；扁耳两对饰辫纹 Drum face: patterns of sun(12rays), water wave, concentric circles, comb line, hooked thunder, transformed feathermen, transformed flying heron mixed Dingsheng; 4 frog statues of 4 feet with braid, comb line and spiracle patterns on back anticlockwise stand on the edge of drum face; Drum body: patterns of comb line, tangent concentric circles, vertical ribbon of straight line and tangent concentric circles, leaf-shape triangle with concentric circle in the middle; Braid patterns on 2 pairs of flat handles.	61	42	冷水冲型 Lengshui-chong Type	
386	0148 号 四官河鼓 No.0148 Bronze Drum Siguan He	横县博物馆 Heng County Museum	1997 年 11 月出土于南宁市横县郁江四官河段 Unearthed in Siguan River, part of Yujiang River, Heng County, Nanning City in November, 1997	鼓面：太阳纹（12 芒）、栉纹、同心圆纹、复线交叉纹、变形羽人纹、变形翔鹭纹间定胜纹、鼓面边缘饰四只逆时针四足素面立体青蛙；鼓身：栉纹、同心圆纹、栉纹同心圆垂直纹带、圆心垂叶纹；扁耳两对饰辫纹 Drum face: patterns of sun(12rays), comb line, circle, crossed double lines, transformed feathermen, transformed flying heron mixed Dingsheng;4 frog statues of 4 feet anticlockwise stand on the edge of drum face; Drum body: patterns of comb line, concentric circle, vertical ribbon of straight lines and circles, leaf-shape triangle with concentric circle in the middle; Braids pattern on 2 pairs of flat handles.	65	40	冷水冲型 Lengshui-chong Type	

序号 N0.	原编号及鼓名 Stock Number & Name	收藏单位 Museum	出土（征集）时间、地点 Time & Spot for discovered or collected	主要装饰 Main Decorations	尺寸（厘米）Size(cm)		类型 Type	图片 Picture
					面径 Face Diameter	身高 Height		
387	横县圭壁鼓 Bronze Drum Guibi	横县博物馆 Hengxian County Museum	1988年出土于南宁市横县板露乡圭壁村 Unearthed at Guibi Village, Banlu, Hengxian County, Nanning City in 1988	鼓面：太阳纹（12芒），四瓣花纹、云纹、四出钱纹、席纹、虫形纹，鼓面边缘饰六组顺时针四足瓣纹立体青蛙，两组为累蹲蛙；鼓身：席纹、四出钱纹、云纹、雷纹、四瓣花填线纹、半同心圆纹、雷纹填线纹、水波纹、四瓣花纹；扁耳两对饰乳钉纹、瓣纹；鼓足环耳一对，饰一怪兽塑像，兽身有双翅，每翅各坐两人 Drum face: patterns of sun(12 rays), quatrefoil, cloud, coin with quadrangle inside, woven mat, insect; 6 frogs with 4 feet and braid patterns on back clockwise stand on the edge, 2 of them are overlap; Drum body: patterns of woven mat, coin with quadrangle inside, cloud, thunder, quatrefoil filled with straight lines, semi-concentric circle, thunder filled with straight lines, water wave, quatrefoil; Braid & nipple protrusion patterns on 2 pairs of flat handles; a beast statue with 4 persons on its' 2 wings, and 2 attached ring handles on the foot.	118	64	灵山型 Lingshan Type	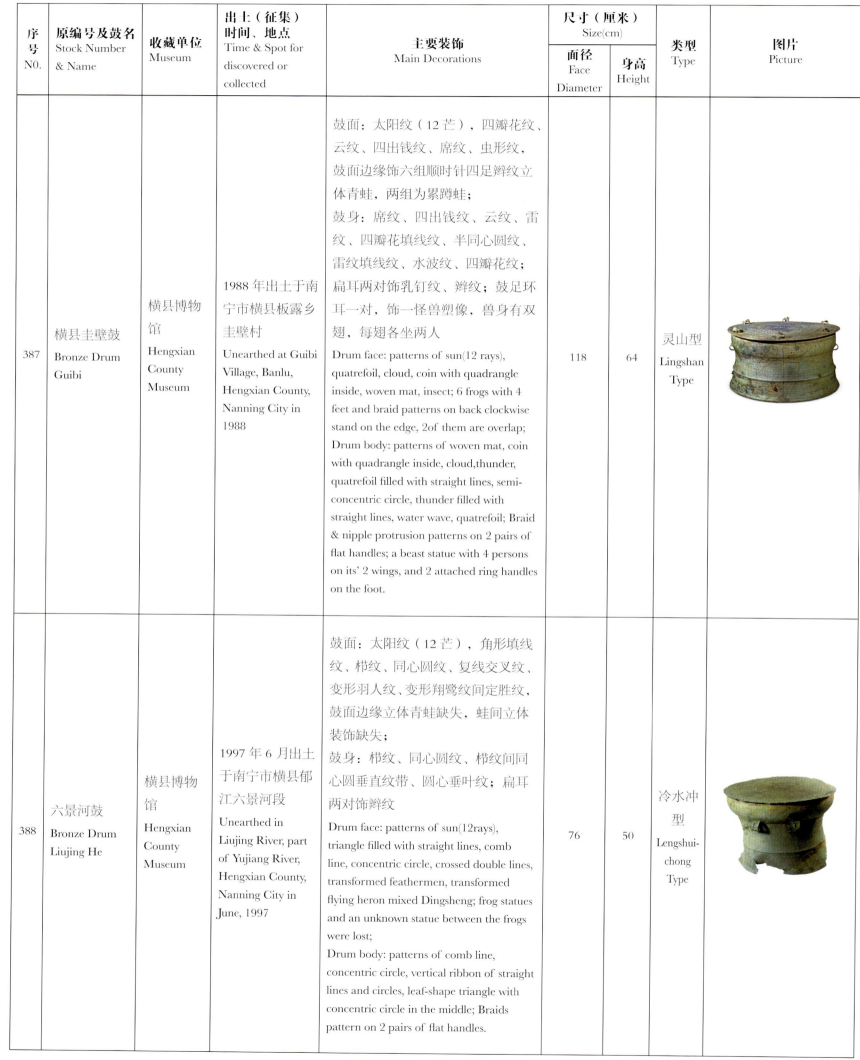
388	六景河鼓 Bronze Drum Liujing He	横县博物馆 Hengxian County Museum	1997年6月出土于南宁市横县郁江六景河段 Unearthed in Liujing River, part of Yujiang River, Hengxian County, Nanning City in June, 1997	鼓面：太阳纹（12芒），角形填线纹、栉纹、同心圆纹、复线交叉纹、变形羽人纹、变形翔鹭纹间定胜纹，鼓面边缘立体青蛙缺失，蛙间立体装饰缺失；鼓身：栉纹、同心圆纹、栉纹间同心圆垂直纹带、圆心垂叶纹；扁耳两对饰瓣纹 Drum face: patterns of sun(12rays), triangle filled with straight lines, comb line, concentric circle, crossed double lines, transformed feathermen, transformed flying heron mixed Dingsheng; frog statues and an unknown statue between the frogs were lost; Drum body: patterns of comb line, concentric circle, vertical ribbon of straight lines and circles, leaf-shape triangle with concentric circle in the middle; Braids pattern on 2 pairs of flat handles.	76	50	冷水冲型 Lengshui-chong Type	

续表

序号 NO.	原编号及鼓名 Stock Number & Name	收藏单位 Museum	出土（征集） 时间、地点 Time & Spot for discovered or collected	主要装饰 Main Decorations	尺寸（厘米） Size(cm)		类型 Type	图片 Picture
					面径 Face Diameter	身高 Height		
389	0008 号 塘红村鼓 No.0008 Bronze Drum Tanghongcun	上林县文物管理所 Shanglin County Cultural Relics Administration	1974 年 11 月 18 日出土于南宁市上林县塘红乡塘红村上营屯南约 1 公里铜鼓岭半山坡 Unearthed at hillside of Tonggu Ling, the south of 1km to Shangying Tun, Tanghong village, Shanglin County, Nanning City on November 18th, 1974	鼓面：太阳纹（12 芒），可辨勾连雷纹、变形羽人纹、变形翔鹭纹、同心圆纹，鼓面边缘饰四只逆时针四足素面立体青蛙； 鼓身：可辨同心圆纹、变形船纹、变形羽人纹、栉纹、同心圆纹；扁耳两对饰辫纹 Drum face: patterns of sun(12rays), hooked thunder, transformed feathermen, transformed flying heron, concentric circle; 4 frog statues of 4 feet anticlockwise stand on the edge of drum face; Drum body: patterns of concentric circle, transformed boat, transformed feathermen, vertical ribbon of comb line and concentric circles; Braid patterns on 2 pairs of flat handles.	91～92.3	66.3	冷水冲型 Lengshui-chong Type	
390	0009 号 万古村鼓 No.0009 Bronze Drum Wangucun	上林县文物管理所 Shanglin County Cultural Relics Administration	1975 年 3 月 20 日出土于南宁市上林县明亮镇万古村安灶山山脚水渠边 Unearthed beside a canal at the foot of Anzao Hill, Wangu Village, Mingliang Town, Shanglin County, Nanning City on March 20th, 1975	鼓面：太阳纹（12 芒）、栉纹、切线同心圆纹、复线交叉夹三角纹、变形羽人纹、变形翔鹭纹间定胜纹、鱼纹，鼓面边缘饰四只逆时针四足线条纹立体青蛙； 鼓身：栉纹、切线同心圆纹、栉纹切线同心圆垂直纹带、羽纹、圆心垂叶纹；扁耳两对饰辫纹 Drum face: patterns of sun(12rays), comb line, tangent concentric circle, crossed double lines, transformed feathermen, transformed flying heron mixed Dingsheng and fish; 4 frog statues of 4 feet and lines on back anticlockwise stand on the edge of drum face; Drum body: patterns of comb line, tangent concentric circle, vertical ribbon of straight lines and concentric circles, feather, leaf-shape triangle with circle in the middle; Braids pattern on 2 pairs of flat handles.	62.5～64.5	38.5	冷水冲型 Lengshui-chong Type	

序号 N0.	原编号及鼓名 Stock Number & Name	收藏单位 Museum	出土（征集）时间、地点 Time & Spot for discovered or collected	主要装饰 Main Decorations	尺寸（厘米） Size(cm)		类型 Type	图片 Picture
					面径 Face Diameter	身高 Height		
391	0204 号 那婆山鼓 No.0204 Bronze Drum Naposhan	上林县文物管理所 Shanglin County Cultural Relics Administration	1991 年 12 月 25 日出土于南宁市上林县三里镇双罗村云聪屯北面约 1 公里处那婆山柑橘园 Unearthed in an orange orchard on Napo Hill, the north of 1km to Yuncong Tun, Shuangluo Village, Sanli Town, Shanglin County, Nanning City on December 25th, 1991	鼓面：太阳纹（12 芒），栉纹、同心圆纹、复线交叉纹、变形羽人纹、变形翔鹭纹间定胜纹、人形纹，鼓面边缘饰四只逆时针四足素面立体青蛙； 鼓身：栉纹、同心圆纹、栉纹同心圆纹垂直纹带、两行相对的圆心垂叶纹；扁耳两对饰辫纹 Drum face: patterns of sun(12rays), comb line, comb line, concentric circle, crossed double lines, transformed feathermen, transformed flying heron mixed Dingsheng, human figure; 4 frog statues of 4 feet and blank back anticlockwise stand on the edge of drum face; Drum body: patterns of comb line, concentric circle, vertical ribbon of straight lines and concentric circles, leaf-shape triangle with circle in the middle; Braids pattern on 2 pairs of flat handles.	81.6－83	54.2	冷水冲型 Lengshui-chong Type	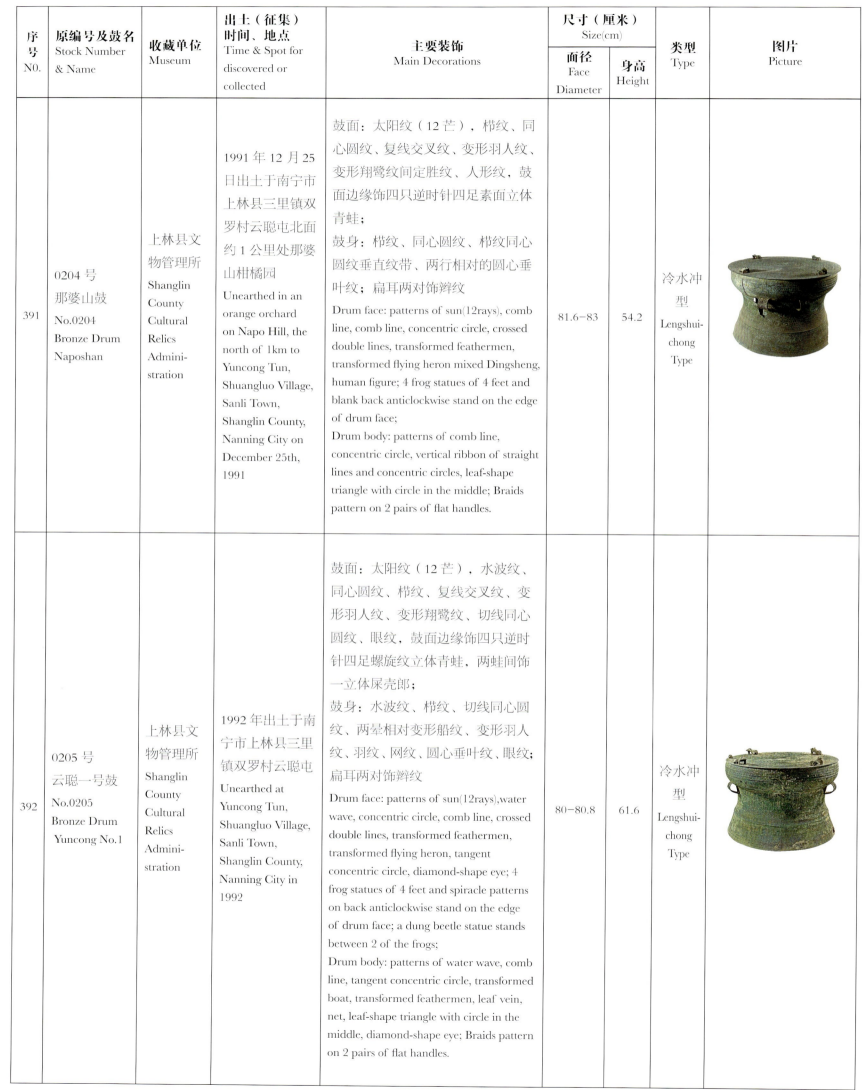
392	0205 号 云聪一号鼓 No.0205 Bronze Drum Yuncong No.1	上林县文物管理所 Shanglin County Cultural Relics Administration	1992 年出土于南宁市上林县三里镇双罗村云聪屯 Unearthed at Yuncong Tun, Shuangluo Village, Sanli Town, Shanglin County, Nanning City in 1992	鼓面：太阳纹（12 芒），水波纹、同心圆纹、栉纹、复线交叉纹、变形羽人纹、变形翔鹭纹、切线同心圆纹、眼纹，鼓面边缘饰四只逆时针四足螺旋纹立体青蛙，两蛙间饰一立体屎壳郎； 鼓身：水波纹、栉纹、切线同心圆纹、两晕相对变形船纹、变形羽人纹、羽纹、网纹、圆心垂叶纹、眼纹；扁耳两对饰辫纹 Drum face: patterns of sun(12rays),water wave, concentric circle, comb line, crossed double lines, transformed feathermen, transformed flying heron, tangent concentric circle, diamond-shape eye; 4 frog statues of 4 feet and spiracle patterns on back anticlockwise stand on the edge of drum face; a dung beetle statue stands between 2 of the frogs; Drum body: patterns of water wave, comb line, tangent concentric circle, transformed boat, transformed feathermen, leaf vein, net, leaf-shape triangle with circle in the middle, diamond-shape eye; Braids pattern on 2 pairs of flat handles.	80－80.8	61.6	冷水冲型 Lengshui-chong Type	

序号 N0.	原编号及鼓名 Stock Number & Name	收藏单位 Museum	出土（征集）时间、地点 Time & Spot for discovered or collected	主要装饰 Main Decorations	尺寸（厘米） Size(cm) 面径 Face Diameter	身高 Height	类型 Type	图片 Picture
393	0206 号 云聪二号鼓 No.0206 Bronze Drum Yuncong No.2	上林县文物管理所 Shanglin County Cultural Relics Administration	1992 年出土于南宁市上林县三里镇双罗村云聪屯 Unearthed at Yuncong Tun, Shuangluo Village, Sanli Town, Shanglin County, Nanning City in 1992	鼓面：太阳纹（12 芒）、角形填线纹、雷纹、栉纹、同心圆纹、复线交叉纹、变形羽人纹、变形翔鹭纹间定胜纹鱼纹鸟形纹、鸟形纹，鼓面边缘饰四只逆时针四足圆点圆圈纹立体青蛙；鼓身：辫纹、栉纹、同心圆纹、变形船纹、变形羽人纹、圆心垂叶纹；扁耳两对饰辫纹 Drum face: patterns of sun(12rays), triangle filled with comb line, thunder, comb line, concentric circle, crossed double lines, transformed feathermen, transformed flying heron mixed Dingsheng, fish and bird, bird; 4 frog statues of 4 feet and circle patterns on back anticlockwise stand on the edge of drum face; Drum body: patterns of braid, comb line, concentric circle, transformed boat, transformed feathermen, leaf-shape triangle with circle in the middle; Braids pattern on 2 pairs of flat handles.	79.8—86	54.5	冷水冲型 Lengshui-chong Type	
394	0207 号 云聪三号鼓 No.0207 Bronze Drum Yuncong No.3	上林县文物管理所 Shanglin County Cultural Relics Administration	1992 年出土于南宁市上林县三里镇双罗村云聪屯 Unearthed at Yuncong Tun, Shuangluo Village, Sanli Town, Shanglin County, Nanning City in 1992	鼓面：太阳纹（12 芒）、水波纹、同心圆纹、栉纹、羽纹、复线交叉纹、变形羽人纹、变形翔鹭纹、眼纹、鼓面边缘饰四只逆时针四足辫纹立体青蛙，其中两只蛙背上负鱼，蛙吻部有两小孔；鼓身：羽纹、同心圆纹、两辈相对变形船纹、水波纹、变形羽人纹、网纹、圆心垂叶纹、眼纹；扁耳两对饰辫纹 Drum face: patterns of sun(12rays), water wave, concentric circle, comb line, feather, crossed double lines, transformed feathermen, transformed flying heron, diamond-shape eye; 4 frog statues of 4 feet and spiracle patterns on back anticlockwise stand on the edge of drum face; 2 of them carrying a fish on their backs and there are 2 holes on the front of the mouths; Drum body: patterns of feather, concentric circles, transformed boat, water wave, transformed feathermen, net, leaf-shape triangle with circle in the middle, diamond-shape eye; Braids pattern on 2 pairs of flat handles.	78.2—78.5	58.2	冷水冲型 Lengshui-chong Type	

序号 N0.	原编号及鼓名 Stock Number & Name	收藏单位 Museum	出土（征集）时间、地点 Time & Spot for discovered or collected	主要装饰 Main Decorations	尺寸（厘米）Size(cm)		类型 Type	图片 Picture
					面径 Face Diameter	身高 Height		
395	0208 号 云聪四号鼓 No.0208 Bronze Drum Yuncong No.4	上林县文物管理所 Shanglin County Cultural Relics Administration	1992 年出土于南宁市上林县三里镇双罗村云聪屯 Unearthed at Yuncong Tun, Shuangluo Village, Sanli Town, Shanglin County, Nanning City in 1992	鼓面：太阳纹（12 芒），水波纹、席纹、栉纹、同心圆纹、复线交叉纹间复线角形纹、羽纹、变形羽人纹、变形翔鹭纹、眼纹，鼓面边缘饰四只逆时针四足辫纹立体青蛙，其中两蛙之间饰人抱龟后腿立体装饰；鼓身：水波纹、栉纹、同心圆纹、两晕相对变形船纹、变形羽人纹、羽纹、网纹、圆心垂叶纹；扁耳两对饰辫纹 Drum face: patterns of sun(12rays),water wave, woven mat, comb line, concentric circle, crossed double lines mixed triangle, feather, transformed feathermen, transformed flying heron, diamond-shape eye; 4 frog statues of 4 feet and spiracle patterns on back anticlockwise stand on the edge of drum face; a statue of a person holding the tortoise' leg between 2 of the frogs; Drum body: patterns of water wave, comb line, concentric circles, transformed boat, transformed feathermen, feather, net, leaf-shape triangle with circle in the middle; Braids pattern on 2 pairs of flat handles.	74-75.6	50	冷水冲型 Lengshui-chong Type	
396	宾阳新宁鼓 Bronze Drum Xinning	宾阳县文物管理所 Binyang County Cultural Relics Administration	1999 年出土于南宁市宾阳县甘棠镇新宁村 Unearthed at Xinning Village, Gantang Town, Binyang County, Nanning City in 1999	鼓面：太阳纹（10 芒），蝉纹、雷纹、四出钱纹、鸟纹、连钱纹、变形羽人纹、兽面纹、席纹、四瓣花纹，鼓面边缘饰六组逆时针三足螺旋纹立体青蛙，三组为累蹲蛙；鼓身：蝉纹、连钱纹、四出钱纹、鸟形纹、兽面纹、虫形纹、席纹、四瓣花纹；扁耳两对饰辫纹，一侧鼓耳下饰一只立体鸟 Drum face: patterns of sun(10rays), cicada, thunder, coin with quadrangle inside, bird, coins part of overlap, transformed feathermen, beast face, woven mat, quatrefoil; 6 frogs with 3 feet and spiracle patterns on back anticlockwise stand on the edge, 3 of them are overlap; Drum body: patterns of cicada, coins part of overlap, coin with quadrangle inside, bird, beast face, insect, woven mat, quatrefoil; Braid patterns on 2 pairs of flat handles; A bird statue stand under one of the handles.	79.8-80.1	45.5	灵山型 Lingshan Type	

续表

序号 N0.	原编号及鼓名 Stock Number & Name	收藏单位 Museum	出土（征集） 时间、地点 Time & Spot for discovered or collected	主要装饰 Main Decorations	尺寸（厘米） Size(cm)		类型 Type	图片 Picture
					面径 Face Diameter	身高 Height		
397	Hg00001 号 南朝变形羽人 纹铜鼓 No.Hg00001 South Dynasty Bronze Drum with transformed feathermen patterns	柳州市博 物馆 Liuzhou Museum	1958 年 12 月从 柳州市文管会接 收，原存江西会 馆内 An old stock of Jiangxi Guildhall, allocated by Liuzhou Cultural Relics Administration in December, 1958	鼓面：太阳纹（12 芒）、栉纹、同 心圆纹、复线交叉纹、变形羽人纹、 变形翔鹭纹间定胜纹，鼓面边缘饰 四只逆时针四足立体素面青蛙； 鼓身：羽纹、栉纹、同心圆纹、羽 纹栉纹同心圆纹垂直纹带、圆心三 角垂叶纹；扁耳两对饰辫纹 Drum face: patterns of sun(12rays), comb line, concentric circles, crossed double lines, transformed feathermen, transformed flying heron mixed Dingsheng, and 4 frog statues of 4 feet with plain back anticlockwise stand on the edge of drum face; Drum body: patterns of feather, comb line, concentric circles, vertical ribbon with straight line and concentric circles, leaf- shape triangle with concentric circles in the middle; Braids pattern on 2 pairs of flat handles.	71.6~72.5	49.5	冷水冲型 Lengshui- chong Type	
398	Hg00002 号 明小铜鼓 No.Hg00002 Ming Dynasty Bronze Drum in small size	柳州市博 物馆 Liuzhou Museum	1959 年柳州市人 民银行副行长陆 昌达赠送 Presented by Lu Changda, the director of Liuzhou People's Bank in 1959	鼓面：太阳纹（11 芒）、乳钉纹、 舌形莲花瓣纹、风火轮纹间钱纹、 云纹、五字椭圆图案纹； 鼓身：乳钉纹、蔓草图案纹、变体 雷纹、三角图案纹；扁耳两对饰 弦纹 Drum face: patterns of sun(11rays), nipple protrusion, flame, wind &fire wheel filled with coin, cloud, 五 -character; Drum body: patterns of nipple protrusion, plants, transformed thunder, triangle; String patterns on 2 pairs of flat handles.	24~24.2	13.3	异型 Abnor- mal	
399	Hg00003 号 明游旗纹铜鼓 No.Hg00003 Bronze Drum with flying flag patterns	柳州市博 物馆 Liuzhou Museum	1961 年征集于柳 州二级站 Collected at Liuzhou Secondary Waste Station in 1961	鼓面：太阳纹（12 芒）、西字纹、 S 形云纹、乳钉纹、游旗纹、栉纹、 云纹； 鼓身：乳钉纹、云纹、回形雷纹、 栉纹、复线角形纹；扁耳两对饰辫 纹 Drum face: patterns of sun(12rays), 西 -character, S-shape cloud, nipple protrusion, flying flag, comb line, cloud; Drum body: patterns of nipple protrusion, cloud, 回 -shape thunder, comb line, double line triangle; Braid patterns on 2 pairs of flat handles.	47	26.5	麻江型 Majiang Type	

序号 N0.	原编号及鼓名 Stock Number & Name	收藏单位 Museum	出土（征集）时间、地点 Time & Spot for discovered or collected	主要装饰 Main Decorations	尺寸（厘米）Size(cm)		类型 Type	图片 Picture
					面径 Face Diameter	身高 Height		
400	Hg00004 号 明云纹铜鼓 No.Hg00004 Ming Dynasty Bronze Drum with cloud pattern	柳州市博物馆 Liuzhou Museum	1961 年征集于柳州二级站 Collected at Liuzhou Secondary Waste Station in 1961	鼓面：太阳纹（12 芒）、西字纹、S 形云纹、乳钉纹、云纹、回形雷纹、棂花纹；鼓身：梅花状乳钉纹、云纹、回形雷纹、复线角形纹；扁耳两对饰回纹、卐字纹 Drum face: patterns of sun(12rays), 西 -character, S-shape cloud, nipple protrusion, cloud, 回 -shape thunder, window lattices; Drum body: patterns of nipple protrusion in plum-blossom shape, cloud, 回 -shape thunder, double line triangle; 回 -character and 卐 -character patterns on 2 pairs of flat handles.	47−47.2	27.1	麻江型 Majiang Type	
401	Hg00005 号 明游旗纹铜鼓 No.Hg00005 Ming Dynasty Bronze Drum with flying flag	柳州市博物馆 Liuzhou Museum	1961 年征集于柳州二级站 Collected at Liuzhou Secondary Waste Station in 1961	鼓面：太阳纹（12 芒）、西字纹、S 形云纹、乳钉纹、游旗纹、云纹、栉纹；鼓身：乳钉纹、如意云纹、云纹、回形雷纹、栉纹、复线角形纹；扁耳两对饰辫纹 Drum face: patterns of sun(12rays), 西 -character, S-shape cloud, nipple protrusion, flying flag, cloud, comb line; Drum body: patterns of nipple protrusion, Ruyi-shape cloud, cloud, 回 -shape thunder, comb line, double line triangle; Braid patterns on 2 pairs of flat handles.	47	26.5	麻江型 Majiang Type	
402	Hg00006 号 清游旗纹铜鼓 No.Hg00006 Qing Dynasty Bronze Drum with flying flag	柳州市博物馆 Liuzhou Museum	1961 年征集于柳州二级站 Collected at Liuzhou Secondary Waste Station in 1961	鼓面：太阳纹（12 芒）、西字纹、乳钉纹、栉纹、游旗纹、云纹；鼓身：栉纹、乳钉纹、云纹、回形雷纹、复线角形纹；扁耳两对饰辫纹 Drum face: patterns of sun(12rays), 西 -character, nipple protrusion, comb line, flying flag, cloud,; Drum body: patterns of comb line, nipple protrusion, cloud, 回 -shape thunder, double line triangle; Braid patterns on 2 pairs of flat handles.	48.5	28	麻江型 Majiang Type	

序号 NO.	原编号及鼓名 Stock Number & Name	收藏单位 Museum	出土（征集） 时间、地点 Time & Spot for discovered or collected	主要装饰 Main Decorations	尺寸（厘米） Size(cm)		类型 Type	图片 Picture
					面径 Face Diameter	身高 Height		
403	Hg00007 号 明游旗纹铜鼓 No.Hg00007 Ming Dynasty Bronze Drum with flying flag	柳州市博物馆 Liuzhou Museum	1961 年征集于柳州二级站 Collected at Liuzhou Secondary Waste Station in 1961	鼓面：太阳纹（12 芒）、回形雷纹、乳钉纹、栉纹、游旗纹、云纹； 鼓身：乳钉纹、四出钱纹、复线角形纹；扁耳两对饰凸棱纹 Drum face: patterns of sun(12rays), 回 -shape thunder, nipple protrusion, comb line, flying flag, cloud; Drum body: patterns of nipple protrusion, coin with quadrangle inside, double line triangle; Raise ridges on 2 pairs of flat handles.	49	29	麻江型 Majiang Type	
404	Hg00008 号 明符箓纹铜鼓 No.Hg00008 Ming Dynasty Bronze Drum with flying flag	柳州市博物馆 Liuzhou Museum	1963 年 11 月在柳州市五里卡仓库拣选 Collected at Liuzhou Wulika Waste Storage in November,1963	鼓面：太阳纹（12 芒）、酉字纹、S 形云纹、乳钉纹、符箓纹、回形雷纹、缠枝纹； 鼓身：乳钉纹、回形雷纹、云纹、复线三角纹；扁耳两对饰回形雷纹 Drum face: patterns of sun(12rays), 西 -character, S-shape cloud, nipple protrusion, Ofuda, 回 -shape thunder, twisted branches; Drum body: patterns of nipple protrusion, 回 - shape thunder, cloud, double line triangle; 回 - shape thunder on 2 pairs of flat handles.	48-48.5	26.7	麻江型 Majiang Type	
405	Hg00009 号 清十二生肖纹铜鼓 No.Hg00009 Qing Dynasty Bronze Drum with Zodiac pattern	柳州市博物馆 Liuzhou Museum	1964 年 1 月在柳州二级馆拣选 Collected at Liuzhou Secondary Waste Station in January,1964	鼓面：太阳纹（12 芒）、乳钉纹、回形雷纹、S 形云纹、十二生肖纹、栉纹、云纹； 鼓身：乳钉纹、云纹、栉纹、复线角形纹；扁耳两对饰回形雷纹 Drum face: patterns of sun(12rays), nipple protrusion, 回 - shape thunder, S-shape cloud, zodiac, comb line, cloud; Drum body: patterns of nipple protrusion, cloud, comb line，double line triangle; 回 - shape thunder on 2 pairs of flat handles.	47.2-47.8	27.8	麻江型 Majiang Type	

序号 NO.	原编号及鼓名 Stock Number & Name	收藏单位 Museum	出土（征集）时间、地点 Time & Spot for discovered or collected	主要装饰 Main Decorations	尺寸（厘米）Size(cm)		类型 Type	图片 Picture
					面径 Face Diameter	身高 Height		
406	Hg00010 号 清游旗纹铜鼓 No.Hg00010 Qing Dynasty Bronze Drum with flying flag	柳州市博物馆 Liuzhou Museum	1964 年 1 月在柳州二级馆拣选 Collected at Liuzhou Secondary Waste Station in January,1964	鼓面：太阳纹（12 芒）、酉字纹、乳钉纹、蝉纹、枊纹间五瓣花纹、游旗纹、同心圆纹、羽纹； 鼓身：同心圆纹、乳钉纹、枊纹、回形雷纹、心形纹、复线角形纹；扁耳两对饰凸棱纹 Drum face: patterns of sun(12rays), 酉 -character, nipple protrusion, cicada, straight line mixed cinquefoil, flying flag, concentric circle, feather; Drum body: patterns of concentric circle, nipple protrusion, comb line, 回 - shape thunder, heart-shape motif, double line triangle; Raise ridges on 2 pairs of flat handles.	47.2~48	29.5	麻江型 Majiang Type	
407	Hg00011 号 清异形游旗纹铜鼓 No.Hg00011 Qing Dynasty Bronze Drum with transformed flying flag	柳州市博物馆 Liuzhou Museum	1964 年 1 月在柳州二级馆拣选 Collected at Liuzhou Secondary Waste Station in January,1964	鼓面：太阳纹（12 芒）、同心圆纹、枊纹、乳钉纹、异形游旗纹、云纹、羽纹； 鼓身：乳钉纹、云纹、回形雷纹、如意云纹、复线角形纹；扁耳两对饰辫纹 Drum face: patterns of sun(12rays), concentric circle, comb line, nipple protrusion, transformed flying flag, cloud, feather; Drum body: patterns of nipple protrusion, cloud, 回 - shape thunder, Ruyi-shape cloud, double line triangle; Braid pattern on 2 pairs of flat handles.	47	28.8	麻江型 Majiang Type	
408	Hg00012 号 清符箓纹铜鼓 No.Hg00012 Qing Dynasty Bronze Drum with ofuda pattern	柳州市博物馆 Liuzhou Museum	1964 年 1 月在柳州二级馆拣选 Collected at Liuzhou Secondary Waste Station in January,1964	鼓面：太阳纹（12 芒）、同心圆纹、回形雷纹、乳钉纹、符箓纹、云纹； 鼓身：云纹、回形雷纹、如意云纹、同心圆纹、复线角形纹；扁耳两对饰辫纹 Drum face: patterns of sun(12rays), concentric circle, 回 - shape thunder , nipple protrusion, Ofuda, cloud; Drum body: patterns of cloud, 回 - shape thunder, Ruyi-shape cloud, concentric circle, double line triangle; Braids on 2 pairs of flat handles.	42.8	26.4	麻江型 Majiang Type	

序号 NO.	原编号及鼓名 Stock Number & Name	收藏单位 Museum	出土（征集） 时间、地点 Time & Spot for discovered or collected	主要装饰 Main Decorations	尺寸（厘米） Size(cm)		类型 Type	图片 Picture
					面径 Face Diameter	身高 Height		
409	Hg00013 号 飞鹅路铜鼓 No.Hg00013 Bronze Drum Fei'e Lu	柳州市博物馆 Liuzhou Museum	1964 年 3 月 25 日出土于柳州市 飞鹅路 Unearthed at Fei'e Road, Liuzhou City on March 25th, 1964	鼓面：太阳纹（12 芒）、栉纹、同心圆纹、复线交叉纹、变形羽人纹、变形翔鹭纹间定胜纹，鼓面边缘饰四只逆时针四足立体青蛙； 鼓身：栉纹、同心圆纹、栉纹同心圆纹垂直纹带、圆心三角垂叶纹；扁耳两对饰辫纹 Drum face: patterns of sun(12rays), comb line, concentric circles, crossed double lines, transformed feathermen, transformed flying heron mixed Dingsheng, and 4 frog statues of 4 feet anticlockwise stand on the edge of drum face; Drum body: patterns of comb line, concentric circles, vertical ribbon with straight line and concentric circles, leaf-shape triangle with concentric circles in the middle; Braids pattern on 2 pairs of flat handles.	70–71	46	冷水冲型 Lengshui- Chong Type	
410	Hg00014 号 清游旗纹铜鼓 No.Hg00014 Qing Dynasty Bronze Drum with flying flag	柳州市博物馆 Liuzhou Museum	1966 年 11 月在 柳州二级站拣选 Collected at Liuzhou Secondary Waste Station in November,1966	鼓面：太阳纹（12 芒）、西字纹、S 形云纹、乳钉纹、游旗纹、栉纹、兽形纹； 鼓身：乳钉纹、栉纹、回形雷纹、云纹、复线角形纹；扁耳两对饰辫纹 Drum face: patterns of sun(12rays), 西 -character, S-shape cloud, nipple protrusion, flying flag, comb line, beast-shape cloud; Drum body: patterns of nipple protrusion, comb line, 回 - shape thunder, cloud, double line triangle; Braids on 2 pairs of flat handles.	47–47.4	26.1	麻江型 Majiang Type	

序号 N0.	原编号及鼓名 Stock Number & Name	收藏单位 Museum	出土（征集）时间、地点 Time & Spot for discovered or collected	主要装饰 Main Decorations	尺寸（厘米）Size(cm)		类型 Type	图片 Picture
					面径 Face Diameter	身高 Height		
411	Hg00015 号 乘骑铜鼓 I No.Hg00015 Bronze Drum with horse-ride statue I	柳州市博物馆 Liuzhou Museum	1973 年 9 月于柳州二级站拣选 Collected at Liuzhou Secondary Waste Station in September,1973	鼓面：太阳纹（12 芒），水波纹、席纹、雷纹填线纹、同心圆纹、复线交叉纹、叶脉纹、变形羽人纹、变形翔鹭纹、眼纹、鼓面边缘饰四只逆时针四足螺旋纹立体青蛙，蛙间饰一妇女怀抱婴儿骑马立体装饰；鼓身：栉纹、同心圆纹、雷纹填线纹、变形船纹、变形羽人纹、叶脉纹、网纹、圆心垂叶纹、眼纹；扁耳两对饰辫纹 Drum face: patterns of sun(12rays), water wave, woven mat, thunder mixed straight line, concentric circles, crossed double lines, leaf vein, transformed feathermen, transformed flying heron, diamond-shape eye; 4 frog statues of 4 feet with spiracles on back anticlockwise stand on the edge of drum face; A statue of a woman holding her baby rides on a horse between the frogs; Drum body: patterns of comb line, concentric circles, thunder mixed straight line, boat, transformed feathermen, leaf vein, net, leaf-shape triangle with concentric circles in the middle,diamond-shape eye; Braids pattern on 2 pairs of flat handles.	73.6－24.9	54	冷水冲型 Lengshui-Chong Type	
412	Hg00016 号 清游旗纹铜鼓 No.Hg00016 Qing Dynasty Bronze Drum with flying flag patterns	柳州市博物馆 Liuzhou Museum	1974 年 2 月柳州市刀片厂赠送 Presented by Liuzhou Blade Factory in February, 1974	鼓面：太阳纹（12 芒），酉字纹、S 形云纹、乳钉纹、游旗纹、栉纹、兽形云纹；鼓身：乳钉纹、如意云纹、回形雷纹、栉纹、云纹、复线角形纹；扁耳两对饰辫纹、回形雷纹 Drum face: patterns of sun(12rays), 酉 -character, S-shape cloud, nipple protrusion, flying flag, comb line, beast-shape cloud; Drum body: patterns of nipple protrusion, Ruyi-shape cloud, 回 - shape thunder, comb line, cloud, double line triangle; Braids and 回 - shape thunder on 2 pairs of flat handles.	46.6－47	26	麻江型 Majiang Type	

续表

序号 NO.	原编号及鼓名 Stock Number & Name	收藏单位 Museum	出土（征集）时间、地点 Time & Spot for discovered or collected	主要装饰 Main Decorations	尺寸（厘米） Size(cm)		类型 Type	图片 Picture
					面径 Face Diameter	身高 Height		
413	Hg00017 号 清游旗纹铜鼓 No.Hg00017 Qing Dynasty Bronze Drum with flying flag patterns	柳州市博物馆 Liuzhou Museum	1974 年 2 月柳州市刀片厂赠送 Presented by Liuzhou Blade Factory in February, 1974	鼓面：太阳纹（12 芒）、西字纹、S 形云纹、乳钉纹、游旗纹、栉纹、兽形云纹、卦纹； 鼓身：乳钉纹、如意云纹、云纹、回形雷纹、栉纹、复线角形纹；扁耳两对饰辫纹 Drum face: patterns of sun(12rays), 西 -character, S-shape cloud, nipple protrusion, flying flag, comb line, beast-shape cloud, divinatory symbol pattern; Drum body: patterns of nipple protrusion, Ruyi-shape cloud, cloud, 回 - shape thunder, comb line, double line triangle; Braids on 2 pairs of flat handles.	49.7−50.4	27.8	麻江型 Majiang Type	
414	Hg00018 号 清游旗纹铜鼓 No.Hg00018 Qing Dynasty Bronze Drum with flying flag patterns	柳州市博物馆 Liuzhou Museum	1974 年 2 月柳州市刀片厂赠送 Presented by Liuzhou Blade Factory in February, 1974	鼓面：太阳纹（12 芒），S 形云纹、乳钉纹、游旗纹、栉纹、兽形云纹； 鼓身：乳钉纹、兽形云纹、雷纹、栉纹、复线角形纹；扁耳两对饰辫纹 Drum face: patterns of sun(12rays), S-shape cloud, nipple protrusion, flying flag, comb line, beast-shape cloud; Drum body: patterns of nipple protrusion, beast-shape cloud, thunder, comb line, double line triangle; Braids on 2 pairs of flat handles.	51−51.5	28.4	麻江型 Majiang Type	
415	Hg00019 号 清游旗纹铜鼓 No.Hg00019 Qing Dynasty Bronze Drum with flying flag patterns	柳州市博物馆 Liuzhou Museum	1979 年 11 月 26 日在柳州地区废品三仓拣选 Collected at Liuzhou the Third Waste Storage on November, 26th, 1979	鼓面：太阳纹（12 芒）、西字纹、S 形云纹、乳钉纹、游旗纹、栉纹、兽形云纹； 鼓身：乳钉纹、回形雷纹、如意云纹、栉纹、云纹、复线角形纹；扁耳两对饰辫纹、回形雷纹 Drum face: patterns of sun(12rays), 西 -character, S-shape cloud, nipple protrusion, flying flag, comb line, beast-shape cloud; Drum body: patterns of nipple protrusion, 回 - shape thunder, Ruyi-shape cloud, comb line, cloud, double line triangle; Braids and 回 - shape thunder on 2 pairs of flat handles.	47	27	麻江型 Majiang Type	

序号 NO.	原编号及鼓名 Stock Number & Name	收藏单位 Museum	出土（征集）时间、地点 Time & Spot for discovered or collected	主要装饰 Main Decorations	尺寸（厘米）Size(cm)		类型 Type	图片 Picture
					面径 Face Diameter	身高 Height		
416	Hg00020 号 明游旗纹铜鼓 No.Hg00020 Ming Dynasty Bronze Drum with flying flag patterns	柳州市博物馆 Liuzhou Museum	1979 年 11 月 26 日在柳州地区废品三仓拣选 Collected at Liuzhou the Third Waste Storage on November, 26th, 1979	鼓面：太阳纹（12 芒），乳钉纹、栉纹、游旗纹、云纹、S 形云纹、蝉纹；鼓身：四出钱纹、乳钉纹、云纹、三角纹间四方纹、蝉纹、回形雷纹、栉纹、复线角形纹；扁耳两对饰辫纹 Drum face: patterns of sun(12rays), nipple protrusion, straight line, flying flag, cloud, S-shape cloud, cicada; Drum body: patterns of coin with quadrangle inside, nipple protrusion, cloud, triangle mixed quadrangle inside, cicada, 回 - shape thunder, comb line, double line triangle; Braids on 2 pairs of flat handles.	46.9~47.2	29	麻江型 Majiang Type	
417	Hg00021 号 东汉观斗蛙变形羽人纹铜鼓（原武宣 I 号鼓）No.Hg00021 The Eastern Han Dynasty Bronze Drum with transformed feathermen patterns and statues of frog-fight watching(Former name:WuXuan NO.1)	柳州市博物馆 Liuzhou Museum	1966 年出土于武宣县车渡码头 Unearthed at Dock Chedu, Wuxuan County in 1966	鼓面：太阳纹（12 芒），水波纹、栉纹、同心圆纹、复线交叉纹、叶脉纹、变形羽人纹、变形翔鹭纹、眼纹，鼓面边缘饰四只逆时针四足立体素面青蛙，蛙间各饰一组观斗蛙立体装饰；鼓身：水波纹、栉纹、同心圆纹、叶脉纹、变形船纹、变形羽人纹、网纹、圆心垂叶纹、眼纹；扁耳两对饰辫纹 Drum face: patterns of sun(12rays), water wave, comb line, concentric circles, crossed double lines, leaf vein, transformed feathermen, transformed flying heron, diamond-shape eye; 4 frog statues of 4 feet with plain back anticlockwise stand on the edge of drum face; Statues of frog-fight watching between the frogs; Drum body: patterns of water wave, comb line, concentric circles, leaf vein, boat, transformed feathermen, net, leaf-shape triangle with concentric circles in the middle, diamond-shape eye; Braids pattern on 2 pairs of flat handles.	89~89.5	66	冷水冲型 Lengshuichong Type	

续表

序号 N0.	原编号及鼓名 Stock Number & Name	收藏单位 Museum	出土（征集） 时间、地点 Time & Spot for discovered or collected	主要装饰 Main Decorations	尺寸（厘米） Size(cm)		类型 Type	图片 Picture
					面径 Face Diameter	身高 Height		
418	Hg00022 号 乘骑铜鼓 II No.Hg00022 Bronze Drum with horse-ride statue II	柳州市博 物馆 Liuzhou Museum	1973 年出土于武 宣县通挽乡龙鹏 村 Unearthed at Longpeng Village, Tongwan, Wuxuan County in 1973	鼓面大部缺失，边沿饰一乘骑立体 装饰； 鼓身：叶脉纹、同心圆纹、变形船纹、 水波纹、变形羽人纹、网纹、圆心 垂叶纹、眼纹；扁耳两对饰辫纹 Most part of the face was lost, only a statue of horse-riding was remained; Drum body: patterns of leaf vein, concentric circles, boat, transformed feathermen, water wave, net, leaf-shape triangle with concentric circles in the middle, diamond-shape eye; braids pattern on 2 pairs of flat handles.	82.5	56.5	冷水冲 型 Lengshui- chong Type	
419	Hg00023 号 清异形游旗纹 铜鼓 No.Hg00023 Qing Dynasty Bronze Drum with transformed flying flag patterns	柳州市博 物馆 Liuzhou Museum	1980 年 3 月 28 日在柳州市黄村 居民家中征集 Collected at the house of a villager of Huang Village, Liuzhou City on March 28th, 1980	鼓面：太阳纹（12 芒）、同心圆纹、 乳钉纹、栉纹、异形游旗纹、羽纹、 绚纹； 鼓身：乳钉纹、绚纹、复线角形纹； 扁耳两对饰辫纹 Drum face: patterns of sun(12rays), concentric circles, nipple protrusion, comb line, transformed flying flag, feather, twisted rope; Drum body: patterns of nipple protrusion, twisted rope, double line triangle; braids on 2 pairs of flat handles.	49	28.5	麻江型 Majiang Type	
420	Hg00024 号 清游旗纹铜鼓 No.Hg00024 Qing Dynasty Bronze Drum with flying flag patterns	柳州市博 物馆 Liuzhou Museum	1965 年征集于柳 州市五里卡废旧 仓库 Collected at Liuzhou Wulika Waste Storage in 1965	鼓面：太阳纹（12 芒）、酉字纹、 S 形云纹、乳钉纹、游旗纹、兽面 云纹； 鼓身：乳钉纹、回形雷纹、如意云 纹、栉纹、云纹、复线角形纹；扁 耳两对饰辫纹、回形雷纹 Drum face: patterns of sun(12rays), 酉 -character, S-shape cloud, nipple protrusion, flying flag, beast face cloud; Drum body: patterns of nipple protrusion, 回 -shape thunder, Ruyi-shape cloud, comb line, cloud, double line triangle; Braids and 回 -shape thunder on 2 pairs of flat handles.	47	27	麻江型 Majiang Type	

序号 N0.	原编号及鼓名 Stock Number & Name	收藏单位 Museum	出土（征集） 时间、地点 Time & Spot for discovered or collected	主要装饰 Main Decorations	尺寸（厘米） Size(cm)		类型 Type	图片 Picture
					面径 Face Diameter	身高 Height		
421	Hg00025 号 东汉大铜鼓 No.Hg00025 East-han Dynasty Bronze Drum in big size	柳州市博物馆 Liuzhou Museum	1983 年 1 月 26 日在柳州市跃进路废旧门市部拣选 Collected at waste shop on Yuejin Road, Liuzhou City on January 26th, 1983	鼓面：太阳纹（12 芒），栉纹、同心圆纹、复线交叉纹、变形羽人纹、变形翔鹭纹间定胜纹，鼓面边缘饰四只逆时针四足素面立体青蛙（缺失）； 鼓身：栉纹、同心圆纹、栉纹同心圆纹垂直纹带、圆心三角垂叶纹；扁耳两对饰辫纹 Drum face: patterns of sun(12rays), comb line, concentric circles, crossed double lines, transformed feathermen, transformed flying heron mixed Dingsheng; 4 frog statues of 4 feet with plain back anticlockwise stand on the edge of drum face; Drum body: patterns of comb line, concentric circles, vertical ribbon with straight line and concentric circles, leaf-shape triangle with concentric circles in the middle; Braids pattern on 2 pairs of flat handles.	64.2~64.5	42	冷水冲型 Lengshui-chong Type	
422	Hg00026 清游旗纹铜鼓 No.Hg00026 Qing Dynasty Bronze Drum with flying flag patterns	柳州市博物馆 Liuzhou Museum	1986 年 10 月 8 日在河池地区土产公司水洞仓库拣选 Collected at Shuidong Storage of Hechi Local Product Company on October 8th, 1986	鼓面：太阳纹（12 芒），西字纹、S 形云纹、乳钉纹、游旗纹、栉纹、兽形云纹； 鼓身：乳钉纹、回形雷纹、如意云纹、栉纹、云纹、复线角形纹；扁耳两对饰辫纹 Drum face: patterns of sun(12rays), 西 -character, S-shape cloud, nipple protrusion, flying flag, comb line, beast-shape cloud; Drum body: patterns of nipple protrusion, 回 -shape thunder, Ruyi-shape cloud, comb line, cloud, double line triangle; Braids on 2 pairs of flat handles.	47	26	麻江型 Majiang Type	

续表

序号 NO.	原编号及鼓名 Stock Number & Name	收藏单位 Museum	出土（征集）时间、地点 Time & Spot for discovered or collected	主要装饰 Main Decorations	尺寸（厘米）Size(cm)		类型 Type	图片 Picture
					面径 Face Diameter	身高 Height		
423	Hg00027 号 南宋异型游旗纹铜鼓 No.Hg00027 South-Song Dynasty Bronze Drum with flying flag patterns in abnormal shape	柳州市博物馆 Liuzhou Museum	1986 年 10 月 8 日在河池地区土产公司水洞仓库拣选 Collected at Shuidong Storage of Hechi Local Product Company on October 8th, 1986	鼓面：太阳纹（12 芒），乳钉纹、菱形填四瓣花纹、异形游旗纹、乍字图案纹；鼓身：乳钉纹、菱形填四瓣花纹、雷纹、回形雷纹、羽纹、复线角形纹；扁耳两对饰辫纹 Drum face: patterns of sun(12rays), nipple protrusion, double-line diamond mixed quatrefoil, flying flag in abnormal shape, 乍 -character mixed thunder; Drum body: patterns of nipple protrusion, double-line diamond mixed quatrefoil, thunder, 回 -shape thunder, feather, double-line triangle; braids on 2 pairs of flat handles.	47.2	26.5	麻江型 Majiang Type	
424	Hg00028 号 明游旗纹铜鼓 No.Hg00028 Ming Dynasty Bronze Drum with flying flag patterns	柳州市博物馆 Liuzhou Museum	1990 年 9 月 10 日在柳州市金融回收公司跃进仓库拣选 Collected at Yuejin Storage of Liuzhou Financial Recycle Company on September 10th, 1990	鼓面：太阳纹（12 芒），西字纹、梳纹、乳钉纹、游旗纹、云纹；鼓身：乳钉纹、梳纹、云纹、回形雷纹、缠枝纹、复线角形纹；扁耳两对饰凸棱纹 Drum face: patterns of sun(12rays), 西 -character, comb line, nipple protrusion, flying flag, cloud; Drum body: patterns of nipple protrusion, comb line, cloud, 回 -shape thunder, twisted branches, double line triangle; Raise ridges on 2 pairs of flat handles.	50	31	麻江型 Majiang Type	
425	Hg00029 号 清波浪纹铜鼓 No.Hg00029 Qing Dynasty Bronze Drum with water wave pattern	柳州市博物馆 Liuzhou Museum	1996 年 9 月 22 日征集于广西鹿寨县凤凰街 Collected at Fenghuang Street, Luzhai County, Guangxi on September 22nd, 1996	鼓面：太阳纹（12 芒），乳钉纹、缠枝纹、回形雷纹、波浪纹；鼓身：乳钉纹、回形雷纹、缠枝纹、波浪纹、复线角形纹；扁耳两对饰凸棱纹 Drum face: patterns of sun(12rays), nipple protrusion, twisted branches, 回 -shape thunder, water wave; Drum body: patterns of nipple protrusion, 回 -shape thunder, twisted branches, water wave, double line triangle; Raise ridges on 2 pairs of flat handles.	47.6 - 47.8	27	麻江型 Majiang Type	

序号 NO.	原编号及鼓名 Stock Number & Name	收藏单位 Museum	出土（征集）时间、地点 Time & Spot for discovered or collected	主要装饰 Main Decorations	尺寸（厘米）Size(cm)		类型 Type	图片 Picture
					面径 Face Diameter	身高 Height		
426	Hg00030 号 清水鸟夹定胜纹铜鼓 No.Hg00030 Qing Dynasty Bronze Drum with waterfowl& Dingsheng patterns	柳州市博物馆 Liuzhou Museum	1996 年 10 月 9 日征集于广西南丹县三口林场 Collected at Sankou Forest Farm, Nandan County, Guangxi on October 9th, 1996	鼓面：太阳纹（12 芒）、乳钉纹、蝉纹、水鸟纹间定胜纹、栉纹；鼓身：栉纹、乳钉纹、回形雷纹、锚形纹、复线角形纹；扁耳两对饰辫纹、回形雷纹 Drum face: patterns of sun(12rays), nipple protrusion, cicada, waterfowl mixed Dingsheng, comb line; Drum body: patterns of comb line, nipple protrusion, 回-shape thunder, anchor, double line triangle; Braids and 回-shape thunder on 2 pairs of flat handles.	47.6	28.5	麻江型 Majiang Type	
427	Hg00031 号 鱼龙纹变形游旗纹铜鼓 No.Hg00031 Bronze Drum with fish, dragon and transformed flying flag patterns	柳州市博物馆 Liuzhou Museum	1997 年 1 月日征集于广西南丹县三口林场 Collected at Sankou Forest Farm, Nandan County, Guangxi in January, 1997	鼓面：太阳纹（12 芒）、同心圆纹、乳钉纹、变形游旗纹、回形雷纹、变体雷纹、鱼龙纹；鼓身：乳钉纹、同心圆纹、回形雷纹、兽形云纹、图案三角纹；扁耳两对饰辫纹、云纹、雷纹 Drum face: patterns of sun(12rays), concentric circles, nipple protrusion, transformed flying flag, 回-shape thunder, transformed thunder, fish& dragon; Drum body: patterns of nipple protrusion, concentric circles, 回-shape thunder, beast-shape cloud, patterning triangle; Braid, cloud and thunder patterns on 2 pairs of flat handles.	36.2-36.5	26.5	麻江型 Majiang Type	
428	Hg00032 号 隋唐灵山型铜鼓 No.Hg00032 Sui & Tang Dynasty Bronze Drum of Lingshan Type	柳州市博物馆 Liuzhou Museum	1997 年 4 月 21 日柳州市阳羊实业有限公司出售，据传横县捞沙所得 Sold by Liuzhou Yangyang Industry Corporation on April 21st, 1997, said it was gained during a sand salvage in Heng County	鼓面：太阳纹（10 芒）、蝉纹、雷纹、鸟形纹、四瓣花纹、连钱纹、四出钱纹、兽形纹、席纹、兽面纹，鼓面边缘饰六组逆时针三足立体青蛙（缺失）；鼓身：蝉纹、连钱纹、四出钱纹、鸟形纹、雷纹、雷纹填线纹、虫形纹、兽形纹、席纹；扁耳两对饰辫纹 Drum face: patterns of sun(10 rays), cicada, thunder, bird, quatrefoil, coins part of overlap, coin with quadrangle inside, beast-shape motif, woven mat, beast face; 6 frogs with 3 feet anticlockwise stand on the edge(lost); Drum body: patterns of cicada, coins part of overlap, coin with quadrangle inside, bird-shape motif, thunder, thunder filled with straight line, insect-shape motif, beast-shape motif, woven mat; Braid patterns on 2 pairs of flat handles.	80.2-80.5	48.4	灵山型 Lingshan Type	

序号 NO.	原编号及鼓名 Stock Number & Name	收藏单位 Museum	出土（征集）时间、地点 Time & Spot for discovered or collected	主要装饰 Main Decorations	尺寸（厘米）Size(cm)		类型 Type	图片 Picture
					面径 Face Diameter	身高 Height		
429	Hg00033 号 清人物纹牛纹水鸟符箓纹铜鼓 No.Hg00033 Qing Dynasty Bronze Drum with man ox and waterfowl patterns	柳州市博物馆 Liuzhou Museum	1998 年 1 月 6 日征集于广西南丹县 Collected in Nandan County, Guangxi on January 6th, 1998	鼓面：太阳纹（12 芒），回形雷纹、S 形云纹、乳钉纹、人物纹牛纹水鸟符箓纹、兽形云纹；鼓身：乳钉纹、如意云纹、回形雷纹、复线角形纹；扁耳两对 Drum face: patterns of sun(12rays), 回 -shape thunder, S-shape cloud, nipple protrusion, man, ox and waterfowl, beast-shape cloud; Drum body: patterns of nipple protrusion, Ruyi-shape cloud, 回 -shape thunder, double line triangle;2 pairs of flat handles.	44.2–44.4	25.5	麻江型 Majiang Type	
430	Hg00034 号 清游旗纹铜鼓 No.Hg00034 Qing Dynasty Bronze Drum with flying flag pattern	柳州市博物馆 Liuzhou Museum	2005 年 10 月 12 日柳州市民出售 Collected from a citizen in Liuzhou on October 12th, 2005	鼓面：太阳纹（12 芒），西字纹、S 形云纹、乳钉纹、栉纹、游旗纹、兽形云纹；鼓身：乳钉纹、雷纹、复线交叉纹、回形雷纹、图案三角纹；扁耳两对饰辫纹 Drum face: patterns of sun(12rays), 西 -character, S-shape cloud, nipple protrusion, comb line, flying flag, cloud; Drum body: patterns of nipple protrusion, thunder, crossed double lines, 回 -shape thunder, patterning triangle; Braids on 2 pairs of flat handles.	46	27.5	麻江型 Majiang Type	
431	Hg00035 号 清龙纹游旗纹铜鼓 No.Hg00035 Qing Dynasty Bronze Drum with dragon and flying flag patterns	柳州市博物馆 Liuzhou Museum	2006 年 12 月 22 日柳州市民出售 Collected from a citizen in Liuzhou on December 22nd, 2006	鼓面：太阳纹（12 芒），同心圆纹、兽形云纹、乳钉纹、缠枝纹、游旗纹、双龙戏珠纹；鼓身：乳钉纹、雷纹、回形雷纹、栉纹、缠枝纹、复线角形纹；扁耳两对饰辫纹 Drum face: patterns of sun(12rays), concentric circle, cloud, nipple protrusion, twisted branches, flying flag, 2 dragons playing with pearl; Drum body: patterns of nipple protrusion, thunder, 回 -shape thunder, comb line, twisted branches, double line triangle; Braids on 2 pairs of flat handles.	55–55.3	29.5	麻江型 Majiang Type	

续表

序号 NO.	原编号及鼓名 Stock Number & Name	收藏单位 Museum	出土（征集） 时间、地点 Time & Spot for discovered or collected	主要装饰 Main Decorations	尺寸（厘米） Size(cm)		类型 Type	图片 Picture
					面径 Face Diameter	身高 Height		
432	Hg00036 号 清十二生肖纹 铜鼓 No.Hg00036 Qing Dynasty Bronze Drum with zodiac patterns	柳州市博物馆 Liuzhou Museum	2008 年 3 月 4 日 征集于广西环江 Collected in Huanjiang County, Guangxi on March 4th, 2008	鼓面：太阳纹（12 芒），酉字纹、兽形云纹、乳钉纹、栉纹、游旗纹、十二生肖纹、雷纹； 鼓身：乳钉纹、同心圆纹、云纹、雷纹、波浪纹、回形雷纹、复线角形纹；扁耳两对饰辫纹 Drum face: patterns of sun(12rays), 酉 -character, cloud, nipple protrusion, comb line, flying flag, zodiac, thunder; Drum body: patterns of nipple protrusion, concentric circle, cloud, thunder, water wave, 回 -shape thunder, double line triangle; Braids on 2 pairs of flat handles.	51.5	29.5	麻江型 Majiang Type	
433	Hg00037 号 清龙纹游旗纹 铜鼓 No.Hg00037 Qing Dynasty Bronze Drum with dragon and flying flag	柳州市博物馆 Liuzhou Museum	2008 年 3 月 4 日 征集于广西环江 Collected in Huanjiang County, Guangxi on March 4th, 2008	鼓面：太阳纹（12 芒），酉字纹、兽形云纹、乳钉纹、雷纹、游旗纹、双龙献寿、牛耕、荷耙人、鹤组合图案； 鼓身：梅花状乳钉纹、云纹、雷纹、回形雷纹、栉纹、复线角形纹；鼓面内壁有铭文印章；扁耳两对饰辫纹 Drum face: patterns of sun(12rays), 酉 -character, cloud, nipple protrusion, thunder, flying flag, complex motif(including 2dragons with 寿 -character, man-plough by using a cattle, hoers, crane); Drum body: patterns of nipple protrusion, cloud, thunder, 回 -shape thunder, comb line, double line triangle; A pair of stamps inside the drum; Braids on 2 pairs of flat handles.	51.8−52	27	麻江型 Majiang Type	
434	Hg00038 号 东汉立蛙铜鼓 No.Hg00038 East-Han Dynasty Bronze Drum with frog statues	柳州市博物馆 Liuzhou Museum	2008 年 3 月 7 日 征集 Collected on March 7th, 2008	鼓面：太阳纹（7 芒），栉纹、同心圆纹、雷纹、变形羽人纹、鸟纹、定胜纹、菱形纹，鼓面边缘饰四只逆时针四足素面立体青蛙； 鼓身：栉纹、同心圆纹，鼓足饰三角垂叶纹；扁耳两对饰辫纹 Drum face: patterns of sun(7rays), comb line, concentric circles, thunder, transformed feathermen, bird, Dingsheng, diamond; 4 frog statues of 4 feet and plain back anticlockwise stand on the edge of drum face; Drum body: patterns of comb line, concentric circles, leaf-shape triangle on the foot; Braids pattern on 2 pairs of flat handles.	43−43.5	28	西盟型 Ximeng Type	

续表

序号 NO.	原编号及鼓名 Stock Number & Name	收藏单位 Museum	出土（征集） 时间、地点 Time & Spot for discovered or collected	主要装饰 Main Decorations	尺寸（厘米） Size(cm)		类型 Type	图片 Picture
					面径 Face Diameter	身高 Height		
435	总 193 号 苗族铜鼓 No.193 Bronze Drum Of Miao Minorities	融水苗族自治县博物馆 Rongshui Miao Autonomous County Museum	80 年代征集于广西融水县 Collected in Rongshui County, Guangxi in 1980s'	鼓面：太阳纹（12 芒）、酉字纹、S 形云纹、乳钉纹、游旗纹、栉纹、兽形云纹、卦纹； 鼓身：乳钉纹、回形雷纹、如意云纹、栉纹、复线角形纹；扁耳两对饰辫纹、回形雷纹 Drum face: patterns of sun(12rays), 酉 -character, S-shape cloud, nipple protrusion, flying flag, comb line, beast face, divinatory symbol pattern; Drum body: patterns of nipple protrusion, 回 -shape thunder, Ruyi-shape cloud, comb line, double line triangle; Braid and 回 -shape thunder on 2 pairs of flat handles.	48	27.5	麻江型 Majiang Type	
436	总 194 号 苗族铜鼓 No.194 Bronze Drum Of Miao Minorities	融水苗族自治县博物馆 Rongshui Miao Autonomous County Museum	80 年代广西融水县物资局征集 Collected by Guangxi Rongshui County Material Bureau in 1980s'	鼓面：太阳纹（12 芒）、S 形云纹、乳钉纹、游旗纹、栉纹、云纹； 鼓身：乳钉纹、如意云纹、栉纹、S 形云纹、回形雷纹、复线角形纹；扁耳两对饰辫纹、弦纹 Drum face: patterns of sun(12rays), S-shape cloud, nipple protrusion, flying flag, comb line, cloud; Drum body: patterns of nipple protrusion, cloud, Ruyi-shape cloud, comb line, S-shape cloud, 回 -shape thunder, double line triangle; Braid and strings on 2 pairs of flat handles.	49–49.2	30.5	麻江型 Majiang Type	
437	总 476 号 苗族铜鼓 No.476 Bronze Drum Of Miao Minorities	融水苗族自治县博物馆 Rongshui Miao Autonomous County Museum	80 年代征集于广西融水县三防镇 Collected in Sanfang Town, Rongshui County, Guangxi in 1980s'	鼓面：太阳纹（12 芒）、酉字纹、S 形云纹、乳钉纹、栉纹、游旗纹、云纹； 鼓身：乳钉纹、云纹、如意云纹、栉纹、回形雷纹、复线角形纹；扁耳两对饰辫纹、回形雷纹 Drum face: patterns of sun(12rays), 酉 -character, S-shape cloud, nipple protrusion, comb line, flying flag, cloud; Drum body: patterns of nipple protrusion, cloud, Ruyi-shape cloud, comb line, 回 -shape thunder, double line triangle; Braid and 回 -shape thunder on 2 pairs of flat handles.	48.2–48.4	22.4	麻江型 Majiang Type	

序号 N0.	原编号及鼓名 Stock Number & Name	收藏单位 Museum	出土（征集）时间、地点 Time & Spot for discovered or collected	主要装饰 Main Decorations	尺寸（厘米）Size(cm)		类型 Type	图片 Picture
					面径 Face Diameter	身高 Height		
438	游旗纹小铜鼓 Bronze Drum with flying flag patterns in small size	融水苗族自治县博物馆 Rongshui Miao Autonomous County Museum	90 年代广西融水县志办移交 Transferred by Guangxi Rongshui County Annals Office in 1990s'	鼓面：太阳纹（12 芒），S 形云纹、乳钉纹、游旗纹、回形雷纹；鼓身：乳钉纹、回形雷纹、四出钱纹、复线三角纹；鼓面内壁有双龙戏珠、鸟、鱼、蝴蝶、人骑牛、树、翎眼、回形雷、桥、人物、房屋、牛、钉耙、谷仓、荷耙人等组合图案纹饰；扁耳两对饰辫纹 Drum face: patterns of sun(12rays), S-shape cloud, nipple protrusion, flying flag, 回-shape thunder; Drum body: patterns of nipple protrusion, 回-shape thunder, coins with quadrangle inside, double line triangle; a complex motifs on the reverse side of drum face(including 2 dragons play with a pearl, bird, fish, butterfly, cattle rider, tree, peacock feather, 回-shape thunder, bridge, person, house, cattle, harrow, garner, hoer); Braids pattern on 2 pairs of flat handles.	32.6—32.9	19.2	麻江型 Majiang Type	
439	总 086 号 拉尧屯铜鼓 No:086 Bronze Drum Larao tun	柳江县文物管理所 Liujiang County Cultural Relics Administration	1980 年 7 月 25 日出土于广西柳江县百朋乡镇西村拉尧屯南 5 公里处 Unearthed in the south of 5km to Larao Tun, Zhenxi Village, Baipeng, Liujiang County, Guangxi on July 25th, 1980	鼓面：太阳纹（12 芒）、栉纹、同心圆纹、复线交叉纹、变形羽人纹、变形翔鹭纹间定胜纹、羽纹、鼓面边缘饰四只逆时针四足立体青蛙；鼓身：羽纹、同心圆纹、栉纹同心圆纹垂直纹带、圆心垂叶纹；扁耳两对饰辫纹 Drum face: patterns of sun(12rays), comb line, concentric circles, crossed double lines, transformed feathermen, flying heron mixed Dingsheng, feather; 4 frog statues of 4 feet anticlockwise stand on the edge of drum face; Drum body: patterns of feather, concentric circles, vertical ribbon with straight line and concentric circles, leaf-shape triangle with concentric circles in the middle; Braids pattern on 2 pairs of flat handles.	81.5—81.6	55.7	冷水冲型 Lengshui-chong Type	

序号 NO.	原编号及鼓名 Stock Number & Name	收藏单位 Museum	出土（征集） 时间、地点 Time & Spot for discovered or collected	主要装饰 Main Decorations	尺寸（厘米） Size(cm)		类型 Type	图片 Picture
					面径 Face Diameter	身高 Height		
440	总110号 流塘村铜鼓 No:110 Bronze Drum Liutangcun	柳江县文物管理所 Liujiang County Cultural Relics Administration	1993年出土于广西柳江县流山乡流塘村 Unearthed at Liutang Village, Liushan, Liujiang County, Guangxi in 1993	鼓面：太阳纹（12芒），水波纹、同心圆纹、栉纹、复线交叉纹、叶脉纹、变形羽人纹、变形翔鹭纹、眼纹，鼓面边缘饰四只逆时针辫纹四足立体青蛙，蛙间各饰一组乘骑立饰； 鼓身：水波纹、叶脉纹、同心圆纹、栉纹、变形船纹、变形羽人纹、网纹、圆心垂叶纹；扁耳两对饰辫纹 Drum face: patterns of sun(12rays), water wave, concentric circles, comb line, crossed double lines, leaf vein, transformed feathermen, transformed flying heron, diamond-shape eye; 4 frog statues of 4 feet and braids on back anticlockwise stand on the edge of drum face; 2 groups of horse-ride statues between the frogs; Drum body: patterns of water wave, leaf vein, concentric circles, comb line, boat, transformed feathermen, net, leaf-shape triangle with concentric circles in the middle; Braids pattern on 2 pairs of flat handles.	65.2−65.6	48	冷水冲型 Lengshui-chong Type	
441	古罗屯铜鼓 （残片） Bronze Drum Guluo tun (Pieces)	鹿寨县文物管理所 Luzhai County Cultural Relics Administration	1986年秋出土于广西鹿寨县拉沟乡背塘村古罗屯 Unearthed at Guluo Tun, Beitang Village, Lagou, Luzhai County, Guangxi in autumn of 1986	仅存鼓面残片，饰太阳纹8芒，栉纹、圆圈纹 Only part of the drum face with 3 strings of motifs is remained： sun(8 rays), comb line, circles.			冷水冲型 Lengshui-chong Type	
442	麻盖岭铜鼓 （残片） Bronze Drum Magailing (Pieces)	鹿寨县文物管理所 Luzhai County Cultural Relics Administration	1997年4月22日出土于广西鹿寨县四排乡那当村桂兰屯麻盖岭 Unearthed at Magai Ling, Guilan Tun, Nadang Village, Sipai, Luzhai County, Guangxi on April 22nd, 1997	仅存鼓面残片，饰太阳纹12芒，栉纹、切线同心圆纹、变形羽人纹、变形翔鹭纹间定胜纹，鼓面边缘立体青蛙已缺失 Only the drum face is remained： sun(12rays), comb line, tangent concentric circles, transformed feathermen, transformed flying herons mixed Dingshengs; 4 frog statues of 4 feet anticlockwise stand on the edge of drum face(lost).	47		冷水冲型 Lengshui-chong Type	

序号 N0.	原编号及鼓名 Stock Number & Name	收藏单位 Museum	出土（征集）时间、地点 Time & Spot for discovered or collected	主要装饰 Main Decorations	尺寸（厘米）Size(cm)		类型 Type	图片 Picture
					面径 Face Diameter	身高 Height		
443	广崖山铜鼓 Bronze Drum Guangyashan	鹿寨县文物管理所 Luzhai County Cultural Relics Administration	1985 年出土于广西鹿寨县中渡镇广崖山 Unearthed at Guangya Hill, Zhongdu Town, Luzhai County, Guangxi in 1985	鼓面：太阳纹（12 芒）、水波纹、栉纹、同心圆纹、复线交叉纹、叶脉纹、变形羽人纹、变形翔鹭纹、眼纹，鼓面边缘饰四只逆时针四足立体青蛙，蛙间各饰一组乘骑立饰；鼓身：叶脉纹、同心圆纹、变形船纹、变形羽人纹、水波纹、网纹、圆心垂叶纹；扁耳两对饰辫纹 Drum face: patterns of sun(12rays), water wave, comb line, concentric circles, crossed double lines, leaf vein, transformed feathermen, transformed flying heron, diamond-shape eye; 4 frog statues of 4 feet anticlockwise stand on the edge of drum face; 2 groups of horse-ride statues between the frogs; Drum body: patterns of leaf vein, concentric circles, boat, water wave, net, leaf-shape triangle with concentric circles in the middle; Braids pattern on 2 pairs of flat handles.	65.5—68.5	45（残）Incomplete	冷水冲型 Lengshuichong Type	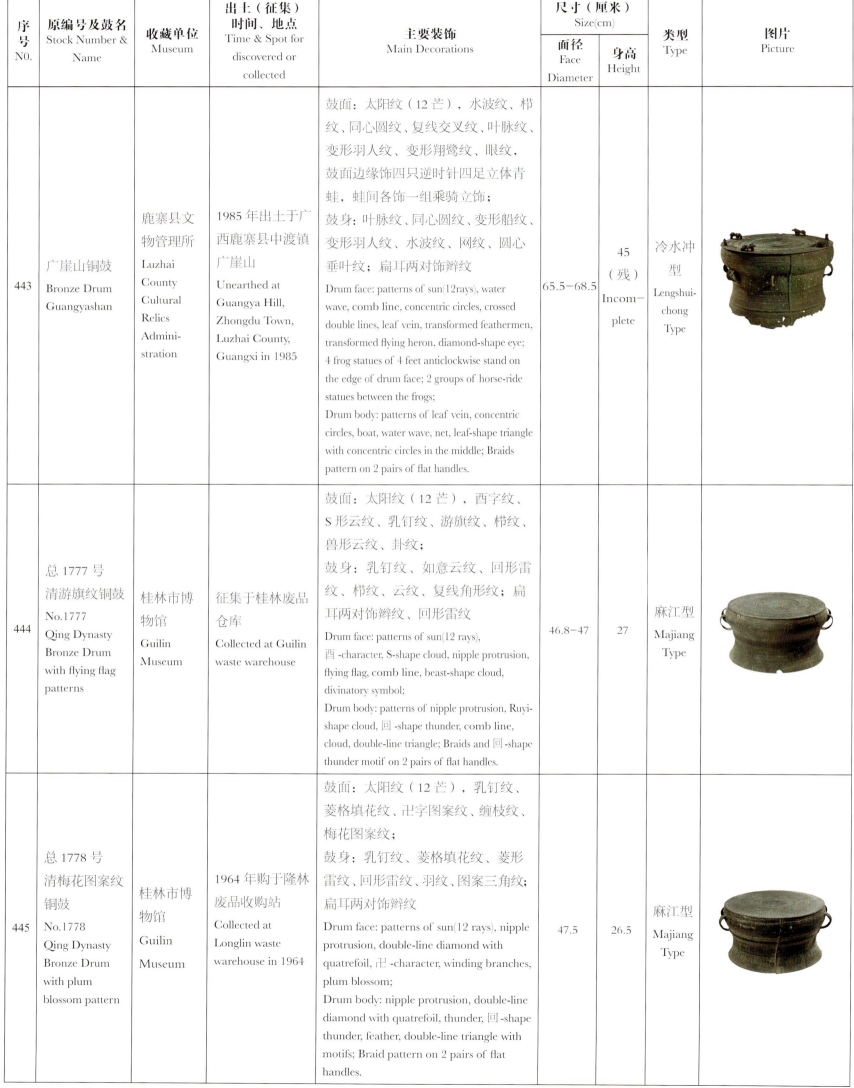
444	总 1777 号 清游旗纹铜鼓 No.1777 Qing Dynasty Bronze Drum with flying flag patterns	桂林市博物馆 Guilin Museum	征集于桂林废品仓库 Collected at Guilin waste warehouse	鼓面：太阳纹（12 芒）、西字纹、S 形云纹、乳钉纹、游旗纹、栉纹、兽形云纹、卦纹；鼓身：乳钉纹、如意云纹、回形雷纹、栉纹、云纹、复线角形纹；扁耳两对饰辫纹、回形雷纹 Drum face: patterns of sun(12 rays), 酉 -character, S-shape cloud, nipple protrusion, flying flag, comb line, beast-shape cloud, divinatory symbol; Drum body: patterns of nipple protrusion, Ruyi-shape cloud, 回 -shape thunder, comb line, cloud, double-line triangle; Braids and 回 -shape thunder motif on 2 pairs of flat handles.	46.8—47	27	麻江型 Majiang Type	
445	总 1778 号 清梅花图案纹铜鼓 No.1778 Qing Dynasty Bronze Drum with plum blossom pattern	桂林市博物馆 Guilin Museum	1964 年购于隆林废品收购站 Collected at Longlin waste warehouse in 1964	鼓面：太阳纹（12 芒），乳钉纹、菱格填花纹、卍字图案纹、缠枝纹、梅花图案纹；鼓身：乳钉纹、菱格填花纹、菱形雷纹、回形雷纹、羽纹、图案三角纹；扁耳两对饰辫纹 Drum face: patterns of sun(12 rays), nipple protrusion, double-line diamond with quatrefoil, 卍 -character, winding branches, plum blossom; Drum body: nipple protrusion, double-line diamond with quatrefoil, thunder, 回 -shape thunder, feather, double-line triangle with motifs; Braid pattern on 2 pairs of flat handles.	47.5	26.5	麻江型 Majiang Type	

续表

序号 N0.	原编号及鼓名 Stock Number & Name	收藏单位 Museum	出土（征集）时间、地点 Time & Spot for discovered or collected	主要装饰 Main Decorations	尺寸（厘米）Size(cm)		类型 Type	图片 Picture
					面径 Face Diameter	身高 Height		
446	总 1779 号 清杂宝花草纹铜鼓 No.1779 Qing Dynasty Bronze Drum with treasures and plants pattern	桂林市博物馆 Guilin Museum	1964 年购于隆林废品收购站 Collected at Longlin waste warehouse in 1964	鼓面：太阳纹（12 芒），乳钉纹、狮子滚绣球纹、杂宝纹（蟾蜍、鲤鱼、螃蟹、田螺、乌龟、荷花、宝伞、法轮、法螺）、花草纹（梅花、菊花、水仙）、同心圆纹；鼓身：乳钉纹、绚纹、菱格填花纹、菱形雷纹、回形雷纹、复线角形纹、同心圆纹；扁耳两对饰弦纹 Drum face: patterns of sun(12 rays), nipple protrusion, lion playing embroidered ball, treasures and animals(toad, carp, crab, field snail, tortoise, lotus, and umbrella, wheel, gong as the symbols of Buddhism),flowers(plum blossom, chrysanthemum, narcissus), concentric circles; Drum body: patterns of nipple protrusion, twisted rope, double-line diamond with 十 -character, thunder, 回 -shape thunder, double-line triangle, concentric circle; Straight line pattern on 2 pairs of flat handles.	45.5	25.3	麻江型 Majiang Type	
447	总 1780 号 清弦纹铜鼓 No.1780 Qing Dynasty Bronze Drum with strings	桂林市博物馆 Guilin Museum	1964 年购于隆林废品收购站 Collected at Longlin waste warehouse in 1964	鼓面：太阳纹（12 芒），通体弦纹；扁耳两对饰辫纹 12- ray-sun pattern on the face and other part is straight line; Braid pattern on 2 pairs of flat handles.	45.9－46	25	麻江型 Majiang Type	
448	总 1781 号 游旗纹铜鼓 No.1781 Qing Dynasty Bronze Drum with flying flag patterns	桂林市博物馆 Guilin Museum	1964 年购于隆林废品收购站 Collected at Longlin waste warehouse in 1964	鼓面：太阳纹（12 芒）、西字纹、S 形云纹、乳钉纹、游旗纹、栉纹、兽形云纹、卦纹，鼓面内部有五个铭文印章；鼓身：如意云纹、兽形云纹、乳钉纹、回形雷纹、栉纹、云纹、复线角形纹；Drum face: patterns of sun(12 rays), 酉 -character, S-shape cloud, nipple protrusion, flying flag, comb line, beast-shape cloud, divinatory symbol, and 5 stamps inside; Drum body: patterns of Ruyi-shape cloud, beast-shape cloud, nipple protrusion, 回 -shape thunder, comb line, cloud, double-line triangle.	48	26.5	麻江型 Majiang Type	

序号 N0.	原编号及鼓名 Stock Number & Name	收藏单位 Museum	出土（征集） 时间、地点 Time & Spot for discovered or collected	主要装饰 Main Decorations	尺寸（厘米） Size(cm)		类型 Type	图片 Picture
					面径 Face Diameter	身高 Height		
449	总 1782 号 人物纹鱼纹铜鼓 No.1782 Qing Dynasty Bronze Drum with figures and fishes pattern	桂林市博物馆 Guilin Museum	1964 年购于隆林废品收购站 Collected at Longlin waste warehouse in 1964	鼓面：太阳纹（12 芒），四出钱纹、如意云纹、乳钉纹、人物纹、鱼纹、云纹； 鼓身：乳钉纹、四出钱纹、回形雷纹、如意云纹、云纹、复线角形纹；扁耳两对饰辫纹 Drum face: patterns of sun(12 rays), coins with quadrangle inside, Ruyi-shape cloud, nipple protrusion, figures, fish, cloud; Drum body: patterns of nipple protrusion, coin with quadrangle inside, 回 -shape thunder, Ruyi-shape cloud, cloud, double-line triangle; Braid pattern on 2 pairs of flat handles.	42.8-43	27	麻江型 Majiang Type	
450	总 1783 号 清游旗纹铜鼓 No.1783 Qing Dynasty Bronze Drum with flying flag patterns	桂林市博物馆 Guilin Museum	废品收购站收购 Collected at waste warehouse	鼓面：太阳纹（12 芒），酉字纹、S 形云纹、乳钉纹、游旗纹、栉纹、兽形云纹、卦纹； 鼓身：乳钉纹、回形雷纹、如意云纹、栉纹、云纹、复线角形纹；扁耳两对饰辫纹； Drum face: patterns of sun(12 rays), 酉 -character, S-shape cloud, nipple protrusion, flying flag, comb line, beast-shape cloud, divinatory symbol; Drum body: patterns of nipple protrusion, 回 -shape thunder, Ruyi-shape cloud, comb line, cloud, double-line triangle; Braid pattern on 2 pairs of flat handles.	47	27	麻江型 Majiang Type	
451	总 1784 号 清缠枝纹莲花纹铜鼓 No.1784 Qing Dynasty Bronze Drum with winding lotus branch patterns	桂林市博物馆 Guilin Museum	1964 年购于隆林废品收购站 Collected at Longlin waste warehouse in 1964	鼓面：太阳纹（12 芒），乳钉纹、缠枝纹、莲花纹、梅花图案纹； 鼓身：乳钉纹、菱格填花纹、雷纹、回形雷纹、图案三角纹；扁耳两对饰辫纹 Drum face: patterns of sun(12 rays), nipple protrusion, winding branches, lotus, tortoise's back with plum blossom; Drum body: nipple protrusion, diamond with quatrefoil, thunder, 回 -shape thunder, double-line triangle with motifs inside; Braid pattern on 2 pairs of flat handles.	47.5	26.8	麻江型 Majiang Type	

续表

序号 NO.	原编号及鼓名 Stock Number & Name	收藏单位 Museum	出土（征集）时间、地点 Time & Spot for discovered or collected	主要装饰 Main Decorations	尺寸（厘米） Size(cm) 面径 Face Diameter	身高 Height	类型 Type	图片 Picture
452	总 1785 号 清游旗纹铜鼓 No.1785 Qing Dynasty Bronze Drum with flying flag patterns	桂林市博物馆 Guilin Museum	1964 年购于隆林废品收购站 Collected at Longlin waste warehouse in 1964	鼓面：太阳纹（12 芒），西字纹、S 形云纹、乳钉纹、游旗纹、栉纹、兽形云纹； 鼓身：如意云纹、回形雷纹、栉纹、复线角形纹；扁耳两对饰辫纹、回形雷纹 Drum face: patterns of sun(12 rays), 西 -character, S-shape cloud, nipple protrusion, flying flag, comb line, beast-shape cloud; Drum body: Ruyi-shape cloud, 回 -shape thunder, comb line, double-line triangle; Braid and 回 -shape thunder patterns on 2 pairs of flat handles.	46	25.8	麻江型 Majiang Type	
453	总 1786 号 清游旗纹铜鼓 No.1786 Qing Dynasty Bronze Drum with flying flag patterns	桂林市博物馆 Guilin Museum	1964 年购于隆林废品收购站 Collected at Longlin waste warehouse in 1964	鼓面：太阳纹（12 芒），西字纹、S 形云纹、乳钉纹、栉纹、游旗纹、兽形云纹、卦纹； 鼓身：乳钉纹、如意云纹、回形雷纹、栉纹、复线角形纹；扁耳两对饰辫纹、回形雷纹 Drum face: patterns of sun(12 rays), 西 -character, S-shape cloud, nipple protrusion, comb line, flying flag, beast-shape cloud, divinatory symbol; Drum body: nipple protrusion, Ruyi-shape cloud, 回 -shape thunder, comb line, double-line triangle; Braid and 回 -shape thunder patterns on 2 pairs of flat handles.	50.2－50.4	28.7	麻江型 Majiang Type	
454	总 1787 号 团花纹铜鼓 No.1787 Qing Dynasty Bronze Drum with flower clump patterns	桂林市博物馆 Guilin Museum	1964 年购于隆林废品收购站 Collected at Longlin waste warehouse in 1964	鼓面：太阳纹（12 芒），乳钉纹、水波纹、席纹、团花纹； 鼓身：乳钉纹、如意云纹、回形雷纹、云纹、复线角形纹；扁耳两对饰弦纹 Drum face: patterns of sun(12 rays), nipple protrusion, water wave, mat, flower clumps; Drum body: nipple protrusion, Ruyi-shape cloud, 回 -shape thunder, cloud, double-line triangle; String patterns on 2 pairs of flat handles.	47.7－48	26.8	麻江型 Majiang Type	

序号 NO.	原编号及鼓名 Stock Number & Name	收藏单位 Museum	出土（征集） 时间、地点 Time & Spot for discovered or collected	主要装饰 Main Decorations	尺寸（厘米） Size(cm)		类型 Type	图片 Picture
					面径 Face Diameter	身高 Height		
455	总1788号 清游旗纹铜鼓 No.1788 Qing Dynasty Bronze Drum with flying flag patterns	桂林市博 物馆 Guilin Museum	1982年桂林市文 管会拨交 Allocated by Guilin Cultural Relic Administration in 1982	鼓面：太阳纹（12芒）、乳钉纹、 西字纹、羽纹、游旗纹； 鼓身：乳钉纹、西字纹、羽纹、复 线角形纹；扁耳两对饰辫纹 Drum face: patterns of sun(12 rays), nipple protrusion, 西-character, feather, flying flag; Drum body: nipple protrusion, 西-character, feather, double-line triangle; Braid patterns on 2 pairs of flat handles.	47.5	25.7	麻江型 Majiang Type	
456	总1789号 鸟纹铜鼓 No.1789 Qing Dynasty Bronze Drum with bird pattern	桂林市博 物馆 Guilin Museum	1964年购于隆林 废品收购站 Collected at Longlin waste warehouse in 1964	鼓面：太阳纹（12芒）、四出钱纹、 S形云纹、乳钉纹、鸟纹、如意云纹、 兽形云纹、绚纹； 鼓身：乳钉纹、如意云纹、回形雷 纹、栉纹、复线三角纹；扁耳两对 饰辫纹 Drum face: patterns of sun(12 rays), coin with quadrangle inside, S-shape cloud, nipple protrusion, birds, Ruyi-shape cloud, beast-shape cloud, twisted rope; Drum body: nipple protrusion, Ruyi- shape cloud, 回-shape thunder, comb line, double-line triangle; Braid patterns on 2 pairs of flat handles.	46.2—46.5	24 （残） Incom- plete	麻江型 Majiang Type	
457	总1790号 清游旗纹铜鼓 No.1790 Qing Dynasty Bronze Drum with flying flag patterns	桂林市博 物馆 Guilin Museum	征购于废品收购 站 Collected at waste warehouse	鼓面：太阳纹（12芒）、S形云纹、 乳钉纹、游旗纹、兽形云纹； 鼓身：乳钉纹、如意云纹、回形雷纹、 栉纹、复线角形纹；扁耳两对饰辫纹、 回形雷纹 Drum face: patterns of sun(12 rays), S-shape cloud, nipple protrusion, flying flag, beast-shape cloud; Drum body: nipple protrusion, Ruyi- shape cloud, 回-shape thunder, comb line, double-line triangle; Braid and 回-shape thunder patterns on 2 pairs of flat handles.	46	26.2	麻江型 Majiang Type	

序号 NO.	原编号及鼓名 Stock Number & Name	收藏单位 Museum	出土（征集） 时间、地点 Time & Spot for discovered or collected	主要装饰 Main Decorations	尺寸（厘米） Size(cm)		类型 Type	图片 Picture
					面径 Face Diameter	身高 Height		
458	总 1791 号 清游旗纹铜鼓 No.1791 Qing Dynasty Bronze Drum with flying flag patterns	桂林市博 物馆 Guilin Museum	1964 年购于隆林 废品收购站 Collected at Longlin waste warehouse in 1964	鼓面：太阳纹（12 芒）、西字纹、 S 形云纹、游旗纹、四出钱纹、栉纹、 兽形云纹； 鼓身：乳钉纹、如意云纹、回形雷纹、 栉纹、复线角形纹；扁耳两对饰辫 纹 Drum face: patterns of sun(12 rays), 西 -character, S-shape cloud, flying flag, coin with quadrangle inside, comb line, beast-shape cloud; Drum body: nipple protrusion, Ruyi- shape cloud, 回 -shape thunder, comb line, double-line triangle; Braid patterns on 2 pairs of flat handles.	47	26	麻江型 Majiang Type	
459	总 1792 号 清游旗纹铜鼓 No.1792 Qing Dynasty Bronze Drum with flying flag patterns	桂林市博 物馆 Guilin Museum	1964 年购于隆林 废品收购站 Collected at Longlin waste warehouse in 1964	鼓面：太阳纹（12 芒）、如意云纹、 S 形云纹、乳钉纹、游旗纹、兽形 云纹； 鼓身：乳钉纹、如意云纹、回形雷 纹、栉纹、云纹、复线角形纹；扁 耳两对饰辫纹、回形雷纹 Drum face: patterns of sun(12 rays), Ruyi-shape cloud, S-shape cloud, nipple protrusion, flying flag, beast-shape cloud; Drum body: nipple protrusion, Ruyi-shape cloud, 回 -shape thunder, comb line, cloud, double-line triangle; Braid and 回 -shape thunder patterns on 2 pairs of flat handles.	47-47.3	26.5	麻江型 Majiang Type	
460	总 1793 号 清游旗纹铜鼓 No.1793 Qing Dynasty Bronze Drum with flying flag patterns	桂林市博 物馆 Guilin Museum	1964 年购于隆林 废品收购站 Collected at Longlin waste warehouse in 1964	鼓面：太阳纹（12 芒）、西字纹、 乳钉纹、S 形云纹、游旗纹、栉纹、 兽形云纹； 鼓身：乳钉纹、如意云纹、回形雷 纹、云纹、复线角形纹；扁耳两对 饰辫纹 Drum face: patterns of sun(12 rays), 西 -character, nipple protrusion, S-shape cloud, flying flag, comb line, beast-shape cloud; Drum body: nipple protrusion, Ruyi-shape cloud, 回 -shape thunder, cloud, double- line triangle; Braid patterns on 2 pairs of flat handles.	46	26	麻江型 Majiang Type	

序号 NO.	原编号及鼓名 Stock Number & Name	收藏单位 Museum	出土（征集） 时间、地点 Time & Spot for discovered or collected	主要装饰 Main Decorations	尺寸（厘米） Size(cm)		类型 Type	图片 Picture
					面径 Face Diameter	身高 Height		
461	总 1794 号 清缠枝纹铜鼓 No.1794 Qing Dynasty Bronze Drum with twisted plants pattern	桂林市博物馆 Guilin Museum	1964 年购于隆林废品收购站 Collected at Longlin waste warehouse in 1964	鼓面：太阳纹（12 芒），乳钉纹、缠枝纹、水波纹； 鼓身：通体弦纹，上下部分界处三条突棱；扁耳两对饰弦纹 Drum face: patterns of sun(12 rays), nipple protrusion, twisted plants, water wave; Drum body: only strings, 3 ridges on the boundary of upper and bottom; String patterns on 2 pairs of flat handles.	47.5~47.7	27.5	麻江型 Majiang Type	
462	总 1795 号 清游旗纹铜鼓 No.1795 Qing Dynasty Bronze Drum with flying flag patterns	桂林市博物馆 Guilin Museum	1964 年购于隆林废品收购站 Collected at Longlin waste warehouse in 1964	鼓面：太阳纹（12 芒）、酉字纹、S 形云纹、乳钉纹、游旗纹、栉纹、兽形云纹； 鼓身：乳钉纹、如意云纹、回形雷纹、云纹、复线角形纹；扁耳两对饰辫纹 Drum face: patterns of sun(12 rays), 酉 -character, S-shape cloud, nipple protrusion, flying flag, comb line, beast-shape cloud; Drum body: nipple protrusion, Ruyi-shape cloud, 回 -shape thunder, cloud, double-line triangle; Braid patterns on 2 pairs of flat handles.	47.2~47.4	26.5	麻江型 Majiang Type	
463	总 1796 号 清游旗纹铜鼓 No.1796 Qing Dynasty Bronze Drum with flying flag patterns	桂林市博物馆 Guilin Museum	1982 年桂林市文管会拨交 Allocated by Guilin Cultural Relic Administration in 1982	鼓面：太阳纹（12 芒）、酉字纹、S 形云纹、乳钉纹、游旗纹、栉纹、兽形云纹、卦纹； 鼓身：梅花状乳钉纹、回形雷纹、云纹、栉纹、复线角形纹；扁耳两对饰辫纹、回形雷纹； Drum face: patterns of sun(12 rays), 酉 -character, S-shape cloud, nipple protrusion, flying flag, comb line, beast-shape cloud, divinatory symbol; Drum body: nipple protrusion in plum-blossom shape, 回 -shape thunder, cloud, comb line, double-line triangle; Braid and 回 -shape thunder patterns on 2 pairs of flat handles.	47.5	26.8	麻江型 Majiang Type	

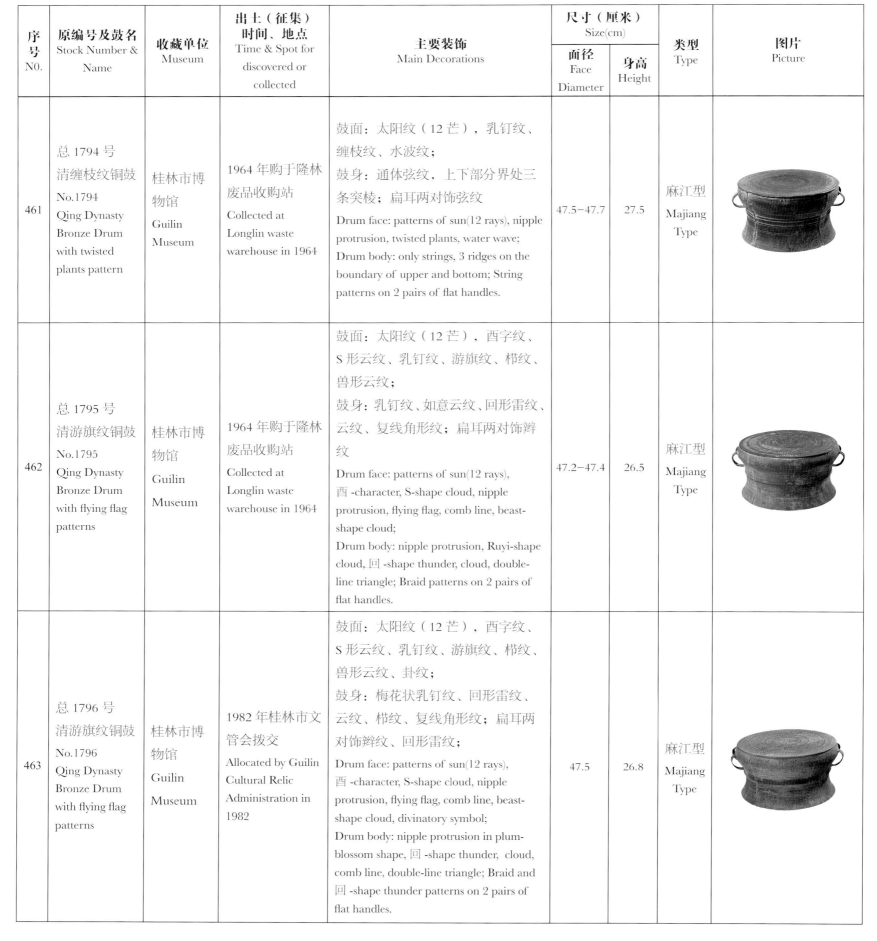

续表

序号 NO.	原编号及鼓名 Stock Number & Name	收藏单位 Museum	出土（征集）时间、地点 Time & Spot for discovered or collected	主要装饰 Main Decorations	尺寸（厘米） Size(cm)		类型 Type	图片 Picture
					面径 Face Diameter	身高 Height		
464	总1797号 游旗纹铜鼓 No.1797 Qing Dynasty Bronze Drum with flying flag patterns	桂林市博物馆 Guilin Museum	不明 Unclear	鼓面：太阳纹（12芒）、西字纹、乳钉纹、游旗纹、如意云纹、回形雷纹； 鼓身：乳钉纹、回形雷纹、如意云纹、复线三角纹；扁耳两对饰回形雷纹 Drum face: patterns of sun(12 rays), 西-character, nipple protrusion, flying flag, Ruyi-shape cloud, 回-shape thunder; Drum body: nipple protrusion, 回-shape thunder, Ruyi-shape cloud, double-line triangle; 回-shape thunder patterns on 2 pairs of flat handles.	49	26.2	麻江型 Majiang Type	
465	总1798号 清团花纹铜鼓 No.1798 Qing Dynasty Bronze Drum with flower clump	桂林市博物馆 Guilin Museum	1982年桂林市文管会拨交 Allocated by Guilin Cultural Relic Administration in 1982	鼓面：太阳纹（12芒）、同心圆纹、回形雷纹、乳钉纹、团花纹； 鼓身：可辨乳钉纹、云纹、回形雷纹、复线角形纹；扁耳两对饰辫纹 Drum face: patterns of sun(12 rays), concentric circle, 回-shape thunder, nipple protrusion, flower clump; Drum body: nipple protrusion, cloud, 回-shape thunder, double-line triangle; Braid patterns on 2 pairs of flat handles.	44.5	25.6	麻江型 Majiang Type	
466	总1799号 清游旗纹铜鼓 No.1799 Qing Dynasty Bronze Drum with flying flag patterns	桂林市博物馆 Guilin Museum	不明 Unclear	鼓面：太阳纹（12芒）、西字纹、S形云纹、乳钉纹、栉纹、游旗纹、兽形云纹； 鼓身：兽形云纹、花枝纹、回形雷纹、云纹、复线角形纹；扁耳两对饰辫纹、回形雷纹 Drum face: patterns of sun(12 rays), 西-character, S-shape cloud, nipple protrusion, comb line, flying flag, Ruyi-shape cloud; Drum body: patterns of Ruyi-shape cloud, plant branch, 回-shape thunder, cloud, double-line triangle; Braid and 回-shape thunder patterns on 2 pairs of flat handles.	51.5~51.7	27.5	麻江型 Majiang Type	

续表

序号 N0.	原编号及鼓名 Stock Number & Name	收藏单位 Museum	出土（征集） 时间、地点 Time & Spot for discovered or collected	主要装饰 Main Decorations	尺寸（厘米） Size(cm)		类型 Type	图片 Picture
					面径 Face Diameter	身高 Height		
467	总 1800 号 清游旗纹铜鼓 No.1800 Qing Dynasty Bronze Drum with flying flag patterns	桂林市博 物馆 Guilin Museum	不明 Unclear	鼓面：太阳纹（12 芒），西字纹、S 形云纹、乳钉纹、游旗纹、栉纹、兽形云纹、卦纹； 鼓身：乳钉纹、回形雷纹、如意云纹、栉纹、云纹、复线角形纹；扁耳两对饰辫纹、回形雷纹 Drum face: patterns of sun(12 rays), 酉 -character, S-shape cloud, nipple protrusion, flying flag, comb line, beast-shape cloud, divinatory symbol; Drum body: patterns of nipple protrusion, 回 -shape thunder, Ruyi-shape cloud, comb line, cloud, double-line triangle; Braid and 回 -shape thunder patterns on 2 pairs of flat handles.	47.5–47.8	26.5	麻江型 Majiang Type	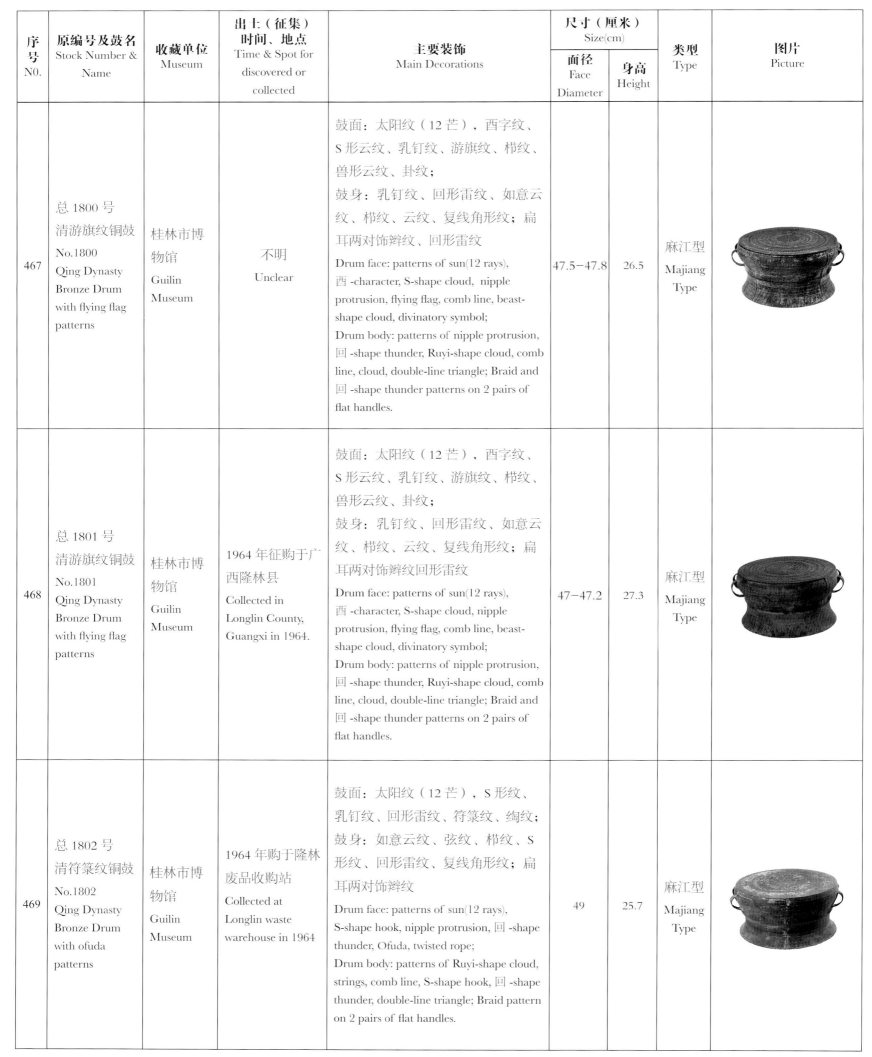
468	总 1801 号 清游旗纹铜鼓 No.1801 Qing Dynasty Bronze Drum with flying flag patterns	桂林市博 物馆 Guilin Museum	1964 年征购于广西隆林县 Collected in Longlin County, Guangxi in 1964.	鼓面：太阳纹（12 芒），西字纹、S 形云纹、乳钉纹、游旗纹、栉纹、兽形云纹、卦纹； 鼓身：乳钉纹、回形雷纹、如意云纹、栉纹、云纹、复线角形纹；扁耳两对饰辫纹回形雷纹 Drum face: patterns of sun(12 rays), 酉 -character, S-shape cloud, nipple protrusion, flying flag, comb line, beast-shape cloud, divinatory symbol; Drum body: patterns of nipple protrusion, 回 -shape thunder, Ruyi-shape cloud, comb line, cloud, double-line triangle; Braid and 回 -shape thunder patterns on 2 pairs of flat handles.	47–47.2	27.3	麻江型 Majiang Type	
469	总 1802 号 清符箓纹铜鼓 No.1802 Qing Dynasty Bronze Drum with ofuda patterns	桂林市博 物馆 Guilin Museum	1964 年购于隆林废品收购站 Collected at Longlin waste warehouse in 1964	鼓面：太阳纹（12 芒），S 形纹、乳钉纹、回形雷纹、符箓纹、绚纹； 鼓身：如意云纹、弦纹、栉纹、S 形纹、回形雷纹、复线角形纹；扁耳两对饰辫纹 Drum face: patterns of sun(12 rays), S-shape hook, nipple protrusion, 回 -shape thunder, Ofuda, twisted rope; Drum body: patterns of Ruyi-shape cloud, strings, comb line, S-shape hook, 回 -shape thunder, double-line triangle; Braid pattern on 2 pairs of flat handles.	49	25.7	麻江型 Majiang Type	

续表

序号 N0.	原编号及鼓名 Stock Number & Name	收藏单位 Museum	出土（征集）时间、地点 Time & Spot for discovered or collected	主要装饰 Main Decorations	尺寸（厘米） Size(cm)		类型 Type	图片 Picture
					面径 Face Diameter	身高 Height		
470	总 1803 号 清游旗纹铜鼓 No.1803 Qing Dynasty Bronze Drum with flying flag patterns	桂林市博物馆 Guilin Museum	1982 年桂林市文管会拨交 Allocated by Guilin Cultural Relic Administration in 1982	鼓面：太阳纹（12 芒）、乳钉纹、酉字纹、S 云纹、游旗纹、云纹； 鼓身：乳钉纹、如意云纹、S 形云纹、回形雷纹，鼓足残缺；扁耳两对饰辫纹 Drum face: patterns of sun(12 rays), nipple protrusion, 酉 -character, S-shape cloud, flying flag, cloud; Drum body: patterns of nipple protrusion, Ruyi-shape cloud, S-shape cloud, 回 -shape thunder, double-line triangle; The foot was lost; Braids pattern on 2 pairs of flat handles.	47	22 （残） Incomplete	麻江型 Majiang Type	
471	总 1804 号 清游旗纹铜鼓 No.1804 Qing Dynasty Bronze Drum with flying flag patterns	桂林市博物馆 Guilin Museum	60 年代征购于广西桂林市 Collected in Guilin in 1960s'	鼓面：太阳纹（12 芒）、酉字纹、S 云纹、乳钉纹、游旗纹、栉纹、兽形云纹、卦纹； 鼓身：乳钉纹、如意云纹、回形雷纹、栉纹、云纹、复线角形纹；扁耳两对饰辫纹 Drum face: patterns of sun(12 rays), 酉 -character, S-shape cloud, nipple protrusion, flying flag, comb line, beast-shape cloud, divinatory symbol; Drum body: patterns of nipple protrusion, Ruyi-shape cloud, 回 -shape thunder, comb line, cloud, double-line triangle; Braid pattern on 2 pairs of flat handles.	48	26.3	麻江型 Majiang Type	
472	总 1805 号 明"王魁"铭符箓纹铜鼓 No.1805 Ming Dynasty Bronze Drum with "王魁" – character and Ofuda patterns	桂林市博物馆 Guilin Museum	1982 年桂林市文管会拨交 Allocated by Guilin Cultural Relic Administration in 1982	鼓面：太阳纹（12 芒）、乳钉纹、栉纹、S 形纹、符箓纹、羽纹、回形雷纹、同心圆纹、云纹、绚纹、铭文（匠人王魁造；正、酒）； 鼓身：乳钉纹、S 形云纹、花枝纹、复线角形纹；扁耳两对饰辫纹 Drum face: patterns of sun(12 rays), nipple protrusion, comb line, S-shape hook, Ofuda, feather, 回 -shape thunder, concentric circle, cloud, twisted rope, characters(name of the maker 王魁 , and characters 正、酒 etc.); Drum body: patterns of nipple protrusion, S-shape cloud, plant branch, double-line triangle; Braid pattern on 2 pairs of flat handles.	49	27.2	麻江型 Majiang Type	

广西铜鼓精华

序号 N0.	原编号及鼓名 Stock Number & Name	收藏单位 Museum	出土（征集） 时间、地点 Time & Spot for discovered or collected	主要装饰 Main Decorations	尺寸（厘米） Size(cm)		类型 Type	图片 Picture
					面径 Face Diameter	身高 Height		
473	总 1806 号 麻江型铜鼓 No.1806 Bronze Drum in Majiang Type	桂林市博物馆 Guilin Museum	不明 Unclear	鼓面缺失； 鼓身：乳钉纹、回形雷纹、如意云纹、兽形云纹、复线角形纹；扁耳两对饰辫纹、回形雷纹 Drum face was lost, only drum body left. Drum body: patterns of nipple protrusion, 回 -shape thunder, Ruyi-shape cloud, beast-shape cloud, double-line triangle; Braids and 回 -shape thunder pattern on 2 pairs of flat handles.	49.3	26.3	麻江型 Majiang Type	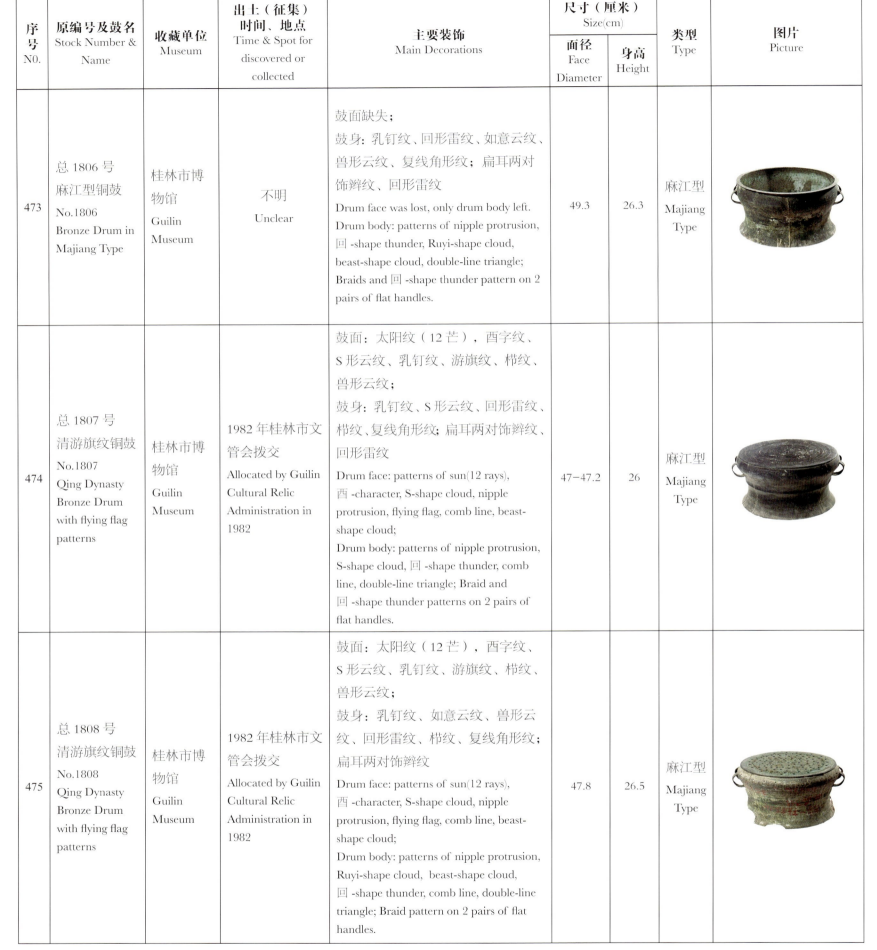
474	总 1807 号 清游旗纹铜鼓 No.1807 Qing Dynasty Bronze Drum with flying flag patterns	桂林市博物馆 Guilin Museum	1982 年桂林市文管会拨交 Allocated by Guilin Cultural Relic Administration in 1982	鼓面：太阳纹（12 芒）、酉字纹、S 形云纹、乳钉纹、游旗纹、栉纹、兽形云纹； 鼓身：乳钉纹、S 形云纹、回形雷纹、栉纹、复线角形纹；扁耳两对饰辫纹、回形雷纹 Drum face: patterns of sun(12 rays), 酉 -character, S-shape cloud, nipple protrusion, flying flag, comb line, beast-shape cloud; Drum body: patterns of nipple protrusion, S-shape cloud, 回 -shape thunder, comb line, double-line triangle; Braid and 回 -shape thunder patterns on 2 pairs of flat handles.	47–47.2	26	麻江型 Majiang Type	
475	总 1808 号 清游旗纹铜鼓 No.1808 Qing Dynasty Bronze Drum with flying flag patterns	桂林市博物馆 Guilin Museum	1982 年桂林市文管会拨交 Allocated by Guilin Cultural Relic Administration in 1982	鼓面：太阳纹（12 芒）、酉字纹、S 形云纹、乳钉纹、游旗纹、栉纹、兽形云纹； 鼓身：乳钉纹、如意云纹、兽形云纹、回形雷纹、栉纹、复线角形纹；扁耳两对饰辫纹 Drum face: patterns of sun(12 rays), 酉 -character, S-shape cloud, nipple protrusion, flying flag, comb line, beast-shape cloud; Drum body: patterns of nipple protrusion, Ruyi-shape cloud, beast-shape cloud, 回 -shape thunder, comb line, double-line triangle; Braid pattern on 2 pairs of flat handles.	47.8	26.5	麻江型 Majiang Type	

408

续表

序号 N0.	原编号及鼓名 Stock Number & Name	收藏单位 Museum	出土（征集） 时间、地点 Time & Spot for discovered or collected	主要装饰 Main Decorations	尺寸（厘米） Size(cm)		类型 Type	图片 Picture
					面径 Face Diameter	身高 Height		
476	总 2811 号 东汉冷水冲型 羽人纹六耳铜鼓 No.2811 East-Han Dynasty Bronze Drum with featherman pattern and 6 handles	桂林市博物馆 Guilin Museum	1982 年桂林市文管会拨交 Allocated by Guilin Cultural Relic Administration in 1982	鼓面：太阳纹（12 芒）、水波纹、栉纹、同心圆纹、复线交叉纹、羽纹、变形羽人纹、变形翔鹭纹、眼纹、鼓面边缘四只逆时针四足立体青蛙（缺失）、蛙间立体装饰缺失； 鼓身：羽纹、栉纹、同心圆纹、变形船纹、水波纹、变形羽人纹、网纹、圆心垂叶纹、眼纹；扁耳两对饰辫纹，另有一对附耳饰辫纹 Drum face: patterns of sun(12 rays), water wave, comb line, concentric circles, crossed double lines, feather, transformed feathermen, transformed flying heron, diamond-shape eye, and 4 frog statues of 4 feet anticlockwise stand on the edge of drum face(lost), between the frogs remains some marks of 2 groups of statues; Drum body: patterns of feather, comb line, concentric circles, boat, water wave, transformed featermen, fishing net, leaf-shape triangle with concentric circles in the middle, diamond-shape eye; Braid pattern on 2 pairs of flat handles and a pair of extra handles.	80.7−81.3	59.5	冷水冲型 Lenshui-chong Type	
477	总 6208 号 变形羽人纹铜鼓 No.6208 Bronze Drum with featherman pattern	桂林市博物馆 Guilin Museum	1988 年 8 月征集于广西巴马县那巴乡那敏村 Collected at Namin Village, Naba, Bama County, Guangxi in August,1988	鼓面：太阳纹（12 芒）、栉纹、同心圆纹、复线交叉纹、变形羽人纹、变形翔鹭纹间定胜纹，鼓面边缘四只逆时针四足立体青蛙（缺失）； 鼓身：栉纹、同心圆纹、栉纹同心圆纹垂直纹带、圆心垂叶纹；扁耳两对饰辫纹 Drum face: patterns of sun(12 rays), comb line, concentric circles, crossed double lines, transformed feathermen, transformed flying heron mixed Dingsheng, and 4 frog statues of 4 feet anticlockwise stand on the edge of drum face(lost); Drum body: patterns of comb line, concentric circles, vertical ribbon with straight line and concentric circles, leaf-shape triangle with concentric circles in the middle; braid pattern on 2 pairs of flat handles.	54.8−55.8	37 （残） Incomplete	冷水冲型 Lenshui-chong Type	

序号 N0.	原编号及鼓名 Stock Number & Name	收藏单位 Museum	出土（征集）时间、地点 Time & Spot for discovered or collected	主要装饰 Main Decorations	尺寸（厘米）Size(cm)		类型 Type	图片 Picture
					面径 Face Diameter	身高 Height		
478	总 202 号 游旗纹铜鼓 No.202 Bronze Drum with flying flag patterns	龙胜各族自治县文物管理所 Longsheng County Cultural Relics Administration	征集于广西龙胜县上孟村 Collected at Shangmeng Village, Longsheng County, Guangxi	鼓面：太阳纹（12 芒）、酉字纹、S 形云纹、乳钉纹、游旗纹、栉纹、兽形云纹、卦纹；鼓身：乳钉纹、回形雷纹、如意云纹、栉纹、复线角形纹；扁耳两对饰辫纹、回形雷纹 Drum face: patterns of sun(12 rays), 酉 -character, S-shape cloud, nipple protrusion, flying flag, comb line, beast-shape cloud, divinatory symbol; Drum body: patterns of nipple protrusion, 回 -shape thunder, Ruyi-shape cloud, comb line, double-line triangle; Braid and 回 -shape thunder patterns on 2 pairs of flat handles.	48.5	27.3	麻江型 Majiang Type	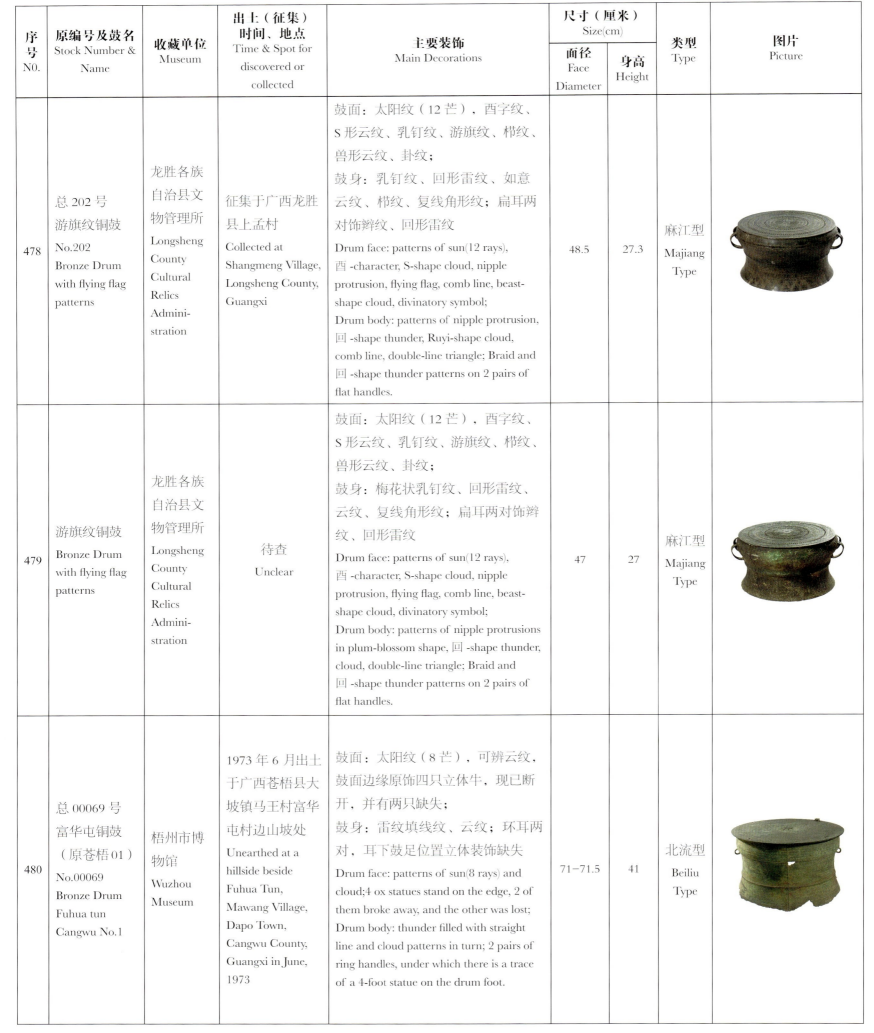
479	游旗纹铜鼓 Bronze Drum with flying flag patterns	龙胜各族自治县文物管理所 Longsheng County Cultural Relics Administration	待查 Unclear	鼓面：太阳纹（12 芒）、酉字纹、S 形云纹、乳钉纹、游旗纹、栉纹、兽形云纹、卦纹；鼓身：梅花状乳钉纹、回形雷纹、云纹、复线角形纹；扁耳两对饰辫纹、回形雷纹 Drum face: patterns of sun(12 rays), 酉 -character, S-shape cloud, nipple protrusion, flying flag, comb line, beast-shape cloud, divinatory symbol; Drum body: patterns of nipple protrusions in plum-blossom shape, 回 -shape thunder, cloud, double-line triangle; Braid and 回 -shape thunder patterns on 2 pairs of flat handles.	47	27	麻江型 Majiang Type	
480	总 00069 号 富华屯铜鼓 （原苍梧 01） No.00069 Bronze Drum Fuhua tun Cangwu No.1	梧州市博物馆 Wuzhou Museum	1973 年 6 月出土于广西苍梧县大坡镇马王村富华屯村边山坡处 Unearthed at a hillside beside Fuhua Tun, Mawang Village, Dapo Town, Cangwu County, Guangxi in June, 1973	鼓面：太阳纹（8 芒）、可辨云纹、鼓面边缘原饰四只立体牛，现已断开，并有两只缺失；鼓身：雷纹填线纹、云纹；环耳两对，耳下鼓足位置立体装饰缺失 Drum face: patterns of sun(8 rays) and cloud;4 ox statues stand on the edge, 2 of them broke away, and the other was lost; Drum body: thunder filled with straight line and cloud patterns in turn; 2 pairs of ring handles, under which there is a trace of a 4-foot statue on the drum foot.	71-71.5	41	北流型 Beiliu Type	

序号 N0.	原编号及鼓名 Stock Number & Name	收藏单位 Museum	出土（征集） 时间、地点 Time & Spot for discovered or collected	主要装饰 Main Decorations	尺寸（厘米） Size(cm)		类型 Type	图片 Picture
					面径 Face Diameter	身高 Height		
481	总 01995 号 "万宝家财" 铭文铜鼓 No.01995 Bronze Drum with the characters 万宝 家财	梧州市博 物馆 Wuzhou Museum	1960 年征集于广 西梧州市废品收 购站 Collected at Wuzhou City waste station in 1960	鼓面：太阳纹（13 芒）、酉字纹、 符篆纹、乳钉纹、游旗间 "万宝家财" 铭文及寿字纹、栉纹、回形雷纹、 云纹； 鼓身：梅花状乳钉纹、回形雷纹、 云纹、符篆纹、复线角形纹；扁耳 两对饰辫纹 Drum face: patterns of sun(13 rays), 酉 -character, Ofuda, nipple protrusion, flying flag mixed characters 万宝家财 & 寿, comb line, 回 -shape thunder, cloud; Drum body: patterns of nipple protrusion in the shape of plum blossom, 回 -shape thunder , cloud, Ofuda, double-line triangle; Braid pattern on 2 pairs of flat handles.	48.8-49.3	27.4	麻江型 Majiang Type	
482	总 02020 号 永固定村铜鼓 No.02020 Bronze Drum Yonggu Dingcun	梧州市博 物馆 Wuzhou Museum	1973 年出土于广 西岑溪南渡镇永 固定村 Unearthed at Yongguding Village, Nandu Town, Cenxi City, Guangxi in 1973	鼓面：太阳纹（11 芒）、栉纹、水 波纹、变形羽人纹、席 / 蝉纹，鼓 面边缘饰四只逆时针四足素面立体 青蛙； 鼓身：栉纹、水波纹、蝉纹、栉纹 同心圆纹垂直纹带；扁耳两对 Drum face: patterns of sun(11rays), comb line, water wave, transformed feathermen, woven mat mixed cicada, 4 frogs with 4 feet and plain back anticlockwise stand on the edge; Drum body: patterns of comb line, water wave, cicada, vertical ribbon with straight lines and concentric circles; 2 pairs of flat handles.	64-64.5	41	冷水冲 型 Lengshui- chong Type	
483	总 03526 号 变形羽人纹铜 鼓 No.03526 Bronze Drum With transformed feathermen patterns	梧州市博 物馆 Wuzhou Museum	旧藏 The old stock	鼓面：太阳纹（12 芒）、栉纹、同 心圆纹、复线交叉纹、变形羽人纹、 变形翔鹭纹间定胜纹，鼓面边缘饰 四只逆时针四足素面立体青蛙； 鼓身：栉纹、同心圆纹、栉纹同心 圆纹垂直纹带、圆心垂叶纹；扁耳 两对饰羽纹 Drum face: patterns of sun(12rays), comb line, concentric circle, crossed double lines, transformed feathermen, transformed flying herons mixed Dingsheng, 4 frogs with 4 feet and plain back anticlockwise stand on the edge; Drum body: patterns of comb line, concentric circle, vertical ribbon with straight lines and concentric circles, leaf- shape triangle with concentric circles in the middle; Feather patterns on 2 pairs of flat handles.	62.6-63.4	41.8	冷水冲 型 Lengshui- chong Type	

411

序号 N0.	原编号及鼓名 Stock Number & Name	收藏单位 Museum	出土（征集）时间、地点 Time & Spot for discovered or collected	主要装饰 Main Decorations	尺寸（厘米）Size(cm)		类型 Type	图片 Picture
					面径 Face Diameter	身高 Height		
484	总 0018 号 雷纹铜鼓 No.0018 Bronze Drum With thunder patterns	岑溪市文物管理所 Cenxi Cultural Relics Administration	1987 年 4 月在广西岑溪县物资局拣选 Collected at Cenxi County Materials Bureau, Guangxi in April, 1987	鼓面：太阳纹（8芒），通体雷纹，鼓面边缘饰四只顺时针四足素面立体青蛙蛙；环耳两对 Drum face: patterns of sun(8rays) and thunder; 4 frogs with 4 feet and plain back clockwise stand on the edge of drum face; 2 pairs of ring handles.	72.6-74	41	北流型 Beiliu Type	
485	总 0019 号 东叶坑鼓 No.0019 Bronze Drum Dongyekeng	岑溪市文物管理所 Cenxi Cultural Relics Administration	1974 年 3 月出土于广西岑溪水汶寨顶东叶坑生产队 Unearthed at Dongyekeng Production Team, the top of Shuiwen Village, Cenxi County in March, 1974	鼓面：太阳纹（8芒），云纹，鼓面边缘饰四只顺时针四足素面立体青蛙；鼓身：云纹、雷纹填线纹，环耳两对 Drum face: patterns of sun(8rays) and cloud; 4 frogs with 4 feet and plain back clockwise stand on the edge; Drum body: cloud and thunder mixed straight line patterns in turn; 2 pairs of ring handles.	76.5-77.4	46.3	北流型 Beiliu Type	
486	总 0020 号 岑 02 号 古藏屯铜鼓 No.0020 Chen No.2 Bronze Drum Gucang tun	岑溪市文物管理所 Cenxi Cultural Relics Administration	1988 年 8 月出土于广西岑溪诚谏镇陀村古藏屯水沟边 Unearthed beside a drain of Gucang Tun, Tuo Village, Chengjian Town, Cenxi County, Guangxi in August,1988	鼓面：太阳纹（8芒），云纹、雷纹、雷纹填线纹，鼓面边缘饰四只两两相对四足立体青蛙；鼓身：雷纹；环耳两对饰缠丝纹、辫纹 Drum face: patterns of sun(8rays), cloud, thunder, thunder filled with straight lines; 4 frogs with 4 feet stand on the edge face to each other in pairs; Drum body: pattern of thunder; Braid & silk-like patterns on 2 pairs of ring handles.	73.1-73.6	41.4	北流型 Beiliu Type	
487	总 01332 号 原苍梧 02 号 广平铜鼓 No.01332 Cangwu No.2 Bronze Drum Guangping	苍梧县文物管理所 Cangwu County Cultural Relics Administration	1973 年 6 月出土于广西苍梧广平镇甘村 Unearthed at Gan Village Guangping Town, Cangwu County, Guangxi in June,1973	鼓面：太阳纹（10芒），云纹、雷纹填线纹，鼓面边缘饰四只逆时针四足立体青蛙；鼓身：云纹，大部残缺 Drum face: patterns of sun(10rays), cloud, thunder filled with straight lines; 4 frogs with 4 feet anticlockwise stand on the edge; Drum body: pattern of cloud. Only drum face and part of drum chest were remained.	87-89	12 （残）Incomplete	北流型 Beiliu Type	

序号 NO.	原编号及鼓名 Stock Number & Name	收藏单位 Museum	出土（征集） 时间、地点 Time & Spot for discovered or collected	主要装饰 Main Decorations	尺寸（厘米） Size(cm)		类型 Type	图片 Picture
					面径 Face Diameter	身高 Height		
488	藤01号 芦塘岗铜鼓 Teng No.1 Bronze Drum Lutang Gang	藤县博物馆 Teng County Museum	1973年9月1日出土于广西藤县天平镇新兴村北芦塘岗山坡 Unearthed at the hillside of Lutang Gang, in the north of Xinxing Village, Tianping Town, Teng County, Guangxi on September 1st, 1973	鼓面：太阳纹（8芒）、云纹、雷纹、雷纹填线纹，鼓面边缘饰四只逆时针四足素面立蛙； 鼓身：云纹、水波纹、大部分残缺；扁耳两对 Drum face: patterns of sun(8rays), cloud, thunder, thunder filled with straight lines; 4 frogs with 4 feet and plain back anticlockwise stand on the edge; Drum body: patterns of cloud, water wave. Only drum face and part of drum chest remained. 2 pairs of flat handles.	61.4−62.4	15 （残） Incomplete	北流型 Beiliu Type	
489	藤02号 甘村鼓 Teng No.2 Bronze Drum Gancun	藤县博物馆 Teng County Museum	1974年6月出土于广西藤县象棋镇甘村东南 Unearthed in the southeast of Gan Village, Xiangqi Town, Teng County, Guangxi in June,1974	鼓面：太阳纹（12芒）、水波纹、同心圆纹、复线交叉纹、变形羽人纹、变形翔鹭纹、羽纹、眼纹，鼓面边缘饰四只逆时针四足谷穗纹立体青蛙，蛙间各饰一组单乘骑立饰； 鼓身：水波纹、同心圆纹、变形船纹、变形羽人纹鼓腰以下大部分残缺；扁耳两对饰辫纹 Drum face: patterns of sun(12rays), water wave, concentric circle, crossed double lines, transformed feathermen, transformed flying heron, feather, diamond-shape eyes; 4 frogs with 4 feet and rice-ear motif on back anticlockwise stand on the edge, 2 groups of horse rider statues between the frogs. Drum body: patterns of water wave, concentric circles, boat, transformed feathermen; most part of the waist and the foot is lost; Braid pattern on 2 pairs of flat handles.	64.6−65	22.2 （残） Incomplete	冷水冲型 Lengshui-chong Type	

413

续表

序号 N0.	原编号及鼓名 Stock Number & Name	收藏单位 Museum	出土（征集） 时间、地点 Time & Spot for discovered or collected	主要装饰 Main Decorations	尺寸（厘米） Size(cm)		类型 Type	图片 Picture
					面径 Face Diameter	身高 Height		
490	藤03号 平福村铜鼓 Teng No.3 Bronze Drum Pingfu	藤县博物馆 Teng County Museum	1974年出土于广西藤县平福乡平福村 Unearthed at Pingfu Village Pingfu, Teng County, Guangxi in 1974	鼓面：太阳纹（12芒），芒间饰翎眼纹、水波纹、同心圆纹、复线交叉纹、羽纹、变形羽人纹、变形翔鹭纹、眼纹，鼓面边缘饰四只逆时针四足谷穗纹立体青蛙，蛙间各饰十字螺旋纹立体龟； 鼓身：水波纹、同心圆纹、栉纹、变形船纹、变形羽人纹、网纹、眼纹、羽纹、圆心垂叶纹、眼纹；扁耳两对饰辫纹 Drum face: patterns of sun(12rays) with feather eye between the rays, water wave, concentric circle, crossed double lines, feather, transformed feathermen, transformed flying heron, diamond-shape eyes; 4 frogs with 4 feet and rice-ear motif on back anticlockwise stand on the edge, 2 groups of tortoise statues with 十-shape motif and spiracle on their back between the frogs. Drum body: patterns of water wave, concentric circles, comb line, boat, transformed feathermen, fishing net, diamond-shape eyes, feather, leaf-shape triangle with concentric circles in the middle, diamond-shape eyes; Braid pattern on 2 pairs of flat handles.	82.1－83.8	60.2	冷水冲型 Lengshui-chong Type	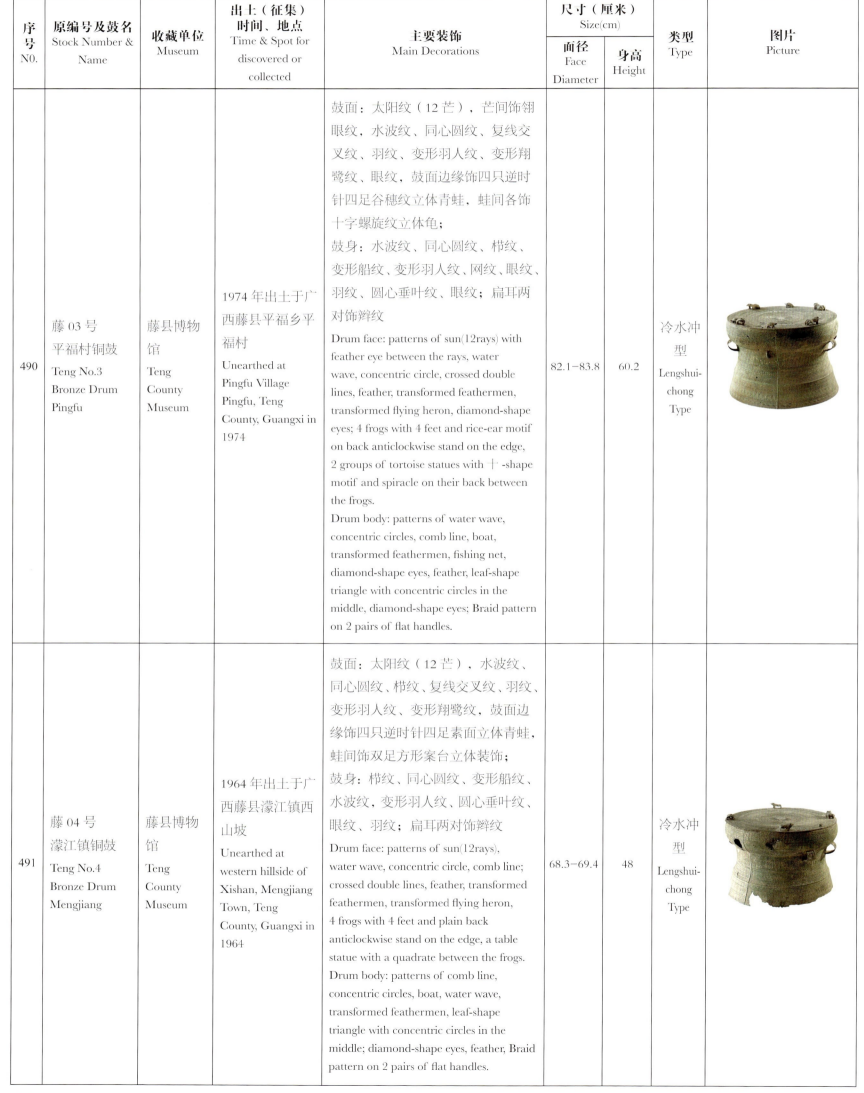
491	藤04号 濛江镇铜鼓 Teng No.4 Bronze Drum Mengjiang	藤县博物馆 Teng County Museum	1964年出土于广西藤县濛江镇西山坡 Unearthed at western hillside of Xishan, Mengjiang Town, Teng County, Guangxi in 1964	鼓面：太阳纹（12芒），水波纹、同心圆纹、栉纹、复线交叉纹、羽纹、变形羽人纹、变形翔鹭纹，鼓面边缘饰四只逆时针四足素面立体青蛙，蛙间饰双足方形案台立体装饰； 鼓身：栉纹、同心圆纹、变形船纹、水波纹、变形羽人纹、圆心垂叶纹、眼纹、羽纹；扁耳两对饰辫纹 Drum face: patterns of sun(12rays), water wave, concentric circle, comb line; crossed double lines, feather, transformed feathermen, transformed flying heron, 4 frogs with 4 feet and plain back anticlockwise stand on the edge, a table statue with a quadrate between the frogs. Drum body: patterns of comb line, concentric circles, boat, water wave, transformed feathermen, leaf-shape triangle with concentric circles in the middle; diamond-shape eyes, feather, Braid pattern on 2 pairs of flat handles.	68.3－69.4	48	冷水冲型 Lengshui-chong Type	

序号 NO.	原编号及鼓名 Stock Number & Name	收藏单位 Museum	出土（征集）时间、地点 Time & Spot for discovered or collected	主要装饰 Main Decorations	尺寸（厘米） Size(cm)		类型 Type	图片 Picture
					面径 Face Diameter	身高 Height		
492	藤 05 号 志成村鼓 Teng No.5 Bronze Drum Zhichengcun	藤县博物馆 Teng County Museum	1951 年出土于广西藤县和平镇志成村山坡 Unearthed at hillside of Zhicheng Village, Heping Town, Teng County, Guangxi in 1951	鼓面：太阳纹（10 芒），水波纹、同心圆纹、栉纹、复线交叉纹、变形羽人纹、变形翔鹭纹、眼纹，鼓面边缘饰四只逆时针四足谷穗纹立体蛙，蛙间分别饰单乘骑、马立体装饰； 鼓身：水波纹、同心圆纹、变形船纹、变形羽人纹、网纹；鼓足大部分缺失，扁耳两对饰辫纹 Drum face: patterns of sun(10rays), water wave, concentric circle, comb line, crossed double lines, transformed feathermen, transformed flying heron, diamond-shape eyes; 4 frogs with 4 feet and rice-ear-decorated back anticlockwise stand on the edge, 2 groups of horse-riding and a horse statues between the frogs. Drum body: patterns of water wave, concentric circles, boat, transformed feathermen, fishing net; Braids pattern on 2 pairs of flat handles.Most of the foot was lost.	63.3—64.1	38.5 （残） Incomplete	冷水冲型 Lengshui-chong Type	
493	藤 06 号 底村屯铜鼓 Teng No.6 Bronze Drum Dicuntun	藤县博物馆 Teng County Museum	1979 年 3 月出土于广西藤县古龙镇木河村底村屯山坡 Unearthed at hillside of Dicun Tun, Muhe Village, Gulong Town, Teng County, Guangxi in March 1979	鼓面：太阳纹（10 芒），水波纹、同心圆纹、栉纹、复线交叉纹、变形羽人纹、变形翔鹭纹、眼纹，鼓面边缘饰四只逆时针四足素面立体蛙，蛙间立体装饰缺失； 鼓身：水波纹、同心圆纹、变形船纹、变形羽人纹、网纹、圆心垂叶纹；扁耳两对饰辫纹 Drum face: patterns of sun(10rays), water wave, concentric circle, comb line, crossed double lines, transformed feathermen, transformed flying heron, diamond-shape eyes; 4 frogs with 4 feet and plain back anticlockwise stand on the edge, mark of statues between the frogs. Drum body: patterns of water wave, concentric circles, boat, transformed feathermen, fishing net, leaf-shape triangle with concentric circles in the middle; Braids pattern on 2 pairs of flat handles.	70—70.6	48.5	冷水冲型 Lengshui-chong Type	

序号 N0.	原编号及鼓名 Stock Number & Name	收藏单位 Museum	出土（征集）时间、地点 Time & Spot for discovered or collected	主要装饰 Main Decorations	尺寸（厘米） Size(cm) 面径 Face Diameter	身高 Height	类型 Type	图片 Picture
494	藤 07 号 杨村鼓 Teng No.7 Bronze Drum Yangcun	藤县博物馆 Teng County Museum	1974 年出土于广西藤县壤南杨村大队 Unearthed at Yangcun production team, Rangnan, Teng County, Guangxi in 1974	鼓面：太阳纹（6 芒），通体雷纹填线纹，鼓面边缘饰四只逆时针四足素面立蛙；环耳两对饰谷穗纹 Drum face: patterns of sun(6rays), thunder filled with straight lines; 4 frogs with 4 feet and plain back anticlockwise stand on the edge; Rice-ear patterns on 2 pairs of ring handles.	83~87.7	44	北流型 Beiliu Type	
495	藤 08 号 陈村铜鼓 Teng No.8 Bronze Drum Chencun	藤县博物馆 Teng County Museum	1979 年 11 月 8 日出土于广西藤县新庆镇庆旺村陈村东北山冲 Unearthed at a small valley in north-east of Chencun, Qingwang Village, Xinqing Town, Teng County, Guangxi on November 8th, 1979	鼓面：太阳纹（8 芒）、席纹、云纹、雷纹、鸟形纹、雷纹填线纹，鼓面边缘饰四只逆时针四足素面立体青蛙； 鼓身：水波纹、雷纹填线纹、云纹、席纹；扁耳两对饰辫纹 Drum face: patterns of sun(8rays),woven mat, cloud, thunder, bird-shape motif, thunder mixed straight line, 4 frogs with 4 feet and plain back anticlockwise stand on the edge; Drum body: patterns of water wave, thunder mixed straight line, cloud, woven mat; Braids pattern on 2 pairs of flat handles.	68.5~68.8	40.5	北流型 Beiliu Type	
496	藤 09 号 福本岗鼓 Teng No.9 Bronze Drum Fubengang	藤县博物馆 Teng County Museum	1981 年 7 月 1 日出土于广西藤县天平镇三益村福本岗 Unearthed at Fubengang, Sanyi Village, Tianping Town, Teng County, Guangxi on July 1st,1981	鼓面：太阳纹（8 芒）、水波纹、变形羽人纹、半同心圆填线纹、复线角形图案纹，鼓面边缘饰六只顺时针三足划线痕立体青蛙； 鼓身：水波纹、变形羽人纹、云纹、四瓣花纹；扁耳两对 Drum face: patterns of sun(8rays),water wave, transformed feathermen, semi-concentric-circle mixed straight lines, double-line triangle with motif, 6 frogs with 3 feet and lineate back clockwise stand on the edge; Drum body: patterns of water wave, transformed feathermen, cloud, quatrefoil; 2 pairs of flat handles.	82.1~83.6	51	灵山型 Lingshan Type	

序号 NO.	原编号及鼓名 Stock Number & Name	收藏单位 Museum	出土（征集） 时间、地点 Time & Spot for discovered or collected	主要装饰 Main Decorations	尺寸（厘米） Size(cm)		类型 Type	图片 Picture
					面径 Face Diameter	身高 Height		
497	总 00166 号 游旗纹铜鼓 N0.00166 Bronze Drum with flying flag patterns	藤县博物馆 Teng County Museum	1975 年从广西壮族自治区博物馆调拨 Allocated from Museum of Guangxi Zhuang Autonomous Region in 1975	鼓面：太阳纹（12 芒）、西字纹、S 形云纹、乳钉纹、游旗纹、栉纹、兽形云纹、卦纹； 鼓身：乳钉纹、回形雷纹、如意云纹、栉纹、复线角形纹；扁耳两对饰辫纹、回形雷纹 Drum face: patterns of sun(12 rays), 酉 -character, S-shape cloud, nipple protrusion, flying flag, comb line, Beast-shape cloud, divinatory symbol pattern; Drum body: patterns of nipple protrusion, 回 -shape thunder, Ruyi-shape cloud, comb line, double-line triangle; Braid and 回 -shape thunder patterns on 2 pairs of flat handles.	47	27	麻江型 Majiang Type	
498	总 02 号 高堆村鼓 No.02 Bronze Drum Gaoduicun	蒙山县文物管理所 Mengshan County Cultural Relics Admini- stration	1990 年 9 月出土于广西蒙山县西河镇高堆村德梗组营盘岭 Unearthed at Yingpan Ling, Degeng team, Gaodui Village, Xihe Town, Mengshan County, Guangxi in September,1990	鼓面：太阳纹（10 芒）、水波纹、同心圆纹、羽纹、复线交叉纹、变形羽人纹、变形翔鹭纹、眼纹，鼓面边缘饰四只逆时针四足谷穗纹立体肯蛙，蛙间各饰一组乘骑立饰； 鼓身：水波纹、同心圆纹、变形船纹、变形羽人纹、网纹、羽纹、圆心三角垂叶纹、眼纹；扁耳两对饰辫纹，合范线附近各一对环附耳饰辫纹 Drum face: patterns of sun(10rays), water wave, concentric circle, feather, crossed double lines, transformed feathermen, transformed flying heron, diamond-shape eyes; 4 frogs with 4 feet and rice-ear-decorated back statues anticlockwise stand on the edge, 2 groups of statues between the frogs. Drum body: patterns of water wave, concentric circles, boat, transformed feathermen, fishing net, feather, leaf-shape triangle with concentric circles in the middle, diamond-shape eyes; Braids pattern on 2 pairs of flat handles, 2 pairs of attached ring handles with braid pattern beside the casting line respectively.	69.4－70.8	47	冷水冲型 Lengshui-chong Type	

序号 N0.	原编号及鼓名 Stock Number & Name	收藏单位 Museum	出土（征集） 时间、地点 Time & Spot for discovered or collected	主要装饰 Main Decorations	尺寸（厘米） Size(cm)		类型 Type	图片 Picture
					面径 Face Diameter	身高 Height		
499	古排前村铜鼓 Bronze Drum Gupai Qiancun	蒙山县文物管理所 Mengshan County Cultural Relics Administration	原存广西蒙山县古排前村村民家中 Originally preserved in the house of a villager of Gupaiqian Village, Mengshan County, Guangxi	鼓面：太阳纹（12 芒），酉字纹、乳钉纹、游旗纹、栉纹、S 形云纹、兽形云纹； 鼓身：乳钉纹、如意云纹、回形雷纹、菱格填四瓣花纹、图案三角纹；扁耳两对饰辫纹、雷纹 Drum face: patterns of sun(12 rays), 酉 -character, nipple protrusion, flying flag, comb line, S-shape cloud, cloud; Drum body: patterns of nipple protrusion, Ruyi-shape cloud, 回 -shape thunder , diamond with quatrefoil, triangle with motifs inside; Braid and thunder patterns on 2 pairs of flat handles.	47.3~47.8	27.5	麻江型 Majiang Type	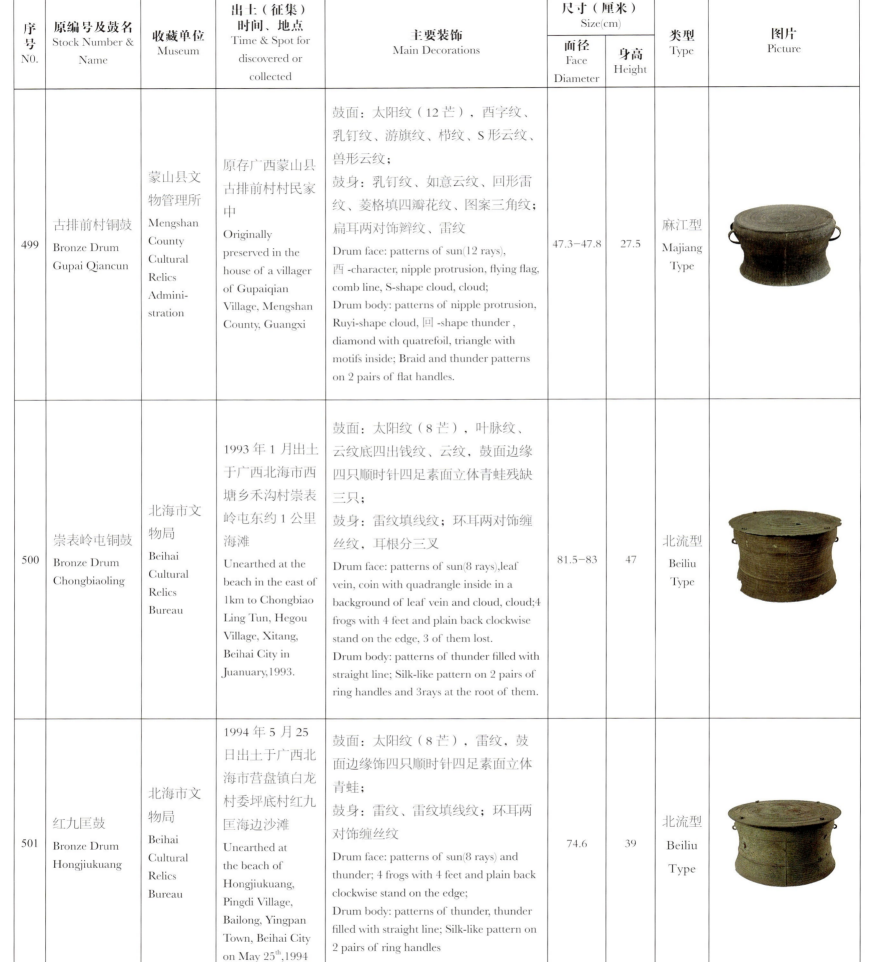
500	崇表岭屯铜鼓 Bronze Drum Chongbiaoling	北海市文物局 Beihai Cultural Relics Bureau	1993 年 1 月出土于广西北海市西塘乡禾沟村崇表岭屯东约 1 公里海滩 Unearthed at the beach in the east of 1km to Chongbiao Ling Tun, Hegou Village, Xitang, Beihai City in Juanuary,1993.	鼓面：太阳纹（8 芒），叶脉纹、云纹底四出钱纹、云纹，鼓面边缘四只顺时针四足素面立体青蛙残缺三只； 鼓身：雷纹填线纹；环耳两对饰缠丝纹，耳根分三叉 Drum face: patterns of sun(8 rays),leaf vein, coin with quadrangle inside in a background of leaf vein and cloud, cloud;4 frogs with 4 feet and plain back clockwise stand on the edge, 3 of them lost. Drum body: patterns of thunder filled with straight line; Silk-like pattern on 2 pairs of ring handles and 3rays at the root of them.	81.5~83	47	北流型 Beiliu Type	
501	红九匡鼓 Bronze Drum Hongjiukuang	北海市文物局 Beihai Cultural Relics Bureau	1994 年 5 月 25 日出土于广西北海市营盘镇白龙村委坪底村红九匡海边沙滩 Unearthed at the beach of Hongjiukuang, Pingdi Village, Bailong, Yingpan Town, Beihai City on May 25th,1994	鼓面：太阳纹（8 芒），雷纹，鼓面边缘饰四只顺时针四足素面立体青蛙； 鼓身：雷纹、雷纹填线纹；环耳两对饰缠丝纹 Drum face: patterns of sun(8 rays) and thunder; 4 frogs with 4 feet and plain back clockwise stand on the edge; Drum body: patterns of thunder, thunder filled with straight line; Silk-like pattern on 2 pairs of ring handles	74.6	39	北流型 Beiliu Type	

序号 N0.	原编号及鼓名 Stock Number & Name	收藏单位 Museum	出土（征集）时间、地点 Time & Spot for discovered or collected	主要装饰 Main Decorations	尺寸（厘米） Size(cm)		类型 Type	图片 Picture
					面径 Face Diameter	身高 Height		
502	竹林鼓 Bronze Drum Zhulin	北海市文物局 Beihai Cultural Relics Bureau	2011 年 4 月 7 日出土于广西北海市银海区福城镇竹林村 Unearthed at Zhulin Village, Fucheng Town, Yinhai District of Beihai City on April 7th, 2011	鼓面：太阳纹（8 芒），兽面纹、雷纹、云纹、鸟形纹、兽形纹，鼓面边缘饰四组顺时针四足立蛙，其中两组为累蹲蛙； 鼓身：席纹、四出钱纹、兽面纹、雷纹、雷纹填线纹、兽形纹、连钱纹；鼓胸内壁饰一只立体牛；扁耳两对饰叶脉纹、乳钉纹 Drum face: patterns of sun(8 rays), beast' face, thunder, cloud, bird, beast, 4 frogs with 4 feet clockwise stand on the edge, 2 of them are overlap; Drum body: patterns of woven mat, coin with quadrangle inside , beast' face, thunder, thunder filled with straight line, beast, coins part of overlap; an ox statue stands on the inside wall of drum breast; Leaf vein and nipple protrusion patterns on 2 pairs of flat handles.	79.7−80	43	灵山型 Lingshan Type	
503	坪底村铜鼓 Bronze Drum Pingdicun	合浦汉代文化博物馆 Hepu Han Culture Museum	1967 年出土于广西合浦县营盘乡坪底村后背岭 Unearthed at Houbeiling, Pingdi Village, Yingpan, Hepu County, Guangxi in 1967	鼓面：太阳纹（8 芒），雷纹地四出钱纹，鼓面边缘饰四只逆时针四足立体青蛙； 鼓身：雷纹填线纹、云纹；环耳两对 Drum face: patterns of sun(8 rays), coin with quadrangle inside in a thunder pattern background; 4 frogs with 4 feet anticlockwise stand on the edge; Drum body: thunder filled with straight line and cloud in turn; 2 pairs of ring handles.	85.3−86.7	48	北流型 Beiliu Type	
504	竹仔塘铜鼓 Bronze Drum Zhuzaitang	合浦汉代文化博物馆 Hepu Han Culture Museum	1980 年 9 月 24 日出土于广西合浦县南康镇雷田村竹仔塘 Unearthed at Zhuzaitang, Leitian Village, Nankang Town, Hepu County, Guangxi on September 24th,1980	鼓面：太阳纹（8 芒），席纹、连钱纹、兽形纹，弦间饰云纹、席纹、四瓣花纹，鼓面边缘饰六只顺时针三足立体青蛙； 鼓身：连钱纹、半圆填线纹、雷纹、云纹（合范线两侧纹饰不一致）；扁耳两对 Drum face: patterns of sun(8 rays), woven mat, coins part of overlap, beast; cloud, woven mat and quatrefoil between the strings and quatrefoil; 6 frogs with 3 feet clockwise stand on the edge; Drum body: patterns of coins part of overlap, half-circle filled with straight line, thunder, cloud(different patterns on two sides of casting line) , 2 pairs of flat handles.	98−98.7	61.5	灵山型 Lingshan Type	

序号 N0.	原编号及鼓名 Stock Number & Name	收藏单位 Museum	出土（征集） 时间、地点 Time & Spot for discovered or collected	主要装饰 Main Decorations	尺寸（厘米） Size(cm)		类型 Type	图片 Picture
					面径 Face Diameter	身高 Height		
505	岑排屯铜鼓 Bronze Drum Cenpaitun	上思县文物管理所 Shangsi County Cultural Relic Administration	1990年出土于广西上思县南屏乡米强村岑排屯 Unearthed at Cenpai Tun, Miqiang Village, Nanping, Shangsi County, Guangxi in 1990	鼓面：太阳纹（8芒），可辨虫形纹、四瓣花纹、兽形纹、四出钱纹、蝉纹，鼓面边缘饰六只逆时针三足螺旋纹立体青蛙； 鼓身：席纹、虫形纹、四瓣花纹、四出钱纹、兽形纹；扁耳两对饰辫纹 Drum face: patterns of sun(8 rays), insect, quatrefoil, beast, coin with quadrangle inside, cicada, and 6 frogs of 3-feet and spiral pattern on the back stand anticlockwise on the edge; Drum body: patterns of woven mat, insect, quatrefoil, coin with quadrangle inside, beast; Braids pattern on 2 pairs of flat handles.	66-66.5	36（残） Incom-plete	灵山型 Lingshan Type	
506	那凤鼓 Bronze Drum Nafeng	上思县文物管理所 Shangsi County Cultural Relic Administration	出土于广西上思县在妙镇那凤屯 Unearthed at Nafeng Tun, Zaimiao Town, Shangsi County, Guangxi	鼓面：太阳纹（8芒），四瓣花纹、虫形纹、四出钱纹、鸟形纹、席纹、兽形纹、蝉纹，鼓面边缘饰六组逆时针三足螺旋纹累蹲立体青蛙； 鼓身：蝉纹、连钱纹、四出钱纹、兽形纹、虫形纹、席纹、鸟形纹、蝉纹、雷纹填线纹；扁耳两对饰辫纹 Drum face: patterns of sun(8 rays), quatrefoil, insect, coin with quadrangle inside, bird, woven mat, beast, cicada, and 6 overlap frogs of 3-feet and spiral pattern on the back stand anticlockwise on the edge; Drum body: patterns of cicada, coins part of overlap, beast, insect, woven mat, bird, cicada, thunder filled with straight line; Braids pattern on 2 pairs of flat handles.	76.8-77.2	46.4	灵山型 Lingshan Type	

续表

序号 No.	原编号及鼓名 Stock Number & Name	收藏单位 Museum	出土（征集） 时间、地点 Time & Spot for discovered or collected	主要装饰 Main Decorations	尺寸（厘米） Size(cm)		类型 Type	图片 Picture
					面径 Face Diameter	身高 Height		
507	094 号 新塘鼓 No.094 Bronze Drum Xintang	钦州市博物馆 Qinzhou City Museum	1993 年出土于广西钦州市板城镇城圩北 1 公里新塘村麓山 Unearthed at Lushan, Xintang Village, about 1km in the north of Chengxu, Bancheng Town, Qinzhou City,Guangxi in 1993	鼓面：太阳纹（12 芒）、连钱纹、蝉纹、四瓣花纹、四出钱纹、鸟形纹、席纹、鼓面边缘饰六组逆时针三足螺旋纹立蛙，其中三组为累蹲蛙；鼓身：蝉纹、四瓣花纹、四出钱纹、鸟形纹、连钱纹、兽面纹、席纹、虫形纹；扁耳两对饰辫纹 Drum face: patterns of sun(12 rays), coins part of overlap, cicada, quatrefoil, coin with quadrangle inside, bird-shape motif, woven mat; 6 frogs with 3 feet and spiracle on their backs anticlockwise stand on the edge, 3 of them are overlap; Drum body: patterns of cicada, quatrefoil, coin with quadrangle inside, bird-shape motif, coins part of overlap, beast face, woven mat, insect-shape motif; Braid patterns on 2 pairs of flat handles.	79.3	47.5	灵山型 Lingshan Type	
508	000127 号 双镇岭铜鼓 No.000127 Bronze Drum Shuangzhen Ling	钦州市博物馆 Qinzhou City Museum	1988 年 6 月出土于广西钦州市那蒙镇四维村崇眼屯南双镇岭 Unearthed at Shuangzhenling, south to Dongyan Tun, Siwei Village, Nameng Town, Qinzhou City, Guangxi in June 1988	鼓面：太阳纹（8 芒）、雷纹、半圆填线纹、虫形纹、变形羽人纹、如意云纹、蝉纹，鼓面边缘饰六组逆时针三足网纹、叶脉纹立蛙；鼓身：鸟形纹、四瓣花纹、如意云纹、席纹、半圆填线、雷纹、蝉纹；扁耳两对饰辫纹 Drum face: patterns of sun(8rays), thunder, half-circle filled with straight lines, insect-shape motif, transformed feathermen, Ruyi-shape cloud, cicada; 6 frogs with 3 feet and net & leaf-vein patterns on back anticlockwise stand on the edge; Drum body: patterns of bird-shape, quatrefoil, Ruyi-shape cloud, woven mat, half-circle filled with straight lines, thunder, cicada; Braid patterns on 2 pairs of flat handles.	80.7-81	52.8	灵山型 Lingshan Type	
509	000129 号 沙坡村铜鼓 No.000129 Bronze Drum Shapo Cun	钦州市博物馆 Qinzhou City Museum	1996 年 4 月 16 日出土于广西钦州市长滩镇那谷村公所沙坡村波学岭 Unearthed at Boxue Ling, Shapo Village, Nagu Changtan Town, Qinzhou City, Guangxi on April 16th, 1996	鼓面：太阳纹（10 芒）、通体四出钱纹、比轮钱纹，鼓面边缘饰六组逆时针三足辫纹累蹲立体蛙；扁耳两对饰辫纹 Drum face: patterns of sun(10rays), coins with quadrangle inside and Bilun Coins cover all the body; 6 overlap frogs with 3 feet and braids on back anticlockwise stand on the edge; Braid patterns on 2 pairs of flat handles.	117-120.3	70.7	灵山型 Lingshan Type	

序号 N0.	原编号及鼓名 Stock Number & Name	收藏单位 Museum	出土（征集） 时间、地点 Time & Spot for discovered or collected	主要装饰 Main Decorations	尺寸（厘米） Size(cm)		类型 Type	图片 Picture
					面径 Face Diameter	身高 Height		
510	000130 号 廷朗山铜鼓 No.000130 Bronze Drum Tinglang Shan	钦州市博物馆 Qinzhou City Museum	1975 年出土于广西钦州市那蒙镇那蒙村廷朗山 Unearthed at Tinglang Hill, Nameng Village, Nameng Town, Qinzhou City, Guangxi in 1975	鼓面：太阳纹（10 芒）、席纹、变形羽人纹、半圆填线纹、蝉纹，鼓面边缘饰六组逆时针三足菱形纹立体蛙； 鼓身：如意云纹、同心圆纹、席纹、半圆填线、变形羽人纹、蝉纹；扁耳两对饰辫纹 Drum face: patterns of sun(10rays), woven mat, transformed feathermen, half-circle filled with straight lines, cicada; 6 frogs with 3 feet and diamond patterns on back anticlockwise stand on the edge; Drum body: patterns of Ruyi-shape cloud, concentric circle, woven mat, half-circle filled with straight lines, transformed feathermen, cicada; Braid patterns on 2 pairs of flat handles.	88.2－89	56	灵山型 Lingshan Type	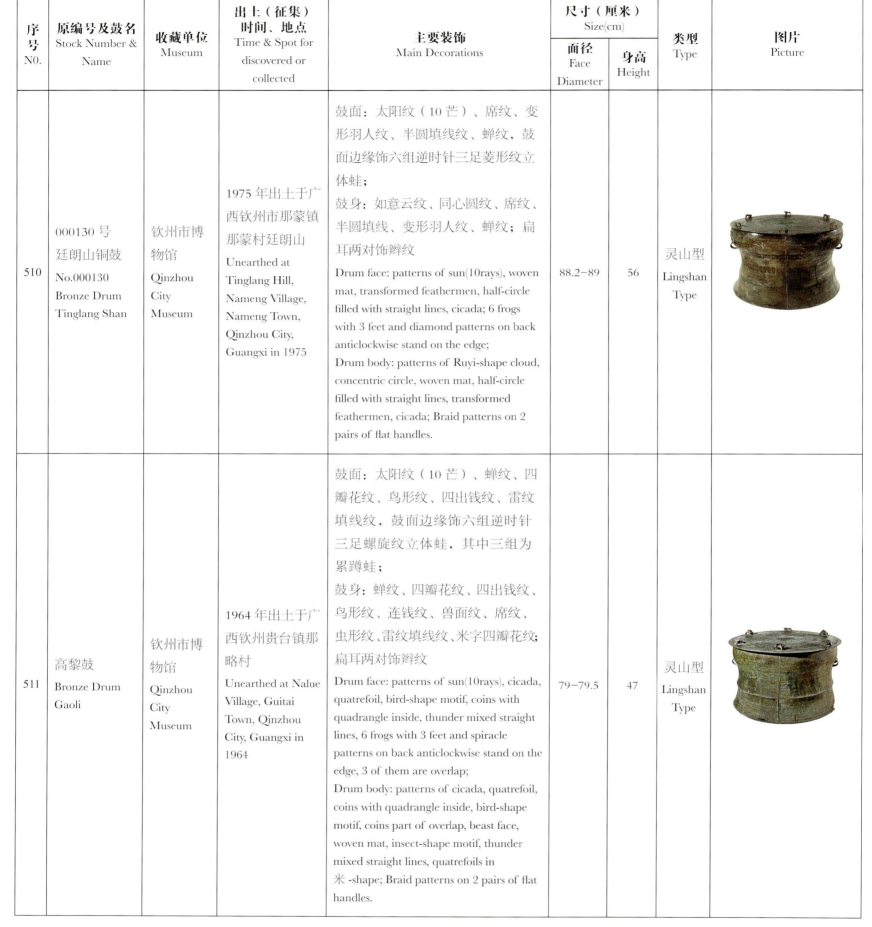
511	高黎鼓 Bronze Drum Gaoli	钦州市博物馆 Qinzhou City Museum	1964 年出土于广西钦州贵台镇那略村 Unearthed at Nalue Village, Guitai Town, Qinzhou City, Guangxi in 1964	鼓面：太阳纹（10 芒）、蝉纹、四瓣花纹、鸟形纹、四出钱纹、雷纹填线纹，鼓面边缘饰六组逆时针三足螺旋纹立体蛙，其中三组为累蹲蛙； 鼓身：蝉纹、四瓣花纹、四出钱纹、鸟形纹、连钱纹、兽面纹、席纹、虫形纹、雷纹填线纹、米字四瓣花纹；扁耳两对饰辫纹 Drum face: patterns of sun(10rays), cicada, quatrefoil, bird-shape motif, coins with quadrangle inside, thunder mixed straight lines, 6 frogs with 3 feet and spiracle patterns on back anticlockwise stand on the edge, 3 of them are overlap; Drum body: patterns of cicada, quatrefoil, coins with quadrangle inside, bird-shape motif, coins part of overlap, beast face, woven mat, insect-shape motif, thunder mixed straight lines, quatrefoils in 米 -shape; Braid patterns on 2 pairs of flat handles.	79－79.5	47	灵山型 Lingshan Type	

续表

序号 N0.	原编号及鼓名 Stock Number & Name	收藏单位 Museum	出土（征集） 时间、地点 Time & Spot for discovered or collected	主要装饰 Main Decorations	尺寸（厘米） Size(cm)		类型 Type	图片 Picture
					面径 Face Diameter	身高 Height		
512	云纹鹿耳环鼓 Bronze Drum Luerhuan with cloud patterns	钦州市博 物馆 Qinzhou City Museum	1988 年出土于广 西钦州市犀牛脚 镇鹿耳环村南海 边沙滩 Unearthed at the sea beach, south to LuerhuanVillage, Xiniujiao Town, Qinzhou City, Guangxi in 1988	鼓面：太阳纹（8 芒）、通体云纹、鼓面边缘饰六只逆时针四足素面立蛙；仅存鼓面及部分鼓胸；环耳两对、残缺一对 Drum face: patterns of sun(8 rays) and cloud; 6 frogs with 4 feet and plain back anticlockwise stand on the edge; only the drum face and part of the chest were remained; 2 pairs of ring handles, one of them lost.	90－91.6	16 （残） Incom- plete	北流型 Beiliu Type	
513	游旗纹铜鼓 Bronze Drum with flying flag patterns	钦州市博 物馆 Qinzhou City Museum	钦州市文化馆 旧藏 The old stock of Qinzhou City Cultural House	鼓面：太阳纹（12 芒）、乳钉纹、游旗纹、回形雷纹、兽形云纹； 鼓身：回形雷纹、兽形云纹、复线三角纹；扁耳两对饰凸棱纹 Drum face: patterns of sun(12 rays), nipple protrusion, flying flag, 回 -shape thunder, beast-shape cloud; Drum body: patterns of 回 -shape thunder, beast-shape cloud, double line triangle; Raise ridges on 2 pairs of flat handles.	46.5－46.8	26	麻江型 Majiang Type	
514	总 0002 号 原 0001 号 高连塘鼓 No.0002(Old No.0001) Bronze Drum Gaoliantang	灵山县博 物馆 Lingshan County Museum	1979 年出土于 广西灵山佛子镇 睦象村公所高联 塘村 Unearthed at Gaoliantang, Muxiang Village, Fozi Town, Lingshan County, Guangxi in 1979	鼓面：太阳纹（8 芒）、四出钱纹、云纹、四瓣花纹、变体雷纹、连钱纹、席纹、鼓面边缘饰六组逆时针三足立蛙； 鼓身：云纹、雷纹、四瓣花纹、四出钱纹、席纹；扁耳两对饰辫纹 Drum face: patterns of sun(8 rays), coins with quadrangle inside, cloud, quatrefoil, transformed thunder, coins part of overlap, woven mat, 6 frogs with 4 feet anticlockwise stand on the edge; Drum body: patterns of cloud, thunder, quatrefoil, coins with quadrangle inside, woven mat; Braid patterns on 2 pairs of flat handles.	68－69.5	39	灵山型 Lingshan Type	
515	总 0014 号 原灵山 10 号 高塘岭鼓 No.0014(Ling- shan No.10) Bronze Drum Gaotangling	灵山县博 物馆 Lingshan County Museum	1983 年 5 月 20 日出土于广西灵 山太平那谐村高 塘岭 Unearthed at Gaotangling, Naxie Village, Taiping, Lingshan County, Guangxi on May 20th, 1983	鼓面：太阳纹（8 芒）、云纹、雷纹、变体雷纹、鼓面边缘饰四只逆时针素面四足立蛙； 鼓身：雷纹、云纹；环耳两对饰缠丝纹 Drum face: patterns of sun(8 rays), cloud, thunder, transformed thunder, 4 frogs with 4 feet and plain back anticlockwise stand on the edge; Drum body: patterns of thunder, cloud; Silk-like patterns on 2 pairs of ring handles.	93.4－93.8	53.5	北流型 Beiliu Type	

序号 N0.	原编号及鼓名 Stock Number & Name	收藏单位 Museum	出土（征集） 时间、地点 Time & Spot for discovered or collected	主要装饰 Main Decorations	尺寸（厘米） Size(cm)		类型 Type	图片 Picture
					面径 Face Diameter	身高 Height		
516	总 0015 号 石基鼓 No.0015 Bronze Drum Shiji	灵山县博物馆 Lingshan County Museum	1984 年 4 月 7 日出土于广西平南县石基屯石基村 Unearthed at Shiji Tun, Shiji Village, Pingnan County, Guangxi on April 7th, 1984	鼓面：太阳纹（10 芒）、虫形纹、四瓣花纹、四出钱纹、鸟形纹、兽形纹、蝉纹，鼓面边缘饰六组逆时针三足螺旋纹累蹲立体蛙； 鼓身：蝉纹、四瓣花纹、四出钱纹、兽面纹、四瓣花填线纹、兽形纹、连钱纹、鸟形纹，一侧鼓耳下鼓足位置饰一只叶脉纹立体鸟；扁耳两对饰辫纹 Drum face: patterns of sun(10 rays), insect-shape motif, quatrefoil, coins with quadrangle inside, bird-shape motif, beast-shape motif, cicada;6 overlap frogs with 3 feet and spiracle patterns on back anticlockwise stand on the edge; Drum body: patterns of cicada, quatrefoil, coins with quadrangle inside, beast face, quatrefoil filled with straight lines, beast-shape motif, coins part of overlap, bird-shape motif; a bird statue with leaf-vein patterns on back stands under one of the handle on the drum foot, Braid patterns on 2 pairs of flat handles.	88.5–89	52.4	灵山型 Lingshan Type	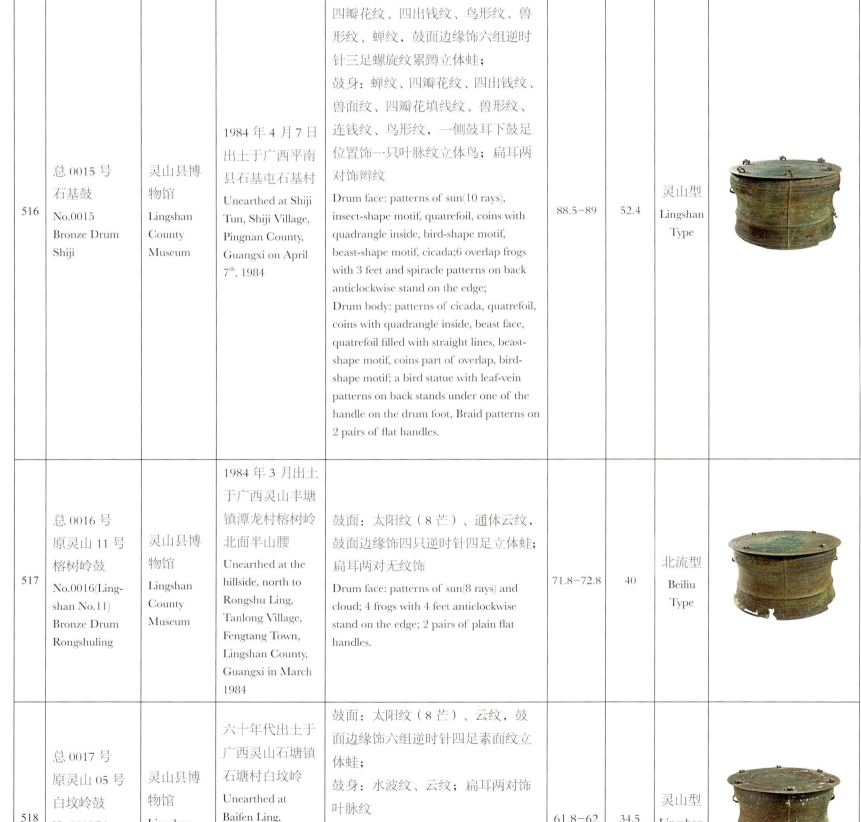
517	总 0016 号 原灵山 11 号 榕树岭鼓 No.0016(Lingshan No.11) Bronze Drum Rongshuling	灵山县博物馆 Lingshan County Museum	1984 年 3 月出土于广西灵山丰塘镇潭龙村榕树岭北面半山腰 Unearthed at the hillside, north to Rongshu Ling, Tanlong Village, Fengtang Town, Lingshan County, Guangxi in March 1984	鼓面：太阳纹（8 芒）、通体云纹，鼓面边缘饰四只逆时针四足立体蛙；扁耳两对无纹饰 Drum face: patterns of sun(8 rays) and cloud; 4 frogs with 4 feet anticlockwise stand on the edge; 2 pairs of plain flat handles.	71.8–72.8	40	北流型 Beiliu Type	
518	总 0017 号 原灵山 05 号 白坟岭鼓 No.0017(Lingshan No.05) Bronze Drum Baifenling	灵山县博物馆 Lingshan County Museum	六十年代出土于广西灵山石塘镇石塘村白坟岭 Unearthed at Baifen Ling, Shitang Village, Shitang Town, Lingshan County, Guangxi in 1960s	鼓面：太阳纹（8 芒）、云纹，鼓面边缘饰六组逆时针四足素面纹立体蛙； 鼓身：水波纹、云纹；扁耳两对饰叶脉纹 Drum face: patterns of sun(8 rays), all are cloud patterns, 6 frogs with 4 feet and plain back anticlockwise stand on the edge; Drum body: patterns of water wave, cloud; Leaf-vein patterns on 2 pairs of flat handles.	61.8–62	34.5	灵山型 Lingshan Type	

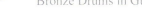

续表

序号 NO.	原编号及鼓名 Stock Number & Name	收藏单位 Museum	出土（征集） 时间、地点 Time & Spot for discovered or collected	主要装饰 Main Decorations	尺寸（厘米） Size(cm)		类型 Type	图片 Picture
					面径 Face Diameter	身高 Height		
519	总 0018 号 原灵山 06 号 稔坡村鼓 No.0018(Ling- shan No.06) Bronze Drum Renpocun	灵山县博 物馆 Lingshan County Museum	出土于广西灵山 新圩镇稔坡村 Unearthed at Renpo Village, Xinxu Town, Lingshan County, Guangxi	鼓面：太阳纹（12 芒）、蝉纹、四瓣花纹、四出钱纹、鸟形纹、连钱纹、席纹，鼓面边缘饰六组逆时针三足螺旋纹立体蛙，其中三组为累蹲蛙； 鼓身：蝉纹、四出钱纹、鸟形纹、连钱纹、兽面纹、席纹、四瓣花纹、一侧鼓耳下鼓足位置饰一对叶脉纹立体鸟；扁耳两对饰叶脉纹 Drum face: patterns of sun(12 rays), cicada, quatrefoil, coins with quadrangle inside, bird-shape motif, coins part of overlap, woven mat; 6 frogs with 3 feet and spiracle patterns on back anticlockwise stand on the edge, 3 of them are overlap; Drum body: patterns of cicada, bird-shape motif, coins part of overlap, beast face, woven mat, quatrefoil; A pair of bird statues with leaf-vein patterns on back stand under one of the handle on the drum foot; Leaf-vein patterns on 2 pairs of flat handles.	69.9~70.2	42.5	灵山型 Lingshan Type	
520	总 0019 号 原灵山 07 号 石塘鼓 No.0019(Ling- shan No.07) Bronze Drum Shitang	灵山县博 物馆 Lingshan County Museum	1984 年广西灵山 县文化馆征集 Collected by Lingshan County Cultural House of Guangxi in 1984	鼓面：太阳纹（10 芒）、四出钱纹、连钱纹，鼓面边缘饰六组逆时针三足叶脉纹、比轮钱纹立体蛙，其中三组为累蹲蛙； 鼓身：兽面纹、连钱纹、比轮钱纹；一侧鼓耳下鼓足位置饰两组乘骑立饰，鼓胸内壁饰一只立体牛；扁耳两对饰叶脉纹、乳钉纹 Drum face: patterns of sun(10 rays), coins with quadrangle inside, coins part of overlap; 6 frogs with 3 feet and leaf-vein & Bilun Coins patterns on back anticlockwise stand on the edge, 3 of them are overlap; Drum body: patterns of beast face, coins part of overlap, Bilun Coins;2 groups of horse-riding statues stand under one of the handle on the drum foot amd an ox statue stands on the inside wall of the chest; Leaf-vein & nipple protrusion patterns on 2 pairs of flat handles.	79.3~80.6	44	灵山型 Lingshan Type	
521	总 0020 号 原灵山 08 号 红尾塘鼓 No.0020(Ling- shan No.08) Bronze Drum Hongweitang	灵山县博 物馆 Lingshan County Museum	出土于广西灵山 伯劳镇六槛村 公所 Unearthed at Liukan Village office, Bolao Town, Lingshan County, Guangxi	鼓面：太阳纹（8 芒）、通体云纹、雷纹，鼓面边缘饰四只顺时针四足素面立体蛙；环耳两对饰缠丝纹 Drum face: patterns of sun(8 rays), cloud and thunder; 4 frogs with 4 feet and plain back clockwise stand on the edge; Silk-like patterns on 2 pairs of ring handles.	60~61	34.5	北流型 Beiliu Type	

425

序号 N0.	原编号及鼓名 Stock Number & Name	收藏单位 Museum	出土（征集） 时间、地点 Time & Spot for discovered or collected	主要装饰 Main Decorations	尺寸（厘米） Size(cm)		类型 Type	图片 Picture
					面径 Face Diameter	身高 Height		
522	总0025号 原灵山09号 拼垌鼓 No.0025(Ling-shan No.09) Bronze Drum Bingdong	灵山县博物馆 Lingshan County Museum	1974年出土于广西灵山武力镇桥山村拼垌屯西北2公里利竹丫 Unearthed at Lizhuya, 2km west-north to Bindong Tun, Qiaoshan Village,Wuli Town, Lingshan County, Guangxi in 1974	鼓面：太阳纹（8芒）、雷纹填线纹、连钱纹、同心圆纹、半同心圆纹、四出钱纹、鸟形纹，鼓面边缘饰六组顺时针三足叶脉纹、席纹立体蛙； 鼓身：鸟形填线纹、四出钱纹、比轮钱纹、连钱纹、同心圆纹、雷纹填线纹、四瓣花纹、蝉纹，扁耳两对饰叶脉纹、乳钉纹 Drum face: patterns of sun(8rays), thunder filled with straight lines, coins part of overlap, concentric circle, half concentric circle, coins with quadrangle inside, bird-shape motif; 6 frogs with 3 feet and leaf-vein & woven mat patterns on back anticlockwise stand on the edge; Drum body: patterns of birds filled with straight lines, coins with quadrangle inside, Bilun Coins, coins part of overlap, concentric circle, thunder filled with straight lines, quatrefoil, cicada; Leaf-vein & nipple protrusion patterns on 2 pairs of flat handles.	81	46.5	灵山型 Lingshan Type	
523	总0036号 原灵山12号 白木鼓 No.0036(Ling-shan No.12) Bronze Drum Baimu	灵山县博物馆 Lingshan County Museum	1986年出土于广西灵山三海镇白木村屋背岭 Unearthed at Wubei Ling, Baimu Village, Sanhai Town, Lingshan County, Guangxi in 1986	鼓面：太阳纹（10芒）、蝉纹、鸟形纹、虫形纹、四出钱纹、兽形纹、四瓣花纹、半圆填线纹、席纹，鼓面边缘饰六组逆时针三足螺旋纹立体蛙；其中三组为累蹲蛙 鼓身：蝉纹、虫形纹、四出钱纹、兽面纹、席纹、重轮钱纹、四瓣花填线纹、半圆填线纹、同心圆纹、连钱纹；一侧鼓耳下鼓足位置饰两只素面立体羊，其中一只头回转向后；扁耳两对饰辫纹 Drum face: patterns of sun(10 rays), cicada, bird-shape motif, insect-shape motif, coins with quadrangle inside, beast-shape motif, quatrefoil, half circle filled with straight lines, woven mat; 6 frogs with 3 feet and spiracle patterns on back anticlockwise stand on the edge; three of them are overlap Drum body: patterns of cicada, insect-shape motif, coins with quadrangle inside, beast face, woven mat, double-ring coin, quatrefoil filled with straight lines, half circle filled with straight lines, concentric circle, coins part of overlap; 2 sheep with plain back statues stand under one of the handle on the drum foot, one of them looking back; Braid patterns on 2 pairs of flat handles.	103.9–104.6	64	灵山型 Lingshan Type	

续表

序号 NO.	原编号及鼓名 Stock Number & Name	收藏单位 Museum	出土（征集） 时间、地点 Time & Spot for discovered or collected	主要装饰 Main Decorations	尺寸（厘米） Size(cm)		类型 Type	图片 Picture
					面径 Face Diameter	身高 Height		
524	总 0040 号 原灵山 13 号 大丰鼓 No.0040(Lingshan No.13) Bronze Drum Dafeng	灵山县博物馆 Lingshan County Museum	1986 年 6 月出土于广西丰塘镇大丰村大丰屯猫岭 Unearthed at Mao Ling, Dafeng Tun, Dafeng Village, Fengtang Town, Guangxi in June 1986	鼓面：太阳纹（10 芒）、蝉纹、四出钱纹、鸟形纹、虫形纹、连钱纹、席纹、兽形纹，鼓面边缘饰六组逆时针三足螺旋纹立体蛙；其中三组为累蹲蛙 鼓身：蝉纹、虫形纹、四出钱纹、连钱纹、兽面纹、雷纹、席纹、雷纹填线纹；一侧鼓耳下鼓足位置饰一对叶脉纹立体鸟；扁耳两对饰凸棱纹 Drum face: patterns of sun(10 rays), cicada, coins with quadrangle inside, bird-shape motif, insect-shape motif, coins part of overlap, woven mat, beast-shape motif; 6 frogs with 3 feet and spiracle patterns on back anticlockwise stand on the edge; three of them are overlap Drum body: patterns of cicada, insect-shape motif, coins with quadrangle inside, coins part of overlap, beast face, thunder, woven mat, thunder filled with straight lines; A pair of bird statues with leaf-vein patterns on back stand under one of the handle on the drum foot; Raise ridges on 2 pairs of flat handles.	99－100.5	59.3	灵山型 Lingshan Type	
525	总 0043 号 原灵山 14 号 石龙鼓 No.0043(Lingshan No.14) Bronze Drum Shilong	灵山县博物馆 Lingshan County Museum	1980 年出土于广西灵山三海镇大武村石龙屯七头岭 Unearthed at Qitou Ling, Shilong Tun, Dawu Village, Sanhai Town, Lingshan County, Guangxi in 1980	鼓面：太阳纹（12 芒）、蝉纹、四瓣花纹、四出钱纹、鸟形纹、虫形纹、连钱纹、席纹，鼓面边缘饰六组逆时针三足螺旋纹累蹲立体蛙； 鼓身：蝉纹、连钱纹、四出钱纹、鸟形纹、四瓣花纹、兽面纹、席纹、虫形纹；一侧鼓耳下鼓足位置饰一只斜线纹立体鸟；扁耳两对饰辫纹 Drum face: patterns of sun(12 rays), cicada, quatrefoil, coins with quadrangle inside, bird-shape motif, insect-shape motif, coins part of overlap, woven mat; 6 overlap frogs with 3 feet and spiracle patterns on back anticlockwise stand on the edge; Drum body: patterns of cicada, coins part of overlap, coins with quadrangle inside, bird-shape motif, quatrefoil, beast face, woven mat, insect-shape motif; A bird statue with oblique lines on back stands under one of the handle on the drum foot; Braid patterns on 2 pairs of flat handles.	79.8－80.2	48	灵山型 Lingshan Type	

序号 N0.	原编号及鼓名 Stock Number & Name	收藏单位 Museum	出土（征集） 时间、地点 Time & Spot for discovered or collected	主要装饰 Main Decorations	尺寸（厘米） Size(cm)		类型 Type	图片 Picture
					面径 Face Diameter	身高 Height		
526	总0065号 原灵山15号 鹿跳山鼓 No.0065(Ling- shan No.15) Bronze Drum Lutiaoshan	灵山县博物馆 Lingshan County Museum	1987年6月1日出土于广西灵山旧州镇长基村尚坪屯鹿跳山 Unearthed at Lutiaoshan, Shangping Tun, Changji Village, Jiuzhou Town, Lingshan County, Guangxi on June 1st, 1987	鼓面：太阳纹（8芒）、四方钱纹、虫形纹、鸟形纹、云纹、兽形纹、半圆填线纹，鼓面边缘饰六组逆时针三足叶脉纹、栉纹立体蛙； 鼓身：四方钱纹、雷纹填线纹、云纹、变体雷纹填线纹、虫形纹、半圆填线纹、席纹、蝉纹；扁耳两对饰辫纹 Drum face: patterns of sun(8 rays), coins with a square inside, insect-shape motif, bird-shape motif, cloud, beast-shape motif, half circle filled with straight lines; 6 frogs with 3 feet and leaf-vein & straight line patterns on back anticlockwise stand on the edge; Drum body: patterns of coins with a square inside, thunder filled with straight lines, cloud, transformed thunder filled with straight lines, insect-shape motif, half circle filled with straight lines, woven mat, cicada; Braid patterns on 2 pairs of flat handles.	82.5	53.4	灵山型 Lingshan Type	
527	总0066号 原灵山16号 富致岭鼓 No.0066(Ling- shan No.16) Bronze Drum Fuzhiling	灵山县博物馆 Lingshan County Museum	1987年8月1日出土于广西灵山旧州镇青松村富致岭屯大坑口 Unearthed at Dakengkou, Fuzhiling Tun, Qingsong Village, Jiuzhou Town, Lingshan County, Guangxi on August 1st, 1987	鼓面：太阳纹（8芒）、通面雷纹、变体云纹，鼓面边缘饰四只逆时针四足素面立蛙； 鼓身：半圆填线纹、雷纹；环耳两对饰缠丝纹 Drum face: patterns of sun(8 rays), thunder, transformed cloud; 4 frogs with 4 feet and plain back anticlockwise stand on the edge; Drum body: patterns of half circle filled with straight lines, thunder; Silk-like patterns on 2 pairs of ring handles.	74.3-75	42.5	北流型 Beiliu Type	

序号 NO.	原编号及鼓名 Stock Number & Name	收藏单位 Museum	出土（征集） 时间、地点 Time & Spot for discovered or collected	主要装饰 Main Decorations	尺寸（厘米） Size(cm)		类型 Type	图片 Picture
					面径 Face Diameter	身高 Height		
528	总 0108 号 原灵山 17 号 华龙鼓 No.0108(Lingshan No.17) Bronze Drum Hualong	灵山县博物馆 Lingshan County Museum	1988 年 3 月 26 日出土于广西灵山丰塘镇高华村公所华龙村华龙水库山坡 Unearthed at the hillside next to Hualong reservoir, Hualong Village, Gaohua Village office, Fengtang Town, Lingshan County, Guangxi on March 26th, 1988	鼓面：太阳纹（8 芒）、云纹，鼓面边缘饰四只顺时针四足素面立体蛙； 鼓身：云纹填线纹、连钱纹、半圆纹、席纹、方孔钱纹；扁耳两对纹饰锈蚀 Drum face: patterns of sun(8 rays) and cloud; 4 frogs with 4 feet and plain back anticlockwise stand on the edge; Drum body: patterns of cloud mixed straight lines, coins part of overlap, half circle, woven mat, coins with a square inside; the patterns on 2 pair flat handles are rusting.	76.1~76.7	44.2	灵山型 Lingshan Type	
529	总 114 号 原灵山 18 号 珠理鼓 No.0114(Lingshan No.18) Bronze Drum Zhuli	灵山县博物馆 Lingshan County Museum	1988 年 4 月出土于广西灵山武利珠理村 Unearthed at Zhuli Village, Wuli, Lingshan County, Guangxi in April, 1988	鼓面：太阳纹（10 芒）、蝉纹、四瓣花纹、四出钱纹、鸟形纹、席纹，鼓面边缘饰六组逆时针三足螺旋纹立体蛙； 鼓身：蝉纹、四出钱纹、鸟形纹、四瓣花纹、连钱纹、虫形纹；一侧鼓耳下鼓足位置饰一只立体鸟；扁耳两对饰辫纹 Drum face: patterns of sun(10 rays), cicada, quatrefoil, coins with quadrangle inside, bird-shape motif, woven mat; 6 frogs with 3 feet and spiracle patterns on back anticlockwise stand on the edge; Drum body: patterns of cicada, coins with quadrangle inside, bird-shape motif, quatrefoil, coins part of overlap, insect-shape motif; A bird statue stands under one of the handle on the drum foot; Braid patterns on 2 pairs of flat handles.	69.5~69.8	41 （残） Incomplete	灵山型 Lingshan Type	

序号 N0.	原编号及鼓名 Stock Number & Name	收藏单位 Museum	出土（征集）时间、地点 Time & Spot for discovered or collected	主要装饰 Main Decorations	尺寸（厘米）Size(cm)		类型 Type	图片 Picture
					面径 Face Diameter	身高 Height		
530	总 0124 号 原灵山 21 号 六颜鼓 No.0124(Lingshan No.21) Bronze Drum Liuyan	灵山县博物馆 Lingshan County Museum	1988 年出土于广西灵山丰塘镇六颜村公所 Unearthed at Liuyan Village office, Fengtang Town, Lingshan County, Guangxi in 1988	鼓面：太阳纹（10 芒）、连钱纹、四出钱纹、鸟纹、鱼纹、席纹、鸟形纹、兽形纹、雷纹填线纹，鼓面边缘饰六组逆时针三足螺旋纹累蹲立体蛙；鼓身：连钱纹、四出钱纹、兽面纹、席纹、同心圆纹、雷纹填线纹、虫形纹、鸟纹、鱼纹、蝉纹；鼓胸内壁饰一组螺旋纹累蹲蛙；扁耳两对饰辫纹 Drum face: patterns of sun(10 rays), coins part of overlap, coins with quadrangle inside, bird, fish, woven mat, bird, beast-shape motif, thunder filled with straight lines; 6 overlap frogs with 3 feet and spiracle patterns on back anticlockwise stand on the edge; Drum body: patterns of coins part of overlap, coins with quadrangle inside, beast face, woven mat, concentric circle, thunder filled with straight lines, insect-shape motif, bird, fish, cicada; A group of overlap frogs with spiracles on back stand on the chest inside; Braid patterns on 2 pairs of flat handles.	81−81.3	50	灵山型 Lingshan Type	
531	总 0143 号 原灵山 19 号 天顶山鼓 No.0143(Lingshan No.19) Bronze Drum Tiandingshan	灵山县博物馆 Lingshan County Museum	1990 年 3 月出土于广西灵山檀圩镇东岸村天顶山屯六局塘岭 Unearthed at Liujutang Ling, Tiandingshan Tun, Dong'an Village, Tanxu Town, Lingshan County, Guangxi in March, 1990	鼓面：太阳纹（12 芒）、蝉纹、四出钱纹、鸟形纹、连钱纹、席纹、四瓣花纹，鼓面边缘饰六组逆时针三足螺旋纹立蛙，其中三组为累蹲蛙；鼓身：蝉纹、四瓣花纹、四出钱纹、连钱纹、席纹、四瓣花填线纹、虫形纹；一侧鼓耳下鼓足位置饰一只螺旋纹、直线纹立体鸟；扁耳两对饰辫纹 Drum face: patterns of sun(12 rays), cicada, coins with quadrangle inside, bird-shape motif, coins part of overlap, woven mat, quatrefoil; 6 frogs with 3 feet and spiracle patterns on back anticlockwise stand on the edge, 3 of them are overlap; Drum body: patterns of cicada, quatrefoil, coins with quadrangle inside, coins part of overlap, woven mat, quatrefoil filled with straight lines, insect-shape motif; A bird with spiracles and straight lines on back stands under one of the handles on the drum foot; Braid patterns on 2 pairs of flat handles.	80−80.5	48.5 （残）Incomplete	灵山型 Lingshan Type	

续表

序号 NO.	原编号及鼓名 Stock Number & Name	收藏单位 Museum	出土（征集）时间、地点 Time & Spot for discovered or collected	主要装饰 Main Decorations	尺寸（厘米） Size(cm)		类型 Type	图片 Picture
					面径 Face Diameter	身高 Height		
532	总0146号 原灵山20号 杉木簏鼓 No.0146(Lingshan No.20) Bronze Drum Shanmulu	灵山县博物馆 Lingshan County Museum	1990年3月出土于广西灵山平南镇岭平村六谭屯杉木簏北山脚 Unearthed at the foot of the hill Shanmulu, Liutan Tun, Lingping Village, Pingnan Town, Lingshan County, Guangxi in March, 1990	鼓面：太阳纹（8芒）、通体雷纹，鼓面边缘饰四只逆时针四足素面立体蛙；扁耳两对饰叶脉纹 Drum face: patterns of sun(8rays) and thunder. Thunders are all over the face and body. 4 frogs with 4 feet and plain back anticlockwise stand on the edge; Leaf-vein patterns on 2 pairs of flat handles.	59.2−59.8	33 （残） Incomplete	北流型 Beiliu Type	
533	总0166号 泥鳅湖鼓 No.0166 Bronze Drum Niqiuhu	灵山县博物馆 Lingshan County Museum	1984年3月30日出土于广西灵山旧州镇青松村宁屋屯泥鳅湖坳 Unearthed at Niqiuhu Ao, Ningwu Tun, Qingsong Village, Jiuzhou Town, Lingshan County, Guangxi on March 30th, 1984	鼓面：太阳纹（10芒）、云纹、雷纹填线纹、席纹、四瓣花纹、变形羽人纹、蝉纹，鼓面边缘饰六组顺时针三足斜线纹立体蛙； 鼓身：同心圆纹、席纹、四瓣花填线纹、兽形纹、虫形纹、方孔钱纹、蝉纹；扁耳两对饰叶脉纹 Drum face: patterns of sun(10 rays),cloud, thunder filled with straight lines, woven mat, quatrefoil, transformed feathermen, cicada; 6 frogs with 3 feet and oblique lines on back anticlockwise stand on the edge; Drum body: patterns of concentric circle, woven mat, quatrefoil filled with straight lines, beast-shape motif, insect-shape motif, coins with a square inside, cicada; Leaf-vein patterns on 2 pairs of flat handles.	80−81	49.6	灵山型 Lingshan Type	
534	总0182号 No.0182	灵山县博物馆 Lingshan County Museum	出土地点不明 The discovered spot is unknown	鼓面：太阳纹（10芒）、蝉纹、虫形纹、鸟形纹、四出钱纹、连钱纹、席纹，鼓面边缘饰六组逆时针三足螺旋纹立蛙； 鼓身：蝉纹、连钱纹、四出钱纹、鸟形纹、席纹、雷纹填线纹、兽面纹、虫形纹、四瓣花纹；扁耳两对饰辫纹 Drum face: patterns of sun(10 rays), cicada, insect-shape motif, bird-shape motif, coins with quadrangle inside, coins part of overlap, woven mat; 6 frogs with 3 feet and spiracles on back anticlockwise stand on the edge; Drum body: patterns of cicada, coins part of overlap, coins with quadrangle inside, bird-shape motif, woven mat, thunder filled with straight lines, beast face, insect-shape motif, quatrefoil; Braid patterns on 2 pairs of flat handles.	80.6−80.8	48.5	灵山型 Lingshan Type	

续表

序号 NO.	原编号及鼓名 Stock Number & Name	收藏单位 Museum	出土（征集）时间、地点 Time & Spot for discovered or collected	主要装饰 Main Decorations	尺寸（厘米）Size(cm)		类型 Type	图片 Picture
					面径 Face Diameter	身高 Height		
535	总0183号 原灵山01号 双凤鼓 No.0183(Lingshan No.01) Bronze Drum Shuangfeng	灵山县博物馆 Lingshan County Museum	1973年出土于广西灵山旧州镇双凤村北约150米 Unearthed in the north,150m to Shuangfeng Village, Jiuzhou Town, Lingshan County, Guangxi in 1973	鼓面：太阳纹（10芒）、云纹、同心圆纹、鸟形纹、雷纹、重轮钱纹、方孔钱纹、虫形纹、四瓣花填线纹、半圆叶脉纹、席纹、蝉纹，鼓面边缘饰六组顺时针三足螺旋纹立体蛙；鼓身：重轮钱、方孔钱纹、四瓣花纹、虫形纹、云纹、半圆填线纹、雷纹、同心圆纹、四瓣花填线纹、兽形纹、席纹、蝉纹；扁耳两对饰辫纹 Drum face: patterns of sun(10 rays), cloud, concentric circle, bird-shape motif, thunder, double-ring coin, coin with a square inside, insect-shape motif, quatrefoil filled with straight lines, half circle mixed leaf vein, woven mat, cicada; 6 frogs with 3 feet and spiracles on back anticlockwise stand on the edge; Drum body: patterns of double-ring coin, coin with a square inside, quatrefoil, insect-shape motif, cloud, half circle filled with straight lines, thunder, concentric circle, quatrefoil filled with straight lines, beast-shape motif, woven mat, cicada; Braid patterns on 2 pairs of flat handles.	103~103.5	62	灵山型 Lingshan Type	
536	总0349号 绿水村二号 No.0349 Lvshuicun No.2	灵山县博物馆 Lingshan County Museum	2000年5月20日出土于广西灵山新圩镇绿水村马麓塘山 Unearthed at Malutang Hill, Lvshui Village, Xinxu Town, Lingshan County, Guangxi on May 20th, 2000	鼓面：太阳纹（8芒）、雷纹，鼓面边缘饰四只顺时针四足素面立蛙；鼓身：云纹、雷纹填线纹；环耳两对无纹饰 Drum face: patterns of sun(8 rays) and thunder; 4 frogs with 4 feet and plain back anticlockwise stand on the edge; Drum body: patterns of cloud, thunder filled with straight lines; 2 pairs of plain ring handles.	78.3~78.6	45.8	北流型 Beiliu Type	

续表

序号 NO.	原编号及鼓名 Stock Number & Name	收藏单位 Museum	出土（征集） 时间、地点 Time & Spot for discovered or collected	主要装饰 Main Decorations	尺寸（厘米） Size(cm)		类型 Type	图片 Picture
					面径 Face Diameter	身高 Height		
537	总 0429 号 长麓岭鼓 No.0429 Bronze Drum Changluling	灵山县博物馆 Lingshan County Museum	2002 年 8 月 10日出土于广西灵山丰塘镇丰塘村村委三叉村长麓岭 Unearthed at Changlu Ling, Sancha Village, Fengtang Village office, Fengtang Town, Lingshan County, Guangxi on August 10th, 2002	鼓面：太阳纹（12 芒）、栉纹、同心圆纹、复线交叉纹、变形羽人纹、变形翔鹭间定胜纹，鼓面边缘饰四只逆时针四足素面立蛙； 鼓身：栉纹、同心圆纹、栉纹同心圆纹垂直纹带、圆心三角垂叶纹；扁耳两对饰辫纹 Drum face: patterns of sun(12 rays), comb line, concentric circle, multiple & crossed line, transformed feathermen, transformed flying heron mixed Dingsheng; 4 frogs with 4 feet and plain back anticlockwise stand on the edge; Drum body: patterns of comb line, concentric circle, vertical ribbon with straight line and concentric circles, leaf-shape triangle with concentric circles in the middle; Braid patterns on 2 pairs of flat handles.	62.3−63	43	冷水冲型 Lengshui-chong Type	
538	大涷村鼓 Bronze Drum Dabingcun	灵山县博物馆 Lingshan County Museum	2010 年出土于广西灵山丰塘镇大涷村 Unearthed at Dabing Village, Fengtang Town, Lingshan County, Guangxi in 2010	鼓面：太阳纹（10 芒）、虫形纹、同心圆纹、席纹、四出钱纹、鸟形纹、兽面纹、云纹、兽形纹、半圆叶脉纹、蝉纹，鼓面边缘饰六组逆时针三足螺旋纹立体蛙； 鼓身：虫形纹、席纹、云纹、四出钱纹、兽面纹、比轮钱纹、四瓣花纹、半圆叶脉纹、蝉纹；扁耳两对饰辫纹 Drum face: patterns of sun(10 rays), insect-shape motif, concentric circle, woven mat, coins with quadrangle inside, bird-shape motif, beast face, cloud, beast-shape motif, half circle in leaf vein, cicada;6 frogs with 3 feet and spiracles on back anticlockwise stand on the edge; Drum body: patterns of insect-shape motif, woven mat, cloud, coins with quadrangle inside, beast face, coin Bilun, quatrefoil, half circle in leaf vein, cicada; Braid patterns on 2 pairs of flat handles.	80−81	47.5	灵山型 Lingshan Type	

序号 N0.	原编号及鼓名 Stock Number & Name	收藏单位 Museum	出土（征集）时间、地点 Time & Spot for discovered or collected	主要装饰 Main Decorations	尺寸（厘米）Size(cm)		类型 Type	图片 Picture
					面径 Face Diameter	身高 Height		
539	总 0025 号 铜鼓形饰件 No.0025 Decoration in Bronze drum shape	灵山县博物馆 Lingshan County Museum	1990 年 1 月出土于广西灵山新圩镇塘排村九都岭一座东汉墓 Unearthed in an East-Han Dynasty grave at Jiudu Ling, Tangpai Village, Xinxu Town, Lingshan County, Guangxi in January, 1990	鼓面有 8 弦，边缘有四蛙痕迹，鼓足边缘有一圈绳纹和铃铛 8 strings on the drum face, marks of 4 frogs on the drum edge, one ring of rope motif on the edge of drum foot and there is a small bell.	2.46~2.48	1.89	饰件 Decoration	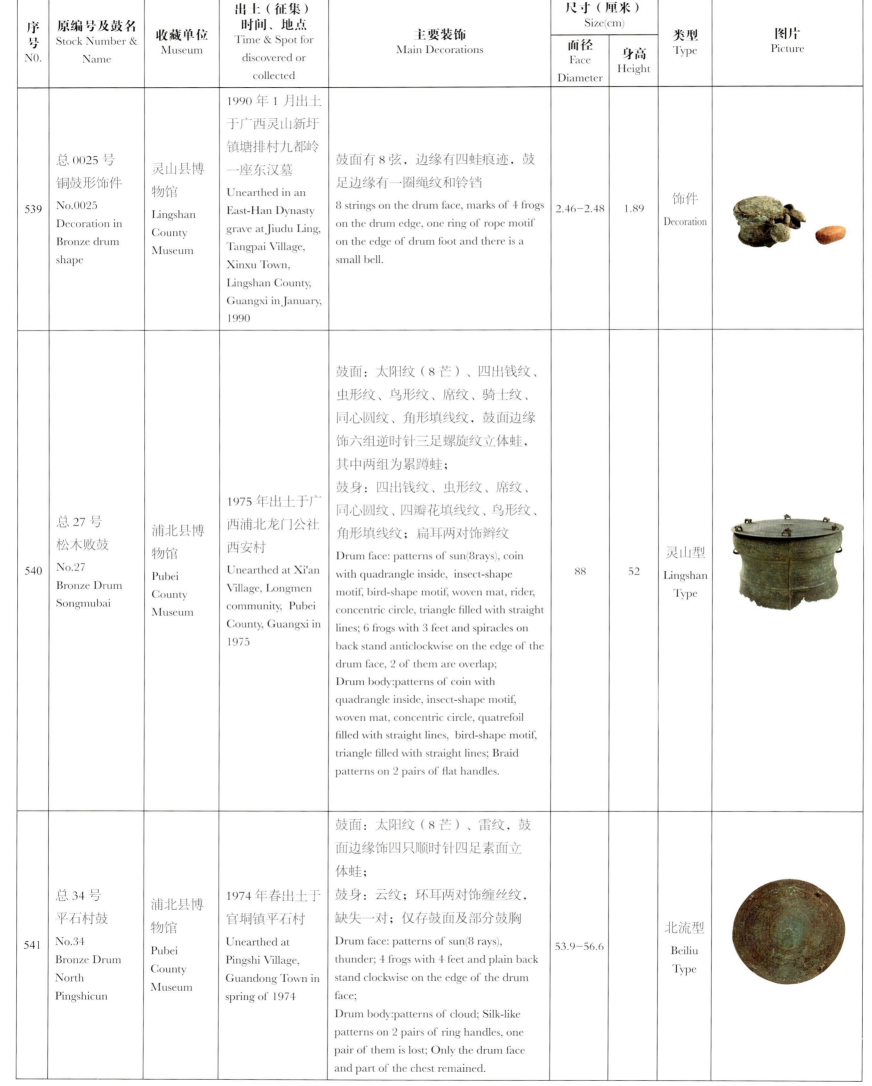
540	总 27 号 松木败鼓 No.27 Bronze Drum Songmubai	浦北县博物馆 Pubei County Museum	1975 年出土于广西浦北龙门公社西安村 Unearthed at Xi'an Village, Longmen community, Pubei County, Guangxi in 1975	鼓面：太阳纹（8 芒）、四出钱纹、虫形纹、鸟形纹、席纹、骑士纹、同心圆纹、角形填线纹，鼓面边缘饰六组逆时针三足螺旋纹立体蛙，其中两组为累蹲蛙；鼓身：四出钱纹、虫形纹、席纹、同心圆纹、四瓣花填线纹、鸟形纹、角形填线纹；扁耳两对饰辫纹 Drum face: patterns of sun(8rays), coin with quadrangle inside, insect-shape motif, bird-shape motif, woven mat, rider, concentric circle, triangle filled with straight lines; 6 frogs with 3 feet and spiracles on back stand anticlockwise on the edge of the drum face, 2 of them are overlap; Drum body:patterns of coin with quadrangle inside, insect-shape motif, woven mat, concentric circle, quatrefoil filled with straight lines, bird-shape motif, triangle filled with straight lines; Braid patterns on 2 pairs of flat handles.	88	52	灵山型 Lingshan Type	
541	总 34 号 平石村鼓 No.34 Bronze Drum North Pingshicun	浦北县博物馆 Pubei County Museum	1974 年春出土于官垌镇平石村 Unearthed at Pingshi Village, Guandong Town in spring of 1974	鼓面：太阳纹（8 芒）、雷纹，鼓面边缘饰四只顺时针四足素面立体蛙；鼓身：云纹；环耳两对饰缠丝纹，缺失一对；仅存鼓面及部分鼓胸 Drum face: patterns of sun(8 rays), thunder; 4 frogs with 4 feet and plain back stand clockwise on the edge of the drum face; Drum body:patterns of cloud; Silk-like patterns on 2 pairs of ring handles, one pair of them is lost; Only the drum face and part of the chest remained.	53.9~56.6		北流型 Beiliu Type	

序号 N0.	原编号及鼓名 Stock Number & Name	收藏单位 Museum	出土（征集） 时间、地点 Time & Spot for discovered or collected	主要装饰 Main Decorations	尺寸（厘米） Size(cm)		类型 Type	图片 Picture
					面径 Face Diameter	身高 Height		
542	总 36 号 搭竹寮鼓 No.36 Bronze Drum Dazhuliao	浦北县博物馆 Pubei County Museum	1972 年秋出土于广西浦北龙门公社莲塘大队搭竹寮岭 Unearthed at Dazhuliao Ling, Liantang production team, Longmen community, Pubei County, Guangxi in the Autumn of 1972	鼓面：太阳纹（10 芒）、雷纹、兽面纹、四瓣花纹、四出钱填线纹、云纹、比轮钱纹，鼓面边缘饰六组逆时针三足叶脉纹立蛙，其中三组为累蹲蛙； 鼓身：雷纹填线纹、四出钱纹、比轮钱纹、兽面纹、云纹、雷纹；扁耳两对饰叶脉纹 Drum face: patterns of sun(10rays), thunder, beast face, quatrefoil, coin with quadrangle inside filled with straight lines, cloud, coin Bilun; 6 frogs with 3 feet and leaf-vein pattern on back stand anticlockwise on the edge of the drum face, 3 of them are overlap; Drum body: thunder filled with straight lines, coin with quadrangle inside, coin Bilun, beast face, cloud, thunder; Leaf-vein patterns on 2 pairs of flat handles.	83—84.2	46.1	灵山型 Lingshan Type	
543	总 42 号 破石山鼓 No.42 Bronze Drum Poshishan	浦北县博物馆 Pubei County Museum	1980 年秋出土于广西浦北大成公社六平大队破石山村屋角岭 Unearthed at Wujiao Ling, Poshishan Village, Liuping production team, Dacheng community, Pubei County, Guangxi in 1980	鼓面：太阳纹（8 芒）、方孔钱纹、席纹、雷纹、团花纹、同心圆交叉纹、云纹、雷纹填线纹，鼓面边缘饰六组顺时针四足立体蛙； 鼓身：云纹、同心圆交叉纹、席纹、团花纹、方孔钱纹、雷纹、雷纹填线纹、连钱纹；扁耳两对无纹饰 Drum face: patterns of sun(8rays), coin with a square inside, woven mat, thunder, flower clump, concentric circles in crossed line, cloud, thunder filled with straight lines; 6 frogs with 4 feet and spiracles on back stand anticlockwise on the edge of the drum face; Drum body:patterns of cloud, concentric circles in crossed line, woven mat, flower clump, coin with a square inside, thunder, thunder filled with straight lines, coins part of overlap; 2 pairs of blank flat handles.	69—69.5	40.5	灵山型 Lingshan Type	

序号 N0.	原编号及鼓名 Stock Number & Name	收藏单位 Museum	出土（征集） 时间、地点 Time & Spot for discovered or collected	主要装饰 Main Decorations	尺寸（厘米） Size(cm)		类型 Type	图片 Picture
					面径 Face Diameter	身高 Height		
544	总45号 佛新村鼓 No.45 Bronze Drum Foxincun	浦北县博物馆 Pubei County Museum	1973年春出土于广西浦北北通乡佛新村 Unearthed at Foxin Village, Beitong, Pubei County, Guangxi in the spring of 1973	鼓面：太阳纹（8芒）、云纹，鼓面边缘饰四只逆时针四足素面立蛙；鼓身：对称半同心圆纹、云纹；扁耳两对无纹饰； Drum face: patterns of sun(8rays), cloud; 4 frogs with 4 feet and plain back stand anticlockwise on the edge of the drum face; Drum body:patterns of half concentric circles in pair, cloud; 2 pairs of blank flat handles.	86.6–86.8	52.3（残）Incomplete	北流型 Beiliu Type	
545	总46号 原浦北03号 北河村鼓 No.46 (Pubei No.3) Bronze Drum Beihecun	浦北县博物馆 Pubei County Museum	1975年秋出土于广西浦北小江公社北河大队大塘鹿生产队曲里塘岭牛角叉鹿 Unearthed at Niujiaocha Lu, Qulitang Ling, Datang Lu production team, Beihe team, Xiaojiang community, Pubei County, Guangxi in the Autumn of 1975	鼓面：太阳纹（8芒）、通体云纹、雷纹，鼓面边缘饰四只顺时针四足素面立蛙；环耳两对缠丝纹 Drum face: patterns of sun(8rays), cloud and thunder; 4 frogs with 4 feet and plain back stand clockwise on the edge of the drum face; Silk-like patterns on 2 pairs of ring handles.	96.7–99	53.4	北流型 Beiliu Type	
546	总48号 公租屯鼓 No.48 Bronze Drum Gongzu Tun	浦北县博物馆 Pubei County Museum	1974年秋出土于广西浦北北通乡中屯大队公租四队 Unearthed at Gongzu Team Four, Zhongtun team, Beitong, Pubei County, Guangxi in the Autumn of 1974	鼓面：太阳纹（8芒）、通体云纹，鼓面边缘饰四只逆时针四足素面立蛙；环耳两对无纹饰；仅存鼓面及部分鼓胸 Drum face: patterns of sun(8rays), cloud; 4 frogs with 4 feet and plain back stand anticlockwise on the edge of the drum face; 2 pairs of plain ring handles; Only the drum face and part of the chest remained.	71–72.5		北流型 Beiliu Type	

续表

序号 N0.	原编号及鼓名 Stock Number & Name	收藏单位 Museum	出土（征集） 时间、地点 Time & Spot for discovered or collected	主要装饰 Main Decorations	尺寸（厘米） Size(cm)		类型 Type	图片 Picture
					面径 Face Diameter	身高 Height		
547	总49号 螺壳埇鼓 No.49 Bronze Drum Luokeyong	浦北县博物馆 Pubei County Museum	1980年秋出土于广西浦北安石公社安石大队螺壳埇村 Unearthed at Luokeyong Village, Anshi team, Anshi community, Pubei County, Guangxi in the Autumn of 1980	鼓面：太阳纹（8芒）、席纹、虫形纹、变形羽人纹、四出钱纹，团花纹、兽面纹，鼓面边缘饰六组顺时针三足螺旋纹、辫纹立体蛙； 鼓身：云纹、四出钱纹、团花纹、虫形纹、席纹、变形羽人纹、兽面纹、蝉纹；扁耳两对饰辫纹 Drum face: patterns of sun(8rays), woven mat, insect-shape motif, transformed feathermen, coins with quadrangle inside, flower clump, beast face; 6 frogs with 3 feet and spiracles & braids on back stand clockwise on the edge of the drum face; Drum body:patterns of cloud, coins with quadrangle inside, flower clump, insect-shape motif, woven mat, transformed feathermen, beast face, cicada; Braid patterns on 2 pairs of flat handles.	87.3-88	53	灵山型 Lingshan Type	
548	总50号 乌石村鼓 No.50 Bronze Drum Wushicun	浦北县博物馆 Pubei County Museum	1965年秋出土于广西浦北寨圩公社乌石大队后土岭 Unearthed at Houtu Ling, Wushi team, Zhaixu community, Pubei County, Guangxi in Autumn of 1965	鼓面：太阳纹（10芒）、席纹、四瓣花纹、虫形纹、雷纹填线纹、十字交叉填线纹、四出钱纹、鸟形纹、四瓣花填线纹、兽形纹、蝉纹，鼓面边缘饰六组逆时针三足螺旋纹立蛙，其中三组为累蹲蛙； 鼓身：蝉纹、四瓣花纹、虫形纹、四出钱纹、兽面纹、连钱纹、雷纹、席纹、兽形纹、鸟形纹；扁耳两对饰凸棱纹 Drum face: patterns of sun(10rays), woven mat, quatrefoil, insect-shape motif, thunder filled with straight lines, crosses mixed straight lines, coins with quadrangle inside, bird-shape motif, quatrefoil filled with straight lines, beast-shape motif, cicada; 6 frogs with 3 feet and spiracles on back stand anticlockwise on the edge of the drum face,3 of them are overlap; Drum body:patterns of cicada, quatrefoil, insect-shape motif, coins with quadrangle inside, beast face, coins part of overlap, woven mat, beast-shape motif, bird-shape motif; Raise ridges on 2 pairs of plat handles.	100.2-101	55 （残） Incom- plete	灵山型 Lingshan Type	

序号 N0.	原编号及鼓名 Stock Number & Name	收藏单位 Museum	出土（征集） 时间、地点 Time & Spot for discovered or collected	主要装饰 Main Decorations	尺寸（厘米） Size(cm)		类型 Type	图片 Picture
					面径 Face Diameter	身高 Height		
549	总51号 大颈塘鼓 No.51 Bronze Drum Dajingtang	浦北县博物馆 Pubei County Museum	1972年8月30日出土于广西浦北小江公社文山大队大颈塘十八鹿 Unearthed at Shibalu, Dajingtang, Wenshan Team, Xiaojiang community, Pubei County, Guangxi on August 30th, 1972	鼓面：太阳纹（10芒）、人形纹、虫形纹、变形羽人纹、四出钱纹、四瓣花纹、蝉纹，鼓面边缘饰六组逆时针三足螺旋纹累蹲立体蛙； 鼓身：席纹、比轮钱纹、四出钱纹、半圆叶脉纹、云纹、鸟形纹、兽形纹、蝉纹；扁耳两对饰辫纹 Drum face: patterns of sun(10rays), human-shape motif, insect-shape motif, transformed feathermen, coins with quadrangle inside, quatrefoil, cicada; 6 overlap frogs with 3 feet and spiracles on back stand anticlockwise on the edge of the drum face; Drum body: patterns of woven mat, coin Bilun, coins with quadrangle inside, half circle in leaf vein, cloud, bird-shape motif, beast-shape motif, cicada; Braid patterns on 2 pairs of flat handles.	114.2–115.4	68	灵山型 Lingshan Type	
550	总166号 华木垌鼓 No.166 Bronze Drum Huamudong	浦北县博物馆 Pubei County Museum	1990年3月12日出土于广西浦北福旺镇新塘村华木垌 Unearthed at Huamudong, Xintang Village, Fuwang Town, Pubei County, Guangxi on March 12th, 1990	鼓面：太阳纹（8芒）、雷纹、四瓣花填线纹、席纹、云纹、蝉纹，鼓面边缘饰四只逆时针三足雷纹立蛙； 鼓身：云纹、四瓣花填线纹、雷纹填线纹、半圆直线纹、虫形纹、席纹；扁耳两对饰辫纹 Drum face: patterns of sun(8rays), thunder, quatrefoil filled with straight line, woven mat, cloud, cicada, 4 frogs with 3 feet and thunder patterns on back stand anticlockwise on the edge of the drum face; Drum body: patterns of cloud, quatrefoil filled with straight lines, thunder filled with straight lines, straight lines in half circle, insect-shape motif, woven mat; Braid patterns on 2 pairs of flat handles.	68.3–69.2	42 （残） Incom-plete	灵山型 Lingshan Type	

续表

序号 N0.	原编号及鼓名 Stock Number & Name	收藏单位 Museum	出土（征集） 时间、地点 Time & Spot for discovered or collected	主要装饰 Main Decorations	尺寸（厘米） Size(cm)		类型 Type	图片 Picture
					面径 Face Diameter	身高 Height		
551	总 255 号 沙梨山鼓 No.255 Bronze Drum Shalishan	浦北县博物馆 Pubei County Museum	1984 年 11 月 11 日出土于广西浦 北北通乡高村沙 梨山 Unearthed at Shali Hill, Xianggao Village, Beitong, Pubei County, Guangxi on November 11th, 1984	鼓面：太阳纹（8 芒）、云纹，鼓面边缘饰四只逆时针四足素面立体蛙；鼓身纹饰锈蚀；扁耳两对饰辫纹 Drum face: patterns of sun(8rays), cloud; 4 frogs with 4 feet and plain back stand anticlockwise on the edge of the drum face; Patterns on the body were rusting; Braid patterns on 2 pairs of flat handles.	78	45.5	北流型 Beiliu Type	
552	总 584 号 上柿子村鼓 No.584 Bronze Drum Shangshizi Cun	浦北县博物馆 Pubei County Museum	1995 年 2 月 18 日出土于广西浦 北民乐镇西角上 柿子村 Unearthed at Shangshizi Village, the west corner of Minle Town, Pubei County, Guangxi on February 18th, 1995	鼓面：太阳纹（10 芒）、栉纹、切线同心圆纹、复线交叉纹、变形羽人纹、复线角形纹、变形翔鹭间定胜纹、蝉纹、鼓面边缘饰四只逆时针三足立蛙； 鼓身：栉纹、同心圆纹、复线角形纹、栉纹同心圆纹垂直纹带、蝉纹；扁耳两对饰辫纹 Drum face: patterns of sun(10rays), comb line, tangent line mixed concentric circle, double feathermen, double line triangle, transformed herons mixed Dingsheng, cicada; 4 frogs with 3 feet stand anticlockwise on the edge of the drum face; Drum body:patterns of comb line, concentric circle, multiple line triangle, vertical ribbon with straight lines and concentric circles, cicada; Braid patterns on 2 pairs of flat handles.	89.5-90	56	冷水冲型 Lengshui- chong Type	

序号 N0.	原编号及鼓名 Stock Number & Name	收藏单位 Museum	出土（征集）时间、地点 Time & Spot for discovered or collected	主要装饰 Main Decorations	尺寸（厘米）Size(cm)		类型 Type	图片 Picture
					面径 Face Diameter	身高 Height		
553	总591号 十字村鼓 No.591 Bronze Drum Shizi Cun	浦北县博物馆 Pubei County Museum	1974年4月21日出土于广西浦北张黄镇东方农场十字分场白坟岭旁 Unearthed beside Baifen Ling, Cross Sub-farm, Eastern Farm, Zhanghuang Town, Pubei County, Guangxi on April 21st, 1974	鼓面：太阳纹（10芒）、同心圆纹、变形鸟纹、虫形纹、兽形纹、席纹、四出钱纹、蝉纹，鼓面边缘饰六组逆时针三足立蛙； 鼓身：四出钱纹、虫形纹、同心圆纹、席纹、变形鸟纹、蝉纹；扁耳两对饰辫纹 Drum face: patterns of sun(10rays), concentric circle, transformed bird, insect-shape motif, beast-shape motif, woven mat, coins with quadrangle inside, cicada; 6 frogs with 3 feet stand anticlockwise on the edge of the drum face; Drum body:patterns of coins with quadrangle inside, insect-shape motif, concentric circle, woven mat, transformed bird, cicada; Braid patterns on 2 pairs of flat handles.	90.5~92	54	灵山型 Lingshan Type	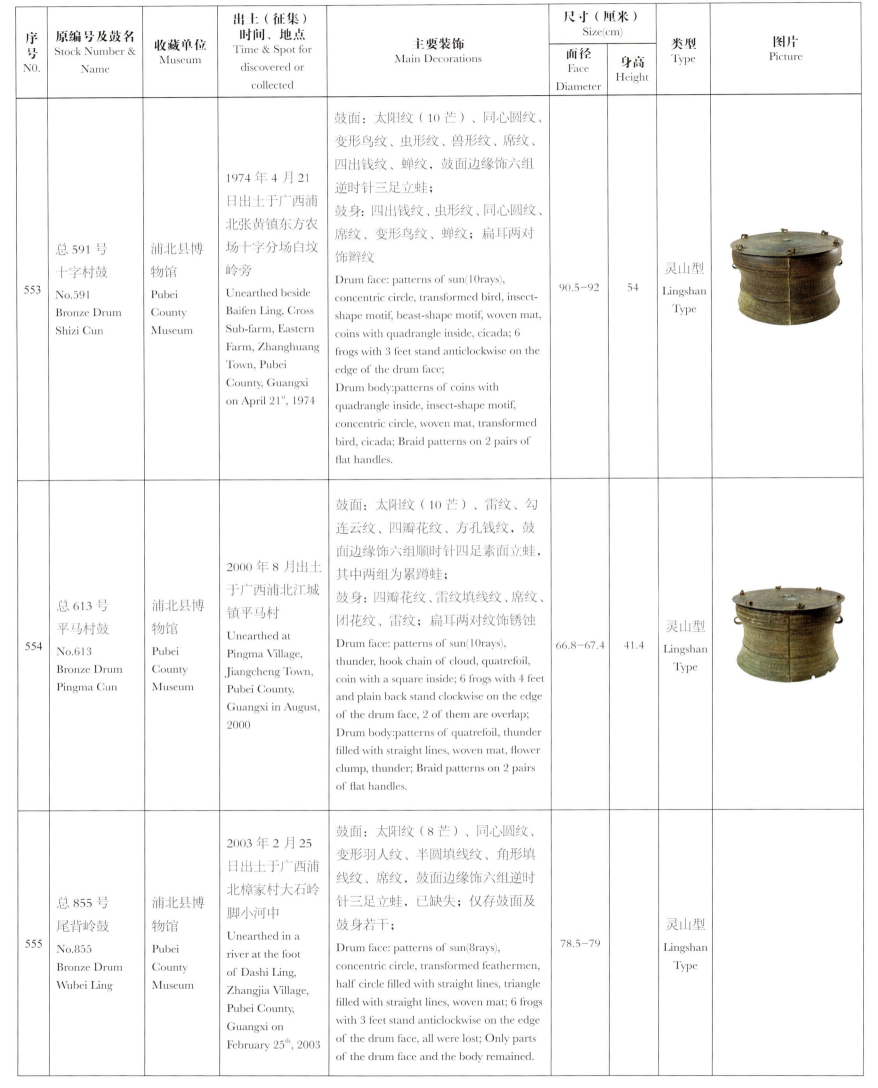
554	总613号 平马村鼓 No.613 Bronze Drum Pingma Cun	浦北县博物馆 Pubei County Museum	2000年8月出土于广西浦北江城镇平马村 Unearthed at Pingma Village, Jiangcheng Town, Pubei County, Guangxi in August, 2000	鼓面：太阳纹（10芒）、雷纹、勾连云纹、四瓣花纹、方孔钱纹，鼓面边缘饰六组顺时针四足素面立蛙，其中两组为累蹲蛙； 鼓身：四瓣花纹、雷纹填线纹、席纹、团花纹、雷纹；扁耳两对纹饰锈蚀 Drum face: patterns of sun(10rays), thunder, hook chain of cloud, quatrefoil, coin with a square inside; 6 frogs with 4 feet and plain back stand clockwise on the edge of the drum face, 2 of them are overlap; Drum body:patterns of quatrefoil, thunder filled with straight lines, woven mat, flower clump, thunder; Braid patterns on 2 pairs of flat handles.	66.8~67.4	41.4	灵山型 Lingshan Type	
555	总855号 尾背岭鼓 No.855 Bronze Drum Wubei Ling	浦北县博物馆 Pubei County Museum	2003年2月25日出土于广西浦北樟家村大石岭脚小河中 Unearthed in a river at the foot of Dashi Ling, Zhangjia Village, Pubei County, Guangxi on February 25th, 2003	鼓面：太阳纹（8芒）、同心圆纹、变形羽人纹、半圆填线纹、角形填线纹、席纹，鼓面边缘饰六组逆时针三足立蛙，已缺失；仅存鼓面及鼓身若干； Drum face: patterns of sun(8rays), concentric circle, transformed feathermen, half circle filled with straight lines, triangle filled with straight lines, woven mat; 6 frogs with 3 feet stand anticlockwise on the edge of the drum face, all were lost; Only parts of the drum face and the body remained.	78.5~79		灵山型 Lingshan Type	

序号 NO.	原编号及鼓名 Stock Number & Name	收藏单位 Museum	出土（征集）时间、地点 Time & Spot for discovered or collected	主要装饰 Main Decorations	尺寸（厘米）Size(cm)		类型 Type	图片 Picture
					面径 Face Diameter	身高 Height		
556	总 1069 号 1069 号鼓 No.1069	浦北县博物馆 Pubei County Museum	2009 年 8 月 14 日出土于广西浦北县新体育馆大门前 Unearthed at front of the gate of new county gymnasium, Pubei County, Guangxi on August 14th, 2009	鼓面：太阳纹（8 芒）、云纹、席纹、鼓面边缘饰六组逆时针三足素面立蛙；鼓身：四出钱纹、席纹、半同心圆纹、四瓣花纹、云纹；仅存鼓面及部分鼓身残片 Drum face: patterns of sun(8rays), cloud, woven mat; 6 frogs with 3 feet and plain back stand anticlockwise on the edge of the drum face; Drum body:patterns of coins with quadrangle inside, woven mat, half concentric circle, quatrefoil, cloud; Only the drum face and parts of the body remained.	56.3		灵山型 Lingshan Type	
557	38 号 古平鼓 No.38 Bronze Drum Guping	贵港市博物馆 Guigang City Museum	1974 年 5 月 3 日出土于广西贵港大岭乡古平村圆圈山脚大路中间 Unearthed in the middle of a road at the foot of Yuanquan Hill, Guping Village, Daling, Guigang, Guangxi on May 3rd, 1974	鼓面：太阳纹（8 芒）、云纹，鼓面边缘饰六只逆时针三足素面立蛙；鼓身：雷纹、水波纹、网纹、云纹；扁耳两对无纹饰 Drum face: patterns of sun(8rays), cloud; 6 frog statues of 3 feet anticlockwise stand on the edge of drum face; Drum body: patterns of thunder, water wave, net, cloud; 2 pairs of blank flat handles.	69.2~70.5	42	灵山型 Lingshan Type	
558	74 号 牛坳山铜鼓 No.74 Bronze Drum Niu'ao shan	贵港市博物馆 Guigang City Museum	1975 年 8 月出土于广西贵港蒙公乡新岭村西牛坳山 Unearthed at the west of Niu'ao Hill, Xinling Village, Menggong, Guigang, Guangxi in August, 1975	鼓面：太阳纹（12 芒）、栉纹、同心圆纹、复线交叉纹、变形羽人纹、变形翔鹭纹间定胜纹、鸟纹，鼓面边缘饰四只逆时针四足素面立蛙；鼓身：栉纹、同心圆纹、栉纹素纹同心圆纹垂直纹带、三角垂叶纹；扁耳两对饰辫纹 Drum face: patterns of sun(12rays), comb line, concentric circles, crossed double lines, transformed feathermen, transformed flying heron mixed Dingsheng, bird;4 frog statues of 4 feet and blank back anticlockwise stand on the edge of drum face; Drum body: patterns of comb line, concentric circles, vertical ribbon of straight line, blank and concentric circles, leaf-shape triangle with concentric circles in the middle; Braids pattern on 2 pairs of flat handles.	71.2~72.5	45.5	冷水冲型 Lengshui-chong Type	

序号 N0.	原编号及鼓名 Stock Number & Name	收藏单位 Museum	出土（征集）时间、地点 Time & Spot for discovered or collected	主要装饰 Main Decorations	尺寸（厘米）Size(cm)		类型 Type	图片 Picture
					面径 Face Diameter	身高 Height		
559	545 号 万新铜鼓 No.545 Bronze Drum Wanxin	贵港市博物馆 Guigang City Museum	1978 年 7 月出土于广西贵港庆丰乡万新村西南约 300 米处 Unearthed in south-west of 300m to Wanxin Village, Qinfeng, Guigang, Guangxi in July, 1978	鼓面：太阳纹（13 芒）、水波纹、叶脉纹、复线交叉纹、变形羽人纹、变形翔鹭纹间同心圆纹、眼纹，鼓面边缘饰四只逆时针四足谷穗纹立蛙，两蛙间饰一乘骑立饰，另两蛙间立饰缺失；鼓身：水波纹、同心圆纹、船纹、变形羽人纹、网纹、三角垂叶纹、眼纹；扁耳两对饰辫纹 Drum face: patterns of sun(13rays), water wave, leaf vein, crossed double lines, transformed feathermen, transformed flying heron mixed concentric circles, diamond-shape eye; 4 frog statues of 4 feet and rice-ears on back anticlockwise stand on the edge of drum face; 2 groups of horse-ride statues between the frogs and one of them lost; Drum body: patterns of water wave, concentric circles, boat, transformed feathermen, net, leaf-shape triangle; diamond-shape eye; Braids pattern on 2 pairs of flat handles.	76—77.7	52.6	冷水冲型 Lengshui-chong Type	
560	547 号 四蛙双兽鼓 No.547 Bronze Drum with 4 frogs and 2 beasts statue	贵港市博物馆 Guigang City Museum	1979 年 10 月 23 日在广西贵港废旧收购部拣选 Collected at Guangxi Guigang Waste Recycle Shop on October 23rd, 1979	鼓面：太阳纹（12 芒）、栉纹、同心圆纹、复线交叉纹、变形羽人纹、变形翔鹭纹间定胜纹，鼓面边缘立饰缺失；仅存鼓面 Only the drum face is remained: patterns of sun(12rays), comb line, concentric circles, crossed double lines, transformed feathermen, transformed flying heron mixed Dingsheng; the edge of the face was lost.	78.8—79.3		冷水冲型 Lengshui-chong Type	

续表

序号 N0.	原编号及鼓名 Stock Number & Name	收藏单位 Museum	出土（征集） 时间、地点 Time & Spot for discovered or collected	主要装饰 Main Decorations	尺寸（厘米） Size(cm)		类型 Type	图片 Picture
					面径 Face Diameter	身高 Height		
561	564 号 摩天岭鼓 No.564 Bronze Drum Motianling	贵港市博物馆 Guigang City Museum	1981 年 6 月 30 日出土于广西贵港奇石镇清潭村摩天岭脚 Unearthed at the foot of Motianling, Qingtan Village, Qishi Town, Guigang, Guangxi on June 30th, 1981	鼓面：太阳纹（12 芒）、栉纹、同心圆纹、复线交叉纹、变形羽人纹、变形翔鹭纹间定胜纹，鼓面边缘饰四只逆时针四足素面立蛙； 鼓身：栉纹、同心圆纹、栉纹素纹同心圆纹垂直纹带、三角垂叶纹；扁耳两对饰辫纹 Drum face: patterns of sun(12rays), comb line, concentric circles, crossed double lines, transformed feathermen, tansformed flying heron mixed Dingsheng; 4 frog statues of 4 feet and blank back anticlockwise stand on the edge of drum face; Drum body: patterns of comb line, concentric circles, vertical ribbon of straight line, blank and concentric circles, leaf-shape triangle; Braids pattern on 2 pairs of flat handles.	81.5—82.3	48 （残） Incomplete	冷水冲型 Lengshui-chong Type	
562	565 号 奇石鼓 No.565 Bronze Drum Qishi	贵港市博物馆 Guigang City Museum	1981 年 6 月 8 日出土于广西贵港奇石镇福庆村古蕉岭中段 Unearthed at the hillside of Gujiao Ling, Fuqing Village, Qishi Town, Guigang, Guangxi on June 8th, 1981	鼓面：太阳纹（12 芒）、叶脉纹、同心圆纹、栉纹、复线交叉纹、变形羽人纹、变形翔鹭纹间定胜纹，鼓面边缘饰四只逆时针四足素面立蛙； 鼓身：叶脉纹、栉纹、同心圆纹、栉纹切线同心圆纹垂直纹带、切线同心圆纹、三角垂叶间同心圆纹；扁耳两对饰辫纹 Drum face: patterns of sun(12rays), leaf vein, concentric circles, comb line, crossed double lines, transformed feathermen, transformed flying heron mixed Dingsheng; 4 frog statues of 4 feet and blank back anticlockwise stand on the edge of drum face; Drum body: patterns of leaf vein, comb line, concentric circles, vertical ribbon of straight line and tangent concentric circles, tangent concentric circles, leaf-shape triangle with concentric circle; Braid patterns on 2 pairs of flat handles.	81.5—82.8	49 （残） Incomplete	冷水冲型 Lengshui-chong Type	

序号 N0.	原编号及鼓名 Stock Number & Name	收藏单位 Museum	出土（征集） 时间、地点 Time & Spot for discovered or collected	主要装饰 Main Decorations	尺寸（厘米） Size(cm)		类型 Type	图片 Picture
					面径 Face Diameter	身高 Height		
563	580 号 长岭铜鼓 No.580 Bronze Drum Changling	贵港市博物馆 Guigang City Museum	1982 年 4 月出土于广西东龙镇柳蓬村东北长岭 Unearthed at Chang Ling, in the North-east of Liupeng Village, Donglong Town, Guangxi in April, 1982	鼓面：太阳纹（12 芒）、谷穗纹、切线同心圆纹、栉纹、复线交叉纹、变形羽人纹、变形翔鹭纹、大鸟间定胜纹、小鸟纹，鼓面边缘饰四只逆时针四足钱纹立蛙； 鼓身：谷穗纹、栉纹、切线同心圆纹、栉纹切线同心圆纹变形羽人纹垂直纹带、三角垂叶纹；扁耳两对饰辫纹 Drum face: patterns of sun(12rays), rice ear, tangent concentric circles, comb line, crossed double lines, transformed feathermen, transformed flying heron, bird; 4 frog statues of 4 feet and coins on back anticlockwise stand on the edge of drum face; Drum body: patterns of rice ear, comb line, tangent concentric circles, vertical ribbon of straight line, tangent concentric circles and transformed feathermen, leaf-shape triangle; Braid patterns on 2 pairs of flat handles.	79.4－77.7	48 （残） Incomplete	冷水冲型 Lengshui-chong Type	
564	896 号 覃塘鼓 No.896 Bronze Drum Qintang	贵港市博物馆 Guigang City Museum	1984 年征集于广西贵港覃塘镇拥兴村莫桂年家 Collected from Mo Guinian, a villager of Yongxing Village, Qintang Town, Guigang, Guangxi in 1984	鼓面：太阳纹（12 芒）、羽纹、栉纹、切线同心圆纹、复线交叉纹、变形羽人纹、变形翔鹭纹间定胜纹，鼓面边缘饰四只逆时针四足素面立蛙； 鼓身：栉纹、切线同心圆纹、栉纹素纹切线同心圆纹垂直纹带（胸腰连接）；扁耳两对饰辫纹 Drum face: patterns of sun(12rays), feather, comb line, tangent concentric circles, crossed double lines, transformed feathermen, transformed flying heron mixed Dingsheng; 4 frog statues of 4 feet and blank back anticlockwise stand on the edge of drum face; Drum body: patterns of comb line, tangent concentric circles, vertical ribbon of straight line, blank and tangent concentric circles(from the chest to the waist); Braid patterns on 2 pairs of flat handles.	67－67.5	37.7 （残） Incomplete	冷水冲型 Lengshui-chong Type	

续表

序号 NO.	原编号及鼓名 Stock Number & Name	收藏单位 Museum	出土（征集）时间、地点 Time & Spot for discovered or collected	主要装饰 Main Decorations	尺寸（厘米） Size(cm)		类型 Type	图片 Picture
					面径 Face Diameter	身高 Height		
565	1056号 马槽山铜鼓 No.1056 Bronze Drum Macaoshan	贵港市博物馆 Guigang City Museum	1984年秋出土于广西贵港东龙镇闭村东北1公里马槽山 Unearthed at Macao Hill, 1km in the North-east to Bi Village, Donglong Town, Guigang, Guangxi in the autumn, 1984	鼓面：太阳纹（12芒）、栉纹、同心圆纹、复线交叉纹、变形羽人纹、变形翔鹭纹间定胜纹、叶脉纹、鱼、兽、燕子纹，鼓面边缘饰四只逆时针四足羽纹、云纹立体蛙，两蛙间有立体装饰痕迹，已缺失；仅存鼓面 Only the drum face is remained: patterns of sun(12rays), comb line, concentric circles, crossed double lines, transformed feathermen, transformed flying heron mixed Dingsheng, leaf vein, fish, beast and swallow; 4 frog statues of 4 feet and feather, cloud patterns on back anticlockwise stand on the edge of drum face; marks of statues between the frogs were lost.	72.2－73	（残） Incomplete	冷水冲型 Lengshui-chong Type	
566	1878号 石卡铜鼓 No.1878 Bronze Drum Shika	贵港市博物馆 Guigang City Museum	1995年12月出土于广西贵港覃塘区石卡镇凤凰林场 Unearthed at Fenghuang Forest Farm, Shika Town, Qintang District, Guigang, Guangxi in December, 1995	鼓面：太阳纹（10芒）、蝉纹、连钱纹、虫形纹、四出钱纹、鸟纹、四瓣花填线纹、席纹、四瓣花纹、兽形纹，鼓面边缘饰8组逆时针三足螺旋纹立蛙，其中四组为累蹲蛙；鼓身：蝉纹、雷纹填线纹、连钱纹、四出钱纹、兽面纹、四瓣花填线纹、席纹、虫形纹；一侧鼓耳下鼓足位置饰一对弦纹立体鸟；扁耳两对饰弦纹 Drum face: patterns of sun(10rays), cicada, coins part of overlap, insect-shape motif, coin with quadrangle inside, bird, quatrefoil filled with straight lines, woven mat, quatrefoil, beast-shape motif; 8 frogs with 3 feet and spiracle patterns on back anticlockwise stand on the edge; 4 of them are overlap; Drum body: patterns of cicada, thunder filled with straight lines, coins part of overlap, coin with quadrangle inside, beast face, quatrefoil filled with straight lines, woven mat, insect-shape motif; a pair of birds with strings on back stand under one of the handles on the foot; Strings on 2 pairs of flat handles.	118.5－119.8	66.4	灵山型 Lingshan Type	

序号 N0.	原编号及鼓名 Stock Number & Name	收藏单位 Museum	出土（征集）时间、地点 Time & Spot for discovered or collected	主要装饰 Main Decorations	尺寸（厘米）Size(cm)		类型 Type	图片 Picture
					面径 Face Diameter	身高 Height		
567	总01号 东胜屯铜鼓 No.01 Bronze Drum Dongshengtun	平南县博物馆 Pingnan County Museum	1979年2月出土于官城镇八宝村东胜屯坡地 Unearthed at the hillside of Dongsheng Tun, Babao Village, Guancheng Town in February, 1979	鼓面：太阳纹（12芒）、水波纹、栉纹、同心圆纹、复线交叉纹、变形羽人纹、变形翔鹭纹间定胜纹、眼纹，鼓面边缘饰四只逆时针四足弦纹、谷穗纹立蛙； 鼓身：水波纹、栉纹、同心圆纹、船纹、变形羽人纹、羽纹、网纹、眼纹、圆心三角垂叶纹；扁耳两对饰辫纹 Drum face: patterns of sun(12rays), water wave, comb line, concentric circles, crossed double lines, transformed feathermen, transformed flying heron mixed Dingsheng, diamond-shape eye; 4 frog statues of 4 feet, strings and rice ears on back, anticlockwise stand on the edge of drum face; Drum body: patterns of water wave, comb line, concentric circles, boat, transformed feathermen, feather, net, diamond-shape eye, leaf-shape triangle with circle in the middle; Braid patterns on 2 pairs of flat handles.	86.3−87.5	59.5	冷水冲型 Lengshui-chong Type	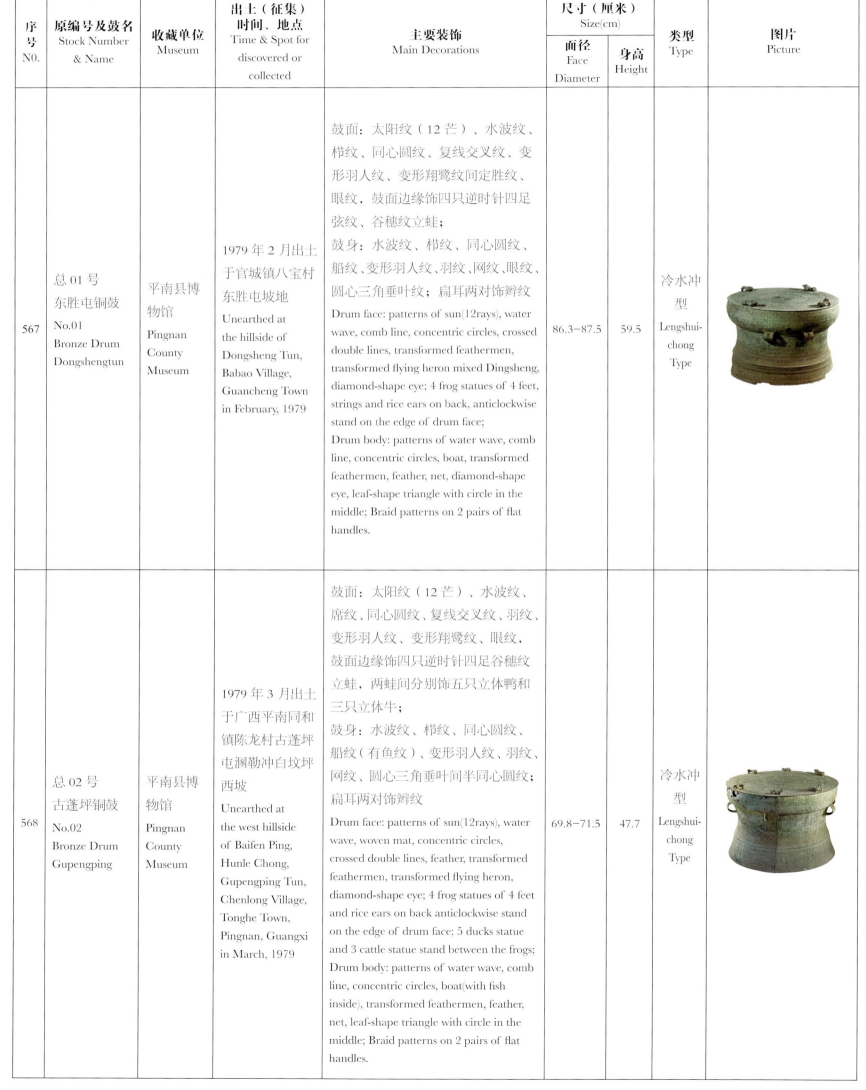
568	总02号 古蓬坪铜鼓 No.02 Bronze Drum Gupengping	平南县博物馆 Pingnan County Museum	1979年3月出土于广西平南同和镇陈龙村古蓬坪屯澇勒冲白坟坪西坡 Unearthed at the west hillside of Baifen Ping, Hunle Chong, Gupengping Tun, Chenlong Village, Tonghe Town, Pingnan, Guangxi in March, 1979	鼓面：太阳纹（12芒）、水波纹、席纹、同心圆纹、复线交叉纹、羽纹、变形羽人纹、变形翔鹭纹、眼纹，鼓面边缘饰四只逆时针四足谷穗纹立蛙，两蛙间分别饰五只立体鸭和三只立体牛； 鼓身：水波纹、栉纹、同心圆纹、船纹（有鱼纹）、变形羽人纹、羽纹、网纹、圆心三角垂叶间半同心圆纹；扁耳两对饰辫纹 Drum face: patterns of sun(12rays), water wave, woven mat, concentric circles, crossed double lines, feather, transformed feathermen, transformed flying heron, diamond-shape eye; 4 frog statues of 4 feet and rice ears on back anticlockwise stand on the edge of drum face; 5 ducks statue and 3 cattle statue stand between the frogs; Drum body: patterns of water wave, comb line, concentric circles, boat(with fish inside), transformed feathermen, feather, net, leaf-shape triangle with circle in the middle; Braid patterns on 2 pairs of flat handles.	69.8−71.5	47.7	冷水冲型 Lengshui-chong Type	

续表

序号 NO.	原编号及鼓名 Stock Number & Name	收藏单位 Museum	出土（征集）时间、地点 Time & Spot for discovered or collected	主要装饰 Main Decorations	尺寸（厘米）Size(cm) 面径 Face Diameter	身高 Height	类型 Type	图片 Picture
569	总03号 西村铜鼓 No.03 Bronze Drum Xicun	平南县博物馆 Pingnan County Museum	1973年7月出土于广西平南环城乡西村岭脚铜鼓岭 Unearthed at Bronze Drum Hill, the foot of Xicun Ling, Huancheng, Pingnan, Guangxi in July, 1973	鼓面：太阳纹（12芒）、水波纹、栉纹、同心圆纹、复线交叉纹、变形羽人纹、变形翔鹭纹、鼓面边缘饰四只逆时针四足素面立体蛙； 鼓身：栉纹、同心圆纹、船纹、羽纹、变形羽人纹、网纹、眼纹、圆心三角垂叶纹；扁耳两对饰辫纹 Drum face: patterns of sun(12rays), water wave, woven mat, concentric circles, crossed double lines, feather, transformed feathermen, transformed flying heron, diamond-shape eye; 4 frog statues of 4 feet and blank back anticlockwise stand on the edge of drum face; Drum body: patterns of comb line, concentric circles, boat, transformed feathermen, feather, net, leaf-shape triangle with circle in the middle; Braid patterns on 2 pairs of flat handles.	63.8－64.6	43.8	冷水冲型 Lengshui-chong Type	
570	总04号 木花屯铜鼓 No.04 Bronze Drum Muhua Tun	平南县博物馆 Pingnan County Museum	1976年4月出土于广西平南六陈镇邦机村木花屯南约500米坡地 Unearthed at the hillside in the south of 500m to Muhua Tun, Bangji Village, Liuchen Town, Pingnan, Guangxi in April, 1976	鼓面：太阳纹（8芒）、云纹、水波纹，鼓面边缘饰六只逆时针三足素面立蛙； 鼓身：雷纹填线纹、云纹；扁耳两对无纹饰 Drum face: patterns of sun(8 rays), cloud, water wave; 6 frog statues of 3 feet and blank back anticlockwise stand on the edge of drum face; Drum body: patterns of thunder filled with straight lines, cloud; 2 pairs of blank flat handles.	59－59.7	31.8（残）Incomplete	灵山型 Lingshan Type	

序号 NO.	原编号及鼓名 Stock Number & Name	收藏单位 Museum	出土（征集） 时间、地点 Time & Spot for discovered or collected	主要装饰 Main Decorations	尺寸（厘米） Size(cm)		类型 Type	图片 Picture
					面径 Face Diameter	身高 Height		
571	总 05 号 花石村铜鼓 No.05 Bronze Drum Huashi Cun	平南县博物馆 Pingnan County Museum	1971 年出土于广西平南思旺镇花石村北 200 米坡地 Unearthed at the hillside in the north of 200m to Huashi Village, Siwang Town, Pingnan, Guangxi in 1971	鼓面：太阳纹（12 芒）、水波纹、羽纹、同心圆纹、栉纹、复线交叉纹、变形羽人纹、变形翔鹭纹，鼓面边缘饰四只逆时针四足谷穗纹立体蛙，两蛙间有立饰痕迹； 鼓身：水波纹、栉纹、同心圆纹、船纹、羽纹、变形羽人纹、网纹、圆心三角垂叶纹；扁耳两对饰辫纹 Drum face: patterns of sun(12rays), water wave, feather, concentric circles, comb line, crossed double lines, transformed feathermen, transformed flying heron; 4 frog statues of 4 feet and rice ears on back anticlockwise stand on the edge of drum face; marks of statues between the frogs; Drum body: patterns of water wave, comb line, concentric circles, boat, feather, transformed feathermen, net, leaf-shape triangle with circle in the middle; Braid patterns on 2 pairs of flat handles.	79.7-80.5	57	冷水冲型 Lengshui-chong Type	
572	总 06 号 第一碑铜鼓 No.06 Bronze Drum Diyibei	平南县博物馆 Pingnan County Museum	1978 年 4 月出土于广西平南富藏乡富藏村第一碑村山坡 Unearthed at the hillside of Diyibei, Fucang Village, Fucang, Pingnan, Guangxi in April, 1978	鼓面：太阳纹（12 芒）、鼓面可辨变形羽人纹、变形翔鹭纹、栉纹、切线同心圆纹，仅存鼓面 Only the drum face is remained: sun(12rays), few motifs are visible, including transformed feathermen, transformed flying heron, comb line, tangent concentric circle.	52.8	（残） Incomplete	冷水冲型 Lengshui-chong Type	

续表

序号 NO.	原编号及鼓名 Stock Number & Name	收藏单位 Museum	出土（征集） 时间、地点 Time & Spot for discovered or collected	主要装饰 Main Decorations	尺寸（厘米） Size(cm)		类型 Type	图片 Picture
					面径 Face Diameter	身高 Height		
573	总 299 号 竹根坪铜鼓 No.299 Bronze Drum Zhugenping	平南县博物馆 Pingnan County Museum	1975 年 3 月出土于广西平南大成乡大成村旺石竹根坪 Unearthed at Zhugen Ping, Wangshi, Dacheng Village, Dacheng, Pingnan, Guangxi in March, 1975	鼓面：太阳纹（12 芒）、水波纹、同心圆纹、羽纹、复线交叉纹、变形羽人纹、变形翔鹭纹，鼓面边缘饰四只逆时针四足谷穗纹立体蛙，两蛙间分别饰一组乘骑立饰； 鼓身：水波纹、羽纹、同心圆纹、船纹、变形羽人纹、网纹、圆心三角垂叶纹、眼纹、席纹；扁耳两对饰辫纹，合范线附近各一只附耳饰辫纹 Drum face: patterns of sun(12rays), water wave, concentric circles, feather, crossed double lines, transformed feathermen, flying heron; 4 frog statues of 4 feet and rice ears on back anticlockwise stand on the edge of drum face; 2 groups of horse-ride statues between the frogs; Drum body: patterns of water wave, feather, concentric circles, boat, transformed feathermen, net, leaf-shape triangle with circle in the middle, diamond-shape eye, woven mat; Braid patterns on 2 pairs of flat handles and 2 attached handles beside the casting line.	74.5~75.2	54.9	冷水冲型 Lengshui-chong Type	

序号 N0.	原编号及鼓名 Stock Number & Name	收藏单位 Museum	出土（征集）时间、地点 Time & Spot for discovered or collected	主要装饰 Main Decorations	尺寸（厘米）Size(cm)		类型 Type	图片 Picture
					面径 Face Diameter	身高 Height		
574	总 1304 号 深塘铜鼓 No.1304 Bronze Drum Shentang	平南县博物馆 Pingnan County Museum	1981 年 11 月出土于广西平南官城镇八宝村深塘屯西北面中央冲鲶鱼岭西北坡 Unearthed at the North-west hillside of Nianyu Ling, Zhongyang Chong, the North-west to Shentang Tun, Babao Village, Guancheng Town, Pingnan, Guangxi in November, 1981	鼓面：太阳纹（12 芒）、栉纹、同心圆纹、复线交叉纹、变形羽人纹、羽纹、变形翔鹭纹，鼓面边缘饰四只逆时针四足谷穗纹立体蛙，两蛙间分别饰一组牛和一组谷仓立饰；鼓身：栉纹、同心圆纹、羽纹、船纹（有鱼纹）、变形羽人纹、网纹、圆心三角垂叶间半圆填线纹、水波纹、眼纹；扁耳两对饰辫纹 Drum face: patterns of sun(12rays), comb line, concentric circles, crossed double lines, feather, transformed feathermen, transformed flying heron; 4 frog statues of 4 feet and rice ears on back anticlockwise stand on the edge of drum face; an ox and a garner statues between the frogs; Drum body: patterns of comb line, concentric circles, feather, boat(with fish inside), transformed feathermen, net, leaf-shape triangle with circle in the middle, diamond-shape eye, water wave; Braid patterns on 2 pairs of flat handles	63.5	43	冷水冲型 Lengshui-chong Type	
575	总 1772 号 龙胆塘铜鼓 No.1772 Bronze Drum Longdan Tang	平南县博物馆 Pingnan County Museum	1987 年 3 月出土于广西平南寺面镇新隆村龙胆塘山坡 Unearthed at the hillside of Longdan Tang, Xinlong Village, Simian Town, Pingnan, Guangxi in March, 1987	鼓面：太阳纹（8 芒）、云纹，鼓面边缘饰四只逆时针四足素面立体蛙；鼓身：雷纹填线纹、云纹、雷纹、水波纹；扁耳两对无纹饰 Drum face: patterns of sun(8rays), cloud; 4 frog statues of 4 feet and blank back anticlockwise stand on the edge of drum face; Drum body: patterns of thunder filled with straight lines, cloud, thunder, water wave; 2 pairs of blank flat handles.	82.7~83.2	47.5	北流型 Beiliu Type	

续表

序号 NO.	原编号及鼓名 Stock Number & Name	收藏单位 Museum	出土（征集）时间、地点 Time & Spot for discovered or collected	主要装饰 Main Decorations	尺寸（厘米）Size(cm)		类型 Type	图片 Picture
					面径 Face Diameter	身高 Height		
576	总 1887 号 上宋铜鼓 No.1887 Bronze Drum Shangsong	平南县博物馆 Pingnan County Museum	1985 年 8 月出土于广西平南思旺镇双上村上宋屯 Unearthed at Shangsong Tun, Shuangshang Village, Siwang Town, Pingnan, Guangxi in August, 1985	鼓面：水波纹、栉纹、同心圆纹、复线交叉纹、羽纹、变形羽人纹、变形翔鹭纹、眼纹、鼓面边缘饰四只逆时针四足谷穗纹立体蛙，两蛙间分别饰一组双乘骑立饰；鼓身：羽纹、同心圆纹、船纹（有鱼纹），仅存鼓面及部分鼓胸 Drum face: patterns of sun(12rays), water wave, comb line, concentric circles, crossed double lines, feather, transformed feathermen, transformed flying heron, diamond-shape eye; 4 frog statues of 4 feet and rice ears on back anticlockwise stand on the edge of drum face; 2 groups of horse-ride statues between the frogs; Drum body: patterns of feather, concentric circles, boat(with fish inside).Only the drum face and part of the chest are remained.	69.5~70.8	12 （残）Incomplete	冷水冲型 Lengshuichong Type	
577	总 1911 号 白面崖铜鼓 No.1911 Bronze Drum Baimian Ya	平南县博物馆 Pingnan County Museum	1988 年 9 月出土于广西平南镇隆镇平界村新地屯白面崖山顶 Unearthed at the top of Baimian Ya, Xindi Tun, Pingjie Village, Zhenlong Town, Pingnan, Guangxi in September,1988	鼓面：太阳纹（12 芒）、栉纹、同心圆纹、复线交叉纹、变形羽人纹、变形翔鹭间定胜纹、鼓面边缘饰四只逆时针四足素面立蛙；鼓身：栉纹、同心圆纹、栉纹同心圆纹垂直纹带、圆心三角垂叶纹；扁耳两对饰辫纹 Drum face: patterns of sun(12rays), comb line, concentric circles, crossed double lines, transformed feathermen, transformed flying heron mixed Dingsheng; 4 frog statues of 4 feet and blank back anticlockwise stand on the edge of drum face; Drum body: patterns of comb line, concentric circles, vertical ribbon of straight line and concentric circle leaf-shape triangle with circle in the middle; Braid patterns on 2 pairs of flat handles.	68.3~70	48	冷水冲型 Lengshuichong Type	

451

序号 N0.	原编号及鼓名 Stock Number & Name	收藏单位 Museum	出土（征集）时间、地点 Time & Spot for discovered or collected	主要装饰 Main Decorations	尺寸（厘米）Size(cm)		类型 Type	图片 Picture
					面径 Face Diameter	身高 Height		
578	总2392号 新和村铜鼓 No.2392 Bronze Drum Xinhe Cun	平南县博物馆 Pingnan County Museum	1990年12月出土于广西平南大新镇新和村大火屯 Unearthed at Dahuo Tun, Xinhe Village, Daxin Town, Pingnan, Guangxi in December, 1990	鼓面：太阳纹（12芒）、水波纹、同心圆纹、栉纹、复线交叉纹、羽纹、变形羽人纹、变形翔鹭纹、眼纹、鼓面边缘饰四只逆时针四足谷穗纹立体蛙，蛙间各饰一组双乘骑立饰；鼓身：水波纹、栉纹、同心圆纹、船纹、变形羽人纹、网纹、圆心三角垂叶纹、羽纹、眼纹；扁耳两对饰辫纹 Drum face: patterns of sun(12rays), water wave, concentric circles, comb line, crossed double lines, transformed feathermen, transformed flying heron, diamond-shape eye; 4 frog statues of 4 feet and rice ears on back anticlockwise stand on the edge of drum face; 2 groups of horse-ride statues between the frogs; Drum body: patterns of water wave, comb line, concentric circles, boat, transformed feathermen, net, leaf-shape triangle with circle in the middle, feather, diamond-shape eye; Braid patterns on 2 pairs of flat handles.	71.4－73.2	50	冷水冲型 Lengshui-chong Type	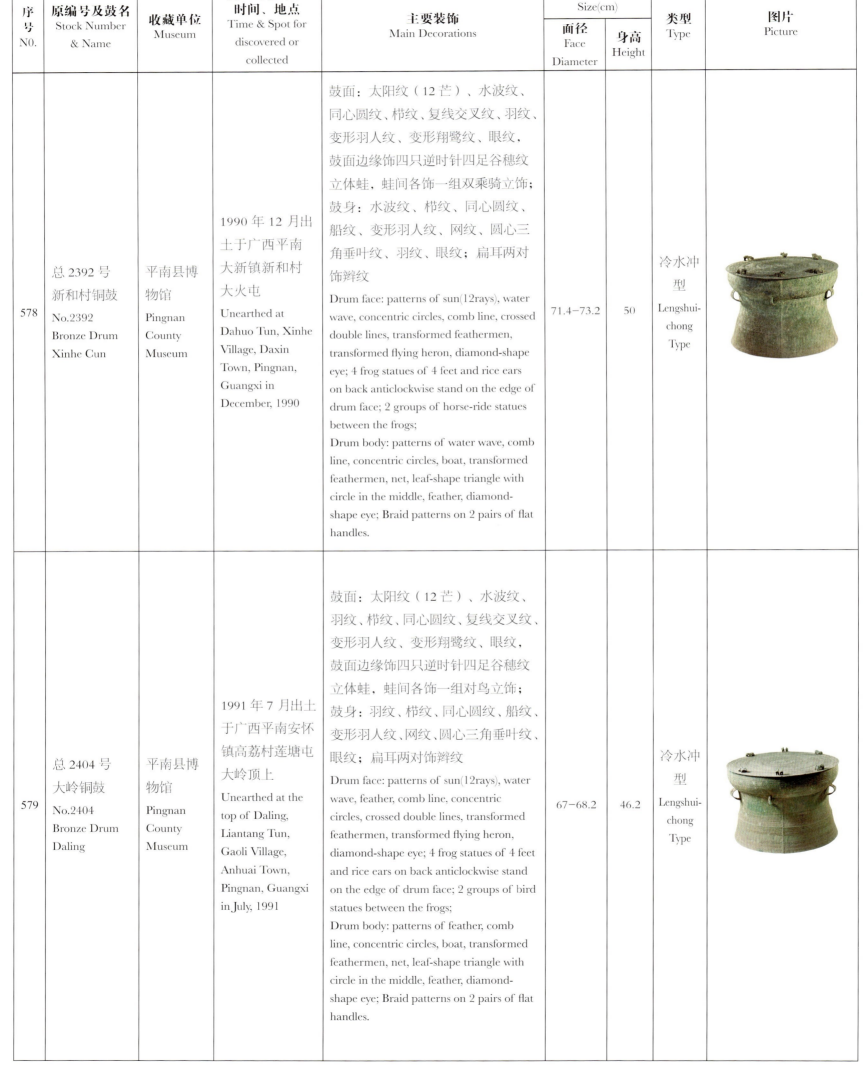
579	总2404号 大岭铜鼓 No.2404 Bronze Drum Daling	平南县博物馆 Pingnan County Museum	1991年7月出土于广西平南安怀镇高荔村莲塘屯大岭顶上 Unearthed at the top of Daling, Liantang Tun, Gaoli Village, Anhuai Town, Pingnan, Guangxi in July, 1991	鼓面：太阳纹（12芒）、水波纹、羽纹、栉纹、同心圆纹、复线交叉纹、变形羽人纹、变形翔鹭纹、眼纹、鼓面边缘饰四只逆时针四足谷穗纹立体蛙，蛙间各饰一组对鸟立饰；鼓身：羽纹、栉纹、同心圆纹、船纹、变形羽人纹、网纹、圆心三角垂叶纹、眼纹；扁耳两对饰辫纹 Drum face: patterns of sun(12rays), water wave, feather, comb line, concentric circles, crossed double lines, transformed feathermen, transformed flying heron, diamond-shape eye; 4 frog statues of 4 feet and rice ears on back anticlockwise stand on the edge of drum face; 2 groups of bird statues between the frogs; Drum body: patterns of feather, comb line, concentric circles, boat, transformed feathermen, net, leaf-shape triangle with circle in the middle, feather, diamond-shape eye; Braid patterns on 2 pairs of flat handles.	67－68.2	46.2	冷水冲型 Lengshui-chong Type	

序号 NO.	原编号及鼓名 Stock Number & Name	收藏单位 Museum	出土（征集）时间、地点 Time & Spot for discovered or collected	主要装饰 Main Decorations	尺寸（厘米）Size(cm) 面径 Face Diameter	身高 Height	类型 Type	图片 Picture
580	总 2406 号武多鼓 No.2406 Bronze Drum Wuduo	平南县博物馆 Pingnan County Museum	2003 年出土于广西平南同和镇武全村武多屯六振冲半山村道旁 Unearthed at the roadside of Banshan Village, Liuzhen Chong, Wuduo Tun, Wuquan Village, Tonghe Town, Pingnan, Guangxi in 2003	鼓面：太阳纹（12 芒）、水波纹、同心圆纹、栉纹、复线交叉纹、羽纹、变形羽人纹、变形翔鹭纹、眼纹、鼓面边缘饰四只逆时针四足谷穗纹立蛙、蛙间各饰一组田螺立饰；鼓身：羽纹、同心圆纹、船纹、变形羽人纹、栉纹、网纹、圆心三角垂叶纹、眼纹；扁耳两对饰辫纹 Drum face: patterns of sun(12rays), water wave, concentric circles, comb line, crossed double lines feather, transformed feathermen, transformed flying heron, diamond-shape eye; 4 frog statues of 4 feet and rice ears on back anticlockwise stand on the edge of drum face; 2 groups of field snail statues between the frogs; Drum body: patterns of feather, concentric circles, boat, transformed feathermen, comb line, net, leaf-shape triangle with circle in the middle, diamond-shape eye; Braid patterns on 2 pairs of flat handles.	68.5-69.4	48	冷水冲型 Lengshui-chong Type	
581	牛栏塘铜鼓 Bronze Drum Niulan Tang	平南县博物馆 Pingnan County Museum	1991 年 6 月出土于广西平南东笋塘小区牛栏塘 Unearthed at Niulan Tang, Suntang Community, Pingnan, Guangxi in June, 1991	鼓面：太阳纹（12 芒）、栉纹、同心圆纹、复线交叉纹、变形羽人纹、变形翔鹭间定胜纹、鼓面边缘饰四只逆时针四足素面立蛙；鼓身：栉纹、同心圆纹、栉纹同心圆纹垂直纹带、鼓足残缺；扁耳两对饰辫纹 Drum face: patterns of sun(12rays), comb line, concentric circles, crossed double lines, transformed feathermen, transformed flying heron mixed Dingsheng; 4 frog statues of 4 feet and blank back anticlockwise stand on the edge of drum face; Drum body: patterns of comb line, concentric circles, vertical ribbon of straight line and concentric circle, the foot was lost; Braid patterns on 2 pairs of flat handles.	71.2-74	27（残）Incomplete	冷水冲型 Lengshui-chong Type	

序号 NO.	原编号及鼓名 Stock Number & Name	收藏单位 Museum	出土（征集） 时间、地点 Time & Spot for discovered or collected	主要装饰 Main Decorations	尺寸（厘米） Size(cm)		类型 Type	图片 Picture
					面径 Face Diameter	身高 Height		
582	总 000434 号 佛子山铜鼓 No.000434 Bronze Drum Fozishan	桂平市博物馆 Guiping Museum	1979 年出土于广西桂平中沙镇太平村西佛子山 Unearthed at the west of Fozi Hill, Taiping Village, Zhongsha Town, Guiping, Guangxi in 1979	鼓面：太阳纹（8 芒）、云纹，鼓面边缘饰四只逆时针四足素面立体蛙； 鼓身：水波纹、雷纹、云纹；扁耳两对无纹饰 Drum face: patterns of sun(8rays), cloud; 4 frog statues of 4 feet and blank back anticlockwise stand on the edge of drum face; Drum body: patterns of water wave, thunder, cloud; 2 pairs of blank flat handles.	102.4− 103.6	57 （残） Incom- plete	北流型 Beiliu Type	
583	总 000435 号 沙岗铜鼓 No.000435 Bronze Drum Shagang	桂平市博物馆 Guiping Museum	1975 年出土于广西桂平蒙圩镇新阳村沙岗朱屋背 Unearthed at Zhuwubei, Shagang, Xinyang Village, Mengxu Town, Guiping, Guangxi in 1975	鼓面：太阳纹（8 芒），通体雷纹，鼓面边缘饰四只逆时针四足素面立体蛙；环耳两对无纹饰 Drum face: patterns of sun(8rays),all are thunders; 4 frog statues of 4 feet and blank back anticlockwise stand on the edge of drum face; 2 pairs of blank ring handles.	62	34.4	北流型 Beiliu Type	
584	总 000436 号 樟村铜鼓 No.000436 Bronze Drum Zhangcun	桂平市博物馆 Guiping Museum	1972 年出土于广西桂平西山镇渡头村樟村屯西浔江岸边 Unearthed beside the Xunjiang River, west to Zhangcun Tun, Dutou Village, Xishan Town, Guiping, Guangxi in 1972	鼓面：太阳纹（12 芒）、水波纹、谷穗纹、同心圆纹、栉纹、复线交叉纹、羽纹、变形羽人纹、变形翔鹭纹、眼纹，鼓面边缘饰四只逆时针四足谷穗纹立蛙，蛙间各饰一只谷穗纹、螺旋纹龟立饰； 鼓身：水波纹、羽纹、同心圆纹、船纹、变形羽人纹、栉纹、网纹、圆心三角垂叶纹、眼纹；扁耳两对饰辫纹 Drum face: patterns of sun(12rays), water wave, rice ear, concentric circles, comb line, crossed double lines, feather, transformed feathermen, transformed flying heron, diamond-shape eye; 4 frog statues of 4 feet and rice ears on back anticlockwise stand on the edge of drum face; 2 tortoise statues with rice- ears and spiracles on back between the frogs; Drum body: patterns of water wave, feather, concentric circles, boat, transformed feathermen, comb line, net, leaf-shape triangle with circle in the middle, diamond-shape eye; Braid patterns on 2 pairs of flat handles.	85−85.5	62	冷水冲型 Lengshui- chong Type	

序号 NO.	原编号及鼓名 Stock Number & Name	收藏单位 Museum	出土（征集）时间、地点 Time & Spot for discovered or collected	主要装饰 Main Decorations	尺寸（厘米）Size(cm)		类型 Type	图片 Picture
					面径 Face Diameter	身高 Height		
585	总 000437 号鸡公山铜鼓 No.000437 Bronze Drum Jigong Shan	桂平市博物馆 Guiping Museum	1974 年出土于广西桂平蒙圩镇新德村西鸡公山 Unearthed at Jigong Hill, Xinde Village, Mengxu Town, Guiping, Guangxi in 1974	鼓面：太阳纹（12 芒）、水波纹、栉纹、同心圆纹、复线交叉纹、变形羽人纹、羽纹、变形翔鹭纹、眼纹，鼓面边缘饰四只逆时针四足谷穗纹立体蛙，蛙间各饰一组乘骑立饰； 鼓身：羽纹、栉纹、同心圆纹、水波纹、船纹、变形羽人纹、网纹、圆心三角垂叶纹；扁耳两对饰羽纹，合范线附近各一只环耳 Drum face: patterns of sun(12rays), water wave, comb line, concentric circles, crossed double lines, transformed feathermen, feather, transformed flying heron, diamond-shape eye; 4 frog statues of 4 feet and rice ears on back anticlockwise stand on the edge of drum face; 2 groups of horse-ride statues between the frogs; Drum body: patterns of feather, comb line, concentric circles, water wave, boat, transformed feathermen, net, leaf-shape triangle with circle in the middle; feather patterns on 2 pairs of flat handles, 2 attached handles stand separately beside the casting line.	72.5–73	52.5	冷水冲型 Lengshui-chong Type	
586	总 000438 号新德村铜鼓 No.000438 Bronze Drum Xinde Cun	桂平市博物馆 Guiping Museum	1974 年出土于广西桂平蒙圩镇新德村东山腰 Unearthed at the hillside in the east of Xinde Village, Mengxu Town, Guiping, Guangxi in 1974	鼓面：太阳纹（12 芒）、水波纹、同心圆纹、栉纹、复线交叉纹、羽纹、变形羽人纹、变形翔鹭间同心圆纹、眼纹，鼓面边缘饰四只逆时针四足谷穗纹立蛙，蛙间分别饰一组单乘骑和一组双乘骑立饰； 鼓身：水波纹、同心圆纹、栉纹、船纹、变形羽人纹、羽纹、网纹、席纹、圆心三角垂叶纹、眼纹；扁耳两对饰辫纹，合范线附近各一只环耳 Drum face: patterns of sun(12rays), water wave, comb line, concentric circles, crossed double lines, transformed feathermen, feather, transformed flying heron, diamond-shape eye; 4 frog statues of 4 feet and rice ears on back anticlockwise stand on the edge of drum face; 2 groups of horse-ride statues between the frogs; Drum body: patterns of water wave, concentric circles, comb line, feather, boat, transformed feathermen, feather, net, leaf-shape triangle with circle in the middle; Feather patterns on 2 pairs of flat handles, 2 attached handles stand separately beside the casting line.	74.3–75	53.5	冷水冲型 Lengshui-chong Type	

序号 N0.	原编号及鼓名 Stock Number & Name	收藏单位 Museum	出土（征集） 时间、地点 Time & Spot for discovered or collected	主要装饰 Main Decorations	尺寸（厘米） Size(cm)		类型 Type	图片 Picture
					面径 Face Diameter	身高 Height		
587	总 000439 号 朱冲铜鼓 No.000439 Bronze Drum zhuchong	桂平市博物馆 Guiping Museum	1978 年出土于广西桂平油麻镇六平村南约 80 米朱冲山 Unearthed at Zhuchong Hill, in the south of 80m to Liuping Village, Youma Town, Guiping, Guangxi in 1978	鼓面：太阳纹（12 芒）、水波纹、同心圆纹、复线交叉纹、变形羽人纹、变形翔鹭纹、羽纹、眼纹，鼓面边缘饰四只逆时针四足谷穗纹立体蛙，蛙间分别饰一只鸟立饰； 鼓身：羽纹、水波纹、同心圆纹、船纹、变形羽人纹、网纹、圆心三角垂叶纹、眼纹；扁耳两对饰辫纹 Drum face: patterns of sun(12rays), water wave, concentric circles, crossed double lines, transformed feathermen, transformed flying heron, feather, diamond-shape eye; 4 frog statues of 4 feet and rice ears on back anticlockwise stand on the edge of drum face; 2 groups of bird statues between the frogs; Drum body: patterns of feather, water wave, concentric circles, boat, transformed feathermen, net, leaf-shape triangle with circle in the middle; Braid patterns on 2 pairs of flat handles.	69.8~71	44.4 （残） Incomplete	冷水冲型 Lengshui-chong Type	
588	总 000440 号 牛巴岭铜鼓 No.000440 Bronze Drum Niuba Ling	桂平市博物馆 Guiping Museum	1977 年出土于广西桂平麻垌镇南桥村北牛巴岭山腰 Unearthed at the hillside of Niuba Ling, the North to Nanqiao Village, Madong Town, Guiping, Guangxi in 1977	鼓面：太阳纹（12 芒）、谷穗纹、栉纹、同心圆纹、复线交叉纹、变形羽人纹、变形翔鹭纹间定胜纹、水波纹，鼓面四蛙已缺失； 鼓身：谷穗纹、栉纹、同心圆纹、谷穗纹栉纹同心圆纹垂直纹带，圆心三角垂叶纹；扁耳两对饰辫纹 Drum face: patterns of sun(12rays), rice ear, comb line, concentric circles, crossed double lines, transformed feathermen, transformed flying heron mixed Dingsheng, water wave; 4 frog statues stand on the edge of drum face; were lost; Drum body: patterns of rice ear, comb line, concentric circles, vertical ribbon of rice ear, straight line and concentric circle, leaf-shape triangle with circle in the middle; Braid patterns on 2 pairs of flat handles.	75.4~75.8	49.5	冷水冲型 Lengshui-chong Type	

序号 NO.	原编号及鼓名 Stock Number & Name	收藏单位 Museum	出土（征集） 时间、地点 Time & Spot for discovered or collected	主要装饰 Main Decorations	尺寸（厘米） Size(cm)		类型 Type	图片 Picture
					面径 Face Diameter	身高 Height		
589	总 000441 号 沙岗朱屋背鼓 No.000441 Bronze Drum Shagang Zhuwubei	桂平市博物馆 Guiping Museum	1975 年 10 月出土于广西桂平蒙圩镇新阳村沙岗朱屋背 Unearthed at Zhuwubei, Shagang, Xinyang Village, Mengxu Town, Guiping, Guangxi in October, 1975	鼓面：太阳纹（12 芒）、水波纹、斜线纹、复线交叉纹、变形羽人纹、变形翔鹭纹、栉纹、同心圆纹，鼓面边缘饰四只逆时针四足素面立体蛙； 鼓身：斜线纹、栉纹、同心圆纹、栉纹同心圆纹垂直纹带、圆心三角垂叶纹；扁耳两对饰辫纹 Drum face: patterns of sun(12rays), water wave, oblique line, crossed double lines, transformed feathermen, transformed flying heron, comb line, concentric circles; 4 frog statues of 4 feet and blank back anticlockwise stand on the edge of drum face; Drum body: patterns of oblique line, comb line, concentric circles, vertical ribbon of straight line and concentric circle, leaf-shape triangle with circle in the middle; Braid patterns on 2 pairs of flat handles.	64-67	40.3	冷水冲型 Lengshui-chong Type	
590	总 000442 号 兽形纹鼓 No.000442 Bronze Drum With beast patterns	桂平市博物馆 Guiping Museum	1978 年征购于广西桂平废品收购站 Collected at Guangxi Guiping Waste Recycle Station in 1978	鼓面：太阳纹（12 芒）、水波纹、切线同心圆纹、栉纹、变形羽人纹、变形翔鹭纹、鼓面边缘立饰缺失；仅存鼓面 Only the drum face is remained：patterns of sun(12rays), water wave, tangent concentric circle, comb line, transformed feathermen, transformed flying heron; the statues on the edge of the face was lost.	52-52.5	（残） Incomplete	冷水冲型 Lengshui-chong Type	

序号 N0.	原编号及鼓名 Stock Number & Name	收藏单位 Museum	出土（征集） 时间、地点 Time & Spot for discovered or collected	主要装饰 Main Decorations	尺寸（厘米） Size(cm)		类型 Type	图片 Picture
					面径 Face Diameter	身高 Height		
591	总000443号 变形翔鹭纹定 胜纹铜鼓 No.000443 Bronze Drum with flying heron and Dingsheng patterns	桂平市博 物馆 Guiping Museum	1978年1月征购 于广西桂平附城 供销社 Collected at Guangxi Guiping Fucheng Supply and Marketing Cooperative in January, 1978	鼓面：太阳纹（12芒）、栉纹、同心圆纹、复线交叉纹、变形羽人纹、变形翔鹭纹间定胜纹，鼓面边缘饰四只逆时针四足素面立蛙； 鼓身：栉纹、同心圆纹、谷穗纹栉纹同心圆纹垂直纹带，鼓足残缺；扁耳两对饰辫纹 Drum face: patterns of sun(12rays), comb line, concentric circles, crossed double lines, transformed feathermen, transformed flying heron mixed Dingsheng; 4 frog statues of 4 feet and blank back anticlockwise stand on the edge of drum face; Drum body: patterns of comb line, concentric circles, vertical ribbon of rice ear and straight line; the foot was lost; Braid patterns on 2 pairs of flat handles.	53-53.5	27.5 （残） Incom- plete	冷水冲 型 Lengshui- chong Type	
592	总000444号 蛙趾游旗纹 铜鼓 No.000444 Bronze Drum with frog toe and flying flag patterns	桂平市博 物馆 Guiping Museum	旧藏 The old stock	鼓面：太阳纹（12芒）、栉纹、同心圆纹、游旗纹、鸟纹间云纹，鼓面边缘有四对蛙爪纹； 鼓身：栉纹、同心圆纹、云纹、图案三角纹；扁耳两对饰辫纹 Drum face: patterns of sun(12rays), comb line, concentric circles, flying flag, bird mixed cloud; 4 pairs of frog toes on the edge of the face; Drum body: patterns of comb line, concentric circles, cloud, triangle with motifs; Braid patterns on 2 pairs of flat handles.	61	35	遵义型 Zunyi Type	

续表

序号 NO.	原编号及鼓名 Stock Number & Name	收藏单位 Museum	出土（征集） 时间、地点 Time & Spot for discovered or collected	主要装饰 Main Decorations	尺寸（厘米） Size(cm)		类型 Type	图片 Picture
					面径 Face Diameter	身高 Height		
593	总000445号 石鼓岭铜鼓 No.000445 Bronze Drum Shiguling	桂平市博 物馆 Guiping Museum	1972年出土于广 西桂平石咀镇石 鼓岭村西南河边 水田 Unearthed in the water field beside a river in southwest to Shiguling Village, Shizui Town, Guiping, Guangxi in 1972	鼓面：太阳纹（12芒）、水波纹、 同心圆纹、栉纹、复线交叉纹、羽纹、 变形羽人纹、变形翔鹭纹、眼纹、 鼓面边缘饰四只逆时针四足螺旋纹 立体蛙，蛙间分别饰一组三棵树和 一组牛拉橇立饰； 鼓身：水波纹、同心圆纹、船纹、 变形羽人纹、羽纹、网纹、切线同 心圆纹、圆心三角垂叶纹、眼纹； 扁耳两对饰辫纹 Drum face: patterns of sun(12rays), water wave, concentric circles, comb line, crossed double lines, feather, transformed feathermen, transformed flying heron, diamond-shape eye; 4 frog statues of 4 feet and spiracles on back anticlockwise stand on the edge of drum face; statues of 3 threes and an ox pulling a cart stand between the frogs; Drum body: patterns of water wave, concentric circles, boat, transformed feathermen, feather, net, tangent concentric circle, leaf-shape triangle with circle in the middle, diamond-shape eye; Braid patterns on 2 pairs of flat handles.	73.3~74.3	48.3	冷水冲 型 Lengshui- chong Type	
594	总000446号 沙岗铜鼓 No.000446 Bronze Drum Shagang	桂平市博 物馆 Guiping Museum	1975年10月出 土于广西桂平蒙 圩镇新阳村沙岗 朱屋 Unearthed at Zhuwu, Shagang, Xinyang Village, Mengxu Town, Guiping, Guangxi in October, 1975	鼓面：太阳纹（12芒）、栉纹、同 心圆纹、复线交叉间同心圆纹、变 形羽人纹、羽纹、变形翔鹭夹定胜纹， 鼓面边缘饰四只逆时针四足素面立 体蛙； 鼓身：羽纹、栉纹、同心圆纹、栉 纹同心圆纹垂直纹带、圆心三角垂 叶纹；扁耳两对纹饰锈蚀 Drum face: patterns of sun(12rays), comb line, concentric circles, crossed double lines, transformed feathermen, feather, transformed flying heron mixed Dingsheng; 4 frog statues of 4 feet and blank back anticlockwise stand on the edge of drum face; Drum body: patterns of feather, comb line, concentric circles, vertical ribbon of straight lines and concentric circles, leaf- shape triangle with circle in the middle; patterns on 2 pairs of flat handles are rusting.	69.8~70.8	49 （残） Incom- plete	冷水冲 型 Lengshui- chong Type	

序号 N0.	原编号及鼓名 Stock Number & Name	收藏单位 Museum	出土（征集）时间、地点 Time & Spot for discovered or collected	主要装饰 Main Decorations	尺寸（厘米）Size(cm)		类型 Type	图片 Picture
					面径 Face Diameter	身高 Height		
595	总000447号 鹤岭铜鼓 No.000447 Bronze Drum Heling	桂平市博物馆 Guiping Museum	1980年6月出土于广西桂平西山乡福山村东屯西南约1公里的鹤岭 Unearthed at Heling, in the southwest of 1km to Dongtun, Fushan Village, Xishan, Guiping, Guangxi in June, 1980	鼓面：太阳纹（12芒）、水波纹、同心圆纹、栉纹、羽纹、复线交叉纹、变形羽人纹、变形翔鹭纹、眼纹，鼓面边缘饰四只逆时针四足谷穗纹立体蛙，蛙间分别饰一组人喂马立饰；鼓身：羽纹、同心圆纹、船纹、变形羽人纹、网纹、水波纹、圆心三角垂叶纹、眼纹；扁耳两对饰辫纹 Drum face: patterns of sun(12rays), water wave, concentric circles, comb line, feather, crossed double lines, transformed feathermen, flying heron, diamond-shape eye; 4 frog statues of 4 feet and rice ears on back anticlockwise stand on the edge of drum face; 2 statue groups of horse-feeding stand between the frogs; Drum body: patterns of feather, concentric circles, boat, transformed feathermen, net, water wave, leaf-shape triangle with circle in the middle, diamond-shape eye; Braid patterns on 2 pairs of flat handles.	80.3－80.8	58.7	冷水冲型 Lengshui-chong Type	
596	总000448号 理塘铜鼓 No.000448 Bronze Drum Litang	桂平市博物馆 Guiping Museum	1983年出土于广西桂平江口镇理塘村西200米半山腰 Unearthed at the hillside in the west of 200m to Litang Village, Jiangkou Town, Guiping, Guangxi in 1983	鼓面：太阳纹（12芒）、栉纹、同心圆纹、复线交叉纹、变形羽人纹、变形翔鹭间定胜纹，鼓面边缘饰四只逆时针四足素面立体蛙；鼓身：栉纹、同心圆纹、栉纹同心圆纹垂直纹带、圆心三角垂叶纹；扁耳两对饰辫纹 Drum face: patterns of sun(12rays), comb line, concentric circles, crossed double lines, transformed feathermen, transformed flying heron mixed Dingsheng; 4 frog statues of 4 feet and blank back anticlockwise stand on the edge of drum face; Drum body: patterns of comb line, concentric circles, vertical ribbon of straight lines and concentric circles, leaf-shape triangle with circle in the middle; Braid patterns on 2 pairs of flat handles.	67.5－68.3	45	冷水冲型 Lengshui-chong Type	

续表

序号 NO.	原编号及鼓名 Stock Number & Name	收藏单位 Museum	出土（征集）时间、地点 Time & Spot for discovered or collected	主要装饰 Main Decorations	尺寸（厘米） Size(cm)		类型 Type	图片 Picture
					面径 Face Diameter	身高 Height		
597	总000449号 寻旺村鼓 No.000449 Bronze Drum Xunwang Cun	桂平市博物馆 Guiping Museum	1983年3月24日出土于广西桂平寻旺村西南 Unearthed in the southwest of Xunwang Village, Guiping, Guangxi on March 24th, 1983	鼓面：太阳纹（12芒）、水波纹、栉纹、同心圆纹、复线交叉纹、羽纹、变形羽人纹、变形翔鹭纹、眼纹、鼓面边缘饰四只逆时针四足谷穗纹立蛙，蛙间分别饰一组双鱼和一组双乘骑立饰； 鼓身：羽纹、栉纹、同心圆纹、船纹(有鱼纹)、变形羽人纹，鼓足残缺；扁耳两对饰辫纹，合范线附近各一只环附耳饰缠丝纹 Drum face: patterns of sun(12rays), water wave, comb line, concentric circles, crossed double lines, feather, transformed feathermen, transformed flying heron, diamond-shape eye; 4 frog statues of 4 feet and rice ears on back anticlockwise stand on the edge of drum face; a group statue of 2 fishes and the other of 2 horse-ride stand between the frogs; Drum body: patterns of feather, comb line, concentric circles, boat(with fish inside), transformed feathermen; the foot was lost; Braid patterns on 2 pairs of flat handles, silk-like patterns on 2 attached ring handles stand separately beside the casting line.	72.6－73.8	40 （残） Incomplete	冷水冲型 Lengshui-chong Type	
598	总000450号 四方墩铜鼓 No.000450 Bronze Drum Sifangdun	桂平市博物馆 Guiping Museum	1984年2月出土于广西桂平金田镇田江村西北四方墩坡地 Unearthed at the hillside of Sifangdun, in Northwest of Tianjiang Village, Jintian Town, Guiping, Guangxi in February, 1984	鼓面：太阳纹（12芒）、水波纹、栉纹、同心圆纹、复线交叉纹、变形羽人纹、变形翔鹭纹间定胜纹，鼓面边缘饰四只逆时针四足素面立体蛙； 鼓身：栉纹、同心圆纹、栉纹同心圆纹垂直纹带、圆心三角垂叶纹；扁耳两对饰辫纹 Drum face: patterns of sun(12rays), water wave, comb line, concentric circles, crossed double lines, transformed feathermen, transformed flying heron mixed Dingsheng; 4 frog statues of 4 feet and blank back anticlockwise stand on the edge of drum face; Drum body: patterns of comb line, concentric circles, vertical ribbon of straight lines and concentric circles, leaf-shape triangle with circle in the middle; Braid patterns on 2 pairs of flat handles.	61.8－62.5	33 （残） Incomplete	冷水冲型 Lengshui-chong Type	

序号 NO.	原编号及鼓名 Stock Number & Name	收藏单位 Museum	出土（征集）时间、地点 Time & Spot for discovered or collected	主要装饰 Main Decorations	尺寸（厘米）Size(cm)		类型 Type	图片 Picture
					面径 Face Diameter	身高 Height		
599	总000451号 理村铜鼓 No.000451 Bronze Drum Licun	桂平市博物馆 Guiping Museum	1982年出土于广西桂平垌心乡理村北约50米坡地 Unearthed at the hillside in north of 50m to Li Village, Dongxin, Guiping, Guangxi in 1982	鼓面：太阳纹（12芒）、S形纹、切线同心圆纹、变形羽人纹、行走鹭鸟间定胜纹、栉纹，仅存鼓面 Only the drum face is remained：patterns of sun(12rays), S-shape motif, tangent concentric circle, transformed feathermen, walking heron mixed Dingsheng, comb line.	36.5~37	（残）Incomplete	冷水冲型 Lengshui-chong Type	
600	总000606号 上江头铜鼓 No.000606 Bronze Drum Shangjiangtou	桂平市博物馆 Guiping Museum	1986年8月12日出土于广西桂平金田镇上江头村北三家下垌 Unearthed at Sanjia Xiadong, Shangjiangtou Village, Jintian Town, Guiping, Guangxi on August 12th, 1986	鼓面：太阳纹（12芒）、水波纹、同心圆纹、栉纹、复线交叉纹、羽纹、变形羽人纹、变形翔鹭纹、眼纹、鼓面边缘饰四只逆时针四足谷穗纹立体蛙，其中两蛙背负田螺立饰；鼓身：羽纹、同心圆纹、船纹，鼓腰以下残缺 Drum face: patterns of sun(12rays), water wave, concentric circles, comb line, crossed double lines, feather, transformed feathermen, transformed flying heron, diamond-shape eye; 4 frog statues of 4 feet and rice ears on back anticlockwise stand on the edge of drum face, 2 of them carrying a field snail on back; Drum body: patterns of feather, concentric circles, boat; Parts under the waist were lost.	59.8~60.3	17.5 （残）Incomplete	冷水冲型 Lengshui-chong Type	

续表

序号 NO.	原编号及鼓名 Stock Number & Name	收藏单位 Museum	出土（征集） 时间、地点 Time & Spot for discovered or collected	主要装饰 Main Decorations	尺寸（厘米） Size(cm)		类型 Type	图片 Picture
					面径 Face Diameter	身高 Height		
601	总 000607 号 黑石岭铜鼓 No.000607 Bronze Drum Heishiling	桂平市博物馆 Guiping Museum	1985 年 6 月 2 日 出土于广西桂平 石龙镇新龙村东 黑石岭 Unearthed at Heishi Ling, in the east of Xinlong Village, Shilong Town, Guiping, Guangxi on June 2nd, 1985	鼓面：太阳纹（12 芒）、栉纹、同心圆纹、复线交叉纹、变形羽人纹、变形翔鹭纹间定胜纹、鼓面边缘饰四只逆时针四足素面立蛙； 鼓身：栉纹、同心圆纹、栉纹同心圆纹垂直纹带、圆心三角垂叶纹；扁耳两对饰辫纹 Drum face: patterns of sun(12rays), comb line, concentric circles, crossed double lines, transformed feathermen, transformed flying heron mixed Dingsheng; 4 frog statues of 4 feet and blank back anticlockwise stand on the edge of drum face; Drum body: patterns of comb line, concentric circles, vertical ribbon of straight lines and concentric circles, leaf-shape triangle with circle in the middle; Braid patterns on 2 pairs of flat handles.	71.5～72	46	冷水冲型 Lengshui-chong Type	
602	总 000611 号 秀南铜鼓 No.000611 Bronze Drum Xiunan	桂平市博物馆 Guiping Museum	1991 年 10 月 20 日出土于广西木根镇秀南村东田鸡头岭西北 Unearthed at northwest of Jitou Ling, Dongtian, Xiunan Village, Mugen Town, Guangxi on October 20th, 1991	鼓面：太阳纹（12 芒）、水波纹、栉纹、同心圆纹、复线交叉纹、变形羽人纹、变形翔鹭纹、切线同心圆纹、鼓面边缘饰四只逆时针四足十字纹立蛙、蛙间饰一只穿山甲立饰； 鼓身：水波纹、栉纹、变形羽人纹、同心圆纹、雷纹、圆心三角垂叶纹；扁耳两对饰羽纹 Drum face: patterns of sun(12rays), water wave, comb line, concentric circles, crossed double lines, transformed feathermen, transformed flying heron, tangent concentric circle; 4 frog statues of 4 feet and cross on back anticlockwise stand on the edge of drum face; a pangolin statue stand between the frogs; Drum body: patterns of water wave, comb line, transformed feathermen, concentric circles, thunder, leaf-shape triangle with circle in the middle; Feather patterns on 2 pairs of flat handles.	84～86	46.8 （残） Incomplete	冷水冲型 Lengshui-chong Type	

续表

序号 N0.	原编号及鼓名 Stock Number & Name	收藏单位 Museum	出土（征集）时间、地点 Time & Spot for discovered or collected	主要装饰 Main Decorations	尺寸（厘米） Size(cm)		类型 Type	图片 Picture
					面径 Face Diameter	身高 Height		
603	总000613号 张凌彭铜鼓 No.000613 Bronze Drum Zhanglingpeng	桂平市博物馆 Guiping Museum	1993年1月31日出土于广西桂平金田镇新燕村张凌彭屯南约50米处 Unearthed in the south of 50m to Zhanglingpeng Tun, Xinyan Village, Jintian Town, Guiping, Guangxi on January 31st, 1993	鼓面：太阳纹（12芒）、水波纹、栉纹、同心圆纹、复线交叉纹、绹纹、变形羽人纹、变形翔鹭纹、眼纹间云纹，鼓面边缘饰四只逆时针四足谷穗纹立蛙，蛙间饰一组孩童抱鸭和一组人拉牛播种立饰； 鼓身：水波纹、同心圆纹、船纹（有鱼纹）、变形羽人纹、网纹、栉纹、圆心三角垂叶纹；扁耳两对饰辫纹 Drum face: patterns of sun(12rays), water wave, comb line, concentric circles, crossed double lines, rope, transformed feathermen, transformed flying heron, diamond-shape eye mixed cloud; 4 frog statues of 4 feet and rice ears on back anticlockwise stand on the edge of drum face; a group statue of a child holding a duck and the other of a man pulling the ox to sow between the frogs; Drum body: patterns of water wave, concentric circles, boat(with fish inside), transformed feathermen, net, comb line, leaf-shape triangle with circle in the middle; Braid patterns on 2 pairs of flat handles.	73-74	48.8（残） Incomplete	冷水冲型 Lengshui-chong Type	
604	总000615号 过山路铜鼓 No.000615 Bronze Drum Guoshanlu	桂平市博物馆 Guiping Museum	1994年7月21日出土于广西桂平南木镇联江下湾村过山路屯黔江南岸 Unearthed at the south bank of Qianjiang, Guoshanlu Tun, Xiawan Village, Lianjiang, Nanmu Town, Guiping, Guangxi on July 21st, 1994	鼓面：太阳纹（8芒）、通体云纹、雷纹，鼓面边缘饰四只逆时针四足素面立体蛙；扁耳两对饰羽纹 Drum face: patterns of sun(8rays), all are clouds and thunders; 4 frog statues of 4 feet and blank back anticlockwise stand on the edge of drum face; Feather patterns on 2 pairs of flat handles.	84.8-85.5	45	北流型 Beiliu Type	

序号 NO.	原编号及鼓名 Stock Number & Name	收藏单位 Museum	出土（征集） 时间、地点 Time & Spot for discovered or collected	主要装饰 Main Decorations	尺寸（厘米） Size(cm)		类型 Type	图片 Picture
					面径 Face Diameter	身高 Height		
605	总000635号 上江铜鼓 No.000635 Bronze Drum Shangjiang	桂平市博物馆 Guiping Museum	1993年2月出土于广西桂平木根乡连平村公所上江村南约400米的耙头顶西侧 Unearthed at the west of Patouding, in south of 400m to Shangjiang Village, Lianping Village office, Mugen, Guiping, Guangxi in February, 1993	鼓面：太阳纹（12芒）、水波纹、谷穗纹、同心圆纹、复线交叉纹、羽纹、变形羽人纹、变形翔鹭纹、眼纹，鼓面边缘饰四只逆时针四足谷穗纹立体蛙； 鼓身：羽纹、同心圆纹、栉纹、船纹、变形羽人纹、网纹、圆心三角垂叶间半同心圆谷穗纹；扁耳两对饰辫纹 Drum face: patterns of sun(12rays), water wave, rice ears, concentric circles, crossed double lines, feather transformed feathermen, transformed flying heron, diamond-shape eye; 4 frog statues of 4 feet and rice ears on back anticlockwise stand on the edge of drum face; Drum body: patterns of feather, concentric circles, comb line, boat, transformed feathermen, net, leaf-shape triangle with circle in the middle mixed half concentric circles and rice ears; Braid patterns on 2 pairs of flat handles.	71.3~71.5	53.3	冷水冲型 Lengshui-chong Type	
606	总000636号 古莲鼓 No.000636 Bronze Drum Gulian	桂平市博物馆 Guiping Museum	2003年7月12日出土于广西桂平江口六保村六队古莲村 Unearthed at Gulian Village, Liubao Team 6, Jiangkou, Guiping, Guangxi on July 12th, 2003	鼓面：太阳纹（12芒）、水波纹、栉纹、同心圆纹、复线交叉纹、变形羽人纹、变形翔鹭纹、眼纹，鼓面边缘饰四只逆时针四足谷穗纹立体蛙，蛙间各饰一组乘骑立饰； 鼓身：水波纹、栉纹、同心圆纹、船纹、变形羽人纹、网纹、圆心三角垂叶间同心圆和羽纹、眼纹；扁耳两对饰辫纹 Drum face: patterns of sun(12rays), water wave, comb line, concentric circles, crossed double lines, transformed feathermen, trnasformed flying heron, diamond-shape eye; 4 frog statues of 4 feet and rice ears on back anticlockwise stand on the edge of drum face; 2 groups of horse-ride statues stand between the frogs; Drum body: patterns of water wave, comb line, concentric circles, boat, transformed feathermen, net, leaf-shape triangle with circle in the middle mixed half concentric circle, feather and diamond-shape eye; Braid patterns on 2 pairs of flat handles.	63.5~64	43.3	冷水中型 Lengshui-chong Type	

序号 NO.	原编号及鼓名 Stock Number & Name	收藏单位 Museum	出土（征集） 时间、地点 Time & Spot for discovered or collected	主要装饰 Main Decorations	尺寸（厘米） Size(cm)		类型 Type	图片 Picture
					面径 Face Diameter	身高 Height		
607	玉林 01 号 新民村铜鼓 Yulin No.01 Bronze Drum Xinmin Cun	玉林市博物馆 Yulin City Museum	1975 年 3 月出土于广西玉林新民村东南约 150 米处 Unearthed in the southeast of 150m to Xinmin Village, Yulin, Guangxi in March, 1975	鼓面：太阳纹（8 芒）、雷纹，鼓面边缘饰六只逆时针四足素面立体蛙； 鼓身：雷纹填线纹、水波纹；扁耳两对无纹饰 Drum face: patterns of sun(8rays), thunder; 6 frog statues of 4 feet and blank back stand anticlockwise on the edge of the face; Drum body: patterns of thunder filled with straight lines, water wave; 2 pairs of blank flat handles.	59.3—60.3	30 （残） Incomplete	北流型 Beiliu Type	
608	玉林 02 号 岭头铜鼓 Yulin No.02 Bronze Drum Lingtou	玉林市博物馆 Yulin City Museum	1977 年 8 月出土于广西玉林小平山乡金华村岭头屯西北约 800 米处 Unearthed in Northwest of 800m to Lingtou Tun, Jinhua Village, Xiaopingshan, Yulin, Guangxi in August, 1977	鼓面：太阳纹（8 芒）、云纹、鸟纹，鼓面边缘饰六只逆时针四足素面立体蛙； 鼓身：云纹、雷纹填线纹；扁耳两对无纹饰 Drum face: patterns of sun(8rays), cloud, bird; 6 frog statues of 4 feet and blank back stand anticlockwise on the edge of the face; Drum body: patterns of cloud, thunder filled with straight lines; 2 pairs of blank flat handles.	71.3—71.7	42.4	北流型 Beiliu Type	
609	000442 号 三龙铜鼓 No.000442 Bronze Drum Sanlong	玉林市博物馆 Yulin City Museum	1984 年 5 月出土于广西玉林石南镇东龙村三龙屯东南约 100 米处 Unearthed in Southeast of 100m to Sanlong Tun, Donglong Village, Shinan Town, Yulin, Guangxi in May, 1984	鼓面：太阳纹（8 芒）、云纹、雷纹、席纹、雷纹填线纹，鼓面边缘饰六组顺时针四足直线纹立体蛙，其中两组为累蹲蛙； 鼓身：席纹、云纹、雷纹填线纹、网纹、比轮钱纹；扁耳两对饰羽纹、乳钉纹 Drum face: patterns of sun(8rays), cloud, thunder, woven mat, thunder filled with straight lines; 6 frog statues of 4 feet and straight line on back stand clockwise on the edge of the face; 2 of them are overlap; Drum body: patterns of woven mat, cloud, thunder filled with straight lines, net, Bilun Coin; Feather and nipple protrusion patterns on 2 pairs of blank flat handles.	95.2—96	52	灵山型 Lingshan Type	

序号 NO.	原编号及鼓名 Stock Number & Name	收藏单位 Museum	出土（征集）时间、地点 Time & Spot for discovered or collected	主要装饰 Main Decorations	尺寸（厘米）Size(cm)		类型 Type	图片 Picture
					面径 Face Diameter	身高 Height		
610	00625 号 浪平铜鼓 No.00625 Bronze Drum Langping	玉林市博物馆 Yulin City Museum	1991 年 3 月 21 日出土于广西玉林小平山乡浪平屯东约 2.5 公里处 Unearthed in the east of 2.5km to Langping Tun, Xiaopingshan, Yulin, Guangxi on March 21st, 1991	鼓面：太阳纹（8 芒）、雷纹、水波纹、席纹、连钱纹，鼓面边缘饰六只逆时针四足辫纹、螺旋纹立蛙；鼓身：席纹、雷纹、雷纹填线纹；环耳两对饰辫纹、直线纹 Drum face: patterns of sun(8rays), thunder, water wave, woven mat, coins part of overlap; 6 frog statues of 4 feet, braids and spiracles on back, stand anticlockwise on the edge of the face; Drum body: patterns of woven mat, thunder, thunder filled with straight lines; Braid and straight line patterns on 2 pairs of ring handles.	123.6–124.6	66.5	北流型 Beiliu Type	
611	00631 号 牛壕塘铜鼓 No.00631 Bronze Drum Niuhao Tang	玉林市博物馆 Yulin City Museum	1992 年 4 月 10 日出土于广西玉林大塘乡阳山村南约 700 米的牛壕塘 Unearthed at Niuhao Tang, in the south of 700m to Yangshan Village, Datang, Yulin, Guangxi on April 10th, 1992	鼓面：太阳纹（8 芒）、云纹、雷纹、方孔钱纹、雷纹填线纹，鼓面边缘饰六组顺时针三足素面立体蛙；鼓身：四瓣花纹、方孔钱纹、雷纹、雷纹填线纹、云纹；扁耳两对无纹饰 Drum face: patterns of sun(8rays), cloud, thunder, coin with a square hole, thunder filled with straight lines; 6 frog statues of 3 feet and blank back stand clockwise on the edge of the face; Drum body: patterns of quatrefoil, coin with a square hole, thunder, thunder filled with straight lines, cloud; 2 pairs of blank flat handles.	58.1–58.9	32（残）Incomplete	灵山型 Lingshan Type	
612	00632 号 古城铜鼓 No.00632 Bronze Drum Gucheng	玉林市博物馆 Yulin City Museum	1992 年 10 月 7 日出土于广西玉林成均镇古城村西三井坑岭 Unearthed at Sanjingkeng Ling, the west to Gucheng Village, Chengjun Town, Yulin, Guangxi on October 7th, 1992	鼓面：太阳纹（10 芒）、通体雷纹，鼓面边缘饰四只逆时针四足叶脉纹立蛙；扁耳两对饰辫纹 Drum face: patterns of sun(10rays), all are thunders; 4 frog statues of 4 feet and leaf vein on back stand anticlockwise on the edge of the face; Braid patterns on 2 pairs of flat handles	85.3–88	47	北流型 Beiliu Type	

序号 N0.	原编号及鼓名 Stock Number & Name	收藏单位 Museum	出土（征集） 时间、地点 Time & Spot for discovered or collected	主要装饰 Main Decorations	尺寸（厘米） Size(cm)		类型 Type	图片 Picture
					面径 Face Diameter	身高 Height		
613	000759 号 莲塘坪铜鼓 No.00759 Bronze Drum Liantangping	玉林市博物馆 Yulin City Museum	1993 年 2 月出土于广西玉林沙田镇六龙村莲塘坪南约 1 公里十五冲山上 Unearthed at Shiwuchong, in the south of 1km to Liantangping, Liulong Village, Shatian Town, Yulin, Guangxi in February, 1993	鼓面：太阳纹（8 芒）、四出钱纹、雷纹填线纹、比轮钱纹，鼓面边缘饰六组顺时针四足羽纹、席纹立蛙，其中四组为累蹲蛙，另外两组蛙负螺； 鼓身：四出钱纹、雷纹填线纹、比轮钱纹、叶纹；一侧鼓耳下鼓足位置饰一只网纹立体虎；扁耳两对饰羽纹、乳钉纹，鼓足合范线附近有一对环形附耳 Drum face: patterns of sun(8rays), coin with quadrangle inside, thunder filled with straight lines, Bilun Coin; 6 frog statues of 4 feet, feather and woven mat patterns on back stand clockwise on the edge of the face, 4 of them are overlap, the other two are statues with field snail on the back of frogs; Drum body: patterns of coin with quadrangle inside, thunder filled with straight lines, Bilun Coin, leaf; a tiger statue with net pattern on back stands under one of the handles on the foot; Feather and nipple protrusion on 2 pairs of blank flat handles, a pair of attached ring handles beside the casting line.	126.2－133.5	66.5	灵山型 Lingshan Type	
614	大岭肚鼓 Bronze Drum Dalingdu	玉林市博物馆 Yulin City Museum	1981 年 1 月出土于广西玉林新桥镇长屏村大岭肚屯东南山坡 Unearthed at the hillside in southeast to Dalingdu Tun, Changping Village, Xinqiao Town, Yulin, Guangxi in January, 1981	鼓面：太阳纹（8 芒）、云纹、连钱纹、鸟纹，鼓面边缘饰六只逆时针四足素面立蛙； 鼓身：连钱纹、席纹、半圆填线纹、云纹、雷纹；扁耳两对无纹饰 Drum face: patterns of sun(8rays), cloud, coins part of overlap, bird; 6 frog statues of 4 feet and blank back stand anticlockwise on the edge of the face; Drum body: patterns of coins part of overlap, woven mat, half circle filled with straight lines, cloud, thunder; 2 pairs of blank flat handles.	66.3－66.5	39.5 （残） Incomplete	灵山型 Lingshan Type	

序号 N0.	原编号及鼓名 Stock Number & Name	收藏单位 Museum	出土（征集）时间、地点 Time & Spot for discovered or collected	主要装饰 Main Decorations	尺寸（厘米） Size(cm)		类型 Type	图片 Picture
					面径 Face Diameter	身高 Height		
615	白坟岭鼓 Bronze Drum Baifenling	玉林市博物馆 Yulin City Museum	2001 年 5 月 20 日出土于广西玉林沙田镇苏立村白坟岭屯 Unearthed at Baifenling Tun, Suli Village, Shatian Town, Yulin, Guangxi on May 20th, 2001	鼓面：太阳纹（12 芒）、雷纹、连钱纹、四出钱纹、雷纹填线纹，鼓面边缘饰六只逆时针四足素面立蛙；仅存鼓面 Drum face: patterns of sun(12rays), thunder, coins part of overlap, coin with quadrangle inside, thunder filled with straight lines; 6 frog statues of 4 feet and blank back stand anticlockwise on the edge of the face; Only the drum face is remained.	114–118	（残） Incomplete	灵山型 Lingshan Type	
616	北流 01 号下浪湾铜鼓 Beiliu No.01 Bronze Drum Xialangwan	北流市博物馆 Beiliu City Museum	1964 年出土于广西北流白马镇大伦农场下浪湾山腰 Unearthed at the hillside of Xialangwan, Dalun Farm, Baima Town, Beiliu, Guangxi in 1964	鼓面：太阳纹（8 芒）、通体云纹、雷纹，鼓面边缘饰四只逆时针四足素面立体蛙；环耳两对饰缠丝纹 Drum face: patterns of sun(8rays), all are clouds and thunders; 4 frog statues of 4 feet and blank back stand anticlockwise on the edge of the face; Silk-like patterns on 2 pairs of ring handles.	90.5–91.5	53	北流型 Beiliu Type	
617	北流 02 号黄叶塘铜鼓 Beiliu No.02 Bronze Drum Huangyetang	北流市博物馆 Beiliu City Museum	1971 年出土于广西北流白马镇玉塘村黄叶塘屯西约 100 米坡上 Unearthed at the hillside in the west of 100m to Huangyetang Tun, Yutang Village, Baima Town, Beiliu, Guangxi in 1971	鼓面：太阳纹（8 芒）、云纹，鼓面边缘立蛙缺失；鼓身：通体雷纹填线纹；环耳两对饰缠丝纹 Drum face: patterns of sun(8rays),cloud; all frog statues are lost; All patterns on the body are thunder filled with straight lines; Silk−like patterns on 2 pairs of ring handles.	70–71	22.5 （残） Incomplete	北流型 Beiliu Type	
618	北流 03 号菠萝根铜鼓 Beiliu No.03 Bronze Drum Boluogen	北流市博物馆 Beiliu City Museum	1972 年出土于广西北流白马镇茶新村菠萝根屯京圩山 Unearthed at Jingxu Hill, Boluogen Tun, Chaxin Village, Baima Town, Beiliu, Guangxi in 1972	鼓面：太阳纹（8 芒）、云纹，鼓面边缘饰四只逆时针四足素面立体蛙；鼓身：雷纹、雷纹填线纹；环耳两对饰缠丝纹 Drum face: patterns of sun(8rays), cloud; 4 frog statues of 4 feet and blank back stand anticlockwise on the edge of the face; Drum body: patterns of thunder, thunder filled with straight lines; Silk-like patterns on 2 pairs of ring handles.	70.5–71.4	33.5 （残） Incomplete	北流型 Beiliu Type	

469

序号 N0.	原编号及鼓名 Stock Number & Name	收藏单位 Museum	出土（征集） 时间、地点 Time & Spot for discovered or collected	主要装饰 Main Decorations	尺寸（厘米） Size(cm)		类型 Type	图片 Picture
					面径 Face Diameter	身高 Height		
619	北流 04 号 白马山铜鼓 Beiliu No.04 Bronze Drum Baimashan	北流市博物馆 Beiliu City Museum	1972 年 11 月出土于广西北流大坡外镇大坡内村西北约 1 公里的白马山半坡 Unearthed at the hillside of Baima Hill, in Northwest of 1km to Daponei Village, Dapowai Town, Beiliu, Guangxi in November, 1972	鼓面：太阳纹（8 芒）、通体纹饰锈蚀，鼓面边缘饰四只逆时针四足素面立蛙；环耳两对残缺 Drum face: patterns of sun(8rays), the whole drum was rusting; 4 frog statues of 4 feet and blank back stand on the edge of the face;2 pairs of ring handles are lost.	69.5～70.8	23（残） Incomplete	北流型 Beiliu Type	
620	北流 05 号 大人岭铜鼓 Beiliu No.05 Bronze Drum Darenling	北流市博物馆 Beiliu City Museum	1973 年 12 月 9 日出土于广西北流清湾镇中龙村东北约 150 米的大人岭 Unearthed at Darenling, in the northeast of 150m to Zhonglong Village, Qingwan Town, Beiliu, Guangxi on December 9th, 1973	鼓面：太阳纹（8 芒）、雷纹，鼓面边缘饰四只逆时针四足素面立体蛙；通体雷纹填线纹；环耳两对饰缠丝纹，耳根开三叉 Drum face: patterns of sun(8rays), thunder; 4 frog statues of 4 feet and blank back stand anticlockwise on the edge of the face; all patterns on the body are thunders filled with straight lines; Silk-like patterns on 2 pairs of ring handles, 3 rays on the roots of all the handles.	77.8～78.4	44	北流型 Beiliu Type	
621	北流 06 号 大屋铜鼓 Beiliu No.06 Bronze Drum Dawu	北流市博物馆 Beiliu City Museum	1974 年 11 月出土于广西北流六靖镇水冲村大屋屯南 60 米岭脚 Unearthed at the foot of a hill in south of 60m to Dawu Tun, Shuichong Village, Liujing Town, Beiliu, Guangxi in November, 1974	鼓面：太阳纹（8 芒）、雷纹，鼓面边缘饰四只两两相对四足素面三爪立蛙； 鼓身：云纹、雷纹；环耳两对饰缠丝纹，耳根开三叉 Drum face: patterns of sun(8rays), thunder; 4 frog statues of 4 feet and blank back stand on the edge of the face, face to each other; Drum body: patterns of cloud and thunder; Silk-like patterns on 2 pairs of ring handles, 3 rays on the roots of all the handles.	91.2～92.5	54	北流型 Beiliu Type	

续表

序号 NO.	原编号及鼓名 Stock Number & Name	收藏单位 Museum	出土（征集） 时间、地点 Time & Spot for discovered or collected	主要装饰 Main Decorations	尺寸（厘米） Size(cm)		类型 Type	图片 Picture
					面径 Face Diameter	身高 Height		
622	北流 07 号 堡山铜鼓 Beiliu No.07 Bronze Drum Baoshan	北流市博物馆 Beiliu City Museum	1975 年出土于广西北流民乐镇了平村鸡头屯堡山 Unearthed at Baoshan, Jitou Tun, Liaoping Village, Minle Town, Beiliu, Guangxi in 1975	鼓面：太阳纹（8 芒）、雷纹、鸟形纹、云纹，鼓面边缘饰四只逆时针三足素面立体蛙； 鼓身：云纹、雷纹填线纹；扁耳两对饰辫纹 Drum face: patterns of sun(8rays), thunder, bird, cloud; 4 frog statues of 3 feet and blank back stand anticlockwise on the edge of the face; Drum body: patterns of cloud and thunder filled with straight lines; braid patterns on 2 pairs of ring handles.	90−91.4	57.4	灵山型 Lingshan Type	
623	北流 08 号 山牛化铜鼓 Beiliu No.08 Bronze Drum Shanniuhua	北流市博物馆 Beiliu City Museum	1975 年出土于广西北流清湾镇龙南村东风屯山牛化 Unearthed at Shanniuhua, Dongfeng Tun, Longnan Village, Qingwan Town, Beiliu, Guangxi in 1975	鼓面：太阳纹（8 芒）、雷纹、云纹、角形填线纹、叶脉纹，鼓面边缘饰四只逆时针四足素面立体蛙；通体雷纹；扁耳两对无纹饰 Drum face: patterns of sun(8rays), thunder, cloud, triangle filled with straight lines, leaf vein; 4 frog statues of 4 feet and blank back stand anticlockwise on the edge of the face; Drum body: all patterns are thunder; 2 pairs of blank flat handles.	76−77	48 （残） Incomplete	北流型 Beiliu Type	
624	北流 09 号 园山铜鼓 Beiliu No.09 Bronze Drum Yuanshan	北流市博物馆 Beiliu City Museum	1975 年出土于广西北流白马镇黄金村龙塘屯园山 Unearthed at Yuanshan, Longtang Tun, Huangjin Village, Baima Town, Beiliu, Guangxi in 1975	鼓面：太阳纹（8 芒）、雷纹，鼓面边缘饰四只两两相对四足素面三爪立体蛙；通体雷纹填线纹；环耳两对饰缠丝纹、耳根开三叉 Drum face: patterns of sun(8rays), thunder; 4 frog statues of 4 feet, 3 toes and blank back stand on the edge of the face, face to each other; Drum body: all patterns are thunder filled with straight lines; Silk-like patterns on 2 pairs of ring handles, 3 rays on the roots of all the handles.	73.5−74	42	北流型 Beiliu Type	
625	北流 10 号 担水岭铜鼓 Beiliu No.10 Bronze Drum Danshuiling	北流市博物馆 Beiliu City Museum	1977 年出土于广西北流六靖镇镇南村长塘屯东北约 2 公里的担水岭 Unearthed at Danshuiling, in the northeast of 2km to Changtang Tun, Zhennan Village, Liujing Town, Beiliu, Guangxi in 1977	鼓面：太阳纹（8 芒）、云纹，鼓面边缘饰四只顺时针四足素面立体蛙； 鼓身：云纹、席纹、雷纹填线纹；扁耳两对无纹饰 Drum face: patterns of sun(8rays), cloud; 4 frog statues of 4 feet and blank back stand clockwise on the edge of the face; Drum body: patterns of cloud, woven mat, thunder filled with straight lines; 2 pairs of blank flat handles.	90.3−92	53.8	北流型 Beiliu Type	

续表

序号 N0.	原编号及鼓名 Stock Number & Name	收藏单位 Museum	出土（征集） 时间、地点 Time & Spot for discovered or collected	主要装饰 Main Decorations	尺寸（厘米） Size(cm)		类型 Type	图片 Picture
					面径 Face Diameter	身高 Height		
626	北流 11 号 Beiliu No.11	北流市博物馆 Beiliu City Museum	旧藏 The old stock	鼓面：太阳纹（8 芒）、雷纹，鼓面边缘饰四只逆时针四足素面立体蛙；仅存鼓面 Drum face: patterns of sun(8rays), thunder; 4 frog statues of 4 feet and blank back stand anticlockwise on the edge of the face; Only the drum face is remained.	69.2-69.8		北流型 Beiliu Type	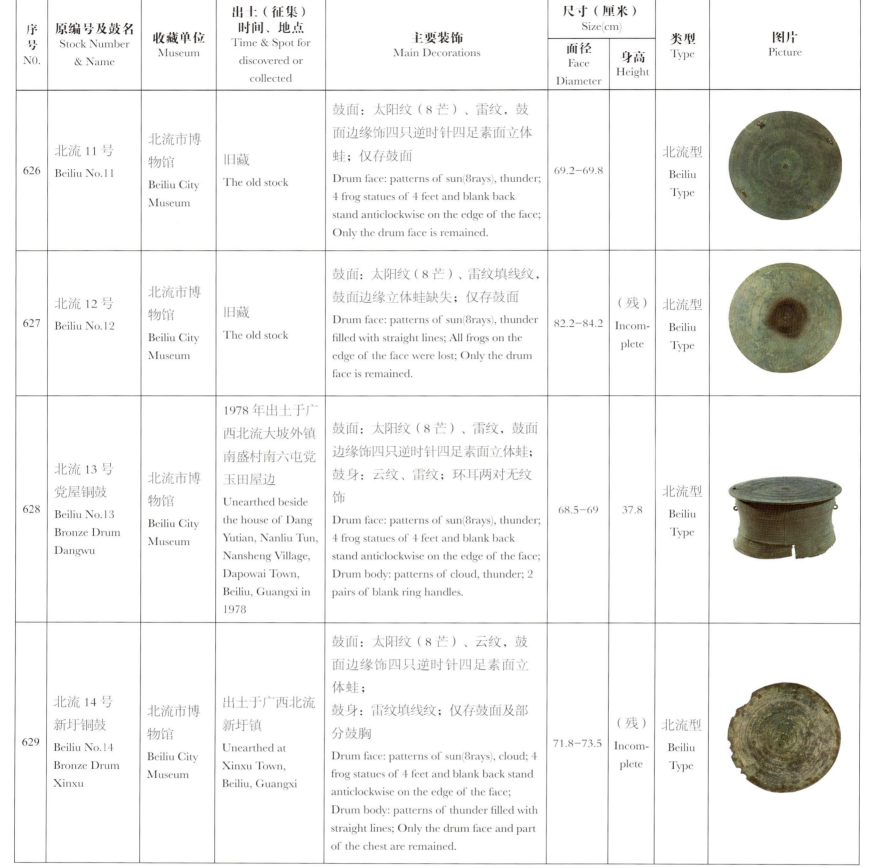
627	北流 12 号 Beiliu No.12	北流市博物馆 Beiliu City Museum	旧藏 The old stock	鼓面：太阳纹（8 芒）、雷纹填线纹，鼓面边缘立体蛙缺失；仅存鼓面 Drum face: patterns of sun(8rays), thunder filled with straight lines; All frogs on the edge of the face were lost; Only the drum face is remained.	82.2-84.2	（残） Incom- plete	北流型 Beiliu Type	
628	北流 13 号 党屋铜鼓 Beiliu No.13 Bronze Drum Dangwu	北流市博物馆 Beiliu City Museum	1978 年出土于广西北流大坡外镇南盛村南六屯党玉田屋边 Unearthed beside the house of Dang Yutian, Nanliu Tun, Nansheng Village, Dapowai Town, Beiliu, Guangxi in 1978	鼓面：太阳纹（8 芒）、雷纹，鼓面边缘饰四只逆时针四足素面立体蛙；鼓身：云纹、雷纹；环耳两对无纹饰 Drum face: patterns of sun(8rays), thunder; 4 frog statues of 4 feet and blank back stand anticlockwise on the edge of the face; Drum body: patterns of cloud, thunder; 2 pairs of blank ring handles.	68.5-69	37.8	北流型 Beiliu Type	
629	北流 14 号 新圩铜鼓 Beiliu No.14 Bronze Drum Xinxu	北流市博物馆 Beiliu City Museum	出土于广西北流新圩镇 Unearthed at Xinxu Town, Beiliu, Guangxi	鼓面：太阳纹（8 芒）、云纹，鼓面边缘饰四只逆时针四足素面立体蛙；鼓身：雷纹填线纹；仅存鼓面及部分鼓胸 Drum face: patterns of sun(8rays), cloud; 4 frog statues of 4 feet and blank back stand anticlockwise on the edge of the face; Drum body: patterns of thunder filled with straight lines; Only the drum face and part of the chest are remained.	71.8-73.5	（残） Incom- plete	北流型 Beiliu Type	

续表

序号 NO.	原编号及鼓名 Stock Number & Name	收藏单位 Museum	出土（征集）时间、地点 Time & Spot for discovered or collected	主要装饰 Main Decorations	尺寸（厘米）Size(cm)		类型 Type	图片 Picture
					面径 Face Diameter	身高 Height		
630	北流 15 号 Beiliu No.15	北流市博物馆 Beiliu City Museum	1980 年 1 月征集于广西玉林市金属材料公司 Collected from Guangxi Yulin City Metal Material Company in January, 1980	鼓面：太阳纹（8 芒）、云纹、雷纹、鼓面边缘饰四只逆时针四足素面立体蛙、缺两只； 鼓身：网纹、雷纹；仅存一对环耳饰缠丝纹；仅存鼓面及部分鼓胸、鼓腰 Drum face: patterns of sun(8rays), cloud, thunder; 4 frog statues of 4 feet and blank back stand anticlockwise on the edge of the face, 2 of them were lost; Drum body: patterns of net and thunder; only one pair of silk-like-pattern decorated ring handles are remained; Only the drum face and part of chest and waist are remained.	79	32.5（残）Incomplete	北流型 Beiliu Type	
631	北流 16 号 玉塘铜鼓 Beiliu No.16 Bronze Drum Yutang	北流市博物馆 Beiliu City Museum	1980 年出土于广西北流白马镇玉塘村边山坡 Unearthed at the hillside beside Yutang Village, Baima Town, Beiliu, Guangxi in 1980	鼓面：太阳纹（8 芒）、云纹、雷纹，鼓面边缘饰四只顺时针四足素面立体蛙； 鼓身：雷纹、雷纹填线纹；环耳两对饰缠丝纹． Drum face: patterns of sun(8rays), cloud, thunder; 4 frog statues of 4 feet and blank back stand clockwise on the edge of the face; Drum body: patterns of thunder, thunder filled with straight lines; Silk-like patterns on 2 pairs of ring handles.	72-73	39（残）Incomplete	北流型 Beiliu Type	
632	北流 17 号 南禄村鼓 Beiliu No.17 Bronze Drum Nanlucun	北流市博物馆 Beiliu City Museum	1989 年 6 月 20 日出土于广西北流隆盛乡南禄村果园 Unearthed at an orchard of Nanlu Village, Longsheng, Beiliu, Guangxi on June 20th, 1989	鼓面：太阳纹（6 芒）、直线分格云纹，鼓面边缘饰四只逆时针四足素面立体蛙； 鼓身：雷纹填线纹；仅存鼓面及部分鼓胸 Drum face: patterns of sun(6rays), cloud divided into grids; 4 frog statues of 4 feet and blank back stand anticlockwise on the edge of the face; Drum body: patterns of thunder filled with straight lines; Only the drum face and part of the chest are remained.	55-56.8	（残）Incomplete	北流型 Beiliu Type	

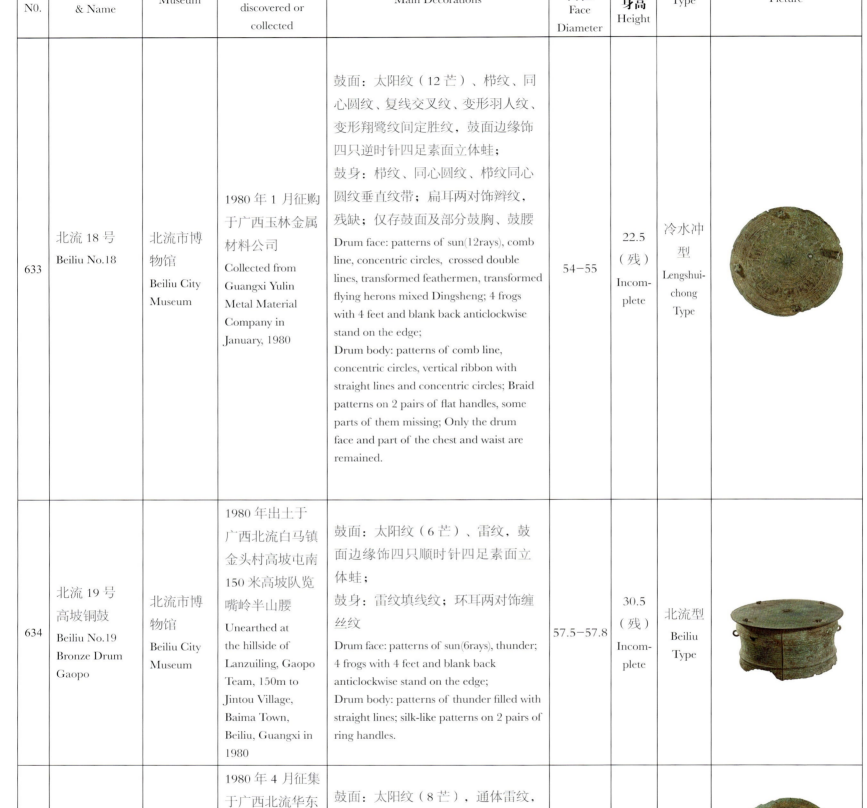

序号 N0.	原编号及鼓名 Stock Number & Name	收藏单位 Museum	出土（征集）时间、地点 Time & Spot for discovered or collected	主要装饰 Main Decorations	尺寸（厘米）Size(cm)		类型 Type	图片 Picture
					面径 Face Diameter	身高 Height		
633	北流 18 号 Beiliu No.18	北流市博物馆 Beiliu City Museum	1980 年 1 月征购于广西玉林金属材料公司 Collected from Guangxi Yulin Metal Material Company in January, 1980	鼓面：太阳纹（12 芒）、栉纹、同心圆纹、复线交叉纹、变形羽人纹、变形翔鹭纹间定胜纹，鼓面边缘饰四只逆时针四足素面立体蛙；鼓身：栉纹、同心圆纹、栉纹同心圆纹垂直纹带；扁耳两对饰辫纹，残缺；仅存鼓面及部分鼓胸、鼓腰 Drum face: patterns of sun(12rays), comb line, concentric circles, crossed double lines, transformed feathermen, transformed flying herons mixed Dingsheng; 4 frogs with 4 feet and blank back anticlockwise stand on the edge; Drum body: patterns of comb line, concentric circles, vertical ribbon with straight lines and concentric circles; Braid patterns on 2 pairs of flat handles, some parts of them missing; Only the drum face and part of the chest and waist are remained.	54-55	22.5（残）Incomplete	冷水冲型 Lengshui-chong Type	
634	北流 19 号 高坡铜鼓 Beiliu No.19 Bronze Drum Gaopo	北流市博物馆 Beiliu City Museum	1980 年出土于广西北流白马镇金头村高坡屯南150 米高坡队览嘴岭半山腰 Unearthed at the hillside of Lanzuiling, Gaopo Team, 150m to Jintou Village, Baima Town, Beiliu, Guangxi in 1980	鼓面：太阳纹（6 芒）、雷纹，鼓面边缘饰四只顺时针四足素面立体蛙；鼓身：雷纹填线纹；环耳两对饰缠丝纹 Drum face: patterns of sun(6rays), thunder; 4 frogs with 4 feet and blank back anticlockwise stand on the edge; Drum body: patterns of thunder filled with straight lines; silk-like patterns on 2 pairs of ring handles.	57.5-57.8	30.5（残）Incomplete	北流型 Beiliu Type	
635	北流 20 号 华东鼓 Beiliu No.20 Bronze Drum Huadong	北流市博物馆 Beiliu City Museum	1980 年 4 月征集于广西北流华东乡供销社 Collected from Guangxi Beiliu Huadong Supply and Marketing Cooperative in April, 1980	鼓面：太阳纹（8 芒），通体雷纹，鼓面边缘有四只立蛙痕迹；仅存一只环耳 Drum face: patterns of sun(8rays), all are thunders; Marks of 4 frog statues on the edge of the face; Only one ring handle is remained.	76-76.5	32（残）Incomplete	北流型 Beiliu Type	

续表

序号 N0.	原编号及鼓名 Stock Number & Name	收藏单位 Museum	出土（征集） 时间、地点 Time & Spot for discovered or collected	主要装饰 Main Decorations	尺寸（厘米） Size(cm)		类型 Type	图片 Picture
					面径 Face Diameter	身高 Height		
636	北流 21 号 垌尾铜鼓 Beiliu No.21 Bronze Drum Dongwei	北流市博 物馆 Beiliu City Museum	1982 年 1 月 7 日 出土于广西北流 白马镇黄金村垌 尾屯 Unearthed at Dongwei Tun, Huangjin Village, Baima Town, Beiliu, Guangxi on January 7th, 1982	鼓面：太阳纹（8 芒）、雷纹，鼓 面边缘饰四只两两相对四足素面立 体蛙； 鼓身：雷纹填线纹；环耳两对饰缠 丝纹、耳根开三义 Drum face: patterns of sun(8rays), thunder; 4 frogs with 4 feet and blank back stand on the edge, face to each other; Drum body: patterns of thunder filled with straight lines; Silk-like patterns on 2 pairs of ring handles, 3 rays on the roots of all handles.	103.5~105	58	北流型 Beiliu Type	
637	北流 22 号 寨顶铜鼓 Beiliu No.22 Bronze Drum Zhaiding	北流市博 物馆 Beiliu City Museum	1983 年 1 月 20 日出土于广西北 流平政镇六沙 村寨顶屯西南约 100 米处 Unearthed at the southwest of 100m to Zhaiding Tun, Liusha Village, Pingzheng Town, Beiliu, Guangxi on January 20th, 1983	鼓面：太阳纹（8 芒）、雷纹、云纹， 鼓面边缘饰四只逆时针四足素面立 体蛙； 鼓身：雷纹、云纹；环耳两对饰缠 丝纹 Drum face: patterns of sun(8rays), thunder, cloud; 4 frogs with 4 feet and blank back stand anticlockwise on the edge; Drum body: patterns of thunder, cloud; Silk-like patterns on 2 pairs of ring handles.	89.5~90.5	51.3	北流型 Beiliu Type	
638	北流 23 号 六月化岭铜鼓 Beiliu No.23 Bronze Drum Liuyuehua Ling	北流市博 物馆 Beiliu City Museum	1983 年 5 月中旬 出土于广西北流 石窝镇煌炉村旺 祖屯西北 1.5 公 里六月化岭 Unearthed at Liuyuehua Ling, the northwest of 1.5km to Wangzu Tun, Huanglu Village, Shiwo Town, Beiliu, Guangxi in May, 1983	鼓面：太阳纹（8 芒）、雷纹、云纹， 鼓面边缘饰四只顺时针四足素面立 体蛙； 鼓身：云纹、雷纹；环耳两对饰缠 丝纹、辫纹 Drum face: patterns of sun(8rays), thunder, cloud; 4 frogs with 4 feet and blank back stand clockwise on the edge; Drum body: patterns of thunder, cloud; Silk-like and braid patterns on 2 pairs of ring handles.	111.1~113	59.8	北流型 Beiliu Type	

序号 N0.	原编号及鼓名 Stock Number & Name	收藏单位 Museum	出土（征集） 时间、地点 Time & Spot for discovered or collected	主要装饰 Main Decorations	尺寸（厘米） Size(cm)		类型 Type	图片 Picture
					面径 Face Diameter	身高 Height		
639	北流 24 号 石径岭铜鼓 Beiliu No.24 Bronze Drum Shijing Ling	北流市博物馆 Beiliu City Museum	1984 年 5 月中旬出土于广西白马镇白马村石屯塘屯石径岭 Unearthed at Shijing Ling, Shituntang Tun, Baima Town, Guangxi in the middle of May, 1984	鼓面：太阳纹（6 芒）、雷纹，鼓面边缘饰四只逆时针四足素面立体蛙； 鼓身：雷纹；环耳两对无纹饰 Drum face: patterns of sun(6rays), thunder; 4 frogs with 4 feet and blank back stand anticlockwise on the edge; Drum body: patterns of thunder; 2 pairs of blank ring handles.	68.8-70	37.8	北流型 Beiliu Type	
640	北流 25 号 屋背山铜鼓 Beiliu No.25 Bronze Drum Wobeishan	北流市博物馆 Beiliu City Museum	1985 年 5 月 18 日出土于广西北流新丰镇大罗垌村屋背山 Unearthed at Wubei Hill, Daluodong Village, Xinfeng Town, Beiliu, Guangxi on May 18th, 1985	鼓面：太阳纹（8 芒）、雷纹，鼓面边缘饰四只逆时针四足素面立体蛙； 鼓身：雷纹填线纹；环耳两对饰缠丝纹 Drum face: patterns of sun(8rays), thunder; 4 frogs with 4 feet and blank back stand anticlockwise on the edge; Drum body: patterns of thunder filled with straight lines; Silk-like patterns on 2 pairs of ring handles.	70.5-71.2	30 （残） Incom-plete	北流型 Beiliu Type	
641	北流 26 号 西岸铜鼓 Beiliu No.26 Bronze Drum Xi'an	北流市博物馆 Beiliu City Museum	1985 年 9 月中旬出土于广西北流隆盛镇中和村西岸屯 Unearthed at Xi'an Tun, Zhonghe Village, Longsheng Town, Beiliu, Guangxi in middle September, 1985	鼓面：太阳纹（8 芒）、雷纹，鼓面边缘饰四只顺时针四足素面立体蛙； 鼓身：云纹、雷纹；环耳两对饰缠丝纹 Drum face: patterns of sun(8rays), thunder; 4 frogs with 4 feet and blank back stand clockwise on the edge; Drum body: patterns of cloud, thunder; Silk-like patterns on 2 pairs of ring handles.	91.2-93	51.3	北流型 Beiliu Type	
642	北流 27 号 六村鼓 Beiliu No.27 Bronze Drum Liucun	北流市博物馆 Beiliu City Museum	1989 年 5 月出土于广西北流隆盛镇南六村 Unearthed at Nanliu Village, Longsheng Town, Beiliu, Guangxi in May, 1989	鼓面：太阳纹（8 芒）、云纹，鼓面边缘饰四只顺时针四足素面立体蛙； 鼓身：雷纹填线纹；环耳两对无纹饰 Drum face: patterns of sun(8rays), cloud; 4 frogs with 4 feet and blank back stand clockwise on the edge; Drum body: patterns of thunder filled with straight lines; 2 pairs of blank ring handles.	70.4-71.1	38 （残） Incom-plete	北流型 Beiliu Type	

续表

序号 N0.	原编号及鼓名 Stock Number & Name	收藏单位 Museum	出土（征集） 时间、地点 Time & Spot for discovered or collected	主要装饰 Main Decorations	尺寸（厘米） Size(cm)		类型 Type	图片 Picture
					面径 Face Diameter	身高 Height		
643	北流 28 号 大伦村鼓 Beiliu No.28 Bronze Drum Daluncun	北流市博物馆 Beiliu City Museum	1991 年 6 月 28 日出土于广西 白马镇大伦村 大塘组 Unearthed at Datang Team, Dalun Village, Baima Town, Beiliu, Guangxi on June 28th, 1991	鼓面：太阳纹（8 芒）、云纹、雷纹，鼓面边缘饰四只逆时针四足素面立体蛙； 鼓身：云纹、雷纹；环耳两对无纹饰 Drum face: patterns of sun(8rays), cloud, thunder; 4 frogs with 4 feet and blank back stand anticlockwise on the edge; Drum body: patterns of cloud, thunder; 2 pairs of blank ring handles.	76.5-77	45	北流型 Beiliu Type	
644	北流 29 号 水垌铜鼓 Beiliu No.29 Bronze Drum Shuidong	北流市博物馆 Beiliu City Museum	1995 年 4 月 11 日出土于广西北 流新丰镇水垌村 南约 1.5 公里横 岭山半山腰 Unearthed at the hillside of Hengling Hill, the south of 1.5km to Shuidong Village, Xinfeng Town, Beiliu, Guangxi on April 11th, 1995	鼓面：太阳纹（8 芒）、雷纹，鼓面边缘饰六只逆时针四足素面立体蛙； 鼓身：雷纹、云纹；环耳两对饰缠丝纹 Drum face: patterns of sun(8rays), thunder; 6 frogs with 4 feet and blank back stand anticlockwise on the edge; Drum body: patterns of cloud, thunder; Silk-like patterns on 2 pairs of ring handles.	97.2-100.3	50.2	北流型 Beiliu Type	
645	北流 30 号 大坡外铜鼓 Beiliu No.30 Bronze Drum Dapowai	北流市博物馆 Beiliu City Museum	1995 年 5 月 17 日出土于广西 北流大坡外镇 大坡外村木鸡 岭半山坳 Unearthed at the hillside of Muji Ling, Dapowai Village, Dapowai Town, Beiliu, Guangxi on May 17th, 1995	鼓面：太阳纹（8 芒）、雷纹、云纹，鼓面边缘饰四只逆时针四足素面立体蛙； 鼓身：雷纹、云纹，一侧鼓耳下鼓足位置饰一立体兽；环耳两对饰缠丝纹 Drum face: patterns of sun(8rays), thunder, cloud; 4 frogs with 4 feet and blank back stand anticlockwise on the edge; Drum body: patterns of cloud, thunder; A beast stand under one of the handles on the foot; Silk-like patterns on 2 pairs of ring handles.	103.2-104.2	56.7	北流型 Beiliu Type	

序号 N0.	原编号及鼓名 Stock Number & Name	收藏单位 Museum	出土（征集） 时间、地点 Time & Spot for discovered or collected	主要装饰 Main Decorations	尺寸（厘米） Size(cm)		类型 Type	图片 Picture
					面径 Face Diameter	身高 Height		
646	北流 33 号 南蛇岭铜鼓 Beiliu No.33 Bronze Drum Nanshe Ling	北流市博物馆 Beiliu City Museum	1997 年 3 月 5 日 出土于广西北流 六麻镇大旺村南 蛇岭半山腰 Unearthed at the hillside of Nanshe Ling, Dawang Village, Liuma Town, Beiliu, Guangxi on March 5th, 1997	鼓面：太阳纹（8 芒）、云纹、雷纹， 鼓面边缘饰四只逆时针四足素面立 体蛙； 鼓身：雷纹、云纹；环耳两对无纹 饰 Drum face: patterns of sun(8rays), thunder, cloud; 4 frogs with 4 feet and blank back stand anticlockwise on the edge; Drum body: patterns of cloud, thunder; 2 pairs of blank ring handles.	77–77.6	46	北流型 Beiliu Type	
647	北流 34 号 凌云冲铜鼓 Beiliu No.34 Bronze Drum Lingyunchong	北流市博 物馆 Beiliu City Museum	1998 年 8 月 5 日 出土于广西北流 平政镇凌云冲 Unearthed at Lingyunchong, Pingzheng Town, Beiliu, Guangxi on August 5th, 1998	鼓面：太阳纹（8 芒）、雷纹，鼓 面边缘饰四只顺时针四足素面立 体蛙； 鼓身：云纹、雷纹；环耳两对饰缠 丝纹 Drum face: patterns of sun(8rays), thunder; 4 frogs with 4 feet and blank back stand clockwise on the edge; Drum body: patterns of cloud, thunder; Silk-like patterns on 2 pairs of ring handles.	69–69.5	37.6	北流型 Beiliu Type	
648	北流 35 号 平山村铜鼓 Beiliu No.35 Bronze Drum Pingshan Cun	北流市博 物馆 Beiliu City Museum	2008 年 4 月 9 日 出土于广西北流 市西垠镇平山村 19 组 Unearthed at Pingshan Village Team 19, Xilang Town, Beiliu, Guangxi on April 9th, 2008	鼓面：太阳纹（8 芒）、雷纹填线纹、 变体云纹、方孔钱纹、角形填线纹， 鼓面边缘饰六只顺时针四足素面立 体蛙； 鼓身：席纹、雷纹填线纹、半圆填 线纹、角形填线纹、云纹、四瓣花纹； 扁耳两对无纹饰，缺一对 Drum face: patterns of sun(8rays), thunder mixed straight line, transformed cloud, coin with square hole inside, triangle filled with straight lines, 6 frogs with 4 feet and blank back clockwise stand on the edge; Drum body: patterns of woven mat, thunder filled with straight lines, half circle filled with straight lines, triangle filled with straight lines, cloud, quatrefoil; 2 pairs of blank flat handles, one pair of them lost.	74.2–74.8	33.5 （残） Incom- plete	灵山型 Lingshan Type	

续表

序号 N0.	原编号及鼓名 Stock Number & Name	收藏单位 Museum	出土（征集）时间、地点 Time & Spot for discovered or collected	主要装饰 Main Decorations	尺寸（厘米） Size(cm)		类型 Type	图片 Picture
					面径 Face Diameter	身高 Height		
649	六楼铜鼓 Bronze Drum Liulou	北流市博物馆 Beiliu City Museum	1995 年 10 月 4 日出土于广西北流六麻镇六楼村西北约 80 米大坟岭 Unearthed at Dafenling, northwest of 80m to Liulou Village, Liuma Town, Beiliu, Guangxi on October 4th, 1995	鼓面：太阳纹（8 芒）、雷纹，鼓面边缘饰四只逆时针四足素面立体蛙； 鼓身：云纹、雷纹；环耳两对饰缠丝纹 Drum face: patterns of sun(8rays), thunder; 4 frogs with 4 feet and blank back stand anticlockwise on the edge; Drum body: patterns of cloud, thunder; Silk-like patterns on 2 pairs of ring handles.	91~92.3	55	北流型 Beiliu Type	
650	上劈岭铜鼓 Bronze Drum Shangpiling	北流市博物馆 Beiliu City Museum	1996 年 7 月 15 日出土于广西北流六麻镇六楼村西约 100 米的上劈岭 Unearthed at Shangpiling, west of 100m to Liulou Village, Liuma Town, Beiliu, Guangxi on July 15th, 1996	鼓面：太阳纹（8 芒）、雷纹，鼓面边缘饰四只顺时针四足素面立体蛙； 鼓身：云雷纹交替；环耳两对饰缠丝纹 Drum face: patterns of sun(8rays), thunder; 4 frogs with 4 feet and blank back stand clockwise on the edge; Drum body: patterns of cloud, thunder; Silk-like patterns on 2 pairs of ring handles.	67.8~68.6	39	北流型 Beiliu Type	
651	容 01 号 大岭岗铜鼓 Rong No.01 Bronze Drum Dalinggang	容县博物馆 Rongxian County Museum	1909 年出土于广西容县六王镇六王村大岭岗 Unearthed at Daling Gang, Liuwang Village, Liuwang Town, Rong County, Guangxi in 1909	鼓面：太阳纹（14 芒）、同心圆纹、复线交叉纹、羽纹、变形羽人纹、变形翔鹭纹，鼓面边缘四蛙已缺失； 鼓身：羽纹、切线同心圆纹、变形羽人纹、圆心三角垂叶纹；扁耳两对饰辫纹 Drum face: patterns of sun(14rays), concentric circle, crossed double lines, feather, transformed feathermen, trnasformed flying heron; 4 frogs on the edge; were lost; Drum body: patterns of feather, tangent concentric circles, transformed feathermen, leaf-shape triangle with concentric circles in the middle; Braids pattern on 2 pairs of flat handles.	78.2~79.5	51.5	冷水冲型 Lengshui-chong Type	

479

序号 N0.	原编号及鼓名 Stock Number & Name	收藏单位 Museum	出土（征集）时间、地点 Time & Spot for discovered or collected	主要装饰 Main Decorations	尺寸（厘米） Size(cm)		类型 Type	图片 Picture
					面径 Face Diameter	身高 Height		
652	容02号 双头岭铜鼓 Rong No.02 Bronze Drum Shuangtouling	容县博物馆 Rongxian County Museum	1975年出土于广西容县灵山镇华琅陈村双头岭 Unearthed at Shuangtou Ling, Hualang, Chen Village, Lingshan Town, Rongxian County, Guangxi in 1975	鼓面：太阳纹（11芒）、如意云纹、雷纹、变形羽人纹、席纹，鼓面边缘饰四只逆时针四足素面立体蛙； 鼓身：如意云纹、雷纹、席纹；扁耳两对无纹饰 Drum face: patterns of sun(11rays), Ruyi-cloud, thunder, transformed feathermen, woven mat; 4 frogs with 4 feet and blank back stand anticlockwise on the edge; Drum body: patterns of Ruyi-cloud, thunder, woven mat; 2 pairs of blank flat handles.	77.4–78	30.2 （残） Incomplete	灵山型 Lingshan Type	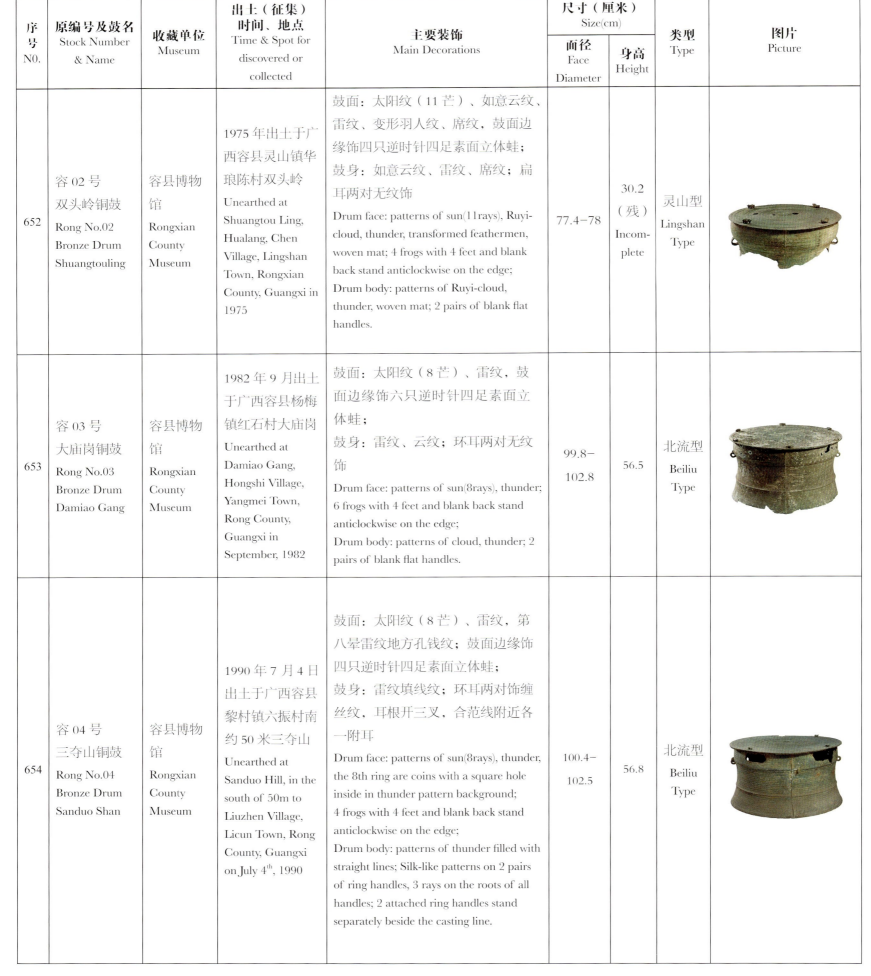
653	容03号 大庙岗铜鼓 Rong No.03 Bronze Drum Damiao Gang	容县博物馆 Rongxian County Museum	1982年9月出土于广西容县杨梅镇红石村大庙岗 Unearthed at Damiao Gang, Hongshi Village, Yangmei Town, Rong County, Guangxi in September, 1982	鼓面：太阳纹（8芒）、雷纹，鼓面边缘饰六只逆时针四足素面立体蛙； 鼓身：雷纹、云纹；环耳两对无纹饰 Drum face: patterns of sun(8rays), thunder; 6 frogs with 4 feet and blank back stand anticlockwise on the edge; Drum body: patterns of cloud, thunder; 2 pairs of blank flat handles.	99.8–102.8	56.5	北流型 Beiliu Type	
654	容04号 三夺山铜鼓 Rong No.04 Bronze Drum Sanduo Shan	容县博物馆 Rongxian County Museum	1990年7月4日出土于广西容县黎村镇六振村南约50米三夺山 Unearthed at Sanduo Hill, in the south of 50m to Liuzhen Village, Licun Town, Rong County, Guangxi on July 4th, 1990	鼓面：太阳纹（8芒）、雷纹，第八晕雷纹地方孔钱纹；鼓面边缘饰四只逆时针四足素面立体蛙； 鼓身：雷纹填线纹；环耳两对饰缠丝纹，耳根开三叉，合范线附近各一附耳 Drum face: patterns of sun(8rays), thunder, the 8th ring are coins with a square hole inside in thunder pattern background; 4 frogs with 4 feet and blank back stand anticlockwise on the edge; Drum body: patterns of thunder filled with straight lines; Silk-like patterns on 2 pairs of ring handles, 3 rays on the roots of all handles; 2 attached ring handles stand separately beside the casting line.	100.4–102.5	56.8	北流型 Beiliu Type	

续表

序号 N0.	原编号及鼓名 Stock Number & Name	收藏单位 Museum	出土（征集）时间、地点 Time & Spot for discovered or collected	主要装饰 Main Decorations	尺寸（厘米） Size(cm)		类型 Type	图片 Picture
					面径 Face Diameter	身高 Height		
655	独山岭鼓 Bronze Drum Dushan Ling	容县博物馆 Rongxian County Museum	2010 年 4 月出土于广西容县灵山镇六良村独山岭 Unearthed at Dushan Ling, Liuliang Village, Lingshan Town, Rongxian County, Guangxi in April, 2010	鼓面：太阳纹（8 芒）、雷纹填线纹；鼓面边缘饰四只两两相对四足素面立体蛙； 鼓身：云纹、雷纹填线纹；环耳两对饰缠丝纹 Drum face: patterns of sun(8 rays), thunder filled with straight lines; 4 frogs with 4 feet and blank back stand anticlockwise on the edge, face to each other; Drum body: patterns of cloud, thunder filled with straight lines; Silk-like patterns on 2 pairs of ring handles.	82.2−84	46.2	北流型 Beiliu Type	
656	清游旗纹铜鼓 Qing Dynasty Bronze Drum with flying flag patterns	容县博物馆 Rongxian County Museum	2003 年征购于广西容县黎村镇 Collected at Licun Town, Rongxian County, Guangxi in 2003	鼓面：太阳纹（12 芒）、酉字纹、S 形云纹、乳钉纹、栉纹、游旗纹、如意云纹、卦纹； 鼓身：乳钉纹、如意云纹、栉纹、兽面云纹、回形雷纹、复线三角纹；扁耳两对饰辫纹 Drum face: patterns of sun(12 rays), 酉 -character, S-shape cloud, nipple protrusion, comb line, flying flag, Ruyi-shape cloud, divinatory symbol; Drum body: patterns of nipple protrusion, Ruyi-shape cloud, comb line, beast-face-shape cloud, 回 -shape thunder, double-line triangle; Braid patterns on 2 pairs of flat handles.	50.7	29	麻江型 Majiang Type	
657	00001 号 谷仰鼓 No.00001 Bronze Drum Guyang	陆川县文管所 Luchuan County Cultural Relics Administration	1974 年 8 月出土于广西陆川县米场镇米场村谷仰屯东北约 500 米十九圹山脚 Unearthed at the hill foot of Shijiu Kuang, northeast of 500m to Guyang Tun, Michang Village, Michang Town, Luchuan County, Guangxi in August, 1974	鼓面：太阳纹（8 芒）、四瓣花纹、方孔钱纹、云纹、雷纹填线纹、半同心圆填线纹，鼓面边缘饰六组顺时针三足素面立体蛙，其中两组为累蹲蛙； 鼓身：方孔钱纹、四瓣花纹、席纹、雷纹填线纹、网纹、雷纹、水波纹；扁耳两对饰辫纹 Drum face: patterns of sun(8 rays), quatrefoil, square-hole coin, cloud, thunder filled with straight lines, half concentric circle filled with straight lines; 6 frogs with 3 feet and blank back stand clockwise on the edge, 2 of them are overlap; Drum body: patterns of square hole coin, quatrefoil, woven mat, thunder filled with straight lines, net, thunder, water wave; Braid patterns on 2 pairs of flat handles.	90.7−91.8	50.3	灵山型 Lingshan Type	

序号 NO.	原编号及鼓名 Stock Number & Name	收藏单位 Museum	出土（征集）时间、地点 Time & Spot for discovered or collected	主要装饰 Main Decorations	尺寸（厘米）Size(cm)		类型 Type	图片 Picture
					面径 Face Diameter	身高 Height		
658	00002号 李屋铜鼓 No.00002 Bronze Drum Liwu	陆川县文管所 Luchuan County Cultural Relics Administration	1976年出土于广西陆川县米场镇李屋村 Unearthed at Liwu Village, Michang Town, Luchuan County, Guangxi in 1976	鼓面：太阳纹（12芒）、雷纹、席纹、比轮钱纹、四瓣花填线纹，鼓面边缘饰六组顺时针三足素面立体蛙；鼓身：叶脉纹、四瓣花填线纹、比轮钱纹、雷纹、四瓣花纹、半同心圆填线纹、席纹；扁耳两对饰羽纹、乳钉纹 Drum face: patterns of sun(12 rays), thunder, woven mat, Bilun coin, quatrefoil filled with straight lines; 6 frogs with 3 feet and blank back stand clockwise on the edge; Drum body: patterns of leaf vein, quatrefoil filled with straight lines, Bilun coin, thunder, quatrefoil, half concentric circle, woven mat; Feather and nipple protrusion patterns on 2 pairs of flat handles.	118-121	60.5（残）Incomplete	灵山型 Lingshan Type	
659	00003号 蛤蟆田铜鼓 No.00003 Bronze Drum Hamatian	陆川县文管所 Luchuan County Cultural Relics Administration	1978年出土于广西陆川县沙坡大队蛤蟆田 Unearthed at Hama Tian, Shapo Team, Luchuan County, Guangxi in 1978	鼓面：太阳纹（8芒）、云纹、雷纹；鼓面边缘饰四只逆时针四足素面立体蛙；鼓身：云纹、雷纹填线纹；环耳两对无纹饰 Drum face: patterns of sun(8rays), cloud, thunder; 4 frogs with 4 feet and blank back stand anticlockwise on the edge; Drum body: patterns of cloud, thunder filled with straight lines; 2 pairs of blank ring handles.	68.5-69	38.8（残）Incomplete	北流型 Beiliu Type	
660	00004号 雅松铜鼓 No.00004 Bronze Drum Yasong	陆川县文管所 Luchuan County Cultural Relics Administration	1977年出土于广西陆川县大桥镇雅松村 Unearthed at Yasong Village, Daqiao Town, Luchuan County, Guangxi in 1977	鼓面：太阳纹（11芒）、半同心圆羽纹、雷纹填线纹；鼓面边缘饰四只顺时针四足素面立体蛙；鼓身：方孔钱纹、雷纹填线纹、云纹；环耳两对饰缠丝纹 Drum face: patterns of sun(11rays), half concentric circle and feather, thunder filled with straight lines; 4 frogs with 4 feet and blank back stand anticlockwise on the edge; Drum body: patterns of square hole coin, thunder filled with straight lines, cloud; Silk-like patterns on 2 pairs of ring handles.	71-72.5	45（残）Incomplete	北流型 Beiliu Type	

序号 NO.	原编号及鼓名 Stock Number & Name	收藏单位 Museum	出土（征集）时间、地点 Time & Spot for discovered or collected	主要装饰 Main Decorations	尺寸（厘米）Size(cm)		类型 Type	图片 Picture
					面径 Face Diameter	身高 Height		
661	00005 号 牛角冲铜鼓 No.00005 Bronze Drum Niujiao Chong	陆川县文管所 Luchuan County Cultural Relics Administration	1991 年 10 月 28 日出土于广西陆川县沙坡镇北安村风塘屯牛角冲 Unearthed at Niujiao Chong, Fengtang Tun, Bei'an Village, Shapo Town, Luchuan County, Guangxi on October 28th, 1991	鼓面：太阳纹（12 芒）、羽纹、四出钱纹、比轮钱纹、席纹、四瓣花纹，鼓面边缘饰六组顺时针三足羽纹立体蛙，其中三组为累蹲蛙； 鼓身：比轮钱纹、羽纹、雷纹填线纹、席纹、复线角形纹、四出钱纹；扁耳两对饰羽纹、乳钉纹，鼓足合范线附近各一只附耳 Drum face: patterns of sun(12 rays), feather, coin with quadrangle inside, Bilun coin, woven mat, quatrefoil; 6 frogs with 3 feet and feather on back clockwise stand on the edge, 3 of them are overlap; Drum body: patterns of Bilun coin, feather, thunder filled with straight lines, woven mat, double line triangle, coin with quadrangle inside; Feather and nipple protrusion patterns on 2 pairs of flat handles, a pair of attached handles stand separately beside the casting line.	100.5～102	56	灵山型 Lingshan Type	
662	00006 号 石垌铜鼓 No.00006 Bronze Drum Shidong	陆川县文管所 Luchuan County Cultural Relics Administration	1973 年出土于广西陆川县良田镇石垌村南 500 米处 Unearthed in the south of 500m to Shidong Village, Liangtian Town, Luchuan County, Guangxi in 1973	鼓面：太阳纹（8 芒）、云纹；鼓面边缘饰四只顺时针四足素面立体蛙； 鼓身：云纹、雷纹填线纹；环耳两对无纹饰 Drum face: patterns of sun(8rays), cloud; 4 frogs with 4 feet and blank back stand clockwise on the edge; Drum body: patterns of cloud, thunder filled with straight lines; 2 pairs of blank ring handles.	77.5～78.5	43.5 （残） Incomplete	北流型 Beiliu Type	
663	00007 号 横山村铜鼓 No.00007 Bronze Drum Hengshan Cun	陆川县文管所 Luchuan County Cultural Relics Administration	1979 年 11 月出土于广西陆川县沙坡横山村 Unearthed at Hengshan Village, Shapo, Luchuan County, Guangxi in November, 1979	鼓面：太阳纹（8 芒）、雷纹填线纹；鼓面边缘饰四只逆时针四足素面立体蛙； 鼓身：云纹填线纹；环耳两对饰缠丝纹 Drum face: patterns of sun(8rays), thunder filled with straight lines; 4 frogs with 4 feet and blank back stand anticlockwise on the edge; Drum body: patterns of cloud filled with straight lines; Silk-like patterns on 2 pairs of ring handles.	54～56	25.9 （残） Incomplete	北流型 Beiliu Type	

序号 N0.	原编号及鼓名 Stock Number & Name	收藏单位 Museum	出土（征集）时间、地点 Time & Spot for discovered or collected	主要装饰 Main Decorations	尺寸（厘米）Size(cm)		类型 Type	图片 Picture
					面径 Face Diameter	身高 Height		
664	00008 吕屋鼓 No.00008 Bronze Drum Lvwu	陆川县文管所 Luchuan County Cultural Relics Administration	1983 年出土于广西陆川县米场镇桥鲁村吕屋屯西100 米山坡 Unearthed at the hillside in the west of 100m to Lvwu Tun, Qiaolu Village, Michang Town, Luchuan County, Guangxi in 1983	鼓面：太阳纹（8 芒）、菱形填线填点纹、雷纹、雷纹填线纹、云纹；鼓面边缘饰四只逆时针四足素面立体蛙；鼓身：雷纹填线纹、半圆填线纹、复线角形同心圆纹、云纹；环耳两对饰缠丝纹 Drum face: patterns of sun(8rays), diamond filled with straight lines and dots, thunder, thunder filled with straight lines, cloud; 4 frogs with 4 feet and blank back stand anticlockwise on the edge; Drum body: patterns of thunder filled with straight lines, half circle filled with straight lines, double line triangle with concentric circle inside, cloud; Silk-like patterns on 2 pairs of ring handles.	71−72.8	41（残）Incomplete	北流型 Beiliu Type	
665	00009 号 旱塘鼓 No.00009 Bronze Drum Hantang	陆川县文管所 Luchuan County Cultural Relics Administration	1978 年出土于广西陆川县大桥镇旱塘 Unearthed at Hantang, Daqiao Town, Luchuan County, Guangxi in 1978	鼓面：太阳纹（8 芒）、雷纹；鼓面边缘饰四只立体蛙，已失；鼓身：雷纹填线纹；环耳两对饰缠丝纹，耳根开三叉 Drum face: patterns of sun(8rays), thunder; 4 frog statues stand on the edge of the face, all are lost; Drum body: patterns of thunder filled with straight lines; Silk-like patterns on 2 pairs of ring handles, 3 rays on the feet of all handles.	71.2−72	40	北流型 Beiliu Type	
666	00010 号 坡尾铜鼓 No.00010 Bronze Drum Powei	陆川县文管所 Luchuan County Cultural Relics Administration	1994 年 1 月 29日出土于广西陆川县乌石镇坡脚村坡尾屯电山坡 Unearthed at the hillside of Powei Tun, Pojiao Village, Wushi Town, Luchuan County, Guangxi on January 29th, 1994	鼓面：太阳纹（8 芒），通体雷纹；鼓面边缘饰四只顺时针四足素面立体蛙；环耳两对饰缠丝纹 Drum face: patterns of sun(8rays), 4 frog statues of 4 feet stand clockwise on the edge of the face; Drum body: all patterns on the body are thunders; Silk-like patterns on 2 pairs of ring handles.	74.2−75.6	42（残）Incomplete	北流型 Beiliu Type	
667	01021 号 沙坡鼓 No.01021 Bronze Drum Shapo	陆川县文管所 Luchuan County Cultural Relics Administration	90 年代出土于广西陆川县沙坡镇 Unearthed at Shapo Town, Luchuan County, Guangxi in 1990s'	鼓面：太阳纹（6 芒）、云纹；鼓面边缘饰四只顺时针四足素面立体蛙；鼓身：雷纹；环耳两对无纹饰 Drum face: patterns of sun(6rays), cloud; 4 frog statues of 4 feet and blank back stand clockwise on the edge of the face; Drum body: patterns of thunder; 2 pairs of blank ring handles.	75.4−78	41.7（残）Incomplete	北流型 Beiliu Type	

续表

序号 NO.	原编号及鼓名 Stock Number & Name	收藏单位 Museum	出土（征集） 时间、地点 Time & Spot for discovered or collected	主要装饰 Main Decorations	尺寸（厘米） Size(cm)		类型 Type	图片 Picture
					面径 Face Diameter	身高 Height		
668	01009 号 蕉豆岭铜鼓 No.01009 Bronze Drum Fandou Ling	陆川县文管所 Luchuan County Cultural Relics Administration	1998 年 12 月 24 日出土于广西陆川县乌石镇坡脚村蕉豆岭东约 80 米兴丰果场 Unearthed at Xingfeng Orchard, in the east of 80m to Fandou Ling, Pojiao Village,Wushi Town, Luchuan County, Guangxi on December 24th, 1998	鼓面：太阳纹（8 芒）、雷纹；鼓面边缘饰两只顺时针、两只两两相对四足素面立体蛙； 鼓身：雷纹、云纹；环耳两对饰缠丝纹 Drum face: patterns of sun(8rays), thunder; 4 frog statues of 4 feet and blank back, 2 of them stand clockwise, 2 of them face to each other; Drum body: patterns of thunder, cloud; Silk-like patterns on 2 pairs of ring handles.	64.4－66	35 （残） Incomplete	北流型 Beiliu Type	
669	013 号 塘排山铜鼓 No.013 Bronze Drum Tangpai Shan	博白县博物馆 Bobai County Museum	1973 年 12 月出土于广西博白县江宁镇江宁村绿屋屯塘排山 Unearthed at Tangpai Hill, Lvwu Tun, Jiangning Village,Jiangning Town, Bobai County, Guangxi in December, 1973	鼓面：太阳纹（8 芒）、雷纹、方孔钱纹；鼓面边缘饰四只立体蛙，已失； 鼓身：雷纹、云纹；环耳两对无纹饰 Drum face: patterns of sun(6rays),thunder; square hole coin; 4 frog statues on the edge of the face, all are lost; Drum body: patterns of thunder, cloud; 2 pairs of blank ring handles.	78.4－79.4	39.7 （残） Incomplete	北流型 Beiliu Type	
670	014 号 铜鼓埇铜鼓 No.014 Bronze Drum Tonggu Yong	博白县博物馆 Bobai County Museum	1973 年 12 月出土于广西博白县新田镇马田村铜鼓埇 Unearthed at Tonggu Yong, Matian Village,Xintian Town, Bobai County, Guangxi in December, 1973	鼓面：太阳纹（10 芒）、蝉纹、四瓣花纹、四出钱纹、鸟纹、席纹、兽面纹、虫形纹、连钱纹，鼓面边缘饰六组逆时针三足螺旋纹立蛙，其中三组为累蹲蛙； 鼓身：蝉纹、连钱纹、四出钱纹、鸟纹、四瓣花纹、兽面纹、席纹、虫形纹；扁耳两对饰辫纹 Drum face: patterns of sun(10 rays), cicada, quatrefoil, coin with quadrangle inside, bird, woven mat, beast face, insect, coins part of overlap; 6 frogs with 3 feet and spiracles on back stand anticlockwise on the edge, 3 of them are overlap; Drum body: patterns of cicada, coins part of overlap, coin with quadrangle inside, bird, quatrefoil, beast face, woven mat, insect; Braid patterns on 2 pairs of flat handles.	69.2－69.5	35 （残） Incomplete	灵山型 Lingshan Type	

序号 N0.	原编号及鼓名 Stock Number & Name	收藏单位 Museum	出土（征集）时间、地点 Time & Spot for discovered or collected	主要装饰 Main Decorations	尺寸（厘米） Size(cm)		类型 Type	图片 Picture
					面径 Face Diameter	身高 Height		
671	015 号 江南岭铜鼓 No.015 Bronze Drum Jiangnan Ling	博白县博物馆 Bobai County Museum	1982 年 1 月出土于广西博白县城厢镇新仲村（博白镇西南约 3.5 公里）江南岭脚 Unearthed at the foot of Jiangnan Ling, Xinzhong Village, Chengxiang Town, in southwest of 3.5km to Bobai Town, Bobai County, Guangxi in January, 1982	鼓面：太阳纹（8 芒）、雷纹；鼓面边缘饰六只顺时针四足素面立体蛙； 鼓身：云纹、雷纹；环耳两对无纹饰 Drum face: patterns of sun(8rays),thunder; 6 frog statues of 4 feet and blank back stand clockwise on the edge of the face; Drum body: patterns of thunder, cloud; 2 pairs of blank ring handles.	89.5－91.2	49.8 （残） Incomplete	北流型 Beiliu Type	
672	016 号 莫屋铜鼓 No.016 Bronze Drum Mowu	博白县博物馆 Bobai County Museum	1982 年 11 月出土于广西博白县宁潭镇大车塘村莫屋屯 Unearthed at Mowu Tun, Dachetang Village, Ningtan Town, Bobai County, Guangxi in November, 1982	鼓面：太阳纹（8 芒）、虫形纹、兽形纹、十字钱纹、四瓣花纹、蝉纹，鼓面边缘饰六组逆时针三足螺旋纹立蛙，其中两组为累蹲蛙； 鼓身：四瓣花纹、兽形纹、十字钱纹、虫形纹、雷纹填线纹、蝉纹；鼓胸内壁饰一对螺旋纹立体蛙；扁耳两对饰辫纹 Drum face: patterns of sun(8 rays), insect, beast-shape pattern, cross coin, quatrefoil, cicada; 6 frogs with 3 feet and spiracles on back stand anticlockwise on the edge, 2 of them are overlap; Drum body: patterns of quatrefoil, camel, cross, insect and horse, thunder filled with straight lines, cicada; a pair of frog statues with spiracles on back stand inside the chest; Braid patterns on 2 pairs of flat handles.	83.9－84.2	49.7	灵山型 Lingshan Type	

续表

序号 NO.	原编号及鼓名 Stock Number & Name	收藏单位 Museum	出土（征集）时间、地点 Time & Spot for discovered or collected	主要装饰 Main Decorations	尺寸（厘米）Size(cm) 面径 Face Diameter	尺寸（厘米）Size(cm) 身高 Height	类型 Type	图片 Picture
673	017 号 冲头塘铜鼓 No.017 Bronze Drum Chongtou Tang	博白县博物馆 Bobai County Museum	1982 年 12 月出土于广西博白县江宁镇木旺村白坟头岭冲头塘 Unearthed at Chongtou Tang, Baifentou Ling, Muwang Village, Jiangning Town, Bobai County, Guangxi in December, 1982	鼓面：太阳纹（8 芒）、椭圆填线纹、鸟形纹、云纹；鼓面边缘饰四只逆时针三足素面立体蛙；鼓身：云纹、椭圆填线纹；扁耳两对无纹饰 Drum face: patterns of sun(8rays), ellipse filled with straight lines, bird, cloud; 4 frog statues of 3 feet and blank back stand anticlockwise on the edge of the face; Drum body: patterns of cloud, ellipse filled with straight lines; 2 pairs of blank ring handles.	66.4-67.2	33.7 （残） Incomplete	灵山型 Lingshan Type	
674	018 号 贞平铜鼓 No.018 Bronze Drum Zhenping	博白县博物馆 Bobai County Museum	1982 年 12 月 3 日出土于广西博白县永安乡永安村贞平屯 Unearthed at Zhenping Tun, Yong'an Village, Yong'an, Bobai County, Guangxi on December 3rd, 1982	鼓面：太阳纹（8 芒）、虫形纹、四瓣花纹、席纹、鸟形纹；鼓面边缘饰六只立蛙，已失；仅存鼓面 Drum face: patterns of sun(8rays), insect, quatrefoil, woven mat, bird;6 frog statues on the edge of the face had lost; only the drum face is remained.	99.7-100.2	（残） Incomplete	灵山型 Lingshan Type	
675	019 号 四方田铜鼓 No.019 Bronze Drum Sifangtian	博白县博物馆 Bobai County Museum	1983 年 3 月 6 日出土于广西博白县那林镇金阵村四方田屯东南约 150 米处 Unearthed in the southeast of 150m to Sifangtian tun, Jinzhen Village, Nalin Town, Bobai County, Guangxi on March 6th, 1983	鼓面：太阳纹（8 芒）、雷纹；鼓面边缘饰四只逆时针四足素面立体蛙；仅存鼓面 Drum face: patterns of sun(8rays), thunder; 4 frog statues of 4 feet and blank back stand anticlockwise on the edge of the face; Only the drum face is remained.	67.4-67.8	（残） Incomplete	北流型 Beiliu Type	

序号 N0.	原编号及鼓名 Stock Number & Name	收藏单位 Museum	出土（征集）时间、地点 Time & Spot for discovered or collected	主要装饰 Main Decorations	尺寸（厘米） Size(cm)		类型 Type	图片 Picture
					面径 Face Diameter	身高 Height		
676	020 号 亚山铜鼓 No.020 Bronze Drum Yashan	博白县博物馆 Bobai County Museum	1986 年 3 月出土于广西博白县亚山镇西约 3 公里农场 Unearthed at the farm in west of 3km to Yashan Town, Bobai County, Guangxi in March, 1986	鼓面：太阳纹（10 芒）、四出钱纹、四瓣花纹、蝉纹填线纹、连钱纹、蝉纹、鸟形纹、席纹、兽形纹，鼓面边缘饰六组逆时针三足螺旋纹立体蛙，其中三组为累蹲蛙，并负田螺；鼓身：蝉纹、连钱纹、四出钱纹、兽面纹、四瓣花填线纹、席纹、雷纹填线纹、兽形纹、鸟形纹、蝉纹填线纹；一侧鼓耳下鼓足位置饰一对立体鸟；扁耳两对饰羽纹 Drum face: patterns of sun(10 rays), coin with quadrangle inside, quatrefoil, cicada filled with straight lines, coins part of overlap, cicada, bird, woven mat, beast; 6 frogs with 3 feet and spiracles on back stand anticlockwise on the edge, 3 of them are overlap and carrying a snail; Drum body: patterns of cicada, coins part of overlap, coin with quadrangle inside, beast face, quatrefoil filled with straight lines, woven mat, thunder filled with straight lines, beast, bird, cicada filled with straight lines; A pair of bird statues stand under one of the handles on the foot; feather patterns on 2 pairs of flat handles.	76.3~76.8	46	灵山型 Lingshan Type	
677	总 001047 龙川鼓 No.001047 Bronze Drum Longchuan	百色起义纪念馆 Baise Uprising Memorial Hall	1977 年出土于广西百色市龙川公社合乐大队 Unearthed at Hele Team, Longchuan Community, Baise City, Guangxi in 1977	鼓面：太阳纹（10 芒）、可辨锯齿纹、同心圆纹；鼓身：可辨锯齿纹、同心圆纹、斜线纹牛纹垂直纹带；扁耳两对饰辫纹 Drum face: patterns of sun(10rays), only saw-tooth and concentric circles can be recognized; Drum body: only saw-tooth, concentric circles and vertical ribbon of oblique line and ox; Braids on 2 pairs of flat handles.	40.8~41.3	29.7	石寨山型 Shizaishan Type	

续表

序号 NO.	原编号及鼓名 Stock Number & Name	收藏单位 Museum	出土（征集）时间、地点 Time & Spot for discovered or collected	主要装饰 Main Decorations	尺寸（厘米） Size(cm)		类型 Type	图片 Picture
					面径 Face Diameter	身高 Height		
678	总 001048 清游旗纹铜鼓 No.001048 Qing Dynasty Bronze Drum with flying flag patterns	百色起义纪念馆 Baise Uprising Memorial Hall	1980 年广西右江革命文物馆从西林县文物管理所借调 Allocated from Xilin County Cultural Relic Administration by Guangxi Youjiang Revolutionary Cultural Relic Hall in 1980	鼓面：太阳纹（12 芒）、S 形云纹、乳钉纹、游旗纹、栉纹、四出钱纹、兽形云纹； 鼓身：乳钉纹、如意云纹、回形雷纹、栉纹、S 形云纹、复线三角纹；扁耳两对饰辫纹 Drum face: patterns of sun(12rays), S-shape cloud, nipple protrusion, flying flag, comb line, coins with quadrangle inside, beast-shape cloud; Drum body:patterns of nipple protrusion, Ruyi-shape cloud, 回 -shape thunder, comb line, S-shape cloud, double line triangle; Braid patterns on 2 pairs of flat handles.	47.3~47.6	26	麻江型 Majiang Type	
679	总 001049 清耕田奔马图铜鼓 No.001049 Qing Dynasty Bronze Drum with plough and galloping horse pattern	百色起义纪念馆 Baise Uprising Memorial Hall	1976 年征集于广西西林县马蚌公社马桑大队田湾志村 Collected at Tianwanzhi Village, Masang Team, Masang Community, Xilin County, Guangxi in 1976	鼓面：太阳纹（12 芒）、乳钉纹、回形雷纹、云纹、水波纹、动物花卉纹； 鼓身：乳钉纹、耕田奔马动物纹、回形雷纹、绚纹、水波纹、复线三角纹；扁耳两对饰弦纹 Drum face: patterns of sun(12rays), nipple protrusion, 回 - shape thunder, cloud, water wave, animal and plant; Drum body: patterns of nipple protrusion, plough, galloping horse and animal, 回 - shape thunder, twisted rope, water wave, double line triangle; Strings on 2 pairs of flat handles.	47.3~47.6	27.2	麻江型 Majiang Type	
680	总 001050 清缠枝纹铜鼓 No.001050 Qing Dynasty Bronze Drum with twisted branches pattern	百色起义纪念馆 Baise Uprising Memorial Hall	1980 年广西右江革命文物馆从西林县文物管理所借调 Allocated from Xilin County Cultural Relic Administration by Guangxi Youjiang Revolutionary Cultural Relic Hall in 1980	鼓面：太阳纹（12 芒）、乳钉纹、缠枝纹、云纹、绚纹、三角填斜线纹； 鼓身：云纹、雷纹、回形雷纹、图案三角纹；扁耳两对饰弦纹 Drum face: patterns of sun(12rays), nipple protrusion, twisted branches, cloud, twisted rope, triangle filled with oblique lines; Drum body: patterns of cloud, thunder, 回 - shape thunder, triangle with motifs; Strings on 2 pairs of flat handles.	47	27	麻江型 Majiang Type	

序号 N0.	原编号及鼓名 Stock Number & Name	收藏单位 Museum	出土（征集）时间、地点 Time & Spot for discovered or collected	主要装饰 Main Decorations	尺寸（厘米）Size(cm)		类型 Type	图片 Picture
					面径 Face Diameter	身高 Height		
681	总 001051 清水波纹卐字纹铜鼓 No.001051 Qing Dynasty Bronze Drum with water wave and 卐 pattern	百色起义纪念馆 Baise Uprising Memorial Hall	1980 年广西右江革命文物馆从西林县文物管理所借调 Allocated from Xilin County Cultural Relic Administration by Guangxi Youjiang Revolutionary Cultural Relic Hall in 1980	鼓面：太阳纹（12 芒）、乳钉纹、卐字纹、缠枝纹；鼓身：弦纹；扁耳两对饰弦纹 Drum face: patterns of sun(12rays), nipple protrusion, 卐 -character, twisted branches; Drum body: patterns of strings; Strings on 2 pairs of flat handles.	48.5－48.7	27	麻江型 Majiang Type	
682	总 001052 清十二芒二道乳钉纹铜鼓 No.001052 Qing Dynasty Bronze Drum with 12 rays and 2 rings of nipple protrusion pattern	百色起义纪念馆 Baise Uprising Memorial Hall	1982 年广西右江革命文物馆从西林县文物管理所借调 Allocated from Xilin County Cultural Relic Administration by Guangxi Youjiang Revolutionary Cultural Relic Hall in 1982	鼓面：太阳纹（12 芒）、酉字纹、S 形云纹、乳钉纹、游旗纹、栉纹、兽面云纹；鼓身：乳钉纹、如意云纹、回形雷纹、栉纹；扁耳两对饰辫纹 Drum face: patterns of sun(12rays), 酉 -character, S-shape cloud, nipple protrusion, flying flag, comb line, beast-face cloud; Drum body: patterns of nipple protrusion, Ruyi-shape cloud, 回 -shape thunder, comb line; Braid patterns on 2 pairs of flat handles.	46.5	19（残）Incomplete	麻江型 Majiang Type	
683	总 001053 清四鸟兽纹铜鼓 No.001053 Qing Dynasty Bronze Drum with 4 birds and beasts pattern	百色起义纪念馆 Baise Uprising Memorial Hall	1980 年广西右江革命文物馆从西林县文物管理所借调 Allocated from Xilin County Cultural Relic Administration by Guangxi Youjiang Revolutionary Cultural Relic Hall in 1980	鼓面：太阳纹（12 芒）、酉字纹、乳钉纹、S 钩纹、游旗纹、羽纹、四鸟兽纹；鼓身：乳钉纹、回形雷纹、如意云纹、栉纹、复线三角；扁耳两对饰辫纹 Drum face: patterns of sun(12rays), 酉 -character, nipple protrusion, S-shape hook, flying flag, feather,4 birds and beasts; Drum body: patterns of nipple protrusion, 回 -shape thunder, Ruyi-shape cloud, comb line, double line triangle; Braid patterns on 2 pairs of flat handles.	47.2	28	麻江型 Majiang Type	

序号 NO.	原编号及鼓名 Stock Number & Name	收藏单位 Museum	出土（征集）时间、地点 Time & Spot for discovered or collected	主要装饰 Main Decorations	尺寸（厘米）Size(cm)		类型 Type	图片 Picture
					面径 Face Diameter	身高 Height		
684	总001054 清十二芒乳钉纹铜鼓 No.001054 Qing Dynasty Bronze Drum with 12 rays and nipple protrusion pattern	百色起义纪念馆 Baise Uprising Memorial Hall	1980年广西右江革命文物馆从西林县文物管理所借调 Allocated from Xilin County Cultural Relic Administration by Guangxi Youjiang Revolutionary Cultural Relic Hall in 1980	鼓面：太阳纹（12芒）、酉字纹、乳钉纹、S形云纹、游旗纹、栉纹、如意云纹、S钩纹； 鼓身：乳钉纹、回形雷纹、如意云纹、栉纹、复线三角；扁耳两对饰辫纹 Drum face: patterns of sun(12rays), 酉-character, nipple protrusion, S-shape cloud, flying flag, comb line, Ruyi-shape cloud, S-shape hook; Drum body: patterns of nipple protrusion, 回-shape thunder, Ruyi-shape cloud, comb line, double line triangle; Braid patterns on 2 pairs of flat handles.	47.2	28	麻江型 Majiang Type	
685	总001055 清变形羽人纹铜鼓 No.001055 Qing Dynasty Bronze Drum with transformed feathermen pattern	百色起义纪念馆 Baise Uprising Memorial Hall	1980年广西右江革命文物馆从西林县文物管理所借调 Allocated from Xilin County Cultural Relic Administration by Guangxi Youjiang Revolutionary Cultural Relic Hall in 1980	鼓面：太阳纹（12芒）、酉字纹、乳钉纹、羽纹、变形羽人纹、栉纹、S形云纹； 鼓身：乳钉纹、同心圆纹、回形雷纹、S形云纹、复线三角；扁耳两对饰叶脉纹、回形雷纹 Drum face: patterns of sun(12rays), 酉-character, nipple protrusion, feather, transformed feathermen, comb line, S-shape cloud; Drum body: patterns of nipple protrusion, concentric circle, 回-shape thunder, S-shape cloud, double line triangle; Leaf vein and 回-shape thunder patterns on 2 pairs of flat handles.	47–47.2	28	麻江型 Majiang Type	
686	总001056 乳钉三角网纹铜鼓 No.001056 Bronze Drum nipple protrusion and triangle net pattern	百色起义纪念馆 Baise Uprising Memorial Hall	1982年广西右江革命文物馆从西林县文物管理所借调 Allocated from Xilin County Cultural Relic Administration by Guangxi Youjiang Revolutionary Cultural Relic Hall in 1982	鼓面：太阳纹（12芒）、乳钉纹、复线三角纹、网格纹； 鼓身：弦纹；扁耳两对饰弦纹 Drum face: patterns of sun(12rays), nipple protrusion, double line triangle, net; Drum body: patterns of string; String patterns on 2 pairs of flat handles.	47.2–47.5	27.5	麻江型 Majiang Type	

序号 N0.	原编号及鼓名 Stock Number & Name	收藏单位 Museum	出土（征集） 时间、地点 Time & Spot for discovered or collected	主要装饰 Main Decorations	尺寸（厘米） Size(cm)		类型 Type	图片 Picture
					面径 Face Diameter	身高 Height		
687	总001057 清乳钉纹雷纹 铜鼓 No.001057 Qing Dynasty Bronze Drum with nipple protrusion and thunder patterns	百色起义 纪念馆 Baise Uprising Memorial Hall	1980年广西右江 革命文物馆从西 林县文物管理所 借调 Allocated from Xilin County Cultural Relic Administration by Guangxi Youjiang Revolutionary Cultural Relic Hall in 1980	鼓面：太阳纹（12芒）、乳钉纹、 雷纹、游旗纹、回形雷纹； 鼓身：乳钉纹、回形雷纹、水波纹、 雷纹填十字纹、复线三角；扁耳两 对饰弦纹 Drum face: patterns of sun(12rays), nipple protrusion, thunder, flying flag, 回-shape thunder; Drum body: patterns of nipple protrusion, 回-shape thunder, water wave, thunder filled with cross, double line triangle; String patterns on 2 pairs of flat handles.	45.5	25.7	麻江型 Majiang Type	
688	总001058 清符箓纹铜鼓 No.001058 Qing Dynasty Bronze Drum with Ofuda patterns	百色起义 纪念馆 Baise Uprising Memorial Hall	1982年广西右江 革命文物馆从西 林县文物管理所 借调 Allocated from Xilin County Cultural Relic Administration by Guangxi Youjiang Revolutionary Cultural Relic Hall in 1982	鼓面：太阳纹（12芒）、乳钉纹、 S钩纹、同心圆纹、符箓纹、羽纹、 回形雷纹、栉纹、绚纹、卦纹； 鼓身：品字形乳钉纹、弦纹、如意 云纹、回形雷纹、S形云纹、复线三角； 扁耳两对饰叶脉纹 Drum face: patterns of sun(12rays), nipple protrusion, S-shape hook, concentric circle, Ofuda, feather, 回-shape thunder, comb line, twisted rope, divinatory symbol; Drum body: patterns of nipple protrusion lay in 品-shape, string, Ruyi-shape cloud, 回-shape thunder, S-shape cloud, double line triangle; Leaf vein patterns on 2 pairs of flat handles.	49—49.5	26.5	麻江型 Majiang Type	
689	总001059 十二芒乳钉纹 回纹铜鼓 No.001059 Qing Dynasty Bronze Drum with 12rays, nipple protrusion, 回—shape patterns	百色起义 纪念馆 Baise Uprising Memorial Hall	广西西林县文物 管理所拨交 Allocated from Xilin County Cultural Relic Administration	鼓面：太阳纹（12芒）、乳钉纹、 团云纹、回形雷纹、绚纹、游旗纹； 鼓身：乳钉纹、回形雷纹、团云纹、 复线三角纹；扁耳两对饰弦纹 Drum face: patterns of sun(12rays), nipple protrusion, cloud cluster, 回-shape thunder, twisted rope, flying flag; Drum body: patterns of nipple protrusion, 回-shape thunder, cloud cluster, double line triangle; String patterns on 2 pairs of flat handles.	47.3	27	麻江型 Majiang Type	

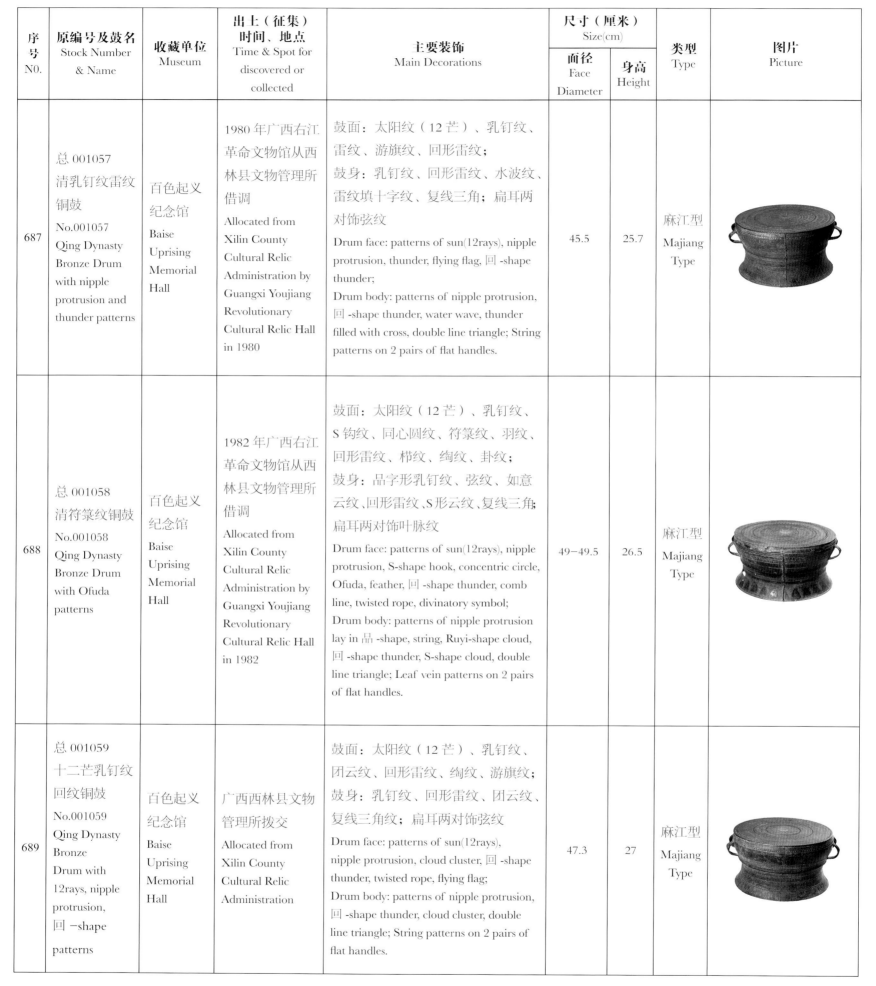

续表

序号 NO.	原编号及鼓名 Stock Number & Name	收藏单位 Museum	出土（征集）时间、地点 Time & Spot for discovered or collected	主要装饰 Main Decorations	尺寸（厘米） Size(cm)		类型 Type	图片 Picture
					面径 Face Diameter	身高 Height		
690	总 001060 清缠枝纹八宝纹铜鼓 No.001060 Qing Dynasty Bronze Drum with twisted branches and eight Buddhist treasures pattern	百色起义纪念馆 Baise Uprising Memorial Hall	1980 年广西右江革命文物馆从西林县文物管理所借调 Allocated from Xilin County Cultural Relic Administration by Guangxi Youjiang Revolutionary Cultural Relic Hall in 1980	鼓面：太阳纹（12 芒）、乳钉纹、花纹、缠枝纹； 鼓身：乳钉纹、水波纹、复线三角纹；扁耳两对饰弦纹 Drum face: patterns of sun(12rays), nipple protrusion, flower, twisted branches; Drum body: patterns of nipple protrusion, water wave, double line triangle; String patterns on 2 pairs of flat handles.	48	26	麻江型 Majiang Type	
691	总 001061 清游旗纹铜鼓 No.001061 Qing Dynasty Bronze Drum with flying flag patterns	百色起义纪念馆 Baise Uprising Memorial Hall	1980 年广西右江革命文物馆从西林县文物管理所借调 Allocated from Xilin County Cultural Relic Administration by Guangxi Youjiang Revolutionary Cultural Relic Hall in 1980	鼓面：太阳纹（12 芒）、西字纹、S 形云纹、乳钉纹、游旗纹、兽形云纹； 鼓身：乳钉纹、如意云纹、回形雷纹、栉纹、云纹、复线三角纹；扁耳两对饰辫纹、回形雷纹 Drum face: patterns of sun(12rays), 西 -character, S-shape cloud, nipple protrusion, flying flag, beast-shape cloud; Drum body: patterns of nipple protrusion, Ruyi-shape cloud, 回 -shape thunder, comb line, cloud, double line triangle; Braid and 回 -shape thunder patterns on 2 pairs of flat handles.	48	26	麻江型 Majiang Type	
692	总 001062 清乳钉人物图铜鼓 No.001062 Qing Dynasty Bronze Drum with nipple protrusion and person patterns	百色起义纪念馆 Baise Uprising Memorial Hall	1980 年广西右江革命文物馆从西林县文物管理所借调 Allocated from Xilin County Cultural Relic Administration by Guangxi Youjiang Revolutionary Cultural Relic Hall in 1980	鼓面：太阳纹（12 芒）、同心圆纹、回形雷纹、乳钉纹、符箓人物纹、云纹； 鼓身：乳钉纹、同心圆纹、如意云纹、回形雷纹、云纹、复线三角纹；扁耳两对饰辫纹 Drum face: patterns of sun(12rays), concentric circle, 回 -shape thunder, nipple protrusion, Ofuda and person, cloud; Drum body: patterns of nipple protrusion, concentric circle, Ruyi-shape cloud, 回 -shape thunder, cloud, double line triangle; Braid patterns on 2 pairs of flat handles.	47	27 （残） Incomplete	麻江型 Majiang Type	

序号 No.	原编号及鼓名 Stock Number & Name	收藏单位 Museum	出土（征集）时间、地点 Time & Spot for discovered or collected	主要装饰 Main Decorations	尺寸（厘米）Size(cm)		类型 Type	图片 Picture
					面径 Face Diameter	身高 Height		
693	总 001063 清游旗纹铜鼓 No.001063 Qing Dynasty Bronze Drum with flying flag patterns	百色起义纪念馆 Baise Uprising Memorial Hall	1980 年广西右江革命文物馆从西林县文物管理所借调 Allocated from Xilin County Cultural Relic Administration by Guangxi Youjiang Revolutionary Cultural Relic Hall in 1980	鼓面：太阳纹（12 芒）、酉字纹、S 形云纹、乳钉纹、游旗纹、栉纹、兽形云纹；鼓身：乳钉纹、回形雷纹、如意云纹、栉纹、云纹、复线三角纹；扁耳两对饰辫纹、回形雷纹 Drum face: patterns of sun(12rays), 酉 -character, S-shape cloud, nipple protrusion, flying flag, comb line, beast-shape cloud; Drum body: patterns of nipple protrusion, 回 -shape thunder, Ruyi-shape cloud, comb line, cloud, double line triangle; Braid and 回 -shape thunder patterns on 2 pairs of flat handles.	47.5	27	麻江型 Majiang Type	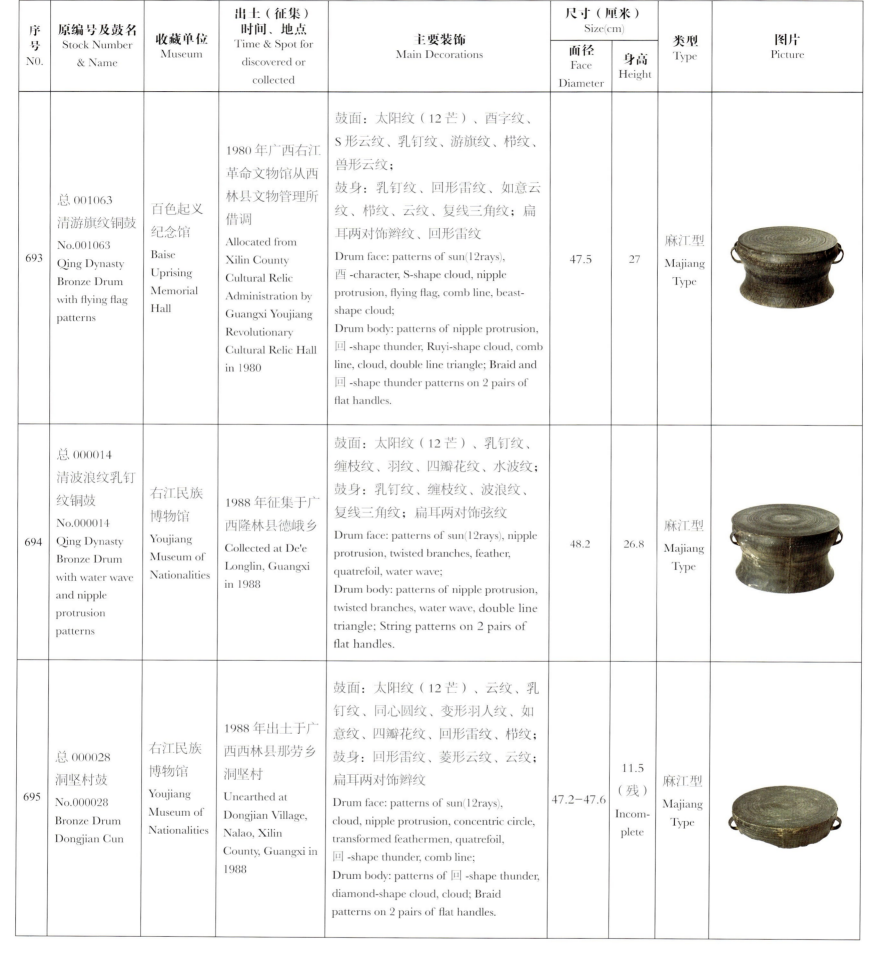
694	总 000014 清波浪纹乳钉纹铜鼓 No.000014 Qing Dynasty Bronze Drum with water wave and nipple protrusion patterns	右江民族博物馆 Youjiang Museum of Nationalities	1988 年征集于广西隆林县德峨乡 Collected at De'e Longlin, Guangxi in 1988	鼓面：太阳纹（12 芒）、乳钉纹、缠枝纹、羽纹、四瓣花纹、水波纹；鼓身：乳钉纹、缠枝纹、波浪纹、复线三角纹；扁耳两对饰弦纹 Drum face: patterns of sun(12rays), nipple protrusion, twisted branches, feather, quatrefoil, water wave; Drum body: patterns of nipple protrusion, twisted branches, water wave, double line triangle; String patterns on 2 pairs of flat handles.	48.2	26.8	麻江型 Majiang Type	
695	总 000028 洞坚村鼓 No.000028 Bronze Drum Dongjian Cun	右江民族博物馆 Youjiang Museum of Nationalities	1988 年出土于广西西林县那劳乡洞坚村 Unearthed at Dongjian Village, Nalao, Xilin County, Guangxi in 1988	鼓面：太阳纹（12 芒）、云纹、乳钉纹、同心圆纹、变形羽人纹、如意纹、四瓣花纹、回形雷纹、栉纹；鼓身：回形雷纹、菱形云纹、云纹；扁耳两对饰辫纹 Drum face: patterns of sun(12rays), cloud, nipple protrusion, concentric circle, transformed feathermen, quatrefoil, 回 -shape thunder, comb line; Drum body: patterns of 回 -shape thunder, diamond-shape cloud, cloud; Braid patterns on 2 pairs of flat handles.	47.2−47.6	11.5 （残）Incomplete	麻江型 Majiang Type	

续表

序号 NO.	原编号及鼓名 Stock Number & Name	收藏单位 Museum	出土（征集）时间、地点 Time & Spot for discovered or collected	主要装饰 Main Decorations	尺寸（厘米） Size(cm)		类型 Type	图片 Picture
					面径 Face Diameter	身高 Height		
696	总 000168 清乳钉卷花纹铜鼓 No.000168 Qing Dynasty Bronze Drum With nipple protrusion and twisted flower patterns	右江民族博物馆 Youjiang Museum of Nationalities	1990 年百色市中级法院没收并转交 Transferred from Baise Intermediate Court in 1990	鼓面：太阳纹（12 芒）、西字纹、花瓣纹、乳钉纹、卷花纹、三瓣花纹、三叶草纹、栉纹、回形雷纹； 鼓身：乳钉纹、三瓣花纹、回形雷纹、卷花纹、花瓣纹、如意纹、圆心复线三角纹；扁耳两对饰辫纹 Drum face: patterns of sun(12rays), 西 -character, flower petal, nipple protrusion, twisted flower, tri-petal flower, clover, comb line, 回 -shape thunder; Drum body: patterns of nipple protrusion, tri-petal flower, 回 -shape thunder, twisted flower, flower petal, Ruyi, double line triangle with circle inside; Braid patterns on 2 pairs of flat handles.	47.8	27	麻江型 Majiang Type	
697	总 000222 清"大吉大利"龙纹铜鼓 No.000222 Qing Dynasty Bronze Drum with "大吉大利" −character and dragon patterns	右江民族博物馆 Youjiang Museum of Nationalities	1990 年征集于广西隆林县者保乡那麻村 Collected at Nama Village, Zhebao, Longlin County, Guangxi in 1990	鼓面：太阳纹（12 芒）、西字纹、云纹、乳钉纹、龙纹、兽面云纹、"大吉大利"铭文； 鼓身：乳钉纹、回形雷纹、如意云纹、栉纹、云纹、复线三角纹；扁耳两对饰辫纹、回形雷纹 Drum face: patterns of sun(12rays), 西 -character, cloud, nipple protrusion, dragon, beast-face cloud, " 大吉大利 "-character; Drum body: patterns of nipple protrusion, 回 -shape thunder, Ruyi-shape cloud, comb line, cloud, double line triangle; Braid and 回 -shape thunder patterns on 2 pairs of flat handles.	47.2	26.8	麻江型 Majiang Type	

序号 NO.	原编号及鼓名 Stock Number & Name	收藏单位 Museum	出土（征集）时间、地点 Time & Spot for discovered or collected	主要装饰 Main Decorations	尺寸（厘米） Size(cm)		类型 Type	图片 Picture
					面径 Face Diameter	身高 Height		
698	总 000682 清游旗纹乳钉纹铜鼓 No.000682 Qing Dynasty Bronze Drum with flying flag and nipple protrusion patterns	右江民族博物馆 Youjiang Museum of Nationalities	1990 年征集于广西隆林县者保乡那麻村 Collected at Nama Village, Zhebao, Longlin County, Guangxi in 1990	鼓面：太阳纹（12 芒）、团花纹、乳钉纹、窗花纹、游旗纹、菱形云纹、雷纹、菱形填四瓣花纹；鼓身：乳钉纹、勾连雷纹、缠枝花纹、菱形云纹、四瓣花纹、团花纹、窗花纹、复线三角纹；扁耳两对饰弦纹、回形雷纹 Drum face: patterns of sun(12rays), flower cluster, nipple protrusion, widow lattices, flying flag, diamond-shape cloud, thunder, diamond filled with quatrefoil; Drum body: patterns of nipple protrusion, hooked thunder, twisted branches, diamond-shape cloud, quatrefoil, flower cluster, widow lattices, double line triangle; String and 回 -shape thunder patterns on 2 pairs of flat handles.	46.2	25.8	麻江型 Majiang Type	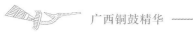
699	总 000857 "盘古至今人望财兴"鼓 No.000857 Bronze Drum with "盘古至今人望财兴" –character	右江民族博物馆 Youjiang Museum of Nationalities	2004 年征集于广西隆林县天生桥 Collected at Tiansheng Qiao, Longlin County, Guangxi in 2004	鼓面：太阳纹（12 芒）、乳钉纹、绚纹、波浪纹、"盘古至今人望财兴"铭文、回形雷纹、团云纹、缠枝纹；鼓身：乳钉纹、马、龙、梅花纹、回形雷纹、团云纹、复线三角纹；扁耳两对饰弦纹 Drum face: patterns of sun(12rays), nipple protrusion, twisted rope, water wave, " 盘古至今人望财兴 "-character, 回 -shape thunder, cloud cluster, twisted branches; Drum body: patterns of nipple protrusion, horse, dragon and plum blossom, 回 -shape thunder, cloud cluster, double line triangle; String patterns on 2 pairs of flat handles.	47.2	27.2	麻江型 Majiang Type	
700	总 001235 桂鱼耕牛纹鼓 No.001235 Bronze Drum with mandarin fish and farm cattle patterns	右江民族博物馆 Youjiang Museum of Nationalities	2012 年 10 月征集于广西隆林县 Collected at Longlin County, Guangxi in October, 2012	鼓面：太阳纹（12 芒）、西字纹、S 形云纹、乳钉纹、梳纹、游旗纹、桂鱼耕牛纹、回形雷纹；鼓身：乳钉纹、如意云纹、对称半同心圆纹、回形雷纹、复线三角纹；扁耳两对饰辫纹、网格纹 Drum face: patterns of sun(12rays), 酉 -character, S-shape cloud, nipple protrusion, comb line, flying flag, mandarin fish and farm cattle, 回 -shape thunder; Drum body: patterns of nipple protrusion, Ruyi-shape cloud, half concentric circle, 回 -shape thunder, double line triangle; Braid and grid patterns on 2 pairs of flat handles.	47.4–47.7	26	麻江型 Majiang Type	

序号 N0.	原编号及鼓名 Stock Number & Name	收藏单位 Museum	出土（征集） 时间、地点 Time & Spot for discovered or collected	主要装饰 Main Decorations	尺寸（厘米） Size(cm)		类型 Type	图片 Picture
					面径 Face Diameter	身高 Height		
701	总076号 塘槐屯鼓 No.076 Bronze Drum Tanghuai Tun	右江革命纪念馆 Youjiang Revolu-tionary Memorial Hall	1983年出土于广西田东县祥周乡康亢村塘槐屯 Unearthed at Tanghuai Tun, Kangkang Village, Xiangzhou, Tiandong County, Guangxi in 1983	鼓面：太阳纹（12芒）、羽纹、栉纹、同心圆纹、复线交叉纹、变形羽人纹、变形翔鹭纹间定胜纹，鼓面边缘饰四只逆时针四足素面立体蛙； 鼓身：羽纹、栉纹、同心圆纹、栉纹切线同心圆纹变形羽人纹垂直纹带、圆心三角垂叶纹；扁耳两对饰辫纹 Drum face: patterns of sun(12rays), feather, comb line, concentric circles, crossed double lines, transformed feathermen, transformed flying heron mixed Dingsheng;4 frog statues of 4 feet and blank back anticlockwise stand on the edge of drum face; Drum body: patterns of feather, comb line, concentric circles, vertical ribbon of straight line, tangent concentric circles and transformed feathermen, leaf-shape triangle with concentric circles in the middle; Braids pattern on 2 pairs of flat handles.	63.7−64	45	冷水冲型 Lengshui-chong Type	
702	总00493号 分0001号 靖安鼓 No.00493 Classified No.0001 Bronze Drum Jing'an	田阳县博物馆 Tianyang County Museum	1986年10月10日出土于广西田阳县洞靖乡靖安村那鸡屯达米山 Unearthed at Dami Hill, Naji Tun, Jing'an Village, Dongjing, Tianyang County, Guangxi on October 10th, 1986	鼓面：太阳纹（12芒）、栉纹、同心圆纹、复线交叉纹、变形羽人纹、变形翔鹭间定胜纹，鼓面边缘饰四只逆时针四足素面立体蛙； 鼓身：栉纹、同心圆纹、栉纹同心圆纹垂直纹带、圆心三角垂叶纹；扁耳两对饰辫纹 Drum face: patterns of sun(12rays), comb line, concentric circles, crossed double lines, transformed feathermen, trnasformed flying heron mixed Dingsheng;4 frog statues of 4 feet and blank back anticlockwise stand on the edge of drum face; Drum body: patterns of comb line, concentric circles, vertical ribbon of straight line and concentric circles, leaf-shape triangle with concentric circles in the middle; Braids pattern on 2 pairs of flat handles.	61.8−63.2	40.8	冷水冲型 Lengshui-chong Type	

序号 NO.	原编号及鼓名 Stock Number & Name	收藏单位 Museum	出土（征集）时间、地点 Time & Spot for discovered or collected	主要装饰 Main Decorations	尺寸（厘米）Size(cm)		类型 Type	图片 Picture
					面径 Face Diameter	身高 Height		
703	总 00747 号 分 0028 号 谷界屯铜鼓 No.00747 Classified No.0028 Bronze Drum Gujie Tun	田阳县博物馆 Tianyang County Museum	1994 年 10 月 21 日出土于广西田阳县那坡镇敢亮村谷界屯落水洞 Unearthed at Luoshui Dong, Gujie Tun, Ganliang Village, Napo Town, Tianyang County, Guangxi on October 21st, 1994	鼓面：太阳纹（12 芒）、乳钉纹、斜线纹、缠枝纹、勾连回形雷纹；鼓身：乳钉纹；扁耳两对饰弦纹 Drum face: patterns of sun(12rays), nipple protrusion, oblique line, twisted branches, hooked thunder in 回 -shape; Drum body: patterns of nipple protrusion; String patterns on 2 pairs of flat handles.	47.8	28	遵义型 Zunyi Type	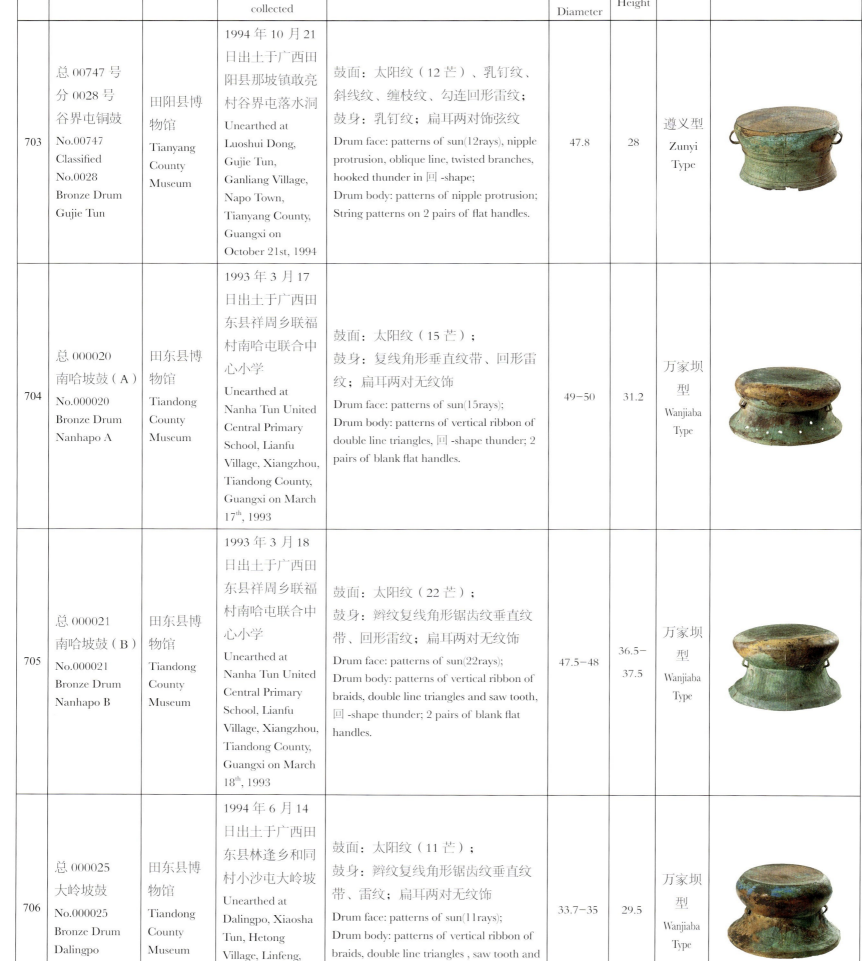
704	总 000020 南哈坡鼓（A） No.000020 Bronze Drum Nanhapo A	田东县博物馆 Tiandong County Museum	1993 年 3 月 17 日出土于广西田东县祥周乡联福村南哈屯联合中心小学 Unearthed at Nanha Tun United Central Primary School, Lianfu Village, Xiangzhou, Tiandong County, Guangxi on March 17th, 1993	鼓面：太阳纹（15 芒）；鼓身：复线角形垂直纹带、回形雷纹；扁耳两对无纹饰 Drum face: patterns of sun(15rays); Drum body: patterns of vertical ribbon of double line triangles, 回 -shape thunder; 2 pairs of blank flat handles.	49−50	31.2	万家坝型 Wanjiaba Type	
705	总 000021 南哈坡鼓（B） No.000021 Bronze Drum Nanhapo B	田东县博物馆 Tiandong County Museum	1993 年 3 月 18 日出土于广西田东县祥周乡联福村南哈屯联合中心小学 Unearthed at Nanha Tun United Central Primary School, Lianfu Village, Xiangzhou, Tiandong County, Guangxi on March 18th, 1993	鼓面：太阳纹（22 芒）；鼓身：辫纹复线角形锯齿纹垂直纹带、回形雷纹；扁耳两对无纹饰 Drum face: patterns of sun(22rays); Drum body: patterns of vertical ribbon of braids, double line triangles and saw tooth, 回 -shape thunder; 2 pairs of blank flat handles.	47.5−48	36.5−37.5	万家坝型 Wanjiaba Type	
706	总 000025 大岭坡鼓 No.000025 Bronze Drum Dalingpo	田东县博物馆 Tiandong County Museum	1994 年 6 月 14 日出土于广西田东县林逢乡和同村小沙屯大岭坡 Unearthed at Dalingpo, Xiaosha Tun, Hetong Village, Linfeng, Tiandong County, Guangxi on June 14th, 1994	鼓面：太阳纹（11 芒）；鼓身：辫纹复线角形锯齿纹垂直纹带、雷纹；扁耳两对无纹饰 Drum face: patterns of sun(11rays); Drum body: patterns of vertical ribbon of braids, double line triangles , saw tooth and thunder; 2 pairs of blank flat handles.	33.7−35	29.5	万家坝型 Wanjiaba Type	

续表

序号 NO.	原编号及鼓名 Stock Number & Name	收藏单位 Museum	出土（征集） 时间、地点 Time & Spot for discovered or collected	主要装饰 Main Decorations	尺寸（厘米） Size(cm)		类型 Type	图片 Picture
					面径 Face Diameter	身高 Height		
707	总 000164 平马镇鼓 No.000164 Bronze Drum Pingmazhen	田东县博物馆 Tiandong County Museum	2004 年 5 月 26 日出土于广西田东县平马镇中山街右江河内 Unearthed in Youjiang River, Zhongshan Street, Pingma Town, Tiandong County, Guangxi on May 26th, 2004	鼓面：太阳纹（8 芒）、三角斜线纹、栉纹、切线同心圆纹、变形羽人纹、翔鹭间切线同心圆纹、切线同心圆纹； 鼓身：切线同心圆纹、同心圆纹、栉纹；扁耳两对饰弦纹 Drum face: patterns of sun(8rays), triangle filled with oblique lines, comb line, tangent concentric circles, transformed feathermen, flying heron mixed tangent concentric circles, tangent concentric circles; Drum body: patterns of tangent concentric circles, concentric circles, comb line; String patterns on 2 pairs of flat handles.	43.5–44.5	33	石寨山型 Shizhai shan Type	
708	总 127–1 号 荷耙人团寿纹铜鼓 No.127-1 Bronze Drum With hoers and round 寿 –character patterns	平果县博物馆 Pingguo County Museum	1985 年 12 月 20 日广西平果县水泥厂群众捐献 Donated by clerk of Guangxi Pingguo County Cement Plant on December 20th, 1985	鼓面：太阳纹（12 芒）、同心圆纹、花纹、乳钉纹、荷耙人、团寿、羽组合纹、游旗纹、兽面纹、勾连工字纹； 鼓身：乳钉纹、花纹、雷纹、栉纹、羽纹、回形雷纹、图案复线三角纹；扁耳两对饰辫纹 Drum face: patterns of sun(12rays), concentric circle, flower, nipple protrusion, patterns group of hoers, round 寿 -character and feather, flying flag, beast face, hooked 工 -character; Drum body: patterns of nipple protrusion, flower, thunder, comb line, feather, 回 -shape thunder, double line triangle with motifs; Braid and grid patterns on 2 pairs of flat handles.	45.5	25.3	麻江型 Majiang Type	
709	总 127–2 号 游旗纹铜鼓 No.127-2 Bronze Drum with flying flag patterns	平果县博物馆 Pingguo County Museum	1985 年 12 月 20 日广西平果县水泥厂群众捐献 Donated by clerk of Guangxi Pingguo County Cement Plant on December 20th, 1985	鼓面：太阳纹（12 芒）、西字纹、S 形云纹、乳钉纹、游旗纹、栉纹、兽面纹、卦纹； 鼓身：乳钉纹、回形雷纹、如意云纹、栉纹、复线三角纹；扁耳两对饰辫纹 Drum face: patterns of sun(12rays), 酉 -character, S-shape cloud, nipple protrusion, flying flag, comb line, beast face, divinatory symbol; Drum body: patterns of nipple protrusion, 回 -shape thunder, Ruyi-shape cloud, comb line, double line triangle; Braid patterns on 2 pairs of flat handles.	46.6–47	27	麻江型 Majiang Type	

序号 N0.	原编号及鼓名 Stock Number & Name	收藏单位 Museum	出土(征集)时间、地点 Time & Spot for discovered or collected	主要装饰 Main Decorations	尺寸(厘米) Size(cm)		类型 Type	图片 Picture
					面径 Face Diameter	身高 Height		
710	立鸟翔鹭纹铜鼓 Bronze Drum with standing bird and heron patterns	靖西县博物馆 Jingxi County Museum	2008年在广西靖西与天等交界的废品收购站拣选 Collected at a waste recycle station on the boundary between Jingxi County and Tiandeng County, Guangxi in 2008	鼓面:太阳纹(12芒)、同心圆纹、立鸟纹、翔鹭纹、栉纹;鼓身:栉纹、栉纹羽纹垂直纹带;扁耳两对饰辫纹;鼓已断裂为若干残片 Drum face: patterns of sun(12rays), concentric circles, standing bird, heron, comb line; Drum body: patterns of comb line, vertical ribbon of straight line and feather; braids pattern on 2 pairs of flat handles. The whole drum body was broken into pieces.		(残) Incomplete	冷水冲型 Lengshui-chong Type	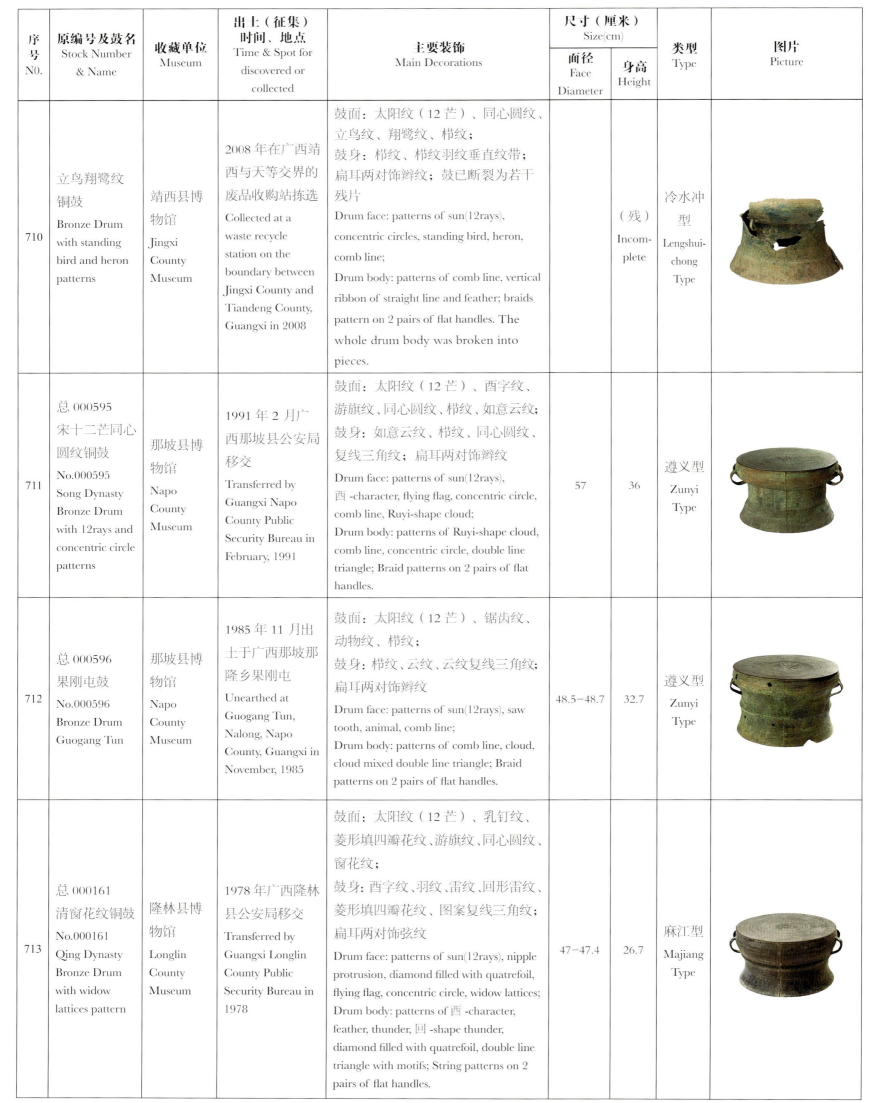
711	总000595 宋十二芒同心圆纹铜鼓 No.000595 Song Dynasty Bronze Drum with 12rays and concentric circle patterns	那坡县博物馆 Napo County Museum	1991年2月广西那坡县公安局移交 Transferred by Guangxi Napo County Public Security Bureau in February, 1991	鼓面:太阳纹(12芒)、酉字纹、游旗纹、同心圆纹、栉纹、如意云纹;鼓身:如意云纹、栉纹、同心圆纹、复线三角纹;扁耳两对饰辫纹 Drum face: patterns of sun(12rays), 酉-character, flying flag, concentric circle, comb line, Ruyi-shape cloud; Drum body: patterns of Ruyi-shape cloud, comb line, concentric circle, double line triangle; Braid patterns on 2 pairs of flat handles.	57	36	遵义型 Zunyi Type	
712	总000596 果刚屯鼓 No.000596 Bronze Drum Guogang Tun	那坡县博物馆 Napo County Museum	1985年11月出土于广西那坡那隆乡果刚屯 Unearthed at Guogang Tun, Nalong, Napo County, Guangxi in November, 1985	鼓面:太阳纹(12芒)、锯齿纹、动物纹、栉纹;鼓身:栉纹、云纹、云纹复线三角纹;扁耳两对饰辫纹 Drum face: patterns of sun(12rays), saw tooth, animal, comb line; Drum body: patterns of comb line, cloud, cloud mixed double line triangle; Braid patterns on 2 pairs of flat handles.	48.5-48.7	32.7	遵义型 Zunyi Type	
713	总000161 清窗花纹铜鼓 No.000161 Qing Dynasty Bronze Drum with widow lattices pattern	隆林县博物馆 Longlin County Museum	1978年广西隆林县公安局移交 Transferred by Guangxi Longlin County Public Security Bureau in 1978	鼓面:太阳纹(12芒)、乳钉纹、菱形填四瓣花纹、游旗纹、同心圆纹、窗花纹;鼓身:酉字纹、羽纹、雷纹、回形雷纹、菱形填四瓣花纹、图案复线三角纹;扁耳两对饰弦纹 Drum face: patterns of sun(12rays), nipple protrusion, diamond filled with quatrefoil, flying flag, concentric circle, widow lattices; Drum body: patterns of 酉-character, feather, thunder, 回-shape thunder, diamond filled with quatrefoil, double line triangle with motifs; String patterns on 2 pairs of flat handles.	47-47.4	26.7	麻江型 Majiang Type	

续表

序号 NO.	原编号及鼓名 Stock Number & Name	收藏单位 Museum	出土（征集）时间、地点 Time & Spot for discovered or collected	主要装饰 Main Decorations	尺寸（厘米）Size(cm) 面径 Face Diameter	身高 Height	类型 Type	图片 Picture
714	总 000162 清寿字纹铜鼓 No.000162 Qing Dynasty Bronze Drum with 寿 –character patterns	隆林县博物馆 Longlin County Museum	1985 年征集 Collected in 1985	鼓面：太阳纹（12 芒）、乳钉纹、回形雷纹、寿字纹、羽纹、窗花纹；鼓身：弦纹；扁耳两对饰弦纹 Drum face: patterns of sun(12rays), nipple protrusion, 回 -shape thunder, 寿 -character, feather, widow lattices; Drum body: patterns of string; String patterns on 2 pairs of flat handles.	47	26.5	麻江型 Majiang Type	
715	总 000164 游旗纹铜鼓 No.000164 Bronze Drum with Flying flag patterns	隆林县博物馆 Longlin County Museum	1994 年 6 月征集于广西隆林县者保乡那平村 Collected at Naping Village, Zhebao, Longlin County, Guangxi in June, 1994	鼓面：太阳纹（12 芒）、酉字纹、S 形云纹、乳钉纹、游旗纹、四出钱纹、栉纹、兽形云纹；鼓身：乳钉纹、如意云纹、回形雷纹、栉纹、云纹、复线三角纹；扁耳两对饰辫纹、回形雷纹 Drum face: patterns of sun(12rays), 酉 -character, S-shape cloud, nipple protrusion, flying flag, coin with quadrangle inside, straight line, beast face; Drum body: patterns of nipple protrusion, Ruyi-shape cloud, 回 -shape thunder, straight line, cloud, double line triangle; Braid and 回 -shape thunder patterns on 2 pairs of flat handles.	46.8–47	26	麻江型 Majiang Type	
716	总 000165 清游旗纹铜鼓 No.000165 Qing Dynasty Bronze Drum with Flying flag patterns	隆林县博物馆 Longlin County Museum	1978 年征集于广西隆林县者保乡 Collected at Zhebao, Longlin County, Guangxi in 1978	鼓面：太阳纹（12 芒）、酉字纹、S 形云纹、乳钉纹、游旗纹、兽形云纹；鼓身：乳钉纹、如意云纹、回形雷纹、栉纹、云纹、复线三角纹；扁耳两对饰辫纹、回形雷纹 Drum face: patterns of sun(12rays), 酉 -character, S-shape cloud, nipple protrusion, flying flag, beast-shape cloud; Drum body: patterns of nipple protrusion, Ruyi-shape cloud, 回 -shape thunder, straight line, cloud, double line triangle; Braid and 回 -shape thunder patterns on 2 pairs of flat handles.	47.2–47.4	26.5	麻江型 Majiang Type	

续表

序号 N0.	原编号及鼓名 Stock Number & Name	收藏单位 Museum	出土（征集） 时间、地点 Time & Spot for discovered or collected	主要装饰 Main Decorations	尺寸（厘米） Size(cm)		类型 Type	图片 Picture
					面径 Face Diameter	身高 Height		
717	总 000166 "虎"字纹 铜鼓 No.000166 Bronze Drum with "虎" – character patterns	隆林县博 物馆 Longlin County Museum	1996 年征集于广 西隆林县德峨乡 Collected at De'e, Longlin County, Guangxi in 1996	鼓面：太阳纹（12 芒）、乳钉纹、绹 纹、U 形纹、缠枝花纹、"虎"字纹； 鼓身：乳钉纹、S 形云纹、云飘带 纹、四出钱飘带纹、波浪纹、复线 三角纹；扁耳两对饰辫纹、弦纹 Drum face: patterns of sun(12rays), nipple protrusion, twisted rope, U-shape, twisted branches," 虎 "-character patterns; Drum body: patterns of nipple protrusion, S-shape cloud, cloud mixed ribbon, coin with quadrangle inside mixed ribbon, water wave, double line triangle; Braid and string patterns on 2 pairs of flat handles.	45	27	麻江型 Majiang Type	
718	总 000167 同心圆纹铜鼓 No.000167 Bronze Drum with concentric circle patterns	隆林县博 物馆 Longlin County Museum	1996 年征集于广 西隆林县者保 Collected at Zhebao, Longlin County, Guangxi in 1996	鼓面：太阳纹（12 芒）、乳钉纹、 同心圆网格组合纹； 鼓身：弦纹；扁耳两对饰辫纹、 弦纹 Drum face: patterns of sun(12rays), nipple protrusion, concentric circle mixed net grids; Drum body: patterns of string; Braid and string patterns on 2 pairs of flat handles.	50.7－51.4	27.2	麻江型 Majiang Type	
719	总 000260 共和村铜鼓 No.000260 Bronze Drum Gonghe Cun	隆林县博 物馆 Longlin County Museum	1990 年 9 月出土 于广西隆林扁牙 乡共和村河岸 Unearthed at the river bank of Gonghe Village, Bianya, Longlin County, Guangxi in September,1990	鼓面：太阳纹（12 芒）、锯齿纹、 切线同心圆纹、翔鹭纹； 鼓身：锯齿纹、切线同心圆纹、锯 齿纹牛纹垂直纹带；扁耳两对饰辫 纹、弦纹 Drum face: patterns of sun(12rays), saw tooth, tangent concentric circles, flying heron; Drum body: patterns of saw tooth, tangent concentric circles, vertical ribbon of saw tooth and cattle; Braid and string patterns on 2 pairs of flat handles.	44.5	28.5	石寨山 型 Shizhai- shan Type	

序号 NO.	原编号及鼓名 Stock Number & Name	收藏单位 Museum	出土（征集）时间、地点 Time & Spot for discovered or collected	主要装饰 Main Decorations	尺寸（厘米）Size(cm)		类型 Type	图片 Picture
					面径 Face Diameter	身高 Height		
720	旧：01 号 游旗窗花纹铜鼓 Old No.01 Bronze Drum with flying flag and widow lattices patterns	西林县博物馆 Xilin County Museum	不明 Unclear	鼓面：太阳纹（12 芒）、乳钉纹、菱形填四瓣花纹、游旗纹、同心圆纹、卐字纹；鼓身：菱形填四瓣花纹、雷纹、同形雷纹、变形寿字纹、图案三角纹；扁耳两对饰弦纹 Drum face: patterns of sun(12rays), nipple protrusion, diamond filled with quatrefoil, flying flag, concentric circle, 卐 -character; Drum body: patterns of diamond filled with quatrefoil, thunder, 回 -shape thunder, transformed 寿 -character, double line triangle with motifs; String patterns on 2 pairs of flat handles.	47	27	麻江型 Majiang Type	
721	旧：02 号 游旗纹铜鼓 Old No.02 Bronze Drum with flying flag patterns	西林县博物馆 Xilin County Museum	不明 Unclear	鼓面：太阳纹（12 芒）、西字纹、乳钉纹、游旗纹、S 形云纹、云纹、兽形云纹；鼓身：乳钉纹、云纹、同心圆纹、回形雷纹、图案三角纹；扁耳两对饰辫纹 Drum face: patterns of sun(12rays), 西 -character, nipple protrusion, flying flag, S-shape cloud, cloud, beast; Drum body: patterns of nipple protrusion, cloud, concentric circle, 回 -shape thunder, double line triangle with motifs; Braid patterns on 2 pairs of flat handles.	48	28	麻江型 Majiang Type	
722	旧：03 号 团云纹铜鼓 Old No.03 Bronze Drum with cloud cluster patterns	西林县博物馆 Xilin County Museum	不明 Unclear	鼓面：太阳纹（12 芒）、乳钉纹、回形雷纹、复线三角纹、团云纹；鼓身：乳钉纹、团云纹、回形雷纹、复线三角纹；扁耳两对饰弦纹 Drum face: patterns of sun(12rays), nipple protrusion, 回 -shape thunder, double line triangle , cloud cluster; Drum body: patterns of nipple protrusion, cloud cluster, 回 -shape thunder, double line triangle; String patterns on 2 pairs of flat handles.	46.8	26.8	麻江型 Majiang Type	

序号 N0.	原编号及鼓名 Stock Number & Name	收藏单位 Museum	出土（征集）时间、地点 Time & Spot for discovered or collected	主要装饰 Main Decorations	尺寸（厘米） Size(cm)		类型 Type	图片 Picture
					面径 Face Diameter	身高 Height		
723	旧：05号 八宝缠枝纹铜鼓 Old No.05 Bronze Drum with eight Buddhist treasures and twisted branches pattern	西林县博物馆 Xilin County Museum	不明 Unclear	鼓面：太阳纹（12芒）、乳钉纹、八宝纹、缠枝纹； 鼓身：复线三角纹；扁耳两对饰弦纹 Drum face: patterns of sun(12rays), nipple protrusion, eight Buddhist treasures, twisted branches; Drum body: patterns of double line triangle; String patterns on 2 pairs of flat handles.	48	29	麻江型 Majiang Type	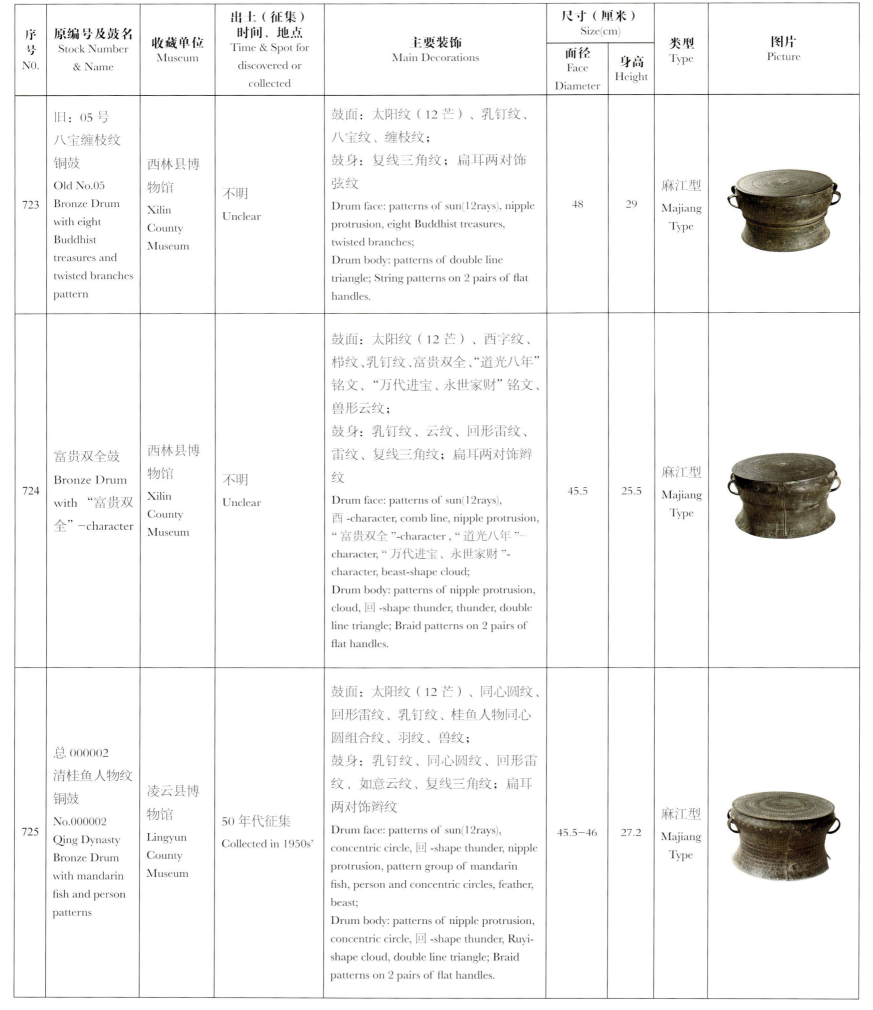
724	富贵双全鼓 Bronze Drum with "富贵双全"–character	西林县博物馆 Xilin County Museum	不明 Unclear	鼓面：太阳纹（12芒）、酉字纹、枇纹、乳钉纹、富贵双全、"道光八年"铭文、"万代进宝、永世家财"铭文、兽形云纹； 鼓身：乳钉纹、云纹、回形雷纹、雷纹、复线三角纹；扁耳两对饰辫纹 Drum face: patterns of sun(12rays), 酉-character, comb line, nipple protrusion, "富贵双全"-character, "道光八年"-character, "万代进宝、永世家财"-character, beast-shape cloud; Drum body: patterns of nipple protrusion, cloud, 回-shape thunder, thunder, double line triangle; Braid patterns on 2 pairs of flat handles.	45.5	25.5	麻江型 Majiang Type	
725	总000002 清桂鱼人物纹铜鼓 No.000002 Qing Dynasty Bronze Drum with mandarin fish and person patterns	凌云县博物馆 Lingyun County Museum	50年代征集 Collected in 1950s'	鼓面：太阳纹（12芒）、同心圆纹、回形雷纹、乳钉纹、桂鱼人物同心圆组合纹、羽纹、兽纹； 鼓身：乳钉纹、同心圆纹、回形雷纹、如意云纹、复线三角纹；扁耳两对饰辫纹 Drum face: patterns of sun(12rays), concentric circle, 回-shape thunder, nipple protrusion, pattern group of mandarin fish, person and concentric circles, feather, beast; Drum body: patterns of nipple protrusion, concentric circle, 回-shape thunder, Ruyi-shape cloud, double line triangle; Braid patterns on 2 pairs of flat handles.	45.5—46	27.2	麻江型 Majiang Type	

序号 N0.	原编号及鼓名 Stock Number & Name	收藏单位 Museum	出土（征集） 时间、地点 Time & Spot for discovered or collected	主要装饰 Main Decorations	尺寸（厘米） Size(cm)		类型 Type	图片 Picture
					面径 Face Diameter	身高 Height		
726	总 000001 清游旗纹铜鼓 No.000001 Qing Dynasty Bronze Drum with flying flag patterns	乐业县博 物馆 Leye County Museum	广西乐业县公安 局移交 Transferred by Guangxi Leye County Public Security Bureau	鼓面：乳钉纹、栉纹、游旗纹、水 波纹、同心圆纹、绚纹； 鼓身：复线三角填斜线纹、缠枝纹、 复线三角纹；扁耳两对饰辫纹、水 波纹 Drum face: patterns of sun(12rays), comb line, water wave, concentric circle, twisted rope; Drum body: patterns of double line triangle filled with oblique lines, twisted branches, double line triangle; Braid and water wave patterns on 2 pairs of flat handles.	47	26.2	麻江型 Majiang Type	
727	总 000002 塘英鼓 No.000002 Bronze Drum Tangying	乐业县博 物馆 Leye County Museum	1985 年出土于广 西乐业县逻沙乡 塘英村 Unearthed at Tangying Village, Luosha, Leye County, Guangxi in 1985	鼓面：太阳纹（12 芒）、可辨变形 羽人纹、定胜纹、栉纹、圆圈纹； 鼓身：可辨栉纹、弦纹；扁耳两对 饰辫纹 Drum face: patterns of sun(12rays), only transformed feathermen, Dingsheng, comb line, circle patterns can be recognized; Drum body: only straight line, string patterns can be recognized; Braid patterns on 2 pairs of flat handles.	38.7－39	19 （残） Incom- plete	冷水冲 型 Lengshui- chong Type	
728	战国竞渡纹牛 纹铜鼓 Warring State Bronze Drum with boat racing and cattle patterns	贺州市博 物馆 Hezhou City Museum	1991 年 7 月 18 日出土于广西贺 县沙田龙中村 Unearthed at Longzhong Village, Shatian, He County, Guangxi on July 18th, 1991	鼓面：太阳纹（12 芒）、突起圆点纹、 锯齿间三角圆点纹、乳钉纹； 鼓身：突起圆点纹、锯齿间三圆点 纹、竞渡纹、圆点斜线牛纹垂直纹带、 锯齿纹；扁耳两对饰辫纹 Drum face: patterns of sun(12rays), dot protrusion, saw tooth mixed triangle and dots, nipple protrusion; Drum body: patterns of dot protrusion, saw tooth mixed 3 dots, boat racing, vertical ribbon of dots, oblique line and cattle, saw tooth; Braid patterns on 2 pairs of flat handle.	36.4－36.5	27.5	石寨山 型 Shizhai- shan Type	

序号 N0.	原编号及鼓名 Stock Number & Name	收藏单位 Museum	出土（征集）时间、地点 Time & Spot for discovered or collected	主要装饰 Main Decorations	尺寸（厘米）Size(cm)		类型 Type	图片 Picture
					面径 Face Diameter	身高 Height		
729	027 号 明游旗纹铜鼓 No.027 Ming Dynasty Bronze Drum with flying flag patterns	河池市文物站 Hechi City Cultural Relic Station	征集于广西河池金城江百货站 Collected at Guangxi Hechi Jinchengjiang Department Store	鼓面：太阳纹（磨蚀）、酉字纹、乳钉纹、栉纹、游旗纹、S 形卷云纹； 鼓身：栉纹、乳钉纹、如意云纹、S 形卷云纹、回形雷纹、复线三角纹；扁耳两对饰辫纹 Drum face: patterns of sun(rusting), 酉-character, nipple protrusion, comb line, flying flag, S-shape cloud, cloud; Drum body: patterns of comb line, nipple protrusion, Ruyi-shape cloud, S-shape cloud cluster, 回-shape thunder, double line triangle; Braid patterns on 2 pairs of flat handles.	48.5	28.5	麻江型 Majiang Type	
730	030 号 清荷耙人纹铜鼓 No.030 Qing Dynasty Bronze Drum with hoer patterns	河池市文物站 Hechi City Cultural Relic Station	1994 年广西环江县龙岩派出所移交 Transferred by Guangxi Huanjiang County Longyan Police Station in 1994	鼓面：太阳纹（12 芒）、同心圆纹、回形雷纹、乳钉纹、荷耙人纹、栉纹； 鼓身：乳钉纹、荷耙人纹、同心圆纹、回形雷纹、复线三角纹；扁耳两对饰辫纹 Drum face: patterns of sun(12rays), concentric circle, 回-shape thunder, nipple protrusion, hoer, comb line; Drum body: patterns of nipple protrusion, hoer, concentric circle, 回-shape thunder, double line triangle; Braid patterns on 2 pairs of flat handles.	32.4	19.5	麻江型 Majiang Type	
731	031 号 明八蛙饰回纹铜鼓 No.031 Ming Dynasty Bronze Drum with 8 frog statues and 回-character patterns	河池市文物站 Hechi City Cultural Relic Station	20 世纪 90 年代中期征集于广西河池凤山县砦牙乡拉英乡那田屯 Unearthed at Natian Tun, Laying, Zhaiya, Fengshan County, Hechi, Guangxi in the middle of 1990s'	鼓面：太阳纹（12 芒）、乳钉纹、花瓣纹、回形雷纹、同心圆纹、绚纹，鼓面边缘饰四只头向鼓心四足立体蛙； 鼓身：乳钉纹、S 钩纹，胸饰四只头向上四足立体蛙；扁耳两对饰辫纹、弦纹 Drum face: patterns of sun(12rays), nipple protrusion, flower petal, 回-shape thunder, concentric circle, twisted rope; 4 frog statues of 4 feet stand on the edge of the drum face, face to the sun pattern; Drum body: patterns of nipple protrusion, S-shape hook; 4 frog statues of 4 feet stand with heads up on the drum's chest; Braid and string patterns on 2 pairs of flat handles.	48.7—49	27.7	麻江型 Majiang Type	

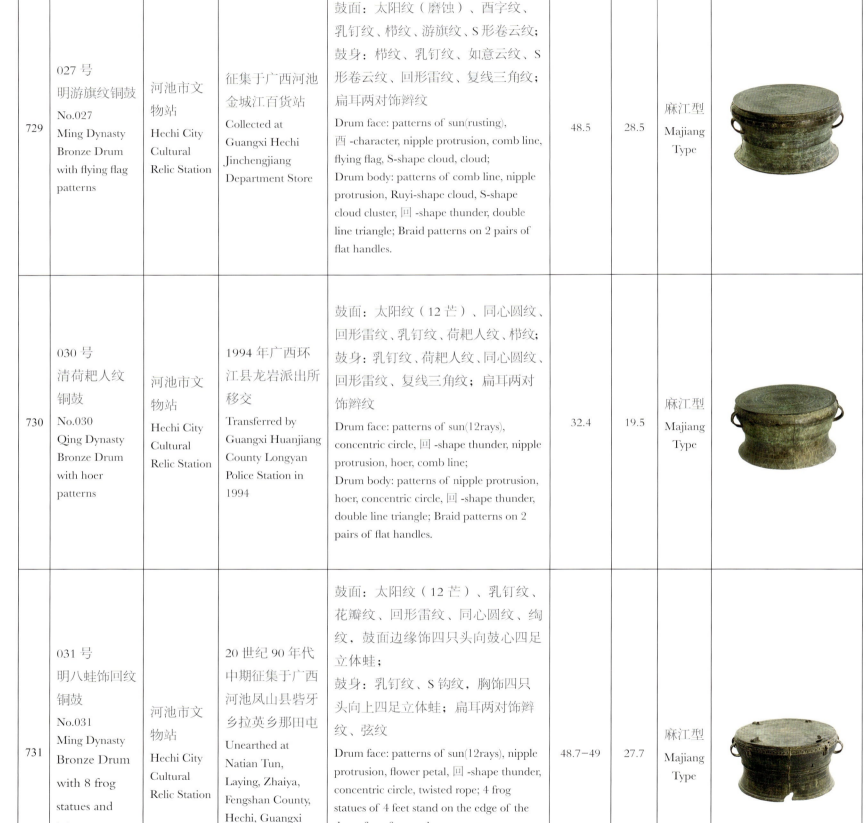

序号 NO.	原编号及鼓名 Stock Number & Name	收藏单位 Museum	出土（征集） 时间、地点 Time & Spot for discovered or collected	主要装饰 Main Decorations	尺寸（厘米） Size(cm)		类型 Type	图片 Picture
					面径 Face Diameter	身高 Height		
732	058 号 清云纹间团寿纹铜鼓 No.058 Qing Dynasty Bronze Drum with cloud mixed round 寿 −character patterns	河池市文物站 Hechi City Cultural Relic Station	征集 collected	鼓面：太阳纹（12 芒）、西字纹、云纹、乳钉纹、云纹间团寿纹、游旗纹、回形雷纹； 鼓身：云纹、回形雷纹、圆心复线三角纹；扁耳两对饰辫纹 Drum face: patterns of sun(12rays), 西 -character, cloud, nipple protrusion, cloud mixed round 寿 -character, flying flag, 回 -shape thunder; Drum body: patterns of cloud, 回 -shape thunder, double line triangle with circle in the middle; Braid patterns on 2 pairs of flat handles.	47.8−48	27.3	麻江型 Majiang Type	
733	059 号 清游旗纹铜鼓 No.059 Qing Dynasty Bronze Drum with flying flag patterns	河池市文物站 Hechi City Cultural Relic Station	征集 collected	鼓面：太阳纹（12 芒）、乳钉纹、如意云纹、雷纹、游旗纹、回形雷纹、同心圆纹； 鼓身：乳钉纹、绹纹、雷纹、回形雷纹、同心圆纹；扁耳两对饰弦纹 Drum face: patterns of sun(12rays), nipple protrusion, Ruyi-shape cloud, thunder, flying flag, 回 -shape thunder, concentric circle; Drum body: patterns of nipple protrusion, twisted rope, thunder, 回 -shape thunder, concentric circle; String patterns on 2 pairs of flat handles.	45.5	25.7	麻江型 Majiang Type	
734	060 号 清游旗纹铜鼓 No.060 Qing Dynasty Bronze Drum with flying flag patterns	河池市文物站 Hechi City Cultural Relic Station	征集 collected	鼓面：太阳纹（12 芒）、S 形云纹、同心圆纹、乳钉纹、雷纹、游旗纹、回形雷纹； 鼓身：乳钉纹、四出钱纹、回形雷纹、S 形云纹、复线三角纹；扁耳两对饰辫纹 Drum face: patterns of sun(12rays), S-shape cloud, concentric circle, nipple protrusion, thunder, flying flag, 回 -shape thunder; Drum body: patterns of nipple protrusion, coin with quadrangle, 回 -shape thunder, S-shape cloud cluster, double line triangle; Braid patterns on 2 pairs of flat handles.	43.5	25	麻江型 Majiang Type	

序号 N0.	原编号及鼓名 Stock Number & Name	收藏单位 Museum	出土（征集） 时间、地点 Time & Spot for discovered or collected	主要装饰 Main Decorations	尺寸（厘米） Size(cm)		类型 Type	图片 Picture
					面径 Face Diameter	身高 Height		
735	083 号 清游旗纹十二 生肖纹铜鼓 No.083 Qing Dynasty Bronze Drum with flying flag and zodiac patterns	河池市文物站 Hechi City Cultural Relic Station	征集于广西河池 东兰县东兰镇 Collected at Donglan Town, Donglan County, Hechi, Guangxi	鼓面：太阳纹（12 芒）、酉字纹、 S 形云纹、乳钉纹、栉纹、游旗纹、 十二生肖纹、云纹； 鼓身：乳钉纹、云纹、如意云纹、 栉纹、回形雷纹、复线三角纹；扁 耳两对饰辫纹 Drum face: patterns of sun(12rays), 酉 -character, S-shape cloud, nipple protrusion, comb line, flying flag, zodiac, cloud; Drum body: patterns of nipple protrusion, cloud, Ruyi-shape cloud, comb line, 回 -shape thunder, double line triangle; Braid patterns on 2 pairs of flat handles.	50.4－50.5	28	麻江型 Majiang Type	
736	代 029 号 荷耙人纹铜鼓 Dai No.029 Bronze Drum with hoer patterns	河池市文物站 Hechi City Cultural Relic Station	广西都安文物馆 委托代管 Manage on behalf of Guangxi Du'an County Cultural Relic House	鼓面：太阳纹（12 芒）、S 钩纹、栉纹、 乳钉纹、荷耙人、回形雷、符箓、团寿、 贝叶、四出钱组合图案纹、蝴蝶花纹、 四出钱纹； 鼓身：乳钉纹、如意云纹、同心圆 纹、贝叶纹、S 钩纹、复线三角纹； 扁耳两对无纹饰 Drum face: patterns of sun(12rays), S-shape hook, comb line, nipple protrusion, patterns group of hoer, 回 -shape thunder, Ofuda, round 寿 -character, shell-shape leaf and coin with quadrangle inside, butterfly, coin with quadrangle inside; Drum body: patterns of nipple protrusion, Ruyi-shape cloud, concentric circle, shell- shape leaf, S-shape hook, double line triangle; 2 pairs of blank flat handles.	45	26.7	麻江型 Majiang Type	
737	代 030 号 双龙献寿人纹 牛纹铜鼓 Dai No.030 Bronze Drum with 2 dragons and 寿 －character patterns	河池市文物站 Hechi City Cultural Relic Station	广西都安文物馆 委托代管 Manage on behalf of Guangxi Du'an County Cultural Relic House	鼓面：太阳纹（12 芒）、酉字纹、 回形雷纹、乳钉纹、双龙献寿、鹤、 荷耙人、牛、组合图案纹、游旗纹； 鼓身：乳钉纹、如意云纹、雷纹、 回形雷纹、图案复线三角纹；扁耳 两对饰辫纹 Drum face: patterns of sun(12rays), 酉 -character, 回 -shape thunder, nipple protrusion, patterns group of 2 dragons and 寿 -character, crane, hoer and cattle, flying flag; Drum body: patterns of nipple protrusion, Ruyi-shape cloud, thunder, 回 -shape thunder, double line triangle with motifs; Braid patterns on 2 pairs of flat handles.	44.9－45	25.4	麻江型 Majiang Type	

续表

序号 NO.	原编号及鼓名 Stock Number & Name	收藏单位 Museum	出土（征集）时间、地点 Time & Spot for discovered or collected	主要装饰 Main Decorations	尺寸（厘米） Size(cm)		类型 Type	图片 Picture
					面径 Face Diameter	身高 Height		
738	代 031 号 游旗纹铜鼓 Dai No.031 Bronze Drum flying flag patterns	河池市文物站 Hechi City Cultural Relic Station	广西都安文物馆委托代管 Manage on behalf of Guangxi Du'an County Cultural Relic House	鼓面：太阳纹（12 芒）、六瓣花纹、同心圆纹、乳钉纹、团寿如意云回形雷、翎眼、同心圆、酉字形纹组合纹、游旗纹、酉字纹； 鼓身：乳钉纹、如意云纹、回形雷纹、雷纹、圆心复线三角纹；扁耳两对饰辫纹 Drum face: patterns of sun(12rays), hexapetalous flower, concentric circle, nipple protrusion, patterns group of round 寿 -character, Ruyi-shape cloud, 回 -shape thunder, peacock feather, concentric circle and 酉 -character, flying flag, 酉 -character; Drum body: patterns of nipple protrusion, Ruyi-shape cloud, 回 -shape thunder, thunder, double line triangle with circle inside; Braid patterns on 2 pairs of flat handles.	44.8-45	25.4	麻江型 Majiang Type	
739	代 032 号 游旗纹铜鼓 Dai No.032 Bronze Drum with flying flag patterns	河池市文物站 Hechi City Cultural Relic Station	广西都安文物馆委托代管 Manage on behalf of Guangxi Du'an County Cultural Relic House	鼓面：太阳纹（12 芒）、酉字纹、乳钉纹、游旗纹、回形雷纹、云纹； 鼓身：乳钉纹、云纹、如意云纹、栉纹、回形雷纹、圆心复线三角纹；扁耳两对饰辫纹 Drum face: patterns of sun(12rays), 酉 -character, nipple protrusion, flying flag, 回 -shape thunder, cloud; Drum body: patterns of nipple protrusion, cloud, Ruyi-shape cloud, straight line, 回 -shape thunder, double line triangle with circle inside; Braid patterns on 2 pairs of flat handles.	47.1	27	麻江型 Majiang Type	
740	代 033 号 人纹铜鼓 Dai No.033 Bronze Drum person patterns	河池市文物站 Hechi City with Cultural Relic Station	广西都安文物馆委托代管 Manage on behalf of Guangxi Du'an County Cultural Relic House	鼓面：太阳纹（12 芒）、可辨同心圆纹、乳钉纹、人物组合纹； 鼓身：乳钉纹、云纹、回形雷纹、四出钱纹、S 钩纹、复线三角纹；扁耳两对饰辫纹 Drum face: patterns of sun(12rays), pattern group of concentric circle, nipple protrusion and persons; Drum body: patterns of nipple protrusion, cloud, 回 -shape thunder, coin with quadrangle inside, S-shape hook, double line triangle; Braid patterns on 2 pairs of flat handles.	45.7-45.9	27.3	麻江型 Majiang Type	

序号 N0.	原编号及鼓名 Stock Number & Name	收藏单位 Museum	出土（征集）时间、地点 Time & Spot for discovered or collected	主要装饰 Main Decorations	尺寸（厘米）Size(cm)		类型 Type	图片 Picture
					面径 Face Diameter	身高 Height		
741	代 034 号 游旗纹铜鼓 Dai No.034 Bronze Drum with flying flag patterns	河池市文物站 Hechi City Cultural Relic Station	广西都安文物馆委托代管 Manage on behalf of Guangxi Du'an County Cultural Relic House	鼓面：太阳纹（12 芒）、四出钱纹、S 形云纹、乳钉纹、游旗纹、栉纹、兽面云纹；鼓身：乳钉纹、如意云纹、回形雷纹、云纹、四出钱纹、复线三角纹；扁耳两对饰辫纹 Drum face: patterns of sun(12rays), coin with quadrangle inside, S-shape cloud, nipple protrusion, flying flag, comb line, beast- face cloud; Drum body: patterns of nipple protrusion, Ruyi-shape cloud, 回 -shape thunder, cloud, coin with quadrangle inside, double line triangle; Braid patterns on 2 pairs of flat handles.	47.1	26.5	麻江型 Majiang Type	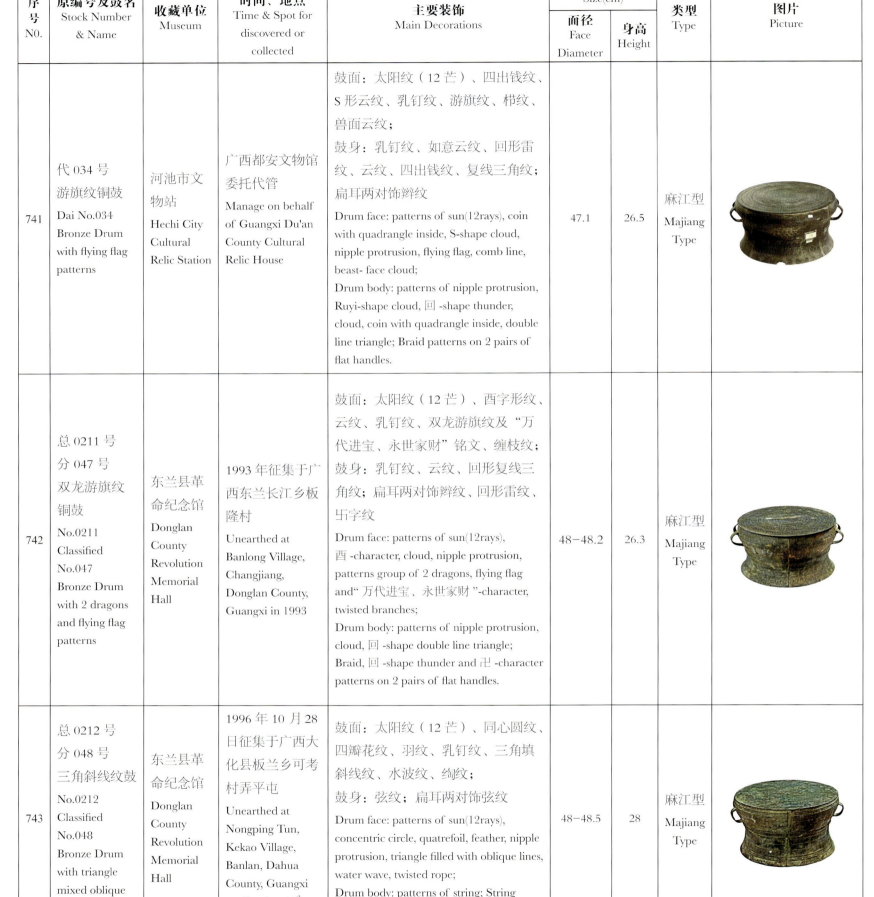
742	总 0211 号 分 047 号 双龙游旗纹铜鼓 No.0211 Classified No.047 Bronze Drum with 2 dragons and flying flag patterns	东兰县革命纪念馆 Donglan County Revolution Memorial Hall	1993 年征集于广西东兰长江乡板隆村 Unearthed at Banlong Village, Changjiang, Donglan County, Guangxi in 1993	鼓面：太阳纹（12 芒）、西字形纹、云纹、乳钉纹、双龙游旗纹及"万代进宝、永世家财"铭文、缠枝纹；鼓身：乳钉纹、云纹、回形复线三角纹；扁耳两对饰辫纹、回形雷纹、卐字纹 Drum face: patterns of sun(12rays), 西 -character, cloud, nipple protrusion, patterns group of 2 dragons, flying flag and"万代进宝、永世家财"-character, twisted branches; Drum body: patterns of nipple protrusion, cloud, 回 -shape double line triangle; Braid, 回 -shape thunder and 卐 -character patterns on 2 pairs of flat handles.	48－48.2	26.3	麻江型 Majiang Type	
743	总 0212 号 分 048 号 三角斜线纹鼓 No.0212 Classified No.048 Bronze Drum with triangle mixed oblique lines pattern	东兰县革命纪念馆 Donglan County Revolution Memorial Hall	1996 年 10 月 28 日征集于广西大化县板兰乡可考村弄平屯 Unearthed at Nongping Tun, Kekao Village, Banlan, Dahua County, Guangxi on October 28th, 1996	鼓面：太阳纹（12 芒）、同心圆纹、四瓣花纹、羽纹、乳钉纹、三角填斜线纹、水波纹、绚纹；鼓身：弦纹；扁耳两对饰弦纹 Drum face: patterns of sun(12rays), concentric circle, quatrefoil, feather, nipple protrusion, triangle filled with oblique lines, water wave, twisted rope; Drum body: patterns of string; String patterns on 2 pairs of flat handles	48－48.5	28	麻江型 Majiang Type	

续表

序号 NO.	原编号及鼓名 Stock Number & Name	收藏单位 Museum	出土（征集）时间、地点 Time & Spot for discovered or collected	主要装饰 Main Decorations	尺寸（厘米） Size(cm)		类型 Type	图片 Picture
					面径 Face Diameter	身高 Height		
744	兰阳一号 Bronze Drum Lanyang No.1	东兰兰阳村韦克锋私藏 Private collection	广西东兰县长江乡兰阳村韦克锋私藏 The private stock of Wei Kefeng, a villager of Lanyang Village, Donglan County, Guangxi	鼓面：太阳纹（12 芒）、同心圆纹、回形雷纹、乳钉纹、桂鱼人物纹、图案云纹、人物、回形雷、同心圆组合图案内壁有房屋等图案； 鼓身：乳钉纹、同心圆纹、回形雷纹、如意云纹、图案云纹、复线三角纹；扁耳两对饰辫纹 Drum face: patterns of sun(12rays), concentric circle, 回 -shape thunder, nipple protrusion, mandarin fish and person, motif cloud, patterns group of person, 回 -shape thunder and concentric circle, there're some pattern like house inside; Drum body: patterns of nipple protrusion, concentric circle, 回 -shape thunder, Ruyi-shape cloud, motif cloud, double line triangle; Braid patterns on 2 pairs of flat handles.	45.5	27.5	麻江型 Majiang Type	
745	046 号 荷耙人纹铜鼓 No.046 Bronze Drum with hoer patterns	金城江文物管理所 Jincheng-jiang Cultural Relics Administration	1991 年原广西县级河池市公安局移交 Transferred by Guangxi Hechi City Public Security Bureau in 1991	鼓面：太阳纹（12 芒）、栉纹、四出钱纹、乳钉纹、荷耙人、回形雷、符篆、团寿、牛、鹤、四出钱组合图案纹、如意云纹、云纹； 鼓身：乳钉纹、如意云纹、云纹、复线三角纹；扁耳两对饰辫纹 Drum face: patterns of sun(12rays), comb line, coin with quadrangle inside, patterns group of hoer, 回 -shape thunder, Ofuda, round 寿 -character, ox, crane and coin with quadrangle inside, Ruyi-shape cloud, cloud; Drum body: patterns of nipple protrusion, Ruyi-shape cloud, cloud, double line triangle; Braid patterns on 2 pairs of flat handles.	47.1−47.4	27.4	麻江型 Majiang Type	
746	105 号 清麻江型铜鼓 No.105 Qing Dynasty Bronze Drum in Majinag Type	南丹县文物管理所 Nandan County Cultural Relics Administration	1992 年征集于吾隘镇独田村 Collected at Dutian Village, Wuai Town, Nandan County in 1992	鼓面：太阳纹（12 芒）、回形雷纹、栉纹、乳钉纹、游旗纹、卦纹； 鼓身：梅花状乳钉纹、四出钱纹、回形雷纹、S 云纹、复线三角纹；扁耳两对饰辫纹 Drum face: patterns of sun(12rays), 回 -shape thunder, comb line, nipple protrusion, flying flag, divinatory symbol; Drum body: patterns of nipple protrusion in plum-blossom shape, coin with quadrangle inside, 回 -shape thunder, S-shape cloud, double line triangle; Braid patterns on 2 pairs of flat handles.	32.8	19	麻江型 Majiang Type	

续表

序号 N0.	原编号及鼓名 Stock Number & Name	收藏单位 Museum	出土（征集） 时间、地点 Time & Spot for discovered or collected	主要装饰 Main Decorations	尺寸（厘米） Size(cm)		类型 Type	图片 Picture
					面径 Face Diameter	身高 Height		
747	汉行走鹭纹铜鼓（大） Han Dynasty Bronze Drum with walking heron patterns (big)	宜州市博物馆 Yizhou City Museum	1995 年出土于广西宜州市西郊约20 公里怀远镇冲英屯 Unearthed at Chongying Tun, Huaiyuan Town, in west of 20km to Yizhou City, Guangxi in 1995	鼓面：太阳纹（12 芒）、复线三角纹、切线同心圆纹、栉纹、复线交叉纹、变形羽人纹、行走鹭鸟纹间定胜纹； 鼓身：栉纹、切线同心圆纹、栉纹切线同心圆纹垂直纹带、羽纹、圆心三角垂叶纹；扁耳两对纹饰磨蚀；鼓断裂为若干残片 Drum face: patterns of sun(12rays), double line triangle, tangent concentric circles, comb line, crossed double lines, transformed feathermen, walking heron mixed Dingsheng; Drum body: patterns of comb line, tangent concentric circles, vertical ribbon of straight line and tangent concentric circles, feather, leaf-shape triangle with concentric circles in the middle; patterns on 2 pairs of flat handles are rusting; The whole drum was broken into pieces.	49－49.7	（残） Incomplete	冷水冲型 Lengshui-chong Type	
748	汉行走鹭纹铜鼓（小） Han Dynasty Bronze Drum with walking heron patterns (small)	宜州市博物馆 Yizhou City Museum	1995 年出土于广西宜州市西郊约20 公里怀远镇冲英屯 Unearthed at Chongying Tun, Huaiyuan Town, in west of 20km to Yizhou City, Guangxi in 1995	鼓面：太阳纹（12 芒）、勾连雷纹、切线同心圆纹、栉纹、行走鹭鸟纹间定胜纹； 鼓身：栉纹、切线同心圆纹、栉纹切线同心圆纹垂直纹带、三角垂叶纹；扁耳两对饰辫纹； Drum face: patterns of sun(12rays), hooked thunder, tangent concentric circles, comb line, walking heron mixed Dingsheng; Drum body: patterns of comb line, tangent concentric circles, vertical ribbon of straight line and tangent concentric circles, leaf-shape triangle with concentric circles in the middle; Braid patterns on 2 pairs of flat handles.	33.2－33.8	24.6 （残） Incomplete	冷水冲型 Lengshui-chong Type	

序号 N0.	原编号及鼓名 Stock Number & Name	收藏单位 Museum	出土（征集）时间、地点 Time & Spot for discovered or collected	主要装饰 Main Decorations	尺寸（厘米）Size(cm)		类型 Type	图片 Picture
					面径 Face Diameter	身高 Height		
749	东汉蹲蛙翔鹭纹铜鼓 East-Han Dynasty Bronze Drum with frog statue and flying heron patterns	宜州市博物馆 Yizhou City Museum	70年代出土于广西原宜山县矮山乡良山屯 Unearthed at Liangshan Tun, Aishan, Yishan County, Guangxi in 1970s'	鼓面：太阳纹（10芒）、水波纹、同心圆纹、栉纹、复线交叉纹、变形羽人纹、变形翔鹭纹、切线同心圆纹，鼓面边缘饰四只逆时针立蛙；鼓身：栉纹、同心圆纹、栉纹同心圆纹垂直纹带、水波纹、圆心三角垂叶纹；扁耳两对饰辫纹；Drum face: patterns of sun(10rays), water wave, concentric circles, comb line, crossed double lines, transformed feathermen, transformed flying heron, tangent concentric circles; 4 frog statues stand anticlockwise on the edge of drum face; Drum body: patterns of comb line, concentric circles, vertical ribbon of straight line and concentric circles, water wave, leaf-shape triangle with concentric circles in the middle; Braids pattern on 2 pairs of flat handles.	66.4~66.8	44.7	冷水冲型 Lengshui-chong Type	
750	宜 A015 清双龙献珠纹铜鼓 Yi No.A015 Qing Dynasty Bronze Drum with 2 dragons playing pearl patterns	宜州市博物馆 Yizhou City Museum	1991年广西宜州市公安局移交 Transferred by Guangxi Yizhou City Public Security Bureau in 1991	鼓面：太阳纹（10芒）、S形云纹、云纹、乳钉纹、双龙献珠纹及"万代进宝、永世家财"铭文、雷纹；鼓身：云纹、回形雷纹、雷纹、复线三角纹；扁耳两对饰辫纹 Drum face: patterns of sun(10rays), S-shape cloud, cloud, nipple protrusion, 2 dragons playing pearl and "万代进宝、永世家财"-character, thunder; Drum body: patterns of cloud, 回-shape thunder, thunder, double line triangle; Braid patterns on 2 pairs of flat handles.	47.3~47.4	26.5	麻江型 Majiang Type	
751	清游旗纹铜鼓 Qing Dynasty Bronze Drum with flying flag patterns	宜州市博物馆 Yizhou City Museum	1988年宜州市纺织机械配件厂征购 Collected at Yizhou City Textile Machinery Accessories Plant in 1988	鼓面：太阳纹（12芒）、西字纹、乳钉纹、游旗纹、回形雷纹、栉纹；鼓身：乳钉纹、云纹、回形雷纹、雷纹、复线三角纹；扁耳两对饰辫纹 Drum face: patterns of sun(12rays), 西-character, nipple protrusion, flying flag, 回-shape thunder, comb line; Drum body: patterns of nipple protrusion, cloud, 回-shape thunder, thunder, double line triangle; Braid patterns on 2 pairs of flat handles.	48.5	27.5	麻江型 Majiang Type	

序号 N0.	原编号及鼓名 Stock Number & Name	收藏单位 Museum	出土（征集）时间、地点 Time & Spot for discovered or collected	主要装饰 Main Decorations	尺寸（厘米）Size(cm)		类型 Type	图片 Picture
					面径 Face Diameter	身高 Height		
752	总0328号 游旗纹铜鼓 No.0328 Bronze Drum with flying flag patterns	环江毛南族自治县博物馆 Huanjiang Maonan Autonomous County	2004年6月14日征集于广西环江驯乐乡平莫村 Collected at Pingmo Village, Xunle, Huanjiang County, Guangxi on June 14th, 2004	鼓面：太阳纹（12芒）、酉字纹、S形云纹、乳钉纹、栉纹、游旗纹、兽面云纹、卦纹； 鼓身：乳钉纹、如意云纹、云纹、回形雷纹、栉纹、复线三角纹；扁耳两对饰辫纹、回形雷纹 Drum face: patterns of sun(12rays), 酉-character, S-shape cloud, nipple protrusion, comb line, flying flag, beast-face cloud, divinatory symbol; Drum body: patterns of nipple protrusion, Ruyi-shape cloud, cloud, 回-shape thunder, comb line, double line triangle; Braid and 回-shape thunder patterns on 2 pairs of flat handles.	50.5	28.5	麻江型 Majiang Type	
753	0132号 游旗纹铜鼓 No.0132 Bronze Drum with flying flag patterns	巴马县文物管理所 Bama County Cultural Relics Administration	1997年5月5日征集于广西东兰县东山乡 Collected at Dongshan, Donglan County, Guangxi on May 5th, 1997	鼓面：太阳纹（12芒）、酉字纹、乳钉纹、游旗纹、回形雷纹、云纹； 鼓身：乳钉纹、回形雷纹、云纹、复线三角纹；扁耳两对饰辫纹、回形雷纹 Drum face: patterns of sun(12rays), 酉-character, nipple protrusion, flying flag, 回-shape thunder, cloud; Drum body: patterns of nipple protrusion, cloud, 回-shape thunder, double line triangle; Braid and 回-shape thunder patterns on 2 pairs of flat handles.	49.3	26.3	麻江型 Majiang Type	

续表

序号 N0.	原编号及鼓名 Stock Number & Name	收藏单位 Museum	出土（征集） 时间、地点 Time & Spot for discovered or collected	主要装饰 Main Decorations	尺寸（厘米） Size(cm)		类型 Type	图片 Picture
					面径 Face Diameter	身高 Height		
754	古防鼓 Bronze Drum Gufang	兴宾区文物管理所 Xingbin District Cultural Relics Administration	1989 年 7 月出土于广西来宾北五乡白山上马寨村西北古防崖容村山东坡 Unearthed at the east hillside of Rong Village, Gufang Ya, in the northwest to Shangmazhai Village, Baishan, Beiwu, Laibin City, Guangxi in July, 1989	鼓面：太阳纹（12 芒）、栉纹、同心圆、复线交叉纹、变形羽人纹、变形翔鹭间定胜纹；鼓面边缘饰四只逆时针四足素面立体蛙；鼓身：栉纹、同心圆纹、栉纹同心圆纹垂直纹带、圆心三角垂叶纹；扁耳两对饰辫纹 Drum face: patterns of sun(12rays), comb line, concentric circles, crossed double lines, transformed feathermen, transformed flying heron mixed Dingsheng; 4 frog statues of 4 feet and blank back stand anticlockwise on the edge of drum face; Drum body: patterns of comb line, concentric circles, vertical ribbon of straight line and concentric circle, leaf-shape triangle with circle in the middle; Braid patterns on 2 pairs of flat handles.	80–81.7	54.2	冷水冲型 Lengshui-chong Type	
755	总 0834 号 分 0030 号 石崖村鼓 No.0834 Classified No.0030 Bronze Drum Shiya	武宣县博物馆 Wuxuan County Museum	1988 年 1 月出土于广西武宣东乡乡石崖村 Unearthed at Shiya Village, Dongxiang, Wuxuan County, Guangxi in January, 1988	鼓面：太阳纹（12 芒）、水波纹、栉纹、同心圆纹、叶脉纹、复线交叉纹、变形羽人纹、变形翔鹭纹、眼纹；鼓面边缘饰四只逆时针四足辫纹立体蛙，两蛙间饰一立体鸟；鼓身：水波纹、叶脉纹、同心圆纹、船纹、变形羽人纹、网纹、圆心三角垂叶纹、眼纹；扁耳两对饰辫纹，有附耳 Drum face: patterns of sun(12rays), water wave, comb line, concentric circles, leaf vein, crossed double lines, transformed feathermen, transformed flying heron, diamond-shape eye; 4 frog statues of 4 feet, braid patterns on back, stand anticlockwise on the edge of drum face; a bird statue stands between the frogs. Drum body: patterns of water wave, leaf vein, concentric circles, boat, transformed feathermen, net, leaf-shape triangle with circle in the middle, diamond-shape eye; Braid patterns on 2 pairs of flat handles; a pair of attached handles.	72.1–72.7	53.4	冷水冲型 Lengshui-chong Type	

序号 NO.	原编号及鼓名 Stock Number & Name	收藏单位 Museum	出土（征集） 时间、地点 Time & Spot for discovered or collected	主要装饰 Main Decorations	尺寸（厘米） Size(cm)		类型 Type	图片 Picture
					面径 Face Diameter	身高 Height		
756	总0060号 分035号 寺村鼓 No.0060 Classified No.035 Bronze Drum Sicun	象州县博物馆 Xiangzhou County Museum	1974年4月7日出土于广西象州寺村镇寺村小学 Unearthed at Sicun Primary School, Sicun Town, Xiangzhou County, Guangxi on April 7th, 1974	鼓面：太阳纹（12芒）、水波纹、同心圆纹、栉纹、复线交叉纹、叶脉纹、变形羽人纹、变形翔鹭纹、眼纹；鼓面边缘饰四只逆时针四足辫纹立体蛙，两蛙间各饰一立体鱼，鱼栓于柱子上； 鼓身：水波纹、同心圆纹、叶脉纹、船纹（有鱼）、变形羽人纹、网纹、圆心三角垂叶纹、眼纹；扁耳两对饰辫纹，有附耳 Drum face: patterns of sun(12rays), water wave, concentric circles, comb line, crossed double lines, leaf vein, transformed feathermen, transformed flying heron, diamond-shape eye; 4 frog statues of 4 feet, braid patterns on back, stand anticlockwise on the edge of drum face; 2 fish statues stand between the frogs, tails tied on a pole. Drum body: patterns of water wave, concentric circles, leaf vein, boat(with fish inside), transformed feathermen, net, leaf-shape triangle with circle in the middle, diamond-shape eye; Braid patterns on 2 pairs of flat handles; a pair of attached handles.	80.2–81	57	冷水冲型 Lengshui-chong Type	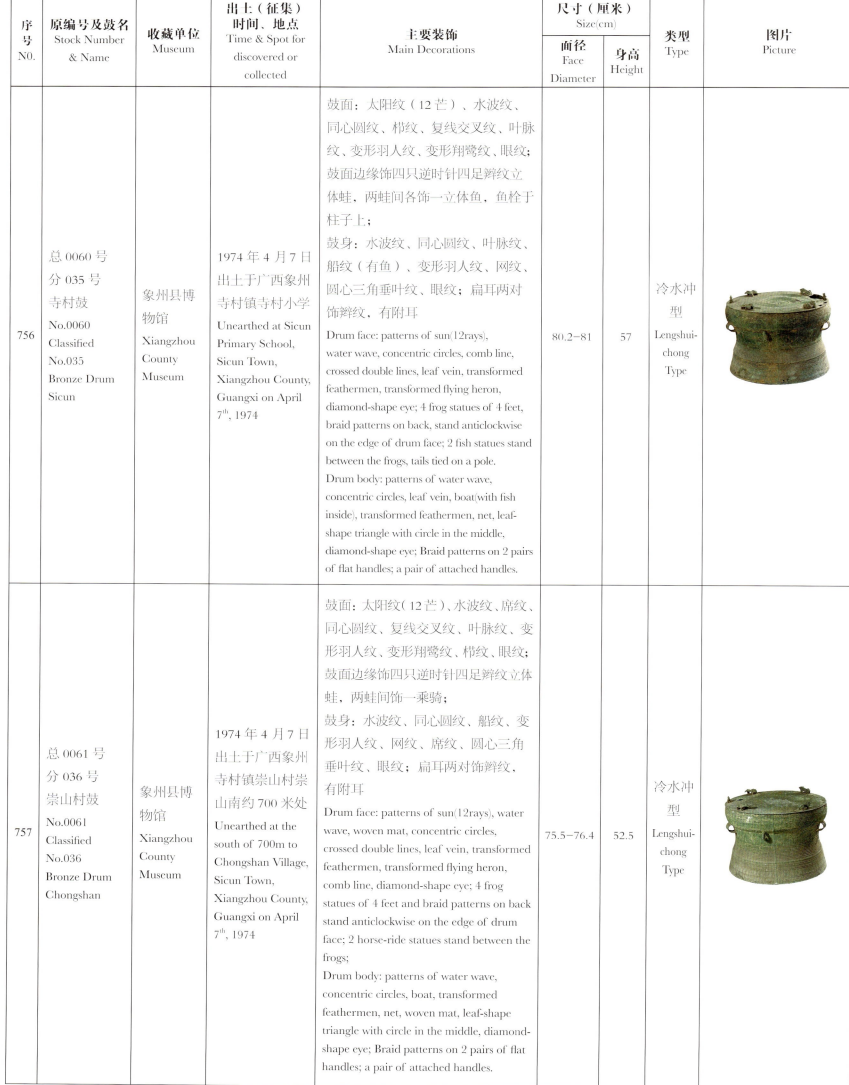
757	总0061号 分036号 崇山村鼓 No.0061 Classified No.036 Bronze Drum Chongshan	象州县博物馆 Xiangzhou County Museum	1974年4月7日出土于广西象州寺村镇崇山村崇山南约700米处 Unearthed at the south of 700m to Chongshan Village, Sicun Town, Xiangzhou County, Guangxi on April 7th, 1974	鼓面：太阳纹（12芒）、水波纹、席纹、同心圆纹、复线交叉纹、叶脉纹、变形羽人纹、变形翔鹭纹、栉纹、眼纹；鼓面边缘饰四只逆时针四足辫纹立体蛙，两蛙间饰一乘骑； 鼓身：水波纹、同心圆纹、船纹、变形羽人纹、网纹、席纹、圆心三角垂叶纹、眼纹；扁耳两对饰辫纹，有附耳 Drum face: patterns of sun(12rays), water wave, woven mat, concentric circles, crossed double lines, leaf vein, transformed feathermen, transformed flying heron, comb line, diamond-shape eye; 4 frog statues of 4 feet and braid patterns on back stand anticlockwise on the edge of drum face; 2 horse-ride statues stand between the frogs; Drum body: patterns of water wave, concentric circles, boat, transformed feathermen, net, woven mat, leaf-shape triangle with circle in the middle, diamond-shape eye; Braid patterns on 2 pairs of flat handles; a pair of attached handles.	75.5–76.4	52.5	冷水冲型 Lengshui-chong Type	

续表

序号 NO.	原编号及鼓名 Stock Number & Name	收藏单位 Museum	出土（征集）时间、地点 Time & Spot for discovered or collected	主要装饰 Main Decorations	尺寸（厘米）Size(cm)		类型 Type	图片 Picture
					面径 Face Diameter	身高 Height		
758	总 0062 号 分 037 号 苏村鼓 No.0062 Classified No.037 Bronze Drum Shucun	象州县博物馆 Xiangzhou County Museum	1989 年 1 月出土于广西象州中平乡苏村约 500 米水田中 Unearthed in a water field,500m beside Su Village, Zhongping, Xiangzhou County, Guangxi in January, 1989	鼓面：太阳纹（12 芒）、栉纹、同心圆纹、复线交叉纹、变形羽人纹、变形翔鹭纹、眼纹；鼓面边缘饰四只逆时针四足辫纹立体蛙、两蛙间分饰一乘骑和一立体马；鼓身：栉纹、同心圆纹、船纹、变形羽人纹、网纹、圆心三角垂叶纹；扁耳两对饰辫纹 Drum face: patterns of sun(12rays), comb line, concentric circles, crossed double lines, transformed feathermen, transformed flying heron, diamond-shape eye; 4 frog statues of 4 feet and braid patterns on back stand anticlockwise on the edge of drum face; a horse-ride statue and a horse statue stand between the frogs; Drum body: patterns of comb line, concentric circles, boat, transformed feathermen, net, leaf-shape triangle with circle in the middle; Braid patterns on 2 pairs of flat handles.	64.2−65	40.8 （残）Incomplete	冷水冲型 Lengshui-chong Type	
759	总 0727 号 分 048 号 罗汉村鼓 No.0727 Classified No.048 Bronze Drum Luohan Cun	象州县博物馆 Xiangzhou County Museum	1976 年 12 月出土于广西象州中平乡罗汉村南约 500 米水田中 Unearthed in a water field, the south of 500m to Luohan Village, Zhongping, Xiangzhou County, Guangxi in December, 1976	鼓面：太阳纹（12 芒）、水波纹、栉纹、同心圆纹、复线交叉纹、叶脉纹、变形羽人纹、变形翔鹭间定胜纹、眼纹；鼓面边缘饰四只逆时针四足辫纹立蛙，两蛙间分饰一单乘骑、一组三乘骑和一组立体牛；鼓身：水波纹、栉纹、同心圆纹、船纹、变形羽人纹、网纹、圆心三角垂叶纹；扁耳两对饰辫纹，有附耳 Drum face: patterns of sun(12rays), water wave, comb line, concentric circles, crossed double lines, leaf vein, transformed feathermen, transformed flying heron mixed Dingsheng, diamond-shape eye; 4 frog statues of 4 feet and braid patterns on back stand anticlockwise on the edge of drum face; a horse-ride by one man statue, 3 horse-riders, and an ox statue stand between the frogs; Drum body: patterns of water wave, comb line, concentric circles, boat, transformed feathermen, net, leaf-shape triangle with circle in the middle; Braid patterns on 2 pairs of flat handles; a pair of attached handles.	88.3−89	53.5 （残）Incomplete	冷水冲型 Lengshui-chong Type	

序号 N0.	原编号及鼓名 Stock Number & Name	收藏单位 Museum	出土（征集）时间、地点 Time & Spot for discovered or collected	主要装饰 Main Decorations	尺寸（厘米）Size(cm)		类型 Type	图片 Picture
					面径 Face Diameter	身高 Height		
760	总0751号 分050号 大普化村鼓 No.0751 Classified No.050 Bronze Drum Dapuhua	象州县博物馆 Xiangzhou County Museum	1991年11月20日出土于广西象州中平乡大普化村北约100米处 Unearthed in the north of 100m to Dapuhua Village, Zhongping, Xiangzhou County, Guangxi on November 20th, 1991	鼓面：太阳纹（12芒）、水波纹、同心圆、栉纹、复线交叉纹、叶脉纹、变形羽人纹、变形翔鹭纹、眼纹；鼓面边缘饰四只逆时针四足辫纹立体蛙，两蛙间各饰一立体鱼，鱼栓于柱子上；鼓身：水波纹、同心圆纹、叶脉纹、船纹（有鱼）、变形羽人纹、网纹、圆心三角垂叶纹、眼纹；扁耳两对饰辫纹，有附耳 Drum face: patterns of sun(12rays), water wave, concentric circles, comb line, crossed double lines, leaf vein, transformed feathermen, transformed flying heron, diamond-shape eye; 4 frog statues of 4 feet and braid patterns on back stand anticlockwise on the edge of drum face; 2 fish statues stand between the frogs, tails tied on a pole; Drum body: patterns of water wave, concentric circles, leaf vein, boat(with fish inside), transformed feathermen, net, leaf-shape triangle with circle in the middle, diamond-shape eye; Braid patterns on 2 pairs of flat handles; a pair of attached handles.	81.6-82	57.5	冷水冲型 Lengshui-chong Type	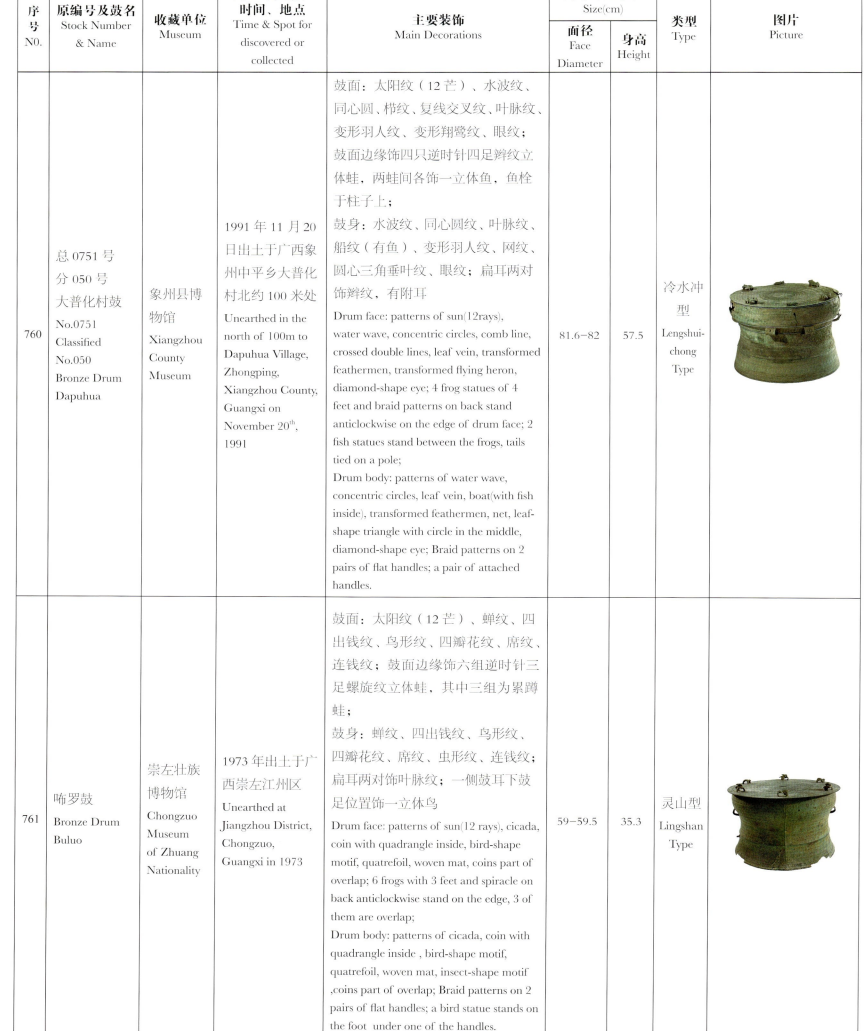
761	咘罗鼓 Bronze Drum Buluo	崇左壮族博物馆 Chongzuo Museum of Zhuang Nationality	1973年出土于广西崇左江州区 Unearthed at Jiangzhou District, Chongzuo, Guangxi in 1973	鼓面：太阳纹（12芒）、蝉纹、四出钱纹、鸟形纹、四瓣花纹、席纹、连钱纹；鼓面边缘饰六组逆时针三足螺旋纹立体蛙，其中三组为累蹲蛙；鼓身：蝉纹、四出钱纹、鸟形纹、四瓣花纹、席纹、虫形纹、连钱纹；扁耳两对饰叶脉纹；一侧鼓耳下鼓足位置饰一立体鸟 Drum face: patterns of sun(12 rays), cicada, coin with quadrangle inside, bird-shape motif, quatrefoil, woven mat, coins part of overlap; 6 frogs with 3 feet and spiracle on back anticlockwise stand on the edge, 3 of them are overlap; Drum body: patterns of cicada, coin with quadrangle inside , bird-shape motif, quatrefoil, woven mat, insect-shape motif ,coins part of overlap; Braid patterns on 2 pairs of flat handles; a bird statue stands on the foot under one of the handles.	59-59.5	35.3	灵山型 Lingshan Type	

续表

序号 NO.	原编号及鼓名 Stock Number & Name	收藏单位 Museum	出土（征集）时间、地点 Time & Spot for discovered or collected	主要装饰 Main Decorations	尺寸（厘米）Size(cm)		类型 Type	图片 Picture
					面径 Face Diameter	身高 Height		
762	慢侣鼓 Bronze Drum Manlv	大新县博物馆 Daxin County Museum	1993年10月22日出土于广西大新县桃城镇大塘村慢侣屯 Unearthed at Manlv Tun, Taocheng Town, Daxin County, Guangxi on October 22nd, 1993	鼓面：太阳纹（12芒）、水波纹、同心圆纹、栉纹、复线交叉纹、变形羽人纹、叶脉纹、变形翔鹭纹；鼓面边缘饰四只逆时针四足线条纹立体蛙，两蛙间有立体装饰痕迹；鼓身：叶脉纹、栉纹、同心圆纹、船纹、变形羽人纹、水波纹、网纹、圆心三角垂叶纹；扁耳两对饰辫纹 Drum face: patterns of sun(12rays), water wave, concentric circles, comb line, crossed double lines, transformed feathermen, leaf vein, transformed flying heron;4 frog statues of 4 feet and strings on back anticlockwise stand on the edge of drum face, other statue marks between them; Drum body: patterns of leaf vein, comb line, concentric circles, boat, transformed feathermen, water wave, net, leaf-shape triangle with concentric circles in the middle; Braids pattern on 2 pairs of flat handles.	69-70	47	冷水冲型 Lengshui-chong Type	
763	麻江型 I 雷纹铜鼓 Bronze Drum with thunder pattern Majiang Type I	大新县博物馆 Daxin County Museum	1995年征集于河池地区 Collected in Hechi area in 1995	鼓面：太阳纹（12芒）、回形雷纹、同心圆纹、乳钉纹、团花纹；鼓身：同心圆纹、回形雷纹、如意云纹、云纹、三角垂叶纹；扁耳两对无纹饰 Drum face: patterns of sun(12rays), 回-shape thunder, concentric circle, nipple protrusion, flower fluster; Drum body: patterns of concentric circle, 回-shape thunder, Ruyi-shape cloud, cloud, leaf-shape triangle; 2 pairs of blank flat handles.	44.5	25.5	麻江型 Majiang Type	
764	麻江型 II 游旗纹铜鼓 Bronze Drum with flying flag pattern Majiang Type II	大新县博物馆 Daxin County Museum	1995年征集于河池地区 Collected in Hechi area in 1995	鼓面：太阳纹（12芒）、西字纹、S形云纹、乳钉纹、游旗纹、栉纹、兽形云纹；鼓身：乳钉纹、回形雷纹、如意纹、栉纹、三角垂叶纹；扁耳两对饰辫纹、回形雷纹 Drum face: patterns of sun(12rays), 西-character, S-shape cloud, nipple protrusion, flying flag, comb line, beast-shape cloud; Drum body: patterns of nipple protrusion, 回-shape thunder, Ruyi, comb line, leaf-shape triangle; Braid and 回-shape thunder on 2 pairs of flat handles.	47.5	27	麻江型 Majiang Type	

序号 N0.	原编号及鼓名 Stock Number & Name	收藏单位 Museum	出土（征集） 时间、地点 Time & Spot for discovered or collected	主要装饰 Main Decorations	尺寸（厘米） Size(cm)		类型 Type	图片 Picture
					面径 Face Diameter	身高 Height		
765	武德鼓 Bronze Drum Wude	龙州红八军纪念馆 Longzhou Memorial Hall for the Eighth Red Army	1996 年 11 月 2 日出土于广西龙州武德村空定屯 Unearthed at Kongding Tun, Wude Village, Longzhou, Guangxi on November 2nd, 1996	鼓面：太阳纹（12 芒）、栉纹、同心圆纹、复线交叉纹、变形羽人纹、变形翔鹭纹间定胜纹；鼓面边缘饰四只逆时针四足素面立体蛙；鼓身：栉纹、同心圆纹、栉纹同心圆纹垂直纹带、圆心三角垂叶纹；扁耳两对饰辫纹 Drum face: patterns of sun(12rays), comb line, concentric circles, crossed double lines, transformed feathermen, transformed flying heron mixed Dingsheng;4 frog statues of 4 feet and blank back anticlockwise stand on the edge of drum face; Drum body: patterns of comb line, concentric circles, vertical ribbon of straight line and concentric circle, leaf-shape triangle with concentric circles in the middle; Braids pattern on 2 pairs of flat handles.	62—63	42（残） Incomplete	冷水冲型 Lengshui-chong Type	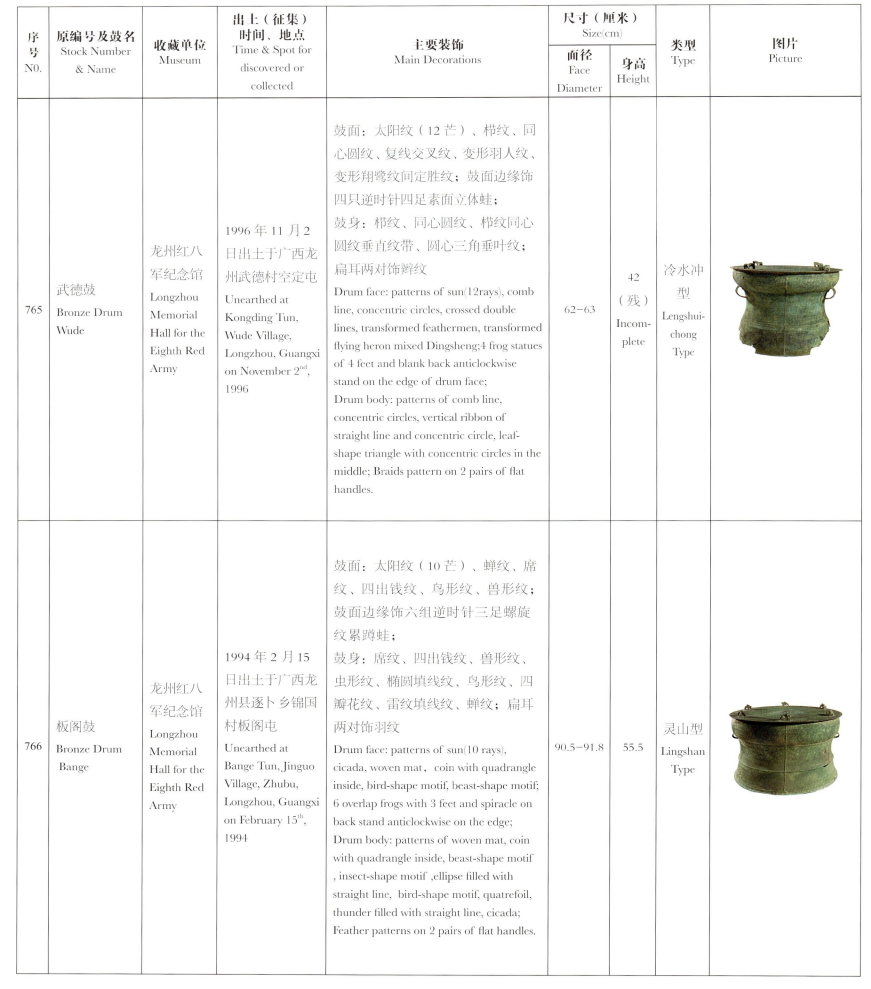
766	板阁鼓 Bronze Drum Bange	龙州红八军纪念馆 Longzhou Memorial Hall for the Eighth Red Army	1994 年 2 月 15 日出土于广西龙州县逐卜乡锦国村板阁屯 Unearthed at Bange Tun, Jinguo Village, Zhubu, Longzhou, Guangxi on February 15th, 1994	鼓面：太阳纹（10 芒）、蝉纹、席纹、四出钱纹、鸟形纹、兽形纹；鼓面边缘饰六组逆时针三足螺旋纹累蹲蛙；鼓身：席纹、四出钱纹、兽形纹、虫形纹、椭圆填线纹、鸟形纹、四瓣花纹、雷纹填线纹、蝉纹；扁耳两对饰羽纹 Drum face: patterns of sun(10 rays), cicada, woven mat, coin with quadrangle inside, bird-shape motif, beast-shape motif; 6 overlap frogs with 3 feet and spiracle on back stand anticlockwise on the edge; Drum body: patterns of woven mat, coin with quadrangle inside, beast-shape motif , insect-shape motif ,ellipse filled with straight line, bird-shape motif, quatrefoil, thunder filled with straight line, cicada; Feather patterns on 2 pairs of flat handles.	90.5—91.8	55.5	灵山型 Lingshan Type	

序号 N0.	原编号及鼓名 Stock Number & Name	收藏单位 Museum	出土（征集） 时间、地点 Time & Spot for discovered or collected	主要装饰 Main Decorations	尺寸（厘米） Size(cm)		类型 Type	图片 Picture
					面径 Face Diameter	身高 Height		
767	五铢钱纹铜鼓 Bronze Drum with Wuzhu coin pattern	国家博物 馆 National Museum of China	广西壮族自治区 博物馆调拨 Allocated from Museum of Guangxi Zhuang Autonomous Region	鼓面：太阳纹（12芒），云纹、水波纹、五铢钱纹；鼓面边缘饰四只素面立体青蛙； 鼓身：水波纹、云纹、五铢钱纹；扁耳两对饰辫纹 Drum face: patterns of sun(12rays), cloud, water wave, Wuzhu Coin;4 frog statues of blank back stand on the edge of drum face; Drum body: patterns of water wave, cloud, Wuzhu Coin; Braids pattern on 2 pairs of flat handles.	90	53	北流型 BeiliuType	
768	土0281 西林281号鼓 Tu No.0281 Bronze Drum Xilin No.281	北京民族 文化宫 Beijing Cultural Palace of Nationalities	1972年7月出土 于百色市西林县 普驮村铜鼓墓葬 Unearthed in bronze drum burials at Putuo Village, Xilin County, Baise City in July,1972	鼓面：太阳纹（12芒），勾连雷纹、圆点圆圈纹、翔鹭纹、栉纹； 鼓身：翔鹭纹、羽人纹、锯齿圆点纹带；扁耳两对饰辫纹 Drum face: patterns of sun(12rays), hooked thunder, dots and circles, flying heron, comb line; Drum body: patterns of flying heron, featherman, saw teeth and dots pattern ribbon; Braids pattern on 2 pairs of flat handles.	72	49	石寨山 型 Shizhai- shan Type	
769	乘骑变形羽人纹铜鼓 Bronze Drum with transformed feathermen patterns and horse-riding statues	北京民族 文化宫 TheCultural Palace of Nationalities	广西壮族自治区 博物馆调拨 Allocated from Museum of Guangxi Zhuang Autonomous Region	鼓面：太阳纹（12芒），水波纹、复线交叉纹、同心圆纹、栉纹、羽纹、变形羽人纹、变形翔鹭纹、眼纹；鼓面边缘饰四只辫纹立体青蛙，蛙间分别饰双乘骑立体装饰 鼓身：栉纹、同心圆纹、变形船纹、变形羽人纹、水波纹、网纹、圆心垂叶纹、眼纹；扁耳两对饰辫纹，另有一对环附耳 Drum face: patterns of sun(12rays), water wave, crossed double lines, concentric circles, comb line, feather, transformed feathermen, transformed flying heron, eyes;4 frog statues with braid patterns on back stand on the edge of drum face, 2 groups statues of double horse-riders between the frogs ; Drum body: patterns of comb line, concentric circles, transformed boat, transformed feathermen, water wave, net, leaf-shape triangle with concentric circles in the middle, eyes; Braids pattern on 2 pairs of flat handles, with a pair of ring handles.	77.5	53.5	冷水冲 型 Lengshui- chong Type	

后　记

　　1979 年至 1980 年，广西壮族自治区博物馆组成中国古代铜鼓调查小组，对全国馆藏铜鼓进行了普查，获得了 1383 面铜鼓的珍贵数据，其中广西各级文物单位所藏铜鼓共 503 面，位居全国第一。在此基础上，1988 年 5 月，广西壮族自治区博物馆对全区馆藏铜鼓以及区外有关单位收藏的广西铜鼓共 610 面进行信息采集，并编辑出版了《广西铜鼓图录》，为铜鼓研究做出了贡献。

　　受限于经费和条件，过去两次调查所采集的照片绝大部分是黑白胶片。再者近十年来，因出土、征集等原因，广西馆藏铜鼓数量有所增长。有鉴于此，中国古代铜鼓研究会理事长覃溥女士提出再开展一次全国铜鼓收藏情况调查，力争全面地将我国铜鼓发现的资料搜集存档。经广西壮族自治区文化厅批准，由中国古代铜鼓研究会、广西民族博物馆牵头，会同广西壮族自治区博物馆组成调查组，开展了广西馆藏铜鼓调查记录项目。项目负责人是中国古代铜鼓研究会理事长覃溥女士。成员共 12 人，其中广西民族博物馆 5 人，分别是农学坚、梁燕理、陆秋燕、刘文毅、陈嘉；广西壮族自治区博物馆 6 人，分别是蒋廷瑜、吴崇基、王梦祥、罗坤馨、蔡荭、李永春。自 2014 年 4 月至 12 月，项目组行程近万公里，调查了广西 14 个设区市，57 个市、县（区），62 家文物收藏单位的 772 面铜鼓，采集了极为珍贵的第一手资料。调查工作结束后，广西民族博物馆的 5 位同志在资料整理和编辑出版过程中承担了大部分重要工作。其中，农学坚副馆长是该项目的执行组织者，负责项目推进；梁燕理同志是该书原始资料的调查者和整理者，铜鼓资料说明及附录部分的第一撰稿人，负责全书的文字撰写和多次校对以及出版相关统筹事宜；陆秋燕同志也是该书原始资料的调查者和整理者，参与铜鼓资料说明的文字撰写，并负责该书全部文字资料的英文翻译及校对；富霞同志承担了该书大部分文字校对工作；刘文毅同志与王梦祥老师一道为该书的铜鼓拍摄做出了贡献。

　　作为该项目的成果之一，本书就广西铜鼓的总体情况进行概述，对 2014 年全区铜鼓调查进行综述，根据铜鼓"八分法"选取出土或征集于广西境内的八大类型、具有代表性和较高历史艺术价值的 167 面铜鼓，配以实物高清全景图和细部图，辅以简单文字说明，并附有按广西行政区划归纳整理的广西馆藏铜鼓一览表（调查的 772 面铜鼓，有 1 面破碎，2 面属于越南铜鼓，故该表共收入 769 面铜鼓）。全书为中英双语，以期通过翔实的资料、高清的图片来展现广西丰富的铜鼓资源，为铜鼓科研和教学提供系统、完善的基本信息。但由于我们水平有限，经验不足，错漏、粗疏之处在所难免，诚恳期待国内外同行和广大读者批评指正。

　　本书编辑出版过程中，得到了社会各界的关注和支持，尤其是广西 62 家文物收藏单位在铜鼓原始资料搜集和实地拍摄中给予了积极协助与配合。北京科技大学硕士研究生邹桂森参与了项目组部分调查工作，并协助铜鼓拍摄和文字录入等工作。广西民族研究所李桐老师、广西壮族自治区博物馆张磊同志等参与了部分铜鼓的拍摄和指导。本书文字与图片的著作权归广西民族博物馆所有。对以上单位、个人所给予的支持和帮助我们在此表示深切的感谢！

本书编委会

2016 年 9 月 21 日